The Internet and Its Protocols

The Morgan Kaufmann Series in Networking

Series Editor, David Clark, M.I.T.

Communication Networking: An Analytical Approach
  Anurag Kumar, D. Manjunath, and Joy Kuri
Wireless Sensor Networks: An Information Processing Approach
  Feng Zhao and Leonidas Guibas
Routing, Flow, and Capacity Design in Communication and Computer Networks
  Michal Pióro and Deepankar Medhi
The Internet and Its Protocols: A Comparative Approach
  Adrian Farrel
Modern Cable Television Technology: Video, Voice, and Data Communications, 2e
  Walter Ciciora, James Farmer, David Large, and Michael Adams
Bluetooth Application Programming with the Java APIs
  C Bala Kumar, Paul J. Kline, and Timothy J. Thompson
Policy-Based Network Management: Solutions for the Next Generation
  John Strassner
Computer Networks: A Systems Approach, 3e
  Larry L. Peterson and Bruce S. Davie
Network Architecture, Analysis, and Design, 2e
  James D. McCabe
MPLS Network Management: MIBs, Tools, and Techniques
  Thomas D. Nadeau
Developing IP-Based Services: Solutions for Service Providers and Vendors
  Monique Morrow and Kateel Vijayananda
Telecommunications Law in the Internet Age
  Sharon K. Black
Optical Networks: A Practical Perspective, 2e
  Rajiv Ramaswami and Kumar N. Sivarajan
Internet QoS: Architectures and Mechanisms
  Zheng Wang
TCP/IP Sockets in Java: Practical Guide for Programmers
  Michael J. Donahoo and Kenneth L. Calvert
TCP/IP Sockets in C: Practical Guide for Programmers
  Kenneth L. Calvert and Michael J. Donahoo
Multicast Communication: Protocols, Programming, and Applications
  Ralph Wittmann and Martina Zitterbart
MPLS: Technology and Applications
  Bruce Davie and Yakov Rekhter
High-Performance Communication Networks, 2e
  Jean Walrand and Pravin Varaiya
Internetworking Multimedia
  Jon Crowcroft, Mark Handley, and Ian Wakeman
Understanding Networked Applications: A First Course
  David G. Messerschmitt
Integrated Management of Networked Systems: Concepts, Architectures, and their Operational Application
  Heinz-Gerd Hegering, Sebastian Abeck, and Bernhard Neumair
Virtual Private Networks: Making the Right Connection
  Dennis Fowler
Networked Applications: A Guide to the New Computing Infrastructure
  David G. Messerschmitt
Wide Area Network Design: Concepts and Tools for Optimization
  Robert S. Cahn

For further information on these books and for a list of forthcoming titles, please visit our website at http://www.mkp.com

The Internet and Its Protocols

A Comparative Approach

ADRIAN FARREL

AMSTERDAM • BOSTON • HEIDELBERG • LONDON
NEW YORK • OXFORD • PARIS • SAN DIEGO
SAN FRANCISCO • SINGAPORE • SYDNEY • TOKYO

Morgan Kaufmann is an imprint of Elsevier

ELSEVIER

MORGAN KAUFMANN PUBLISHERS

Acquisitions Editor Rick Adams
Publishing Services Manager Simon Crump
Developmental Editor Karyn Johnson
Cover Design Yvo Riezebos Design
Cover Image Getty Images
Composition Integra Software Services Pvt. Ltd.
Copyeditor Sherri Dietrich
Proofreader Jacqui Brownstein
Indexer Sharon Hilgenberg
Interior printer The Maple-Vail Book Manufacturing Group
Cover printer Phoenix Color Corp.

Morgan Kaufmann Publishers is an imprint of Elsevier.
500 Sansome Street, Suite 400, San Francisco, CA 94111

This book is printed on acid-free paper.

Library of Congress Cataloging-in-Publication Data

Farrel, Adrian.
    The Internet and its protocols : a comparative approach / Adrian Farrel.
      p. cm.
    Includes bibliographical references and index.
    ISBN 1-55860-913-X (hardcover : alk. paper)
    1. Computer network protocols 2. Internet. I. Title.
TK5105.55.F37   2004
004.6—dc22   2003027812

For information on all Morgan Kaufmann publications,
visit our Web site at *www.mkp.com*.

Printed in the United States of America
04 05 06 07 08 5 4 3 2 1

For Eleanor and Elliot.
In the hope that they need never read it.

Contents

Preface   xix

About the Author   xxix

Chapter 1   Overview of Essentials   1
          1.1   Physical Connectivity   1
          1.2   Protocols and Addressing   2
          1.3   The OSI Seven-Layer Model   4
          1.4   An Architecture for the Network   7
          1.5   Packaging Data   9
          1.6   Data-Link Protocols   10
                1.6.1   Ethernet   10
                1.6.2   Token Ring   12
                1.6.3   Asynchronous Transfer Mode   14
                1.6.4   Packet over SONET   16
                1.6.5   Dial-Up Networking   18
                1.6.6   802.2 and Logical Link Control   18
          1.7   The Protocols at a Glance   19
          1.8   Further Reading   20

Chapter 2   The Internet Protocol   23
          2.1   Choosing to Use IP   24
                2.1.1   Connecting Across Network Types   24
          2.2   IPv4   25
                2.2.1   IP Datagram Formats   26
                2.2.2   Data and Fragmentation   30
                2.2.3   Choosing to Detect Errors   34
          2.3   IPv4 Addressing   37
                2.3.1   Address Spaces and Formats   37
                2.3.2   Broadcast Addresses   39
                2.3.3   Address Masks, Prefixes, and Subnetworks   39
                2.3.4   Network Address Translation (NAT)   41
          2.4   IP in Use   42
                2.4.1   Bridging Function   42
                2.4.2   IP Switching and Routing   44
                2.4.3   Local Delivery and Loopbacks   46
                2.4.4   Type of Service   47

	2.4.5	Address Resolution Protocol	49
	2.4.6	Dynamic Address Assignment	53
2.5	IP Options and Advanced Functions		59
	2.5.1	Route Control and Recording	61
2.6	Internet Control Message Protocol (ICMP)		64
	2.6.1	Messages and Formats	64
	2.6.2	Error Reporting and Diagnosis	65
	2.6.3	Flow Control	70
	2.6.4	Ping and Traceroute	70
	2.6.5	Discovering Routers	74
	2.6.6	Path MTU Discovery	75
	2.6.7	Security Implications	76
2.7	Further Reading		77

Chapter 3 Multicast   79

3.1	Choosing Unicast or Multicast		79
	3.1.1	Applications That Use Multicast	83
3.2	Multicast Addressing and Forwarding		84
3.3	Internet Group Management Protocol (IGMP)		87
	3.3.1	What Are Groups?	87
	3.3.2	IGMP Message Formats and Exchanges	88
3.4	Further Reading		91

Chapter 4 IP Version Six   93

4.1	IPv6 Addresses		94
	4.1.1	IPv6 Address Formats	95
	4.1.2	Subnets and Prefixes	99
	4.1.3	Anycast	99
	4.1.4	Addresses with Special Meaning	100
	4.1.5	Picking IPv6 Addresses	101
4.2	Packet Formats		102
4.3	Options		103
4.4	Choosing Between IPv4 and IPv6		110
	4.4.1	Carrying IPv4 Addresses in IPv6	110
	4.4.2	Interoperation Between IPv4 and IPv6	111
	4.4.3	Checksums	111
	4.4.4	Effect on Other Protocols	112
	4.4.5	Making the Choice	113
4.5	Further Reading		113

Chapter 5 Routing   115

5.1	Routing and Forwarding		116
	5.1.1	Classless Interdomain Routing (CIDR)	116
	5.1.2	Autonomous Systems	118
	5.1.3	Building and Using a Routing Table	119
	5.1.4	Router IDs, Numbered Links, and Unnumbered Links	122

5.2	Distributing Routing Information		124
	5.2.1	Distance Vectors	125
	5.2.2	Link State Routing	131
	5.2.3	Path Vectors and Policies	137
	5.2.4	Distributing Additional Information	141
	5.2.5	Choosing a Routing Model	141
5.3	Computing Paths		142
	5.3.1	Open Shortest Path First (OSPF)	143
	5.3.2	Constrained Shortest Path First (CSPF)	145
	5.3.3	Equal Cost Multipath (ECMP)	146
	5.3.4	Traffic Engineering	146
	5.3.5	Choosing How to Compute Paths	147
5.4	Routing Information Protocol (RIP)		147
	5.4.1	Messages and Formats	148
	5.4.2	Overloading the Route Entry	150
	5.4.3	Protocol Exchanges	151
	5.4.4	Backwards Compatibility with RIPv1	153
	5.4.5	Choosing to Use RIP	154
5.5	Open Shortest Path First (OSPF)		155
	5.5.1	Basic Messages and Formats	155
	5.5.2	Neighbor Discovery	157
	5.5.3	Synchronizing Database State	159
	5.5.4	Advertising Link State	161
	5.5.5	Multi-Access Networks and Designated Routers	167
	5.5.6	OSPF Areas	170
	5.5.7	Stub Areas	172
	5.5.8	Not So Stubby Areas (NSSAs)	172
	5.5.9	Virtual Links	174
	5.5.10	Choosing to Use Areas	175
	5.5.11	Other Autonomous Systems	177
	5.5.12	Opaque LSAs	178
5.6	Intermediate-System to Intermediate-System (IS-IS)		179
	5.6.1	Data Encapsulation and Addressing	180
	5.6.2	Fletcher's Checksum	181
	5.6.3	Areas	181
	5.6.4	IS-IS Protocol Data Units	184
	5.6.5	Neighbor Discovery and Adjacency Maintenance	185
	5.6.6	Distributing Link State Information	190
	5.6.7	Synchronizing Databases	195
5.7	Choosing Between IS-IS and OSPF		196
5.8	Border Gateway Protocol 4 (BGP-4)		199
	5.8.1	Exterior Routing and Autonomous Systems	199
	5.8.2	Basic Messages and Formats	200
	5.8.3	Advanced Function	214
	5.8.4	Example Message	217
	5.8.5	Interior BGP	217
	5.8.6	Choosing to Use BGP	222

5.9		Multicast Routing	223
	5.9.1	Multicast Routing Trees	224
	5.9.2	Dense-Mode Protocols	225
	5.9.3	Sparse-Mode Protocols	227
	5.9.4	Protocol Independent Multicast Sparse-Mode (PIM-SM)	227
	5.9.5	Multicast OSPF (MOSPF)	231
	5.9.6	Distance Vector Multicast Routing Protocol (DVMRP)	232
	5.9.7	The MBONE	234
	5.9.8	A New Multicast Architecture	236
	5.9.9	Choosing a Multicast Routing Protocol	239
5.10		Other Routing Protocols	241
	5.10.1	Inter-Gateway Routing Protocol (IGRP) and Enhanced Inter-Gateway Routing Protocol (EIGRP)	242
	5.10.2	ES-IS	242
	5.10.3	Interdomain Routing Protocol (IDRP)	243
	5.10.4	Internet Route Access Protocol	243
	5.10.5	Hot Standby Router Protocol (HSRP) and Virtual Router Redundancy Protocol (VRRP)	243
	5.10.6	Historic Protocols	245
5.11		Further Reading	246

Chapter 6   IP Service Management   249

6.1		Choosing How to Manage Services	251
6.2		Differentiated Services	253
	6.2.1	Coloring Packets in DiffServ	253
	6.2.2	DiffServ Functional Model	255
	6.2.3	Choosing to Use DiffServ	257
6.3		Integrated Services	257
	6.3.1	Describing Traffic Flows	258
	6.3.2	Controlled Load	260
	6.3.3	Guaranteed Service	260
	6.3.4	Reporting Capabilities	262
	6.3.5	Choosing to Use IntServ	264
	6.3.6	Choosing a Service Type	265
	6.3.7	Choosing Between IntServ and DiffServ	266
6.4		Reserving Resources Using RSVP	266
	6.4.1	Choosing to Reserve Resources	267
	6.4.2	RSVP Message Flows for Resource Reservation	267
	6.4.3	Sessions and Flows	270
	6.4.4	Requesting, Discovering, and Reserving Resources	271
	6.4.5	Error Handling	272
	6.4.6	Adapting to Changes in the Network	274
	6.4.7	Merging Flows	277
	6.4.8	Multicast Resource Sharing	280

	6.4.9	RSVP Messages and Formats	281
	6.4.10	RSVP Objects and Formats	286
	6.4.11	Choosing a Transport Protocol	296
	6.4.12	RSVP Refresh Reduction	297
	6.4.13	Choosing to Use Refresh Reduction	303
	6.4.14	Aggregation of RSVP Flows	304
6.5	Further Reading		304

Chapter 7 Transport Over IP | 307

7.1	What Is a Transport Protocol?		307
	7.1.1	Choosing to Use a Transport Protocol	308
	7.1.2	Ports and Addresses	309
	7.1.3	Reliable Delivery	311
	7.1.4	Connection-Oriented Transport	312
	7.1.5	Datagrams	312
7.2	User Datagram Protocol (UDP)		313
	7.2.1	UDP Message Format	313
	7.2.2	Choosing to Use the UDP Checksum	314
	7.2.3	Choosing Between Raw IP and UDP	316
	7.2.4	Protocols That Use UDP	316
	7.2.5	UDP Lite	317
7.3	Transmission Control Protocol (TCP)		318
	7.3.1	Making IP Connection Oriented	318
	7.3.2	TCP Messages	318
	7.3.3	Connection Establishment	319
	7.3.4	Data Transfer	322
	7.3.5	Acknowledgements and Flow Control	324
	7.3.6	Urgent Data	329
	7.3.7	Closing the Connection	330
	7.3.8	Implementing TCP	331
	7.3.9	TCP Options	334
	7.3.10	Choosing Between UDP and TCP	336
	7.3.11	Protocols That Use TCP	337
7.4	Stream Control Transmission Protocol (SCTP)		337
	7.4.1	SCTP Message Formats	339
	7.4.2	Association Establishment and Management	341
	7.4.3	Data Transfer	348
	7.4.4	SCTP Implementation	352
	7.4.5	Choosing Between TCP and SCTP	353
	7.4.6	Protocols That Use SCTP	353
7.5	The Real-Time Transport Protocol (RTP)		354
	7.5.1	Managing Data	354
	7.5.2	Control Considerations	358
	7.5.3	Choosing a Transport for RTP	363
	7.5.4	Choosing to Use RTP	363
7.6	Further Reading		364

Chapter 8		Traffic Engineering	367
	8.1	What Is IP Traffic Engineering?	367
	8.2	Equal Cost Multipath (ECMP)	369
	8.3	Modifying Path Costs	369
	8.4	Routing IP Flows	371
	8.5	Service-Based Routing	372
	8.6	Choosing Offline or Dynamic Traffic Engineering	373
	8.7	Discovering Network Utilization	374
		8.7.1 Explicit Congestion Notification	375
	8.8	Routing Extensions for Traffic Engineering	376
		8.8.1 OSPF-TE	377
		8.8.2 IS-IS TE	379
	8.9	Choosing to Use Traffic Engineering	381
		8.9.1 Limitations of IP Traffic Engineering	382
		8.9.2 Future Developments in Traffic Engineering	382
	8.10	Further Reading	383
Chapter 9		Multiprotocol Label Switching (MPLS)	385
	9.1	Label Switching	386
		9.1.1 Choosing between Routing and Switching	387
	9.2	MPLS Fundamentals	388
		9.2.1 Labeling Packets	388
		9.2.2 Label Swapping and the Label Switched Path (LSP)	389
		9.2.3 Inferred Labels in Switching Networks	390
		9.2.4 Mapping Data to an LSP	391
		9.2.5 Hierarchies and Tunnels	393
		9.2.6 Choosing MPLS Over Other Switching Technologies	396
	9.3	Signaling Protocols	397
		9.3.1 What Does a Signaling Protocol Do?	397
		9.3.2 Choosing an IP-Based Control Plane	397
		9.3.3 Routing-Based Label Distribution	398
		9.3.4 On-Demand Label Distribution	399
		9.3.5 Traffic Engineering	399
		9.3.6 Choosing to Use a Signaling Protocol	400
	9.4	Label Distribution Protocol (LDP)	401
		9.4.1 Peers, Entities, and Sessions	403
		9.4.2 Address Advertisement and Use	409
		9.4.3 Distributing Labels	411
		9.4.4 Choosing a Label Distribution Mode	417
		9.4.5 Choosing a Label Retention Mode	418
		9.4.6 Stopping Use of Labels	419
		9.4.7 Error Cases and Event Notification	423
		9.4.8 Further Message Flow Examples	426
		9.4.9 Choosing Transport Protocols for LDP	429
		9.4.10 Surviving Network Outages	429
		9.4.11 LDP Extensions	430

9.5	Traffic Engineering in MPLS	431
	9.5.1 Explicit Routes	433
	9.5.2 Reserving Resources and Constraint-Based Routing	436
	9.5.3 Grooming Traffic	437
	9.5.4 Managing the Network	437
	9.5.5 Recovery Procedures	438
	9.5.6 Choosing to Use a Constraint-Based Signaling Protocol	438
9.6	Constraint-Based LSP Setup Using LDP (CR-LDP)	439
	9.6.1 Adding Constraints to LDP	439
	9.6.2 New TLVs	440
	9.6.3 New Status Codes	451
	9.6.4 CR-LDP Messages	452
9.7	Extensions to RSVP for LSP Tunnels (RSVP-TE)	456
	9.7.1 Reuse of RSVP Function	457
	9.7.2 Distributing Labels	458
	9.7.3 Identifying LSPs	458
	9.7.4 Managing Routes	459
	9.7.5 Resource Requests and Reservation	464
	9.7.6 Priorities, Preemption, and other Attributes	465
	9.7.7 Coloring the LSP	466
	9.7.8 Detecting Errors and Maintaining Connectivity	466
	9.7.9 Summary of Messages and Objects	468
	9.7.10 Choosing a Transport Protocol	470
	9.7.11 Security, Admission Control, and Policy Considerations	471
	9.7.12 New Error Codes and Values	471
	9.7.13 Message Flows	472
	9.7.14 Sample Messages	476
9.8	Choosing Between CR-LDP and RSVP-TE	479
	9.8.1 Why Are There Two Protocols?	479
	9.8.2 Applicability and Adoption	479
	9.8.3 Comparison of Functionality	480
9.9	Prioritizing Traffic in MPLS	481
	9.9.1 Inferring Priority from Labels	482
	9.9.2 Inferring Priority from Experimental Bits	483
	9.9.3 New Error Codes	484
	9.9.4 Choosing Between L-LSPs and E-LSPs	485
9.10	BGP-4 and MPLS	486
	9.10.1 Distributing Labels for BGP Routes	486
	9.10.2 New and Changed Message Objects	488
	9.10.3 Constructing MPLS VPNs	489
9.11	Further Reading	489
Chapter 10	Generalized MPLS (GMPLS)	491
10.1	A Hierarchy of Media	492
	10.1.1 Layer Two Switching	492
	10.1.2 Packet Switching	492
	10.1.3 Time Division Multiplexing	492

	10.1.4	Lambda Switching	493
	10.1.5	Waveband Switching	493
	10.1.6	Fiber and Port Switching	493
	10.1.7	Choosing Your Switching Type	493
	10.1.8	What Is a Label?	494
10.2	Generic Signaling Extensions for GMPLS		494
	10.2.1	Generic Labels	494
	10.2.2	Requesting Labels	496
	10.2.3	Negotiating Labels	497
	10.2.4	Bidirectional Services	502
	10.2.5	Protection Services	503
	10.2.6	Managing Connections and Alarms	504
	10.2.7	Out of Band Signaling	505
	10.2.8	Choosing to Use GMPLS Signaling	507
10.3	Choosing RSVP-TE or CR-LDP in GMPLS		508
10.4	Generalized RSVP-TE		509
	10.4.1	Enhanced Route Control	509
	10.4.2	Reducing Protocol Overheads	511
	10.4.3	Notification Requests and Messages	512
	10.4.4	Graceful Restart	513
	10.4.5	New and Changed Message Objects	514
	10.4.6	Message Formats	516
	10.4.7	Message Exchanges	516
10.5	Generalized CR-LDP		520
	10.5.1	New TLVs	521
	10.5.2	Message Formats	521
10.6	Hierarchies and Bundles		521
10.7	OSPF and IS-IS in GMPLS		523
	10.7.1	A New Meaning for Bandwidth	524
	10.7.2	Switching and Protection Capabilities	524
	10.7.3	Shared Risk Link Groups	525
	10.7.4	OSPF Message Objects	526
	10.7.5	IS-IS Message Objects	528
	10.7.6	Choosing Between OSPF and IS-IS in GMPLS	529
10.8	Optical VPNs		530
10.9	Link Management Protocol (LMP)		531
	10.9.1	Links, Control Channels, and Data Channels	533
	10.9.2	Discovering and Verifying Links	537
	10.9.3	Exchanging Link Capabilities	542
	10.9.4	Isolating Faults	544
	10.9.5	Authentication	545
	10.9.6	Choosing to Use LMP	546
10.10	Further Reading		547

Chapter 11	Switches and Components	549
	11.1 General Switch Management Protocol (GSMP)	549
	11.1.1 Distributed Switches	550
	11.1.2 Overview of GSMP	551
	11.1.3 Common Formats	551
	11.1.4 Establishing Adjacency	554
	11.1.5 Switch Configuration	556
	11.1.6 Port Management	560
	11.1.7 Connection Management	561
	11.1.8 Prereservation of Resources	562
	11.1.9 Events, State and Statistics	563
	11.1.10 Choosing to Use GSMP	565
	11.2 Separating IP Control and Forwarding	566
	11.2.1 The ForCES Working Group and Netlink	566
	11.3 LMP-WDM	569
	11.3.1 Distributed WDM Architectures	569
	11.3.2 Control Channel Management	569
	11.3.3 Link Management	569
	11.3.4 Fault Management	571
	11.4 Further Reading	572
Chapter 12	Application Protocols	575
	12.1 What Is an Application?	576
	12.1.1 Clients and Servers	576
	12.1.2 Ports	576
	12.2 Choosing a Transport	578
	12.2.1 Choosing to Use Sockets	579
	12.3 Domain Name System (DNS)	579
	12.3.1 Host Names	579
	12.3.2 The DNS Protocol	582
	12.3.3 Distribution of DNS Databases	582
	12.3.4 DNS Message Formats	584
	12.3.5 Extensions to DNS	588
	12.4 Telnet	588
	12.4.1 Choosing Between Character and Graphical Access	590
	12.4.2 Network Virtual Terminal	590
	12.4.3 How Does Telnet Work?	591
	12.4.4 Telnet Authentication	595
	12.4.5 Telnet Applications	597
	12.5 File Transfer Protocol (FTP)	598
	12.5.1 A Simple Application Protocol	598
	12.5.2 Connectivity Model	600
	12.5.3 FTP Message Format	601
	12.5.4 Managing an FTP Session	602
	12.5.5 Data Connection Control	603

12.5.6	Moving Files in FTP	607
12.5.7	FTP Replies	608
12.5.8	Could It Be Simpler? Trivial FTP	611
12.5.9	Choosing a File Transfer Protocol	614
12.6	Hypertext Transfer Protocol (HTTP)	615
12.6.1	What Is Hypertext?	616
12.6.2	Universal Resource Locators (URLs)	617
12.6.3	What Does HTTP Do?	618
12.6.4	Multipurpose Internet Message Extensions (MIME)	621
12.6.5	HTTP Message Formats	622
12.6.6	Example Messages and Transactions	625
12.6.7	Securing HTTP Transactions	628
12.7	Choosing an Application Protocol	630
12.8	Further Reading	631

Chapter 13   Network Management   635

13.1	Choosing to Manage Your Network	635
13.2	Choosing a Configuration Method	637
13.2.1	Command Line Interfaces	637
13.2.2	Graphical User Interfaces	638
13.2.3	Standardized Data Representations and Access	639
13.2.4	Making the Choice	641
13.3	The Management Information Base (MIB)	641
13.3.1	Representing Managed Objects	644
13.4	The Simple Network Management Protocol (SNMP)	646
13.4.1	Requests, Responses, and Notifications	646
13.4.2	SNMP Versions and Security	647
13.4.3	Choosing an SNMP Version	648
13.5	Extensible Markup Language (XML)	648
13.5.1	Extensibility and Domains of Applicability	649
13.5.2	XML Remote Procedure Calls	650
13.5.3	Simple Object Access Protocol (SOAP)	650
13.5.4	XML Applicability to Network Management	652
13.6	Common Object Request Broker Architecture (CORBA)	652
13.6.1	Interface Definition Language (IDL)	652
13.6.2	The Architecture	653
13.6.3	CORBA Communications	656
13.7	Choosing a Configuration Protocol	660
13.8	Choosing to Collect Statistics	660
13.9	Common Open Policy Service Protocol (COPS)	663
13.9.1	Choosing to Apply Policy	663
13.9.2	The COPS Protocol	666
13.9.3	COPS Message Formats	668
13.9.4	The Policy Information Base	672
13.10	Further Reading	674

Chapter 14	Concepts in IP Security	677
	14.1	The Need for Security	678
		14.1.1	Choosing to Use Security	679
	14.2	Choosing Where to Apply Security	681
		14.2.1	Physical Security	681
		14.2.2	Protecting Routing and Signaling Protocols	682
		14.2.3	Application-Level Security	682
		14.2.4	Protection at the Transport Layer	684
		14.2.5	Network-Level Security	684
	14.3	Components of Security Models	684
		14.3.1	Access Control	685
		14.3.2	Authentication	687
		14.3.3	Encryption	688
	14.4	IPsec	689
		14.4.1	Choosing Between End-to-End and Proxy Security	689
		14.4.2	Authentication	690
		14.4.3	Authentication and Encryption	692
	14.5	Transport-Layer Security	695
		14.5.1	The Handshake Protocol	697
		14.5.2	Alert Messages	701
	14.6	Securing the Hypertext Transfer Protocol	701
	14.7	Hashing and Encryption: Algorithms and Keys	703
		14.7.1	Message Digest Five (MD5)	704
		14.7.2	Data Encryption Standard (DES)	709
	14.8	Exchanging Keys	710
		14.8.1	Internet Key Exchange	711
	14.9	Further Reading	716
Chapter 15	Advanced Applications	719
	15.1	IP Encapsulation	719
		15.1.1	Tunneling Through IP Networks	720
		15.1.2	Generic Routing Encapsulation	721
		15.1.3	IP in IP Encapsulation	722
		15.1.4	Minimal IP Encapsulation	724
		15.1.5	Using MPLS Tunnels	725
		15.1.6	Choosing a Tunneling Mechanism	726
	15.2	Virtual Private Networks (VPNs)	726
		15.2.1	What Is a VPN?	727
		15.2.2	Tunneling and Private Address Spaces	728
		15.2.3	Solutions Using Routing Protocols	728
		15.2.4	Security Solutions	731
		15.2.5	MPLS VPNs	731
		15.2.6	Optical VPNs	733
		15.2.7	Choosing a VPN Technology	733

15.3	Mobile IP	734
	15.3.1 The Requirements of Mobile IP	735
	15.3.2 Extending the Protocols	736
	15.3.3 Reverse Tunneling	741
	15.3.4 Security Concerns	741
15.4	Header Compression	742
	15.4.1 Choosing to Compress Headers	742
	15.4.2 IP Header Compression	743
	15.4.3 MPLS and Header Compression	747
15.5	Voice Over IP	748
	15.5.1 Voice Over MPLS	749
15.6	IP Telephony	749
	15.6.1 The Protocols in Brief	750
15.7	IP and ATM	752
	15.7.1 IP Over ATM (IPOA)	752
	15.7.2 Multiprotocol Over ATM (MPOA)	753
	15.7.3 LAN Emulation	755
	15.7.4 MPLS Over ATM	756
15.8	IP Over Dial-Up Links	756
	15.8.1 Serial Line Internet Protocol (SLIP)	756
	15.8.2 Point-to-Point Protocol	758
	15.8.3 Choosing a Dial-Up Protocol	759
	15.8.4 Proxy ARP	759
15.9	Further Reading	760

Concluding Remarks	**763**
Index	**769**

Preface

The Internet is now such a well-known concept that it no longer needs introduction. Yet only a relatively small proportion of people who make regular use of email or the World Wide Web have a clear understanding of the computers and telecommunications networks that bring them together across the world. Even within this group that understands, for example, that a router is a special computer that forwards data from one place to another, there is often only a sketchy understanding of what makes the routers tick, how they decide where to send data, and how the data is packaged to be passed from one computer to another.

The Internet is a mesh of computer networks that spans the world. Computers that connect to the Internet or form part of its infrastructure use a common set of languages to communicate with each other. These are the Internet protocols. These languages cover all aspects of communication, from how data is presented on the link between two computers so that they can both have the same understanding of the message, to rules that allow routers to exchange and negotiate capabilities and responsibilities so that the network becomes a fully connected organism. Internet protocols are used to establish conversations between remote computers. These conversations, or logical connections, may span thousands of miles and utilize many intervening routers. They may make use of all sorts of physical connections, including satellite links, fiber-optic cables, or the familiar twisted-pair telephone wire. The conversations may be manipulated through Internet protocols to allow data traffic to be placed within the Internet to optimize the use of resources, to avoid network congestion, and to help network operators guarantee quality of service to the users. In short, the Internet without protocols would be a very expensive and largely useless collection of computers and wires.

The protocols used in the Internet are, therefore, of special interest to everyone concerned with the function of the Internet. Software developers and vendors making web browsers, email systems, electronic commerce packages, or even multiuser domain games, must utilize the protocols to run smoothly over the Internet and to ensure that their products communicate successfully with those from other vendors. Equipment manufacturers need to implement the protocols to provide function and value to their customers and to offer solutions that interoperate with hardware bought from other suppliers. Network operators and managers need to be especially aware of how the protocols function so that they can tune their networks and keep them functioning, even through dramatic changes in traffic demand and resource availability.

There are already a large number of books devoted to descriptions of the protocols that run the Internet. Some describe a cluster of protocols with a view to showing how a particular service (for example, Virtual Private Networks) can be provided across and within the Internet. Others take a field of operation (such as routing) and discuss the specific protocols relevant to that area. Still more books give a highly detailed anatomy of an individual protocol, describing all of its features and foibles.

The aim of this book is to give a broader picture, showing all of the common Internet protocols and how they fit together. This lofty aim is, of course, not easily achieved without some compromises. In the first instance, it is necessary to include only those protocols that receive widespread and public use—there are over one thousand protocols listed by the Internet Assigned Numbers Authority (IANA) and clearly these could not all be covered in a single work. Second, some details of each individual protocol must be left out in order to fit everything between the covers. Despite these constraints, this book gives more than an overview of the established protocols. It examines the purpose and function of each and provides details of the messages used by the protocols, including byte-by-byte descriptions and message flow examples.

The Internet is a rapidly evolving entity. As the amount of traffic increases and advances in hardware technology are made, new demands are placed on the inventors of Internet protocols—the Internet Engineering Task Force (IETF)—leading to the development of new concepts and protocols. Some of these recent inventions, such as Multiprotocol Label Switching (MPLS), are already seeing significant deployment within the Internet. Others, such as Generalized MPLS (GMPLS), are poised to establish themselves as fundamental protocols within the Internet's transport core. This book recognizes the importance of these new technologies and gives them their appropriate share of attention.

Underlying the whole of this book is a comparative thread. Deployment of Internet protocols is fraught with decisions: How should I construct my network? Which protocol should I use? Which options within a protocol should I use? How can I make my network perform better? How can I provide new services to my customers? At each step this book aims to address these questions by giving guidance on choices and offering comparative analysis.

It would not have been possible to write this book without reference to many of the existing texts that provide detailed descriptions of individual protocols. At the end of each chapter some suggestions for further reading are made to point the reader to sources of additional information.

Audience

This book is intended to be useful to professionals and students with an interest in one or more of the protocols used in the Internet. No knowledge of the Internet is assumed, but the reader will find it helpful to have a general understanding of the concepts of communication protocols.

Readers will probably have varying degrees of familiarity with some of the protocols described in this book. This book can be used to learn about unfamiliar protocols, as a refresher for rusty areas, or as a reference for well-known protocols.

Software and hardware developers, together with system testers, will find this book useful to broaden their understanding and to give them a solid grounding in new protocols before they move into new areas or start new projects. It will help them understand how protocols relate to each other and how they differ while providing similar functions.

Network operators are often required to adopt new technologies as new equipment is installed, and must rapidly come up to speed on the new and different protocols. New developments such as MPLS are making a strong impression in the Internet, and technologies like GMPLS are bringing IP-based control protocols into core transport networks. This book should appeal to the many core network operators who suddenly discover that IP is invading their world.

A third category of readers consists of decision makers and managers tasked with designing and deploying networks. Such people can be expected already to have a good understanding of the use and purpose of many protocols, but they will find the comparison of similar protocols useful and will be able to update their knowledge from the description of the new protocols.

Organization of This Book

Network protocols are often considered with respect to a layered model. Applications form the top layer and talk application-level protocols to each other. In doing so, they utilize lower-layer protocols to establish connections, encapsulate data, and route the data through the network.

This book is organized by layer from the bottom up so that network-layer protocols precede transport protocols, and application protocols come last. Like all good generalizations, the statement that protocols fit within layers is badly flawed, and many protocols do not fit easily into that model. MPLS, for example, has often been described as a "layer two-and-a-half" protocol. With these difficult cases, the protocols are described in chapters ordered according to where the functional responsibility fits within a data network.

Chapter 1 provides an overview of essentials designed to consolidate terminology within the rest of the book and to bring readers who are unfamiliar with communication protocols up to speed. It introduces the OSI seven-layer model, describes some common data link protocols, and presents a picture of how the Internet protocols described in this book all fit together.

Chapter 2, The Internet Protocol (IP), introduces the essential data transfer protocol on which all other Internet protocols are built. It discusses addressing and describes the most popular form of the Internet Protocol, IPv4. This chapter also includes information about the Internet Control Message Protocol (ICMP), which is fundamental to the operation of IP networks.

Chapter 3 provides a short overview of multicast. Techniques for mass distribution of IP messages are covered together with the Internet Group Management Protocol (IGMP). The topic of multicast routing is deferred to Chapter 5.

Chapter 4 outlines the next generation of the Internet Protocol, IPv6, and looks at the problems it sets out to solve.

Chapter 5 introduces routing as a concept and describes some of the important routing protocols in use within the Internet. This is the largest chapter in the book and covers a crucial topic. It details the four most deployed unicast routing protocols: the Routing Information Protocol (RIP), the Open Shortest Path First protocol (OSPF), the Intermediate System to Intermediate System protocol (IS-IS), and the Border Gateway Protocol (BGP). Chapter 5 also includes an introduction to some of the concepts in multicast routing and gives an overview of some of the multicast routing protocols.

Chapter 6 is devoted to IP service management and describes how services and features are built on top of IP using Differentiated Services (DiffServ), Integrated Services (IntServ), and the Resource Reservation Protocol (RSVP).

Chapter 7 addresses the important area of transport over IP. Transport protocols are responsible for delivering end-to-end data across the Internet, and they provide different grades of service to the applications that use them. This chapter describes the User Datagram Protocol (UDP), the Transmission Control Protocol (TCP), the Streams Control Transmission Protocol (SCTP), and the Real-Time Transport Protocol (RTP).

Chapter 8 is a digression into the field of traffic engineering. It describes some of the important concepts in optimal placement of traffic within a network and outlines the extensions to routing protocols to provide some of the information that a traffic engineering application needs to do its job. This chapter also sets out the extensions to the OSPF and IS-IS routing protocols in support of traffic engineering.

Chapters 9 and 10 describe Multiprotocol Label Switching (MPLS) and Generalized MPLS (GMPLS). These important new technologies utilize IP to establish data paths through networks to carry traffic that may or may not itself be IP. Chapter 9 explains the fundamentals of MPLS before giving details of three MPLS signaling protocols: the Label Distribution Protocol (LDP), Constraint-Based LSP Setup Using LDP (CR-LDP), and traffic engineering extensions to the Resource Reservation Protocol (RSVP-TE). Chapter 10 explains how the MPLS protocols have been extended to use an IP infrastructure to manage network hardware that might switch optical data rather than IP packets. Chapter 10 also includes a description of the Link Management Protocol (LMP).

Chapter 11 is devoted to managing switches and components. Although switches and components are at the lowest level in the layered protocol model, their management is an application-level issue and the protocols used utilize IP and many of the other features already described. The General Switch

Management Protocol (GSMP) and extensions to LMP for managing optical components (LMP-WDM) are described, and there is a brief introduction to the work of the IETF's Forwarding and Element Control Separation (ForCES) Working Group.

Chapter 12 brings us at last to application protocols. Applications are what it is all about; there is no point in any of the other protocols without applications that need to exchange data between different sites. This chapter describes a few of the very many protocols that applications use to talk amongst themselves across the Internet. The Domain Name System protocol (DNS), Telnet, the File Transfer Protocol (FTP), the Trivial File Transfer Protocol (TFTP), and the Hypertext Transfer Protocol (HTTP) are used as examples.

Chapter 13 develops the previous two chapters to discuss network management. The control protocols used to gather information about the network and to control the resources are increasingly important in today's complex networks. This chapter includes an overview of the Management Information Base (MIB) that acts as a distributed database of information on all elements of a network. There is also a description of three important techniques for distributing management information: the Simple Network Management Protocol (SNMP), the Extensible Markup Language (XML), and the Common Object Request Broker Architecture (CORBA). The chapter concludes with some comments on managing policy within a network, and with a description of the Common Open Policy Service protocol (COPS).

Chapter 14 looks at the important subject of IP Security and how messages can be authenticated and protected when they are sent through the Internet. Special attention is given to the ways in which security can be applied at the network layer (IPsec), at the transport layer using the Transport Layer Security protocol (TLS) and the Secure Sockets Layer (SSL), and at the application layer, with security techniques for HTTP providing an example.

Chapter 15 briefly dips into some advanced applications such as IP Encapsulation, Virtual Private Networks, Mobile IP, and Voice over IP. Some of these topics are new uses of IP that are requiring the development of new protocols and extensions to existing protocols. Others are almost as old as IP itself and are well-established techniques.

Finally, the closing remarks look toward future developments and attempt to predict the next steps in the development and standardization of Internet protocols.

Each chapter begins with a brief introduction that lists the topics that will be covered and explains why the material is important. The chapters all end with suggestions for further reading, pointing the reader to books and other material that cover the topics in greater detail.

Throughout the book, comparisons are made between protocols, and between implementation/deployment options, in the form of sections with titles such as Choosing Between TCP and SCTP, or Choosing Between CR-LDP and RSVP-TE.

Conventions Used in This Book

A byte is an 8-bit quantity, sometimes known as an octet. Bits are numbered within a byte in the order that they would arrive in a transmission. The first bit is numbered 0 (zero) and is the most significant bit.

Where integers are transmitted as part of a protocol, they are sent in "line format"—that is, with the most significant bit first. This can most easily be seen by converting the number into binary representation with the right number of bits (that is, padding with zeros on the left) and numbering the bits from left to right starting with zero. Thus, the number 26,025 (which is 0x65A9 in hexadecimal) is represented as a 16-bit binary number as 0110010110101001. Bit zero has value 0 and bit 15 has value 1.

Diagrammatic representation of messages is achieved by showing bits running from left to right across the page with bit zero of byte zero in the top left corner. Thirty-two bits (4 bytes) are shown in a row. For example, Figure 0.1 shows the Protocol Data Unit (PDU) header used to prefix all messages in the Label Distribution Protocol (LDP). The header is 10 bytes long and comprises four fields: the Version, the PDU Length, an LSR Identifier, and a Label Space Identifier. The Version field is 16 bits (2 bytes) long and is transmitted (and received!) first.

Sample networks are shown in figures using some of the symbols shown in Figure 0.2. A distinction is made between IP routers and Multiprotocol Label Switching (MPLS) Label Switching Routers (LSRs). Multi-access networks are typically represented as Ethernets, and more general IP networks are shown as "clouds." Users' computers and workstations (hosts) attached to the networks are usually shown as personal computers with monitors. Larger computers that may act as application servers are represented as tower systems.

Protocol exchanges are shown diagrammatically using vertical lines to represent network nodes and horizontal lines to represent messages with the message name written immediately above them. Time flows down the diagram; in Figure 0.3, which illustrates the events and exchange of messages between two RSVP-TE LSRs, the first events are Path messages that are passed from one LSR to the next. Dotted vertical lines are used to illustrate the passing of time, such as when waiting for a timer to expire or waiting for application instructions.

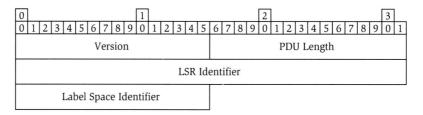

Figure 0.1 LDP PDU header.

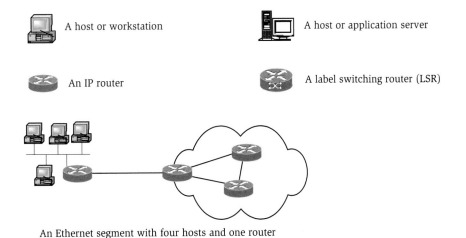

Figure 0.2 Some of the symbols used in the figures in this book.

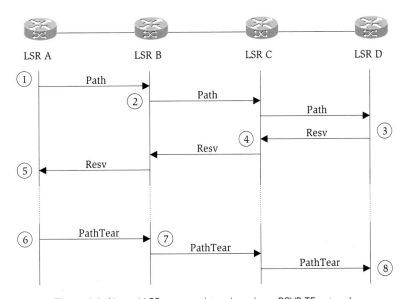

Figure 0.3 Normal LSP setup and teardown in an RSVP-TE network.

The *Backus Naur Form* (BNF) is sometimes used to describe message formats when the messages are built from component parts. Each component is identified by angle brackets < as here > and optional components are placed in square brackets [< like this >]. The other symbol used is the pipe "|", a vertical bar that

```
< Decision Message > ::=      < Common Header >
                              < Client Handle >
                              < Decisions >  |  < Error >
                              [ < Integrity > ]
```

Figure 0.4 The COPS protocol decision message represented in BNF.

indicates an exclusive or, so that < either this component is present > | < or this one >. Figure 0.4 shows the COPS Decision message that is built from two mandatory components (the common header and the client handle), a choice between the Decisions component and the Error component (exactly one of which must be present), and an optional Integrity component.

About the IETF

The *Internet Engineering Task Force* (IETF) is the principle standards-making body documenting standards for use in the Internet and in relation to the Internet Protocol, IP. The body is a loose collection of individuals who supposedly eschew their corporate affiliations and work together to produce the best technical solutions in a timely manner. Membership doesn't exist as such, and everyone is free to participate in the discussions of new standards and problems with existing ones.

Most of the work of the IETF is carried out within Working Groups, each chartered to address a reasonably small set of problems. At the time of writing there are 133 active Working Groups in operation. Each Working Group maintains an email list that is used for discussions and holds a meeting once every four months when the IETF meets up "in the flesh."

Standards are developed through a process of drafting. Internet Drafts may be the work of groups of individuals or of a Working Group, and are published and republished until they are acceptable or until everyone loses interest and they are dropped. Acceptable drafts are put to *last call* within the Working Group and then again across the whole IETF to allow everyone to express any last-minute objections. If all is well and the draft is approved by the Internet Engineering Steering Group (IESG), it is published as a Request for Comment (RFC).

An RFC is not automatically a standard. It must go through a process of implementation, deployment, and assessment before it is given that mark of approval. There are more than 3500 RFCs published to date, but only 62 of those have been certified as standards.

For the sake of clarity, RFCs and Standards are referred to only through their RFC number within this book.

Most of the protocols described in this book are the subject of more than one RFC. The Further Reading sections at the end of each chapter list the relevant RFCs, which can be found through the IETF's web site.

Two other important groups contribute to the IETF's success. The RFC editor is responsible for formatting, checking, and publishing RFCs. The Internet Assigned Numbers Authority (IANA) maintains a repository of all allocated protocol numbers and values so that there is no risk of accidental double usage of the same value.

The IETF maintains a web site at http://www.ietf.org from where links exist to each of the Working Groups, to IANA, to a list of all of the published RFCs, and to a search engine to search the repository of Internet Drafts. The IETF publishes a useful document, *RFC 3160—The Tao of the IETF*, that serves as an introduction to the aims and philosophy of the IETF; it can be found at http://www.ietf.org/rfc/rfc3160.txt.

A Note on Gender

Within this book it is occasionally necessary to refer to an individual (for example, a network operator or the implementer of a software component) using a third-person pronoun. The word *he* is used without prejudice and is not intended to imply that a disproportionate number of techno-nerds are male nor that women are too clever to waste their time in such jobs.

Acknowledgements

I wrote this book while working for a startup company making high-tech optical switches for the Internet during a severe downturn in the telecoms market, and living in a country that was new and strange to me during a time of heightened security and stress caused by terrorism and war. There was never a dull moment, and very few that were dedicated to sleep.

Most of my writing time was squeezed into spare moments in evenings or weekends that should have been spent being a house-husband or a tourist. My thanks go, therefore, to my wife Catherine and dog Bracken for putting up with my turned back as I sat typing, and for amusing each other without my input.

I am grateful, too, to my reviewers who took such pains to wade through the manuscript, making helpful suggestions and factual changes. Loa Andersson, Paul Turcotte, Judith M. Myerson, and Y. Reina Wang all contributed significantly to the form of the book and to my comfort level as I wrote it. Thanks also to Phillip Matthews for stepping in to provide prompt, substantial, and detailed feedback on Chapter 5. My gratitude goes to the team at Morgan Kaufmann for all their hard work: especially Karyn Johnson and Marcy Barnes-Henrie.

Finally, special thanks to Philip Yim for providing encouragement at a difficult time.

About the Author

Adrian Farrel has almost 20 years of experience designing and developing portable communications software ranging from various aspects of SNA and OSI through ATM and into IP. At Data Connection Ltd., he was MPLS Architect and Development Manager, leading a team that produced a carrier-class MPLS implementation for customers in the router space, while their GMPLS implementation pioneered the protocols working closely with optical companies that were developing the standards. As Director of Protocol Development for Movaz Networks Inc., Adrian had the opportunity to build a cutting-edge system integrating many IP-based protocols to control and manage optical switches offering wavelength services.

Adrian is very active within the IETF, where he is co-chair of the Common Control and Measurement Plane (CCAMP) Working Group that is responsible for the GMPLS family of protocols. He has coauthored and contributed to numerous Internet Drafts and RFCs on MPLS, GMPLS, and related technologies. He was a founding board member of the MPLS Forum, frequently speaks at conferences, and is the author of several white papers on GMPLS.

He lives in North Wales, from where he runs an Internet Protocols consultancy, Old Dog Consulting, and lives the good life with his wife Catherine and dog Bracken.

Chapter 1
Overview of Essentials

This first chapter provides an overview of some of the essentials for discussion of the Internet and its protocols. It may safely be skipped by anyone with a good background in computers and networking, or skimmed by those who want to check that they have the right level of information to tackle the remainder of the book. The chapter examines aspects of physical connectivity before looking at the fundamentals of communications protocols. The Open Systems Interconnection (OSI) seven-layer architectural model for communication protocols is introduced and used to reference some of the protocols described in this book. There follows a brief examination of how data is packaged and exchanged, and a description of some of the common link level protocols that are hardware dependent and provide essential support for the Internet. The chapter concludes with an overview of network layer addressing, a chart showing how the protocols discussed in this book fit together, and some suggestions for further reading.

1.1 Physical Connectivity

What is the point of connecting two computers together? Why do we go to such lengths to invent languages to allow computers to communicate? The answer is simply to enable the distribution of data of all forms both between computers and between users. It has been suggested (by Robert Metcalfe, former chief of 3Com) that the value of a network increases as the square of the number of computers in the network. If that is true, linking two computers together doubles their value, and linking one hundred computers in an office achieves a 10,000 percent increase in value.

But we should recall that linking computers together has only recently become a simple concept. These days nearly every office computer ships with an Ethernet card built in and most home or portable computers include modems—it is relatively simple to achieve physical connectivity by plugging in the right cable and performing simple configuration. Other local area network (LAN) technologies do still have their footholds and many offices use Token Ring or FDDI in place of Ethernet. Similarly, there are other wide area networking technologies that may be used to connect computers at remote sites in place of dial-up links—these include ISDN, SDLC, and X.25.

The immediate connection between a computer and its network is only the first step in connecting a computer to a remote partner. There may be many computers on the path from data source to destination and these computers may be linked together using a variety of technologies, some of which are designed specifically for bulk data transfer and for building links between computers that run in the core of the network. Increasingly, such technologies utilize fiber optics and rely on special encodings (ATM, SONET, SDH, etc.) to carry data. Of course, as wireless networking grows in popularity there is no obvious physical linkage between computers, but they are still linked and exchanging data on point-to-point connections made across the airwaves.

So the physical links traversed by data exchanged between computers may vary widely. Each link between a pair of directly connected computers is of just one type, but there may be multiple parallel links of different (or the same) types between computers. The physical connection is responsible for delivering bits and bytes from one end of the link to another and for reassembling them in the same order as they were presented for dispatch. There are no further rules that can be applied universally, and each medium has a different way of ensuring that the signal can be clearly and unambiguously converted from and to data (for example, consider how data bits are converted to line voltages using NRZI, or how photons are used to represent electrical signals).

In order to manage the way that data is run across these links, computers employ *data-link level protocols*. These are specific communication languages designed to address the requirements of individual physical networking constraints, and are largely concerned with packaging of data so that it can be recognized and delivered to the correct user at the other end of the link. For the data to be delivered to the correct user, it is necessary to have some form of addressing that identifies computers and users within the network.

1.2 Protocols and Addressing

Computer protocols can be said to serve four purposes. Chiefly, they exist to encode and transfer data from one point to another. To enable this primary function they may need to control how the data is distributed by designating paths that the data must follow, and in order to achieve this they may need to exchange network state information. Finally, the protocols may be needed to manage network resources (computers and links) in order to control their behavior.

Data transfer protocols may be the most important from the user's perspective since all they want to do is send their data, but these protocols are relatively simple and also form only a small percentage of the protocols actually needed to build and maintain the infrastructure of a network. The information distribution, control, and management protocols that serve the other three purposes described in the preceding paragraph are often far more complex and sophisticated.

For any of these protocols to operate, they must have a way to identify the source and destination of messages. Just as the sender of a letter must write the recipient's address on the front of the envelope, the sender of a protocol message must provide the address for the remote computer that is the desired destination. Similarly, if a letter writer wishes to receive a response, he is well advised to supply his name and return address, and so should the sender of a protocol message. It should be clear that computers need names and addresses to identify themselves.

At a physical level, computers and devices are usually identified by unique numbers burned in to ROM. These numbers often identify the equipment manufacturer, and the product type and version, and have a component that is unique to each individual item to come off the production line. An increasingly common format for identifiers is the Media Access Control (MAC) address shown in Figure 1.1, and these are used by several data-link layer protocols to directly identify the computer or interface card that is communicating. Other data-link layer protocols, however, have different addressing schemes ranging from simple 16-bit integers to complex 40-byte structures, and these rely on careful configuration policies to ensure that everyone has a unique address (just as two people with the same name living on the same street will lead to fun and games in an Italian farce, so two computers with the same address in the same network will result in chaos and confusion).

A protocol message, then, has three components: addressing information to define the source and destination of the data, control information to regulate the flow and manner of distribution of the data, and payload data. The payload data is, from the user's perspective, the important part—the information being transferred—although, if the message is being exchanged between control

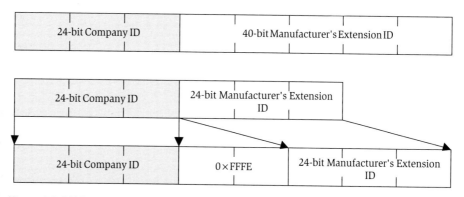

Figure 1.1 MAC addresses may be encoded as 60 bits or 48 bits. The 48-bit variety can be mapped into a 64-bit address by inserting $0 \times FFFE$.

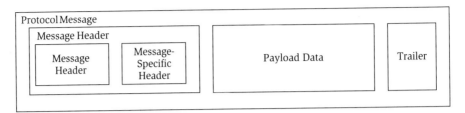

Figure 1.2 A protocol message may be comprised of a header, payload data, and a trailer.

programs on the two communicating computers, the payload data may be control state information such as instructions to regulate the flow of user data, to exchange addresses, or to establish connections over which to exchange user data.

Protocol messages are usually constructed as a *header* followed by data. The header contains the addressing and control information and is, itself, sometimes broken into two parts: a *standard header* that has a well-known format for all messages within a protocol, and *header extensions* that vary per message. Sometimes messages will also include a *trailer* that comes after the payload data. Usually the standard message header includes a length field that tells the protocol how many bytes of message are present. This structure is represented in Figure 1.2.

1.3 The OSI Seven-Layer Model

It is apparently impossible to write a book about networking protocols without reference to the seven-layer architectural model devised by the International Standards Organization (ISO) and used to classify and structure their protocol suite, the Open Systems Interconnection (OSI) protocols. The seven-layer model includes many useful concepts, although it is not as applicable to the entire Internet Protocol suite as it might once have been, with many protocols sitting uncomfortably on the architectural fence. Figure 1.3 shows the seven layers and how they are used in communication between two computers across a network of devices. The lowest layer, the *physical layer*, provides connectivity between devices. The next layer up, the *data-link layer*, is responsible for presenting data to the physical layer and for managing data exchanges across the physical media. Data-link exchanges are point-to-point between computers that terminate physical links, although the concept of *bridging* (see Chapter 2) offers limited forwarding capabilities within the data-link layer. The *network layer* is responsible for achieving end-to-end delivery of data (that is, from source to destination), but achieves it in a hop-by-hop manner (that is, by passing it like a hot potato from one node to the next). Examples of network layer protocols include X.25, CLNP, and IP (the Internet Protocol). An important fact about the network layer is that it aims to be independent of the underlying data-link technology—this has been achieved with varying degrees of success, but the designers of IP are proud of the fact that it can be run over any data-link type from the most sophisticated free-space optics to the less-than-reliable tin cans and string.

Above the network layer comes the *transport layer*. Transport protocols, described in Chapter 7, manage data in a strictly end-to-end manner and are responsible for providing predictable levels of data-delivery across the network. Examples from the IP world include TCP, UDP, and SCTP. Next up the stack comes the *session layer*, which manages associations (or sessions) between applications on remote computers using the transport layer to deliver data from site to site. The *presentation layer* contains features such as national language support, character buffering, and display features. It is responsible for converting data into the right format to be transmitted across the network and for receiving the data and making it available to applications which make up the top layer of the model, the *application layer*.

As shown in Figure 1.3, protocol message exchanges are between entities at the same level within the protocol stack. That is, application layer protocols are used to communicate between applications on different computers, and they send their messages as if they were colocated (along the dotted lines in Figure 1.3). In fact, however, they achieve this communication by passing the messages to the next lower layer in the stack. So with each layer in the stack, the protocol code communicates directly with its peer, but does so by passing the message down to the next layer, and it is only when the data reaches the physical layer that it is actually encoded and put on the "wire" to reach the next node.

As described earlier in this section, physical communications are hop-by-hop and are terminated at each node, but at each node the protocols are terminated only if they are relevant to the type of node and the layer in the protocol stack.

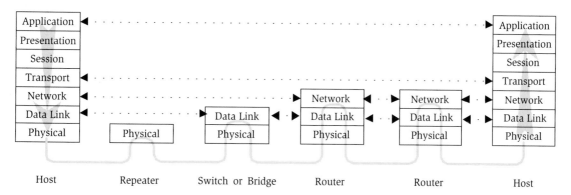

Figure 1.3 Connectivity within the seven-layer model allows neighboring entities at the same level of the stack to consider themselves adjacent regardless of the number of intervening hops between lower layer entities. End-to-end connectivity is, in fact, achieved by passing the data down the stack.

So, as shown by the gray line in Figure 1.3, at some nodes the data may rise as far as the network layer while at others it only reaches the data-link layer.

The IP protocols do not sit particularly well in the seven-layer model, although the concepts illustrated in the diagram are very useful. The lower layers (one through four) are well matched, with IP itself fitting squarely in the network layer and the transport protocols situated in the transport layer. Many of the protocols that support applications (such as HTTP, the Hypertext Transfer Protocol) encompass the session and presentation layers and also stray into the application layer to provide services for the applications they support.

Matters get more fuzzy when we consider the routing protocols. Some of these operate directly over data-link layer protocols, some use IP, and others utilize transport protocols. Functionally, many routing protocols maintain sessions between adjacent or remote computers, making matters still more confusing. Operationally, however, the routing protocols are network layer commodities.

The world is really turned on its head by the Multiprotocol Label Switching (MPLS) protocols described in Chapter 9. These are often referred to as "layer two-and-a-half protocols" because they exist to transport network protocol data over the data-link layer connections, and MPLS relays data in a hop-by-hop way and delivers it end-to-end. However, the MPLS protocols themselves are responsible for installing the forwarding rules within the network, and they operate more at the level of routing protocols running over IP or making use of the transport protocols and establishing sessions between neighbors.

Figure 1.4 shows some of the IP protocols in the context of the OSI seven layers. Note that there is no implied relationship between the protocols in the figure—they are simply placed in the diagram according to their position in

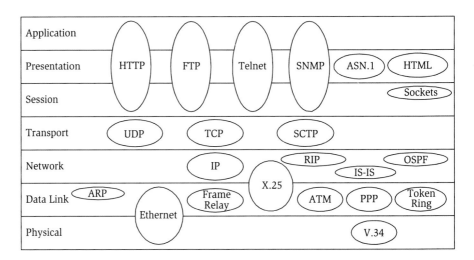

Figure 1.4 Some of the Internet protocols as they fit within the OSI seven-layer model.

the seven-layer model. Refer to Figure 1.17 for a more comprehensive view of how the protocols described in this book fit together.

Some people, it should be pointed out, don't see much point in the seven-layer model. In some cases a five-layer IP model is used that merges the top three OSI layers into a single application layer, but others choose to discard the model entirely after introducing it as a concept to explain that features and functions are provided by protocols in a layered manner. This book takes a middle road and only uses the architectural model loosely to draw distinctions between the data-link protocols that are responsible for transporting IP data, the IP protocol itself as a network protocol, and the transport protocols that provide distinctive services to application programs.

1.4 **An Architecture for the Network**

It is sometimes convenient to consider network computers as split into distinct components, each with a different responsibility. One component might handle management of the router, another could have responsibility for forwarding data, and yet another might be given the task of dealing with control protocol interactions with other computers in the network.

When a network is viewed as a collection of computers partitioned in this way, it can be seen that messages and information move around the network between components with the same responsibility. For example, one computer might process some data using its dedicated data-processing component. The first computer sends the data on to another computer where it is also processed by the dedicated data-processing component, and so on across the network. This view builds up to the concept of processing *planes* in which networked computers communicate for different purposes. Communications between computers do not cross from one plane to another, so that, for example, the management component on one computer does not talk to the control protocol component on another computer. However, within a single computer there is free communication between the planes.

Figure 1.5 displays how this model works. Four planes are generally described. The *Data Plane* is responsible for the data traffic that passes across the network. The *Management Plane* handles all management interactions such as configuration requests, statistics gathering, and so forth. The *Control Plane* is where the signaling and control protocols operate to dynamically interact between network computers. The *Routing Plane* is usually considered as distinct from the Control Plane simply because the routing protocols that dynamically distribute connectivity and reachability information within the network are usually implemented as separate components within network computers.

Some people like to add a fifth plane, the *Application Plane*. However, application transactions tend to be end-to-end and do not require any interaction

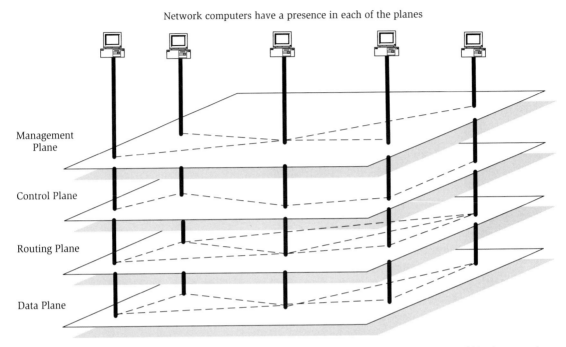

Figure 1.5 The network may be viewed as a set of planes passing through all of the computers within the network.

from other computers in the network, so there is not much benefit in defining a separate plane in the model.

Of course, the key interaction at each computer is that every other plane uses the Data Plane to transfer data between computers. Other interactions might include the Routing Plane telling the Data Plane in which direction to send data toward its destination, the Data Plane reporting to the Management Plane how much data is being transmitted, and the Management Plane instructing the Control Plane to provision some resources across the network.

In Figure 1.5, the vertical lines represent each network computer's presence in all of the planes. The dotted lines within each plane indicate the communication paths between the computers. In the Data Plane, the communication paths map to the physical connections of the network, but in the other planes the communications use *logical connections* and the underlying Data Plane to form arbitrary associations between the computers. The connectivity can be different in each plane.

The *Transport Plane* is sometimes shown as separate from the Data Plane. This allows a distinction between the physical transport network which may include fiber rings, repeaters, and so forth, and the components such as the Internet Protocol and data-link layer software that manage the data transfer between computers.

1.5 Packaging Data

In a full protocol stack the effect of all the protocols is quite significant. An application generates a stream of data to be sent to a remote application (for example, the contents of a file being sent across FTP) and hands it to the presentation layer for buffering, translation, and encoding into a common format. This "network-ready" stream of data is passed to the session layer for transmission. There is then a pause while the session layer sets up an end-to-end connection.

The session layer passes its connection requests and the application's data (usually prepended by a session protocol message header) to the transport layer as buffers or byte streams. The transport layer chops this data up into manageable pieces for transmission and prepends a header to give coordinates to the remote transport component, and then passes the data to the network layer. The network layer chops up the data again according to the capabilities of the underlying data link, making it ready for transmission, and adds its own header to give

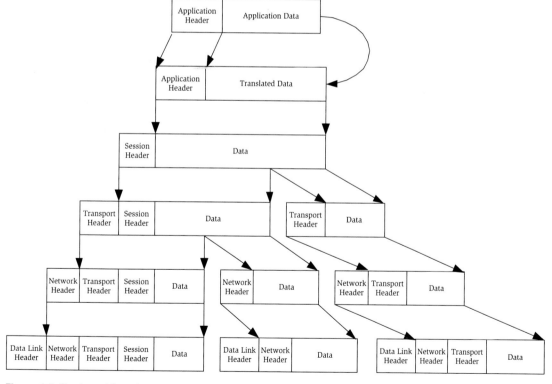

Figure 1.6 The imposition of message headers at each layer in the protocol stack can create a large protocol overhead relative to the amount of application data actually transferred.

hop-by-hop and end-to-end information before passing it to the data-link layer. The data-link layer prepends its own header and may also chop the data up further, if necessary. The data-link layer presents the data to the physical layer, which encodes it for transmission as a bit stream according to the physical medium.

The effect of this is that a considerable amount of protocol overhead may be needed to transmit some data end to end, as shown in Figure 1.6.

At the data-link layer, protocol and data messages are known as *frames*. At the network and transport layers they are called *packets*. At higher layers they are known simply as *messages*. The term *Protocol Data Unit* (PDU) can be applied at any level of the protocol stack, is synonymous with *message*, and may carry control information and/or data. One last term, *Maximum Transmission Unit* (MTU), is also applicable: it is usually applied only at the network and data-link layers, and refers to the largest packet or frame that can be supported by a link, network, or path through a network. An MTU at the network layer, therefore, describes the largest network layer packet that can be encapsulated into a data-link layer frame. The MTU at the data-link layer describes the largest frame that can be supported by the physical layer.

1.6 Data-Link Protocols

This book is about Internet protocols, and these can loosely be defined as those protocols that utilize IP, make IP possible, or are IP. This means that the operational details of the data-link layer protocols are beyond the scope of the book. However, the following short sections give an overview of some of the important data-link technologies and provide useful background to understanding some of the reasons behind the nature of IP and its related protocols. It is important to understand how IP is encapsulated as a payload of data-link protocols and also how data-link technologies are used to construct networks of differing topologies. This can help when decoding packet traces and can explain why IP packets are a particular size, why the Internet protocols have their specific behaviors, and how IP networks are constructed from a collection of networks built from different data-link technologies.

There is a very large number of data-link layer protocols. The five (Ethernet, Token Ring, Asynchronous Transfer Mode, Packet over SONET, and dial-up networking) introduced in the following sections constitute some of the most common for specific uses, but this does not invalidate other protocols such as Frame Relay, FDDI, X.25 and so on.

1.6.1 Ethernet

Ethernet is the most popular office or home networking system. The specifications include the physical and data-link layer, with the IEEE's 802.3 standard being the most common and most familiar. Normal data speeds are either 10 or 100

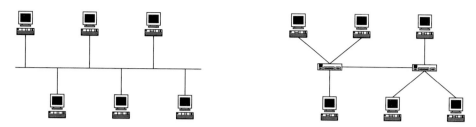

Figure 1.7 An Ethernet network showing logical connectivity and usual notations on the left, and actual physical connectivity using two hubs on the right.

megabits per second and are run over copper wires; more recent developments have led to gigabit and 10-gigabit Ethernet run over fiber.

Ethernet is a point-to-point or multi-access technology. A pair of nodes may be connected by a single cable, or multiple nodes may participate in a network. In the latter case, the network is typically drawn as on the left-hand side of Figure 1.7, with each of the nodes attached to a common cable. In practice, however, connectivity is provided through *hubs*, which allow multiple nodes to connect in. A hub is not much more than a cable splitter: each junction in the network on the left of Figure 1.7 could be a hub, but a more likely configuration is shown on the right side of the figure.

Ethernet messages, as shown in Figure 1.8, carry source and destination addresses. These are 6-byte (48-bit) MAC addresses that uniquely identify the sender and intended recipient. When a node wants to send an Ethernet message it simply formats it as shown and starts to send. This can cause a problem (called a *collision*) if more than one node sends at once. Collisions result in lost frames because the signal from the two sending nodes gets garbled. This is often given as a reason not to use Ethernet, but a node that wants to send can perform a simple test to see if anyone else is currently sending to considerably reduce the chance of a collision. This can be combined with a random delay if someone is sending so that the node comes back and tries again when there is silence on the wire. The risk of collisions can be further reduced by the use of Ethernet *switches* that replace hubs in Figure 1.7 and are configured to terminate one network and only forward frames into another network if the destination is not in the source network.

As can be seen in Figure 1.8, an Ethernet frame begins with seven bytes of preamble and a start delimiter byte containing the value $0 \times AB$. These fields together allow the receiver to synchronize and know that a data frame is coming. The first proper fields of the frame are the destination and source addresses.

In the 802.3 standard, the next field gives the length of the payload in bytes. The minimum frame length (not counting preamble and start delimiter) is 64 bytes, so the minimum payload length is 46 bytes. If fewer bytes need to be sent, the data is padded up to the full 46 bytes. The maximum payload length is

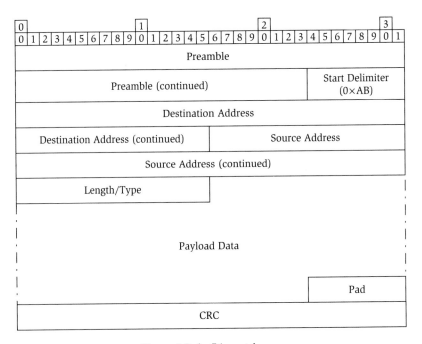

Figure 1.8 An Ethernet frame.

1,500 bytes. The 802.3 standard specifies that the payload data is encoded according to the 802.2 standard, so that the receiving node can determine the application to which the data should be delivered (see Section 1.6.6).

Ethernet differs from 802.3 in that 802.2 is not used to wrap the data. Instead, the length field is reinterpreted as a payload type indicator. Values greater than 1,500 (that is values that could not be misinterpreted as lengths) are used to indicate the type of the payload (for example, IP) so that the receiver can deliver the data to the right application. In this format, the payload length is still constrained to be between 46 and 1,500 bytes. The last 4 bytes of the message carry a *cyclic redundancy check* (CRC). The CRC is a simple checksum computed on the whole frame to protect against accidental corruption.

It is worth noting that the simplicity, stability, and relative cheapness of Ethernet lead not only to its popularity as a networking protocol but also to its use as a communications infrastructure in compound devices, allowing line cards and central processors to communicate across a bus or backplane.

1.6.2 Token Ring

Another popular local area networking protocol is Token Ring, for many years the principal local area networking technology promoted by IBM and documented by the IEEE as the 802.5 standard. As its name suggests, the

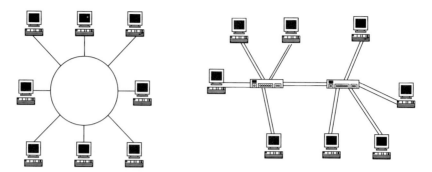

Figure 1.9 A Token Ring network showing logical connectivity and usual notation on the left, and actual physical connectivity using two MAUs on the right.

computers attached to a Token Ring are arranged in a ring, as shown on the left of Figure 1.9. A *token* passes around the ring from node to node, and when a node wishes to transmit it must wait until it has the token. This prevents the data collisions seen in Ethernet, but increases the amount of time that a node must wait before it can send data.

As with Ethernet, Token Ring is a multi-access network, meaning that any node on the ring can send to any other node on the ring without assistance from a third party. It also means that each node sees data for which it is not the intended recipient. In Ethernet, each node discards any frames that it receives for which it is not the destination, but in Token Ring the node must pass the frame further around the ring, and it is the responsibility of the source node to intercept frames that it sent to stop them from looping around the ring forever.

Of course, a major disadvantage of a ring is that it is easily broken by the failure of one node. To manage this, Token Rings are actually cabled as shown on the right-hand side of Figure 1.9. Each computer is on a twin cable spur from a Multiple Access Unit (MAU), making the network look like a hub-and-spoke configuration. The MAU is responsible for taking a frame and sending it to a node; the node examines the frame and passes it on along the ring by sending it back to the MAU on its second cable; the MAU then sends the frame to the next node on the ring. MAUs contain relays, and can detect when any node on the ring is down and can "heal" the break in the ring. MAUs may also be chained together (as shown in Figure 1.9) to increase the size of the ring.

The twin cables and the sophistication of MAUs make Token Rings notably more expensive to deploy than Ethernet.

Token Ring frames are not substantially different from Ethernet frames because they have to do the same things: identify source and destination, carry data, and check for corruption. There are three fields that comprise the token (shown in gray in Figure 1.10) when there is no data flowing; the token still circulates on the ring as a simple 3-byte frame (start delimiter, access control,

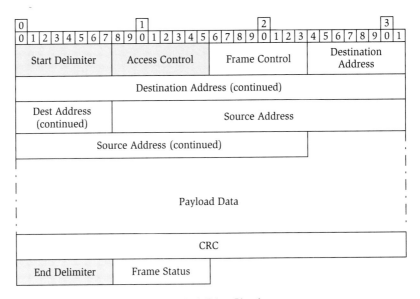

Figure 1.10 A Token Ring frame.

and end delimiter) so that any node that wishes to transmit can receive the token and start to send.

1.6.3 Asynchronous Transfer Mode

The Asynchronous Transfer Mode (ATM) is an end-to-end data transfer protocol. It is connection-oriented, meaning that data between two end points flows down the same path through transit nodes in a regulated way. The connections may be *switched virtual circuits* (SVCs), which are established using a control protocol such as Private Network to Node Interface (PNNI) or Multiprotocol Label Switching (MPLS, see Chapter 9). Alternatively, the connections may be preestablished through management or configuration actions, in which case they are known as *permanent virtual circuits* (PVCs).

The links in an ATM network are point-to-point, with each ATM switch responsible for terminating a link and either switching the ATM frames (called *cells*) on to the next link or delivering the data to the local application. ATM nodes are often shown connected together in a ring topology. This has nothing to do with the data-link or physical layer technologies but much to do with the economics and the applications that can be built. A full mesh of point-to-point links connecting each pair of nodes in a network would be very expensive since it requires a lot of fiber, as shown in the network on the left of Figure 1.11. Full internode connectivity can be achieved through a much more simple network since ATM can switch cells along different paths to reach the right destination. However, as shown in the network in the center of Figure 1.11, a simply

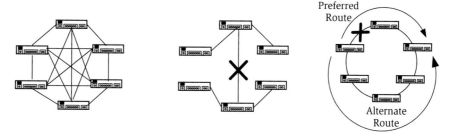

Figure 1.11 Full mesh topologies require a large amount of fiber, but simply-connected networks are vulnerable to single failures. ATM networks are often fibered as rings, providing cheap resilience.

connected network is vulnerable to a single point of failure. The network on the right-hand side of Figure 1.11 demonstrates how a ring topology provides an alternative route between all nodes, making it possible to survive single failures without requiring substantial additional fiber.

ATM cells are all always exactly 53 bytes long. The standard data-bearing cell, as shown in Figure 1.12, has 5 bytes of header information, leaving 48 bytes to carry data. This is a relatively high protocol overhead (15 percent) and is known by ATM's detractors as the *cell tax*. The header information indicates whether flow control is used on the connection (Generic Flow Control field), the destination address of the connection (Virtual Path Indicator and Virtual Channel Indicator), how the cell should be handled in case of congestion (the Cell Loss Priority field), and the Header Error Control field.

The last remaining field (the Payload Type field) indicates how the data is wrapped. For packet data, the payload type normally indicates ATM Adaptation Layer 5 (AAL5), meaning that no further wrapping of data is performed. Note that since the cells are always 53 bytes long, the data portion may need to be

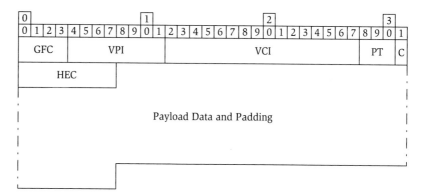

Figure 1.12 An ATM cell as used to carry simple data.

padded and it is the responsibility of the network level protocol (for example, IP) to supply enough information in length fields to determine where the data ends and where the padding starts.

1.6.4 Packet over SONET

Synchronous Optical Network and Synchronous Digital Hierarchy (SONET and SDH) are two closely related specifications for carrying data over fiber-optic links. Originally intended as ways of carrying multiple simultaneous voice connections (telephone calls) over the same fiber, SONET and SDH use a technique known as *time division multiplexing* (TDM) to divide the bandwidth of the fiber between the data streams so that they all get a fair share and so that they all deliver data at a steady rate (voice traffic is particularly sensitive to data that arrives in fits and starts).

SONET links (henceforth we will say *SONET* to cover both SONET and SDH) are very common because of their use for voice traffic, so it should be no surprise to discover that much of the Internet is built on SONET links. Data may be efficiently transported over SONET links using a technique called Packet over SONET (PoS) which is flexible and offers high bandwidth while still allowing voice data to be carried on the same fibers at the same time. PoS has been one of the factors enabling the rapid growth of the Internet because it makes use of existing infrastructure, allows high bandwidth, and offers relatively long (hundreds of kilometers) links. TDM makes it possible for several smaller data flows to be combined on a single fiber, allowing several data streams to share a single physical link. SONET traffic may be further combined using different wavelengths on a single fiber through *wave division multiplexing* (WDM) to increase the amount of traffic carried.

Figure 1.13 shows how a PoS network may be constructed with low-bandwidth links at the edges (OC3 is 155.5 Mbps which gives an effective data rate of 149.76 Mbps), medium bandwidth links approaching the core (OC48 is 2,488 Mbps), and a core trunk link (OC192 is 9,953 Mbps). Connections to desktop computers (that is, hosts) very rarely use PoS. Instead, they are connected to dedicated routers using local area network technologies such as Ethernet or Token Ring. The routers are responsible for directing traffic between areas of the network and for aggregating the low-bandwidth traffic onto high-bandwidth links.

The IETF has specified a way to carry data packets over SONET in RFC 2615. This technique uses a general data framing technique for point-to-point links called the Point-to-Point Protocol (PPP), which is itself described in RFC 1661. The PPP frame, shown in Figure 1.14, is a pretty simple encapsulation of the data, using a 2-byte field to identify the payload protocol so that the packet can be delivered to the right application. Before a PPP frame can be sent over a SONET link it is also encapsulated within a pair of start/end frame bytes

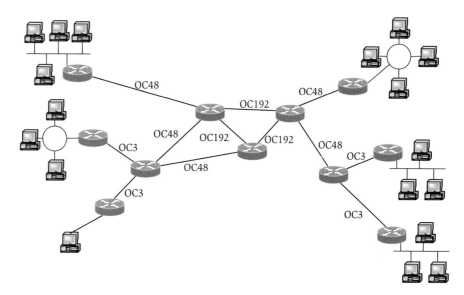

Figure 1.13 A PoS network.

0									1										2										3	
0	1	2	3	4	5	6	7	8	9	0	1	2	3	4	5	6	7	8	9	0	1	2	3	4	5	6	7	8	9	0	1

Flag	Address	Control	Protocol

Protocol (continued)

Payload Data

CRC	Flag

Figure 1.14 A PPP frame encapsulated between start and end frame bytes.

as described in RFC 1662 (shown in gray in Figure 1.14). This makes it easy for the receiver to spot when a frame starts and to distinguish data from an idle line.

The frame is now ready to be sent on the SONET link. Note that the overhead of control information to data for PoS is very low (about 3 percent for large packets) compared with the other chief technique for sending data over fiber-optic links (Asynchronous Transfer Mode [ATM]), where the overhead is as much as 15 percent of the data transmitted.

1.6.5 Dial-Up Networking

Dial-up networking is a familiar way of life for many people who use home computers to access the Internet. A dial-up connection is, of course, point-to-point with the user's computer making a direct connection to a dedicated computer at their Internet Service Provider (ISP). These connections run over normal phone lines and, just as in Packet over SONET, use the Point-to-Point Protocol with start and end flags to encapsulate the frames. Dial-up networking should be considered to cover communications over any link that is activated for the duration of a transaction and then is dropped again. This includes phone lines, ISDN, cable modems, and so on.

Dial-up networking poses particular challenges in IP and is discussed at greater length in Chapter 15.

1.6.6 802.2 and Logical Link Control

Within networking protocols such as Ethernet and Token Ring, it is often useful to employ a simple data wrapper to help determine the type and purpose of the data. The IEEE defines the 802.2 standard, which inserts three bytes (shown in gray in Figure 1.15) before the payload data. The Destination Service Access Point (DSAP) and Source Service Access Point (SSAP) are used to identify the service (the data application or network layer) to which the data should be delivered.

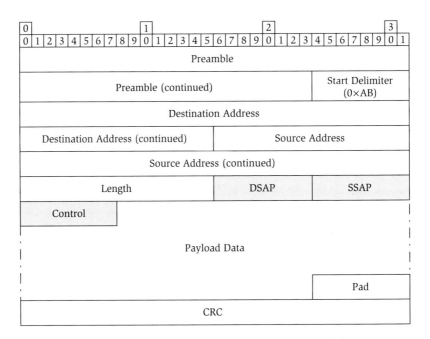

Figure 1.15 An 802.3 frame showing 802.2 data encapsulation.

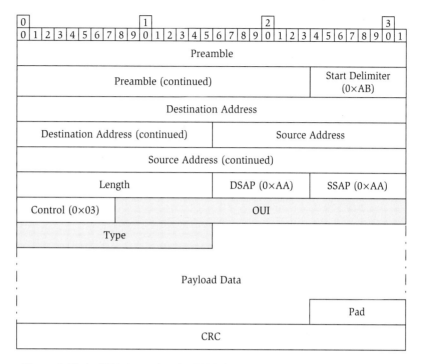

Figure 1.16 An 802.3 frame showing 802.2 data encapsulation with a SNAP header.

Another important encapsulation is the Subnetwork Access Protocol (SNAP) header. This may be used on its own or in association with an 802.2 header, as shown in Figure 1.16. When a SNAP header is used with 802.2, the DSAP and SSAP are set to $0\times AA$ and the control byte is set to 0×03 to indicate that the SNAP header follows.

The SNAP header fields are used to identify the payload protocol. The Organizationally Unique Identifier (OUI) provides a way to manage different sets of payload types. When the OUI is set to zero, the Type field shows the payload type using a set of values known as the *EtherTypes*. The EtherTypes are maintained by the IEEE and mirrored by IANA, and the EtherType value for IPv4 is 0×800.

The encapsulation syntaxes and any associated semantics are known as Logical Link Control (LLC) protocols.

1.7 The Protocols at a Glance

Figure 1.17 shows how the main protocols described in this book are related. Where one protocol is shown vertically above another, it means that the higher

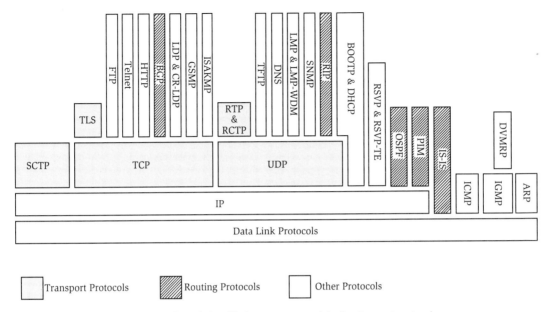

Figure 1.17 The relationship between some of the key Internet protocols.

protocol is used encapsulated in the lower. Thus, for example, FTP messages are sent encapsulated within TCP messages, which are themselves wrapped in IP messages.

The transport protocols are shown in gray. There is a clear demarcation between those protocols that use TCP as their transport protocol and those that use UDP. SCTP is a relatively new transport protocol and currently only a few new protocols utilize it, but there is no technical reason (apart from inertia caused by the existing deployed implementations) why protocols that use TCP should not use SCTP.

The routing protocols are shown with a cross-hatched background. Note that they are distributed across the figure and use different transport mechanisms. See also Figure 15.24 for a similar diagram showing how the IP telephony protocols fit together.

Further Reading

Background material to some of the key networking technologies can be found in the following books:

Ethernet Networking Clearly Explained, by Jan Harrington (1999). Academic Press.

Token Ring: Principles, Perspectives and Strategies, by Hans-George Gohring and
   Franz-Joachim Kauffels (1992). Addison-Wesley.

Broadband Networking: ATM, SDH and SONET by Mike Sexton and Andy Reid
   (1997). Artech House.

The IEEE 802 series of standards can be obtained from http://standards.
ieee.org/getieee802. Some of the pertinent standards are:

802—Overview and Architecture
802.2—Logical Link Control
802.3—CSMA/CD Access Method
802.5—Token Ring Access Method

The EtherType registry can be found at http://standards.ieee.org/regauth/
ethertype/ and similar information is maintained by IANA at http://www.iana.org.

The following IETF RFCs also provide important information.

RFC 1661—The Point-to-Point Protocol (PPP)
RFC 1662—PPP in HDLC-like Framing
RFC 2615—PPP over SONET/SDH

Chapter 2
The Internet Protocol

This chapter describes the Internet Protocol (IP), which is the fundamental building block for all control and data exchanges across and within the Internet. There is a chicken-and-egg definition that describes the Internet as the collection of all networked computers that interoperate using IP, and IP as the protocol that facilitates communication between computers within the Internet. IP and the Internet are so closely woven that the ordering of the definition doesn't really matter, but it is indubitable that the Internet is deeply dependent on the definition and function of IP. IP version four (IPv4) is the most common version of the protocol in use, and this chapter focuses on that version.

This chapter includes a brief section that examines the motivation for IP before moving on to examine the format of IPv4 messages, the meanings of the standard fields that they carry, and the checksum algorithm used to safeguard individual messages against accidental corruption. The way data is packaged into individual messages is explained.

Fundamental to the operation of IP are the addresses that are used to identify the senders and receivers of individual messages. IPv4 addressing is the subject of Section 2.3. There is information on how the address space is subdivided for ease of management and routing.

Section 2.4 describes the basic operation of IP. It shows how messages are delivered based on the destination IP addresses and introduces three protocols designed to help discover and manage IP addresses within a network: the Address Resolution Protocol (ARP), the Bootstrap Protocol (BOOTP), and the Dynamic Host Configuration Protocol (DHCP).

IP also defines some optional fields that may be included in IP messages as needed. These fields manage a set of advanced features that are not used in standard operation but may be added to data flows to enhance the function provided to the applications that are using IP to transfer their data. Section 2.5 describes some of the common IP options, including those to manage and control the route taken by an IP message as it traverses the network.

Finally, there is a section explaining the Internet Control Message Protocol (ICMP). ICMP is a separate protocol and is actually carried as a payload by IP. However, ICMP is fundamental to the operation of IP networks and is so closely related to IP that it is not possible to operate hosts within an IP network without supporting ICMP.

2.1 Choosing to Use IP

It is pretty central to the success of this book that IP is chosen as the core network protocol for your network. Everything else in this book depends on that choice since all of the many protocols described utilize IP to carry their messages, use IP addresses to identify nodes and links, and assume that data is being carried using IP.

Fortunately, IP has already been chosen as the network protocol for the Internet and we don't have to decide for ourselves whether to use IP. If we want to play in the Internet we must use IP. It is, however, worth examining some of the motivation behind IP to discover why it was developed, what problems it solves, and why it continues to be central to the Internet.

2.1.1 Connecting Across Network Types

Hosts on a network use the data-link layer to move data between them in *frames* across the physical network. Each type of physical network has a different data-link layer protocol (Ethernet, Token Ring, ATM, etc.) responsible for delivering the data. Each of these protocols has different formats for its frames and addresses (as described in the previous chapter), and these formats are not interchangeable. That is, you cannot pick up a frame from a Token Ring network and drop it onto an Ethernet—it doesn't belong there and will not work.

As long as all hosts are attached to the same physical medium there is no issue, but as we begin to construct networks from heterogeneous physical network types we must install special points of connection that convert from one data-link protocol to another. There are some issues that immediately raise their heads when we try to do this.

First, the addressing schemes on the two connected networks are different. When a frame with an Ethernet address is moved to a Token Ring the addresses must be mapped. As the number of network types increases, this addressing mapping function gets ever more complicated. A simpler solution is to provide an overarching addressing scheme that requires every node to implement just one address mapping function between the local physical addressing and the systemwide IP addressing.

The next problem is that the different networks do not all support the same size data frame. To demonstrate this in an extreme case, if a Token Ring network sends frames to an X.25 network the interconnecting node may receive a frame of 17,756 bytes and not be able to present it to the X.25 network because that can only support frames of 512 bytes. What is needed is a higher-level protocol that can be invoked to fragment the data into smaller pieces.

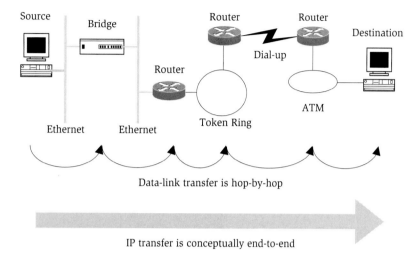

Figure 2.1 IP provides a uniform network layer protocol to operate over any collection of data-link protocols and physical links.

Many physical link types and data-link layer protocols are fundamentally unreliable—that is, they may drop frames without warning. Some are capable of detecting and reporting errors, but few can recover from such problems and retransmit the lost data such that the higher-layer protocols (that is, the transport and application protocols that use the links) are protected from knowledge of the problems. This means that a protocol must be run at a higher level to reliably detect and report problems. IP does this, but does not attempt to recover from problems—this function is devolved further up the stack to become the responsibility of transport or application layer protocols.

Ultimately, we need a single protocol that spans multiple physical network types to deliver data in a uniform way for the higher-level protocols. The path taken by the data is not important to the higher-level protocols (although they may wish to control the path in some way) and individual pieces of data are free to find their different ways across the network as resources are available for their transmission.

IP provides all of these functions, as shown in Figure 2.1.

2.2   IPv4

The Internet Protocol went through several revisions before it stabilized at version four. IPv4 is now ubiquitous, although it should be noted that version six of the protocol (IPv6; see Chapter 4) is gaining support in certain quarters.

IP is a protocol for universal data delivery across all network types. Data is packaged into *datagrams* that comprise some control information and the *payload data* to be delivered. (Datagram is a nice word invented to convey that this is a record containing some data, and with overtones from telegram and aerogram it gives a good impression that the data is being sent from one place to another.) Datagrams are *connectionless* because each is sent on its own and may find its own way across the network independent of the other datagrams. Each datagram may take a different route through the network.

Note a very subtle difference between a packet and a datagram: A packet is any protocol message at the network or transport layer, and a datagram is any connectionless protocol message at any protocol layer, but usually at the network, transport, or session layers. Thus, in IPv4, which is a connectionless protocol, the words *packet* and *datagram* may be used interchangeably.

The control information in an IP datagram is necessary to identify the sender and recipient of the data and to manage the datagram while it is in transit. The control information is grouped together at the start of the datagram in a *header*. It is useful to place the header at the start of the datagram to enable a computer to access it easily without having to search through the entire datagram. All of the datagram headers are formatted in the same way so that a program processing the datagrams can access the information it needs with the minimum of fuss.

The remainder of this section is dedicated to a description of the IPv4 header and to details of how IPv4 carries data within datagrams.

---

data \'dā-tə, 'dat-, 'dät-\ *n pl but sing or pl in constr* [pl. of *datum* L, fr. neut. of *datus*]: factual information (as measurement or statistics) used as a basis for reasoning, discussion, or calculation.
-gram \₁gram\ *n comb form* [L. –gramma, fr. Gk., fr. *gramma*]: drawing: writing: record < chrono*gram* > < tele*gram* > < aero*gram* >

2.2.1 IP Datagram Formats

Each IP datagram begins with a common header. This is shown as a byte-by-byte, bit-by-bit structure in Figure 2.2. The first nibble shows the protocol version (version four indicates IPv4; a value of 6 would be used for IPv6—see Chapter 4). The next nibble gives the length of the header, and because there are only 4 bits available in the length field and we need to be able to have a header length of more than 15, the length is counted in units of 4-byte words. The length field usually contains the value 5 because the count includes all bytes of the header (that is, 20), but may be greater if IP options are included in the header (see Section 2.5). The Type of Service byte is used to classify the datagram for prioritization, use of network resources, and routing within the network; this important function is described further in Section 2.4.4. Next comes a 2-byte field that gives the length of the entire datagram. The length of the data carried by the datagram can be calculated by subtracting the header length from the

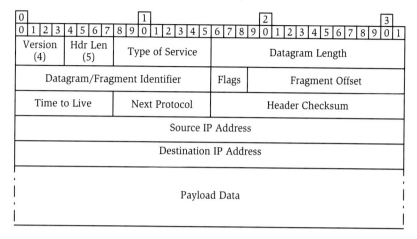

Figure 2.2 The IP datagram header.

length of the entire datagram. Obviously, this places a limit on the amount of data carried by one IP datagram to 65,535 bytes less the size of the header.

The next three fields are concerned with how a datagram is handled if, part way across the network, it reaches a hop that must break the datagram up into smaller pieces to forward it. This process is called *fragmentation* and is covered in the next section. The fields give an identifier for the original datagram so that all fragments can be grouped together, flags for the control of the fragmentation process, and an offset within the original datagram of the start of the fragment.

The next field is called Time to Live (TTL). It is used to prevent datagrams from being forwarded around the network indefinitely through a process called *looping*, as shown in Figure 2.3. The original intent of the TTL was to measure the number of seconds that a datagram was allowed to live in the network, but this quickly became impractical because each node typically forwards a datagram within 1 second of receiving it and there is no way to measure how long a packet took to be transmitted between nodes. So, instead, the TTL is used as a count of the number of hops the datagram may traverse before it is timed out. Each node decrements the TTL before it forwards the packet and, to quote RFC 791, "If the time to live reaches zero before the Internet datagram reaches its destination, the Internet datagram is destroyed." This is generally interpreted as meaning that a datagram may not be transmitted with a TTL of zero. Implementations vary as to whether they decrement the TTL for the first hop from the source. This is important since it controls the meaning of the value 1 in the TTL when a datagram is created; it may mean that the packet may traverse just one hop, or it may mean that the packet is only available for local delivery to another application on the source node (see Section 2.4 for a description of local delivery). In Figure 2.3 a datagram is created with a TTL of 7 and is forwarded through node A to node B. Node B is misconfigured

and, instead of passing the datagram to the destination, it forwards it to node C—
a forwarding loop exists. When the datagram arrives at node C for the second
time, node C prepares to forward it to node A. But when it decrements the TTL
it sees that the value has gone to zero so it discards the packet.

Many higher-layer protocols recommend initial values for the TTL field.
These recommendations are based on some understanding of the scope of the
higher-layer protocol, such as whether it is intended to operate between adjacent
nodes or is supposed to span the entire network. For example, the Transmission
Control Protocol (TCP) described in Section 7.3 recommends a relatively high
starting value of 60 since the protocol is used to carry data between nodes that
may be situated on the extreme edges of the Internet.

After the TTL, the IP header carries a protocol identifier that tells the receiving node what protocol is carried in the payload. This is important information
as it tells the receiver to which application or software component the datagram
should be delivered. Table 2.1 lists the protocol identifiers of some of the common
protocols. Note that there are only 256 values that can be defined here and,
although obviously when IP was invented this was thought to be plenty, the list
of protocols defined and maintained by the Internet Assigned Numbers Authority

Table 2.1 Some Common IP Payload Protocols and Their Identifiers

Protocol Number	Protocol	RFC	Reference
1	Internet Control Message Protocol (ICMP)	RFC 792	2.6
2	Internet Group Message Protocol (IGMP)	RFC 1112	3.3
4	IP encapsulated within IP	RFC 2003	15.1.3
6	Transmission Control Protocol (TCP)	RFC 793	7.3
17	User Datagram Protocol (UDP)	RFC 768	7.2
46	Resource Reservation Protocol (RSVP)	RFC 2205	6.4
47	General Routing Encapsulation (GRE)	RFC 2784	15.1.2
89	Open Shortest Path First (OSPF)	RFC 2328	5.5
124	OSI IS-IS Intradomain Routing Protocol (IS-IS)	RFC 1142	5.6
132	Stream Control Transmission Protocol (SCTP)	RFC 2960	7.4

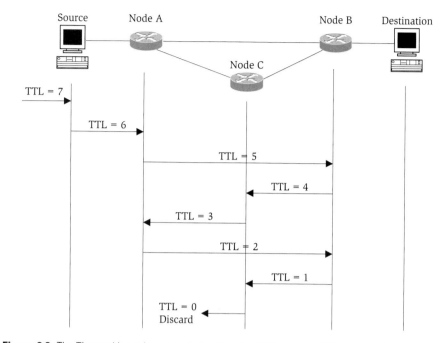

Figure 2.3 The Time to Live value controls the life of an IP datagram within a network and prevents packets from looping forever.

(IANA) at their Web site (http://www.iana.org/assignments/protocol-numbers) has grown to 135, giving rise to serious concerns that they may soon run out of identifiers for protocols that can be carried by IP. The current solution to this is to make new protocols use a transport protocol such as UDP (see Chapter 7), which has the facility to carry far more client protocols.

After the protocol identifier comes a 2-byte field that carries the Header Checksum used to verify that the whole of the header has been received without any accidental corruption. The checksum processing is described in greater length in Section 2.2.3.

Finally, within the standard IP header come two address fields to identify the sender of the message and its intended destination. IP addresses are 4-byte quantities that are usually broken out and expressed as 4-decimal digits with dots between them. Thus, the IP address field carrying the hexadecimal number 0xac181004 would be represented as 172.24.16.4. The choice of addresses for nodes within the network is not a random free-for-all because structure is needed both to ensure that no two nodes have the same address and to enable the address to be used for directing the datagram as it passes through the network. Section 2.3 expands upon IP addressing, and the whole of Chapter 5 is dedicated to routing protocols that make it possible for transit nodes to work out which way to forward datagrams based on the destination address they carry.

After the end of the 20-byte standard header there may be some IP options. IP options are used to add selective control to datagrams and are optional. Section 2.5 describes some of the common IP options. Finally, there is the payload data that IP is carrying across the network.

2.2.2 Data and Fragmentation

Chapter 1 examined some of the different network technologies that exist. Each has different characteristics that affect the way IP is used. For example, each has its own Protocol Data Unit (PDU) maximum size (the largest block of data that can be transmitted in one shot using the network technology). For X.25 this value is 576 bytes, for Ethernet it is 1,500 bytes, for FDDI it is 4,352 bytes, and a 16 Mbps Token Ring can manage a PDU of up to 17,756 bytes. IP itself allows a datagram of up to 65,535 bytes, as we have already seen, but some action has to be taken if the amount of data presented to the IP layer for transmission is greater than the maximum PDU supported by the network. Some network technologies support breaking the packet up into smaller pieces and reassembling it at the destination. ATM is an example of this, which is a good thing since the ATM cell allows for only 48 bytes of data—if IP datagrams had to be made to fit inside ATM cells there would only be 28 bytes of data in each datagram!

Other technologies, however, cannot segment and reassemble data, so there is a need for IP to limit the size of packets that are presented to the network. Figure 2.4 shows how data presented to IP by the application may be

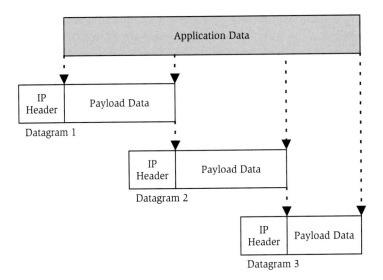

Figure 2.4 Application data may be segmented into separate datagrams.

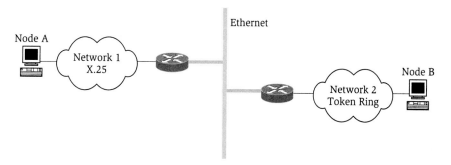

Figure 2.5 The need for fragmentation.

chopped up and transmitted in a series of IP datagrams. Each datagram is assigned a unique Datagram Identifier which is placed in the IP header. This field might have been used to allow the datagrams to be reordered or to detect lost datagrams, and so it would not be unreasonable to make the value increase by one for each datagram, but this is not a requirement in RFC 791 and must not be assumed. The real purpose of this field comes into play if a datagram must be fragmented part-way across the network.

Some applications may not be willing to have their data chopped up into separate datagrams—it may cause them a problem if they have to wait for all of the datagrams in a sequence to arrive before they can start to process the first one. This may be more of an issue for control protocols than it is for data transfer, since a control message must be processed in its entirety but data can simply be written to the output device as it arrives. Applications that don't want their messages broken up need to agree with the IP layer what the maximum PDU is for the attached network, and must present the data in lumps that are small enough to be carried within one IP datagram (taking into account the bytes needed for the IP header).

Consider the network shown in Figure 2.5. Here Node A is attached to an X.25 network where the maximum PDU is 576 bytes. When Node A sends packets to Node B it makes sure that no packet is larger than 512 bytes. As the packet progresses, it traverses the X.25 network and encounters an Ethernet. Since the maximum PDU for the Ethernet is 1,500 bytes, the IP datagrams can simply be forwarded. When they transition to the Token Ring where the maximum PDU is 17,756 bytes, the packets can continue to be forwarded to the destination.

However, suppose Node B wishes to send a reply to Node A. Since Node B is attached to the Token Ring it may prepare IP datagrams up to 17,756 bytes long. These are forwarded toward Node A until they encounter the Ethernet, where they are too large. For the datagram to be forwarded, it must be fragmented into pieces that are no larger than 1,500 bytes. Again, when the fragments reach the X.25 network they must be fragmented still further to be carried across the network. The process of fragmentation is illustrated in Figure 2.6.

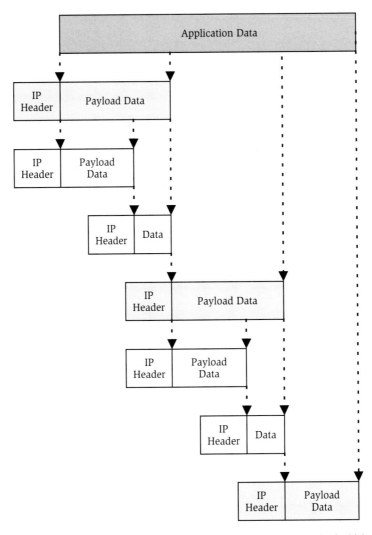

Figure 2.6 Application data may be segmented into separate datagrams, each of which may later require further fragmentation.

When data is presented to IP by an application it is broken up to be carried in separate datagrams, as already described. When the datagrams reach a network where the maximum PDU is smaller than the datagram size, they are fragmented into smaller datagrams. The IP header of each of the fragments is copied from the original datagram so that the TTL, source, and destination are identical. The datagram identifier of each of the fragments is the same so that all fragments of the original datagram can be easily identified.

Fragment reassembly is necessary at the destination. Each of the fragments must be collected and assembled into a single data stream to be passed to the application as if the whole original datagram had been received intact. This should simply be a matter of concatenating the data from the fragments, but there are two issues caused by the fact that datagrams might arrive out of order because of different paths or processing through the network. We need to know where each fragment fits in the original datagram. This is achieved by using the Fragment Offset field in the IP header. Note that the offset field is only 13 bits long, so it can't be used as a simple offset count since the datagram itself may be 2^{16} bytes long. This is handled by insisting that fragmentation may only occur on 8-byte boundaries. There are 2^{13} (that is 8,191) possible values here, and $2^{13} * 8 = 2^{16}$ so all of the data is covered. If fragmentation of the data into blocks of less than 8 bytes were required, performance would be so bad that we might as well give up anyway.

So, as fragments arrive they can be ordered and the data can be reassembled. Implementations typically run a timer when the first fragment in a series arrives so that sequences that never complete (because a datagram was lost in the network) are not stored forever. A reasonable approach would be to use the remaining TTL measured in seconds to define the lifetime of the fragments pending reassembly, giving a maximum life of up to 4 ½ minutes, but many implementations don't use this and actually run timers of around 15 seconds, as recommended by RFC 791. Many applications do not support receipt of out-of-order fragments and will reject the whole datagram if this happens, but they still use the fragment Offset and the Datagram Length to reassemble fragments and to detect when fragments are out of order. Failed reassembly results in discarding of the entire original datagram.

The second issue is determining the end of the original datagram. Initially, this was obvious because the Datagram Length less the Header Length indicated the size of the Payload Data, but each fragment must carry its own length. When the fragments are reassembled there is no way of knowing when to stop. We could wait for the receipt of a fragment with a different Datagram Identifier, but this would not help us if a fragment was lost or arrived out of order. The problem is solved by using the third bit of the Flag field to indicate when there are more fragments—the More Fragments (MF) bit is set to 1 whenever there is another fragment coming and to zero on the last fragment. Note that the rule for fragmenting existing fragments is that if the original datagram has the MF bit set to 1, then all resultant fragments must also have this bit set to 1. If the original fragment has the bit set to zero, then all fragments except the last must have the MF bit set to 1 (the last must retain the zero value).

Unfragmented datagrams carry a Fragment Offset of zero and the MF bit set to zero. Note that IP uses lazy reassembly of fragments. That is, reassembly is only done at the destination node and not at transit nodes within the network even if the datagrams are passing from a network with small PDUs to one that can handle larger PDUs. This is a pragmatic reduction in processing since it is unclear to a transit node that further fragmentation will not be needed further along the path. It also helps to reduce the buffer space that would be needed on transit nodes to store and reassemble fragments.

An application may want to prevent fragmentation within the network. This is particularly useful if it is known that the receiving node does not have the ability or resources to handle reassembly, and is achieved by setting the second bit of the Flags field in the IP header (that first bit is reserved and should be set to zero, and the third bit is the MF bit already described). The Don't Fragment (DF) bit is zero by default, allowing fragmentation, and is set to 1 to prevent fragmentation. A transit node that receives a datagram with the DF bit set to 1 must not fragment the datagram, and may choose a route that does not require fragmentation of the packet or must otherwise discard any datagram that cannot be forwarded because of its size.

Alternatively, fragmentation can be avoided by discovering the *Maximum Transmission Unit* (MTU) between the source and destination. This is the lowest maximum PDU on all the links between the source and destination. Some higher-level protocols attempt to discover this value through information exchanges between the nodes along the route. They then use this information to choose specific routes or to present the data to IP in small enough chunks that will never need to be fragmented.

2.2.3 Choosing to Detect Errors

Whenever messages are transmitted between computers they are at risk of corruption. Electrical systems, in particular, are subject to bursts of static that may alter the data before it reaches its destination. If the distortion is large, the receiver will not be able to understand the message and will discard it, but the risk is that the corruption is only small so that the message is misunderstood but treated as legal. IP needs a way to protect itself against corrupt messages so that they may be discarded or responded to with an error message.

There are several options to safeguard messages sent between computers. The first is to place *guard bytes* within the message. These bytes contain a well-known pattern and can be checked by the receiver. This approach is fine for catching major corruptions, but works only if the guard bytes themselves are damaged—if the error is in any other part of the message, no problem will be detected.

A better approach is to perform some form of processing on all of the bytes in the message and include the answer in the transmitted message. The receiver can perform the same processing and verify that no corruption has occurred. Such processing needs to be low cost if it is not to affect the throughput of data. The simplest method is to sum the values of the bytes, discarding overflow, and to transmit the total to the receiver, which can repeat the sum. This technique is vulnerable on two counts. First, it is sensitive only within the size of the field used to carry the sum. That is, if a 1-byte field is used, there are only

Table 2.2 To Perform the IP Checksum, a Stream of Bytes Is Broken into
16-Bit Integers

Byte Stream	Sequence of Integers
A, B, C, D, ..., W, X, Y, Z	$[A,B] + [C,D] + \cdots + [W,X] + [Y, Z]$
A, B, C, D, ..., W, X, Y	$[A,B] + [C,D] + \cdots + [W,X] + [Y, 0]$

256 possible values of the sum and so there is a relatively high chance that data
corruptions will result in the same sum being generated. Second, such a simple
sum is also exposed to self-canceling errors, such as, a corruption that adds one
to the value of one byte and subtracts one from the value of another byte.

A slight improvement to the simple sum is achieved using the *one's complement checksum* that has been chosen as the standard for IP. In this case, overflows
(that is, results that exceed the size of the field used to carry the sum within the
protocol) are "wrapped" and cause one to be added to the total.

In IP, the checksum is applied to the IP header only. The transport and
application protocols are responsible for protecting their own data. This has the
benefit of reducing the amount of checksum processing that must be done at
each step through the network. It places the responsibility for detection and
handling of errors firmly with the protocol layer that is directly handling a
specific part of the data. If that layer does not need or choose to use any error
detection, then no additional processing is performed by the lower layers.

The standard IP checksum is performed on a stream of bytes by breaking
them up into 16-bit integers. That is, the pair of bytes (a, b) is converted into
the integer $256*a+b$, which is represented by the notation [a, b]. Table 2.2
shows how byte streams are broken into integers depending on whether there is
an even or an odd number of bytes.

These integers are simply added together using 1's complement addition
to form a 16-bit answer. The answer is logically reversed (that is, the 1's
complement of the sum is taken), and this is the checksum. One's complement
addition is the process of adding two numbers together and adding one to the
result if there is an overflow (that is, if the sum is greater than 65,535). The consequence of this is that if the checksum value is added using 1's complement
addition to the 1's complement sum of the other integers, the answer is all
ones (0xffff). Figure 2.7 works a trivial example to show how this operates.

Now, for the checksum to be of any use, it has to be transmitted with the
data. There is a field in the IP header to carry the checksum. When the checksum is computed on the header, this field is set to zero so that it has no effect
on the computed checksum. The computed value is inserted into the header
just before it is transmitted. When the IP packet is received, the checksum is
calculated across the whole header and the result is compared with 0xffff to see
whether the header has arrive uncorrupted.

Consider the byte stream (0x91, 0xa3, 0x82, 0x11)

This is treated as two integers 0x91a3 and 0x8211

$\quad$ 0x91a3 + 0x8211 = 0x113b4

So the one's complement sum is 0x13b4 + 0x01 = 0x13b5

Now 0x13b5 = 0b0001001110110101

So the one's complement of 0x1365, is 0b1110110001001010 = 0xec4a

Thus the checksum is 0xec4a

See that the one's complement sum of the integers and the checksum is as follows:

$\quad$ 0xec4a + 0x91a3 + 0x8211 = 0x17ded + 0x8211

$$= \text{0x7ded} + \text{0x01} + \text{0x8211}$$

$$= \text{0xffff}$$

Figure 2.7 A simple example of the 1's complement checksum and the way it can be checked to show no accidental corruption.

Note that some implementations choose to process a received header by copying out the received checksum, setting the field to zero in the packet, computing the checksum, and comparing the answer with the saved value. There is no difference in the efficacy of this processing.

One of the benefits of this checksum algorithm is that it does not matter where in the sequence the checksum value itself is placed. It doesn't even matter if the checksum field starts on an odd or an even byte boundary. There are even some neat tricks that can be played on machines on which the native integer size is four bytes (32 bits) to optimize checksum calculations for native processing. Essentially, the one's complement sum can be computed using 32-bit integers and the final result is then broken into two 16-bit integers, which are summed.

A further benefit is that it is possible to handle modifications to the IP header without having to recompute the entire checksum. This is particularly useful in IP as the packet is passed from node to node and the TTL field is decremented. It would be relatively expensive to recompute the entire checksum each time, but knowing that the TTL field value has decreased by one and knowing that the field is placed in the high byte of a 16-bit integer, the checksum can be decremented by 0x0100 (taking care of underflow by subtracting 0x0001). Some implementations may prefer to stick to 1's complement addition, in which case the minus 0x0100 is first represented as 0xff00 and then added.

This checksum processing effectively protects the header against most random corruptions. There are some situations that are not caught. For example, if a bit that was zero in one 16-bit integer is corrupted to one, and the same bit in another 16-bit integer that was one is corrupted to zero, the problem will not be detected. It is statistically relatively unlikely that such an event will occur.

And what happens if an error is detected? Well, IP is built on the assumption that it is an unreliable delivery protocol, and that datagrams may be lost. Bearing this in mind, it is acceptable for a node that detects an error to silently discard a packet. Transit nodes might not detect errors because they can simply use the checksum update rules when modifying the TTL to forward a datagram, so it may be that checksum errors are not noticed until the datagram reaches the egress. But wherever the problem is first noticed it will be helpful to distinguish discarded packets from packet loss, and to categorize the reasons for discarding packets (contrasting checksum errors with TTL expiration). Nodes typically retain counters of received and transmitted packets and also count errors by category, but more useful is to notify the sender of the problem so that it can take precautions or actions to avoid the problem. The Internet Control Message Protocol (ICMP) described in Section 2.6 can be used to return notifications when packets are discarded.

2.3   IPv4 Addressing

Every node in an IP network is assigned one or more IP addresses. These addresses are unique to the node within the context of the network and allow the source and destination of packets to be clearly identified. The destination addresses on packets tell nodes within the network where the packets are headed and enable them to forward the packets toward their destinations.

2.3.1 Address Spaces and Formats

All IPv4 addresses are four bytes long (see Figure 2.2). This means that they are not large enough to hold common data-link layer addresses, which are often six bytes and must be assigned from a different address space. The four bytes of the address are usually presented in a *dotted decimal* notation which is easy for a human operator to read and remember. Table 2.3 illustrates this for a few sample addresses.

Table 2.3 IPv4 Addresses Presented in Dotted Decimal Format

Hexadecimal IP Address	Dotted Decimal Representation
0x7f000001	127.0.0.1
0x8a5817bf	138.88.23.191
0xc0a80a64	192.168.10.100

Some structure is applied to IPv4 addresses, as we shall see in subsequent sections, and in that context the bits of the address are all significant, with the leftmost bit carrying the most significance just as it would if the address were a number.

IP addresses are assigned through national registries, each of which has been delegated the responsibility for a subset of all the available addresses by the overseeing body, the Internet Corporation for Assigned Names and Numbers (ICANN). This function is critical to the correct operation of the Internet because if there were two nodes with the same IP address attached to the Internet they would receive each other's datagrams and general chaos would ensue.

To that extent, an IP address is a sufficiently unique identifier to precisely point to a single node. But just as people have aliases and family nicknames, so a single node may have multiple addresses and some of these addresses may be unique only within limited contexts. For example, a node may have an IP address by which it is known across the whole Internet, but use another address within its local network. If the node were to publicize its local address, it would discover that many other nodes in the wider Internet are also using the same alias within their local networks.

The address space 0.0.0.0 to 255.255.255.255 is broken up into bands or *classes* of address. The idea is to designate any network as belonging to a particular class determined by the number of nodes in the network. The network is then allocated an address range from the class and can administratively manage the addresses for its nodes. Table 2.4 shows the five address classes. The table shows the range of addresses from which class ranges will be allocated, an example class range, the number of ranges within the class (that is, the number of networks that can exist within the class), and the number of addresses within a class range (that is, the number of nodes that can participate in a network that belongs to the class). Examination of the first byte of an IP address can tell us to which class it belongs.

Table 2.4 IPv4 Address Classes

Class	Address Range	Example Class Range	Networks in Class	Hosts in Network
A	0.0.0.0 to 127.255.255.255	100.0.0.1 to 100.255.255.254	126	16,777,214
B	128.0.0.0 to 191.255.255.255	181.23.0.1 to 181.23.255.254	16,384	65,534
C	192.0.0.0 to 223.255.255.255	192.168.20.1 to 192.168.20.254	2,097,152	254
D	224.0.0.0 to 239.255.255.255	Addresses reserved for multicast (see Chapter 3)		
E	240.0.0.0 to 247.255.255.255.255	Reserved for future use		

2.3.2 Broadcast Addresses

Some addresses have special meaning. The addresses 0.0.0.0 and 255.255.255.255 may not be assigned to a host. In fact, within any address class range the equivalent addresses with all zeros or all ones in the bits that are available for modification are not allowed. So, for example, the Class C address range shown in Table 2.4 runs from 192.168.20.1 to 192.168.20.254, excluding 192.168.20.0 and 192.168.20.255. The "dot zero" address is used as a shorthand for the range of addresses within a class so that the Class C address range in Table 2.4 can be expressed as 192.168.20.0.

The addresses ending in 255 are designated as broadcast addresses. The broadcast address for the Class C range 192.168.20.0 is 192.168.20.255. When a packet is sent to a broadcast address it is delivered to every host within the network, that is, every host that belongs to the address class range. The broadcast address is a wild card.

Broadcasts have very specific uses that are advantageous when one host needs to communicate with all other hosts. A particular use can be seen in ICMP in Section 2.6, where a host needs to find any routers on its network and so issues a broadcast query to all stations on the network asking them to reply if they are routers. On the other hand, broadcast traffic must be used with caution because it can easily gum up a network.

2.3.3 Address Masks, Prefixes, and Subnetworks

A useful way to determine whether an address belongs to a particular network is to perform a logical AND with a *netmask*. Consider again the example Class C network from Table 2.4 that uses the addresses in the range 192.168.20.1 to 192.168.20.254. To determine whether an address is a member of this network we simply AND it with the value 255.255.255.0 and compare the answer with 192.168.20.0. So in Figure 2.8, 192.168.20.99 is a member of the network, but 192.169.20.99 is not.

The netmask value chosen is based on the class of the address group, that is, the number of trailing bits that are open for use within the network. In this case, the Class C case, the last eight bits do not factor into the decision as to whether the address belongs to the network and are available for distinguishing the nodes within the network.

With this knowledge, the network address can be represented as 192.168.20.0/24, where the number after the forward slash is a count of the

> 192.168.20.99 & 255.255.255.0 = 192.168.20.0
>
> 192.169.20.99 & 255.255.255.0 = 192.169.20.0

Figure 2.8 Use of the netmask to determine whether an address belongs in a network.

number of bits in the address that define the network. In other words, it is a count of the number of ones set in the netmask. The network is said to have a *slash 24* address. The part of the address that is common to all of the nodes in the network is called the *prefix* and the number after the slash gives the *prefix length*.

This may all seem rather academic because we already know from the first byte of the address which class it falls into and so what the prefix length is. Class A addresses are slash 8 addresses, Class B addresses are slash 16s, and Class C gives us slash 24 addresses. But the segmentation of the IPv4 address space doesn't stop here, because there is an administrative need to break the address space up into smaller chunks within each of the address groups. This process is called *subnetting*.

Consider an Internet Service Provider (ISP) that applies to its local IP addressing authority for a block of addresses. It doesn't expect to have many customers, so it asks for three Class C address groups (a total of 762 hosts). As customers sign up with the ISP it needs to allocate these addresses to the hosts in the customers' networks. Obviously, if it allocates each customer a whole Class C address group it will run out of addresses after just three customers. This wastes addresses if each customer has only a few hosts.

A more optimal way for the ISP to allocate its addresses is to break its address groups into smaller groups, one for each subnetwork that it manages. This can be done in a structured way, as shown in Table 2.5, although some care has to be taken that the blocks of addresses carved out in this way fit together correctly without leaving any unused addresses.

Table 2.5 An Example of Subnetting an Address Group

Address Range	Subnet	Subnet Mask	Number of Hosts
192.168.20.1 to 192.168.20.14	192.168.20.0/28	255.255.255.240	14
192.168.20.17 to 192.168.20.30	192.168.20.16/28	255.255.255.240	14
192.168.20.33 to 192.168.20.40	192.168.20.32/30	255.255.255.252	6
192.168.20.41 to 192.168.20.48	192.168.20.40/30	255.255.255.252	6
192.168.20.49 to 192.168.20.112	192.168.20.48/26	255.255.255.192	62

In each subnet, we can start numbering the hosts from 1 upwards. So, for example, in the subnet represented by the second row in Table 2.5, the first host has the address 192.168.20.16+1, that is, 192.168.20.17. Recall that in each subnetwork the zero address (for example, 192.168.20.16) and the all ones address (for example, 192.168.20.15) are reserved.

2.3.4 Network Address Translation (NAT)

Some groups of addresses are reserved for use in private networks and are never exposed to the wider Internet. The ranges appear to be random and have historic reasons for their values, but note that there is one address range chosen from each of Class A, B, and C. They are shown in Table 2.6.

Of course, in a genuinely private network any addresses could be used, but it is a good exercise in self-discipline to use the allocated ranges. Further, if the private network does become attached to the public Internet at some point, it is much easier to see whether internal addresses are leaking into the Internet and simple for the ISP to configure routers to filter out any packets to or from the private address ranges.

If a network using one of the private address ranges is connected to the Internet, Network Address Translation (NAT) must be applied to map local addresses into publicly visible addresses. This process provides a useful security barrier since no information about the internal addressing or routing structure will leak out into the wider Internet. Further, the private network can exist with only a small number of public addresses because only a few of the hosts in the private network will be attached to the Internet at any time.

This scheme and the repeated use of private address ranges across multiple networks is an important step in the conservation of IP addresses. As more and more devices from printers and photocopiers to heating systems and refrigerators were made IP-capable for office or home networking, there was a serious concern that all of the 2^{32} IPv4 addresses would be used up. However, by placing hosts within private networks the speed of the address space depletion has been dramatically reduced.

Table 2.6 Addresses Reserved for Use on Private Networks

Address Range	Subnet
10.0.0.0 to 10.255.255.255	10.0.0.0/8
172.16.0.0 to 172.31.255.255	172.16.0.0/12
192.168.0.0 to 192.168.255.255	192.168.0.0/16

2.4   IP in Use

This section examines how IP is used to deliver datagrams to their target hosts. This is largely an issue of addressing since, on the local network segment, IP datagrams are encapsulated in data-link layer frames that are delivered according to their Media Access Control (MAC) addresses. This section looks at how network segments can be extended by devices called *bridges*, which selectively forward frames based on their MAC addresses.

IP has its own addressing, which was introduced in the previous section. When bridges don't provide sufficient function, devices called *routers* are used to direct IP datagrams based on the destination IP addresses they contain. Routers may perform direct routing using look-up tables such as the one produced by ARP (see Section 2.4.5) to map IP addresses to MAC addresses and so package the IP datagrams into frames that are addressed to their ultimate destinations. Direct routing is useful on a single physical network such as an Ethernet, but is impractical when many separate networks are linked together.

Indirect routing lets routers forward IP datagrams based on their destination IP addresses. For any one datagram, a router determines the *next hop* router along the path to the destination and packages the datagram in a data-link level frame addressed to that router. The next hop router is the gateway into the next segment of the network.

Routers determine the next hop router by using routing tables that may be statically configured or dynamically computed using the information distributed by the routing protocols described in Chapter 5.

2.4.1 Bridging Function

The reach of a network such as an Ethernet can be extended by joining two segments together with a *repeater*. A repeater is simply a piece of equipment that listens on one port and regenerates everything it hears, indiscriminately, out of another port. Repeaters usually help overcome the effects of signal distortion, attenuation, and interference from noise by regenerating a clean signal.

Repeaters do not, however, solve the problem of congestion that can occur as the number of nodes on a network grows, because repeaters forward all traffic between the network segments. On an Ethernet this gives rise to an unacceptable number of collisions, and on a Token Ring or FDDI network the amount of "jitter" may become excessive as each node must wait longer for the token.

The solution is to segment the network and filter the traffic that passes through the connections between the segments. The function of connecting segments and filtering traffic is provided by a *bridge*, which is a sort of intelligent repeater. Bridges act by learning which MAC addresses exist on each segment. They build a table that associates each MAC address with one of the bridge's output ports according to which segment it belongs to. When a bridge receives a frame it first looks up the source MAC address and if it hasn't seen it before it adds an entry to its bridging table saying that the address can be reached through the port on which the frame was received. Second, it forwards the frame according to the entry for the destination address in its bridging table. If the destination address is not in its bridging table or if the address is a broadcast address, the bridge simply acts as a repeater and sends the frame out of all of the ports except the one through which the frame was received. Further, if the bridge receives a frame and notices that the destination address is reachable through the port on which the frame was received, the bridge simply discards the frame. In this way, once the network has been run for a while, the bridge effectively filters the traffic that it receives and only forwards traffic onto the correct network segments. Figure 2.9 shows a simple network segmented with the use of a bridge and also shows the view that a host might have of the same network. Table 2.7 shows the bridging table that the bridge would construct after listening to the network for a while.

Bridges can be daisy-chained so that the network can be broken up still further, but great care must be taken to avoid building looped network segments. This would result in broadcast traffic looping forever and also could result in targeted frames looping. This is a network planning issue—there must be no loops in bridged networks.

Note that while bridges facilitate smoother operation of IP, they are in no way involved in the protocol or in IP addressing.

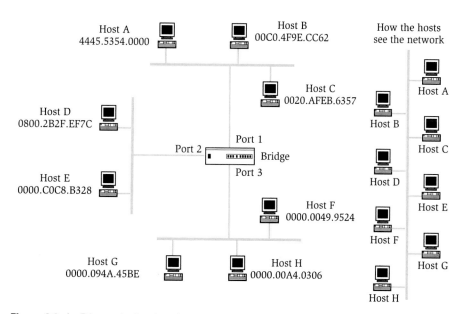

Figure 2.9 An Ethernet broken into three segments by a bridge still appears to be a single Ethernet when viewed by the attached hosts.

Table 2.7 The Bridging Table for the Router in Figure 2.9

Hardware Address	Bridge Port
0000.0049.9524	3
0000.00A4.0306	3
0000.094A.45BE	3
0000.C0C8.B328	2
0020.AFEB.6357	1
00C0.4F9E.CC62	1
0800.2B2F.EF7C	2
4445.5354.0000	1

2.4.2 IP Switching and Routing

Although bridges greatly improve the scalability of networks, they aren't a complete solution. As described in the previous section, bridges have an intrinsic risk of looping so that frames circulate forever if the network is not connected correctly. Further, they don't even handle scaling completely, since all broadcast frames must be copied on to every segment of the network.

Gateways were introduced as smart bridges that act on the network layer (that is, IP) addressing rather than on the data-link layer. The network is still segmented as before, but packets are only forwarded between network segments by the gateway if the IP address meets certain criteria. The addresses on one network segment are usually assigned as a subnetwork so that the gateway can easily determine which packets to forward in which direction.

Gateways are now called *routers*, which is a pretty good name for what they do. Bridges simply choose the next network fragment onto which to send a frame, but routers have a wider view and can see a logical, multi-hop path to the destination, which they use to choose the next router to which to forward the packet. In this way, routers can safely be built into a *mesh network*, which has loops and multiple alternative paths. Using the properties of IP and their broad view of the network, routers can select preferred paths based on many factors, of which path length is usually the most important.

Routers get their knowledge of the network topology from *routing protocols* (see Chapter 5). These protocols allow routers to communicate with each other, exchanging information such as connectivity and link types so that they build up a picture of the whole network and can choose the best way to forward a packet. A key distinction should be made between hosts and routers since both

```
C:\> route print
Active Routes:
Network Address     Netmask             Gateway Address     Interface           Metric
0.0.0.0             0.0.0.0             138.88.23.191       138.88.23.191       1
127.0.0.0           255.0.0.0           127.0.0.1           127.0.0.1           1
138.88.0.0          255.255.0.0         138.88.23.191       138.88.23.191       1
138.88.23.191       255.255.255.255     127.0.0.1           127.0.0.1           1
138.88.255.255      255.255.255.255     138.88.23.191       138.88.23.191       1
224.0.0.0           224.0.0.0           138.88.23.191       138.88.23.191       1
255.255.255.255     255.255.255.255     138.88.23.191       138.88.23.191       1
```

Figure 2.10 The output from a standard route table application on a dial-up PC.

include a routing function: A router is capable of forwarding received packets, but a host is only capable of originating or terminating packets.

The routing function within a host determines what the host does with a packet it has built and needs to send. Typically, a host is directly attached to a router or is connected to a network segment with only one router attached. In this case, the host has a very simple route table like the one shown in Figure 2.10 for a dial-up host. The output from a standard route table application shows us how the host must operate. If the host had a packet to send to the destination address 192.168.20.59, it would start at the top of the table and work down the Network Address column using the Netmask to compare entries with the destination address. Most of the table entries are concerned with connections to the local PC itself (through its address 138.88.23.191 or local host address 127.0.0.1—see the next section), or with delivery to the directly attached subnet 138.88.0.0/16. It is only the last line in the table that tells the host how to handle its packet. This line represents the *default route* since it catches every IP address that has not been handled by another line in the table. It tells the host that it must forward the packet through the gateway 138.88.23.191 (that is, itself) and out of the interface 138.88.23.191 (that is, the modem providing dial-up connectivity).

Routers have similar but far more complex routing tables built by examining the information provided by the routing protocols.

IP switches are a hybrid of bridging and routing technology. They operate by building a table of IP addresses mapped to outgoing interfaces, and look up the destination address of a packet to determine the interface out of which to forward the packet. They switch the packet from one interface to the next at a network level in the same way that a bridge switches a packet at a data-link level. Switches are explicitly programmed to forward traffic on specific paths either through configuration and management options or through special protocols devised to distribute this information. Refer to Multiprotocol Label Switching (MPLS) in Chapter 9 and the General Switch Management Protocol (GSMP) in

Chapter 11. Switches do not learn network topology through routing protocols and do not calculate their routing tables dynamically.

For a while, IP switches were the shining hope of the Internet. They did not require continual calculation of routes each time the routing protocols distributed new information, and they could place their switching table in integrated circuitry (ASICs) for much more rapid forwarding. However, it soon became apparent that a new generation of routers could be built that also used ASICs for forwarding while retaining the flexibility and reactivity of the routing protocols. IP switches have pretty much died out except for simple programmable switches that offer a level of function somewhere between a bridge and a router (popular in home networking). However, packet switching is alive and well in the form of MPLS (described in Chapter 9).

2.4.3 Local Delivery and Loopbacks

The routing table in Figure 2.10 contains some unexpected entries as well as the more obvious ones for the directly connected network and the default route. The entry for the subnet 127.0.0.0/8 says that all matching addresses should be forwarded out of the interface 127.0.0.1. What is more, addresses matching 138.88.23.191/32, the host's own address, should also be forwarded out of the same interface.

127.0.0.1 is the address used to represent the *localhost*. Any packet carrying this address will be delivered to the local IP stack without actually leaving the host. So, any packet addressed to the host's external IP address 138.88.23.191 will be delivered to the local IP stack. Try typing "ping 127.0.0.1" on a PC that is not connected to the network and you will see that you get a response.

When a node (host or router) has many interfaces, each is assigned its own external IP address known as the interface address. In this case it is useful to assign another address that represents the node itself and is not tied to a specific interface. We are looking for an address that has external scope but that applies to the whole of the node (that is, an address that is not limited to the identification of a single interface). Such addresses are known as *loopback* addresses because if a node sends an IP packet to its own loopback address, the packet is looped back and returned up its own IP stack. The concept of loopbacks is useful not just in providing an external view of the whole node, but also in allowing client and server applications to be run on one node and use the same processing that would be used if one of the applications (say the server) were located on a remote box. This similarity of processing extends through all of the application and transport software, right up to the IP stack which, when it is asked to send a packet to a loopback address, turns the packet around as if it had just been received. This is illustrated in Figure 2.11. Note that 127.0.0.1 is a loopback address, but it is not an externally visible loopback address, that is, it cannot be used by a remote node to send a packet to this node because all nodes use the same value, 127.0.0.1, as their localhost loopback address. An individual node may define as many loopback addresses as it wishes.

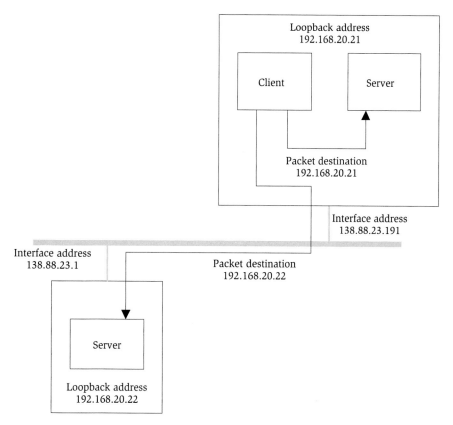

Figure 2.11 Loopback addresses enable a host to use exactly the same software to send a packet to a remote or a local application.

Great care must be taken to distinguish between a loopback address and a router ID. Router IDs are used to distinguish and identify routers in a network, and the concept is important in the routing protocols described in Chapter 5. Since router IDs and IPv4 addresses are both 32-bit fields, it is common practice to assign the router ID to be the first defined loopback address, but this need not be the case and the router ID should not be assumed to be an IP address.

2.4.4 Type of Service

The routing tables just described provide a simple address-based way of forwarding packets. The destination address of the packet is checked against each entry in the table in turn until a match is made, identifying the interface out of which the packet should be forwarded.

Routing allows an extra level of flexibility so that packets may be forwarded based on the service type requested by the application and may be prioritized for

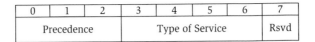

0	1	2	3	4	5	6	7
Precedence			Type of Service				Rsvd

Figure 2.12 The IP type of service byte.

Table 2.8 IP Precedence Values

Precedence Value	Meaning
0	Routine (normal)
1	Priority data
2	Immediate delivery required
3	Flash
4	Flash override
5	Critical
6	Internetwork control
7	Local network control

Table 2.9 IP Type of Service Values

ToS Value	Meaning
0	Normal service. In practice almost all IP datagrams are sent with this ToS and with precedence zero.
1	Minimize delay. Select a route with emphasis on low latency.
2	Maximize throughput. Select a route that provides higher throughput.
4	Maximize reliability. Choose a route that offers greater reliability as measured by whatever mechanisms are available (such as bit error rates, packet failure rates, service up time, etc.).
8	Minimize cost. Select the least expensive route. Cost is usually inversely associated with the length of the route and this is the default operating principle of the algorithms that routers use to build their routing tables.
15	Maximize security. Pick the most secure route available.

processing within the routers that handle the packets. The service level requested by the application is carried in the Type of Service (ToS) byte in the IP header.

The ToS byte is broken into three fields, as shown in Figure 2.12. The Precedence field defines the priority that the router should assign to the packet. This allows a high-priority packet to overtake lower-priority packets within the router, and allows the higher-priority packets better access to constrained resources such as buffers. The list of precedence values is shown in Table 2.8, in which priority seven is the highest priority. A router can use the value of the Type of Service field to help it select the route based on the service requirements. Values of the ToS field are maintained by IANA: the current values are listed in Table 2.9.

Type of Service is now largely deprecated in favor of Differentiated Services (DiffServ), described in Chapter 6. This deprecation and reinterpretation of the ToS field is possible because nearly all datagrams were always sent using precedence zero and ToS zero.

2.4.5 Address Resolution Protocol (ARP)

Suppose a router receives an IP packet. The router looks up the destination IP address carried by the packet and determines the next hop to which to forward the packet—perhaps the destination is even directly attached to the router. This tells the router out of which interface it should send the packet.

If the link from the router is point-to-point, everything is simple and the router can wrap the packet in the data-link layer protocol and send it. However, if the link is a multidrop link such as Ethernet (that is, it is a shared-medium link with multiple attached nodes) the router must also determine the data-link layer address (such as the MAC address) to forward the packet to the right node. If we could simply make the IP address of a node equal to its MAC address there would be no issue, but MAC addresses are typically 6 bytes, which cannot be carried in the 4-byte IP address field. Besides, in IP we like to be able to assign multiple addresses to a single node.

An option would be to broadcast the packet on the link and let the receiving nodes determine from the IP address of the packet whether it is for them. This might be acceptable when all of the attached nodes are hosts, but if any node was a router it would immediately try to forward the packet itself. What is really required is a way of resolving the data-link layer address from the next hop IP address.

The simple solution is to configure the router with a mapping table. This certainly works, but adds configuration overhead and is inflexible, and the whole point of a network such as a multidrop Ethernet is that you can simply plug in new nodes and run with the minimum of fuss. If you had to visit every node on the network and add a configuration item it would be a nuisance.

The Address Resolution Protocol (ARP) defined in RFC 826 solves this problem for us by allowing nodes to announce their presence on a network and also to query MAC addresses based on given IP addresses. When a node is plugged into an Ethernet it announces its presence by advertising the IP address of its

Table 2.10 ARP Operation Codes

Operation Code	Meaning
1	ARP Request. Please supply the IP address corresponding to the requested target MAC address.
2	ARP Reply. Here is a mapping of target MAC address to target IP address.
3	RARP Request. Please supply my IP address given my MAC address.
4	RARP Reply. Here is your IP address given your MAC address.
8	InARP Request. Please supply the MAC address corresponding to the target IP address.
9	InARP Reply. Here is a mapping of target IP address to target MAC address.

attachment to the Ethernet together with its MAC address in a process known as *gratuitous ARP*. This advertisement message is broadcast at the Ethernet level using the MAC address 0xFFFFFFFFFFFF so that all other nodes on the network receive it and can add the information to their mapping tables or *ARP caches*. When a node sends an IP packet to this host it can look up the address of the host in its cache and determine the correct MAC address to use.

The format of all ARP messages is shown in Figure 2.13. The ARP message is illustrated encapsulated in an Ethernet frame shown in gray, which indicates that the payload protocol is ARP (0x0806). The ARP message indicates the hardware type (Ethernet) and the protocol type (IP). Next it gives the lengths of the hardware address (6 bytes for a MAC address) and the protocol address (4 bytes for IPv4). Including these address length fields makes ARP applicable to any data-link layer and any network protocol. The next field in the ARP message identifies the ARP operation—in this case it is set to 2 to indicate an ARP Reply. Table 2.10 lists the full set of ARP operation codes.

The last four fields in the ARP message carry the ARP information. The source MAC and IP addresses are always present and give the information about the sender of the message. The target MAC and IP addresses are set according to the Operation code. If the operation is an ARP Request the target MAC address is zero, because a request is being made to resolve the target IP address into a MAC address. But when the operation is an ARP Reply both the target MAC and IP addresses are present.

A node that receives an ARP Reply message extracts the address mapping information and stores it in its *ARP cache*. It uses the ARP cache information for all subsequent IP messages that it sends. But this process causes a raft of issues, largely associated with what happens when an entry in the cache is wrong or absent.

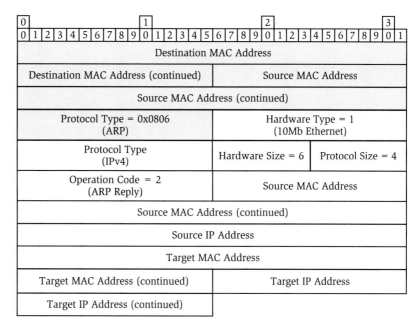

Figure 2.13 The format of an ARP message encapsulated in an Ethernet frame.

The cache might not contain the mapping for a particular host simply because the local host booted more recently than the remote host and so has not heard an ARP reply from the remote host. Alternatively, the cache may be of limited size so that entries are discarded based on least use or greatest age. Further, it may be considered wise to time out cache entries regardless of how much use they are getting so that stale and potentially inaccurate information does not persist. In any of these cases, the local host cannot send its IP packet because it doesn't have a mapping of the next hop address.

A solution is to have all nodes periodically retransmit their IP to MAC address mapping. This would mean that a node only had to wait a well-known period of time before it had an up-to-date entry in its ARP cache. But we would need to keep this time period quite small, perhaps in the order of 10 seconds, and that would imply an unacceptable amount of traffic on an Ethernet with 100 stations. Besides, if the reason the entry is missing from the cache is that the cache is smaller than the number of nodes on the Ethernet, this approach would not work.

What is needed instead is the ability for a node to query the network to determine the address mapping. To do this, a node that cannot map the next hop IP address of a packet to a MAC address discards the IP packet and sends an ARP Request (Operation code one) instead. The ARP Request is broadcast (as are all ARP messages) and contains the target IP address for resolution—the target MAC address is set to zero. All nodes on the local network receive the broadcast ARP Request, but only the one that matches the target MAC address responds—it builds an ARP reply and broadcasts it on the Ethernet. All nodes see the ARP Reply because it is broadcast, and can use the Reply to update their caches. The originator of the Request will collect the information from the Reply and hold it ready for the next IP packet it has to send in the same direction.

Note that this process can cause a "false start" in a flow of IP packets as a few packets are discarded along the path while addresses are resolved. Applications or transport protocols that are sensitive to packet loss may notice this behavior and throttle back the rate at which they send data, believing the network to be unreliable.

Diskless workstations may use *Reverse ARP* (RARP) to discover their own IP address when they are booted. Typically a node knows its own MAC address from a piece of hardwired information built into its hardware. RARP requests use the Ethernet protocol identifier 0x0835, but are otherwise identical to ARP requests and use operation codes taken from Table 2.10. Obviously, in a RARP request the target MAC address is supplied but the IP address is set to zero. Essential to the operation of RARP is that there is at least one node on the network that operates as a RARP server keeping a record of manually configured MAC address to IP address mappings.

A third variant, *Inverse ARP* (InARP), allows a node that knows another node's MAC address to discover its IP address. Again, message formats are identical and operation codes are listed in Table 2.10. InARP is particularly useful in data-link networks such as Frame Relay and ATM where permanent virtual circuits may already exist between known data-link end points and where there is a need to discover the IP address that lives at the other end of the link.

The extended use of the ARP operation code is a good example of how a well-designed protocol can be extended in a simple way. If the original protocol definition had assigned just one bit to distinguish the request and reply messages, it would have been much harder to fit RARP and InARP into the same message formats.

Most operating systems give the user access to the ARP cache and allow the user to manually add entries and to query the network. Figure 2.14 shows the options to a popular ARP application.

```
c:\> arp
ARP -a [inet_addr] [-N if_addr]
ARP -d inet_addr [if_addr]
ARP -s inet_addr eth_addr [if_addr]
-a Displays current ARP cache. If inet_addr is specified, only
   the specified entry is displayed. If -N if_addr is used the
   ARP entries for the network interface are displayed.
-d Deletes the ARP cache entry specified by inet_addr.
-s Sets an entry in the ARP cache modifying any existing entry.
```

Figure 2.14 The options to a popular ARP application.

Although ARP request messages are broadcast, they must be responded to only by the node that matches the target address. This is important because if a response is generated by every node that knows the answer to the query there will be a large burst of responses. Obviously, this rule is bent for RARP, in which it is the RARP server that responds.

One last variation on ARP is *proxy* ARP, where ARP requests are answered by a server on behalf of the queried node. This is particularly useful in bridged and dial-up networks. See Chapter 15 for more discussion of proxy ARP.

Note finally that ARP can be used to help detect the problem of two nodes on a network having the same IP address. If a node receives an ARP response that carries its own IP address but a MAC address that is not its own, it should log messages to error logs and the user's screen, and should generally jump up and down and wave its hands in the air.

2.4.6 Dynamic Address Assignment

Reverse ARP offers a node the opportunity to discover its own IP address given its MAC address. This useful feature is extended by the Bootstrap Protocol (BOOTP) defined in RFC 951 and RFC 1542. This allows a diskless terminal not only to discover its own IP address, but to download an executable image. Such a device can be built with a small program burned into a chip containing BOOTP and the Trivial File Transfer Protocol (TFTP) described in Chapter 12. Upon booting, the node broadcasts the message shown in Figure 2.15 with most fields set to zero and the operation code set to 1 to show that this is a request. If the node has been configured (perhaps in a piece of flash RAM called the BootPROM) with the BOOTP server's address, the message is sent direct and is not broadcast. The BOOTP server fills in the message and returns it to the requester, which is able to initiate file transfer and so load its real executable image. The returned message is usually broadcast as well since the client does not yet know its own IP address and so cannot receive unicast messages, but if the client fills its address into the BOOTP Request and that address matches the one supplied by the server in the BOOTP Response, the response may be unicast.

Note that the information fields are fixed length, so a length field is needed to indicate how many bytes of the hardware address are relevant. There is an option for the client to fill in its IP address if it believes it knows the address and if the node is really just soliciting the boot information.

BOOTP messages are sent encapsulated in IP and UDP (see Chapter 7), so BOOTP is really an application protocol.

The boot-time function of BOOTP is enhanced by the Dynamic Host Configuration Protocol (DHCP) defined in RFC 2131. DHCP is backwards compatible with BOOTP but adds further facilities for remote configuration of the network capabilities of a booting node. DHCP uses the same message structure as BOOTP, but the Reserved field is allocated for use as flags and the Vendor-Specific field is used for passing configuration options. This is illustrated in Figure 2.16.

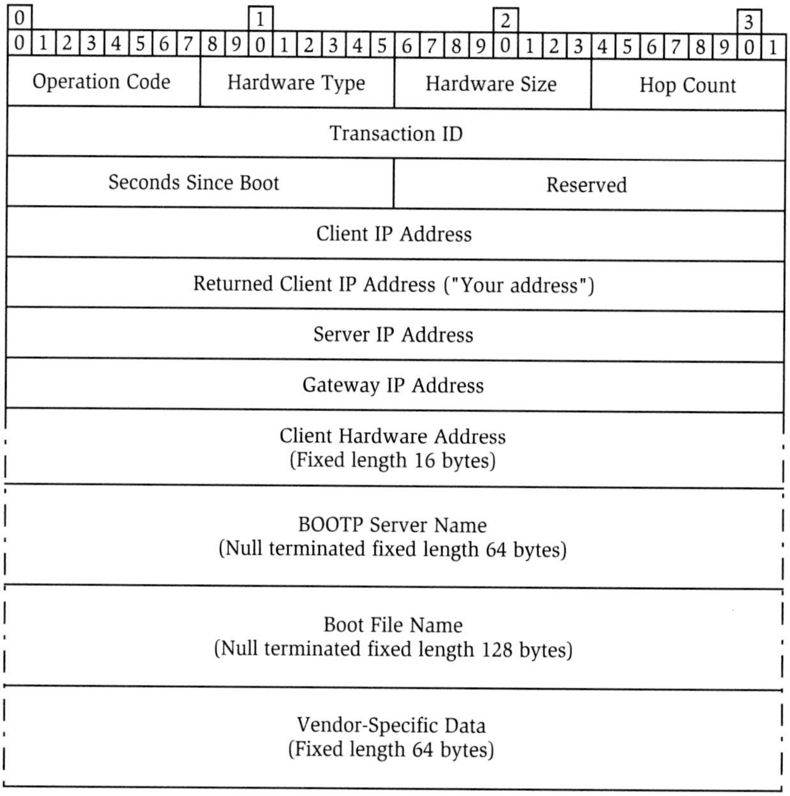

```
 0                      1                     2                    3
 0 1 2 3 4 5 6 7 8 9 0 1 2 3 4 5 6 7 8 9 0 1 2 3 4 5 6 7 8 9 0 1
```

Operation Code	Hardware Type	Hardware Size	Hop Count

Transaction ID

Seconds Since Boot	Reserved

Client IP Address

Returned Client IP Address ("Your address")

Server IP Address

Gateway IP Address

Client Hardware Address (Fixed length 16 bytes)

BOOTP Server Name (Null terminated fixed length 64 bytes)

Boot File Name (Null terminated fixed length 128 bytes)

Vendor-Specific Data (Fixed length 64 bytes)

Figure 2.15 The BOOTP message format.

Currently, only one flag, the most significant bit (bit 16 of the third word), is defined. This bit indicates that DHCP replies must be broadcast to the requesting client. All of the other flag bits must be set to zero. The variable length Options field may be up to 312 bytes long, meaning that the packet may be up to 548 bytes long (add to this the UDP and IP headers). This can be problematic to some data-link types such as X.25 unless packet fragmentation is supported.

The initial client request message carries the operation code value 1, indicating a BOOTP Request. To indicate that the client is DHCP capable, the first 4 bytes of the Options field are set to the magic value 0x63825363 (decimal 99, 130, 83, 99) and all subsequent messages use the same value in those bytes. Options are defined in RFC 1533 and are encoded as type-length-variable (TLV) structures, where the first byte indicates the type of the option and the next byte counts how many bytes of data follow before the end of the option. A large number of options are defined and maintained by IANA, some of which are listed in Table 2.11, and only a few of which are commonly used.

Table 2.11 DHCP Options

DHCP Option	Meaning
1	Subnet mask
2	Time offset
3	Router addresses
6	Domain name server addresses
12	Client host name
13	Size of boot file
18	File containing further DHCP options
19	Enable/disable IP forwarding
23	Default TTL for IP packets
26	MTU for this interface
28	IP broadcast address
33	Static routes
35	ARP cache time-out
37	TCP default TTL
43	Vendor-specific information
50	DHCP Requested IP Address
51	DHCP IP Address Lease Time
52	DHCP Option Overload
53	DHCP Message Type
54	DHCP Server Identifier
55	DHCP Parameter Request List
56	DHCP Error Message
255	Pad (no length or variable field is present)

Two ugly option fields exist. Option 18 points the client at a file on the server that it can download (using TFTP) and interpret as more DHCP options. Option 52 tells the client that it should interpret the Server Name and/or the File Name fields as further DHCP options and not as defined.

For DHCP, the most important option is number 53, the DHCP Message Type option. This allows DHCP to use the two BOOTP messages (Request and Reply) to carry a series of messages that are exchanged between the client

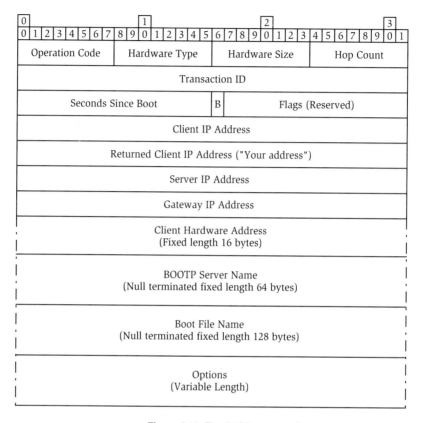

Figure 2.16 The DHCP message format.

and server. The message type is encoded as a single byte using the values listed in Table 2.12. Message exchanges are used to discover DHCP servers and for servers to offer their services (there may be several available on a network), and to exchange configuration information.

RFC 2131 contains an exciting state transition diagram to explain the full operation of DHCP on a client as it sends and receives DHCP messages. The message exchange for the simple case of a client discovering and choosing between two DHCP servers and allocating an IP address can be seen in Figure 2.17. A DHCP client attached to an Ethernet boots up and broadcasts a DHCP Discover message (step 1). Both servers respond with Offer messages (steps 2 and 3) and the client waits a respectable period to make sure it has received all offers (step 4). After the client has waited, it selects its preferred server and issues a Request—this is a broadcast message, so it tells the unwanted server that it doesn't need to do any more work (step 5) and at the same time asks the selected server for configuration information (step 6). The selected server responds with an Ack message carrying the requested information.

Table 2.12 DCP Message Type Values

Value	Message
1	DHCPDISCOVER Client request to discover DHCP servers.
2	DHCPOFFER DHCP server offers to act for a client.
3	DHCPREQUEST Client requests parameters from its chosen server.
4	DHCPDECLINE Client rejects a supplied IP address because it is already in use.
5	DHCPACK Server supplies configuration parameters in response to a request.
6	DHCPNAK Server declines to supply configuration parameters in response to a request.
7	DHCPRELEASE A client that knows it is going away releases the use of an assigned IP address.
8	DHCPINFORM Like a DHCPREQUEST message but issued by a client that already knows its IP address and just wishes to obtain additional configuration parameters.

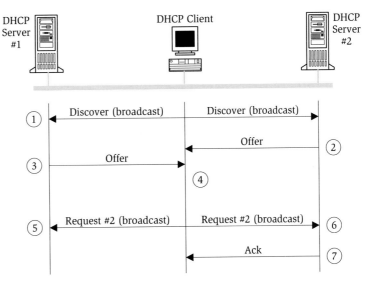

Figure 2.17 DHCP message exchange.

```
C:\> ipconfig /all
Windows 98 IP Configuration
        Host Name.................: OEMCOMPUTER
        DNS Servers...............:
        Node Type.................: Broadcast
        NetBIOS Scope ID..........:
        IP Routing Enabled........: No
        WINS Proxy Enabled........: No
        NetBIOS Resolution Uses DNS: No
0 Ethernet adapter:
        Description...............: PPP Adapter.
        Physical Address..........: 44-45-53-54-00-00
        DHCP Enabled..............: Yes
        IP Address................: 0.0.0.0
        Subnet Mask...............: 0.0.0.0
        Default Gateway...........:
        DHCP Server...............: 255.255.255.255
        Primary WINS Server.......:
        Secondary WINS Server.....:
        Lease Obtained............:
        Lease Expires.............:
```

Figure 2.18 Default IP configuration of an isolated home PC.

```
C:\> ipconfig /all
Windows 98 IP Configuration
        Host Name.................: OEMCOMPUTER
        DNS Servers...............: 199.45.32.43
                                    199.45.32.38
        Node Type.................: Broadcast
        NetBIOS Scope ID..........:
        IP Routing Enabled........: No
        WINS Proxy Enabled........: No
        NetBIOS Resolution Uses DNS: No
0 Ethernet adapter:
        Description...............: PPP Adapter.
        Physical Address..........: 44-45-53-54-00-00
        DHCP Enabled..............: Yes
        IP Address................: 138.88.23.228
        Subnet Mask...............: 255.255.0.0
        Default Gateway...........: 138.88.23.228
        DHCP Server...............: 255.255.255.255
        Primary WINS Server.......:
        Secondary WINS Server.....:
        Lease Obtained............: 01 01 80 00:00:00
        Lease Expires.............: 01 01 80 00:00:00
```

Figure 2.19 IP configuration of any home PC connected to the Internet after running DHCP.

DHCP has a further use in dial-up networking for discovering the IP address and network configuration parameters a computer should use when it is attached to the Internet. The same technique is used more generally for any dynamic assignment of IP addresses such as in DSL or cable modem connectivity. Figure 2.18 shows the default output from the ipconfig program of a home computer that is isolated from the Internet—note that most of the fields are blank even though the MAC address is known. Figure 2.19 shows the output of the same command when the PC is connected to the network through a dial-up link—an IP address has been assigned and DNS servers have been assigned. In a sense this use of DHCP is deferring part of the boot process.

2.5   IP Options and Advanced Functions

IP allows for the inclusion of some option fields between the mandatory 20-byte IP header and the payload data. These are additional fields that form part of the IP header (that is, are included in the length given by the Header Length field) and describe extra features that must be applied to the datagram. "Optional," therefore, refers to the fact that the parameters are optionally present in the IP packet—it is mandatory for a node that receives a packet containing optional parameters to act on those parameters.

The options are encoded as type-length-variable (TLV) structures. Each option begins with a type identifier that indicates which option is present. There follows a length field that says how many bytes make up the option (including the type and length fields). Finally comes the variable—the data specific to the option.

Note that there is a hard limit of 60 bytes on the size of an IP header imposed by the fact that the IP header length is specified using a 4-bit field to count the number of quartets of bytes present ($15 * 4 = 60$). Since the mandatory part of the header is 20 bytes long, there are just 40 bytes left to encode all of the options on a datagram. Note also that since the header length is a count of 4-byte units, the last option present must be padded out to a 4-byte boundary.

Figure 2.20 shows the format of the common part of an IP Option, as previously described. The option type field is itself subdivided into three fields, as shown. The first bit is called the Copy Bit and tells transit nodes that may perform fragmentation whether this option must be copied to each fragment that is produced or whether it may be discarded—since the datagram will be reassembled at the destination, options that apply only to the destination may be left out of subsequent fragments. The next two bits provide a subcategory or Class of the option type (only two classes are defined, zero is used for network control and two is used for debugging). The final five bits are used to identify the option type within its class. Table 2.13 lists the option classes and types.

Table 2.13 The IP Options

Copy	Class	Type	Option Length	Meaning
yes	0	0	N/A	End of Option list. This option occupies only one byte and has no length field or variable field.
N/A	0	1	N/A	No Operation. This option occupies only one byte and has no length field or variable field.
yes	0	2	11	Security. Used to carry security information compatible with U.S. Department of Defense requirements.
yes	0	3	variable	Loose Source Routing. Contains IP addresses supplied by the source and used to route the datagram toward the destination.
no	0	7	variable	Record Route. Used to trace the path of a datagram as it traverses the network.
yes	0	8	4	Stream ID. Used to carry a stream identifier associated with a series of datagrams.
yes	0	9	variable	Strict Source Routing. Contains IP addresses supplied by the source and used to route the datagram toward the destination.
yes	0	20	4	Router Alert. Used to cause the router to pass the received datagram to higher layer software for inspection even though the datagram is not addressed to this router. This option is used particularly by the Resource Reservation Protocol (RSVP) described in Chapter 6.
no	2	4	variable	Internet Timestamp. Records the time at which a router processed a datagram.

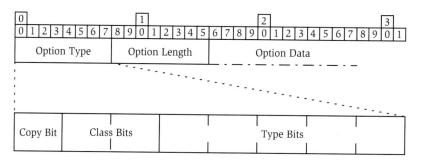

Figure 2.20 IP Options are encoded as TLVs. The Option Type field is broken out into three separate bit fields.

Options zero and one are used to delimit the sequence of options in the header. These are special options since they don't use the TLV encoding properly and are present as single-byte option types with neither length nor variable. Option zero is, perhaps, unnecessary given the presence of the header length field, but is used in any case as the last option in the list. Option one is used to provide padding so that the header is built up to a 4-byte boundary.

2.5.1 Route Control and Recording

Option seven can be used to track the path datagrams follow through the network. This will tell the destination how the packet got there, but it won't tell the sender a thing since the datagram is a one-way message. The sender may place the TLV shown in Figure 2.21 into the IP options field. The sender must leave enough space (set to zero) for the nodes along the path to insert their addresses since they cannot increase the size of the IP header (this might otherwise involve memory copying and so forth).

Each node that receives a datagram with the *Record Route* option present needs to add its IP address to the list in the TLV. The Pointer field is used to tell the node where it should place its address within the option, so initially the pointer field is set to 4—the fourth byte is the first available byte in which to record a hop. As each hop address is added, the pointer field is increased by four to point to the next vacant entry. When the option is received and the pointer value plus four exceeds the option length, the receiving node knows that there is not enough space to record its own address and it simply forwards the datagram without adding its address.

Options three and nine are used to allow the source node to have some control over the path taken by a datagram, thereby overriding the decisions that would otherwise be made by routers within the network. There may be many motivations for this—some are tied to the discussion of fragmentation and may allow a source node to direct datagrams through networks that will not need to fragment the data. Other motivations are related to traffic engineering, described in Chapter 8.

The *Source Route* is a series of IP addresses that identify the routers that must be visited by the datagram on its way through the network. Two alternatives

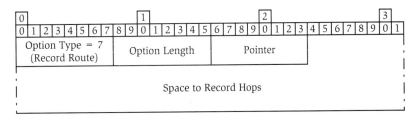

Figure 2.21 IP Record Route option.

exist: A *strict route* is a list of routers that must be visited one at a time, in the specified order and without using any intervening routers. The Record Route generated as a result of using a strict route would show exactly the same series of addresses. The second alternative is a *loose route*, which lists routers that must be visited in order, but allows other routers to be used on the way. The Record Route in this case would be a superset of the source route.

The strict and loose route options use the same format as the Record Route shown in Figure 2.21. That is, the route is expressed as a list of 32-bit IP addresses. The pointer field is used to indicate the address that is currently being processed—that is, it indicates the target of the current hop. When a datagram is sent out using a Source Route, the datagram is addressed not to the ultimate destination, but to the first address in the Source Route. When the datagram is received at the next router it compares the destination address, the next address pointed to in the route, and its own address. If the route is a strict route, all three must be equal. If it is not, an ICMP error is generated (see Section 2.6). If the route is a loose route and the current node is not the current destination of the datagram, the datagram is forwarded. When the datagram is received by a node that is the current destination, it copies the next address from the route to the destination field in the IP header, increments the pointer, and forwards the datagram. The last entry in the Source Route is the real destination of the datagram. Figure 2.22 shows this process at work.

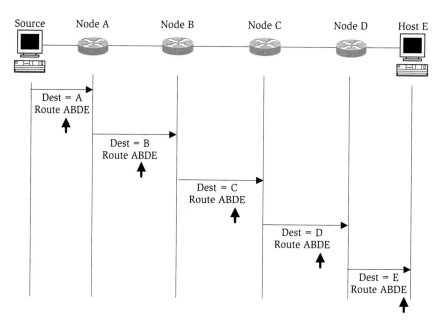

Figure 2.22 A loose source route in use.

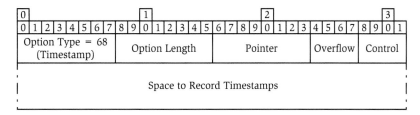

Figure 2.23 IP Timestamp option.

It should be clear that a strict route effectively records the route without using a Record Route option. This is good because it would be hard to fit both into the limited space available for IP options. Note that there is an issue with using loose route to record the path of the datagram because it may take in additional nodes along the way. This is somewhat ambiguously described in RFC 791, but it is clear that there is no place to insert the Record Route to track each node along the path.

There are several concerns with the Source Route options, including the fact that an intruder may contrive to get datagrams that are sent between nodes in one network to be routed through another network. This would allow the intruder to get access to the datagrams. In any case, many network operators don't like the idea of a user having control of how their traffic is carried through the network—that is their responsibility and the job of the routing protocols. In consequence, support for source routing is often disabled.

Given the size limitations of the IP header, these three options are not considered very useful. At best, the Record Route option can gather nine addresses. Although it may once have been considered remarkable to have three or four routers between source and destination, there are now often many more than nine. Further, many IP implementations have some trouble managing source routes correctly and do not always manage to forward the datagrams properly.

The Timestamp option is similar to the Record Route option. As shown in Figure 2.23, it includes two additional 4-bit flags (so the first value of the pointer field is five) to control the behavior of the option. The Control Flag field has three settings—zero means that each node visited by the datagram should insert a timestamp, one means that each node should insert its address and a timestamp, three means that the option already includes a list of IP addresses and space for the specified nodes to fill in their timestamps. The other 4-bit field is the Overflow field. This is used to count the number of nodes that are unable to supply a timestamp because there is no more space in the option.

Even with the Overflow field the Timestamp option runs up against the same space problems as Record Route. The option to record timestamps selectively (option three) may be used to mitigate this to some extent, but can't be used unless the source knows which nodes the datagram will visit.

2.6 Internet Control Message Protocol (ICMP)

The Internet Control Message Protocol (ICMP) is a funny animal. It is used to report errors in IP datagrams, which can be useful to the sender and to transit nodes because they can discover and isolate problems within the network and possibly select different paths down which to send datagrams. At the same time, ICMP supports two very useful applications, *ping* and *traceroute*, that are used to discover the reachability of remote IP addresses and to inspect the route that datagrams follow to get to their destinations. Further, ICMP contains the facility to "discover" routers within the network, which is useful for a host to discover its first hop to the outside world.

These features mean that ICMP is sometimes described as a routing protocol, but because it predates the fully fledged routing protocols and it may be used in a very selective way, it is described here rather than in Chapter 5.

To quote from RFC 1122, the standard that defines what a host attached to the Internet must be capable of doing, "ICMP is a control protocol that is considered to be an integral part of IP." This says that any node that professes to support IP must also support ICMP.

2.6.1 Messages and Formats

ICMP messages are carried as the payload of IP datagrams with the Next Protocol field set to 1 to indicate that the data contains an ICMP message, as shown in Figure 2.24. Each ICMP message begins with three standard fields: the Message Type indicates which ICMP message is present, and the Message Code qualifies this for meaning specific to the type of message. Table 2.14 lists the ICMP message types.

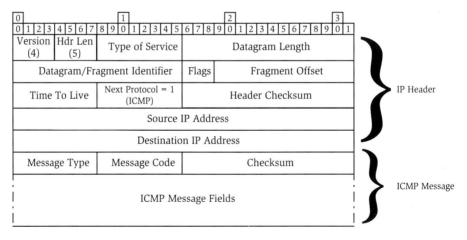

Figure 2.24 An ICMP message is encapsulated in an IP datagram and begins with three common fields and then continues according to the message type.

Table 2.14 The ICMP Messages

Message Type	Message
0	Echo Reply. Sent in direct response to an ICMP Echo Request message.
3	Destination Unreachable. An error message sent when a node cannot forward any IP datagram toward its destination.
4	Source Quench. Sent by a destination node to slow down the rate at which a source node sends IP datagrams.
5	Redirect. Used to tell a source node that there is a better first hop for it to use when trying to send IP datagrams to a given destination.
8	Echo. Sent by a node to probe the network for reachability to a particular destination.
9	Router Advertisement. Used by a router to tell hosts in its network that it exists and is ready for service.
10	Router Solicitation. Used by a host to discover which routers are available for use.
11	Time Exceeded. An error message generated by a router when it cannot forward an IP datagram because the TTL has expired.
12	Parameter Problem. An error sent by any node that discovers a problem with an IP datagram it has received.
13	Timestamp Request. Used to probe the network for the transmission and processing latency of messages to a given destination.
14	Timestamp Reply. Used in direct response to a Timestamp Request message.
15	Information Request. Used by a host to discover the subnet to which it is attached.
16	Information Reply. Used in direct response to an Information Request message.
17	Address Mask Request. Used by a host to discover the subnet mask for the network to which it is attached.
18	Address Mask Reply. Used in direct response to an Address Mask Request message.

The third common ICMP message field is a checksum. This is calculated across the whole ICMP message, including the three common fields but not including the IP header, using the algorithm described in Section 2.2.3. After the checksum are found fields specific to the type of message. These are described later in this section.

2.6.2 Error Reporting and Diagnosis

ICMP can be used to report errors with the delivery or forwarding of IP datagrams. The intention is to report only nontransient errors. Transient errors (that is, those that are likely to be resolved) are not reported because such error reports would congest the network and cause unnecessary concern to the original data sender.

What constitutes a transient error? Recall that IP is built on the precept that it is an unreliable delivery mechanism, making it acceptable that some messages may be lost or discarded, and that it is the responsibility of the higher layer protocols to detect and manage this situation through sequence numbers and retransmissions. What we are looking for, then, is a distinction between events that cause the occasional discard of packets and those events that will result in frequent or persistent packet discards.

A good line to draw here is between a TTL failure and a checksum error. The former indicates that any further datagrams sent with the same source TTL are likely to be discarded in the same way either because the TTL was not set to a high enough value or because there is a forwarding loop—it is possible that no datagrams are reaching the destination and the sooner this is reported, the better. On the other hand, a checksum error on an individual datagram is not very significant and is even statistically predictable given the known characteristics of the links between the nodes. It is not necessary to report every checksum error since usually they represent quirks that are not persistent; a receiving node might implement a threshold and report checksum errors if they indicate more than a certain proportion of the received datagrams. A very important note, however, is that there is no way to know the source address of an IP datagram with a corrupt header because it may be the source IP address field itself that has been corrupted. Extreme caution should be exercised when responding to corrupt IP datagrams with ICMP error messages, and nodes are generally recommended to discard such datagrams without sending any errors.

In fact there is such a long list of reasons not to send an ICMP error message that it looks like there is hardly any point in thinking about sending an error! First, as just mentioned, there is no point in sending an error message if it is unclear to whom it should be sent—this covers not only checksum errors, but received IP datagrams that carry generic source addresses (such as broadcast or multicast addresses). Similarly, if the destination address in the IP header or in the data-link frame is a broadcast or multicast address, no ICMP error should be sent for fear that many nodes might all send the same error message. Next, it is important not to send an ICMP error message in response to a received ICMP error message since this might cause an endless exchange of messages. Finally, there is no need to send an error for any fragment other than the first in a sequence—this is an issue because the sender will not be aware that fragment-ation occurred and is not responsible for the error.

Four of the ICMP messages are used to report errors: Destination Unreachable, Redirect, Time Exceeded, and Parameter Problem. These need to be examined one at a time as their semantics are different.

All four ICMP error messages use the format shown in Figure 2.25. As can be seen, the error messages begin with the standard 4 bytes of an ICMP message. Afterwards comes a Message Data field, which is used differently

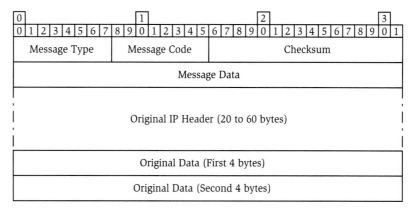

Figure 2.25 All ICMP error messages use the same format.

according to the Message Type and Message Code. The ICMP error messages conclude with a copy of the IP header as received, and the first 8 bytes of the payload of the IP datagram. This copy of the received datagram can be useful to highlight the specific error and to relate the error back to individual data flows.

Time Exceeded

There are two time-related errors that may arise within the IP layer. First, the TTL of an IP datagram may expire before it is delivered to the destination. Alternatively, the datagram may be fragmented and may expire while it is waiting to be reassembled.

Timer problems are reported using the ICMP Time Exceeded message (message type 11). The message code is set to zero to indicate that the TTL expired in transit, and to 1 to indicate that the datagram expired while waiting to be reassembled. The message data is unused and must be set to zero.

Parameter Problem

IP encoding problems can be reported using the Parameter Problem message (message type 12). The message type is set to 12 to indicate Parameter Problem, and the Message Code is used to identify the type of problem being reported, as listed in Table 2.15.

Redirect

The ICMP Redirect message is used by one router to inform the sender of a datagram that a better route exists toward the destination. Note that this is not used for communication between routers, but to tell a host (that is, the source of the datagram) that it has not chosen the best first hop in the path of the datagram that it sent. The only routers that should generate ICMP Redirect messages are the first hop routers that know that they are directly attached to the source node.

In general, the term "better route" is taken to mean shorter path. That is, the alternative router to which the host is referred is able to provide a more direct route to the destination. An example of redirect in operation is shown in Section 2.6.5.

Several message codes are defined for the Redirect message to indicate the scope of the redirect information, as shown in Table 2.16. In all cases, the message

Table 2.15 ICMP Parameter Problem Messages Carry Message Codes to Indicate the Problem Type

Message Code	Meaning
0	No specific error is indicated, but the first byte of the message data is a zero-based offset in bytes into the returned original IP header and data that points to the byte that is in error. In this way, an error in the Type of Service byte can be reported by an offset value of one. Note that although some bytes in the IP header contain more than one field, there are separate error codes or messages to cover these parameters.
1	A required IP header option is missing. The first byte of the Message Data field indicates which option is missing using the option class and number. Perhaps the most important option that may be required by the receiver is the security option indicated by the value 130 (0x82).
2	The header or datagram length is invalid or appears to be at fault. There is some overlap here and it may be impossible to tell whether the complaint is about the header length or the datagram length, but the return of the entire header should make it possible to determine if there is a problem with the header length itself. Any other problem must be with the datagram length.

Table 2.16 ICMP Redirect Messages Carry Message Codes to Give Scope to the Redirect Information

Message Code	Meaning
0	Redirect for Destination Network. All traffic for the destination network should be sent through another first hop router.
1	Redirect for Destination Host. All traffic for the destination host should be sent through another first hop router.
2	Redirect for Destination Network based on Type of Service. All traffic carrying this Type of Service value for the destination network should be sent through another first hop router.
3	Redirect for Destination Host based on Type of Service. All traffic carrying this Type of Service value for the destination host should be sent through another first hop router.

Table 2.17 ICMP Destination Unreachable Messages Carry Message Codes to Indicate the Reason for the Delivery Failure

Message Code	Meaning
0	Network Unreachable. This error is returned by a router that cannot forward an IP packet because it doesn't have an entry in its routing table for any subnet that contains the destination address. This error is advisory and does not immediately require that the source node take any action.
1	Host Unreachable. This error is slightly different from the previous error. It is intended to be returned by what should be the final hop router when it identifies an attachment to the correct subnet but doesn't recognize the destination IP address as one of the hosts on that network. This error is also advisory and indicates that the destination host cannot be reached at the moment, not that it doesn't exist.
2	Protocol Unreachable. This error is returned by the destination host to say that it has received the IP datagram correctly but that it has no application registered to handle the payload protocol. The error may be transitory (the application may be reloading).
3	Port Unreachable. This error relates to the transport protocols discussed in Chapter 7. The IP datagram has been correctly received at the destination and the payload transport protocol targets a specific port which is not bound to any application.
4	Fragmentation Required but Don't Fragment Set. Transit routers generate this error when the IP datagram would need to be fragmented to be forwarded, but the Don't Fragment (DF) bit is set in the IP header. This error also uses the Message Data field to return the maximum PDU of the next hop so that the sender may reduce the size of the IP datagrams that it sends. See Section 2.6.6 for a discussion of how the Path MTU size can be found out in advance of data transmission.
5	Source Route Failed. The router reporting the error was unable to use the source route specified. In other words, the next hop in the source route was unreachable from the reporting router.
6	Destination Network Unknown. This error compares with Network Unreachable and means that the reporting router is certain that the destination network does not exist rather than is currently unreachable.
7	Destination Host Unknown. This error compares with Host Unreachable and means that the reporting router is certain that the destination host does not exist and is not simply currently unreachable.
11	Network Unreachable for Type of Service. If Type-of-Service routing is in use, this error is returned if the router is unable to forward the IP datagram toward the destination using links that provide the required Type of Service.
12	Host Unreachable for Type of Service. This error is generated by the last hop router if it cannot provide the required Type of Service on the final link to the destination host.
13	Communication Administratively Prohibited. This error response is usually used in conjunction with security configuration at the destination host or the hop router when datagrams from the sender are rejected as a matter of policy. See Section 2.6.7 for more details of ICMP and security.

Table 2.17 *Continued*

Message Code	Meaning
14	Host Precedence Violation. The precedence value set on the IP datagram is not supported by the destination host or by some node on the path through the network.
15	Precedence Cutoff In Effect. The IP datagram is rejected because its precedence is not high enough to pass through some transit network.

data field is used to carry the IP address of the router that can provide the better route. Now ICMP is really in the routing business!

Destination Unreachable

The most common reasons for the failure to deliver an IP datagram fall into the category of an unreachable destination—that is, the datagram reached some node in the network that was unable to forward the datagram further. It is at this point that ICMP begins to perform like a routing protocol since the information returned may be used to help identify routing problems within the network. Table 2.17 lists sixteen message code values used with the Destination Unreachable message.

2.6.3 Flow Control

If a destination host is receiving data faster than it can process it, the host can send an ICMP Source Quench message to the sender to ask it to slow down. This is a warning to the sender that if it continues to transmit at this rate it is probable that datagrams will be discarded. The receiver of a Source Quench message should notify the application so that it can slow down the rate at which it provides data to the IP layer—the IP layer itself is not required to apply any flow control.

The Source Quench message type is four. No messages codes are defined, and the Message Code field must be set to zero. The message is formatted as an ICMP error message, but no message data is used. The returned IP header is an example from the flow that needs to be throttled back.

2.6.4 Ping and Traceroute

Two applications that form the mainstay of the network operator's toolkit are ping and traceroute. Ping is used to test the network to discover whether a host is reachable and to record characteristics of the route to that host. The traceroute application is used to discover the route to a host. These tools are particularly useful during network configuration or when packets are not reaching their destination correctly. Ping can be used to verify connectivity and configuration—if

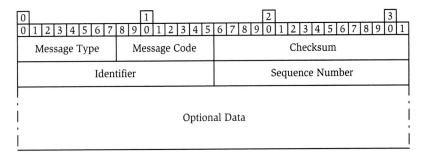

Figure 2.26 ICMP Echo Request and Reply messages have the same format.

ping works, the network is functional and any problems must lie with the transport or application software. The route recording properties of ping and traceroute can be used to determine where a network is broken (the route will be recorded as far as the breach) or where packets are being discarded by a router (perhaps because it cannot route them any further).

Ping uses the ICMP Echo Request and Echo Reply messages. These messages begin in the standard way for all ICMP messages with Message Type, Message Code, and Checksum fields, as shown in Figure 2.26. There is then an Identifier to group together a series of Echo Request/Replies and a Sequence Number to uniquely identify a Request/Reply pair. The Optional Data is optional! It is present to allow the user to verify that data can be successfully exchanged, and the receiver must echo the data back in the Reply unchanged. This process also allows the user to test whether datagrams of a specific size can be supported across the network (see Section 2.6.6).

Figure 2.27 shows the options for a popular implementation of the ping application. A user may choose to set a wide array of options to control the

```
c:\> ping
Options:
    -t              Ping the specified host until stopped.
    -a              Resolve addresses to hostnames.
    -n count        Number of echo requests to send.
    -l size         Send buffer size.
    -f              Set Don't Fragment (DF) flag.
    -i TTL          Initial TTL.
    -v TOS          Set the ToS on all datagrams.
    -r count        Record the route for <count> hops.
    -s count        Record timestamps for <count> hops.
    -j host-list    Loose source route along host-list.
    -k host-list    Strict source route along host-list.
    -w timeout      Time to wait for each reply (milliseconds).
```

Figure 2.27 The options to a popular ping implementation.

```
C:\> ping www.mkp.com
Pinging www.mkp.com [213.38.165.180] with 32 bytes of data:
Reply from 213.38.165.180: bytes=32 time=223 ms TTL=112
Reply from 213.38.165.180: bytes=32 time=215 ms TTL=112
Reply from 213.38.165.180: bytes=32 time=220 ms TTL=112
Reply from 213.38.165.180: bytes=32 time=205 ms TTL=112
Ping statistics for 213.38.165.180:
   Packets: Sent=4, Received=4, Lost=0 (0% loss).
Approximate round trip times in milliseconds:
   Minimum=205 ms, Maximum=223 ms, Average=215 ms
```

Figure 2.28 An example use of ping.

behavior and information returned by the application. Some of these map to application characteristics (such as the number of times to ping, how long to wait for a response, and how to map addresses for display to the user). Others control the fields set in the IP header that carries the ICMP Echo Request (such as the DF bit, the TTL, the ToS, and the source routing options).

The remaining flags describe how ping uses ICMP and allow control of the size of the Optional Data or request reporting information back from the network.

Figure 2.28 shows the output from an execution of ping using the default options. The default in this instance is to send 32 bytes of data and to ping just four times. The output shows four replies, each received a little over 200 milliseconds after the request was sent. The TTL value shows the contents of the TTL field from the IP header of the received reply, so it is helpful to know that the reply originated with a TTL of 128, and we can calculate that the packet has traversed 26 hops. The output continues with a summary of the results.

So how does the route recording and timestamp recording work? Suppose you send a sequence of ICMP Echo Requests to the destination starting with a TTL of 1 and increasing the TTL by one for each request in the sequence. When you do this, the TTLs will expire at successive hops along the path to the destination, and when they expire they will return an ICMP Time Exceeded error (see Section 2.6.2). Examining the list of nodes that return errors gives us the path through the network to the destination. At the same time, examining the turnaround time for the error messages gives a measure of which hops in the network are consuming how much time.

The traceroute application is specifically designed to provide this last piece of ping function—that is, to plot the route through the network of IP datagrams targeted at a specific destination. Figure 2.29 shows the options available in a popular traceroute implementation.

Traceroute can be implemented using the ICMP echo Request/Replies as already described for ping, although some implementations choose to use UDP datagrams using the same philosophy of incrementing the TTL in the IP header and expecting an ICMP Time Expired error message. For more details of UDP, see Chapter 7.

```
c:\> tracert
Options:
-d                 Do not resolve addresses to hostnames.
-h maximum-hops  Maximum number of hops to search for target.
-j host-list     Loose source route along host-list.
-w timeout       Time to wait for each reply (milliseconds).
```

Figure 2.29 The options to a popular traceroute implementation.

Still other implementations of traceroute and the route recording process in ping use the IP Record Route option (see Section 2.5.1) to gather the addresses of the nodes that the datagram passes through on its way to the destination. The recorded information is returned in application data on the response. The implementations can be easily spotted because they limit the number of hops that can be recorded to nine—the maximum that will fit in the Record Route option.

An alternative way to measure the time taken for a datagram to travel across the network is provided by the ICMP Timestamp Request and Reply messages shown in Figure 2.30. These messages also begin with the standard ICMP message fields, and then continue with an Identifier and Sequence Number just like the Echo messages. The messages continue with three timestamps expressed as the system time in milliseconds.

The sender of a Timestamp request is able to measure the total round-trip time by comparing the Originate Timestamp it set on the request message with the time at which it received the reply message. It can do this without storing information for each request that it sent—a minor advantage over the use of the Echo messages. Unfortunately, no conclusions can be drawn from the specific value of the Receive Timestamp used in the Timestamp Reply to say when the original request arrived at the destination because the clocks on the two machines are likely not in synch. However, the Receive Timestamp and the Transmit Timestamp can be compared to discover how long the request took to be processed in the destination node before it was turned around and transmitted

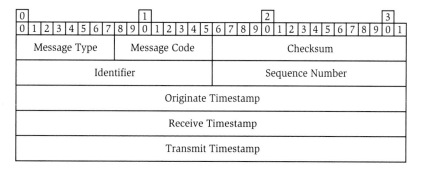

Figure 2.30 ICMP Timestamp Request and Reply messages have the same format.

as a reply. This helps pin down how much of the round-trip time is attributable to network latency and how much to processing on the destination node.

2.6.5 Discovering Routers

A computer attached to a network can discover how to reach other computers directly attached to the same network using the Address Resolution Protocol (ARP) described in Section 2.4.5. So, if a computer has a packet to send to an address that matches the local address mask, it issues an ARP Request, extracts the MAC address from the response, and sends the IP packet to the correct recipient.

If the IP packet is not destined for a recipient in the local network it must be passed to a router for forwarding into the wider Internet. But how does a host know the address of the router on its network? There are several possibilities, including static configuration of router addresses on the host and discovery of configured router addresses through DHCP (see Section 2.4.6). These options, however, don't easily handle the situation where multiple routers exist on a multi-drop network and may come and go as they are installed, decommissioned, or crash.

Figure 2.31 shows just such a network with three routers providing access to external networks. In order to function correctly and optimally, Host A needs to know which routers are operational and to which external networks they provide access.

ICMP offers router discovery function and feedback on which routers are most suitable for a particular destination address. A host that wishes to find out about

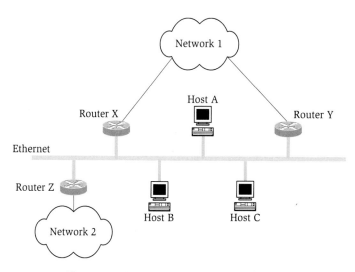

Figure 2.31 Multiple routers on a single network.

all directly attached routers simply sends an ICMP Router Solicitation message to the broadcast address of the local network. All active routers respond with a Router Advertisement message to let the host know that they are ready for service.

Initially, the host will simply pick one router (presumably the first to respond) and use it as the default router. This might mean that in Figure 2.31, Host A would attempt to send packets destined to Network 2 via Router X. This is perfectly functional, because Router X knows to forward them to Router Z, but it is not optimal. So, when Router X receives a packet targeted at a host in Network 2 from any of the hosts on the local network, it forwards the packet to Router Z as it should, but it also sends an ICMP Redirect message back to the originating host to tell it to install a better route (via Router Z) to the destination address or a more general network address.

Note that the routers attached to a network also use this process to discover each other, and that when a router boots up it sends an unsolicited Router Advertisement to tell all the other nodes on the network (hosts and routers) that it exists.

2.6.6 Path MTU Discovery

As mentioned in Section 2.2, IP datagrams may need to be fragmented as they traverse the network. It is not always desirable to perform fragmentation because of the additional processing required and because of the impact it may have on the way the applications function. Fragmentation can be avoided if it is known in advance what the maximum size of datagram supported on the path to the destination is—this is called the *Maximum Transmission Unit* (MTU).

Some higher-level protocols include functions to discover and negotiate the MTU for a path between source and destination, but the same function can be achieved using the ICMP Echo Request message in conjunction with the ICMP Destination Unreachable error message.

Initially, an Echo Request is sent carrying as much Optional Data as is allowed by the limits of the maximum PDU of the local network. The destination is set to the intended destination of the data flow, and the DF bit is set in the IP header to prevent fragmentation. If an Echo Reply is received, then the message has reached the destination and all is well. But if fragmentation is required somewhere in the network, a Destination Unreachable message will be returned by the router that needed to fragment the datagram—it will supply the smaller maximum PDU needed by the next network. The source node reduces the size of the Optional data and tries again.

Consider the example network in Figure 2.5. If Node B wishes to discover the MTU for the path to Node A it sends out an Echo Request with a lot of Optional Data to make the datagram size up to 17,756 bytes, and it sets the DF bit. The request reaches the first router, which determines that it must forward the datagram over the Ethernet. Since fragmentation is not allowed, the router returns a Destination Unreachable message with the message Data carrying the value 1,500 (the maximum PDU for the Ethernet).

Node B tries again, sending an Echo Request made up of just 1,500 bytes, and this time the datagram makes it across the Ethernet to the second router, which discovers that it needs to forward the datagram onto the X.25 network. But fragmentation is still not allowed, so it too returns a Destination Unreachable message, this time with the Message Data carrying the value 512.

Finally, Node B sends a much smaller Echo Request totaling only 512 bytes. This makes it through to the destination (Node A), which responds with an Echo Reply letting Node B know that all will be well if it keeps its datagrams down to just 512 bytes.

2.6.7 Security Implications

ICMP can be used to report security problems through the Communication Administratively Prohibited code of the Destination Unreachable error message (see Section 2.6.2). If an IP datagram cannot be forwarded because of security rules configured at a router or at the destination host, this error message may be returned. Similarly, the Parameter Problem message with message code 1 and message data set to 130 indicates that the security option was required but not found in the received IP datagram.

However, these ICMP error messages might, themselves, be considered as a security weakness since they convey to the originator of the IP datagram some information about how security is being implemented on the target system. For this reason many security gateways simply discard IP datagrams that do not meet the security requirements and do not return any ICMP error.

Further, many administrators consider that the route tracing facilities of ICMP tell people outside their network far too much about the internal connectivity of the network. Through resourceful use of ping, someone can discover a lot about the link types and node connectivity within a network. One answer is to disable the ICMP server function so that Echo Requests do not generate a response, meaning that the node cannot be pinged. But an imaginative person can quickly find ways to cause IP errors and get ICMP error messages sent back to them. So a lot of gateways entirely block ICMP messages from passing from one network to another.

Although such ICMP blockades are effective at protecting the details of the internals of a network, they can have some nasty consequences for applications trying to send data from one network to another. For example, if a sender builds large IP datagrams and sends them toward a destination using the DF bit to prevent fragmentation, it would expect to hear back if the datagram is too large. But if the requirement to fragment happens within the second network, an ICMP Destination Unreachable error message with the message code Fragmentation Required but Don't Fragment Set will be generated. The ICMP error will trace its way back across the second network until it reaches the gateway where it is dropped. This leaves the sender believing that the data has been delivered. The only solution to this is for the gateway node to generate statistics and alarm messages to the network operators informing them of the errors so that they can take manual action to correct any problems.

2.7 Further Reading

IP and IP Addressing

There are more good introductions to IP addressing and the Internet Protocol than it is possible to mention. Several excellent texts are suggested here.

Interconnections: Bridges and Routers, by Radia Perlman (1999). Addison-Wesley. This is an excellent, thorough, and readable text that will explain all of the details.

TCP/IP Clearly Explained, by Pete Loshin (2002). Morgan Kaufmann. A straightforward introduction to the subject as a gateway to explaining some of the protocols that use IP.

The following lists show specific RFCs and other standards broken down by topic.

The Internet Protocol and ICMP

RFC 791—Internet Protocol
RFC 792—Internet Control Message Protocol
RFC 896—ICMP Source Quench
RFC 1191—ICMP Router Discovery

Discovering Addresses and Configuration

RFC 826—An Ethernet Address Resolution Protocol or Converting Network Protocol Address to 48.bit Ethernet Address for Transmission on Ethernet Hardware
RFC 903—A Reverse Address Resolution Protocol
RFC 951—Bootstrap Protocol (BOOTP)
RFC 1533—DHCP Options and BOOTP Vendor Extensions
RFC 1534—Interoperation Between DHCP and BOOTP
RFC 1542—Clarifications and Extensions for the Bootstrap Protocol
RFC 2131—Dynamic Host Configuration Protocol
RFC 2390—Inverse Address Resolution Protocol

Rules for Building Hosts and Routers

RFC 1122—Requirements for Internet Hosts—Communication Layers
RFC 1812—Requirements for IP Version 4 Routers

Chapter 3

Multicast

The previous chapter discussed IP datagram delivery. The normal datagram is addressed to a single station using its IP address, which is unique either across the whole Internet or within the context of a private network. This is known as *unicast* traffic—each datagram is sent to a single destination.

The concept of *broadcast* datagrams was also introduced. Using a special "all nodes" IP address, a sender is able to direct a datagram to all nodes on a subnet. This is particularly useful when a host needs to find a router or server on the local network, or when it has an emergency message that it needs to send to everyone.

But broadcast and unicast delivery represent an all or (nearly) nothing approach. Broadcasting delivers a packet to every node in a single subnet, but does not deliver the packet outside the subnet. Unicast, of course, delivers the packet to just one destination somewhere in the Internet. What if I want to send a message to a collection of some of the hosts on a network, but I don't want to send it to all of them? What if I want to distribute a message to multiple nodes outside my network?

This chapter introduces the concept of multicast IP delivery, in which datagrams are delivered to groups of nodes across the Internet regardless of the subnets to which the individual group members belong. The Internet Group Management Protocol (IGMP) used to manage the groups of hosts is also described.

The mechanism by which routers decide how to propagate multicast IP datagrams routed through a network is fundamental to its success in more complex networks. Such routing decisions are based on information distributed by multicast routing protocols, which are discussed in Chapter 5.

3.1 Choosing Unicast or Multicast

Figure 3.1 shows an Ethernet. The host on the left-hand side wishes to send a datagram to four of the other stations on the Ethernet. The figure shows how it is possible for the source host to make four copies of the datagram and to send them onto the network. This is clearly perfectly functional, but it places an overhead on the source node, which must either manage a cyclic way of sending

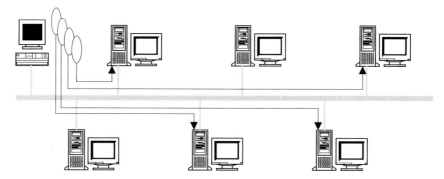

Figure 3.1 The same packet can be delivered to multiple hosts by sending multiple copies.

the datagrams or use additional buffers to make local copies of the data. Additionally, this technique puts stress on the network because an increased amount of data is sent.

Figure 3.2 shows an alternative way of distributing the data. The packet is sent as a broadcast datagram to all the other hosts on the network. Exactly how this is achieved is up to the data-link layer implementation, but most data-link layers such as Ethernet include the concept of a broadcast MAC address (usually $0\times$FFFFFFFFFFFF) so that only one frame has to be placed on the physical medium for all nodes to pick it up. This approach saves a lot of data transmission compared with Figure 3.1, but has the issue that the data is delivered to all nodes, even those that don't want or need to see it. At best, this is an inconvenience to the higher-layer protocols, which must work out which data is wanted and which should be discarded (note that the destination IP address cannot be used to do this since it is set to the broadcast address for the subnet), but at worst it places an unacceptable processing overhead on the nodes that receive

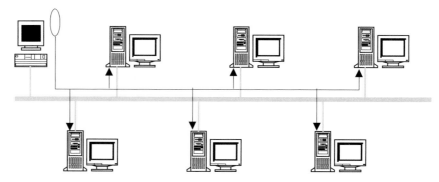

Figure 3.2 A packet can be broadcast within a single subnet, although this means that every host in the subnet receives a copy.

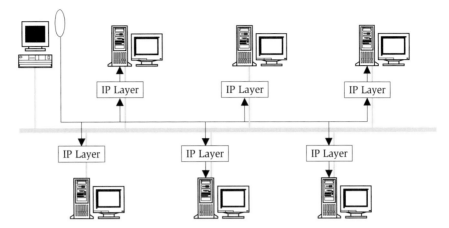

Figure 3.3 IP multicast on an Ethernet still involves broadcast of frames at the data-link layer, but the datagrams are filtered on the basis of their multicast addresses.

the unwanted datagrams. It is even possible that this approach would constitute a security vulnerability because data is delivered to nodes that shouldn't see it.

In multicast, data is sent out to a special address that represents the group of all intended recipients. Stations that wish to receive multicast traffic for a particular distribution listen for datagrams targeted to that address in addition to those sent to their own addresses. In practice, on many data-links the multicast IP datagram is actually broadcast in a frame to all stations on the network, but because the datagram now has a more specific address than the broadcast address for the subnetwork, the hosts are able to discriminate against unwanted packets within their IP code, throwing them away before too much processing has been done. This is illustrated in Figure 3.3. Note that some data-link layers include the multicast concept, in which case it is possible to map IP multicast to data-link multicast and possibly reduce the number of frames received and the amount of processing done for unwanted datagrams.

This is all very well, but the broadcast techniques used within networks don't work across connected networks. Routers are forbidden to forward datagrams carrying IP broadcast addresses. Data-link layer broadcasts are not forwarded across routers since they are not bridges and they act on the datagrams rather than the frames. This could reduce us to sending multiple copies of datagrams as illustrated in Figure 3.4.

However, IP multicast can solve the problem. As illustrated in Figure 3.5, the source sends a single datagram into the network that travels through the network, being fanned out only where necessary according to the intended recipients. The main challenges of IP multicast are in determining which hosts are the intended recipients of the multicast datagram and where the fan-out should happen. These issues are discussed in later sections of this chapter.

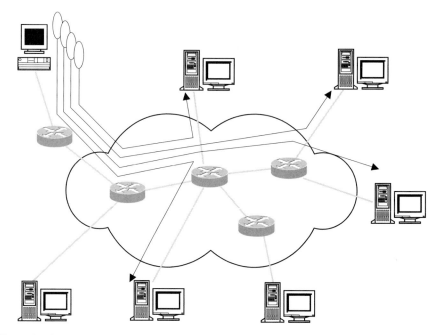

Figure 3.4 In a more general network, broadcasting is not available, but multiple packets can still be sent.

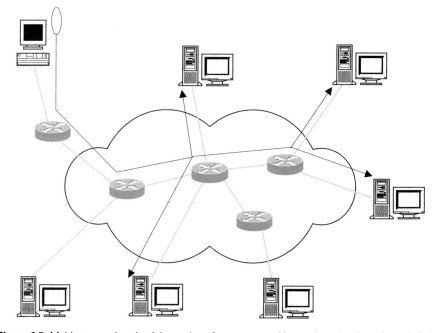

Figure 3.5 Multicast uses just the right number of messages, making copies only where the path forks.

There are, however, still reasons to favor unicast over multicast. Multicast imposes an additional management overhead, and, worse, it requires new forwarding paradigms in routers and special routing protocols to distribute the information about which hosts should receive which multicast packets. There is an interesting scalability issue to these routing and forwarding procedures because multicast addresses do not have the same geographic implications of unicast addresses—two unicast addresses from the same subnet can be handled the same way within a remote part of the network, but each multicast address must be seen as a slash 32 address that needs its own entry (or, in fact, multiple entries since the datagrams may need to be fanned out) in every routing table.

Multicast also raises security concerns as an interloper only has to get himself subscribed as a multicast recipient to receive all of the traffic.

Finally, consideration must be given to the fact that IP is an unreliable protocol. In unicast data exchanges, this problem is handled by the higher-level protocols that can detect missing, out of order, or corrupt data and request that it be resent. But in multicast, if one recipient sees a problem and asks for a retransmission the data will be sent to everyone, causing confusion since most destinations have already seen the data once.

Nevertheless, the key advantages of traffic reduction and better bandwidth utilization make multicast popular in some applications described in the next section.

3.1.1 Applications That Use Multicast

The most common use of multicast is to simultaneously distribute data to multiple recipients. There are some very simple applications involving data distribution. Consider, for example, a supermarket chain that sends a data file to each outlet every night to update the pricing and product descriptions for every item of stock. Historically these price files were distributed to one store at a time, and since they are quite large files, it wasn't long before the head office had to install multiple connections so that they could send to several stores at once in order to get through them all before morning. With multicast, the data is sent just once and is fanned out to all of the sites that need to receive it.

A variant on this theme might be used to upgrade the software load on multiple computers at the same time. Again, there is a need to distribute a potentially large file to many locations, and multicast can do this for us.

Another data distribution service that operates in real time is called *data streaming*. The best-known example would be the up-to-date distribution of commodity or stock prices or exchange rates to traders or, indeed, to the general public, which has recently recast itself as an army of day traders. Again, multicast can be used to ensure that the data is sent out as smoothly as possible.

Audio and video streaming can also be facilitated by multicast. A single site has audio or video information to share with many recipients and multicasts it to them. This would be useful for a press conference or a briefing by the CEO.

Even the IETF, in an attempt to embrace its own technology, multicasts some of the sessions of its triannual meetings. Multicast could also be used for services such as video-on-demand.

A new and increasingly popular use of multicast IP is in voice, video, and data conferencing—collectively known as *multimedia conferencing*. This is an extension of the multiparty telephone call, which can also include live video distribution and application sharing and is offered as a desktop application for most home and office computers. Even conference calls, which are fundamentally not unidirectional, may operate using a single multicast group where any participant can transmit to the group at any time. However, in operations such as voice over IP (see Chapter 15) this may not work well because voice fragments will get interspersed and everyone will hear garbage. This is perhaps what you would expect when more than one person talks at once, but the network can do better by using a conference center. Each participant unicasts his contribution to the call to the conference center, which picks the winner at any moment (using some algorithm such as first speaker) and multicasts that person's voice to all of the participants.

Refer to Section 7.5 for a description of the Real-Time Transport Protocol that is used in unicast and multicast environments to distribute multimedia data with an awareness of the requirements of such systems for smooth and high-quality delivery.

3.2 Multicast Addressing and Forwarding

In multicast, data is sent out to a special address that represents the group of all intended recipients. Recall from Chapter 2 that Class D addresses in the range 224.0.0.0 to 239.255.255.255 are reserved for multicast. Each address in this range represents a multicast *group*—a collection of recipients who all wish to receive the same datagrams. Each host retains its unique IP address and also subscribes to any number of groups. To send to every host in the group, any node (in or out of the group) simply addresses the datagrams to the group address.

Just as routers must maintain routing tables to tell them where to send unicast datagrams based on their address, so these devices also need to know how to distribute multicast datagrams. In this case, however, as shown in Figure 3.5, a router may need to send a multicast datagram in more than one direction at once. This makes the routing tables a little more complex to construct and maintain.

Fortunately, all multicast addresses are Class D addresses and can be recognized from the first nibble, which is $0 \times E$. Addresses that match that characteristic can be passed off to a separate piece of forwarding code. Note that, just as care must be taken to ensure that unicast addresses are unique within their context, so multicast addresses must be kept from clashing and must be carefully and correctly assigned. It is worth noting that some Class D addresses have been

Table 3.1 IP Multicast Address Ranges

Address Range	Usage
224.0.0.1	All systems (all hosts and routers)
224.0.0.2	All routers
224.0.0.5–224.0.0.6	Used by the OSPF routing protocol
224.0.0.1–224.0.0.255	Local segment only (that is, to not forward through a router)
239.0.0.0–239.255.255.255	Administratively scoped (that is, restricted to private networks)
239.192.0.0–239.195.255.255	Administratively scoped for organizations
239.255.0.0–239.255.255.255	Administratively scoped for local segments

allocated by the Internet Assigned Numbers Authority (IANA) for specific applications—there are no fewer than 279 of these defined at the time of writing. Table 3.1 shows how these Class D addresses are broken up to have specific meanings.

The ideal forwarding paradigm for multicast traffic is a logical tree built so that datagrams flow from the root along the trunk and up the branches to the destinations at the leaves. Such a tree can be formed to reduce the length that any datagram travels to any destination, or to reduce the amount of data in the network. These options are illustrated in Figure 3.6.

The routing model gets considerably more complex if there are multiple data sources sending to a multicast tree. Without care, the network reverts to a broadcast mesh and everybody gets every datagram multiple times. Figure 3.7 illustrates this problem for a very simple network in which Host X multicasts to Hosts Y and Z. Router A fans the datagrams out toward Routers B and C to correctly distribute them to their destinations. But when Router B processes a datagram it will send it to Host Y and to Router C, so Router C will see two copies of the datagram and could forward both to Host Z. Similarly, Router C will forward the datagram received from Router A to Router B. And now things could get really nasty, because Router B will forward the datagram received from Router B to Router A, which will deliver it to Host X (the origin of the datagram) and to Router C. Only the TTLs on the datagrams prevent them from looping forever.

Of course, this is not how multicast operates. Each router uses a process called *reverse path lookup* (RPL) to determine which datagrams it should forward and which it should discard. The procedure operates on the source and destination addresses carried in the datagrams. If a router receives a datagram on an interface, it performs a routing lookup on the source address from the datagram and forwards the datagram only if the best (that is, preferred by the routing

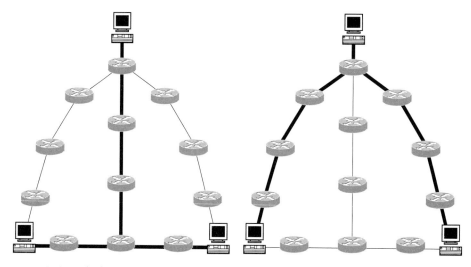

Optimize for fewest datagram hops.
Total of eight datagram hops.
Each destination receives a datagram that has
travelled a total of six hops.

Optimize for shortest paths.
Each destination receives a datagram that has
travelled five hops.
A total of nine datagram hops are executed.

Figure 3.6 Multicast paths may be optimized according to different factors.

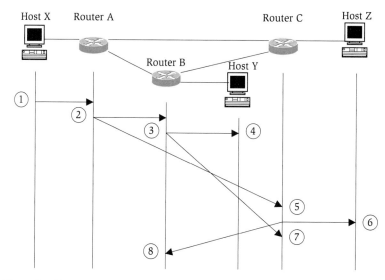

Figure 3.7 Reverse path lookup is used to limit the distribution of multicast datagrams.

algorithm—for example, shortest) route to the source is through the interface that delivered the datagram. Otherwise the datagram is silently discarded. This procedure is demonstrated in Figure 3.7.

In step 1, Host X sends a multicast datagram that should be delivered to both Host Y and Host Z. Router A performs the RPL at step 2 and sees that the datagram has been received on the best path from Host X, so it forwards to both Router B and Router C. At step 3, Router B also does the RPL on the source of the datagram (Host X) and sees that the datagram has come by the best path, so it also forwards it out of every other interface—that is, to Host Y and to Router C. Step 4 shows that the datagram has been delivered to Host Y—it should not receive any further copies.

Step 5 shows the datagram arriving at Router C from Router A. RPL at Router C shows that this datagram came along the best route, so Router C sends a copy out of each of its interfaces—to Host Z and to Router B. Step 6 shows that the datagram has been delivered to Host Z—both of the intended recipients have now received the data, but the datagram is still alive in the network.

Router C receives a second copy of the datagram at step 7. This time the RPL fails because the best route back to the source (Host X) is direct to Router A and this datagram has come from Router B, so Router C discards the copy. Similarly, at step 8 Router B receives a second copy and discards it because it has not come along the best path. Finally, everything goes quiet and only single copies have been delivered to the hosts.

Note that the ordering of events may vary in practice and a router may receive a datagram that fails the RPL before it sees the copy that it should forward. Instinctively, one might want to forward such a datagram anyway, because the copy on the best path may have been lost. But there is no easy way to track this behavior and it would require that transit routers maintain state for all datagrams that they handle in this way if they were to avoid sending duplicates.

3.3 Internet Group Management Protocol (IGMP)

The Internet Group Management Protocol (IGMP) is one of the early IP protocols and was assigned the protocol identifier value of 2. This means that when IGMP messages are carried within IP datagrams the Next Protocol field within the IP header is set to the number 2. IGMP is used to manage which hosts receive datagrams that are sent to multicast addresses. This allows routers to build a picture of where they must send multicast datagrams and so construct their routing trees.

3.3.1 What Are Groups?

In IGMP a *multicast group* is a collection of hosts or routers that wish to receive the same set of multicast IP datagrams. The group needs a group identifier and an IP multicast address, and there being no reason not to, these two concepts are united so that the multicast address uniquely identifies the group.

IGMP is used to allow hosts to register and withdraw their membership of a group, and to discover whether there are any other hosts in the group (that is, whether anyone is listening to the multicast address).

3.3.2 IGMP Message Formats and Exchanges

IGMP is carried as a payload of IP datagrams. As shown in Figure 3.8, each IGMP message is packaged with an IP header into a single datagram. IP uses the protocol identifier value 2 to indicate that the payload is IGMP.

IGMP messages all have the same format within the IP datagram. As shown in Figure 3.9, the messages are made up of just 8 bytes. The first byte is a message type code that tells the recipient what message is being sent—the possible values are listed in Table 3.2. The second field is a timer measured in tenths of seconds that tells the recipient of an IGMP Group Membership Query message (see the following paragraphs) how quickly it must respond. The checksum field uses the standard checksum algorithm described in Section 2.2.3 to protect the entire IGMP message against accidental corruption—the checksum is run across the whole IGMP message, but not the IP header since this is protected by its own checksum. The last field is an IPv4 address that identifies the multicast group.

Note that this description applies to messages for IGMP version two. IGMP version one differs in two ways. The Message Type field was originally specified as two nibbles rather than a single byte—the top nibble gave a protocol

Table 3.2 IGMP Message Types

Protocol Version	IGMPv1 Message Type	IGMPv2 Message Type	Hex	Meaning
1	1	17	0×11	Group Membership Query. Discover which nodes are members of this group.
1	2	18	0×12	IGMP v1 Group Membership Report. Respond to a Group Membership Query or announce that a node has joined a group.
1	6	22	0×16	IGMP v2 Group Membership Report. Respond to a Group Membership Query or announce that a node has joined a group.
1	7	23	0×17	IGMP v2 Leave Group Report. Announce that a node has left a group.

Figure 3.8 Each IGMP message is encapsulated within an IP datagram.

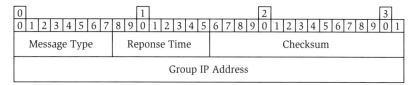

Figure 3.9 The IGMP version two message.

version (version one) and the second nibble defined the message type. The message type values shown in Table 3.2 take this old format into account, allowing IGMP versions one and two to interoperate using the mapping shown in Figure 3.10. The second difference is simply that in version one the Response Time field was undefined and was set to zero—for backwards compatibility, IGMP version two implementations interpret a zero response time as the value 100 (that is, 10 seconds).

A quick inspection of Table 3.2 reveals three curiosities. First, there is no change in protocol version number for IGMP v2—this is consistent with the protocol version field having been retired and provides backwards compatibility between the versions. Second, there are two IGMP Group Membership Report messages—there is no difference between these messages except that the choice of message indicates whether the reporting node implements IGMP v1 or v2. The last point of note is that the Leave Group Report message exists only in IGMP version two—in IGMP version one, nodes silently left groups, which probably meant that they continued to receive and discard multicast datagrams for the group.

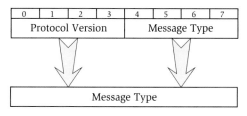

Figure 3.10 In IGMP version one there were separate protocol version and message type fields each comprising four bits, but these are merged into a single message type field in IGMP version two.

Table 3.3 shows the standard operations for IGMP and how they map to the IGMP messages. The use of the three address fields (source and destination in the IP datagram, and Group Address in the IGMP message) are crucial to the way IGMP works. Note the use of the two special addresses *All Systems* and *All Routers*. These addresses have the values 224.0.0.1 and 224.0.0.2, respectively, and are special multicast groups in their own right. All hosts (including routers) are automatically members of the All Systems group, and all routers (but no hosts) are members of the All Routers group. By sending to these groups, IGMP can ensure that all nodes that need to know about an IGMP event receive the message. (Note some implementations send the Group Leave Report to the group being left.)

When joining a group, the Group Membership Report is sent in an IP datagram with TTL set to 1. This means that the message will not be forwarded beyond the first hop routers and hosts on the local network. When a host or a router receives a Group Membership Report from a router or host on its network it makes a note that it must send packets targeted to the group address to the reporting node. In practice this may be achieved at the data-link layer using the data-link equivalent of a multicast address, or by the host sending a specific copy of each datagram to the reporting node. In addition, the router must register with its adjacent routers so that all datagrams addressed to the group address get forwarded to it and then by it to the group members. Routers could simply "pass on" Group Membership Reports to all routers that they know about, effectively registering their membership, but the effect of this in a mesh network would be that every router would participate in every group, which would not serve to reduce the number of datagrams transmitted through the network. What is more, routers must be sophisticated about how they forward multicast datagrams—they can't simply send them out of every interface or the network will be swamped by an exponentially growing amount of traffic. Instead, routers

Table 3.3 How IGMP Messages and Address Fields Are Used

Action	Message	Source Address	Destination Address	IGMP Group Address Field
I want to join a group	Group Membership Report	Host address	Group address	Group address
I want to find out who is in a group	Group Membership Query	Host address	Group address	Group address
I want to find out about all existing groups	Group Membership Query	Host address	All systems	Zero (0.0.0.0)
I want to respond to a Group Membership Query	Group Membership Report (for each group I'm in)	Host address	Group address	Group address
I want to leave a group	Group Leave Report	Host address	All routers	Group address

use multicast routing protocols such as Protocol-Independent Multicast—Sparse Mode (PIM-SM) to announce their requirement to see multicast messages for a specific group and to determine how best to forward multicast packets. Multicast routing is discussed in Chapter 5.

Note that a node responding to an All Systems Group Membership Query sends a Group Membership Report for each group that it is a member of, and sends the response to the group address. It is not actually necessary for every router to respond to a membership query since the network only needs to know that some host is listening to the network. Since the membership report is multicast to the group, each host runs a random timer after receiving a membership request and knows that if it sees a membership report before the timer expires it doesn't have to send a report itself. The Response Time field in the IGMP Group Membership Query message is used to place an upper bound on the time that hosts wait before responding.

3.4 Further Reading

TCP/IP Clearly Explained, by Pete Loshin (2002). Morgan Kaufmann. This provides a good introduction to the concepts of multicast.

Three RFCs cover the function of IGMP. See Chapter 5 for a discussion of multicast routing protocols.

RFC 1112—Host Extensions for IP Multicasting
RFC 1812—Requirements for IP Version 4 Routers
RFC 2236—Internet Group Management Protocol, Version 2

Chapter 4
IP Version Six

Around 1990 the IETF started to get worried that the IPv4 address space was too small. There is scope for a maximum of 2^{32} addresses, but the way in which the addresses are divided into classes can lead to significant wastage as large ranges of addresses are assigned and only partially used. Further, 2^{28} of these addresses are reserved for multicast (Class D) and another 2^{27} are unused (Class E).

The situation was exacerbated both by the success of the Internet and by the dramatic growth in use of personal computers in the office and at home. Additionally, as routers became more sophisticated and networks more complex, the number of IP addresses assigned to identify interfaces rather than nodes was growing at the square of the rate of new routers. And then, in the early 1990s, people started to talk about networking everything—the home would be run as a network with the heating, air conditioning, and lighting systems available for external control. The dream was that you could sit in the office and send a request to your stove to start preparing dinner. Refrigerators would scan items going in and out and would place orders with the supermarket to replenish stocks. All of these domestic appliances would be assigned IP addresses for their communications with the outside world.

These dreams have not come to much, but one device, the mobile phone, has become ubiquitous. As the popularity of cell phones grew, the functions they could provide were extended and it became common for these devices to provide access to email or to the Web. This represented a dramatic growth in the demand for IP addresses, and various charts at the time predicted that we would run out of IP addresses somewhere between 1998 and 2004. By 1994 the projections of the IETF had extended the likely lifetime of the IPv4 address space to somewhere between 2005 and 2011. Although the rate of growth has slowed, the number of addresses in use does continue to grow steadily and IPv4 will eventually need to be replaced or supplemented to increase the size of the address space.

Various schemes were worked on in the early 1990s, but none proved entirely satisfactory, and so the IETF wrote RFC 1752 to summarize the requirements for a next-generation Internet Protocol. This allowed the developers of the new protocol to consider all of the limitations of IPv4 at the same time. Some of these constraints were:

- Provide an unreliable datagram service (as IPv4)
- Support unicast and multicast
- Ensure that addressing is adequate beyond the foreseeable future
- Be backwards compatible with IPv4 so that existing networks do not need to be renumbered or reinstalled, yet provide a simple migration path from IPv4 to IPv6
- Provide support for authentication and encryption
- Architectural simplicity should smooth out some of the "bolt-on" features of IPv4 that have been added over the years
- Make no assumptions about the physical topology, media, or capabilities of the network
- Do nothing that will affect the performance of a router forwarding datagrams
- The new protocol must be extensible and able to evolve to meet the future service needs of the Internet
- There must be support for mobile hosts, networks, and internetworks
- Allow users to build private internetworks on top of the basic Internet infrastructure

The IPv6 Working Group was chartered, and in December 1995 RFC 1883 was published to document IPv6. Since then, work has continued to refine the protocol—initially through experimental networks and more recently with some Service Providers turning over parts of their networks to IPv6. The protocol is now described by RFC 2460, with a raft of other documents defining additions and uses.

Although the majority of the Internet still uses IPv4, its days are numbered and at some point more and more networks will move over to IPv6. In preparation for this, all new IETF protocols must include support for IPv6, and plenty of effort has been devoted to fixing up preexisting protocols so that they, too, support IPv6.

This book is predominantly concerned with the protocols in use on the Internet today. This chapter provides an introduction to IPv6, examining the addressing structure and the messages. Since the higher-level protocols (routing, signaling, and applications) largely view addresses as opaque byte sequences, the other chapters stick with IPv4 as a consistent example with which the readers are more likely to be familiar.

4.1 IPv6 Addresses

One of the big differences between IPv4 and IPv6 is the size of the IP address. The IPv4 address is limited to 32 bits, which are treated as a homogenous

```
2033:0000:0123:00FD:000A:0000:0000:0C67

2033:0:123:FD:A:0:0:C67

2033:0:123:FD:A::C67
```

Figure 4.1 A human-readable IPv6 address can be expressed in compact forms by omitting leading zeros or whole zero words.

although hierarchical unit. The IPv6 address is 128 bits (16 bytes) long, which affords the possibility for encoding all sorts of additional and interesting information within the address.

A 128-bit address obviously allows scope for 2^{128} distinct addresses. That is a very large number—roughly $5 * 10^{28}$ addresses for every human on earth today (IPv4 has scope for just two-thirds of an address per person). How could we possibly need that many addresses? The answer is that we don't, but we may eventually need more than the current IPv4 addressing scheme allows. Having decided to increase the size of the address space, the designers of IPv6 resolved not to get caught out again, and invented addressing that was safely large enough to facilitate partitioning without significantly curtailing the addresses available in any partition.

IPv6 addresses are represented for human manipulation using hexadecimal encoding with a colon placed between each 16-bit word. In Figure 4.1 an IPv6 address is shown as eight words separated by colons. Laziness rapidly led to the omission of leading zeros in any one word, and then to the entire removal of multiple zero words that can be represented by just a single pair of colons—note that this form of compression can only be used once in a single address—otherwise it would be impossible to work out how many zero words should be placed in which position.

The first bits of an IPv6 address, called the *Format Prefix* (FP), indicate the use to which the address is put and the format of its contents. They were initially defined in RFC 2373 and are now managed by the Internet Assigned Numbers Authority (IANA). The number of FP bits varies from usage to usage, but can always be determined by the pattern of the early bits. Table 4.1 lists the currently defined FP bit settings. As can be seen, even with the subdivision of the address space that accounts for only an eighth of the feasible addresses available for use as IP unicast addresses, there is still scope for 2^{125} of them—plenty.

4.1.1 IPv6 Address Formats

The structure of an IPv6 address is defined in RFC 2373. There are five address types identified by the Format Prefix bits shown in Table 4.1. Each address type has a different format governed by the information that needs to be encoded in the address. Global unicast addresses are formatted as shown in Figure 4.2. The

Table 4.1 The IPv6 Address Space Is Divided According to the Format Prefix

FP Bits	Usage	Number of Addresses
0000 0000	Reserved	2^{120}
0000 0001	Unassigned	2^{120}
0000 001	NSAPs	2^{121}
0000 01	Unassigned	2^{122}
0000 1	Unassigned	2^{123}
0001	Unassigned	2^{124}
001	Global unicast addresses	2^{125}
01	Unassigned	2^{126}
10	Unassigned	2^{126}
110	Unassigned	2^{125}
1110	Unassigned	2^{124}
1111 0	Unassigned	2^{123}
1111 10	Unassigned	2^{122}
1111 110	Unassigned	2^{121}
1111 1110 0	Unassigned	2^{119}
1111 1110 10	Link local unicast addresses	2^{118}
1111 1110 11	Site local unicast addresses	2^{118}
1111 1111	Multicast addresses	2^{120}

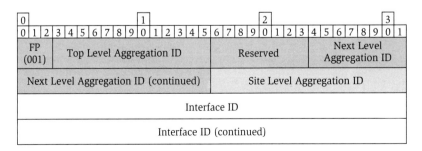

Figure 4.2 The format of a global unicast IPv6 address.

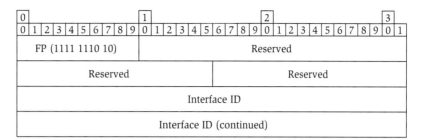

Figure 4.3 The format of a link local unicast IPv6 address.

address is broken into three topology-related segments. The first, shown with a gray background, is called the Public Topology and contains information about the address type (the Format Prefix), the Top Level Aggregation ID (TLA ID), and the Next Level Aggregation ID (NLA ID). The 13-bit TLA ID is used by the naming authorities to identify up to 8192 major ISPs or carriers. The 24-bit NLA ID is used by an individual major ISP to subdivide its address space for administrative purposes or for assignment to small ISPs or customer networks that get their IPv6 Internet attachment through the larger ISP. Note that the 8 reserved bits between the TLA ID and NLA ID make it possible to extend the range of either of these fields in the future if necessary.

The second topological subdivision of the address is the Site Topology, shown in the stippled background in Figure 4.2. This part of the address contains just the 16-bit Site Level Aggregation ID (SLA ID), which is used by an ISP or organization to break their network up into as many as 65,536 smaller administrative chunks. The last 64 bits of the address are the Interface ID, used to identify an individual router, host, or interface—the equivalent of an IPv4 address. So, in IPv6 there is scope for 2^{32} times more hosts or interfaces within one administrative domain of one organization than there can be hosts or interfaces in the whole IPv4 Internet.

In this way, it can be seen that an ordinary global unicast address is built from a hierarchical set of fields derived from the topology. This makes it possible to aggregate the address into subnetworks of varied size, as described in the next section.

Link Local Unicast Addresses (see Figure 4.3) are used between neighbors on the same link. Their scope is limited to the link and they are not distributed more widely. This is useful for dial-up devices or for hosts on a local network.

Site Local Unicast Addresses are equivalent to the three reserved address ranges 10.0.0.0/8, 172.16.0.0/12, and 192.168.0.0/16 in IPv4. They are addresses that are allocated within an organization but are not distributed more widely. Hosts using site local addresses rely on Network Address Translation (see Section 2.3.4) to access the wider Internet. As shown in Figure 4.4, the site local address includes a subnetwork ID which can be used in a hierarchical manner within the organization's network in the same way as the SLA ID in the global address.

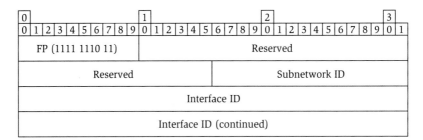

0										1										2										3	
0	1	2	3	4	5	6	7	8	9	0	1	2	3	4	5	6	7	8	9	0	1	2	3	4	5	6	7	8	9	0	1

FP (1111 1110 11) | Reserved

Reserved | Subnetwork ID

Interface ID

Interface ID (continued)

Figure 4.4 The format of a site local unicast IPv6 address.

0										1										2										3	
0	1	2	3	4	5	6	7	8	9	0	1	2	3	4	5	6	7	8	9	0	1	2	3	4	5	6	7	8	9	0	1

FP (1111 1111) | Rsvd | T | Scope | Group ID

Group ID (continued)

Group ID (continued)

Group ID (continued)

Figure 4.5 The format of an IPv6 multicast address.

IPv6 also supports multicast addressing through the multicast address format shown in Figure 4.5. The T-bit flag is used to indicate that the address is transient (set to 1) or is permanently assigned (set to zero). The 4-bit scope field indicates how the group ID should be interpreted and how widely it applies— only a few values have been defined so far, as shown in Table 4.2. The rest of the address carries the group identifier which is otherwise unstructured.

Table 4.2 Values of the Scope Field in an IPv6 Multicast Address Identify the Scope of Applicability of the Address

Scope Value	Meaning
0	Reserved
1	Node-local scope
2	Link-local scope
5	Site-local scope
8	Organization-local scope
E	Global scope
F	Reserved

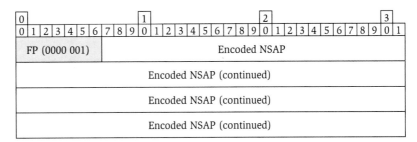

Figure 4.6 The format of an IPv6 NSAP address.

An important feature of IPv6 is that it can transport Network Service Access Point (NSAP) addresses. An NSAP is a generalized address format defined by the International Standards Organization (ISO) for use in a variety of networks. Section 5.6 delves a little into the format of an NSAP when it describes the routing protocol IS-IS, which was developed by ISO and can be used to distribute routing information in IP networks. For now, it is enough to observe that the NSAP address is encoded into 121 bits within the IPv6 address, as shown in Figure 4.6. Further details of the way in which NSAPs are placed into these 121 bits can be found in RFC 1888.

4.1.2 Subnets and Prefixes

Figure 4.2 shows how an IPv6 unicast address is constructed in a hierarchical way. This helps to provide structure that lends itself to subnetting. Subnet prefixes are expressed (just as in IPv4) as a count of the leading bits that identify the subnet. Subnet masks are not explicitly used in IPv6 but can be deduced from the prefix if required by an implementation.

Since the low-order 64 bits of an IPv6 address are designated as the interface address, and the previous 16 bits as the Site Level Aggregation ID or subnetwork address, a prefix of exactly 64 indicates the lowest level of a subnetwork. Within a subnetwork there is scope for prefixes of less than 64, which may allow routing protocols to form a routing hierarchy based on addresses aggregated together into prefixes. Within a site (that is, within an organization) subnets may also be grouped using prefixes greater than 64, and this technique can be applied through the public Next Level Aggregation ID to improve routing within the backbone. It is unlikely that prefixes would be applied to the Top Level Aggregation ID simply because of the topology of the network, but it is by no means forbidden.

4.1.3 Anycast

Anycast addresses are somewhere between node addresses and interface addresses. A datagram targeted at a node address can be routed through the network and arrive at the destination node through any interface on that node.

An interface address in IPv4 used to refer only to a specific interface so that a datagram targeted at the interface could only arrive at the destination node on the link that terminated at the specified interface. This rapidly became overly restrictive, and IPv4 allowed the delivery of a datagram targeted at an interface through any interface on the destination node. Multicast and broadcast addresses result in datagrams being delivered to multiple destinations.

In IPv6, an anycast address identifies a set of interfaces or hosts. A datagram addressed to an anycast address is delivered to just one member of the set, selecting the closest as the favorite. Typically, each member of an anycast address set is on a different destination node.

Anycast addresses use the same formats as unicast addresses described in the previous sections. They are indistinguishable from unicast addresses, except within the context of routing tables and advertisements by routing protocols, which allow a router to choose to forward a datagram along whichever path provides the shortest path to some router that supports the anycast address.

4.1.4 Addresses with Special Meaning

The IPv6 address 0:0:0:0:0:0:0:0, which can also be shown as ::, represents "no address" or "unknown address" as 0.0.0.0 does in IPv4. The IPv4 localhost address 127.0.0.1 is replaced by 0:0:0:0:0:0:0:1, also shown as ::1.

Several addresses are reserved from the multicast group identifiers to indicate "all hosts" and "all routers" within the network. The scope field of the multicast address (see the previous section) indicates the extent of the broadcast. Table 4.3 lists the well-known broadcast addresses.

This model is extended so that for the group ID FF00::500, FF02::501 means all hosts in the group on the same link as the sender. Some common group IDs are assigned as in IPv4 to identify well-known applications of multicast. For example, the group ID FF00::100 is used to multicast to Network Time Protocol (NTP) servers—the address FF0E::1 would mean all NTP servers in the entire Internet.

For a given subnet address, for example FEC0:0000:0000:A123::/64, the "all zeros" member of the subnet is reserved as an anycast address that means

Table 4.3 The IPv6 Broadcast Addresses

Address	Meaning
FF01::1	All addresses on the node
FF02::1	All addresses on the link
FF01::2	All router addresses on the node
FF02::2	All routers on the link
FF05::2	All routers in the organization

"reach any address in the subnet." In this example, FEC0:0000:0000:A123:: is the anycast address for the subnet.

4.1.5 Picking IPv6 Addresses

The interface ID component of an IPv6 unicast address is assigned according to the underlying data-link layer address. This guarantees uniqueness (because MAC addresses are unique), means that IP addresses are automatically known with no requirement for configuration, and means that the mapping of next hop IP address to data-link address can be achieved without the need for an address resolution scheme such as ARP.

The IEEE defines two formats of MAC address using 48 or 64 bits—this is what drove the IETF to assign a full 64 bits for the interface identifier. Both addresses begin with 24 bits that are administered by the IEEE and assigned uniquely to equipment manufacturers. The remaining 24 or 40 bits may be freely assigned by the manufacturer to encode product ID, version number, date of manufacture, and so on, so long as the final MAC address is unique to an individual device across the manufacturer's entire manufacturing range. As shown in Figure 4.7, there are two special bits within the 24-bit range. The U-bit indicates whether the company ID is administered by the IEEE (set to zero) or whether the entire MAC address has been overridden by the network adminis-trator (set to 1). The U-bit effectively allows the network administrator to apply an addressing scheme (perhaps hierarchically) within the network and to administer temporary addresses. The G-bit is used to support multicast addresses and is set to zero for unicast or 1 for multicast.

Figure 4.7 also shows how 48-bit MAC addresses are mapped into 64-bit MAC addresses. The 2-byte word 0xFFFE is inserted into the 48-bit address between the company identifier and the manufacturer's extension ID.

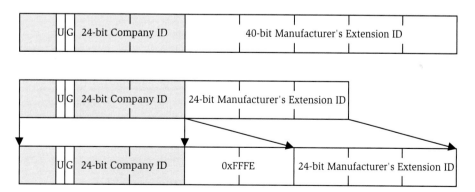

Figure 4.7 MAC addresses may be encoded as 60 bits or 48 bits. The 48-bit variety can be mapped into a 64-bit address by inserting 0xFFFE.

The interface ID component of an IPv6 unicast address was sized at 64 bits to be able to hold both varieties of MAC address. The mapping is relatively simple—all MAC addresses are converted to their 64-bit format and are copied into the interface ID fields with the sense of the U-bit reversed so that a value of zero represents a locally assigned address. This reversal of meaning is done to facilitate address compression of locally assigned addresses, which normally use only the bottom few bits of the whole address and so can now have the upper bytes set to all zeros.

4.2 Packet Formats

Just as with IPv4, the IPv6 datagram is built up of a common header and payload data. The IPv6 header, shown in Figure 4.8, is somewhat larger than the IPv4 address because of the size of the addresses it must carry, but the rest of the header is simpler than the header in IPv4, with the result that the header has a well-known fixed size (40 bytes). IPv6 packets are identified at the data-link layer by an Ethertype of 0x86DD (compare with IPv4, 0x0800), and so

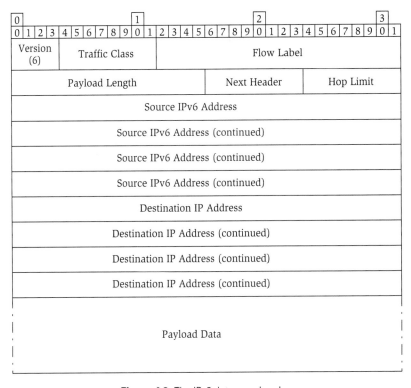

Figure 4.8 The IPv6 datagram header.

the protocol version number is present only as a consistency check. The Traffic Class is used in a similar way to IPv4's Type of Service, and can be mapped to the Differentiated Services colors (see RFC 2474 and Chapter 6).

The Flow Label is a useful addition to IPv6 which helps to identify all datagrams between a source and destination that should be treated in the same way. Alternatively, it could be used in a networkwide context to indicate all datagrams that require the same quality of service processing. At present, the use of the Flow Label is experimental, but it may be used in the future to help integrate IPv6 with routing decisions (see Chapter 5) or with traffic engineering (see Chapter 8).

The Payload Length gives the length in bytes of the remainder of the datagram. There are three things to note. First, it is not necessary to give a length of the header because it has a well-known, fixed format. Second, it is possible to insert options headers between the fixed header and the real data (see Section 4.3), in which case this length field covers the whole of the remainder of the datagram and not just the data being transported. Third, it is possible to use an option header to pass datagrams that are larger than 65,535 bytes, in which case this length is set to zero.

The Next Header field indicates the protocol of the payload data, as does the Protocol field in IPv4. If, as described in Section 4.3, there are option headers between the fixed header and the payload, this field identifies the first of those headers. The Hop Limit is used the same way that the TTL field is used in IPv4, but it is strictly limited to a measure of the number of hops the datagram traverses and does not make any pretence at counting the lifetime in seconds.

4.3 Options

Having removed all of the options from the IPv4 header to achieve a regular, fixed-length header, IPv6 has to solve the problem of carrying the same information in another way. It uses the Next Header field to indicate that there is more information between the standard header and the payload data. Each distinct piece of information is carried in an *extension header*, as shown in Figure 4.9. Each extension header carries information for a specific purpose and is assigned a distinct header type identifier from the list shown in Table 4.4. The order of extension headers (if present) is not mandatory but is strongly recommended to follow the numeric order in Table 4.4 so that nodes receiving an IPv6 datagram encounter the information in the order in which they need to process it.

There are several key advantages to the use of IPv6 extension headers. First, no artificial limit on their size is imposed by the size of the standard header, as it is in IPv4. This means that the extension headers are much more able to carry sufficient information for their purposes—in particular, the facility for source route control in IPv6 supports up to 128 addresses, whereas IPv4

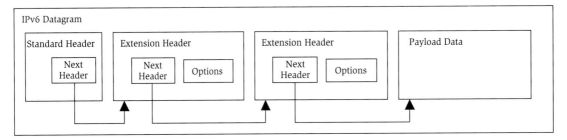

Figure 4.9 Extension Headers can be chained together in between the IPv6 standard header and the payload data.

Table 4.4 The IPv6 Extension Header Types

Type	Use
0	Hop-by-hop options. Carries information that applies equally to each hop along the path.
60	Intermediate destination options. Used to carry information that applies to the next targeted destination from the source route.
43	Source route. Lists a series of IPv6 addresses that must be navigated in order by the datagram.
44	Fragmentation. Used to manage fragmentation of the datagram if it cannot be supported by the MTU on a link.
51	Authentication. Provides scope for authentication services.
50	Encapsulating Security Payload. Facilitates data encryption.
60	Destination options. Carries information that applies specifically to the ultimate destination.
59	No payload. The end of the header has been reached and no payload is included.
41	IPv6 encapsulation (tunneling).
58	ICMPv6 payload.

supports just nine. Equally important is that the structure of the extension headers makes them highly extensible both for the addition of new information within an individual header and for the definition of new headers.

Each extension header begins with a 1-byte field that identifies the next header using the values from Table 4.4 or using the usual protocol identifiers if the next piece of information is the payload data. Otherwise, the format of the extension headers varies from one to another. The hop-by-hop extension header shown in Figure 4.10 consists of the next header indicator, a length

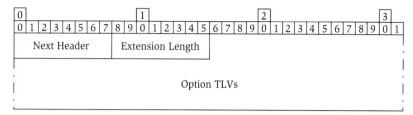

Figure 4.10 Hop-by-hop and destination options are carried as a series of TLVs within the extension header.

field, and a series of options encoded as type-length-variable (TLV) structures. The length field in the extension header gives the length of the entire extension header as a count of 8-byte units. This means that the options TLVs may need to be padded up to an 8-byte boundary.

The two destination options extension headers (see Table 4.4) are identified by the same next header value and are distinguished by whether they are placed immediately before a source route extension header. These two extension headers have the same format as the hop-by-hop extension header shown in Figure 4.10 and also carry a series of option TLVs.

The options TLVs themselves consist of a single option byte type, an option length showing the size of the option variable counted in bytes, and the variable option data. Table 4.5 lists the defined option types, which are managed by IANA, and shows which ones may be present in which extension header. The apparently strange choice of values for the option type is governed by additional meaning applied to the two most significant bits. These bits encode instructions for a receiving node that doesn't recognize the option type and needs to know what it should do. The settings of these bits are shown in Table 4.6, and make the options readily extensible. The third bit indicates whether the option may be modified by intermediate routers (set to 1) or must remain constant (set to zero).

Note that, in addition to the padding requirements to make an extension header up to a multiple of 8 bytes, each option has its own requirement to start on a particular byte boundary so that its value field can conveniently be extracted from a data buffer without the need to move data around in memory. Two special options (Pad and PadN) are used to force options to start on the required boundaries.

The routing extension header shown in Figure 4.11 is used to proscribe the route of a datagram much as the source route does in IPv4. One value of the Routing Type field is defined; zero means that the route is a loose route—that is, that the datagram must pass through the nodes or links identified by the addresses in the extension header in order, but may pass through other nodes on the way. The Segments Left counts the number of addresses in the list remaining to be processed. Thus, the Segments Left field is initially set to the number of addresses in the list, the destination of the datagram is set to the first

Table 4.5 The IPv6 Extension Header Option Types Showing Their Use in the Hop-by-Hop (H), Intermediate Destination (ID), and Destination (D) Extension Headers

Option Type	Offset Requirement	Extension	Use
0	None	H, ID, D	Pad. Exceptionally, this option does not have a length or a data value. It is used as a single byte of pad to make the options data up to an 8-byte boundary.
1	None	H, ID, D	PadN. Also used to pad the options data. There may be zero or more bytes of option data which are ignored.
194	$4n+2$	H	Jumbo Payload. The length indicator in the standard header limits the size of an IPv6 datagram to 65,535 bytes. If the data-link layer supports it, there is no reason not to have larger datagrams called *jumbograms*, and this is enabled by this option. The option data is always a 4-byte value containing the actual length of the datagram in bytes. This value overrides the value in the standard header, which should be set to zero. Defined in RFC 2675.
195	None	H, ID, D	NSAP Address. RFC 1888 describes how ISO addresses, NSAPs, can be encoded and carried within IPv6 addresses. In some cases, the IPv6 address is not large enough for this purpose and this option is used to carry the overflow information for both source and destination addresses.
5	$2n$	H	Router Alert. The presence of this option serves the same purpose as the router alert in IPv4—to deliver the datagram to the higher-layer software on a router even though it is not the destination. The option has 2 bytes of data that define the router alert reason. The option is defined in RFC 2711 and additional reason codes can be found in RFC 3175.
198	$4n+2$	D	Binding Update. This option is used by IPv6 in support of mobile IP (see Chapter 15). It allows a node to update another with its new "care-of" address.
7	$4n+3$	D	Binding Acknowledgement. Used in support of mobile IP, this option acknowledges a previous Binding Update option.
8	None	D	Binding Request. Also for mobile IP support, this allows a mobile node to request to be bound to a Foreign Agent.
201	$8n+6$	D	Home Address. The last of four options used for mobile IP, this option carries the Home Address of the mobile node when it is out and about.

Table 4.6 The Top Two Bits of an Extension Header Option Type Define the Behavior of a Node That Does Not Recognize the Option

Option Type	Action if Option Is Not Recognized
00bbbbbb	Ignore option. An intermediate router should propagate the option.
01bbbbbb	Silently discard the datagram and do not raise any warnings.
10bbbbbb	Discard the datagram and return an ICMP Parameter Problem message to the source.
11bbbbbb	Discard the datagram and return an ICMP Parameter Problem message to the source if (and only if) the destination is not a multicast address.

address (an *intermediate destination*), and the datagram is sent. When a datagram arrives at an intermediate destination, the Segments Left value is decremented and a new destination is set on the datagram using the next entry in the list.

IPv6 supports fragmentation of datagrams for the same reasons as IPv4—if the MTU on some intermediate link is smaller than the datagram size it must be fragmented so that it can be transmitted. Note that IPv6 mandates that datagrams do not need to be segmented into smaller than 1,280 byte packets. If the data-link layer uses smaller frames, IPv6 requires that segmentation be done at the data-link layer and managed with reassembly also at the data-link layer

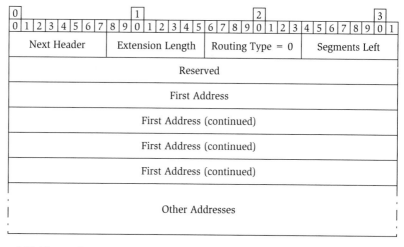

Figure 4.11 The routing extension header allows the path of the datagram to be controlled by specifying the addresses that the datagram must pass through.

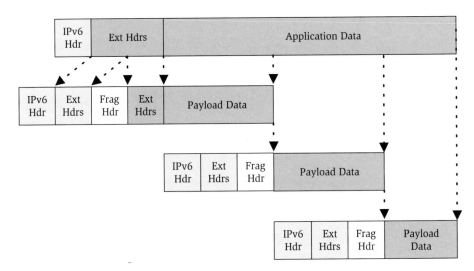

Figure 4.12 Fragmentation in IPv6 is managed using the fragmentation extension header.

without any impact or knowledge in IPv6. Further, IPv6 assumes that end-to-end MTU values are known to data sources, and that all requisite fragmentation is done at the source so that transit routers do not need to perform fragmentation. In consequence, IPv6 bans fragmentation at transit routers and does not need to support the Don't Fragment (DF) bit from IPv4.

Fragmentation in IPv6 is described using the fragmentation extension header. This is inserted into each datagram to identify the datagram that the fragment belongs to, and to show the offset of the data within the whole. Figure 4.12 shows how the fragmentation extension header is placed into each fragment. Note that the standard IPv6 header must be present in each fragment and that the other extension headers are split so that some (hop-by-hop and destination, for example) are present on each fragment and others (authentication and encapsulating security payload, for example) are present only once. The order of precedence of extension headers shown in Table 4.4 shows how to choose which headers are present just once and which are included in each fragment.

Figure 4.13 shows the format of the IPv6 fragmentation header. The fragment offset shows the offset of the first byte of data as a zero-based count of

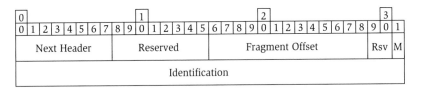

Figure 4.13 Fragmentation is managed using the fragmentation extension header that is only present if the original datagram has been fragmented.

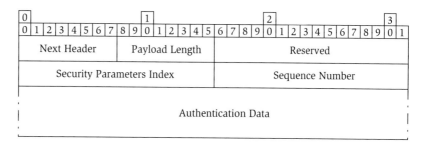

Figure 4.14 The authentication extension header.

8-byte blocks. Thus, the data must be fragmented into units of 8 bytes and the management of fragments is limited to original datagrams no larger than 65,535 bytes, which means that fragmentation of jumbograms is not supported. The M-bit indicates whether this is the last fragment of the series (zero) or more fragments follow (1).

IP security is described in some detail in Chapter 14. IPv6 builds in the facility for authentication and encryption using concepts and techniques developed for IPv4. Authentication is supported using the authentication extension header shown in Figure 4.14, which includes the length of the authenticated data, a Security Parameters Index, a Sequence Number, and Authentication Data used as in IPv4 and described in Chapter 14. Note that the length of the authentication data is known by the sender and receiver through the context of the Security Association they maintain and does not need to be encoded in the message. Only those extension headers occurring after the authentication extension header are authenticated.

Encryption in IPv6 is performed as for IPv4 and as described in Chapter 14. Encryption is achieved by encapsulating the encrypted data between a header and a trailer. Note that the next extension header after the encapsulating security payload (ESP) extension header is identified from within the trailer, as shown in Figure 4.15. Only those extension headers occurring after the ESP extension

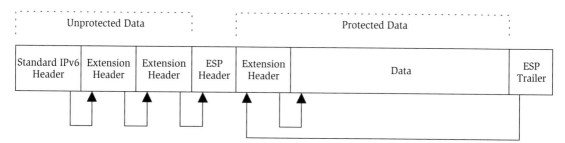

Figure 4.15 Encryption services are provided by the encapsulating security payload extension header and trailer that wrap around the payload header and any extension headers that come after the encapsulating security extension header.

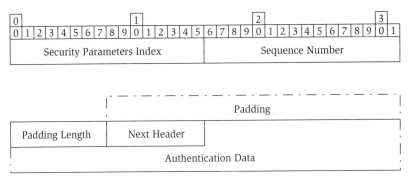

Figure 4.16 The encapsulating security payload extension header and trailer.

header are encrypted, and these cannot include headers accessed at transit nodes because those nodes do not know how to decrypt the datagram.

Figure 4.16 shows the format of the ESP extension header and the trailer. Note that the trailer includes padding up to an 8-byte boundary, and so must be read from the end of the datagram to determine how much padding is actually present.

4.4   Choosing Between IPv4 and IPv6

IPv6 is an emerging protocol. It has undergone considerable testing in development and experimental networks and is being deployed increasingly widely within public and private networks. The U.S. government has recently announced that support for IPv6 should be a major factor in procurement decisions.

Nevertheless, IPv4 continues to be extensively popular, and support for IPv6 at a service provider or home computer level is very limited. This is not surprising, because the core requirement for the adoption of IPv6 is the roll-out of support within key networks—once this is operational, services can be pushed out toward the user. In this matter, the U.S. government is future-proofing itself as much as setting a trend.

This gradual deployment of IPv6 relies heavily on the ability of "islands" of IPv6 routers being able to support IPv4 addressing and function. The next two sections describe how this is achieved.

4.4.1 Carrying IPv4 Addresses in IPv6

IPv4 addresses can be carried in IPv6 address fields in a number of ways. This makes it very easy for an IPv4 datagram to pass through an IPv6 network and for an IPv6 core network to maintain routes out into peripheral IPv4 networks. Some addressing schemes also make it possible for IPv6 nodes to select IPv6 addresses which can be mapped easily into IPv4 addresses so that IPv4 routers

Table 4.7 Two Ways to Encode IPv4 Addresses in an IPv6 Domain

Name	Format	Example	Utility
IPv4-Compatible Address	::a.b.c.d	::881D:C01	This address format allows an IPv6 node to present an address that can be mapped directly to an IPv4 address. The dotted format represents the IPv4 32-bit address.
IPv4-Mapped Address	::FFFF:a.b.c.d	::FFFF:881D:C01	This format is used to represent an IPv4 node within an IPv6 network. Again, the IPv4 32-bit address is easily mapped, but the two bytes of 0xFF indicate to the IPv6 network that the node is not capable of handling IPv6.

and hosts can "see" IPv6 nodes. Table 4.7 shows two ways that IPv4 addresses are carried in the IPv6 world.

4.4.2 Interoperation Between IPv4 and IPv6

Direct interoperation between IPv4 and IPv6 is not so much of an issue. Where it needs to occur, addresses must be represented as described in the previous section so that they may be readily mapped to and from the IPv4 domain. Mapping of datagrams must also be performed, and this must be achieved by special code at the router that provides the link between the IPv4 and IPv6 domains.

Of more interest is the carrying of IPv4 traffic across IPv6 domains, or the transfer of IPv6 traffic across IPv4 domains. This is usually achieved by *tunneling* one type of traffic encapsulated in the headers of the other protocol. Thus, IPv4 has a value in the Protocol header field that indicates that the payload is IPv6, and IPv6 has a value in the Next Header field that indicates that the payload is IPv4. Special addressing formats are used for different tunneling techniques, as shown in Table 4.8.

4.4.3 Checksums

One point of note is that IPv6 does not include any checksum processing. The assumption is that the checks performed at the data-link layer and at the transport layer (see Chapter 7) are sufficient, and that the network layer itself does not need to perform any additional checks to detect accidental corruption of packets. Note that in the worst case, the data-link layer will not detect a problem

Table 4.8 Two Ways to Encode IPv4 Addresses in an IPv6 Domain

Name	**6over4**
Format	< 64-bit prefix > :0:0:a.b.c.d
Example	2033:0:123:FD::881D:C01
Utility	The tunneling technique, 6over4, brings IPv4 addresses into the IPv6 space by including full prefix information but retaining the Interface ID to carry the IPv4 address.
Name	**6to4**
Format	2002:a.b.c.d: < SLA > : < Interface >
Example	2002:881D:C01:37:C200:E1FF:FE00:124B
Utility	This tunneling technique recognizes the need to identify the node through SLA ID and Interface ID. It encodes the IPv4 address in the public topology part using a special reserved prefix (2002).
Name	**ISATAP**
Format	< 64-bit prefix > :0:5EFE:a.b.c.d
Example	2033:0:123:FD::5EFE:881D:C01
Utility	A new protocol, the Intra-Site Automatic Tunnel Addressing Protocol (ISATAP), can be used to exchange IPv4 addresses for use as tunnel end points in IPv6. They use the special value 0:5EFE within the Interface ID.

and the IPv6 datagram will be processed as though it contained valid data. With modern data-link layers this is highly unlikely.

4.4.4 Effect on Other Protocols

A large number of the older IP protocols were devised specifically to handle IPv4 and have no provision to cope with the larger IPv6 address. This effectively means that those protocols cannot be used in IPv6 networks, and so new versions (for example ICMPv6) have been developed. Other protocols such as ARP are rendered redundant by the addressing schemes in IPv6 and are not required at all.

Many other protocols (such as the routing protocols) have been extended to carry IPv6 addresses. Some, such as IS-IS, were able to do this in a relatively graceful way because their address format was already generic. Others, such as OSPF, needed a little more tweaking before they could work with IPv6 addresses. See Chapter 5 for more details of the routing protocols.

More recent additions to the IP suite of protocols (such as MPLS—see Chapter 9) were designed to handle both IPv4 and IPv6. These protocols either have generic addressing fields or can manage addresses according to their types.

4.4.5 Making the Choice

With IPv6, as with all other choices between protocols, what you decide depends on what you are trying to achieve. For simple, small-scale, low-function networks or devices there seems little reason to contemplate IPv6. However, as the device or the network gets more complex and greater levels of function are required, IPv6 gets more interesting.

It is probably true that core network devices such as routers will not be able to restrict themselves to just IPv6 for many years to come without curtailing their market severely. At the same time, a router manufacturer that doesn't offer IPv6 along with IPv4 will definitely lose out in that portion of the Internet that operates IPv6 and also—and more important—with those customers who want to proof themselves against future migrations to IPv6.

Network operators considering deploying IPv6 within their networks obviously have to ensure that all of the devices within a domain support the protocol before they move to using it. This is clearly considerably easier for those deploying new networks than for those migrating existing hardware. At the same time, operators must make sure that all the applications they want to run in their network are available using IPv6 addressing or suitable address mapping.

In the end, the reasons for development of IPv6 have proven to be exaggerated. The IPv4 address space is not depleting as quickly as was predicted, partly owing to the success of Classless Inter-Domain Routing (CIDR—see Chapter 5), partly because of better management of the Class A address spaces allocated in the early days of the Internet, and also through the success of Network Address Translation (NAT—see Chapter 2). The other concern prevalent in the Internet—that routing tables on core routers are growing beyond a manageable size—is not solved by IPv6, although if the allocation of addresses is made very carefully, better aggregation may be possible (not through any feature of the protocol, but solely through better management of the resources). In fact, IPv6 has been described as "an attempt to capture the current IPv4 usage" [John Moy, 1998] and to express it as a new protocol.

The road to full adoption of IPv6 is still very long. Existing IPv6 networks have proven the technology, but conservative service providers who have successful IPv4 networks are likely to migrate to IPv6 only when the need becomes overwhelming. Perhaps the strongest drive will come from large purchasing bodies (such as the U.S. government), whose requirement for IPv6 will prove irresistible to manufacturers and vendors.

4.5   Further Reading

IPv6: Theory, Protocol, and Practice (2004). Morgan Kaufmann. This book contains all of the basics and details of IPv6.

Understanding IPv6, by Joseph Davies (2002). Microsoft Press International. A thorough overview of IPv6, albeit with a heavy bias toward a certain family of operating systems. This book contains some useful sections describing the effect of IPv6 on other protocols in the IP family.

More information about IPv6 can be found at the IETF's IPv6 Working Group web site at http://www.ietf.org/html.charters/ipv6-charter.html.

IPv6 Architecture

RFC 1752—The Recommendation for the IP Next Generation Protocol

IPv6 Addressing

RFC 1881—IPv6 Address Allocation Management
RFC 1887—An Architecture for IPv6 Unicast Address Allocation
RFC 1888—OSI NSAPs and IPv6
RFC 1924—A Compact Representation of IPv6 Addresses
RFC 2374—An IPv6 Aggregatable Global Unicast Address Format
RFC 2375—IPv6 Multicast Address Assignments
RFC 2851—Textual Conventions for Internet Network Addresses
RFC 3513—Internet Protocol Version 6 (IPv6) Addressing Architecture
RFC 3177—IAB/IESG Recommendations on IPv6 Address Allocations to Sites
RFC 3307—Allocation Guidelines for IPv6 Multicast Addresses

IPv6: The Protocol

RFC 1809—Using the Flow Label Field in IPv6
RFC 1981—Path MTU Discovery for IP Version 6
RFC 2460—Internet Protocol, Version 6 (IPv6) Specification
RFC 2461—Neighbor Discovery for IP Version 6 (IPv6)
RFC 2675—IPv6 Jumbograms
RFC 2711—IPv6 Router Alert Option

Related Protocols

RFC 1886—DNS Extensions to Support IP Version 6
RFC 2428—FTP Extensions for IPv6 and NATs
RFC 2463—Internet Control Message Protocol (ICMPv6) for the Internet Protocol Version 6 (IPv6)
RFC 2474—Definition of the Differentiated Services Field (DS Field) in the IPv4 and IPv6 Headers

Migration of IPv4 to IPv6

RFC 2529—Transmission of IPv6 over IPv4 Domains without Explicit Tunnels
RFC 2893—Transition Mechanisms for IPv6 Hosts and Routers
RFC 3056—Connection of IPv6 Domains via IPv4 Clouds
RFC 3142—An IPv6-to-IPv4 Transport Relay Translator

Chapter 5

Routing

This chapter on routing and routing protocols is the longest in the book. It covers a large amount of material, from the basics of routing and the techniques used to distribute routing information, to the protocols that realize these techniques. Along the way there is an examination of the methods used to compute routes from the available network information.

Routing and forwarding is what the Internet is all about: How can an IP packet from one host be delivered to the destination host? Within an individual router, the answer lies in a routing table which is accessed through a look-up function. This function maps the destination address carried in a datagram to the address of the next hop along the path (the *next hop address*) and the interface on the router through which the datagram should be forwarded (the *outgoing interface*).

In simple networks, routing tables can be manually configured or learned from the configuration of interfaces on the router. In more complex networks in which there are many routers arranged in a mesh with lots of links between routers, each link having different capabilities, manual configuration becomes onerous. More important, however, is the need to react dynamically to changes in the network—when a link or a router fails, we need to update all of the routing tables across the whole network to take account of the change. Similar changes are desirable when failures are repaired or when new links and nodes are added. It is possible to conceive of a system of alarms and trouble tickets that are sent to a central location which builds new routing tables and sends them out to the routers, but this would be cumbersome and prone to exactly the failures we need to handle. Instead, we rely on *routing protocols* to collate and distribute information about network connectivity.

As with all complex problems, there are a multitude of solutions. Each solution has its advantages and disadvantages, each its advocates and disparagers, and each a specific applicability. There are three chief ways of propagating connectivity information, and these are described in detail in Section 5.2. Once the connectivity information has been distributed, there still remains the question of how to use it to compute the best path. Some knowledge of the best path is implicit in the way the information is gathered and distributed, but there are also sophisticated *routing algorithms* that can be run against the view of the network to determine the best path along which to forward a datagram. These algorithms are discussed in Section 5.3.

The actual protocols (*routing protocols*) used to distribute the connectivity information make up the core of the chapter. The Routing Information Protocol (RIP) is simple and ubiquitous. The Open Shortest Path First (OSPF) protocol is very popular and has a close rival, Intermediate System to Intermediate System (IS-IS), that performs a similar function. The Border Gateway Protocol (BGP) is important for hooking together the many Service Provider networks into a single Internet. These four protocols are described in detail.

The chapter then includes a section that outlines some of the issues of routing for multicast IP traffic. IP multicast is described in Chapter 3, but that material only explains how individual hosts may join multicast groups and how traffic is targeted at group addresses rather than to individual hosts. Central to how multicast IP works in an IP network built from multiple routers and subnetworks is the ability to determine along which paths multicast traffic should be sent. Multicast routing is a very complex topic with many solutions under development and several protocols proposed for each solution. Consequently, the section in this chapter that deals with multicast routing provides only an overview of the issues and solutions and uses several of the protocols to illustrate the techniques.

The final section summarizes some of the routing protocols that are not mentioned elsewhere in the chapter. There are many routing protocols. Some provided essential evolutionary experience and form the foundation of today's routing protocols. Others solved particular problems at the time, but were never adopted widely. Some routing protocols are outside the mainstream, but see continued use in specific circumstances, particularly in networks constructed from a single vendor's equipment.

5.1 Routing and Forwarding

There are a few essential concepts to describe before embarking on a wider discussion of routing techniques and protocols. This section describes Classless Inter-Domain Routing (CIDR), a simple idea that has made routing more scalable and more granular at the same time. It goes on to explain how networks and the Internet are broken up into administratively distinct segments called autonomous systems. There follows a brief discussion of how the routing table that tells each router how to forward every IP packet must be constructed using whatever routing information is available. Finally, the side issue of unnumbered links is introduced.

5.1.1 Classless Interdomain Routing (CIDR)

Chapter 2 introduced IP addresses and explained how those addresses are grouped into classes. The class to which an address belongs can be determined from the most significant nibble of the address and defines how the address is split to identify the network to which a host belongs, and to identify the host within that network.

For example, a Class B address has the most significant bits set to 10, with the high-order 16 bits to designate the network and the low-order 16 bits to identify the host. Thus, the address 176.19.168.25 is a Class B address for host 168.25 in network 176.19. A network mask can be used to derive the network address from an IP address by performing a logical AND operation. In this case, the Class B network mask is 255.255.0.0. The network mask can also be represented by indicating the number of bits that identify the network part of the address, the *prefix length*. For a Class B address the prefix length is 16.

Early routing between networks was based entirely on the network address. When a router had an IP datagram to forward, it examined the destination address and determined its class. It then applied the appropriate mask to determine the network to which the destination host belonged, and looked that network up in its routing table.

Subnetting, the process of dividing a network into smaller segments as described in Chapter 2, made it possible for the managers of networks to break up their address spaces and assign addresses to third parties in well-known and easily recognized batches. Although it was always possible to simply assign a set of addresses to a dependent network under separate administration, the management of a disparate list of addresses would have made the routing tables within a network a nightmare—each destination address would have been represented in the routing table on each router. Assigning ranges of addresses could have significantly improved the situation, but the subnetting process goes one step further by defining the address range assigned to a subnetwork according to the prefix length. The prefix length can now be any value from 8, for a Class A address, up to 30, for the smallest subnetwork.

Routing using subnetwork addresses is not quite as simple as routing using class addresses, because the knowledge of the network mask (prefix length) is not encoded in the address itself. The routing table must consist of a list of subnetwork addresses (that is, addresses and prefix lengths), each mapping to a route or path along which packets for that subnetwork should be forwarded. The destination address of a packet must be compared against entries in the table until a match is made. This is classless routing, and since we are forwarding packets between subnetworks or management domains, it is termed *Classless Inter-Domain Routing* (CIDR).

Although CIDR solves some of the issues of routing table size by managing lists of addresses within each subnetwork as a single routing table entry, there could still be a very large number of subnetworks, each requiring an entry in the routing table of every router in the Internet. Consider that there are a potential 2^{22} 30-bit prefix subnetworks within a single Class A network, and there are a possible 128 Class A networks. The solution within the Internet is to route at an appropriate level of granularity through address *aggregation*.

Table 5.1 Route Aggregation Allows Several Subnetworks to Be Represented by a Single Routing Table Entry within the Network

Subnetwork	Subnetwork Mask	Address Range
172.19.168.16/28	255.255.255.240	172.19.168.16–172.19.168.31
172.19.168.32/28	255.255.255.240	172.19.168.31–172.19.168.47
172.19.168.32/27	255.255.255.224	172.19.168.16–172.19.168.47

The first stage of aggregation is to fall back to class-full routing—that is, to route from one network to the next based on the class to which the destination address belongs. But the way in which subnetworks are formed means that route aggregation can be performed at any level within the network. For example, the two subnetworks 176.19.168.16/28 and 176.19.168.32/28 may be combined and represented as a single subnetwork 176.19.168.32/27, as shown in Table 5.1.

By carefully choosing how subnetwork addresses are assigned to domains and customer networks, network operators may significantly reduce the routing table entries required on the routers in the core of their networks. This choice is really a matter of geography (or topology) and suggests that subnetworks that can easily be aggregated should be accessed through the same router. The assignment of subnetwork addresses within a large network becomes a hierarchical distribution problem. Route aggregation is described further in Section 5.2.3.

5.1.2 Autonomous Systems

The Internet is one happy family! The infrastructure of the Internet is owned by a wide variety of organizations, including national governments, large Internet Service Providers (ISPs), and telephone companies with a wide geographic footprint. There are also smaller ISPs with only local presence or with limited market niches, educational establishments and consortia, corporations that run their own private networks, and even individuals with home computers. Since the whole point of the Internet is to provide full connectivity between all participating computers, it is good news that all of these bodies have fabulously happy relationships with each other, fully trust each other, and cheerfully share their most intimate operational information.

In the real world, however, each organization wants the largest possible amount of control and secrecy. Each organizational grouping of computers defines itself as an *autonomous system* (AS), that is, a system that can operate in isolation from all other groupings. Within an AS, routing information is generally widely distributed and one router can clearly see the path through the AS network to another router within the same AS. Protocols that distribute routing information within an AS are referred to as *Interior Gateway Protocols* (IGPs). The word *gateway* is the old name for a router.

Organizations, and therefore ASs, obviously require interconnectivity to make the Internet work. This connectivity operates in a largely hierarchical way with home users and small companies paying the smaller ISPs for private access (dial-up, wireless, leased line, etc.). The small ISPs and larger corporations buy access to the *backbone* networks operated by the larger ISPs. The large ISPs create *peering agreements* with each other to glue the whole thing together.

But connectivity is not enough. We need to be able to route from a router in one AS to a router in another AS. Central to this are the routers that sit on the links between ASs. These *autonomous system border routers* (ASBRs) are responsible for leaking routing information from one AS to another. Obviously, they don't want to disclose too much information about the internals of the AS because that might reveal just how frail the ISP's infrastructure is; on the other hand, they must supply enough information to allow IP packets to be routed to the hosts the AS supports.

In a simple hierarchical AS model, the relationship of routers within the AS to the ASBR is similar to the relationship between hosts on a multi-access network to their router. That is, packets that a router within the AS cannot route within the network can be sent to the ASBR by default. Similarly, the ASBR can take advantage of CIDR to advertise a single aggregated address to the neighboring AS.

Life, however, is not this simple for the larger ISPs higher up the food chain that interconnect multiple ASs. These ASs need routing protocols that exchange information between the ASBRs so that packets can be routed across rather than into ASs. Such routing protocols are called *Exterior Gateway Protocols* (EGPs), and they distribute reachability information in terms of subnetted and aggregated IP addresses and unique AS identifiers called *AS numbers*. Figure 5.58 gives an overview of how autonomous systems fit together and how EGPs and IGPs are used.

5.1.3 Building and Using a Routing Table

A router only has to answer a very simple question—given an IP datagram carrying a specific destination host address, out of which interface should the datagram be sent, and to which next hop? Note that the second half of this question is really necessary only on interfaces that lead to multi-access links where the data-link layer is called on to deliver the datagram to the correct next hop router or host.

A routing table, therefore, is some form of look-up algorithm that takes an IP address and derives an interface identifier and a next hop IP address. The implementation of routing tables varies significantly from one router manufacturer to another, and the conflicting requirements of performance and data occupancy drive the competitive advantages they claim. There are, nevertheless, some common abstract themes that run through all implementations and that can be seen when a routing table is examined at a user interface.

First, the routing table is in some sense an ordered list. That is, when the table is searched for a particular address there may be several entries that match the address, but only one of the entries can be chosen and used for any one packet. The most obvious example is a router that has two routes; the first shows how to reach a directly attached host and the second is a default route (see Chapter 2) to an attached router. When the router is asked to route a packet that is addressed to the host, it must choose between the two routes, both of which provide a match for the destination address. The usual solution is to search for the route that matches the longest prefix from the destination address—the explicit route to the directly attached host matches all 32 bits and is selected in preference to the default route which has a netmask of 0.0.0.0 or a prefix match of zero bits. In this way, there is an implicit ordering within the routing table, and by listing entries for longer prefixes higher up the table a first-match rule can be applied with the router selecting the first route that matches the destination address.

At the same time, a routing table could be very large and include many subnetwork routes. A search through the table from top to bottom to match a destination address against a routing entry could take a long time, especially since we have just decided to put all of the directly attached routes at the top of the table. Clearly, it is advantageous to arrange the table so that it can be searched most efficiently by IP address. This sort of problem is a delight to mathematicians, and an array of solutions have been developed. The most common solution is the Patricia Tree, which combines the concepts of best match with binary ordering to solve both requirements at once. For more information about searching and ordering algorithms see the books listed in the Further Reading section at the end of this chapter.

Construction of a routing table within a router becomes an issue of taking information from all sources (manual configuration, IGPs, and EGPs) and populating whatever structure is used to supply efficient storage and lookup. Updating this table from the routing information supplied to a router is neither a quick nor a trivial process. Building a new routing table can divert significant CPU cycles from the function of forwarding packets and may lock the routing table, preventing any lookups. For this reason, routing tables are often recalculated on a timer or when a threshold amount of network change has been observed. Where possible, these calculations are performed in the background and swapped in to replace the old routing table.

Routing table look-up times can be reduced using a route cache. This is simply a smaller copy of the routing table that stores the most recently used routes from the main routing table. Since IP packets do not arrive in isolation, but typically form part of a stream, the same lookup is likely to be performed many times in a short period—the cache recognizes this and stores those lookups in a quickly accessed list. Route caches are particularly suitable for use on distributed forwarding processors in a multiprocessor system, but care must be

taken not to cache only a generic route when more specific routes also exist—
because this might lead to misrouting. Note also that in very busy routers that
see a lot of traffic for many destinations, caches may not work very well
because they quickly grow to be as large as the main routing table.

In practice, the internals of a router are slightly more complex than a single
routing table. As shown in Figure 5.1, the router may take its input from a variety
of sources, including operator configuration, discovery through protocols such
as ICMP, route information sharing with IGP networks, and route distribution
from peer routers running an EGP. Routes learned through routing protocols are
usually subject to some form of route import filtering according to the configured
preferences of the local router. All of the acceptable routes from the routing
protocols are combined with the configured static routes and discovered direct
routes into one large assemblage of information, the *routing information base*
(RIB). From an implementation perspective, the RIB may be stored as one database with suitable tags to indicate how the information was learned, or may be
comprised of multiple separate tables of data according to the source.

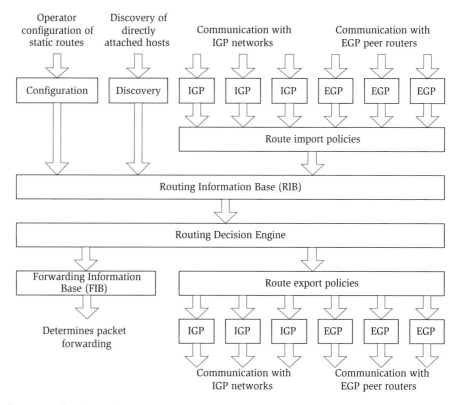

Figure 5.1 The internals of a router showing the distinction between the routing information base
and the forwarding information base.

The RIB is full of all sorts of information about routes available through the network. Some of this information may suggest multiple routes to a single destination, and a routing decision engine applies routing policies to determine the best routes. The processing required to determine the best route depends on how the information was gathered and what the definition of "best" is. Section 5.3 looks at this process in a little more detail.

The output of the routing decision engine is the *forwarding information base* (FIB). The FIB gives unambiguous instructions to the component of the router that forwards data packets. Given a destination address, the FIB will tell the router out of which interface to forward the packet and what the address of the next hop is. In many implementations, the FIB will also contain other useful information such as the MAC address of the next hop so that the forwarding component has to perform only one look-up operation per packet.

The FIB contains the definitive best routes according to the local routing decision policies, and the router needs to share this information with the other routers in the networks to which it belongs. However, routing protocols concern themselves not just with the best routes, but with all available routes. This means that the router uses the output from the routing decision engine to tell it about every possible route. Just as there are policy-based filters for routes arriving into the router, it is important also to apply filters to the information that is shared with other routers.

When we talk about the routing table or issue a command to show the routes present in a router, we are really examining the RIB. We can see all of the routes that have been installed on the router. However, the routing table is ordered to give it the feel of the FIB with a precedence of applicability of routes.

5.1.4 Router IDs, Numbered Links, and Unnumbered Links

Multi-access links are associated with a subnetwork address that provides a collective identification for the hosts on the link. So, for example, the hosts and router attached to the Ethernet in Figure 5.2 belong to the subnet 172.168.25.0/28, and each host's connection to the Ethernet can be identified by the host's IP address. But Router X is also connected to Router Y and Router Z with point-to-point connections—it has more than one link, and these links need to be identified so that they can be represented within the routing and topology information shared through the network.

One convention is to designate each point-to-point link as a subnetwork with a 30-bit prefix (that is, with two valid, assignable addresses). Each router has one address on the subnetwork and this is used to identify the router's connection to its neighbor. In Figure 5.2, Router X and Router Y are in the subnet 172.168.25.24/30 and use 172.168.25.25 and 172.168.25.26 as their link addresses. The link between the two routers is called a *numbered link* because IP addresses (numbers) have been assigned to it. Router X now has two addresses, 172.168.25.4 and 172.168.25.25, both of which identify the router, but which also provide more specific routing information since they also identify links.

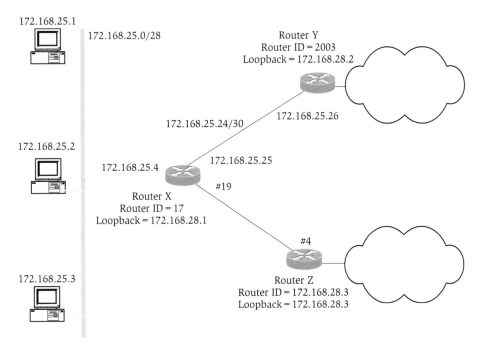

172.168.25.1

172.168.25.0/28

Router Y
Router ID = 2003
Loopback = 172.168.28.2

172.168.25.26

172.168.25.24/30

172.168.25.2

172.168.25.4

172.168.25.25

#19

Router X
Router ID = 17
Loopback = 172.168.28.1

#4

172.168.25.3

Router Z
Router ID = 172.168.28.3
Loopback = 172.168.28.3

Figure 5.2 A simple network showing a multi-access link, a numbered point-to-point link, and an unnumbered link.

So what if we don't care which link is used, but we want to refer to Router X more generically? If we need to do this, we assign a loopback address (see Section 2.4.3) to Router X—in the example, this is 172.168.28.1. This loopback address is known as a routable router identifier because it is an IP address that can be installed in the routing tables at other routers. At the same time, we also need an abstract way of referring to a router within the network so that we know from which router a route was advertised, or so that we can map alert messages to a specific piece of hardware. This identifier, the *router ID*, does not need to be routable, but must be unique within the network if it is to be used successfully to identify a single router. A common deployment is to define a loopback address for each router and to use this address as the router ID of the router— this is very useful because it reduces the name spaces in use and makes all router IDs routable, but note that it is not a requirement to configure a network in this way and there is no reason to believe that a router ID is a routable IP address.

Assigning subnets to each link in the network is an arduous manual process. Core routers may each have a large number of links and the same subnet must be configured at the router at each end of the link, although each must be assigned a different address on the link. No negotiation protocol can be used to perform this task because the routers can't possibly know the available set of network-unique subnetworks. If we want to reduce the configuration effort we must use the concept of *unnumbered links*. An unnumbered link does not have a subnetwork assigned to it but (confusingly!) has a number instead. Each router knows of a list of interfaces and simply numbers them according to its favorite numbering scheme—either according to the order in which the interfaces were manually configured or through automatic discovery of hardware. The router refers to the links externally using any routable address that identifies the router (usually the loopback address) and its own link identifier. Then it is easy for a pair of adjacent routers, such as Router X and Router Z in Figure 5.2, to establish their connectivity—Router X would send a message along the link to Router Z saying, "Hello, my router ID is 17, my address is 172.168.28.1, I call this link number 19," and Router Z can respond with, "Hello, my router ID is 172.168.28.3, my address is 172.168.28.3, I call this link number 4."

5.2   Distributing Routing Information

The routing table described in the previous section can be constructed in a large number of ways. For simple, static networks a manually configured routing table may be adequate. Consider the network in Figure 5.3. This simple star

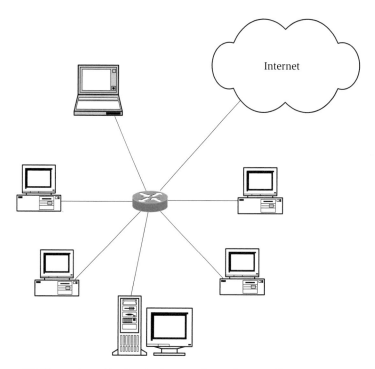

Figure 5.3 The routing tables for simple networks can be manually configured with ease.

network needs very little configuration; each host is given a default route to the central router and sends all nonlocal packets to the router. The router itself knows each link, so its routing table is no more than a list of the subnets or remote link addresses followed by a default route pointing to the Internet.

But not all networks are as simple as the one shown in Figure 5.3. When the network is more complex we need an automated and reactive way to distribute information about the connectivity within the network. The routing protocols that do this work operate according to the principles set out in the following sections.

5.2.1 Distance Vectors

The simplest and most intuitive way to distribute network connectivity information also makes the construction of routing tables particularly easy. Protocols that work in this way are called *distance vector protocols*. Sometimes called routing by rumor, the basic premise is that the routers chatter to each other, exchanging all the information about the routes through the network that they know about, and so distributing, in time, all of the best paths.

The network of routers in Figure 5.4 can be used to illustrate how this works. The first thing any router does is announce itself to its neighbors; in Figure 5.4, Router A would send a message down each of its attached links saying, "I am

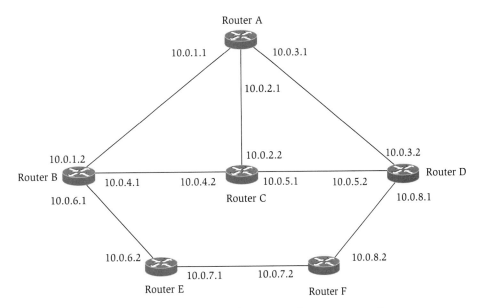

Figure 5.4 Example network to demonstrate distance vector routing.

here and I am directly attached to this link." It does not know who or what is at the other end of the link, but that doesn't worry it. The receivers of the message now all know that if they have any message for Router A they can send it down the link on which they received the message. This forms an entry in the routing table; so, for example, Router B would have a single entry in its table that says, "Send to Router A out of interface 10.0.1.2."

Now, when each router receives this fragment of routing information from Router A, it passes the information on to everyone it knows. So, for example, Router C hears from Router A and tells Routers B and D, "I am here and I am directly connected to you. Also, I am one hop away from Router A." Now Router B knows how to reach Router C and also knows two ways to reach Router A. Which should it install in its routing table? Well, it simply looks at how far away Router A is on each of the routes—in other words, how many hops would a datagram travel in each case? This is information it knows from the messages it receives and so it can select the optimum route and install it in its routing table.

If, for whatever reason, Router B first heard about Router A through Router C (perhaps the link between Routers A and B was down for a while), Router B would install in its routing table a route to Router A through Router C and would advertise this information to Router E: "I am here and I am directly connected to you. Also, I am one hop away from Router C, and two hops away from Router A."

But Router E may already have heard from Router F: "I am here and I am directly connected to you. Also, I am one hop away from Router D, two hops away from Router C, and two hops from Router A." The new information about a path to Router A is not interesting to it—it is the same distance (three) as a route it already knows about—but the new paths to Routers B and C are better than those it previously had, so it installs them in its routing table and informs Router F, "I am here and I am directly connected to you. Also, I am one hop away from Router B, two hops away from Router C, and three hops from Router A." Router F knows that it can reach Router C in just two hops on a different route, so it discards this new route, but would still pass on the information about the connectivity to Routers E and B. At this point Router E's routing table might look like Table 5.2.

If the link between Routers A and B is restored, Router B becomes aware of a better route to Router A. Router B updates its routing table and informs its neighbors about the new route. Router C is not interested because it is, itself, just one hop away from Router A, but for Router E the new route is an improvement, and it updates its routing table and passes the information on. Router F is not impressed since it already has a two-hop route to Router A and so it discards the new information. Router E's routing table has become that shown in Table 5.3 for the fully converged network.

After the routing information has converged, the network is stable and all routers can successfully forward data. But suppose there is a network error—the link between Routers B and C fails and the failure is detected by Router B.

Table 5.2 Routing Table at Router E in Figure 5.4 After Initial Routing Distribution with the Link Between Routers A and B Disabled

Destination	Outgoing Interface	Distance	Next Hop
E	127.0.0.1	0	–
B	10.0.6.2	1	B
F	10.0.7.1	1	F
C	10.0.6.2	2	B
D	10.0.7.1	2	F
A	10.0.7.1	3	F

Table 5.3 Routing Table at Router E in Figure 5.4 After Full Distribution

Destination	Outgoing Interface	Distance	Next Hop
E	127.0.0.1	0	–
B	10.0.6.2	1	B
F	10.0.7.1	1	F
C	10.0.6.2	2	B
D	10.0.7.1	2	F
A	10.0.6.2	2	B

Obviously, Router B can retire any routes that use that link, although it has no alternatives, but it must immediately stop advertising those routes to its neighbors. There are two possibilities: First, Router B may receive an advertisement from Router A that says, "I am here and I am directly connected to you. Also, I am one hop away from Router C." This gives Router B a new route to Router C and it can now advertise to Router E, "I am here and I am directly connected to you. Also, I am one hop away from Router A, and two hops away from Router C." Router E might want to discard the new route to Router C because the distance is greater than the route it currently has in its table, but it notices that the advertisement has come from the same place (the same next hop router) and so it uses the new information to update its routing table, discarding the old route. The second alternative upon link failure is that Router B sends an advertisement to revoke or withdraw the previous information. It would send, "I am here and I am directly connected to you. Also, I am one hop away from Router A. I can no longer reach Router C." Router E would update its router table to show that it can no longer reach Router C after this remote link failure (see Table 5.4), and would also advertise this fact to Router F.

Table 5.4 Routing Table at Router E After Router B Has Withdrawn Its Route to Router C

Destination	Outgoing Interface	Distance	Next Hop
E	127.0.0.1	0	–
B	10.0.6.2	1	B
F	10.0.7.1	1	F
C	10.0.6.2	no route	B
D	10.0.7.1	2	F
A	10.0.6.2	2	B

After route withdrawal, the routing tables can become repopulated if each of the routers re-advertises its routing table. As the withdrawal ripples outwards from the failure, so new routes spread inwards. In distance vector routing, every router runs a timer and periodically re-advertises all of its routing information—this can fill in the gaps left by the withdrawn route. So, for example, after a failure of the link between Routers B and E, when its re-advertisement timer pops, Router D would re-advertise, "I am here and I am directly connected to you. Also, I am one hop away from Routers A and C, and two hops away from Router B." This would replace the withdrawn route to Router B in Router F's routing table. Later, when Router F's re-advertisement timer expires it sends, "I am here and I am directly connected to you. Also, I am one hop away from Router D, two hops away from Routers A and C, and three hops away from Router B."

In the simple example just cited, Router E's routing table takes two timer periods to repair. In a larger, more complex network it might take many re-advertisement cycles before every router had a working routing table, leading to an unacceptably long time between network failures and full routing. One answer might be to reduce the re-advertisement time so that routers update their information very frequently—this would, of course, place an unacceptable load on the network when there are no problems. The alternative is to allow *triggered updates*, so that whenever a router detects any change in its routing table it immediately re-advertises the entire routing table. The same number of exchanges is needed to repair the routing tables, but the time taken is much shorter. Note that one consequence of triggered updates is that distance vector protocols are very chatty immediately after a failure as they spread the rumor of the problem.

Even when triggered updates are in use, re-advertisement on a timer is still useful. It supplies a way to ensure that everyone's routing table is up-to-date and also helps to detect network errors. For example, suppose that Router B in Figure 5.4 fails: the link to Router E remains active, and so Router E continues to send all data for Router A toward Router B, where it is lost. However, because Router E knows that Router B should re-advertise its routing information periodically, it can spot that Router B has gone quiet and time-out all routes that were previously advertised by Router B. To effect this, each router runs a timer for each route in its routing table and, if the timer expires, it treats that event as a route withdrawal or link failure, marking the route unavailable and immediately passing on the rumor. This process is far from ideal since the timer must be large enough not to overreact to occasional packet loss (that is, lost advertisements) and must take account of how frequently (or infrequently) the routers perform background re-advertisements—it can take quite a while for a distance vector routing protocol to notice a network problem.

When a router or link comes back, the router can simply wait for re-advertisements, but most distance vector protocols allow routers to immediately solicit routing information from their neighbors to expedite the building of new routing tables without having to wait for periodic retransmissions from the neighbors.

A classic problem with distance vector routing protocols is shown in Figure 5.5. In steps 1 through 4 the simple network topology is exchanged and the routers

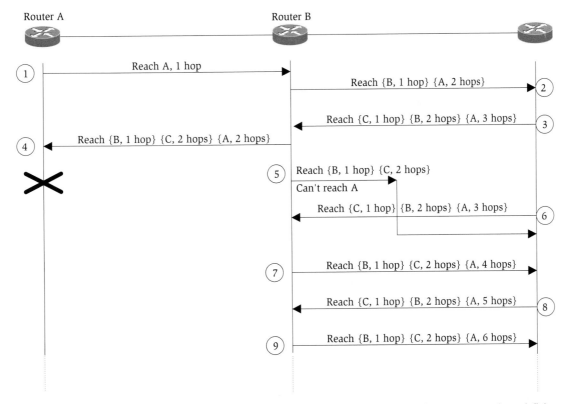

Figure 5.5 In even a simple topology, a distance vector routing protocol may exchange redundant routes, counting to infinity.

build their routing tables, but at step 5 Router A fails and Router B withdraws its route to Router B. At the same time, Router C still knows of a route to Router A and advertises that it is two hops away (step 6). "Great," thinks Router B, "there is a new route to Router A," and it advertises it (step 7). Router C gets this advertisement and replaces the route that it had (same interface, same next hop) and re-advertises (step 8) a five-hop route. The process continues, with the hop count increasing toward infinity. This problem is referred to as *counting to infinity*.

The solution to the problem of counting to infinity is to operate a *split horizon*. A horizon defines the range of an observer's perception, and in a distance vector routing protocol it is used to limit the visibility of one router into another router's routing table. This is usually implemented by a simple rule that says that no router may advertise out of an interface a route that it learned through that interface. So, in Figure 5.5, Router C would not advertise reachability to Routers A and B back along the link to Router B. This completely solves the problem as expressed in the example.

An even more effective measure is for a router to explicitly disqualify a route back along the interface on which it learned the route. In *poison reverse split horizon*, Router C would advertise, "Reach {C, 1 hop}, Can't reach A or B," at step 6. This variant makes sure that routing tables are explicitly flushed of bad routes.

But split horizons don't completely solve the problem of counting to infinity. Consider the network in Figure 5.6. This is not much more complex than the network in Figure 5.5, but when Router A fails a counting loop is built between the other three routers and the hop count continues to increase toward infinity. There is a simple solution to this: the distance vector protocol stops counting hops and circulating routes when the count reaches a predefined threshold. At this point, the destination is flagged as unreachable and advertised accordingly, which puts the routing tables right.

Distance vector routing protocols may combine the concept of a counting threshold and an unreachable flag by designating a specific hop count value to be effectively infinity. If a route is advertised with this hop count value it is equivalent to saying that the destination is unreachable.

There remain some problems with distance vector protocols. There is an issue with how quickly all of the routers in the network can discover changes in the network such as router failures. The redefinition of infinity to a finite number limits the size of the distance vector network because at a certain point a long route will be declared as unreachable. These problems can't be solved in distance vector routing and are handled by other routing methods.

There is one last note on the distance advertised by distance vector routing protocols. In the previous discussion, the distance was equated to the number of hops on the route—that is, the distance increased by exactly one for each hop. It is possible to favor certain routes, or more precisely, to disdain other routes by configuring a *routing metric* for each link. In the previous examples

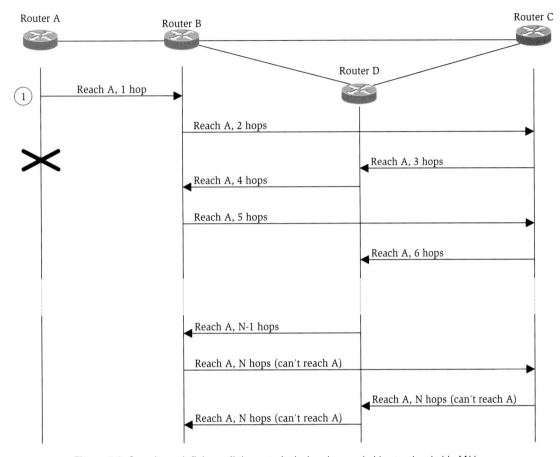

Figure 5.6 Counting to infinity until the route is declared unreachable at a threshold of N hops.

all of the routing metrics were set to 1, but had one of them been set to 3, the advertised route would have been shown with a distance that had increased by three rather than by one. This is a way to mark certain links as less favorable to carry traffic—perhaps because the link is known to be unreliable or to have a low bandwidth. The effect is simply to make routes that use the link with a higher metric appear to be longer routes and so make them less likely to be chosen.

RFC 1058, which defines the Routing Information Protocol (a distance vector protocol), also provides a good introduction to distance vector routing.

5.2.2 Link State Routing

The distance vector routing described in the previous section applies an incremental approach to the construction and distribution of path information. Each router distributes whole routes and its neighbors select from them before passing on a set of routes to their own neighbors.

Link state routing does not distribute any routes, but exchanges topology information that describes the network. Each node is responsible for advertising the details of the links it supports, and for passing on similar information that it receives from other routers. In this way each router in the network builds up a complete database of the available links and which nodes they interconnect. In effect, each router has a full and identical map of the network.

Just as distance vector routing provides a standard way for selecting between routes, link state routing requires a coherent policy for route selection. In link state routing, this process is necessarily more complex because the router must start from the link state database rather than simply compare routes that it receives from other routers. A host of algorithms exists to plot a path through a network (of roads or data links), but it is critical that all of the routers reach consistent conclusions and forward data based on the same paradigms to prevent development of routing loops. For this reason, although the path computation algorithms do not form part of the protocols used to distribute link state routing information, they are usually mandated as part of specification of those protocols. Section 5.3 investigates some of the ways paths are computed.

In distance vector routing, each router sends routing information out over its links—it doesn't much matter whether there is a router on the link to receive the information or not. In link state routing there is a closer bond between neighboring routers; they need to become *peers*, to establish a peer relationship for the purpose of exchanging link state information. This first step is achieved through a *Hello protocol* in which each router sends a Hello message on each link to introduce itself to its neighbors. The format and precise content of the Hello message is, of course, dependent on the link state routing protocol in use, but it must uniquely identify the link on which the message was sent (using an IP address) and the router that sent the message (using a network-unique router ID). The receiver of a Hello message responds with its own Hello so that the routers both know about each other.

The Hello protocol is also useful to monitor the liveliness of the links between routers. The Hello message is periodically retransmitted by both routers, and if a router does not hear from its neighbor for a number of retransmission periods it declares the link to have failed. In this matter, it may be overenthusiastic—the link could actually be just fine and it may be the routing protocol process on the adjacent router that has failed. But it is also quite possible that the routing table will have been lost, making it unwise to continue to forward data along the failed link.

After the initial Hello exchange, the routers exchange and negotiate the parameters they will use to manage their association (such as timer values) and then they declare themselves to be peers. The first thing that peers do is synchronize their *link state databases* by exchanging messages that report on each link that they know about. For a new router, this will start with just the local links that they know to be active—the links to attached subnetworks and the newly opened link to the peer—but if the router has already received information from other routers the synchronization will include information about other links within the network. The information about each link is sent as a *link state advertisement* (LSA) or *link state packet* (LSP) which is formatted and built into a message according to the rules of the specific routing protocol.

In this way two routers that become peers rapidly reach a position of having identical link state databases; that is, they both know about the same list of links within the network. From then on, whenever one of the routers learns about a new link from another of its peers, it *floods* this information to its new peer. The flooding process is simple: The router receives an LSA and searches its link state database to determine whether it already knows about the link; if it does it discards the new LSA, but if it does not it adds the link to its database and sends the new LSA out of each of its interfaces except the interface on which the LSA was originally received (there being no point in telling the news to the router that already knows it).

The flooding process could potentially occupy a large amount of network bandwidth and result in LSAs being sent to routers that already have the information. The procedure described here serves to significantly reduce the flooding overhead compared with a solution that calls for all LSAs always to be re-advertised on all links. Further optimizations of the flooding process are specific to the routing protocols.

Once an LSA has been distributed and the link is established in the link state databases of the routers in the network, the link can be considered in the path computations that operate on the link state database. This means that if the link fails, it must be withdrawn from the network. Link failure can be detected at a hardware level, at the data-link layer, or by failure of the Hello protocol. In any event, the router that notices that a link is down removes the failed link from its own link state database and sends a new LSA to withdraw the link—it reports the change in state of the link, hence, the name *link state routing*. Flooding of link withdrawal is similar to flooding of new links. If a router receives an LSA withdrawing a link, it checks for the link in its link state database and only if it actually finds the link in the database does it forward the withdrawal LSA on its other interfaces and remove the link from its database.

Figure 5.7 shows how neighbors discover each other, negotiate their operational parameters (steps 1 and 2), and synchronize link state (steps 3 and 4) when the link between Routers C and D comes up. The information flooded between Routers C and D is forwarded into the network (steps 4 and 5) but not to Router B, which is currently down. Later, when Router B comes up, a new link between Routers B and C becomes available (step 6) and the link is advertised through the network (steps 7 and 8). Finally, a link fails (step 9) and the link state is withdrawn through the network (steps 10 and 11).

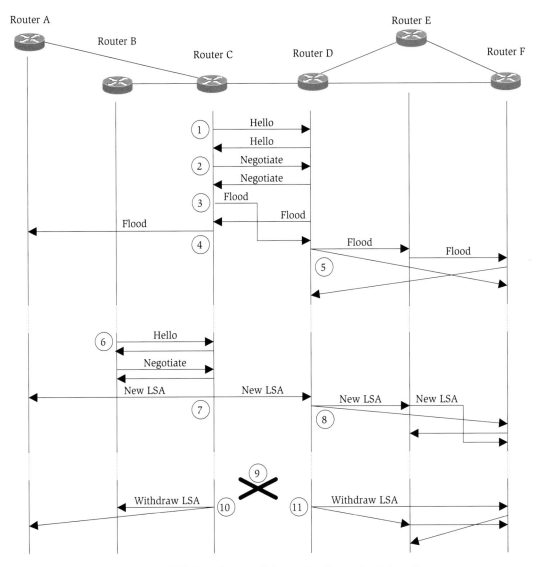

Figure 5.7 Neighbor discovery, link state flooding, and withdrawal.

Note that at this point Router A knows about all of the links on the other side of the network and still has them in its link state database. These links (such as the one between Routers D and E) would not be used by Router A when it builds its routing table since there is no connectivity through the network to reach them, so they sit in the database wasting space. One solution is to process the link state database immediately upon receiving the LSA that withdraws the link between Routers C and D, to also remove any links that are now unreachable, but this would be a CPU-intensive task. Besides, if a new link—say between Routers A and E—was suddenly discovered, the information about the other links would immediately be useful. The solution applied by link state routing is to put an age limit on all information advertised by an LSA and to withdraw that information when the LSA times out.

LSA aging creates its own problems because the routers must now take action to keep their link state databases from emptying. This is achieved by periodically refreshing (flooding) the contents of the link state database of one router to its peers. Since a batch refresh would probably clog the network, individual timers are maintained for each LSA.

One final operational point in link state routing is that the routers must be able to distinguish between LSAs that refer to the same link. Since the LSAs can arrive along different paths through the network, it is important to be able to sequence them to determine whether the link went down and then came up or vice versa. Time stamps don't help, because the originating router might reset its clock at any moment, so simple sequence numbers are used. Various counting schemes are used in the link state routing protocols to generate LSA sequence numbers and to handle the fact that old LSAs may persist in the network for a long time. A further issue that must be resolved with sequence numbers is the fact that when a router restarts it will start counting again at the origin, giving the impression that old LSAs retained in the network are more accurate than the new ones advertised on restart. Further, simple linear counting has an inherent problem in that the integer value used to hold and exchange the sequence number will, at some point, fill up and need to wrap back to the starting point.

These counting issues are resolved in some link state routing protocols by using a lollipop-shaped sequence number space. As illustrated in Figure 5.8, when a router restarts it begins counting at a well-known origin value (n). The sequence numbers increment linearly until they reach the start of a counting

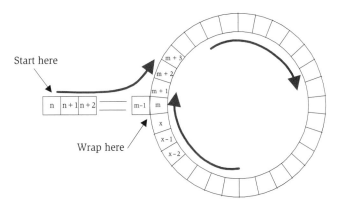

Figure 5.8 Lollipop-shaped sequence number counting.

loop (m). Once on the loop, counting continues incrementally, but resets back to the loop starting value when the maximum is reached (x). OSPF, a link state protocol described in Section 5.5, uses negative numbers for the stick of the lollipop and positive numbers for the head of the lollipop. This means that counting starts at $n=0\times80000001$ and increases through 0×800000002 until it reaches $m=0$. Counting continues through 1, 2, 3, and so on until it reaches $x=0\times7fffffff$. The next value wraps the counter back to $m=0$.

Despite the many advantages that link state protocols have over distance vector protocols, they too have issues with scaling. The memory and processing required to handle large link state databases are not insignificant. The memory requirements grow linearly with the number of links in the network, but the processing is somewhere between $n * log(n)$ and n^2 for a network with n links. Additionally, the amount of link state information that must be exchanged in a large network is a cause for concern because it can swamp the links that should be carrying data traffic.

The solution employed in networks that use link state routing is to group the routers together into *areas*. An area is no more than a collection of routers running the same link state protocol. Where areas meet, they are joined by area border routers (ABRs), and it is here that scaling optimizations are made. While each router in an area exchanges full link state information with the other routers in the area, the ABR passes only a summary of the link state information from one area into the other.

Figure 5.9 shows how a network may be broken into areas connected by ABRs. Note that each ABR is actually present in both areas and needs to maintain a separate routing table for each area to which it belongs. In the example,

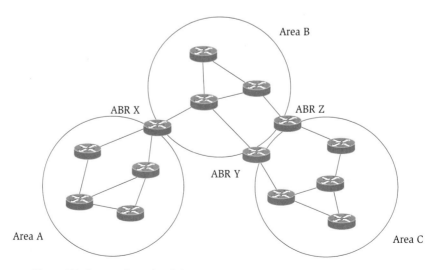

Figure 5.9 A network running link state routing protocols can be broken into areas.

routers in Area A are fully aware of all the links within the area, but perceive all routers in other areas to be just one additional hop away through ABR X. Areas are structured in a hierarchical way and connectivity between two areas at the same level in the hierarchy can be achieved only by moving up one level in the hierarchy—thus, there can be no connection between Areas A and C in Figure 5.9. This restriction is important to eliminate routing loops between the areas. It is, however, possible to install multiple connections between a pair of areas, as shown by ABRs Y and Z.

Link state routing can technically support any depth of hierarchy, although opinion varies about the utility of more than two levels (Figure 5.9 shows just two levels of hierarchy). Some link state routing protocols allow many levels of hierarchy but others retain a limit of just two levels.

When networks grow so large that the number of areas becomes hard to administer, they are broken into distinct autonomous systems, as described earlier in this chapter. Each AS runs an IGP and may be broken into areas in its own right. The ASs exchange routing information using some other means, such as a path vector routing protocol, as described in the next section.

5.2.3 Path Vectors and Policies

Path vector routing is in many ways similar to distance vector routing, but it is considerably enhanced by the inclusion of the entire path in the route advertisements. This allows routers to easily identify routing loops and so removes any problems with counting to infinity. The down side is that the route advertisements are much larger because each route may include multiple hops.

A significant advantage of a path vector protocol is that it allows a router to choose a route based not simply on the distance or cost associated with the route, but by examination of the routers and links that comprise the path. For example, *policy-based routing* decisions can be made using local rules based on knowledge of links that are error prone, vulnerable to security attack, or expensive financially—routes can be chosen or excluded to utilize or avoid specific links. Similarly, the distributed routing information allows policy decisions to be made to exclude resources owned or managed by a particular company.

In fact, policy-based routing cuts both ways since a router may also restrict or modify the routing information it advertises to other routers. This can be done to increase the apparent cost to certain routers of accessing a particular set of resources, or to hide those resources entirely. For example, a Service Provider may provide connectivity to a customer site, but may have a contract to carry traffic only to one specific remote site—it can limit the routing information it advertises to the customer to show only the routes to the remote site. If the contract also allows for expensive backup connections to other sites in case of failure of the customer's primary access through another Service Provider, this can be managed by advertising all routes to the customer, but with a large cost added.

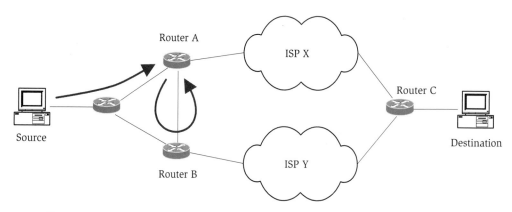

Figure 5.10 Simple policy-based routing can easily lead to forwarding loops if the policy is not balanced across the routers.

One serious problem with policy-based routing is that each router in the network may apply different policies. Distance vector and link state routing are policy-based routing techniques, but they use a simple policy (least cost) and all routes in the network use the same policy—this means that it is possible to predict the behavior of the network and to know the route a datagram will follow in a stable network once it has been launched. It is not hard to see how this predictability could be catastrophically broken as soon as the routers apply policies that are either different from each other or simply different from the least cost policy. Consider the network in Figure 5.10; if Router A has a policy that says, "Avoid using ISP X if at all possible," and Router B's policy says, "Avoid using ISP Y," routes will be successfully distributed, but datagrams will loop forever between Routers A and B.

A path vector routing protocol can resolve this problem, or at least identify it. Router A learns from ISP X that there is connectivity to the destination with a path {ISP X, Router C, Destination}. It would rather not use this route because it requires the packets to traverse ISP X, but because it knows of no other route it advertises to everyone (including Router B), "There is a valid route: {Router A, ISP X, Router C, Destination}." When Router B hears from ISP Y that there is connectivity to the destination with a path {ISP Y, Router C, Destination} it looks at its routing table and finds that there is already a route that does not use the less-favored ISP Y, and so it simply ignores the new route.

The biggest problem of a path vector protocol still remains the amount of information that needs to be propagated. There are two aspects to this and two corresponding solutions. First, as the length of the route grows, the size of the path vector also grows, and this may become unmanageable. Fortunately, routers outside of an autonomous system (AS) don't need to know or understand the routes within the autonomous system, and so the path across the AS can be advertised as a single step. This *route summarization* is shown in Figure 5.11.

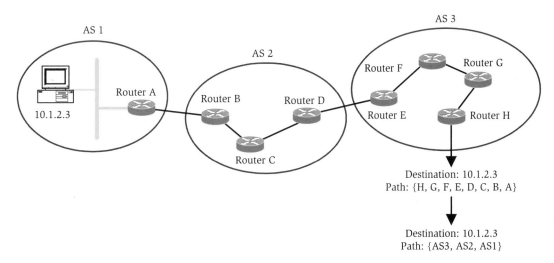

Figure 5.11 Route summarization reduces the information distributed by a path vector protocol.

Distance vector and link state protocols that have already been described tend to be used within a single autonomous system and are consequently called *Interior Gateway Protocols* (IGPs)—recall that gateway is the old name for a router. Within the Internet, there is a requirement to connect the disparate networks and autonomous systems that make up the whole Internet and this is done using *Exterior Gateway Protocols* (EGPs). EGPs use the route summarization property of path vector routing protocols to enable autonomous systems to feature within the routes that are advertised, making them far more scalable and flexible. Note that one feature of this flexibility is the ability to hide the internal workings of one AS from the view of another—this proves to be very popular between rival ISPs who don't want to show each other how they have built their networks.

The second way that the quantity of routing information affects a path vector protocol is in the number of destinations, each of which needs an advertised route. This problem is exactly the same in all routing techniques, but path vector routing protocols tend to be applied across wider networks and so must represent routes to a far larger number of destinations. The solution to this problem is to group IP addresses into subnetworks using IP prefixes and then to continue to aggregate those prefixes.

For example, the subnet prefix address 10.1.2.0/28 represents the set of host addresses 10.1.2.0 through 10.1.2.15. If all the hosts in this set lie on the same subnetwork, then a path vector routing protocol need only advertise a route to the subnetwork—a single advertisement instead of sixteen. Clearly, this saving gets better as the prefix length gets smaller, so that class A addresses can be used to save advertising over 16 million individual routes. Unfortunately, the Internet isn't arranged perfectly and it is often necessary to advertise a collection

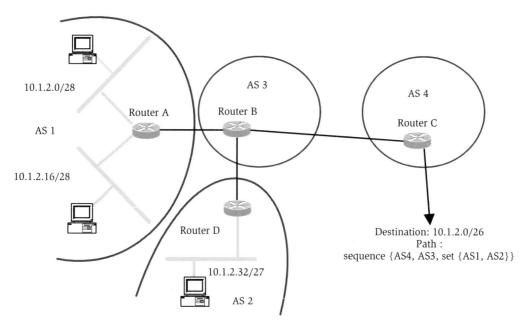

Figure 5.12 Route aggregation reduces the information a path vector routing protocol advertises.

of small subnetworks rather than a single class A address; nevertheless, the routers can often optimize their advertisements through the process of *route aggregation*.

Route aggregation is simply the recognition that subnetworks can be grouped together to construct a new subnetwork that can be represented using a shorter prefix. To illustrate this, look at the network in Figure 5.12. The two subnetworks 10.1.2.0/28 and 10.1.2.16/28 can be reached through Router A. Router A could advertise two routes to its upstream network, but it can also observe that the combination of the two subnetworks can be represented as the prefix 10.1.2.0/27 and advertise just this route to Router B.

In Figure 5.12, Router B can also provide a route to the subnet 10.1.2.32/27, so it can advertise a single route to the prefix 10.1.2.0/26. But suddenly this is no longer a pure path vector distribution—Router B is hiding from Router C the fact that the path is bifurcated when it should be indicating two distinct paths. Advertising two paths doesn't help the information overload problem at Router C, but advertising a single path would be a lie.

The solution to this problem lies in the invention of *path sets*. All routes so far have been advertised as *path sequences*—for example, reach 10.1.2.0/27 along the sequence AS4, AS3, AS1. But with path sets we can define an advertisement that says reach 10.1.2.32/26 through AS4, AS3, set {AS1, AS2}. To be absolutely clear, this is represented as

Destination: 10.1.2.32/26   **Path**: sequence {AS4, AS3, set {AS1, AS2}}

The constructs *sequence* and *set* may be arbitrarily nested within each other, but note that nesting sequence within sequence, or set within set, is a null operation.

5.2.4 Distributing Additional Information

Because routing protocols are running in the network and are distributing connectivity or reachability information between the routers, they have been the easy choice for use by protocol engineers who need to distribute some additional piece of information. In many cases—such as traffic engineering, described in Chapter 8, and multiprotocol label switching, described in Chapter 9—extending the routing protocol is a good choice since the information distributed is directly relevant to the capabilities of the links, and affects how routes are chosen. Link state protocols are particularly amenable to this sort of extension. For example, the link state protocols OSPF and IS-IS have been extended to carry not only the metric or cost of the link, but details of the available resources such as bandwidth. This allows programs that compute end-to-end paths or select traffic placement within the network to consider the best way to spread traffic across the network, utilizing bandwidth evenly and not overburdening any one link or section of the network.

Other information distributed by piggybacking it on routing protocols is less pertinent to the primary function of the routing protocol. Such extensions tend to be proprietary to individual router manufacturers and are usually the product of expediency. That is, the router manufacturer discovered a need (usually commercial) to quickly deploy some function to distribute information between the nodes in a customer's network. Faced with the choice of implementing a new information distribution protocol or bolting a new piece of information onto their routing protocol, the quick and easy solution is always to reuse what already exists.

An example of this might be an application that catalogs the phone number of the operator responsible for each router. When the operator at one router spots a problem with another router, the operator would immediately have the right contact information available. Such additional information could easily be included in the router advertisements of a link state protocol.

5.2.5 Choosing a Routing Model

The choice of routing model goes a long way toward forcing the choice of path computation technique (discussed in the next section) and to limiting the choice of routing protocol used to distribute the routing information. There are some general trends in the features offered by each of the routing models, although it should be noted that when a deficiency in one model is identified, work begins to produce a routing protocol that solves the problem. Table 5.5 compares some of the attributes of the three routing models described in the

Table 5.5 A Comparison of the Attributes of Different Routing Techniques

Attribute	Static Routes	Distance Vector	Link State	Path Vector
Implementation complexity	Trivial	Simple	Complex	Medium
Processing requirements	Low	Medium	High	Medium
Memory requirements	Low	Low	High	Medium
View of network	Adjacent links	Adjacent links and nodes	Full	Adjacent links and nodes and some paths
Path computation	Manual	Iterative and distributed	Shortest Path First on each node	Iterative and distributed
Metric support	None	Basic	Complex	Basic
Policy support	Complex	Simple	Complex	Medium
CIDR support	Yes	Yes	Yes	Yes
Convergence time	Manual	Slow	Fast	Slow
Loop detection	None	Poor to medium	Good	Good
Hierarchical routing	No	Unusual	Yes	Yes
Typical network size/complexity	Small	Small/medium	Medium/large	Medium
Usual role	Small networks	IGP	IGP	EGP

previous sections; it also includes a column for static routes (that is, the manual provisioning of routing tables), which should not arbitrarily be rejected in favor of a routing protocol.

5.3   Computing Paths

The discussion in the previous sections covers techniques for distributing routing information, but the purpose is, of course, to derive routing paths. In the Internet, most forwarding is hop-by-hop. This means that each router is only responsible for forwarding a datagram to some other router. This process continues until the datagram reaches its destination or times out because its path is too long.

Random-walk routing techniques are not particularly reliable, and so it is important that the routers in a network have a coordinated approach to deciding which is the next hop along the path to a destination. The distance vector and path vector techniques essentially pass information between neighboring routers and use this data to build the shortest paths to all destinations. These are then installed in a routing table and passed on to the router's neighbors. The path computation model deployed in distance vector protocols and path vector protocols is iterative and distributed—each router is responsible for performing a piece of computation and for distributing the results.

Link state protocols ensure that all routers in the network have the same view of the network's resources, but do not distribute path information. It is the responsibility of each router to use the link state information that it receives to calculate the shortest paths through the network.

5.3.1 Open Shortest Path First (OSPF)

Before embarking on a discussion of how to select the shortest path across a network, we must establish what we mean by "shortest." As we have seen in distance vector protocols and link state protocols, the advertised connectivity is associated with a metric. In most simple cases this metric is set to 1 for each hop or link, so the total metric for a path is the number of hops. It is possible, however, to set the metric for any one hop to be greater than 1; this increases the distance, as it were, between a pair of adjacent routers. Another way to look at this is to say that an increased *cost* has been assigned to the link. In this case, when the total metric for a path is computed, it is the sum of the link metrics along the path.

Open Shortest Path First (OSPF) computation selects the least cost path across a network from source to destination using only active (open) links. What might initially seem a simple problem does not scale well with an increase in the number of routers and links in a network. It is the sort of problem the human brain can solve relatively accurately by looking at a scale map, but it is hard to convert to an abstract problem for a computer. Even using some clever approaches outlined in the following sections, the challenge is sufficiently time-consuming that it would be chronically inefficient to calculate the path for each datagram as it arrives and requires to be forwarded. Instead, it is necessary to summarize the available network information into a routing table providing a rapid look-up to forward each datagram.

An additional issue for IP forwarding is that the forwarding choice is made at each router along the path. This makes it critical that the same basis for the routing choice is used at each router; if this were not the case it would be very possible for a datagram to be forwarded from one router to another in a loop, doomed to circle forever like the Flying Dutchman in search of a destination until its TTL expired. The routing protocol ensures that each router has consistent information on which to base its routing decisions, but it remains an essential part of the process that the routers should also use the same mechanism to operate on this information to build a routing table.

In distance vector routing, the distribution of routing information is nearly 100 percent of the work. Full routes are distributed with end-to-end metrics. The only computation a router must perform is a comparison of metrics—the higher-cost path is discarded and the lower-cost path is installed in the routing table and advertised to other routers.

In path vector routing the operation is similar. Although end-to-end metrics are not usually distributed with routes in such routing schemes, the full path is passed from router to router, and each router can count the hops and determine the least cost path.

Link state routing presents a whole different problem. Here each router has a complete view of the network supplied by information from all of the routers in the network, but the routers must construct their routing tables from scratch using just this information. It is not a requirement that the routers all use the same mechanism to compute the shortest paths, simply that they all arrive at consistent results. This consistency is, nevertheless, so important that the two principal link state routing protocols (OSPF and IS-IS—see Sections 5.5 and 5.6) mandate the use of the Dijkstra Shortest Path First algorithm invented by Dutch physicist and computer scientist E. W. Dijkstra.

The Dijkstra algorithm is a relatively efficient and significantly simple way to build a routing table from a set of link state information. It is an important point that the algorithm fully populates the routing table in one go by simultaneously calculating the shortest paths to all destinations. Starting at a specific node, each neighboring router is added to a *candidate list*, which is ordered by cost (metric) of the links to the neighbors with the least cost link first. The algorithm then builds a *routing tree* rooted at the local router by selecting the neighboring router with the least cost link to be the next node in the tree.

The algorithm then moves on to examine the neighbors of the tip of the tree branch, making a candidate list and selecting the least cost neighbor that is not already in the tree. By repeating this process, a single-limb tree is built that gives the shortest path to a set of hosts. The algorithm now discards the head of the candidate list at the tip of the branch and processes the next list member. This forks the tree and visits the neighbors until the routes to a new set of hosts have been completed.

This iteration repeats until the candidate list for the branch tip is empty. At this point, the algorithm backs up one node in the tree and continues to work through the candidate list there. The algorithm is complete when the candidate list on the base node is empty. At this point a tree has been built in which each branch represents the shortest path to the host at the tip of the tree. No router appears in the tree twice, and there is only one route to each host.

Note that any router within the link state network is capable of computing the routing table used by any other router—it simply runs the Dijkstra algorithm starting at that router.

It is worth noting that the Dijkstra algorithm examines each link in the network precisely once as it builds the routing tree. Each time a link is examined a new neighbor is found and this neighbor must be compared with the entries in the candidate list to check that it is not already there, and to insert the neighbor into the list at the correct point. If there are l links from a router and n neighbors (l does not necessarily equal n), the sorting process will be a function of the order $log(n)$ and the algorithm has an efficiency the order of $l * log(n)$ for each node. Since each link is visited just once during the whole algorithm, we can sum this efficiency across all nodes to reach an overall efficiency of the order of

$$\Sigma(l * \log(n)) = L * \log(N)$$

where L is the total number of links in the network and N is the total number of nodes. Clearly, in a fully connected mesh network, $L=N(N-1)/2$ and the efficiency is closer to N^2.

5.3.2 Constrained Shortest Path First (CSPF)

Shortest Path First (SPF) algorithms, such as the Dijkstra algorithm, apply a single constraint to the choice of a route: The resulting path must be the shortest. Allowing links to be configured with metric values other than 1 skews the effect of the SPF calculation, but as far as the algorithm is concerned it is still making an SPF choice.

There are occasions, however, when it is appropriate to make SPF calculations that also consider other attributes of the traffic and the available links. These other considerations provide *constraints* to the SPF algorithm, turning it into a Constrained Shortest Path First (CSPF) computation.

The most obvious constraint is already built into OSPF—that is, only available, "open" links are considered within the computation. Other constraints can be handled in a similar way by excluding links that do not meet the requirements of the traffic to be carried. For example, if it is known which links are reliable and which less reliable, mission-critical traffic can be routed over reliable links by simply *pruning* the unreliable links from the routing tree. This approach, however, has the drawback that if there are not enough suitable links, the traffic cannot be delivered at all.

An alternative way of applying CSPF is to use the constraints to generate a new cost metric for each link. The function used to generate this new metric might, for example, operate on the advertised metric, the link's bandwidth, and the known mean-time between failure.

In reality, most CSPF routing engines are a compromise between these two options. Some links are pruned from the routing tree as unsuitable for the traffic that is being routed, and then the constraints are mapped to cost for each remaining link as the routing tree is built.

There are two chief reasons why CSPF is not widely used within IP networks. As described in the previous section, it is crucial to routed IP networks that the same basis for routing decisions is used at each router in the network. This would require an agreement between routers on exactly how they determine the constraints applicable to each datagram, and how they apply the constraints to compute paths.

The second problem that limits the use of CSPF is the availability of sufficient information describing the capabilities of the links in the network. The current routing protocols distribute a single metric along with the link state, and this metric is already used by SPF. In order to be useful for CSPF, the link state advertisements would also need to include information about bandwidth, reliability, and so forth.

In the short term, the solution to both of these issues has been to apply the knowledge of each link's capabilities when setting the metric for the link. This can then feed back into the SPF calculation and apply a modicum of constraint awareness. The next two sections examine other ways to apply constraints to IP routing.

5.3.3 Equal Cost Multipath (ECMP)

It is possible that SPF or CSPF calculations will result in more than one path with the same cost. In normal SPF routing, there is no reason to distinguish between the routes and it is usual to use the first one discovered. CSPF routing may distinguish between equal cost paths using constraints other than the cost metric, but nevertheless may derive multiple paths that equally satisfy all of the constraints.

A router may choose to offer Equal Cost Multipath (ECMP) routing services. This feature serves to load-balance traffic across the paths and so distribute it better over the network—when only the first shortest path to be discovered is used, all traffic is sent the same way, overusing the chosen path and completely ignoring the other paths.

When ECMP solutions exist, the router can choose to forward datagrams alternately on the available paths. Although this guarantees absolutely equitable load balancing, it runs the risk of delivering all packets out of order—consider what would happen if the end-to-end latency on one path was slightly higher than on another path. Similarly, this form of load balancing would result in packet loss for all data flows in the event of a link failure on any one of the paths.

Instead, ECMP routers usually apply some other way to load balance, identifying whole traffic flows and placing them on individual paths. Traffic flows may be categorized by any number of means, including source address, application protocol, transport port number, and DiffServ Color (see Chapter 6). The router assigns a categorization to the equal cost paths and places all matching traffic onto the appropriate path.

The only other change required within an ECMP router is that its routing algorithm should discover all equally priced paths and not discard those that are not cheaper than the best path selected. This can be achieved with a very simple modification to the Dijkstra algorithm.

5.3.4 Traffic Engineering

Traffic engineering (TE), described in Chapter 8 of this book, is the process of predetermining the path through the network that various flows of data will follow. These paths can diverge from the shortest paths for a variety of reasons, including operator choice or the application of constraints to the routing decision. Fundamental to the way TE works is the fact that packets are not routed at each router in the network, but the path is specified from the outset and provided as a series of IP addresses (links) that the traffic must traverse. How these paths accompany the data to prevent it from being routed using SPF at each router is discussed in Chapters 8 and 9.

CSPF is particularly relevant for TE path computation. The path is usually computed to place a well-qualified data flow through the network, so the characteristics of the flow are known. This enables the CSPF algorithm to select only those links that meet the requirements of the flow.

For TE CSPF computations to be made at a single point, the common link state routing protocols in use in the Internet (OSPF and IS-IS) have been extended to carry basic resource availability information describing the total bandwidth available and currently in use on each link. This, too, is described further in Chapter 8.

5.3.5 Choosing How to Compute Paths

The choice of path computation is forced by the decision to use a distance vector, path vector or link state routing protocol. The first two employ a distributed computation technique, but link state protocols require some form of full computation on each node. The advantages of the link state approach are that the protocol has a full view of the network and can perform sophisticated policy-based routing, and even compute paths to remote nodes. On the other hand, the amount of information required can quickly grow large, which may place an effective limit on the size of the network that can be supported. At the same time, the complexity of the path computation does not scale well and needs a serious CPU in a large network.

For the majority of applications, a simple shortest path first approach provided by any of the three routing techniques is adequate. Each can be enhanced by simple metrics to skew the cost of traversing specific links. For more complex applications, especially for traffic engineering using IP or MPLS tunnels, Constrained Shortest Path First computations are very common, and these rely on additional information that is typically only shared by link state protocols. Indeed, if a distance vector or path vector protocol were to try to distribute full details for a CSPF computation it would quickly become overloaded. (Note, however, that Cisco's EIGRP is a distance vector protocol that goes a long way toward bridging this gap.)

5.4 Routing Information Protocol (RIP)

Routing Information Protocol (RIP) version two is a distance vector routing protocol used widely in simple IP networks. It stems from Xerox's XNS protocol suite, but was quickly adopted for IP and published as the Routing Information Protocol in RFC 1058. RIPv2 (RFC 1723) adds some necessary features to RIP to help routers function correctly and to provide some basic security options.

Although RIP has now been replaced, RIPv2 was carefully designed to be backwards compatible with RIP routers and also to operate in small networks or larger internetworks where other routing protocols are used.

Most of the operation of RIPv2 follows the classic behavior of a distance vector protocol and is, therefore, covered only briefly below.

5.4.1 Messages and Formats

RIP messages are carried within UDP datagrams using port 520 (see Chapter 7). UDP offers basic delivery and checksum protection for its payload. RIP uses a single message format, as shown in Figure 5.13. Each message consists of a single 4-byte header and between 1 and 25 route entries. The header identifies the RIP command using a single-byte command code value selected from the values shown in Table 5.6 to indicate what purpose the message serves. There is also a protocol version indicator that carries the value 2 to show that it is RIPv2.

The body of the message is made up of route entries. The number of route entries can be determined from the length of the UDP datagram and there is no other length indicator. Each route entry carries information about one route that can be reached through the reporting node, so to report a full routing table may require more than one message. The Address Family Indicator (AFI) indicates the type of addressing information that is being exchanged and is set to 2 to indicate IPv4—the interface address being reported is carried in the IP Address field in network byte order (note that unnumbered links are not supported by RIP). The Metric is the cost of reaching the destination through the reporting router—the distance.

The other fields build more information into the basic distance vector distribution. The Route Tag allows a 16-bit attribute or identity to be associated with each route and must accompany the route if it is advertised further by the receiving router. The intention here is to allow all routes advertised from one

Table 5.6 The RIP Message Command Codes. Other Command Codes Are Either Obsolete or Reserved for Private Implementations

Command Code	Meaning
1	Request. A request to solicit another router to send all or part of its routing table.
2	Response. The distribution of all or part of the sending router's routing table. This message may be unsolicited, or may be sent in response to a Request command.

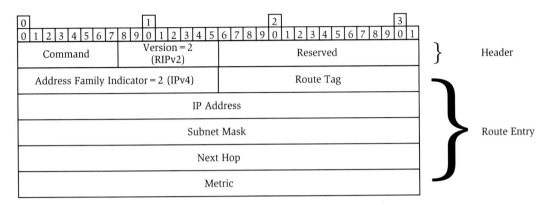

Figure 5.13 RIP version two message consists of a 4-byte header followed by from 1 to 25 route entries.

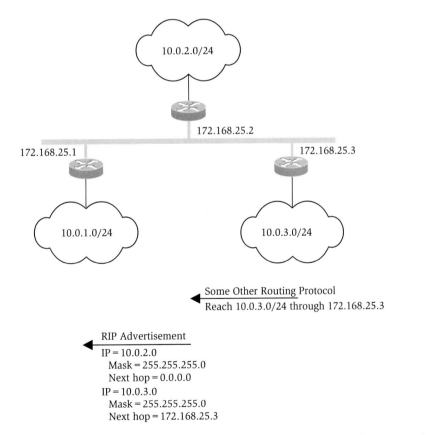

Figure 5.14 RIP may be used to pass on routing information on behalf of statically configured routers or other routing protocols. The Next Hop field indicates where packets should be sent.

domain or autonomous system to be easily recognized. Route tagging is not special to RIP, and other routing protocols use it equally; there is good scope for using route tags to integrate RIP with other routing protocols.

The Subnet Mask identifies the network address for the route being advertised when applied to the IP address carried in the route entry. A zero value means that the address is a host address (that is, no subnet mask has been supplied).

The Next Hop field announces the next hop router that should be used to satisfy this route. That is, the route advertisement may advertise a route on behalf of another node on the directly connected network. This may be particularly useful if RIP is not being run on all of the routers on a network, as indicated in Figure 5.14. A value of 0.0.0.0 indicates that routing should be via the originator of the RIP advertisement.

5.4.2 Overloading the Route Entry

Security is an issue for routers using RIPv2, not because the information they exchange is sensitive, but because severe damage can be done by an intruder who injects false routing information into the network. By doing this, a malicious person is able to trick RIP routers into believing that routes exist when they don't. This can cause the data to be sent down the wrong links (perhaps to a host that will simply discard it) or around in loops until its TTL expires and the data is dropped.

RIP authentication validates that the sender of a RIP message is truly who it claims to be. Three options are provided, as listed in Table 5.7. Note that only option three provides a full check on the authenticity of the message sender.

Table 5.7 RIP Message Authentication Using Three Options

Authentication Type	Usage
1	Message Digest. Placed at the start of the series of route entries, the authentication information contains the 16-byte output from the MD5 algorithm applied to the entire message. This application of a hashing algorithm ensures that accidental changes to the content of the message are detected, but intruders can still change the message and recompute the hash. For more details of the MD5 algorithm see Chapter 14.
2	Password. A 6-byte password is placed in the initial bytes of the authentication information in an entry at the start of the sequence of route entries. This is not a very secure technique since the password can be intercepted by an intruder and used in subsequent fake messages.
3	Message Digest Key and Sequence Number. For full authentication security, the initial route entry carries a message length and sequence number. It also contains the index into a list of secret keys known only to the sender and receiver of the message. The key is combined with the entire RIP message and passed through the MD5 hashing algorithm and the resulting 16-byte output is placed in a second authentication information route entry placed at the end of the message. This is more secure since no intruder knows the value of the key to use when computing the MD5 hash.

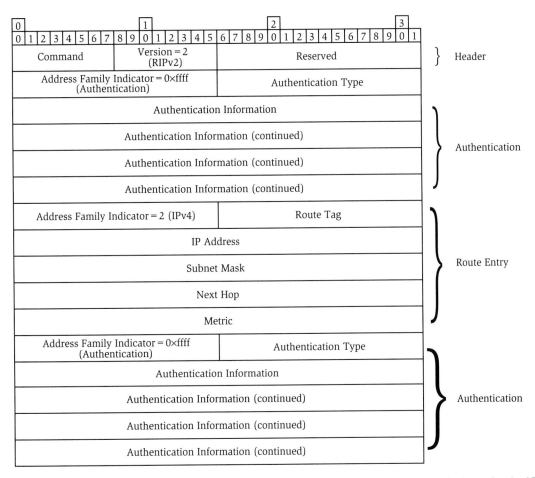

Figure 5.15   RIP messages may contain authentication information within the first and last route entries by setting the AFI to 0xffff.

The authentication information for RIP messages is placed in special route entries within the messages. The AIF is set to 0xffff, which has special meaning and is interpreted according to Figure 5.15 and Table 5.7. As shown in Figure 5.15, the authentication information route entries come either at the start or the end (or both) of the series of route entries. One minor negative consequence of this overloading of route entries is that fewer routes can be carried by a single message.

5.4.3 Protocol Exchanges

In the first version of RIP, response messages were broadcast on the local network. This meant that all nodes on the network received and processed the UDP datagrams before discovering that the payload was for port 522 (RIP) and dropping them if they did not support RIP. Hosts and routers that don't run RIP are not interested in receiving such messages, so RIPv2 improves efficiency by defining a multicast address (224.0.0.9) to which messages are sent. Because these are interrouter messages, which are processed by the routers and not forwarded, IGMP is not needed.

RIP uses the Response message to distribute routing information, following the patterns explained in the description of distance vector routing in Section 5.2.1. Allowing multiple routes on a single message helps improve efficiency when there are multiple routes to be distributed at once.

Infinity is set to 16 in RIP—thus, routes are marked as invalid by a router sending a RIP Response message showing the route metric as 16. A small value of infinity is important because it catches problems quickly, but 16 may seem a very small value to use for infinity, and indeed it is deliberately chosen to be as small as possible without compromising real RIP routes—the *diameter* (the longest route) of a RIP network can be no more than 15 hops. The designers of RIP considered that the protocol would not be effective in networks with a larger diameter partly because the convergence times would be too great and partly because the network complexity would require too many route advertisements.

A router that wishes to solicit routing table updates from its peers does so by sending a Request message using UDP multicast targeted at port 520. Every RIP router that receives one of these messages responds with a RIP Response sent direct to the requesting node. Note, however, that hosts may participate in a RIP network by listening to distributed RIP information but not distributing any information of their own—such hosts are described as *silent* and do not respond to RIP Requests that are sent from port 520, but should respond if the source port is other than 520.

Each RIP Request lists the network or host addresses in which the sender is interested, and the Response can simply use the same message buffer to respond by filling in the appropriate information. If the responder does not have a route to the requested address and subnet mask, it simply sets the metric in the Response to infinity (16). If the requester wishes to see all the information in the responder's routing table it includes a single Route entry with address set to 0.0.0.0 and metric set to 16.

In RIP, several timers are run to manage the exchanges. The full routing table is refreshed to every neighboring router every 30 seconds. On multidrop networks with multiple routers, such timers tend toward coincidence, so this timer is jittered by a small random amount each time it is set to avoid all of the routers generating bursts of messages at the same time.

Additionally, each route on a RIP router is managed by two timers. Whenever a route is added, updated, or refreshed, a 180-second timer is started or restarted for it. If this timer expires, it means that the route is no longer being advertised—perhaps the neighboring router has gone down—and the route is no longer valid. The router immediately starts to advertise the route as withdrawn and, after a further 120 seconds, the route is removed from the local routing table and it is as if it never existed.

Route withdrawal is achieved as expected. A RIP Response is sent for the affected route with metric 16. Note that a router that receives a route withdrawal takes the same action as if the route had timed out. That is, it immediately withdraws the route from its neighbors and starts the 120 second cleanup timer.

---

in-fin-i-ty \in-¹fin-ət-ē\ *n.* **1 a**: the quality of being infinite **b**: unlimited extent of time, space, or quantity: BOUNDLESS **2**: an indefinitely great number or amount

---

5.4.4 Backwards Compatibility with RIPv1

In a remarkable piece of sound protocol design and with a modicum of luck, the initial version of RIP included a significant amount of padding in the route entries it defined. This makes it very easy for RIP versions one and two to interoperate. As can be seen by comparing Figure 5.16 with Figure 5.13, the RIP version one message is identical to that used in version two except that some of the reserved fields have meanings assigned in version two.

In fact, RIPv1 and RIPv2 routers can coexist successfully by the application of a few simple rules on the RIPv2 routers. First, the use of multicast or broadcast must be configurable per interface—this ensures that the RIPv2 router will send and receive messages compatible at a UDP level with the RIPv1 router.

Second, RIPv2 routers must accept RIPv1 Requests and Responses. The way the RIPv2 fields are defined and the fact that the RIPv1 reserved fields are transmitted as zero means that a RIPv2 router can successfully process a RIPv1 message as though it were a RIPv2 message. Nevertheless, a RIPv2 router should issue RIPv1 Responses in reply to RIPv1 Requests if possible. Note, however,

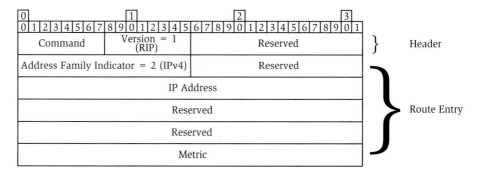

Figure 5.16 A RIP version one message is the same size as the messages used in RIP version two.

that the RIPv1 router will ignore the fields it doesn't understand so that it will actually process a RIPv2 message correctly.

Authentication is the chief feature that will not operate successfully between different protocol versions. The RIPv1 router will ignore all authentication information since it does not recognize the AFI value 0xffff, making it no more vulnerable to attack than it was when talking with another RIPv1 router. The RIPv2 router will, of course, receive RIPv1 messages that do not contain authentication and is free to accept them. However, note that this creates a vulnerability in RIPv2 networks where an interloper may use RIPv1 messages to trick a RIPv2 router. The best strategy is to define RIP version level support on an interface-by-interface basis and to allow only RIPv2 with full authentication on any interface that is not configured as being shared with a RIPv1 router.

5.4.5 Choosing to Use RIP

RIP has two things going for it: it is widely deployed, and it is extremely simple to implement. Although it is true that the IGP protocols described in Sections 5.5 and 5.6 (OSPF and IS-IS) are far more sophisticated and flexible, RIP is still attractive in small networks because of its simplicity and wide availability. Additionally, RIP uses very little bandwidth in a small, stable network (it is less chattery than some of the newer protocols), and can also be configured more simply.

RIP does, however, have some considerable drawbacks. On the whole these issues are unavoidable because RIP is a distance vector protocol. First, RIP has set infinity to the value 16, and cannot support a network with diameter greater than 15. In addition to the obvious limitation of network size, this also forces certain configuration limitations on the network since any attempt to assign costs other than 1 to a link (perhaps to make poor-quality, low-bandwidth links less preferable) immediately reduces the maximum diameter that can be supported—the total diametric cost must be no greater than 15.

Although RIP responds well to link failures with the routers at the ends of the links able to withdraw routes using immediate updates, RIP relies for this process on the data-link or physical layers detecting the link failures. This means that where the lower layers cannot detect link failures or where the link is up but the neighboring router is down (perhaps a software or component failure) RIP must fall back on its own detection methods. RIP's responsiveness to this sort of failure is poor—it takes 180 seconds for a route to time out and a lot of data can be lost in that time.

An increasing concern in modern networks is the fact that RIP includes no support for multicast routing. This function is present in several of the new routing protocols and facilitates the distribution of routes to support multicast traffic (described in Chapter 3).

Finally, RIP is not a very secure protocol, although some security mechanisms can be applied.

Despite all of these concerns, RIP is still a good starting point for a routing protocol in a small network.

5.5   Open Shortest Path First (OSPF)

Open Shortest Path First (OSPF) is a link state, interior gateway protocol developed by the IETF with a good look over the fence at IS-IS (see Section 5.6). We are now at version two of OSPF, version one having lasted only two years from its publication as an RFC to its eclipse by the RFC for OSPFv2. There have been several republications of the OSPFv2 standard over the years, culminating in the current version in RFC 2328, but each change has done little more than fix minor bugs and clarify frequently asked questions or deployment and implementation issues. Further RFCs and drafts have been published to handle specific extensions to OSPF to handle additional requirements such as support for IPv6 and MPLS traffic engineering. OSPFv3 is currently under development within the IETF.

Whether there was ever any need for OSPF to be invented is fortunately a question that does not need to be answered—we are where we are. At the time, IS-IS seemed, no doubt, to be too general and outside the control of the IETF. OSPF was developed with a very IPv4-centric outlook and was certainly aimed at being *the* link state IGP for the Internet. For a comparison of OSPF and IS-IS and a glance at whether it achieved this aim, refer to Section 5.7.

Before embarking on the remainder of this section, you should familiarize yourself with the overview of link state routing protocols contained in Section 5.2.2.

5.5.1 Basic Messages and Formats

OSPF messages are carried as the payload of IP datagrams using the protocol identifier value 89 (0×59) in the next protocol field in the IP header. All OSPF messages begin with a common message header, as shown in Figure 5.17. The version identifier shows that this is OSPF version two, and the message type indicates what the body of the message is used for, using a value from Table 5.8.

Table 5.8 OSPF Message Types

Type	Message
1	Hello. Used to discover neighbors and to maintain a relationship with them.
2	Database Description. Lists the link state information available without actually supplying it.
3	Link State Request. Requests one or more specific pieces of link state information.
4	Link State Update. The primary message in OSPF—used to distribute link state information.
5	Link State Acknowledgement. Acknowledges the safe receipt of link state information.

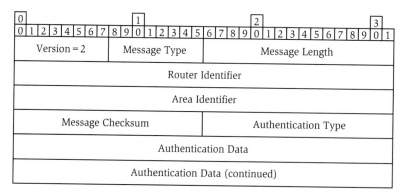

Figure 5.17 The OSPF common message header.

The message length gives the length in bytes of the whole message, including the common message header.

The Router Identifier field provides a unique identifier of the router within the autonomous system to which it belongs. Note two points:

1. It is not sufficient for the OSPF router identifier to be unique within the area to which the router belongs. It must be unambiguous across the whole autonomous system.
2. The router identifier may be set to be one of the IP addresses of the router (perhaps a loopback address or the lowest value interface address), but this is not a requirement. The router identifier may be set as any unique 32-bit number and is not necessarily a routable address.

The next field gives an area identifier for the area to which the router belongs. OSPF areas are discussed in more detail in Section 5.5.6, but for now note that the only constraints on this field are that the area identifiers must be unique within an autonomous system. The message checksum is a standard IP checksum (see Chapter 2) applied to the whole of the OSPF message—it is not computed and set to zero if cryptographic authentication is used.

The Authentication Type field indicates what authentication is in use for the message. An OSPF router is configured to use only one type of authentication on each interface and should discard any OSPF messages it receives that use any other type of authentication. Note that this introduces some ambiguity with multi-access interfaces since authentication operates between router peers—some implementations allow authentication to be configured for explicitly configured peers, but most require that all routers on the same multi-access network use the same authentication type. Null authentication (type zero) does not apply any additional safeguards to the messages and requires that the message checksum is used. Password authentication (type 1) does not provide any additional security since an 8-byte (null padded) password is transported

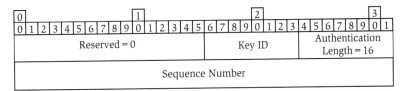

Figure 5.18 The OSPF authentication data when cryptographic authentication is in use.

"in the clear" in the Authentication Data field of each message, but it does offer a degree of protection against misconfiguration or accidental misconnection of routers that would otherwise discover each other and distribute OSPF link state information. Cryptographic authentication (type 2) uses the MD5 algorithm (see Chapter 14) to ensure that the data delivered is unchanged from the data that was sent and so to validate that it arrived from the real sender. For cryptographic authentication, the authentication data field is broken up into four subfields, as shown in Figure 5.18. The Key ID allows each router to maintain a list of encryption keys and algorithms and to select between them at will—although MD5 is the only algorithm in common use, many routers allow multiple keys to be configured. The Authentication Length field states the length of the authentication information that was generated by the authentication algorithm and which is appended to the OSPF message—for MD5 this length is always 16. The fourth field is a sequence number, which helps protect OSPF against replay attacks. The sequence number is incremented for each packet sent, ensuring that no two packets will ever be identical even if they carry the same information.

5.5.2 Neighbor Discovery

The first job of an OSPF router is to discover its neighbors. It uses a Hello exchange as described in Section 5.2.2 to establish an *adjacency* with each of its OSPF peers, and the Hello message continues to be used to keep these adjacencies alive. In OSPF, a fair amount of parameter negotiation is also carried out on the Hello message, although some of this is deferred to the Database Description message described in Section 5.5.3. The Hello message begins with the common message header and then continues as shown in Figure 5.19.

The Network Mask field gives the router's opinion of the network mask that applies to the network on which the message was issued. The Hello Interval states how often in seconds the router will retransmit a Hello message to keep the adjacency alive, and the Router Dead Interval says how long this router will wait without hearing from its neighbor before declaring the neighbor dead. When a router responds to a Hello, it may take this value into account in setting its own Hello Interval, although most routers use the default times of 10 seconds for the Hello Interval and 40 seconds (that is, four times the Hello Interval) for the Router Dead Interval, removing any need for negotiation.

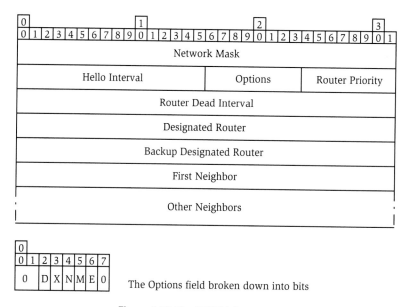

Figure 5.19 The OSPF Hello message.

Table 5.9 The OSPF Router Option Flags

Flag	Meaning
D	If set to 1, this router intends to treat this interface as a *demand circuit*, that is, one for which traffic is charged by the byte and where reducing traffic is, therefore, important. On a demand circuit link, OSPF does not retransmit Hello messages but relies on the data-link layer to report network failures. Similarly, OSPF does not retransmit link state advertisements on demand circuits in stable networks, and the link state database information must be prevented from timing out.
X	If set to 1, the router is willing to receive and handle link state advertisements that carry private data for autonomous systems, as described in Section 5.5.11.
N	If set to 1, the router is willing to receive and handle link state advertisements that describe Not So Stubby Areas (NSSAs), as described in Section 5.5.8.
M	If set to 1, this router will forward IP multicast datagrams and can handle group membership advertisements, as described in Section 5.9.5.
E	If set to 1, the router is willing to receive and handle link state advertisements that pertain to external links, that is links that connect this autonomous system to another, as described in Section 5.5.11.

The Options byte can be broken down into separate bit flags, described in Table 5.9. These bits indicate the capabilities of the router and its willingness to participate in certain subsets of OSPF function.

The Router Priority byte indicates the router's willingness (or desire) to be a designated router. When there are multiple routers on a multi-access network, the one with the highest priority value becomes the router for the network and is called the *designated router*. If two routers have the same priority, the one with the numerically larger router ID gets the job. Two fields are dedicated to identifying the designated router and backup designated router if this Hello message is issued on a multi-access link. Multi-access interfaces and designated routers are discussed in Section 5.5.5.

The remainder of the Hello message lists all the routers the sender already knows about and with which it has established OSPF adjacencies. The number of routers listed here is governed by the length of the Hello message. Each router is identified by its router ID.

Note that the demand circuit option (the D-flag) is particularly useful on slow links and dial-up links. This mixes the concepts of cost and bandwidth. The original intention of the demand circuit option was to limit the number of bytes sent by the protocol to keep the connection active when there are other ways to detect connection failure and when there is a direct cost associated with the number of bytes transmitted. In this case, the Hello messages are expensive and unnecessary. The same logic applies on dial-up links on which bandwidth is limited—Hello messages are not used because they would congest the connection. Further, where dial-up connections are charged according to the amount of time for which the link is connected, it is useful to be able to tear down the physical connection (that is the phone call) while continuing to pretend to the routing protocol that the connection is active. If there is a need to distribute traffic, the physical connection can be reestablished "on demand." Clearly, if Hello messages were used, the disruption to the physical connection would cause OSPF to detect a failure and report the link as down, so the demand circuit option is used.

5.5.3 Synchronizing Database State

Having discovered a neighbor and introduced itself, the first job of an OSPF router is to synchronize its link state database with that of its neighbor. In practice, this means that each router must send a copy of its entire database to its new neighbor and both routers must merge the received information with their own databases. This is all well and good when one of the routers has just rebooted and has an entirely empty database, but it is more likely that routers are participating in well-connected networks and already have substantial databases when they discover each other. Further, the databases on the two routers will typically have many entries in common and to exchange them would be a waste of bandwidth.

This situation is improved by the Database Description and Link State Request messages. Instead of sending the full contents of its link state database, a router sends a Database Description message that supplies a list of the available database entries without including the data from the entries. A router that receives a Database Description message can search its own database for the

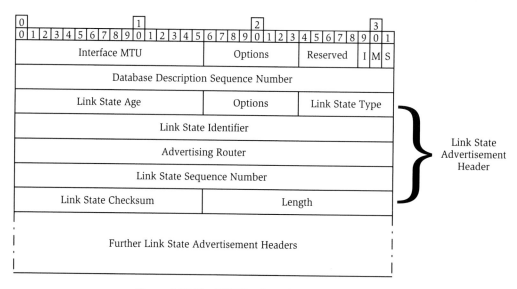

Figure 5.20 The OSPF Database Description message.

listed entries and use the Link State Request message to request that the other router send it specific link state information that is missing from its database.

The link state database entries are described in the Database Description message, as shown in Figure 5.20, using the link state advertisement header—a piece of descriptive control information advertised with the link state information as it is distributed through the network. The link state advertisement header is described more fully in Section 5.5.4.

The Database Description message also contains a few additional fields to describe its operation on the link. The Interface MTU describes the size in bytes of the largest MTU the router can send on this interface—larger datagrams will require fragmentation. The Options reflect the router's capabilities and intentions and are as described for the Hello message in the previous section. Their presence on the Database Description message allows for a degree of negotiation after the Hello exchange.

The Database Description message contains a Database Description Sequence Number to sequence a series of Database Description messages if all the information cannot fit into a single message. The initial Database Description message is sent with the I-bit set, and each message has the M-bit set to show whether or not more Database Description messages will follow. Thus, only the last Database Description message has the M-bit clear, and only the first has the I-bit set.

The S-bit in the Database Description message is used to define the slave/master relationship between the routers during the database exchange process. If the bit is clear, the router is the slave. This uneven relationship is used to send and acknowledge Database Description messages. Acknowledgements are important

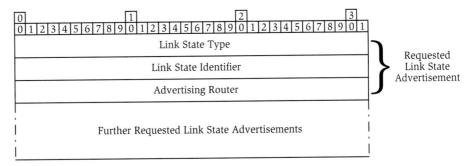

Figure 5.21 The OSPF Link State Request message.

to ensure that the other router knows about the whole of a sending router's database. A Database Description message is sent with the M-bit set and is acknowledged by simply turning the message around with the M-bit clear. Using this process, both routers can be master for their own database resynchronizations at the same time.

If a router decides that it wants to see a piece of link state information listed in a Database Description message, it sends a Link State Request message. As shown in Figure 5.21, this message lists the link state database entries that it wants to see using a summarized form of the link state advertisement header. It can do this because it is not interested in the link state age or sequence number—even if the link state information has been replaced by more up-to-date information, the router still wants to see it. A router that receives a Link State Request responds by distributing the requested link state information just as though it had been locally generated or received from another adjacent router for the first time, as described in the next section.

5.5.4 Advertising Link State

The job of OSPF is to advertise information from one router to another. The routers need to know about routers, links, and networks. It may also be necessary for them to communicate about links to ASBRs (the routers that sit on the boundary to other autonomous systems), about links out of this AS, and about multicast capabilities.

Each piece of this information is carried by OSPF in a Link State Advertisement (LSA) and each LSA is represented by an entry in OSPF's Link State Database. An OSPF router advertises LSAs to its neighbors using the Link State Update message shown in Figure 5.22. Each Link State Update message may carry more than one LSA, as indicated by the 32-bit count field.

Each LSA is made up of a standard header and advertisement-specific data. We have already seen the LSA header in the Database Description message in

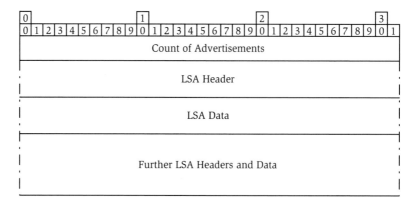

Figure 5.22 An OSPF Link State Update message contains a sequence of link state advertisements, each constructed as a header followed by LSA data.

0										1										2										3	
0	1	2	3	4	5	6	7	8	9	0	1	2	3	4	5	6	7	8	9	0	1	2	3	4	5	6	7	8	9	0	1

Link State Age	Options	Link State Type
Link State Identifier		
Advertising Router		
Link State Sequence Number		
Link State Checksum	Length	

Figure 5.23 The OSPF Link State Advertisement header.

the previous section; it gives all the information necessary to uniquely identify an LSA and to explain what information the LSA is advertising, so the Link State Database entry for the LSA can be referenced by the LSA header. As shown in Figure 5.23, the LSA header contains three fields to uniquely identify the piece of link state information: The Advertising Router provides the router ID of the router that first advertised this piece of information and is not updated as other routers redistribute the LSA around the network; the Link State Identifier uniquely references this piece of link state information within the context of the advertising router; and the Link State Sequence Number makes it possible for the advertising router to update the LSA without having to assign a new link state identifier (note that the sequence numbers are assigned using a lollipop number space [see Section 5.2.2] starting at 0×80000001 and running up to zero on the lollipop stick, and running from zero to 0×7fffffff with wrap-back to zero on the head of the lollipop).

Table 5.10 Timers and Actions Associated with Link State Advertisement in OSPF

Time	Action
1 second	Default amount by which the LS age is incremented for each hop over which the LSA is transmitted.
5 seconds	The shortest interval between LSA updates on the originating router. This protects the network against flapping resources which might cause a very fast rate of LSA generation.
5 minutes	The rate at which a router recomputes the Fletcher checksum on its stored LSAs. This particularly pessimistic feature protects a router against memory overwrites, static electricity, and meteor strikes so that LSAs that are corrupted within the link state database do not get used to compute routes.
15 minutes	If the LS Age on two LSAs with the same sequence number differs by at least this amount, the more recent LSA replaces the old one.
30 minutes	When the age reaches 30 minutes the originating router reissues the LSA with an incremented sequence number. This keeps the LSA alive in all the routers in the network. A small percentage of dither is usually applied to this timer to prevent all LSAs from being refreshed at once, which would cause a burst of traffic in the network.
60 minutes	When an LSA reaches this age it is no longer used for route computation (note that this never happens at the originating router). The LSA is re-advertised to all neighbors and then discarded from the database. The re-advertisement is to ensure that the LSA is also removed from the link state databases on other routers using a rule that says that an LSA received with age 60 minutes is immediately updated in the local database to replace any younger entries. This feature is used by OSPF when an originating router wishes to withdraw a piece of link state information—it simply re-advertises the LSA with the LS Age set to 60 minutes.

The Link State Age is used to age out old state from the database. It is set to zero by the originator and grows in seconds in real time while it is stored in a link state database or when it is passed between routers. Table 5.10 shows the actions and times associated with the Link State Age.

The top bit of the LS Age field can be used in conjunction with the demand circuit option (see the D-bit in Table 5.9) to mean that the LSA should not age out of the link state database. The LSA continues to age in the same way, using the lower bits of the age field to track the age, and all other actions are employed, but when the age reaches 60 minutes (with the top bit set) the LSA remains in the database. The originating LSA uses the same mechanism to withdraw an LSA, that is, it re-advertises it with the LS Age set to 60 minutes (without the top bit set).

The Options byte in the Link State Advertisement Header has the same interpretation it has in the Hello message (see Table 5.9) but applies to the router that originated the advertisement, not to the router that is forwarding it. The Link State Type field indicates the type of information (and, hence, the formatting) carried in the LSA. The standard LSA types are listed in Table 5.11. Three other types are defined for opaque LSAs and are described in Section 5.5.12.

Table 5.11 OSPF Has Eight Standard Types of Information That Are Advertised in LSAs. Further LSA Types Can Be Added Easily to the Protocol

LSA Type	Meaning
1	Router Link. Carries information about each of a router's interfaces that connect to other routers or hosts within the area. This LSA is not advertised outside the area.
2	Network Link. Used for multi-access links (see Section 5.5.5) to list all the routers present on the network. This LSA is not advertised outside the area.
3	Summary Link to Network. Used by an area border router to describe a route to a network destination in another area (but still within the AS). These LSAs report information across area borders, but are only advertised within a single area. OSPF areas are described further in Section 5.5.6.
4	Summary Link to ASBR. Like LSA type 3, this LSA is used to advertise a summary route into another area, but these LSAs describe routes to remote ASBRs. These LSAs report information across area borders, but are advertised only within a single area. OSPF interactions with other ASs are described in Section 5.5.11.
5	External Link. These LSAs are originated by ASBRs to describe routes to destinations in other autonomous systems. These LSAs are exchanged across area borders. OSPF interactions with other ASs are described in Section 5.5.11.
6	Group Membership. This LSA is used to support multicast group membership in Multicast OSPF (MOSPF). Multicast routing is discussed further in Section 5.9.5.
7	NSSA Link. This is used to describe links into Not So Stubby Areas. See Section 5.5.8 for more details.
8	External Attributes. Now generally deprecated, but originally used to carry opaque information across the OSPF AS on behalf of exterior routing protocols (such as BGP—see Section 5.8). OSPF interactions with other ASs are described in Section 5.5.11.

The Link State Checksum is applied to the whole LSA except for the Link State Age (which may change) and is used to verify that the contents of the LSA have not been inadvertently modified. OSPF does not use the standard IP checksum, but instead utilizes *Fletcher's checksum*, which is a compromise between the CPU-intensive cyclic redundancy check and the cheap to compute but non-robust IP checksum. Fletcher's checksum was popular in the International Standards Organization (ISO) when OSPF was being developed, and is used by IS-IS and other ISO protocols (see Section 5.6.2). Note that the checksum is computed by the originator of the LSA and is never updated as the LSA is forwarded. It can be used as a quick way to determine whether two instances of the same LSA received from different neighbors are identical.

The final LSA header field, the Length field, gives the length in byes of the entire LSA including the LSA header.

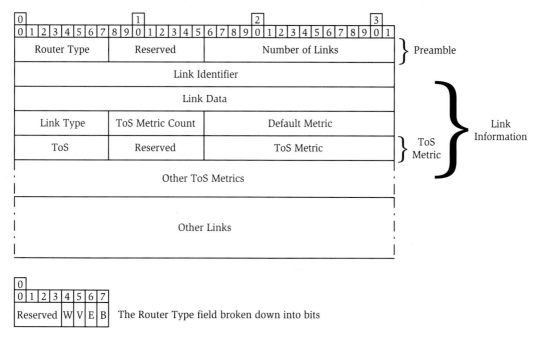

Figure 5.24 The router link state advertisement.

Table 5.12 Router Type Bits Used in a Router Link State Advertisement in OSPF

Router Type Bit	Meaning
W	The router is a wildcard router for multicast support and will accept all packets.
V	The router is an end point of a virtual link that crosses an area.
E	The router is an ASBR (E is for external).
B	The router is an ABR (B is for border).

The principal advertisement OSPF uses is the Router LSA shown in Figure 5.24. If OSPF operates within a single area with point-to-point links, only this LSA is ever used. The Router LSA indicates the router type and then presents counted list links. The Router Type field consists of a series of bits, as shown in Figure 5.24—these are explained in Table 5.12. Each link has two fields to identify it: the Link Identifier and the Link Data. A Link Type field is provided to indicate the type of link and identify the contents of these two identity fields, as shown in Table 5.13.

The remainder of the link information provides metrics on a per ToS (Type of Service) basis. A count says how many ToS metrics are present, and a default metric is provided for all ToS values that are not listed. In practice, networks

Table 5.13 Link Type Field in the Router Link State Advertisement Indicates the Type of the Link Being Advertised and Gives Meaning to the Link Identifier and Link Data Fields

Link Type	Meaning	Link Identifier	Link Data
1	Point-to-Point Link	Router ID at the other end of the link.	For numbered links, the IP address of the link at the local router; for unnumbered links, the interface index at the local router.
2	Connection to Multi-Access Network (see Section 5.5.5)	Designated router's IP interface address on this network.	The IP address of the link at the local router.
3	Connection to Stub Network (see Section 5.5.7)	Network address.	Network mask.
4	Virtual Link (see Section 5.5.9)	Router ID at the other end of the link.	The IP address of the link at the local router.

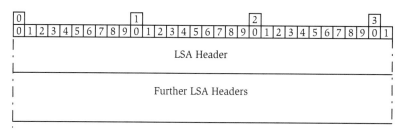

Figure 5.25 The Link State Acknowledgement message contains a simple list of link state advertisement headers.

that offer ToS-based routing are quite uncommon, so the ToS Metric Count would usually be set to zero. If ToS-based routing is used, a more complex routing table must be built to take into account the different metrics associated with each ToS value. Note that 4 bits are assigned to the ToS value in the IP header—OSPF encodes a ToS value by taking the value represented by these bits and multiplying by two (left shift) so that, for example, the ToS bits 0100 (maximize throughput) are represented as the number eight.

A router that sends an LSA to its neighbor wants to know that it arrived safely—if it didn't, the sender can retransmit it. The receiver of a Link State Update message responds with one or more Link State Acknowledgement messages. As shown in Figure 5.25, these messages are simply a list of the LSA headers from the LSAs carried in the Link State Update message. The sender of the Link State Update message can wait a short time (five seconds is the recommended interval on LANs), and if no acknowledgment is received, can retransmit the LSAs.

5.5.5 Multi-Access Networks and Designated Routers

Consider the network illustrated in Figure 5.26. Six routers at the center of the diagram are interconnected by a multi-access, broadcast network (for example, an Ethernet). The routers provide connectivity to other routers and networks. On such a network there are $n * (n—1)/2$ (that is, 15) OSPF adjacencies possible, which should require of the order of n^2 (that is, 36) Hello messages to be sent out every Hello interval. This situation is improved by making use of the broadcast capabilities of the network such that each router multicasts its Hello message to the well-known address 224.0.0.5. As shown in Figure 5.19, the Hello message can list a series of neighbors, so each router on the network can tell whether the sender of the Hello has heard from it. This reduces the number of Hello messages to n (that is, 6) every Hello interval.

The reduction in Hello messages may not make much difference if the routers go on to form a full mesh of OSPF adjacencies, as shown in Figure 5.27. Every time an LSA is advertised on the network it must bounce around between the routers, repeatedly being transmitted on the same network. Since all of the routers are on the same physical network, there is no need for each router to send every advertisement to every other router, which would then send it on to every other router, resulting in $(n—1) * (n—2)$ (that is, 20) advertisements each time a new LSA arrived at a router in the network. Instead, the

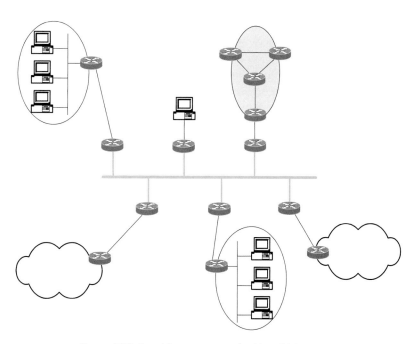

Figure 5.26 A multi-access network with multiple routers.

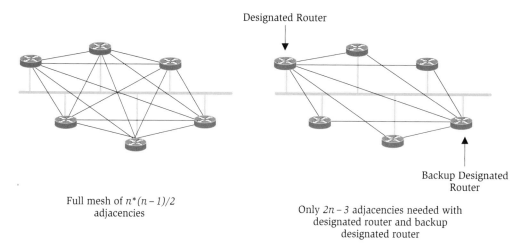

Full mesh of $n*(n-1)/2$
adjacencies

Only $2n-3$ adjacencies needed with
designated router and backup
designated router

Figure 5.27 The full mesh of adjacencies for the routers on a multi-access network can be reduced significantly by using a designated router.

routers elect a *designated router* to act for them—each new LSA is sent to the designated router, which then distributes the information to the other routers in the network, requiring only n (that is, 6) Link State Update messages. The process for electing a designated router is described in Section 5.5.2.

The amount of traffic can be reduced still further if the designated router multicasts its advertisement rather than unicasting it to each router. The multicasts are sent to the special address 224.0.0.5 as used for Hellos. Now we need only two Link State Update messages to tell all routers about a new LSA regardless of the size of network.

The designated router has, however, introduced a single point of failure in the network. Although the routers could quickly conspire to elect a new designated router, there would be a gap during which LSAs might be lost. A common approach is to use a *backup designated router* to cover this potential hole. When a new LSA is received into the network the router must send a Link State Update message to both the designated router and the backup designated router—it uses a special multicast address 224.0.0.6 to achieve this so that it still needs to send only one message. The backup designated router receives and processes the LSA, but does not send it out unless it doesn't hear it from the designated router within five seconds (the LSA retransmission interval).

When a router that is part of a multi-access network sends advertisements to routers beyond the local network it needs to let everyone else know that it provides access to a multi-access network. The responsibility for this is taken by the designated router, which sends a Network LSA, as shown in Figure 5.28. This LSA (type two) includes the network mask and a list of attached routers.

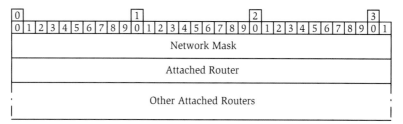

Figure 5.28 The network link state advertisement.

The Link State ID field in the LSA header carries the address of the designated router, which can be combined with the netmask to identify the subnet.

Unfortunately, not all multi-access networks are capable of broadcast (or multicast) techniques. Networks such as X.25, ATM, and Frame Relay provide a "cloud" to which many routers can connect and over which any two routers may form an adjacency through their single point of attachment, yet no one router can send to all of the other routers without setting up individual connections to each one. Such networks are called *nonbroadcast multi-access* (NBMA) networks—the core of the network in Figure 5.29 illustrates such a network.

OSPF adjacencies in NBMA networks must be discovered through configuration as they would be for point-to-point links since there is no broadcast facility. Designated router election can proceed as for a broadcast network, although there is more motivation to configure only a few routers with nonzero priorities. If a router does not want to be a designated router (has priority of zero) it exchanges Hello messages only with the designated router and the backup designated router. Other routers must continue to maintain adjacencies. Note that since links in NBMA networks are often charged by the packet, Hello intervals are set to larger values than in point-to-point or broadcast networks, and when a remote router is not responding, its neighbor will gradually decay its Hello poll rate to as much as two minutes.

Once the designated router and backup designated router have been elected, only adjacencies to those two routers need to be maintained, requiring a total of $2n - 3$ adjacencies as shown in Figure 5.27. Database synchronization must happen on each of these adjacencies, and since the designated router cannot multicast link state update messages there are n link state messages sent for each change rather than just two.

Although the use of designated routers offers a significant reduction in traffic, it is not always considered the best solution for NBMA networks because the designated router can easily become unreachable for one or more of the other routers attached to the NBMA network. Since there is usually a full mesh of underlying logical connections (as shown in Figure 5.29) many operators choose to run point-to-point adjacencies between the routers to achieve a more robust solution.

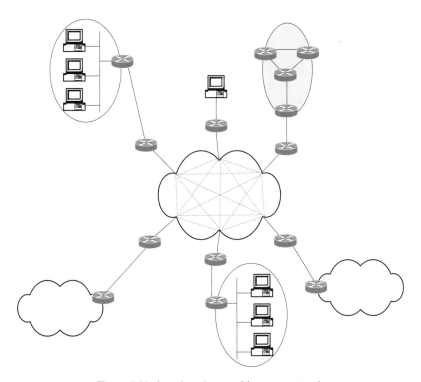

Figure 5.29   A nonbroadcast multi-access network.

5.5.6 OSPF Areas

Section 5.2.2 introduced the concept of areas within a single autonomous system to help break up the routing space to make it more manageable and to reduce the size of the routing tables and link state databases at individual routers. In OSPF, areas are arranged in a two-level hierarchy: area zero provides the *backbone* of the AS and the other areas are nested within area zero. No other nesting of areas is supported and areas are interconnected only through area zero, although any area may support connections out of the AS. The network in Figure 5.30 shows some of the possible arrangements of areas. Observe that, although there is a link between a router in area one and a router in area two, the link is entirely within area zero, and Router X is an ABR sitting on the boundary between area one and area zero, as Router Y is on the boundary between area two and area zero.

ABRs do not distribute full routing information from one area to another, but must *leak* enough information so that routers within an area can know that it is possible to reach addresses outside their area. Where an area has more than one ABR, the information distributed by the ABRs must allow routers within the

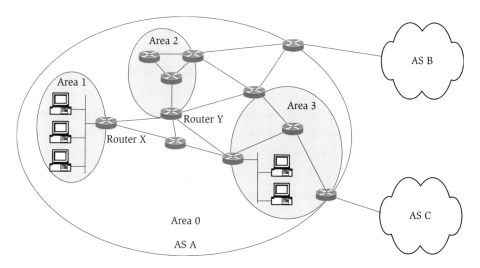

Figure 5.30 A possible arrangement of areas in an OSPF autonomous system.

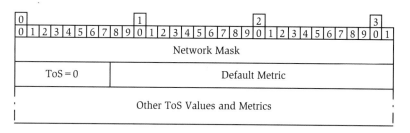

Figure 5.31 The Summary Link State Advertisement.

network to select which ABR to use to route datagrams to destinations outside the area. They use the Summary LSA (type three), as shown in Figure 5.31. The network (or host) address is carried in the Link State Identifier of the LSA header, and the network mask narrows the address down to a specific subnetwork or host. A default ToS and metric must always be supplied, and more metrics (as governed by the length of the LSA) may also be supplied.

ABRs can aggregate addressing information using CIDR so that they reduce the number of advertisements across the area border. Note, however, that aggregation at area borders is usually disabled by default on routers so that they advertise in greater detail. This behavior differs from that at AS boundaries (see later in this chapter) where aggregation is important. It turns out to be particularly important in Multiprotocol Label Switching networks that run the Label Distribution Protocol (LDP) that aggregation is not enabled at area borders. LDP (described in Chapter 9) has a mode of operation called *downstream unsolicited independent mode*, which can operate particularly badly in conjunction with route aggregation.

The metrics advertised by the ABRs into the backbone area are fundamental to how OSPF areas work. OSPF uses the summary LSA to operate in a hybrid of link state and distance vector modes. A router in one area does not know the routes within another area, but it does understand the cost to reach a particular network through one ABR compared with another. It can then select the shortest route to the right ABR. Of course, it must factor in the cost of that route and add it to the metric in the summary LSA to determine whether the route through the cheapest ABR is actually the cheapest route across the whole network.

Clearly, when area zero distributes area one's summary LSAs into area two, it must update the metrics to take account of the cost of traversing the backbone area.

5.5.7 Stub Areas

Small, low-powered routers are popular at the edges of the Internet and in small, company networks. These routers have neither the memory capacity nor the CPU horsepower to handle large routing tables and need to be protected from the flood of link state information inherent in being part of a large OSPF network. Isolating these routers in an OSPF area helps to reduce the information through aggregation and summary, but there still might be a very large number of networks advertised through the ABR into the area.

A stub area recognizes that routers in peripheral areas do not need to know routes to subnets in other areas—a default route to the ABR will suffice. This is particularly relevant to areas that have just one ABR.

A stub area is configured principally at the ABR, which can absorb all summary LSAs from outside the area and generates a default route which it advertises as an LSA into the stub area. The routers within a stub area can optionally be statically configured with a default route to the ABR. If a stub area has more than one ABR, suboptimal routes out of the area may be chosen because of the nature of the default routes used. This is a price that must be paid for reducing the amount of routing information in the network.

5.5.8 Not So Stubby Areas (NSSA)

The poetically named not so stubby area (NSSA) arose to address a specific need in a stub area. As illustrated in Figure 5.32, an area on the edge of an OSPF AS may be connected to an external network that is not of the OSPF area, and in fact does not run OSPF at all. This appended network might be statically configured or might run a simple routing protocol such as RIP, but the area needs to pick up the fact that the external routes exist and advertise them both into the area and into the wider OSPF network.

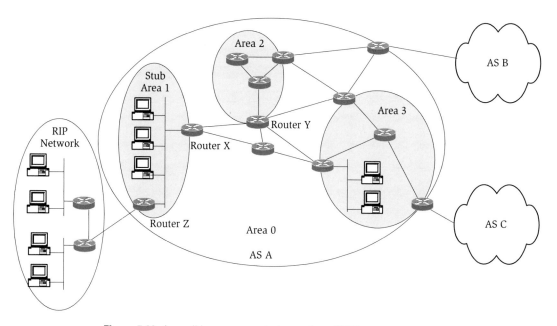

Figure 5.32 A possible arrangement of areas in an OSPF autonomous system.

In Figure 5.32, Area 1 is a stub area. Router X only distributes a default route to represent all of the routing information received from outside the area. However, Router Z needs to inject routing information from the RIP network. It can't advertise a default route as Router X does because the RIP network does not provide a gateway to the rest of the Internet; instead it needs a sort of summary LSA that can be used within the network and converted to a normal summary LSA when it is sent out into the wider world by Router X.

The NSSA LSA shown in Figure 5.33 serves this purpose. The Link State Identifier in the LSA header holds the network address, which is qualified by the network mask in the LSA itself. A default metric is mandatory and other metrics may be appended to the LSA. The Forwarding Address field allows the LSA to identify a router other than the advertising router that should be used as the forwarding address to reach the subnet—it can be set to zero to indicate that the advertising router is the gateway to the subnet. The External Route Tag can be used to supply correlation information provided by other routing protocols.

The E-bit in the top of the ToS byte is used to indicate whether the metric is a type-1 (bit clear) or type-2 (bit set) metric. Type-1 metrics are handled on equal terms as OSPF metrics, effectively integrating the external network into the area. Type-2 metrics are considered as more significant by an order of magnitude, as might be the case if the external routing protocol was BGP and the metric was a count of ASs crossed.

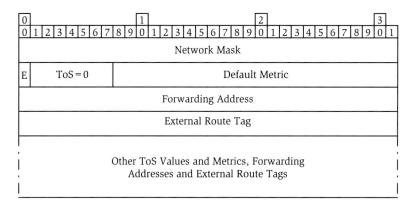

Figure 5.33 The NSSA link state advertisement.

5.5.9 Virtual Links

As mentioned in Section 5.5.6, all ABRs lie on the edge of their area and connect to the backbone area, area zero. This is a fine principle that keeps the topology of the AS manageable, but it does not always fit well with the requirements of the network. For example, part of the network in Figure 5.34 is "long and thin" and needs to be split into Area 1 and Area 2, as shown, but only Area 1 has an ABR (Router Y) with a connection into Area 0.

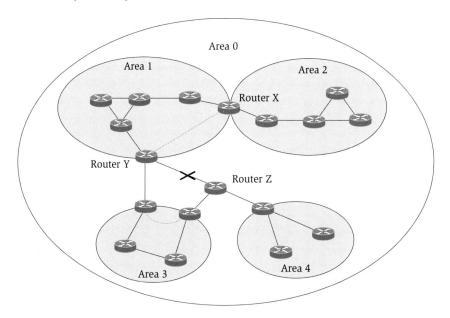

Figure 5.34 Virtual links can be used to connect an area to the backbone and repair a problem in the backbone.

To allow Area 2 to be split from Area 1 with a connection at Router X, Router X must be connected to the backbone by a *virtual link*. In the figure, the virtual link is shown by a dotted line between Router X and Router Y. It does not matter that a direct physical link does not exist between the two end points of a virtual link; the association is only logical and provides an OSPF *virtual adjacency* between the routers for the exchange of OSPF packets. Data packets continue to follow the data links. A virtual link is a network type as advertised by the router LSA, showing an unnumbered link between a pair of ABRs. This means that the ABRs exchange Hello messages and Link Update messages as though they were connected, but they do not advertise a physical connection (unless one exists!), so their adjacency does not find its way into the routing table.

One interesting use of virtual links is to connect two ABRs within the same area to circumvent a problem in the backbone area. This type of virtual link would be a short-lived configuration fix while the problem in the backbone was fixed. Referring to Figure 5.34, observe that Area 3 has two ABRs connected to the backbone. If the link between Router Y and Router Z fails there is no longer any connectivity from Area 1 and Area 2 across to Area 4, but if a virtual link is installed between Area 3's two ABRs, as shown by the dotted line, connectivity can be restored.

In fact, virtual links can be utilized more widely than for simply partitioning the network into convenient areas. In many traffic engineering solutions, such as MPLS, it is desirable to establish virtual adjacencies between two remote routers that are connected by a traffic engineering tunnel such as an LSP. If it is possible to run OSPF through the tunnel (the routers are effectively adjacent through the tunnel although the operator's mind may get warped by considering this). OSPF will be happy to view the tunnel as a real link complete with interfaces installed at the routers and to advertise its existence using the appropriate metrics. If OSPF cannot be run down the tunnel (perhaps because the router can only switch traffic into the tunnel, not add or terminate packets—as might be the case in an optical router), then the routers can establish a virtual adjacency.

5.5.10 Choosing to Use Areas

OSPF areas provide many advantages, from management and configuration simplifications to operational reductions in memory and path computation times. In addition, the use of areas increases the robustness of the routing protocol because the advertisements of link failures are dampened, being contained for the most part within the area. Similarly, routing decisions within the area are protected from strangeness outside the area since routes that are wholly within the area are always preferred by OSPF over routes that leave and reenter the area. It is also possible to use OSPF areas to keep parts of the network hidden or secret simply by configuring the ABR to not publicize certain prefixes in summary LSAs.

These benefits are offset by a decrease in performance of the SPF algorithm as information is summarized at ABRs. In complex networks this manifests as suboptimal inter-area routes being selected, but in normal networks the effect is not significant.

Ten years or more ago, the general opinion was that a single OSPF area should not contain more than 200 routers if the SPF calculation was to be kept to a reasonable time period. Increases in the capabilities of CPUs and the general availability of cheap memory mean that this suggestion has been surpassed by deployed networks. On the other hand, simple low-end routers are still popular because of their price, and these are candidates for far smaller areas or even stub networks. Such configurations may be particularly useful for devices in which the routing capabilities are secondary to some other function, such as might be the case in an optical switch.

Note that the increased benefit of reduced routing information achieved by using a stub area is offset by a further decrease in the quality of routing decisions that can be made. Again, for the simplest networks, this is not significant.

The discussion on the value of areas has recently received further input from an Internet Draft presented to the IETF. This draft (draft-thorup-ospf-harmful) argues that instead of solving scalability issues, areas may exacerbate them. The main thesis of the draft is that imposing an area structure on a backbone network increases the amount of information that is flooded as the network converges after a link failure. The problem arises when a network has a considerable number of ABRs. Each ABR advertises a distance metric for each router in the area—so in an area with n routers and m ABRs the number of pieces of information advertised out of the area is given as

$$N_o = m + m(n-m)$$

This number should be compared with the number of pieces of information advertised within an area, which is the sum of the number of links on each router. So in a network in which the area has more ABRs than the average connectivity of any router in the area, there is more information advertised into the backbone than there would have been if the two areas had been merged. This theory, however, holds up only in precisely those conditions, making the decision point the number of ABRs in the area and the structure of the network as a whole.

A further complaint also applies to areas that have multiple ABRs. If a shortest path passes through an ABR that is in the destination area, the ABR will immediately choose to route the traffic wholly within the destination area, regardless of the actual shortest path. This is demonstrated in Figure 5.35, where the preferred route from Router A in Area 0 to Router Z in Area 1 is {A, B, C, D, Z}. This is both the path with the fewest hops and also the best path since the links in the backbone area typically have higher bandwidth. However, when a packet reaches Router B, a strict adherence to the area routing rules means that the packet has now entered Area 1 (all ABRs are in both areas) and the packet must now be fully routed within Area 1, giving the undesirable path {A, B, U, V, W, X, Y, Z}. It is not hard to invent a processing rule to avoid this

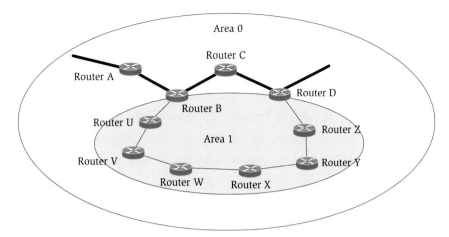

Figure 5.35 Area processing rules may result in undesirable, long paths being selected by ABRs that happen to lie on the preferable path.

issue and favor the path through the backbone area, but existing OSPF implementations will stick to the protocol standards and select the less desirable route.

There is also a suggestion that the use of areas increases the management complexity of the network because operators must place each router within an area and must configure the ABRs. The argument is that this increase in complexity overrides any savings from breaking the network into smaller areas which can be managed as distinct entities. It is, of course, true that the more complex an object is to manage, the more chance there is of a management error.

Finally, the draft points out that IS-IS networks are mainly run using a single area (see Section 5.6), and that if there are scaling problems with OSPF, these problems might be better solved by improving the quality of the implementations rather than by using areas.

5.5.11 Other Autonomous Systems

OSPF also must be able to interact with other autonomous systems. In particular, it must be able to receive routes from external sources and advertise them into the OSPF AS. ABSRs have this responsibility, and use the external LSA and the ASBR summary LSA to represent external routes. The external LSA has exactly the same format as the NSSA LSA, but uses the LS Type value of five, and the ASBR summary LSA is identical in format to the summary LSA, but carries an LS Type of four. Note that the E-bit at the top of the ToS byte in the external LSA can be used to distinguish the precedence of the metric just as it does in the NSSA LSA.

An additional LSA exists to carry information across the OSPF AS on behalf of external routing protocols. In practice, this LSA is rarely used to distribute

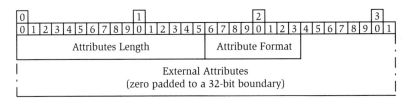

Figure 5.36 The external attributes link state advertisement.

exterior gateway routing information (such as from the Border Gateway Protocol, BGP), and the use of the LSA is limited to the distribution of manually configured routes (that is, static routes). The external attributes LSA shown in Figure 5.36 is entirely opaque to OSPF. It has length and type fields to allow the consumer of the information to decide how to interpret it.

5.5.12 Opaque LSAs

The external LSA described in the previous section is an example of a need to distribute information that is not directly relevant to the SPF calculations performed by OSPF, but that can be carried easily by OSPF because it must be widely distributed. This concept is expanded by an extension to OSPF described in RFC 2370 and called the opaque LSA.

Figure 5.37 shows the opaque LSA in conjunction with the LSA header, which is slightly modified so that the Link State Identifier field is replaced by the Opaque LSA Type and Opaque LSA Identifier fields. The Opaque LSA Type field indicates to the receiver what the LSA contains and so how the information should be treated. Routers that do not understand the Opaque LSA Type ignore

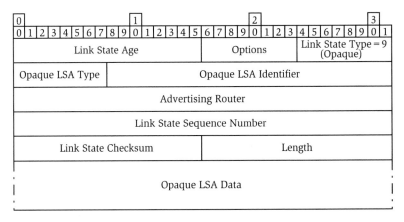

Figure 5.37 The OSPF opaque link state advertisement with the modified link state advertisement header.

its contents, but still install it in their link state databases, advertise it to other routers, and generally treat the LSA as they would any other LSA.

Three Link State Types are defined to control how the opaque LSAs are propagated. This is an important feature because we cannot rely on other routers to interpret the Opaque LSA Type and make the decision based on that field. The Link State Types are 9 (do not advertise beyond the local network), 10 (do not advertise beyond the originating area), and 11 (advertise fully throughout the AS).

Opaque LSAs have come into their own recently as a way of advertising traffic engineering information (such as bandwidth usage and availability) in OSPF—see Chapter 8.

5.6   Intermediate-System to Intermediate-System (IS-IS)

Lovers of acronyms read on! Intermediate-System to Intermediate-System (IS-IS) is a link state routing protocol used between routers in the Open Systems Inter-connection (OSI) network protocols devised by the International Standards Organization (ISO). Since this comes from a different standards body, we must brace ourselves for a new set of terms, concepts, and acronyms. We can also expect to see some variations in spelling, because ISO tends to write in British English—foremost among these are *neighbour* and *routeing*, even though the latter is not in common usage in the United Kingdom. One other quirk is that ISO numbers their bits and bytes differently so that the first byte seen is byte one, but the high-order bit is bit eight and the low-order bit is bit one. For the sake of sanity and consistency, this book retains the IETF bit and byte numbering scheme.

In OSI, terminating equipment and hosts are referred to as *end systems* (ESs) and routers are known as *intermediate systems* (ISs). Thus, the routing protocol that runs between routers is IS-IS. Specified in ISO 10589, IS-IS is targeted at ISO's Connectionless Network Protocol (CLNP) based on the routing protocol developed by DEC for incorporation in DECnet Phase 5. It is a link state protocol with many of the capabilities of OSPF, which is not surprising because the development of OSPF was informed by the work done in ISO.

IS-IS was extended to support TCP/IP and CLNP simultaneously as separate addressing spaces within the same network, so that TCP/IP applications might migrate to CLNP. This form of IS-IS was known as Dual IS-IS or *Integrated IS-IS*. RFC 1142 is essentially copied from ISO 10589, but RFC 1195 focuses on the use of Integrated IS-IS solely in an IP environment. For brevity, the term IS-IS is used from here on to refer to that portion of Integrated IS-IS that applies to routing within IP networks.

Before embarking on the remainder of this section, you should familiarize yourself with the overview of link state routing protocols contained in Section 5.2.2, and it would also be worth being familiar with OSPF as described in Section 5.5.

> **route** *rōōt* (formerly, and still in the army, *rowt*), *n.* a way, course that is or may be traversed: marching orders: —*v.t.* to fix the route of: to send by a particular route: —*pr.p.* **route**(e) **¹ing**; *pa.t.* and *pa.p.* **rout¹ed**.

5.6.1 Data Encapsulation and Addressing

IS-IS messages are not carried in IP datagrams, unlike all other IP protocols. The messages, called *Protocol Data Units* (PDUs), are encapsulated directly in Data Link Layer frames and so IS-IS runs alongside IP at the network layer.

An interface in IS-IS is referred to as a *Subnetwork Point of Attachment* (SNPA) and is much closer to the concept of a physical interface than is an IP interface, which may be logically stacked on other interfaces. ISO addressing uses a generic format and a hierarchical model that lends itself to describing areas, routers, interfaces, and protocol services on a node. Figure 5.38 shows how the generic ISO address is composed of two parts: the Initial Domain Part (IDP) and the Domain Specific Part (DSP). The IDP is used to pin down the context of the addressing scheme used and is strictly standardized and administered by ISO. The Authority and Format Identifier (AFI) indicates the structure and encoding of the address, and the Initial Domain Identifier (IDI) specifies the individual addressing domain to which the address belongs. The format of the DSP is open for specification by the authority indicated by the AFI that owns the addressing domain given by the IDI. The DSP is used to identify the routing area, router, and target application, and is broken up into three fields for this

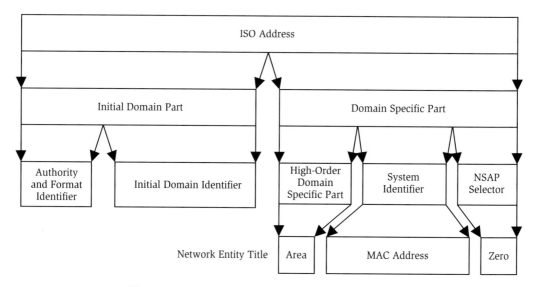

Figure 5.38 The ISO hierarchical address format used in IS-IS.

purpose. The high-order DSP (HO-DSP) is used in IS-IS for IP to hold the Area ID, and the System ID identifies the router or interface within the area. The final field, the NSAP Selector is used to select a specific recipient application on the target node—when the NSAP Selector is set to a nonzero value, the address is referred to as a *Network Service Access Point* (NSAP) and identifies a program that should process a PDU much as the combination of IP address and protocol ID do in an IP network.

Within the scope of IP routing, the entire IS-IS IDP is superfluous because the IP data will never leave the addressing domain. A short-form address is used to represent the routers and is called a *Network Entity Title* (NET). The NET comprises an Area ID, a System ID, and a single-byte NSAP selector that is always set to zero. Although the format of the NET is technically open to the administrative domain, much is dictated by deployed Cisco routers that use a single-byte Area ID and a 6-byte System ID. Further, since the System ID needs to be unique across all routers and hosts, and since IS-IS operates immediately over the data link layer, the System ID is conventionally set to a Media Access Control (MAC) address.

5.6.2 Fletcher's Checksum

IS-IS (and, indeed, OSPF) uses Fletcher's checksum to guard against accidental corruption of data in transit or when stored in the link state database. It is more efficacious than the simple checksum used by IP, but not as painful to compute as the cyclic redundancy check used in data-link layer protocols—the intention is increased detection of errors with only a small increase in computation time.

The algorithm for Fletcher's checksum can be found in Annex B to RFC 905 and is set out in a sample "C" function in Figure 5.39. It is based on a rolling sum of bytes and a rolling sum of the sum of bytes. When the checksum is being validated, these sums should both come out as zero. This is achieved by a little magic when filling in the checksum into the transmitted or stored message.

5.6.3 Areas

Areas are built into the protocol details of IS-IS a little more closely than they are in OSPF, so it is valuable to discuss them before describing how the protocol works. IS-IS supports two levels of hierarchy, as in OSPF: the backbone area is known as Level Two (L2) and other areas are Level One (L1). As shown in Figure 5.40, IS-IS makes a great play of putting area boundaries on links and not on ABRs—that is, any one router lies exclusively in a single area. Nevertheless, L1 routers that provide access into the backbone area are special and are identified as L1/L2 routers and serve as ABRs.

The backbone area (the L2 area) must be well-connected in IS-IS. This means that it must be possible to reach any L2 router from any other L2 router

```
/* Compute Fletcher's Checksum                        */
/*                                        */        */
/* Parameters                            */
/* msg — The message buffer over which to compute the checksum /*
/* msg len — The length of the buffer */
/* store checksum — The offset in the buffer at which to store the checksum */
/*          The offset is one-based.              */
/*          If this parameter is supplied as zero, compute and test */
/*          the checksum rather than storing it.           */
/* Returns                               */
/* TRUE — The checksum has been computed and stored or has been validated—  */
/* FALSE — The checksum validation has failed              */
int caculate fletcher (char *msg, u int16 msg len, u int16 store checksum)
{
    int ii=0;
    int fletcha=0; /* This is really a byte but we allow overflow */
    int fletchb=0; /* This is really a byte but we allow overflow */
    int fletch tmp;
    if (store checksum !=0)
  {
    /* If we are adding a checksum to a message,
     * zero the place where it will be stored.
     */
    msg[store checksum]=0;
    msg[store checksum+1]=0;
  }
    while (ii<msg len)
    {
    /* fletcha holds a rolling byte sum through the bytes
     * in the message buffer. Overflow is simply wrapped.
     */
    if ((fletcha+=msg[ii++])>254)
    {
    fletcha-=255;
    }
    /* fletchb holds a rolling byte sum of fletcha with
     * a similar approach to overflow.
     */
    if ((fletchb+=fletcha)>254)
    {
    fletchb-=255;
    }
  }
  if (store_checksum != 0)
  {
    /* Now store the checksum in the message.
     * Special magic of Fletcher!
     */
    bytes_beyond = msg_len - store_checksum - 1;
    fletch_tmp = ((bytes_beyond * fletcha) - c1) % 255;
    if fletch_tmp < 0
    {
      fletch_tmp += 255;
    }
```

```
  /* Store the lsb */
  msg[store_checksum] = (char)fletch_tmp;
  fletch_tmp = (fletchb - ( (bytes_beyond + 1) * fletcha)) % 255;
  if fletch_tmp < 0
  {
    fletch_tmp += 255;
  }
  /* Again store the lsb */
  msg[store_checksum + 1] = (char)fletch_tmp;
  /* Return success */
  return (TRUE);
}
else
{
  if ((fletcha | fletchb)==0)
  {
   /* Both bytes have arrived at zero.
    * All is well.
    */
   return (TRUE);
  }
  else
  {
    /* The checksum has failed! */
    return (FALSE);
  }
 }
}
```

Figure 5.39 A sample C function to compute Fletcher's checksum.

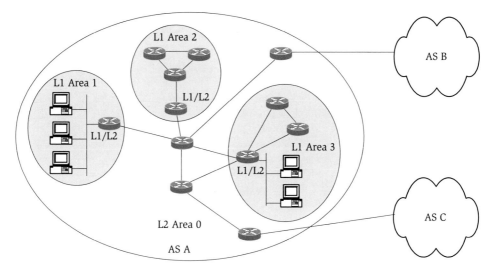

Figure 5.40 A possible arrangement of areas in an IS-IS autonomous system.

without leaving the L2 area, that is, without entering an L1 area or leaving the AS. Only L2 routers may support external links to other ASs.

L1 routers know only about routes within their own area, but maintain a default route to the L1/L2 ABR for all external addresses. The L1/L2 routers have some knowledge of routes outside the area so that they can choose the best attached L2 router. Within the L2 area, the routers have knowledge of the connectivity and routes within the area and know about all of the attached L1/L2 routers. In this way, IS-IS areas are similar to OSPF stub areas.

As a point of note, L1 areas are quite rare in deployed IS-IS IP networks. The trend is to use a single, large L2 network.

5.6.4 IS-IS Protocol Data Units

IS-IS PDUs all have a common format, as shown in Figure 5.41. They begin with 8 bytes of common header and then contain additional fields specific to the PDU type. The PDUs are completed by a series of variable-length fields encoded in type-length-variable (TLV) format. Some of the TLVs are specific to certain PDUs, but others may be carried by multiple PDUs.

The first field in an IS-IS PDU is the Intradomain Routing Protocol Discriminator (IRPD), which identifies the protocol as IS-IS by carrying the value 0×83 (131). The Header Length field indicates the length in bytes of the whole header, including the common fields and the PDU-specific fields, but not including the TLVs—the length of the whole PDU can be derived from the data-link layer frame and is also carried in the PDU-specific fields, and the TLVs carry their own length indicators. Two fields are provided for future protocol and PDU versions, but are both currently set to 1. The System Identifier Length is an important field because it identifies the length of the System ID within any NETs carried in the PDU, allowing them to be correctly parsed—note that a value of zero indicates the default System ID length of 6 bytes that is used in most IP deployments.

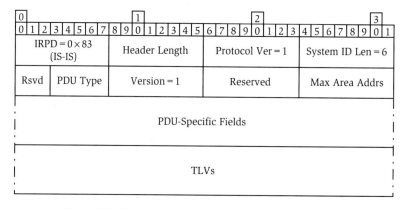

Figure 5.41 The common format of the IS-IS protocol data unit.

Table 5.14 The IS-IS PDU Types

PDU Type	Meaning
15	Multi-access Hello PDU in an L1 area
16	Multi-access Hello PDU in the L2 area
17	Point-to-point Hello PDU in or between any area
18	Link State PDU originated from an L1 area
20	Link State PDU originated from the L2 area
24	Complete sequence Number PDU originated from an L1 area
25	Complete sequence Number PDU originated from the L2 area
26	Partial sequence Number PDU originated from an L1 area
27	Partial sequence Number PDU originated from the L2 area

The use to which the PDU is put is indicated by the PDU Type field. Possible values for use in IP systems are shown in Table 5.14. The choice of value dictates which PDU-specific fields will be present at the end of the header, and which TLVs are allowed to be included in the PDU. Finally, the Maximum Area Addresses field indicates how many area addresses the router can support. This does not mean that the router is intended to reside in multiple areas at once for any length of time, but rather that the router can be migrated from one area to another by adding it to its new home before removing it from its old area. This may seem esoteric, but it allows a router to be moved logically from one area to another, or an area to be renumbered without interruption to services. The default maximum number of area addresses indicated by a value of zero is three, and this is the normal value supported in IP deployments.

Table 5.15 lists the TLVs used for IS-IS in IP systems and indicates on which PDUs they can (O is for optional) or must (M is for mandatory) be carried. The TLVs are described in later sections according to their usage.

The TLVs with numerically low type codes are defined in ISO 10589, and the higher values are defined specifically for IP and are found in RFC 1195. Note that RFC 1195 specifies an alternative Authentication TLV code of 133, but Cisco has used the value 10 from ISO 10589, and where Cisco leads, the IP world has been observed to follow.

5.6.5 Neighbor Discovery and Adjacency Maintenance

The first job of a link state router is to discover its neighbors. IS-IS uses a Hello PDU to discover and maintain adjacencies. There are three distinct types of Hello PDU for use in different circumstances. Each carries several additional header fields, as shown in the following figures.

The Point-to-Point Hello PDU (type 17) shown in Figure 5.42 is used between routers on point-to-point links. The Hello can be exchanged within areas or across area borders. The Circuit Type field is a 2-bit field that indicates whether the circuit (that is link) is originated by an L2, L1, or L1/L2 router (the bits are set to 01, 10, and 11 respectively). The Source ID is the System ID of the originating router—the length of this field is governed by the ID Length field in the common header. The Holding Time is the number of seconds that the neighbor should wait without hearing a Hello before declaring the originator of the Hello dead—it is up to the originator to retransmit Hellos sufficiently frequently to keep the adjacency active, taking into account the possibility of lost or delayed messages. The PDU length is measured in bytes and includes the whole header and the subsequent TLVs. The final field, the Local Circuit ID, is a unique identifier for the link at the originating router—this might be the interface index.

If the link is a multi-access broadcast link, the routers must send a different format Hello PDU to carry additional information needed in the multi-access environment. Since broadcast domains must not span area boundaries, two distinct PDU types are provided to help detect any configuration problems. The L1 Multi-Access Hello PDU (type 15) and the L2 Multi-Access Hello PDU (type 16) are otherwise identical, and the additional header fields are shown in Figure 5.43. The initial fields are the same as those for the Point-to-Point Hello. The 7-bit

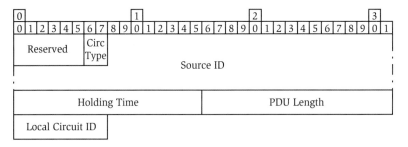

Figure 5.42 The PDU-specific header fields for a Point-to-Point Hello PDU.

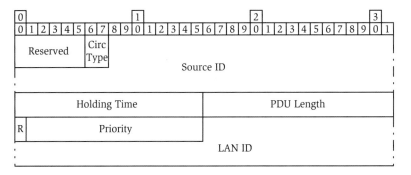

Figure 5.43 The PDU-specific header fields for a Multi-Access Hello PDU.

Table 5.15 Mandatory and Optional Presence of IS-IS TLVs on IS-IS PDUs in IP Systems

TLV	Type	PDU Type (see Table 5.14)								
		15	16	17	18	20	24	25	26	27
Area Addresses	1	M	M	M	M	M				
IS Link State Neighbors	2				O	O				
IS Hello Neighbors	6	M	M							
Padding (Null TLV)	8	O	O	O						
Link State	9						M	M	M	M
Authentication	10	O	O	O	O	O	O	O	O	O
Checksum	12	O	O	O			O	O	O	O
IP Internal Reachability	128				O	O				
Protocols Supported	129	M	M	M	O	O				
IP External Reachability	130					O				
IDRP Information	131					O				
IP Interface Addresses	132	M	M	M	M	M				

Priority field is used for negotiating the Designated Router on the network, just as described for OSPF in Section 5.5.5. The priority can range from 0 to 127 and the router with the highest priority is elected Designated Router; in the event of a tie, the router with the numerically higher Source ID is elected.

The final field identifies the LAN (that is broadcast network) to which the PDU applies. The network gets its identifier from the System ID of the Designated Router with the addition of one further byte, the Pseudonode ID, which is used to distinguish the different broadcast networks for which the Designated Router may act. The Pseudonode ID operates a little like the Local Circuit ID does in the Point-to-Point Hello PDU.

As shown in Table 5.15, the Hello PDUs carry several TLVs to convey additional, variable-length information. The Area Addresses TLV (type 1) indicates the address (or addresses) of the area in which the originating router resides. Figure 5.44 shows the format of this TLV, which must contain at least one area address and may contain up to the maximum number specified in the Maximum Area Addresses field in the common header. As well as the overall TLV length, each area address is prefixed by its own length field.

The IP Interface Addresses TLV (type 132) shown in Figure 5.45 carries the IP address of the interface out of which the Hello was sent. The structure of the TLV allows each interface to have multiple addresses simply by increasing the length of the TLV, but note that the addresses do not have their own length indicators, so only 4-byte IPv4 addresses can be supported.

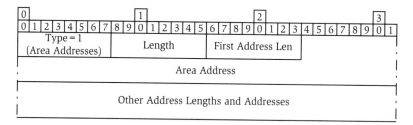

Figure 5.44 The Area Addresses TLV.

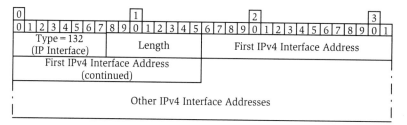

Figure 5.45 The IP Interface Addresses TLV.

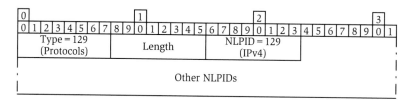

Figure 5.46 The Protocols Supported TLV.

The Protocols Supported TLV (type 129) is important in the context of IP systems because it indicates which network level protocols the originating router supports. The TLV shown in Figure 5.46 consists of a list of 1-byte Network Layer Protocol Identifiers (NLPIDs) that show the capabilities of the router. The value 0×81 (129) is used to indicate support of IPv4.

On a multi-access network, the Hello PDU must also list all of the other routers on the network from which a Hello has been heard within the last hold time period. This provides a way for the Designated Router to tell the other routers who is on the network and who has been lost. Since all routers in this list are attached to the multi-access network they have the same address length; this is known by the sending and receiving routers, so it does not need to be encoded anywhere. This will usually be a MAC address, which is 6 bytes in length. The Intermediate Systems Neighbors TLV (type 6) shown in Figure 5.47 fulfills this requirement and is carried only on L1 and L2 Multi-Access Hello PDUs.

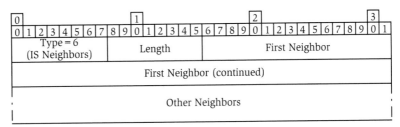

Figure 5.47 The Intermediate Systems Neighbors TLV.

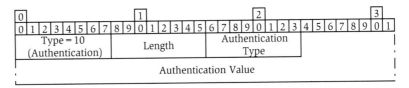

Figure 5.48 The Authentication TLV.

Authentication may optionally be configured for use between routers. If it is, the Authentication Information TLV (type 10) shown in Figure 5.48 is included in the Hello PDUs. The Authentication Type field indicates what type of authentication is in use and the Authentication Value contains the information necessary to validate the originator and integrity of the message. ISO 10589 defined a single authentication type for a clear text password. As observed for the similar function in OSPF (see Section 5.5.1), the clear text password provides no security at all, but does help to avoid configuration errors. Implementations do exist, however, that use MD5 or stronger authentication, placing the authentication value in the Authentication TLV. RFC 1195 specifies an alternative Authentication TLV code of 133, but the value 10 from ISO 10589 is in current usage.

RFC 3358 observes that not all data-link layers provide the same level of reliable data transfer and that accidental corruption of PDUs may occur without detection since only the link state information is explicitly protected by its own checksum. To better detect such errors, an optional Checksum TLV (type 12) may be included in all PDUs. The PDU, shown in Figure 5.49, carries the result of applying Fletcher's algorithm to the entire PDU including the Checksum TLV.

One final TLV is used in the Hello PDUs to pad them up to a well-defined size. To implicitly communicate the lesser of the MTU of the link, and the router's

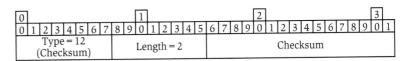

Figure 5.49 The Checksum TLV.

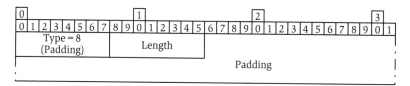

Figure 5.50 The Padding TLV.

maximum receive buffer size, ISO 10589 requires that the Hello PDU be either this limit or 1 byte smaller. Why 1 byte smaller? The Padding TLV has a minimum size of 2 bytes and it may not be possible to exactly hit the required size, but going over the limit would result in an error in the data-link layer. Since the Padding TLV (type 8) shown in Figure 5.50 has a maximum size of 255 bytes governed by the size of the Length field, it may be necessary to include multiple Padding TLVs in a Hello PDU to bring it up to the required size. The contents of the padding are ignored and can be set to any value.

You might reasonably assert that a better way of communicating the MTU would be to have a field or TLV within the Hello PDU that defines this value. This would reduce the overhead in every Hello PDU sent, but ISO 10589 prefers the full PDU because it is seen as a way of testing links against fringe failure conditions that allow small frames to be transmitted but drop larger frames. In practice, however, many IS-IS implementations ignore this feature of the ISO standard and stop padding the Hello PDU once the adjacency is established, thus reducing the number of bytes sent over the link to keep the adjacency active.

One other use of the Padding TLV can be made. If a part of a PDU is to be removed without shuffling the remaining contents in memory, a Padding TLV can be superimposed on the piece of PDU to be expunged.

5.6.6 Distributing Link State Information

Link state information is distributed in Link State PDUs. There are two distinct PDU types (18 and 20) to help distinguish link state originated from an L1 area from that originated from the L2 area.

In OSPF, each piece of link state information (each LSA) represents a separately transmittable item that can be arbitrarily collected with other such pieces of information and sent in a single message (the Link Update message). It is the individual LSAs that are managed, timed out, and withdrawn. In IS-IS the clustering of information is a little more rigid.

Each piece of IS-IS link state information is encoded in a TLV and these TLVs can be arbitrarily combined to form a Link State PDU (LSP), but it is this entire LSP that is managed for retransmission, timeout, and withdrawal. In implementation terms, this means a reduction in the number of timers that a router must run to manage its link state database, but it also requires a little more care and consistency on the part of the originator of link state information.

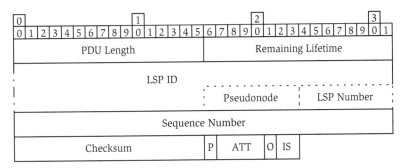

Figure 5.51 The PDU-specific header fields for a Link State PDU.

Figure 5.51 shows the PDU-specific header fields that are present in both of the LSPs. Note first that the LSP is identified using a field that contains a System ID to specify the originating router, a pseudonode ID in case the router is present on multiple networks, and a 1-byte LSP Number. This means that a single router can originate only 255 LSPs and so it will often be the case that a router must combine multiple pieces of link state information into a single LSP (even were that not a good idea).

The LSP additional header fields begin with a PDU Length field that gives the length in bytes of the entire PDU, including the header—note that this field is not in the same position in the header as it is in the Hello PDU. The next field gives the remaining lifetime of the LSP in seconds. Unlike OSPF, IS-IS counts down the life of an LSP from the initial value set by the originator—this is slightly more flexible since it allows the originator to vary the intended lifetime of an advertisement, but otherwise it is functionally equivalent to OSPF. However, IS-IS places a maximum limit on the lifetime of an LSP of 1200 seconds (20 minutes) and requires that a router retransmit its LSPs every 15 minutes (with a randomized jitter of up to 25 percent) to ensure that they do not timeout.

The Sequence number is used, as in OSPF, to distinguish between different versions of the same LSP. Although the lollipop sequence number space is widely attributed to Radia Perlman who worked on IS-IS when it was being developed as part of DECnet, IS-IS uses a linear sequence number space. This starts at 1 and counts up to 4,294,967,295. Since the LSP Numbers are so limited, it is not outside the bounds of possibility that an IS-IS router will stay up for long enough for the sequence number to reach its maximum. If the sequence number increments were solely due to retransmission every 15 minutes, it would be unlikely that the router would last the requisite 122,489 years, but rapid changes in the network (perhaps because of a flapping resource) might require the LSP to be re-advertised more frequently. Since a re-advertisement every second would take only 136 years to exhaust the sequence number space, the designers of IS-IS specified a procedure to handle sequence number wrapping back to 1 by shutting down for 21 minutes and restarting. The real enthusiast might like to note that this represents six nines reliability!

A checksum is provided to ensure the integrity of the contents of the LSP PDU in transit and when stored in the link state database. It is computed using Fletcher's algorithm and applied to the entire PDU from the LSP ID onward. The checksum is not applied to any earlier fields so that the remaining lifetime value can be decremented without affecting the checksum. The Checksum TLV should not be applied to the LSP.

The final fields in the LSP are a series of bit-fields that are shown in Table 5.16.

Table 5.15 shows which TLVs can be included in L1 and L2 LSPs. The chief TLVs for conveying link state are the Intermediate System Neighbors TLV (type 2) and the IP Internal Reachability Information TLV (type 128). The former is conceptually similar to the IS Neighbors Hello TLV (type 6), but as shown in Figure 5.52, it includes much more information about each neighbor. To start

Table 5.16 The Bit Fields in the Link State PDU Header

Bit Field	Usage
P	Partition repair bit. Set to indicate that the originating L2 router supports a sophisticated technique for repairing around problems that have partitioned the L2 area into two component areas. Usually left clear (zero).
ATT	The attachment bits. Apply only to LSPs originated by L1/L2 routers. Each of the 4 bits indicates a metric type supported by the router. The four metric types are a crude form of the ToS routing available in OSPF. The bits are (from left to right) the error metric, the expense metric, the delay metric, and the default metric. It is common to find only the default metric bit set.
O	The Link State Overload bit. This single bit is set only if the originating router is experiencing memory constraint and may have jettisoned part of its link state database. Other routers seeing this bit will attempt to find routes that avoid the reporting router.
IS	The Intermediate System Type bits. Two bits are provided to identify whether the originating router is in an L1 area or the L2 area. Note that 2 bits are not needed for this purpose. Bits 01 are used to indicate an L1 router and bits 11 show an L2 router. L1/L2 routers set the bits according to whether they are sending an L1 Link State PDU (type 18) or an L2 Link State PDU (type 20).

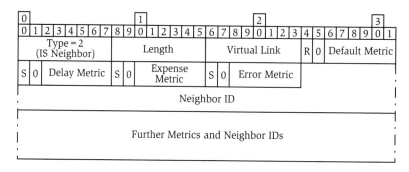

Figure 5.52 The Intermediate System Neighbors TLV.

with, the IS Neighbors TLV has a 1-byte flag to indicate whether the link to the router is real or virtual—virtual links are used much as in OSPF to provide tunnels and to heal breaks in the L2 network. Then, for each router there are 4 bytes that give the metric (that is cost) of the link for each of the metric types. Two bits are held back from the metric value, so the greatest cost that can be assigned to an IS-IS link is 63. The first bit is not used for the mandatory default metric, and for the other three metrics is set to zero if the metric is not supported. The second bit indicates whether the metric is external to the IS-IS addressing domain or not—since IS-IS for IP does not support links to other non-IP addressing domains, this bit is always zero. Note that there is a hard limit on path lengths/costs imposed in IS-IS of 1024—this is supposed to improve the effectiveness of the Dijkstra algorithm since it can exclude any path that reaches this length without computing further, but it does impose some constraints on the metric settings within large networks.

The final field, the Neighbor ID, is the System ID of the neighboring router with an appended Pseudonode ID or a zero byte.

IP Internal Reachability Information TLV (type 128) shown in Figure 5.53 has a similar format to the IS neighbors TLV but is used to carry IP addresses and subnet masks for directly attached routers, hosts, and subnetworks. This TLV is used only within an area, not across area borders.

The IP External Reachability Information TLV is identical in format to the IP Internal Reachability Information TLV, but uses TLV type 130. This TLV is used only in the L2 area to show routes out of the AS. The second bit of each metric byte is set to 1 to show that the metric applies to an external route and is, therefore, an external metric which may have a different weighting from internal metrics.

The Inter-Domain Routing Protocol Information TLV (type 131) shown in Figure 5.54 allows ASBRs to transfer information transparently across the IS-IS routing domain much as the OSPF External Links Attribute does. The TLV contains a 1-byte code to help the receiver determine the nature of the contents,

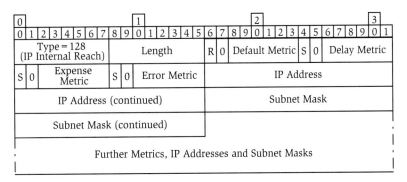

Figure 5.53 The IP Internal Reachability Information TLV.

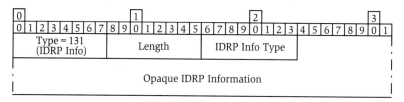

Figure 5.54 The Inter-Domain Routing Protocol Information TLV.

but the rest of the TLV is opaque with one exception: if the IDRP Info Type code is 2, the contents of the TLV are a 2-byte AS number.

Note that an implementation may choose to send one large TLV in a single Link State PDU, multiple TLVs of the same type in a single LSP, or multiple LSPs. The only constraints are the maximum size of the PDU and the limit of 255 LSPs. A router wanting to advertise new routing information either creates and sends a new LSP, or adds the information as a new TLV or an addition to an existing TLV to an existing LSP and re-advertises it with an incremented sequence number. Similarly, to withdraw some link state information, the router removes the details from the TLV (possibly removing the entire TLV) and re-advertises the LSP with an incremented sequence number. If a router wants to withdraw the entire LSP it re-advertises it with the Remaining Time field set to zero.

Reliable exchange of LSPs between routers is as important in IS-IS as it is in OSPF. The checksum ensures that any LSPs that make it between the routers are intact, and the lifetime timer makes sure that lost withdrawals do not result in LSPs persisting in other routers' link state databases, but some form of acknowledgement of LSPs is required if the routing information is to converge in less than the normal fifteen minute retransmission time.

The Partial Sequence Number PDU (PSNP) is used to acknowledge LSPs. The PDU has two additional header fields, as shown in Figure 5.55, to give the PDU length and to identify the sender of the PSNP. The PSNP may include one or more of the LSP Entries TLVs shown in Figure 5.56. These TLVs provide a list of acknowledged LSPs showing the current remaining lifetime, the LSP ID and sequence number, and the checksum value that applies to the LSP. If a router does not receive an acknowledgement of an LSP that it has sent within a small time period (usually 10 seconds) it retransmits the LSP.

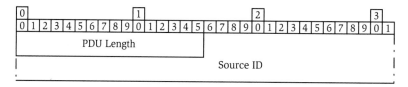

Figure 5.55 The PDU-specific header fields for a Partial Sequence Number PDU.

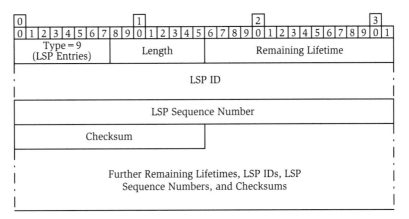

Figure 5.56 The LSP Entries TLV.

5.6.7 Synchronizing Databases

When two routers first form an IS-IS adjacency they must synchronize their link state databases. As in OSPF, the simple approach of flooding the entire contents of the database is rejected as placing too much load on the network. In OSPF one router summarizes the information it has available and the other requests re-advertisement of specific pieces of information. In IS-IS, partially because the granularity of advertised information is coarser, one router announces the contents of its database and the other re-advertises to fill the gaps.

The announcement takes the form of a Complete Sequence Number PDU (CSNP). The CSNP is similar to the PSNP but includes a reference to each of the LSPs in the sender's link state database—hence, the difference in name of Complete and Partial. The CSNP may have to array a large amount of data which might not fit into a single PDU. To handle this, the header of the CSNP shown in Figure 5.57 contains two extra fields to indicate the start point and end point of a range of LSPs that are being announced. There is a requirement that the

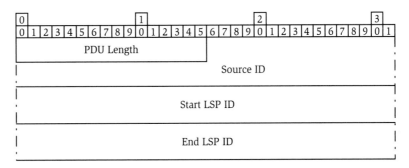

Figure 5.57 The PDU-specific header fields for a Complete Sequence Number PDU.

LSPs are reported in order—the LSP ID is taken as a numeric value for the sake of ordering and the lowest value is sent first. When a CSNP is sent with the End LSP ID set to all 0xff bytes, it is the last in the sequence.

The contents of the CSNP, like the PSNP, is a series of one or more LSP Entries TLVs. Each reported LSP must fall within the range indicated in the PDU header. It might also be reasonable to assume that the LSPs are listed in order within the TLVs, but this is not actually a requirement.

If a router receives a CSNP advertising an LSP about which it knows nothing, it does not need to take any further action. It will have sent its own CSNP, which does not include the LSP, and its neighbor will spot this and re-advertise the missing LSP.

5.7 Choosing Between IS-IS and OSPF

Assuming the decision has been made to use a link state routing protocol within a network (see Section 5.2.5), the question is: How do you choose between two high-function, link state IGPs, especially when any new feature added to one is immediately picked up and added to the other? To answer this is to step into a political minefield, or to venture into the middle of a religious war! OSPF and IS-IS have entrenched supporters who will not hear a word said against their favorite routing protocol.

The first decision point is easy—if you are deploying a router within an existing network, you must participate in the IGP used by the other routers in that network. Although it is possible to switch a network from using one IGP to another, it would be a brave network operator who made that choice for a large network carrying revenue-earning traffic. If or when such migration is done, it would be wise to break the network up into autonomous systems and migrate these one at a time.

But for a new network, or a network that is small enough to be migrated, the question still remains: Which link state routing protocol to use? At a high level there are only a few differences between the protocols, with conceptually the same link state information being distributed by each and the same routing tables being generated as a result of running the Dijkstra algorithm. Both protocols support areas and hierarchy, each uses a Hello mechanism to discover and maintain a relationship with its neighbors, both OSPF and IS-IS support the concept of a designated router on a multi-access link, and both protocols are extensible to encompass future requirements such as traffic engineering. None of this is surprising since OSPF was developed with IS-IS as a base, and the two protocols have evolved in competition side by side, so that whenever a feature is added to one protocol a group rushes off to add the same feature to the other protocol.

The main differences lie in the details of how the protocols achieve these similar ends. The differences are summarized in Table 5.17.

Table 5.17 A Summary of the Differences Between OSPF and IS-IS

Feature	OSPF	IS-IS
Distribution Protocol	Operates over IP.	Runs as a network protocol alongside IP.
Routes Which Protocol?	Designed for IPv4. Now supports IPv6 although in a slightly clumsy way.	Doesn't really care. Can easily be made to support any protocol, including IPv4 and IPv6.
Data on the Wire	Everything is aligned to 32-bit boundaries, making packets a bit larger than they need to be. LSAs are mostly quite small, allowing better granularity on the wire and less data to reflect a network change.	Byte alignment keeps packets small but LSPs are large and triggered in their entirety by even small topology changes.
Scalability Database Refresh	LSAs are age-limited to one hour, giving a high level of background traffic in a large network.	Database information can last more than 18 hours, producing a significant (although not astounding) improvement.
Scalability Network Size	Does not scale well in large, well-connected networks. The only option is to break the network into areas or autonomous systems.	Does not scale well in large, well-connected networks, but the use of mesh groups can avoid the need to use areas or autonomous systems.
Support for Areas	Easily understood two-level hierarchy with area border routers lying in both areas. Extensive multi-area deployment experienced (partly forced by the scalability issues above).	Routers are resident in precisely one area with links between the areas. This makes areas fit more closely with the concept of autonomous systems, but in practice leads to the requirement for virtual routers so that a single physical router can establish a presence in two areas as an ABR. Very limited deployment experience of multi-area IP systems.
Advanced Features	Includes a large number of advanced features for handling specific requirements. Stub areas, not so stubby areas, demand circuits, and backup designated routers are all available should the need arise.	Design is limited to the core requirements with none of the advanced features of OSPF.
Security	More vulnerable to security attacks because OSPF messages can be injected into the network using IP, but can be protected using cryptographic authentication and packet filtering.	Somewhat less vulnerable because IS-IS PDUs are not themselves routed since they do not use IP as a network protocol. This means that it is hard to inject bogus PDUs into the network. The protocol operations can also be protected.
Implementation Simplicity	Quite a complex protocol when all of the options and features are considered. This complexity may be reflected in implementations.	A relatively simple protocol, in part because it is missing many of the advanced features of OSPF. This should lead to more robust implementations.

It is notable that although there are IETF Working Groups dedicated to the development of both OSPF and IS-IS, only the OSPF Working Group is a standards making group. IS-IS is owned by the International Standards Organization (ISO), and the IS-IS Working Group concerns itself with representing the IS-IS developments to the IETF while developing IS-IS solutions for IP requirements and feeding them back to ISO for standardization.

Significantly, both OSPF and IS-IS have good deployment experience and are run successfully in very large networks within the Internet. Although IS-IS was invented first (in 1987) and OSPF took two versions to get it right, OSPF gained the stronger foothold in IP networks, partly because it was shipped by Cisco a year before their IS-IS implementation supported IP. It may, in fact, only be due to some suspect field experience with early OSPF implementations and a rewrite of IS-IS by Cisco that some ISPs deployed IS-IS in extensive networks in 1995. Even though OSPF's popularity has grown ever since, IS-IS has both a deployed base and a strong supporters' club, to the extent that no router manufacturer would be considered serious unless it offered both protocols on its entire product range.

The deployment pattern for the two protocols shows that IS-IS is generally used by the very large "tier one" Internet Service Providers in which the whole AS is usually managed as a single area. OSPF is used in most of the other networks that often use multiple areas. Although it is unusual for a network operator to migrate from one routing protocol to another, there have been a few recent cases of major Service Providers switching from OSPF to IS-IS.

Scalability remains a concern for both protocols, particularly pertaining to the large number of database updates generated when a link or router goes down. For example, a fully meshed OSPF network with n routers would generate of the order of n^2 messages upon link failure and n^3 messages when a router failed. IS-IS suffers because the LSPs are large and must be fully refreshed when there is a failure. This problem is exacerbated in networks that have rapid link failure detection and is a particular issue in environments such as IP over ATM. For both protocols, one of the solutions is to divide the network into areas. This is frequently done for OSPF, but is less common for IS-IS. Note that there is some concern that areas with more than four ABRs may actually cause an increase rather than a decrease in the amount of information propagated and stored. The IS-IS scalability solution of mesh groups is generally considered to be not very robust.

None of the points listed in Table 5.17 is really much to base a decision on. In very large networks with a high degree of interconnectivity, IS-IS may prove slightly more scalable. IS-IS might be slightly more adaptable to changes in requirements over the years, although no new requirement in the last 15 years has proven insurmountable for OSPF. So the choice comes down to pragmatics—as stated at the start of this section, if one of the two protocols is already deployed in your network, the choice is easy. Beyond that it boils down to comfort, understanding, availability of trained resources, and the level of support and experience your router supplier can offer. If you are making a router you have no choice—you must implement both protocols.

5.8   Border Gateway Protocol 4 (BGP-4)

The Border Gateway Protocol is a path vector routing protocol. Version four of the protocol is defined in RFC 1771 and extended with optional features in a series of additional RFCs listed in the Further Reading section at the end of the chapter.

BGP has a long history, but it is now an essential part of the Internet, allowing each Internet Service Provider (ISP) to operate their network as an autonomous routing cloud and only expose to other ISPs the reachability across their network.

5.8.1 Exterior Routing and Autonomous Systems

If we were to operate the entirety of the Internet as a single network and run one instance of an IGP throughout the whole, we would rapidly run into problems. The most significant of these problems would be the size of the link state databases routers would be required to maintain for route calculation, and the rate of change of link state information as changes occurred in the network. Additionally, the many ISPs that cooperate to form the Internet would be required to share their routing information, which would expose their network topology to their competitors.

It is desirable, therefore, to try to segment the Internet into separate domains under the management of the ISPs and to limit the information passed between these domains. This turns out to be relatively simple to achieve since a router in ISP A that wants to route data across the network owned by ISP B to a host attached to ISP C need not be concerned with how the data is routed across ISP B's network. It needs to know only that there is connectivity across ISP B's network to reach the target host. Ideally, it would also have some high-level view of the path the data will take—will it also pass through the networks belonging to ISPs D, E, and F?

The networks managed by the ISPs are designated as *autonomous systems* (ASs), and routing is achieved within each AS by running an Interior Gateway Protocol (IGP). The IGPs are unaware of the topology of the Internet outside of the AS, but do know how to route traffic to any node in the AS and to the nodes that lie on the edge of the AS: the *autonomous system border routers* (ASBRs). The ASBRs provide connectivity to ASs under separate management.

The issue arises of how to route traffic between ASs. In effect, out of which ASBR should an AS route traffic for a target host that lies in some other AS? It is feasible to configure this information manually and to inject it into the IGP running in the AS, but the number of ASs in the Internet has grown quite large, the interconnections between ASs are numerous, and such manual configuration would be very hard to maintain accurately. The answer is to run a routing protocol between the ASs. Such a protocol is described as an *Exterior Gateway Protocol* (EGP). The Border Gateway Protocol is an EGP.

To some extent, each AS can be treated as a virtual node connected to other AS virtual nodes by links. By viewing the network in this way, the EGP can

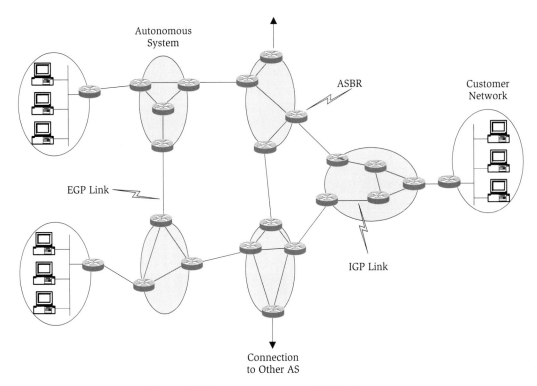

Figure 5.58 Autonomous systems within the Internet.

manage the routes between ASs without worrying about the details of the routes across the ASs. It is up to the AS itself to make sure that connectivity across the AS that it advertises through the EGP is actually available. There is, therefore, a two-way exchange of information between the IGP and EGP at each ASBR. Figure 5.58 shows a picture of part of the Internet built up of ISP networks and customer networks.

5.8.2 Basic Messages and Formats

BGP messages as shown in RFC 1771 use a method of representation different from many other protocols documented by the IETF. For the sake of consistency, the BGP messages in this book have been converted into the format used throughout the rest of this book.

BGP is carried by the Transmission Control Protocol (TCP), which is a reliable transport protocol (see Chapter 7). Using this protocol means that BGP is able to concentrate on routing and leave issues of reliable delivery, retransmission, and detection of connection failure to the underlying transport protocols. On the other hand, a consequence of using TCP is that each BGP router must be configured with the address details of its peers so that it can initiate connectivity.

Each of the five BGP messages begins with a standard header consisting of just three fields, as shown in Figure 5.59. The Marker field is a 16-byte field that is a good example of how protocols degrade and can't dispense with obsolete fields. Originally intended to carry authentication data, each byte of the Marker field on an Open message must be set to contain 0xff, is usually set the same way on other messages, and is not used—the field cannot simply be removed from the message header since deployed implementations are expecting it to be there, so 16 unused bytes are transmitted in every BGP message. The Length gives the length of the entire BGP message (including the header) in bytes, but note that a constraint is placed on BGP messages and the length must never exceed 4096 bytes. The final field of the header indicates the message type using the values listed in Table 5.18.

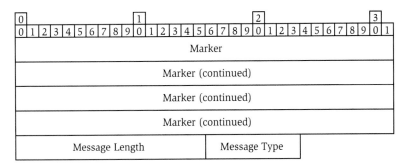

Figure 5.59 The common BGP message header.

Table 5.18 BGP Message Types

Message Type	Meaning
1	Open: Initiates a BGP session between a pair of BGP routers. Allows routers to introduce themselves and to announce/negotiate their capabilities and the optional BGP features to be used on the session.
2	Update: The BGP message that is used to advertise routing information from one BGP router to another.
3	Notification: Used to report an error. Chiefly used to reject an Open message or to report a problem with an Update message.
4	KeepAlive: Exchanged on the BGP session when there is no other traffic to allow the BGP routers to distinguish between a failed connection and a BGP peer that has nothing to say (that is, no new routes to advertise).
5	Route-Refresh: A specific request to a BGP router for it to re-advertise all of the routes in its routing table using Update messages. This message is not defined in the original BGP-4 RFC (RFC 1771), but was added in RFC 2918.

Before proceeding, it is worth establishing some terminology. A router that is aware of BGP and can send and receive BGP messages is referred to as a *BGP speaker*. BGP is a point-to-point protocol that operates between pairs of routers— a pair of routers that exchange BGP messages are described as *BGP peers*. A TCP connection is an end-to-end, bidirectional transport connection between two computers that uses the TCP protocol. BGP peers communicate with each other using a TCP connection over which they establish a peering or *session* that is an explicit relationship between the routers for the purpose of BGP information exchange. A BGP speaker may have multiple peers at any time, each connected through a different session.

When a BGP router wishes to establish a peering with another router it opens a TCP connection using port 179. The remote router is listening on the same port and so a connection is established. See Chapter 7 for a description of ports and TCP itself.

Once the connection is established the routers can exchange BGP messages. The first thing they do is establish a BGP session by exchanging Open BGP messages. The initiator of the TCP connection sends an Open message, as shown in Figure 5.60 and, if the message is acceptable to the other router, it responds

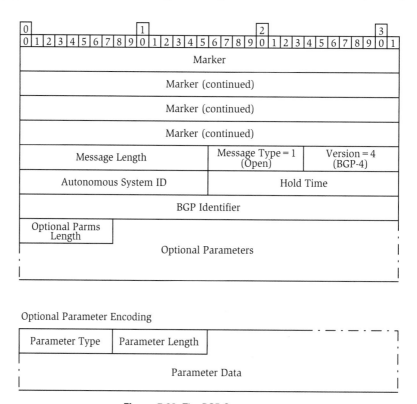

Figure 5.60 The BGP Open message.

with its own Open message. If either router finds the received Open message unacceptable it responds with a Notification message and closes the TCP connection.

The Open message starts with a standard BGP message header and then contains five standard fields followed by optional parameters that define additional capabilities of the router. The standard fields indicate the protocol version supported (version 4 shows BGP-4), and the AS number of the BGP speaker. Just as each BGP router is configured with the IP address of its peers so that it can establish a TCP connection, the routers are configured with their own and their neighbors' AS numbers. This allows the routers to perform an additional sanity check when they first set up a new session.

The standard fields also contain the Hold Time expressed in seconds. This is the time that the BGP speaker will wait before declaring the session dead because it has received no messages from its peer. When there are no other messages to send, a BGP speaker sends a KeepAlive message approximately once every third of the hold time in order to keep the session active. A Keep-Alive message consists of just a BGP message header with message type 4—no other fields are carried in the message. The Hold Time is negotiated between the BGP peers using the Open message—the value used by both peers on a session is the lesser of the two values exchanged. A value of zero is used to indicate that the session should be kept alive even through long periods of silence and KeepAlive messages should not be used; otherwise the smallest legal value for the Hold Time is 3 seconds.

The next field in the Open message is the BGP Identifier of the sender of the message. This value is required to be unique and to be the same for each session in which the speaker participates, but it has no particular semantics. For convenience and ease of management (not to say, ease of maintaining uniqueness) the BGP Identifier is usually set to one of the IP addresses of the router, and often one of the loopback addresses.

The final field gives the length of the options that follow, excluding the field itself. That is, if no options follow, the Optional Parameters Length field contains the value zero.

The optional parameters on a BGP Open message are encoded in type-length-variable (TLV) format. A sequence of TLVs are present up to the length indicated by the Optional Parameters Length field. The Type field identifies the optional parameter and the Length gives the subsequent parameter data in bytes (excluding the Type and Length fields). Using this format, parameters may themselves be constructed from subparameters that are also expressed as TLVs.

RFC 1771 defines only one optional parameter (Type 1, Authentication) and this is left open for future study, but the construct is deliberately generalized and was picked up by RFC 2842 (now made obsolete by RFC 3392) to carry general BGP router capabilities. When the Parameter Type has the value 2 the parameter data is made up of a series of subparameter TLVs, each of which indicates a different capability. The subparameter type Capability Codes are managed by IANA; the values currently registered are shown in Table 5.19.

Table 5.19 The BGP Capability Codes Used in the Capabilities Optional Parameter on a BGP Open Message

Capability Code	Meaning
0	Reserved.
1	Multiprotocol Extensions (see RFC 2858). Used to show that the BGP speaker can distribute routes for routing tables other than IPv4. This is particularly useful for IPv6, but is also used in MPLS to distribute labels in association with routes, as described in Chapter 9.
2	Route Refresh Capability (see RFC 2918). The BGP speaker is capable of handling and responding to the Route Refresh message.
5–63	Unassigned.
64	Graceful Restart Capability. The BGP speaker supports a graceful restart procedure currently under development that allows the router to restart and reestablish sessions with its peers without discarding forwarding state that may be installed in hardware modules.
65	Support for 4-byte AS number capability. The sender of the Open message supports an extension to allow AS numbers to be expressed in 4 bytes rather than the current 2-byte limit.
68–127	Unassigned.
128–255	Vendor Specific. Available for vendors to define their own capabilities.

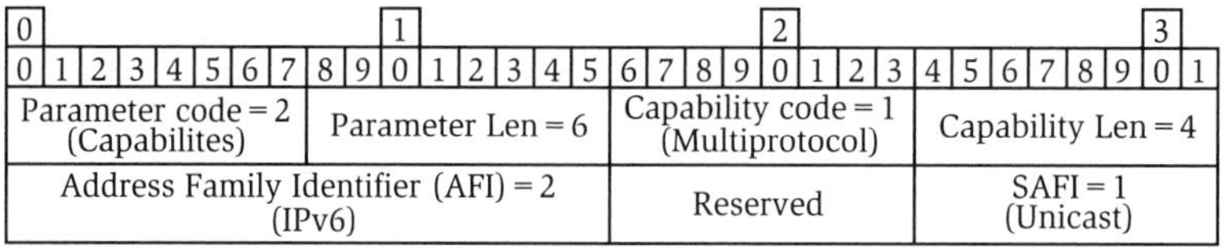

Figure 5.61 The BGP Capabilities optional parameter, including a multiprotocol capability subparameter indicating support of IPv6 routes.

Codes in the range 1 to 63 are available for IETF standards, the range 64 to 127 are available for anyone who registers with IANA, and codes between 128 and 255 are freely available for router vendors to use as they like.

The BGP capabilities appear as a list within the Capabilities optional parameter on the Open message. Each subparameter defines a capability of the BGP speaker, and several subparameters with the same capability code may be present if each defines an additional capability of the speaker. Some subparameters, such as the Route Refresh Capability (code 2), need to convey no additional information and are present with Capability Length zero and no subparameter data. Others, such as the Multiprotocol Capability (code 1) shown in Figure 5.61, carry subparameter data.

The Multiprotocol Capability is used to show that the BGP speaker can handle routes for a variety of protocols and uses. The protocols are expressed using an Address Family Indicator (AFI). An AFI of 1 indicates IPv4 and an AFI of 2 shows support for IPv6. Other AFIs are defined for network service access points (NSAPs), Novel IPX, AppleTalk, and so forth. A further code, the Subsequent Address Family Identifier (SAFI), qualifies the AFI by showing to what use the routing information for the AFI can be put by the BGP speaker. The defined SAFI values are shown in Table 5.20—note that, in general, if a single address family can be used for two purposes it is necessary to include two subparameters with the same AFI but different SAFI values. A special SAFI value was defined to cover routers that can handle unicast and multicast routes for addresses in the same family, but this is deprecated in favor of using two subparameters.

The BGP Notification message shown in Figure 5.62 is used by one BGP peer to report an error to another. The message contains an error code to indicate the high-level error, and a subcode to qualify the error. Some errors also require that error data is supplied to help the receiver understand the exact nature of the error. Table 5.21 lists the error codes and subcodes defined for BGP; note that

Table 5.20 BGP Subsequent Address Family Identifiers (SAFIs)

SAFI Value	Meaning
1	Routes for unicast forwarding.
2	Routes for multicast forwarding.
3	Deprecated (used to mean routes for unicast and multicast forwarding).
4	Labels for MPLS forwarding.

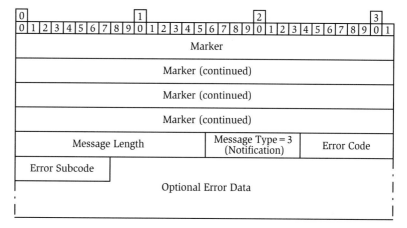

Figure 5.62 The BGP Notification message.

Table 5.21 BGP Notification Message Error Codes and Subcodes

Error Code	Subcode	Meaning
1		Message Header Error. There is an error with the header of a received BGP message. The subcode qualifies the error.
	1	Connection Not Synchronized. The marker field contains an unexpected value. Probably never used.
	2	Bad Message Length. The message length is less that 19 or greater than 4096 bytes, or the message is too short or too long for the specific message type. The error data is used to return a 2-byte field containing the bad length value.
	3	Bad Message Type. The message type value is not recognized. The error data is used to return a single-byte field containing the bad message type value.
2		Open Message Error. There is an error with an Open message that is not a message header problem. The subcode qualifies the error.
	1	Unsupported Version Number. The Open message contains an unsupported protocol version number. The error data is used to return a 2-byte field containing the largest supported version number.
	2	Bad Peer AS. The Open message contains an unacceptable AS number. This is probably because the receiving BGP peer has been configured to expect a different AS number from the one supplied.
	3	Bad BGP Identifier. RFC 1771 says that this error code is used if the BGP identifier in the Open message is syntactically incorrect and that the BGP identifier is not a valid IP address. This apparently contradicts the definition of BGP identifier which may be any unique 32-bit number. Note also that this subcode would be used if the BGP identifier was not as expected through configuration, or matched the local identifier.
	4	Unsupported Optional Parameter. One of the optional parameters is not recognized or is unsupported. Although RFC 1771 says nothing on the subject, the error data usually contains an entire copy of the unsupported optional parameter TLV.
	5	Authentication Failure. Unused since BGP authentication is not used.
	6	Unacceptable Hold Time. Used to reject hold time values of 1 or 2 seconds, which are illegal. May also be used to reject a timer value (especially zero) that is unacceptable to the receiver.
	7	Unsupported Capability. One of the capability subparameters of the capabilities optional parameter is unrecognized or unsupported. The error data field contains the entire subparameter TLV that is in question, and may contain a sequence of unsupported subparameters.
3		Update Message Error. There is an error with an Update message that is not a message header problem. The subcode qualifies the error.
	1	Malformed Attribute List. Parsing of the Withdrawn Routes or Path Attributes has failed because of length, construction, or syntax problems. This includes the presence of multiple copies of a single attribute.

2   Unrecognized Well-known Attribute. An unexpected, unsupported, or unrecognized Path Attribute was encountered. The error data field contains the whole erroneous Attribute TLV.

3   Missing Well-known Attribute. A mandatory Path Attribute is missing. The error data contains a single byte field showing the Path Attribute Code of the missing attribute.

4   Attribute Flags Error. Some Path Attribute is present with flag settings that are incompatible with the attribute itself. The error data field contains the whole erroneous Attribute TLV.

5   Attribute Length Error. The length of a Path Attribute is not as expected from its type. The error data field contains the whole erroneous Attribute TLV.

6   Invalid Origin Attribute. The Origin Attribute contains an undefined value. The error data field contains the whole erroneous Attribute TLV.

7   AS Routing Loop. This error is not described in RFC 1771. In general, routes that contain AS routing loops are simply discarded by the receiver, but this subcode can be used to report the problem to the sender.

8   Invalid Next Hop Attribute. The Next Hop Attribute contains a value that is not syntactically correct. Syntactical correctness means that the attribute contains a valid IPv4 address. The error data field contains the whole erroneous Attribute TLV.

Note that if the Next Hop is semantically incorrect (that is, contains a valid IPv4 address that does not share a common subnet with the receiver, or is equal to one of the addresses of the receiver itself, no Notification message is sent and the advertised route is ignored.

9   Optional Attribute Error. An optional attribute is recognized but fails to parse or contains an unsupported value. The erroneous optional attribute is skipped, but the remainder of the message is processed. The error data field contains the whole erroneous Optional Attribute TLV.

10   Invalid Network Field. The NLRI value in the MP Reach NLRI Attribute or the MP Unreach NLRI Attribute is syntactically incorrect.

11   Malformed AS Path. The AS Path Attribute is malformed or syntactically incorrect.

4   Hold Timer Expired. The hold timer has expired without the receipt of an action message or a KeepAlive message. The sender closes the TCP connection immediately after the message has been sent.

5   Finite State Machine Error. This error may represent an internal implementation issue or the receipt of an unexpected message (for example, an Update message received before the Open message exchange has completed). The Notification can only tell the receiver that something may have gone horribly wrong—nothing can be done except holding on and hoping for the best or closing the session and starting again.

6   Cease. The sender wishes to close the BGP session. The TCP connection would normally (although not necessarily) be closed after this message has been sent. Note that this error code must not be used in place of a more helpful error code when a problem has been detected.

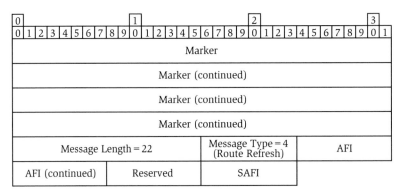

Figure 5.63 The BGP Route Refresh message.

most of the errors are concerned with the receipt of badly formatted messages or message fields with invalid or unsupported values. Note that Notification messages are not sent to report errors in Notification messages.

The Route Refresh message shown in Figure 5.63 can be used by a BGP speaker to request a complete and immediate update of all the routes known by its peer. This enables it to get its routing table up-to-date quickly. It is particularly useful for an implementation that has had to jettison its routing table because of an error, but doesn't want to close and reopen the session. Additionally, route refresh may be required by a system that retains only certain routes and discards the rest according to a locally configured route import policy (see the discussion in Section 5.1.3). If the import policy is changed the router has no idea which routes it has discarded, and must request that its peers resend all of the routes that they know about.

The Route Refresh message was not present in the original BGP specification, but was added by RFC 2918. For backwards compatibility, it must be used only if the receiver indicated support for the message by including a Route Refresh Capability subparameter to the Capabilities Optional Parameter on its Open message. The sender of the Route Refresh can restrict the routing tables it wants to see by setting an AFI and SAFI as previously defined for the Multiprotocol Capability optional subparameter.

The meat of BGP comes with the Update message. This is used to distribute routes between BGP peers, and to withdraw routes that have previously been advertised. After the common message header, the Update message consists of the three distinct blocks of information shown in Figure 5.64: the Withdrawn Routes, the Path Attributes, and the advertised routes known as the Network Layer Reachability Information (NLRI).

IPv4 routes that are being withdrawn are listed in the Withdrawn Routes section of the message. This section begins with a 2-byte length field that is always present and indicates how many bytes of withdrawn route information follow—if there are no withdrawn routes, the length field carries the value zero.

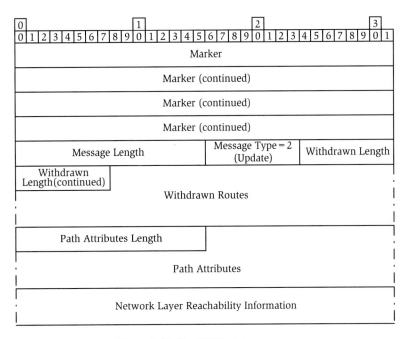

Figure 5.64 The BGP Update message.

Prefix Length = 28	Prefix = 0xaca819 (172.16.25.0)		
Prefix (cont) = 0x00	Prefix Length = 18	Prefix = 0xaca8 (172.16.32)	
Prefix (cont) = 0x20	Prefix Length = 29	Prefix = 0xaca8 (172.168.64.16)	
Prefix (cont) = 0x4010			

Figure 5.65 Withdrawn routes as carried on a BGP Update message.

Each withdrawn route is expressed as a single byte that encodes the prefix length, followed by just enough bytes to carry the prefix itself. This format is shown in Figure 5.65, where the three prefixes 172.168.25.0/28, 172.168.32.0/18, and 172.168.64.16/29 are encoded ready for withdrawal.

The next block of data in the Update message contains parameters called Path Attributes that apply to all of the routes that are being added by this advertisement. In other words, they do not apply to the withdrawn routes, but apply equally to each of the new routes present in the NLRI field. Note that if some route does not fit with the attributes of the other routes it must be the subject of a separate Update message. The Path Attributes are prefixed by a mandatory length field that says how many bytes of Path Attribute information follow, but the routes to which the attributes apply do not qualify for a length field since their length can be deduced from the overall message length and the two other length fields. The new routes in the NLRI field are encoded the same as the withdrawn routes described in the preceding paragraphs and illustrated in Figure 5.65.

The Path Attributes field is constructed of a series of attributes of a standard format (assuming the length is not set to zero). There are two variants of the format, allowing an attribute to be encoded with a 1- or 2-byte length field—the single-byte length field should be used whenever it is adequate. The format of each attribute is Flags-Type Length-Data where the initial flags field includes a flag (the fourth bit—that is, bit 3) that indicates whether the long or short length field is in use. This is illustrated in Figure 5.66.

There are three other flags defined in the flags field of the Path Attributes. The O-flag describes whether the attribute is optional (set to 1) and therefore may be unsupported by the receiver, or *well known* and must be supported by the receiver (set to zero). The T-flag describes how the receiver must redistribute the Path Attribute if it forwards the route to another BGP peer—if the attribute is *transitive* the bit is set to 1 and the attribute must be passed on, but if the bit is set to zero the attribute is not passed on. All well-known attributes must have the transitive bit set. The final bit, the P-flag, indicates whether the information in an optional transitive attribute was added at the source of the announcement of the prefixes in the NLRI (set to zero), or whether it is *partial* (set to 1) and was added at a later stage.

It is important to give another dimension to the O-bit. All well-known attributes must be supported by the receiver of an Update message, but not all such attributes need to be present on each Update message. Each attribute may also be defined as mandatory or optional in the context of the sender. This information does not form part of the Update message, but is included in the definition of the attributes. It follows that all mandatory attributes are well known.

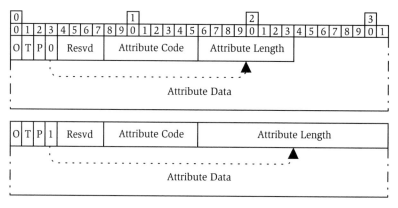

Figure 5.66 BGP Path Attributes are encoded with 1- or 2-byte length fields according to the setting of bit 4 of the flags field.

There are many attributes that may be present on an Update message. Table 5.22 lists the standard attributes defined in RFC 1771. The extension attributes defined in subsequent RFCs are described in Section 5.8.3. Recall that all attributes on one message apply equally to each prefix advertised in the NLRI field.

The term *multihoming* is used to describe multiple connections to or from a host or an autonomous system. A host is described as multihomed if it is

Table 5.22 The Standard BGP Path Attributes Used in Update Messages

Type	O-Bit	Mandatory	T-Bit	Meaning
1	0	Yes	1	Origin. This attribute describes how the routes being advertised were learned by (or *injected into*) BGP. Three values are used, encoded as a single byte of data: 1 indicates that the route was learned from an IGP (such as OSPF), 2 shows that the route came from the EGP (that is, the protocol called EGP—see Section 5.10.6), and 3 indicates that it used some other means. Routes that are statically configured are indicated using the value 3.
2	0	Yes	1	AS Path. This provides a list of autonomous systems through which the route has been advertised to reach the current node. The ASs are represented by their AS numbers which are each 2-byte numbers. The list is well ordered, starting with the first AS in the progression.
				As described in Section 5.2.3, the AS Path needs to support the concept of a sequence and a set. This is handled in BGP by encoding the AS Path as a series of *path segments*. Each segment is a sequence or a set and is formatted as 1 byte type (type 1 for a sequence, type 2 for a set), a 1-byte length field indicating how many bytes of value follow, and the value itself, which is constructed as a series of AS numbers.
				Note that this attribute is not a candidate for the P-bit since the attribute is well known and transitive.
3	0	Yes	0	Next Hop. This is the IP address of the node to which the receiver of the advertisement should forward traffic that matches the routes. In the usual case, the address is an address of the BGP speaker advertising the route, but this does not need to be the case if one speaker advertises routes on behalf of another node—perhaps not all exit points from an AS are BGP enabled. The value field carries the 4-byte IP address.
4	0	No	0	Multi-Exit Discriminator. This attribute is used to help choose between multiple parallel connections between a pair of ASs. Two destinations may be reachable over both of the inter-AS connections, but one connection should be preferred for each of the destinations (see Figure 5.67). The Multi-Exit Discriminator is advertised out of the AS to enable routing decisions to be made by external routers. The advertising AS can set a metric or cost for each of the routes so that the receiving AS can make a choice. The value of the metric may be derived from the cost of the IGP path across the advertising AS. The value field of this attribute is a 4-byte integer.

Table 5.22 *Continued*

Type	O-Bit	Mandatory	T-Bit	Meaning
5	0	No	0	Local Preference. The Multi-Exit Discriminator helps external routers choose from parallel paths between a pair of ASs. The Local Preference attribute helps routers choose routes within their own networks to select from parallel paths that involve multiple ASs such as in the network in Figure 5.68. This attribute has a 4-byte attribute value that expresses the advertiser's preference for a route, with the higher value indicating a higher preference.
				Note that Local Preference can also be used in place of the Multi-Exit Discriminator, but has a subtly different meaning. Local Preference provides additional guidance to the nodes choosing routes, whereas the Multi-Exit Discriminator is closer to an instruction.
6	0	No	0	Atomic Aggregate. If an advertising router wishes to indicate that a route must not be de-aggregated it attaches the Atomic Aggregate attribute. This prevents nodes further upstream from splitting the prefix into several longer prefixes routed in different ways.
				The Atomic Aggregate attribute is just a flag and carries no data, and so has a length of zero.
7	0	No	1	Aggregator. This attribute allows a node to indicate that it is responsible for address aggregation within the advertised route. Note that if successive aggregation is performed this attribute may be confusing or misleading.
				The Aggregator attribute is encoded as a 2-byte AS number followed by a 4-byte IPv4 address to uniquely identify the aggregator node in the context of the whole network.
19–254				Unassigned.
255				Reserved for development.

connected to two networks. An AS is described as multihomed if it has more than one connection to one or more other ASs. Since BGP is primarily concerned with the advertisement of routes between ASs we will concern ourselves only with AS multihoming.

Figure 5.67 shows how the Multi-Exit Discriminator attribute may be used to help routers in one AS distinguish between a pair of parallel routes across another AS. ASs C and D contain the prefix routes 172.168.10.0/28 and 172.168.10.16/28. Both ASs connect to AS B, which has two connections to AS A through Routers X and Y. We need to consider the BGP routes that Routers X and Y advertise to AS A. In option 1, the two routers perform route aggregation and both advertise reachability to 172.168.10.0/27. This is perfectly correct, but doesn't help AS A distinguish the possible routes across AS B. In option 2, the routers keep the prefixes separate and advertise two routes each. This makes it

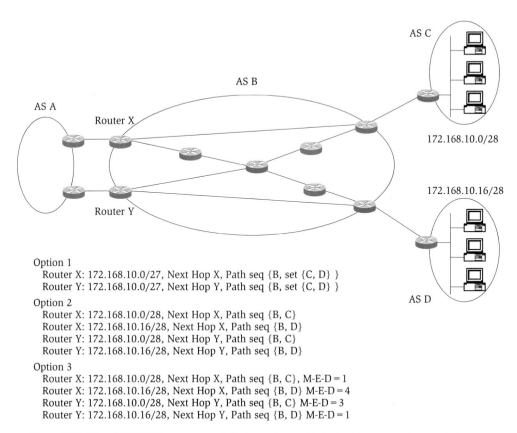

Option 1
  Router X: 172.168.10.0/27, Next Hop X, Path seq {B, set {C, D} }
  Router Y: 172.168.10.0/27, Next Hop Y, Path seq {B, set {C, D} }

Option 2
  Router X: 172.168.10.0/28, Next Hop X, Path seq {B, C}
  Router X: 172.168.10.16/28, Next Hop X, Path seq {B, D}
  Router Y: 172.168.10.0/28, Next Hop Y, Path seq {B, C}
  Router Y: 172.168.10.16/28, Next Hop Y, Path seq {B, D}

Option 3
  Router X: 172.168.10.0/28, Next Hop X, Path seq {B, C}, M-E-D = 1
  Router X: 172.168.10.16/28, Next Hop X, Path seq {B, D} M-E-D = 4
  Router Y: 172.168.10.0/28, Next Hop Y, Path seq {B, C} M-E-D = 3
  Router Y: 172.168.10.16/28, Next Hop Y, Path seq {B, D} M-E-D = 1

Figure 5.67 The Multi-Exit Discriminator attribute can be used to help pick between two parallel routes.

clear that the routes are distinct and indicates which ASs lie on each path, but still doesn't help AS A decide whether to use the link to Router X or to Router Y.

In the third option, Routers X and Y assign metrics from the IGP (counting one for each hop) and signal these using the Multi-Exit Discriminator attribute. Now (all other things being equal) AS A knows that to reach 172.168.10.0/28 it is better to use the link to Router X, but for 172.168.10.16/28 it should use Router Y.

Contrast this with the network shown in Figure 5.68. Here there are no parallel links between AS pairs, but there are two possible routes from AS A to the prefix 172.168.10.0/28. What should be advertised within Area A to help Router X distinguish the routes? Suppose that AS C has a pairing contract with AS A that offers far cheaper traffic distribution than that available through AS B. Alternatively, it is possible that AS A knows that AS B has unreliable routers provided by a well-known, but little-trusted equipment vendor. In these cases, AS A can use the Local Preference attribute to assign a preference to each of the paths—the path with the higher preference value is preferred.

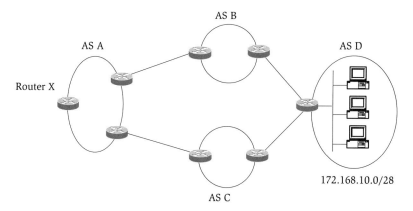

Router X: 172.168.10.0/28, Next Hop X, Path seq {A, B, D}, Local Pref = 12
Router X: 172.168.10.0/28, Next Hop X, Path seq {A, C, D}, Local Pref = 79

Figure 5.68 The Local Preference attribute is used to help choose between parallel paths in more complex networks.

5.8.3 Advanced Function

A series of additional requirements have emerged and BGP has been extended to address them. Many of these new needs have arisen through operational experience with BGP as it has evolved from being used mostly in small networks to being the ubiquitous EGP within the Internet. This represents an interesting and correct evolution of the protocol in the real world.

Communities

A community is simply a set of routes that are treated administratively in the same way. This property is sometimes referred to as *route coloring*. The treatment of each community is a local (AS-wide) configuration issue, and when communities are exposed to other ASs a degree of configuration is required if the other ASs are to make full use of the information since the community numbers do not have the same meaning in different ASs.

Three well-known community identifiers apply to all ASs. The value 0xffffff01 indicates that the route must not be exported beyond the AS. 0xffffff02 is used to indicate that the route must not be advertised beyond the receiving router. 0xffffff03 describes routes that may be advertised, but only within the confines of the current AS confederation.

The Community attribute, introduced in RFC 1997, provides a list of communities to which a route belongs. Each community identifier is a 4-byte integer and is conventionally broken up into 2 bytes of AS number and 2 bytes indicating the community within the AS. The Community attribute has type 8, it is optional (O-bit set to 1) and transitory (T-bit set to 1).

Multiprotocol Support

Up to this point, BGP has been described only for IPv4 routes. Clearly, to be fully useful within the Internet, BGP must also support IPv6 addressing; however, there are backwards compatibility issues with simply allowing the NLRI to contain 16-byte prefixes since deployed implementations expect to find only IPv4 prefixes in that field.

The solution, described in RFC 2283, is to introduce two new path attributes. The Multiprotocol Reach NLRI and Multiprotocol Unreach NLRI attributes carry conceptually the same information as the NLRI and Withdrawn Routes fields, respectively, but these attributes define the address space to which they refer before listing a series of routes or addresses. Note that, as with the NLRI and Withdrawn Routes fields, all other path attributes apply equally to each route listed in the Multiprotocol Reach NLRI attribute, and all routes listed in the Multiprotocol Unreach NLRI are uniformly withdrawn.

The Multiprotocol Reach NLRI has type 14 and the Multiprotocol Unreach NLRI has type 15. Both attributes are optional and nontransitive. The Multiprotocol Reach NLRI shown in Figure 5.69 encodes the AFI and SAFI of the subsequent addresses using the same values used in the Capabilities subparameter (see Table 5.20). Each attribute contains the Next Hop address (the usual Next Hop attribute cannot be used because it encodes only an IPv4 address), one or

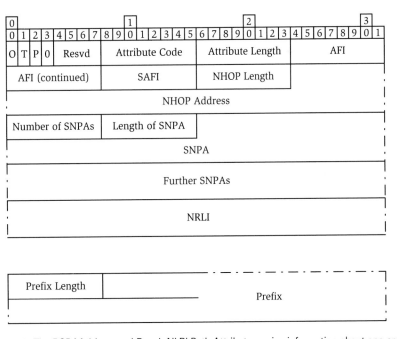

Figure 5.69 The BGP Multiprotocol Reach NLRI Path Attribute carries information about one or more non-IPv4 routes of the same type.

more Subnetwork Point of Attachment (SNPA) addresses to indicate connectivity to the next hop, and one or more NLRIs. Each NLRI is expressed as before as a prefix length in bits and only enough bytes to carry the prefix.

Note that the length fields in the Multiprotocol Reach NLRI attribute all have different forms. The Next Hop Length is in bytes, the SNPA length is in half bytes (nibbles) and the SNPA address itself is padded with zero bits up to a full byte boundary, and the prefix length is in bits with the prefix itself padded with zero bits up to a full byte boundary.

Route withdrawal works in a similar way. Each entry in the Multiprotocol Unreach NLRI path attribute consists of an AFI, SAFI, and a list of prefix lengths and prefixes, each encoded as before.

The multiprotocol extensions to BGP are now used to associate MPLS labels with routes that are distributed across an AS. See Chapter 9 for further details.

Virtual Private Networks

Virtual Private Networks (VPNs) are discussed in detail in Chapter 15. The requirement is to carry IP connectivity for several private networks across a common public network without leaking routes (or traffic) from one customer network to another. Further, the customer networks may choose to use overlapping address spaces.

The solution to this is to define a new multiprotocol address family: the VPN IPv4 address. The AFI indicates that the address in the NLRI of the Multiprotocol Reach attribute is a VPN address and must only be leaked into the correct VPN. The VPN routes are carried in up to 6-bytes of NLRI data (with a single length byte). The first 2 bytes represent a VPN identifier or *route distinguisher* which is an arbitrary but unique indicator of the VPN. The remaining bytes carry the prefix. The prefix length still indicates the length of the prefix, so the 2 bytes of route distinguisher are not included in the length.

Dampening Route Flap

When a link or node in the BGP network fails, the neighboring peers withdraw the routes that used the failed resource. This route withdrawal is propagated through the network and traffic is rerouted along another path to avoid the problem. When the resource is repaired the neighbors will reestablish their BGP sessions and will exchange routes again. These routes are advertised through the network and reclaim the traffic for which they are shorter or better routes. This is BGP working correctly.

However, some hardware problems are transient and repetitive. Interface cards and links are notorious for a type of error called *flapping*, in which the link status goes up and down repeatedly in a relatively short time. Each time the link comes back, BGP sessions are reestablished and routes are redistributed only to have the link fail again and the routes be withdrawn. Such behavior causes a large amount of churn in the BGP network with an outwards ripple of advertised and withdrawn routes. But not only is the BGP traffic and consequent processing unacceptable, the associated *route flap* in the BGP routers' routing tables causes traffic to be repetitively switched from one route to another. This is highly undesirable since traffic on the vulnerable route will be lost when the interface goes down again.

Route flap is circumvented by an operational extension to BGP called *route flap dampening*. When a route is withdrawn it is held by a router in a withdrawn routes list for a period of time. If the route is re-advertised to the router while the route is still in the withdrawn list it is held and not distributed further until a second period of time has elapsed to prove that the route is stable. Many implementations configure these timers as a function of prefix length so that short prefixes are dampened less than long prefixes. This appears attractive since it restores the bulk routes quickly after failure, but this is actually the action we want to avoid. The only real benefit to such a scheme for choosing timer values is that the BGP message exchange and processing is reduced—there are likely to be only a few routes with short prefixes and very many with longer prefixes, so if flap occurs it is less damaging to BGP to favor the bulk routes.

5.8.4 Example Message

Figure 5.70 shows a simple BGP Update message. It shows a single route (172.16.10.0/24) being withdrawn and two prefixes (172.168.11.16/27 and 172.168.11.32/28) being advertised. The basic minimum Path Attributes are present. The route was originated by 172.168.11.253, and the next hop for the route is 172.222.16.1. The route has been distributed through three ASs: 1962, 15, and 10.

5.8.5 Interior BGP

Although the introduction to this section on BGP concentrated on BGP as an Exterior Gateway Protocol, it can also be used as an Interior Gateway Protocol for route exchange between routers within an autonomous system or for transporting exterior routes across an AS to advertise them into the next AS. This second use has clear benefits because it significantly simplifies the interactions between the IGP and BGP and removes any requirement for the IGP to transport information across the AS on behalf of BGP. Run as an IGP, BGP is referred to as *Interior BGP* (I-BGP).

In fact, the previous BGP examples have been somewhat simplistic, and have treated each AS as though it had just one ASBR providing connectivity to other ASs. In practice, many ASs at the core of the Internet carry transit traffic from one AS to another, and have many ASBRs each providing connectivity to other ASs. Figure 5.71 shows five autonomous systems joined together to form a larger network. AS D and AS E are able to communicate directly and would use BGP (that is, E-BGP) to exchange routing information, but traffic to and from ASs A and B must traverse AS C. Each of the ASs runs an IGP internally, but this only provides routing information within the AS. The question must be asked: How does a router at the core of an AS know how to forward packets out of the AS? For the routers in the peripheral ASs, this is not a significant issue because they

0										1										2										3	
0	1	2	3	4	5	6	7	8	9	0	1	2	3	4	5	6	7	8	9	0	1	2	3	4	5	6	7	8	9	0	1

Marker
Marker (continued)
Marker (continued)
Marker (continued)

Message Length = 60	Message Type = 2 (Update)	Withdrawn Len = 4
Withdrawn Length(continued)	Prefix length = 24	Prefix = 172.168.10	
Prefix (continued)	Path Attributes Length = 23	0	1	0	0	Resvd
Attribute Code = 1 (Origin)	Attribute Len = 4	Origin = 172.168.11.253
Origin (continued)	0	1	0	0	Resvd	Attribute Code = 2 (AS Path)
Attribute Len = 6	AS Number = 1962	AS Number = 15
AS Number (continued)	AS Number = 10	0	0	0	0	Resvd
Attribute Code = 3 (Next Hop)	Attribute Len = 4	Next Hop = 172.222.16.1
Next Hop (continued)	Prefix length = 27	Prefix = 172.168.11.16
Prefix (continued)	Prefix length = 28
Prefix = 172.168.11.32

Figure 5.70 An example BGP Update message.

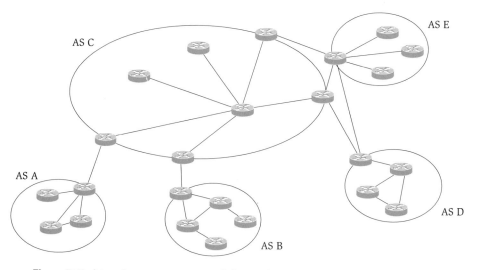

Figure 5.71 A transit autonomous system links together several other autonomous systems.

have only one ASBR and this is obviously the gateway out of the AS. But for routers in AS C the choice is more difficult. Routers that only have one other adjacent router can handle the problem using default routes, but routers with more than one adjacent router (*transit routers*) must make an informed routing decision.

Since the ASBRs have learned about external routes from the BGP sessions with their peers, one option would clearly be for the ASBRs to leak the external routing information to their IGPs and allow the information to be distributed across their network. But this is exactly what ASs were created to avoid! It causes the IGP to distribute very large amounts of information and forces each router to retain a huge amount of routing state, and when the information reaches another ASBR it will be distributed as though the destination were within the wrong AS.

The solution is to use BGP to distribute the external routing information. This information is needed not just at the ASBRs, but at every transit router in the AS because it is important that all transit routers have a consistent view of all the paths to the external networks, so each transit route must be a BGP speaker.

There are some important differences between the form of BGP run across AS borders and that run within an AS. Consider, for example, how each BGP speaker adds its AS number to the routes it propagates. This feature, designed to detect routing loops, breaks down within an AS because all of the routers are in the same AS. To handle this, I-BGP does not prepend the AS number to the routes. This might create a risk of looping within an AS, but since there is a full mesh of I-BGP sessions, each router is fully aware of all the BGP speakers in the AS and there is no problem with loops.

There is a basic rule that states that I-BGP peers must not re-advertise routes within the AS that they learned from other peers within the AS. This means that a BGP speaker must maintain a session with each other BGP-capable router in the AS to know all of the I-BGP routes. A *full mesh* of sessions is needed. This corresponds to $n(n - 1)/2$ sessions where there are n BGP speakers. This is illustrated in Figure 5.72, where the transit routers in AS C all

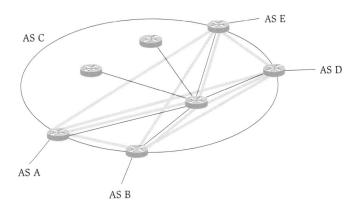

Figure 5.72 I-BGP connectivity is overlaid on the AS network to provide a full mesh of BGP peerings between all transit routers.

have BGP sessions with each other. Note that this full mesh of BGP sessions exists regardless of the underlying physical links. This is possible because each BGP session uses a TCP connection that may span multiple hops in the underlying network. Perhaps confusingly, each BGP message within the AS may require input from the IGP to correctly route it to its destination.

Clearly, as the number of BGP speakers grows, this may result in an unmanageably large number of sessions as each BGP speaker must maintain $n - 1$ sessions. I-BGP presents a serious scaling issue as the size of an AS grows. There are several common solutions to this problem.

Scaling I-BGP: Route Reflection

Route reflection is achieved by imposing a client–server relationship between BGP speakers within an AS. Route reflector clients are implemented with no change from the original specification, but with a configuration change so that each client need only attach to a single route reflector. The client depends on the route reflector to re-advertise its routes to the rest of the AS, and requires the route reflector to deliver to it all of the routes from the AS. The route reflectors themselves break the I-BGP rules and do redistribute routes within the AS—this redistribution is limited to the server–client relationship so that each route reflector only redistributes to other route reflectors those routes learned from a client, while it also redistributes all routes, however learned, to each client. The route reflectors must be arranged in a full mesh, but the clients may hang off this mesh using just a single session. Figure 5.73 shows how such a network might be built.

Note that the connectivity shown in a route reflection diagram does not refer to the connectivity between the routers—they may be connected together in any arbitrary way. The route reflector diagrams such as that in Figure 5.73 show only the BGP sessions between routers.

Route reflection opens up a problem that the original I-BGP rules were designed to eradicate. Now that routes can be re-advertised within the AS, there is a risk of routing loops. Two new path attributes are introduced in RFC 2796 to enable the BGP routers to control this issue. The Originator ID path attribute (type 9, optional, nontransitive) carries the 4-byte router ID of the router that originated the route. The attribute is not added by a reflector client (since reflector clients do not understand route reflection extensions), but is inserted by the route reflector itself. Additional rules are:

- The Originator ID is not forwarded out of the AS.
- A route reflector must not replace an Originator ID if one already exists.
- A route reflector never advertises a route back to the router indicated by the Originator ID.

The risk of looping is further reduced by the Cluster ID path attribute (type 10, optional, nontransitive) which tracks the route reflectors for each route as it is

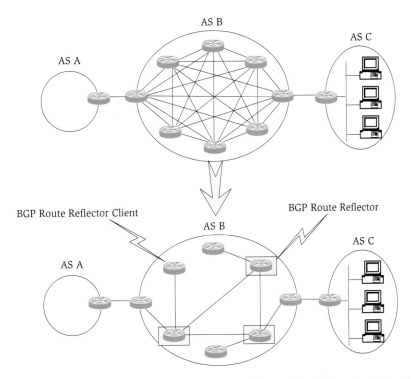

Figure 5.73 Route reflection reduces the full-mesh connectivity problem by imposing a hierarchy on the BGP speakers within an AS.

distributed within the AS. This acts a little like the AS Path attribute, but operates on individual BGP routers. Each route reflector that forwards a route within the AS adds the identity of its cluster to the Cluster ID attribute. When a route is distributed into a cluster, the receiving router checks to see whether the route has been advertised into the cluster before and drops it if it has. Note that the normal case is that a cluster contains just one route reflector, in which case the cluster ID is set to the router's router ID; however, it is acceptable to build a cluster that contains more than one route reflector, in which case a shared unique cluster ID must be configured at each of the route reflectors in the cluster.

Scaling I-BGP: AS Confederations

An alternative approach to solving the I-BGP scaling problems is to divide the AS into sub-ASs and group these sub-ASs together as a *confederation*. The confederation formed in this way is the same size and contains exactly the same routers as the original AS, but is administratively broken into sub-ASs, each of which acts as an AS in its own right. An important point, however, is that the confederation continues to represent itself externally as a single AS—this

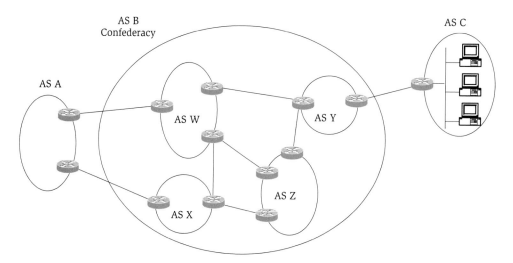

Figure 5.74 A large AS can be managed as a confederacy of sub-ASs.

protects the rest of the network from having to handle the topology of multiple sub-ASs but allows the large, problematic AS to divide itself. Clearly, once the large AS has been broken up, the rules about distributing routes within the AS no longer apply and all of the usual inter-AS features of E-BGP, including route exchange, can be applied to the sub-ASs. Figure 5.74 shows how an AS might be managed as a confederacy of sub-ASs: ASs A, B, and C are the top-level autonomous systems, but AS B is actually a confederacy of ASs W, X, Y, and Z. AS A and AS C run E-BGP sessions with AS B. The sessions within AS B are broken into two groups: those within a sub-AS (such as AS W) are still called I-BGP sessions, but those between sub-ASs are called *EI-BGP* sessions.

The passage of a route advertisement through the confederacy needs to be tracked sub-AS by sub-AS just as the passage of the route is tracked through the wider network by recording each AS in the AS Path attribute. However, since the confederacy wants to represent itself externally as a single AS, the sub-ASs are flagged in the AS Path attribute using two new segment identifiers: AS-Confederacy-Sequence (type 3) and AS-Confederacy-Set (type 4). When a BGP router is about to advertise a route out of the confederacy, it strips the sub-AS information from the AS Path and replaces it with a single AS element.

5.8.6 Choosing to Use BGP

In many circumstances, the choice to use BGP is simple. If you want to interconnect one autonomous system to another and want to avoid manual configuration, you must use an Exterior Gateway Protocol. Although there are other EGPs (see Section 5.10), the *de facto* standard choice within the Internet is BGP-4.

The other EGPs can be used freely for connecting ASs within private networks. However, BGP-4 is fast becoming the common choice because of its widespread availability on routers, the extensive deployment experience that has been gained within the Internet, and the way it opens up future seamless connectivity to the Internet should it be required.

Within an AS, or rather, across the AS, it is not necessary to run I-BGP to distribute routes between ASBRs; any interior routing protocol could be used, but there can be disastrous consequences for the IGP if this is not managed very carefully. This makes I-BGP a sensible choice.

Note that recent developments with Multiprotocol Label Switching (MPLS, see Chapter 9) may offer an alternative to running I-BGP on core routers. The ASBRs set up MPLS tunnels across the AS so that traffic that transits the AS does not need to be routed internally, but is switched from one edge of the AS to another. This idea has yet to see much deployment and so it is not possible to judge how feasible or popular it will turn out to be.

5.9   Multicast Routing

Multicast IP is described in Chapter 3, and that material is a prerequisite to understanding this section. The ability to multicast IP traffic has distinct advantages for a select set of applications, and can reduce the amount of traffic in the network. But multicast presents routers with a challenge—they need to distribute the data down only those links that lead to routers that belong to the multicast group, and not down other links since this would constitute broadcast traffic. To send the data in only the right directions, a router must know either which hosts and router are subscribed to a group or have the group itself advertised along the links of the network. This is achieved using a multicast routing protocol.

Multicast routing is an extremely complex area that is still under development. Several approaches have been suggested, and a large set of multicast routing protocols has been developed. Each protocol attempts to address specific needs and distribute multicast group information in a different way. Because of this complexity, and because multicast routing is still not established as an everyday feature of all IP networks, this section provides only an overview of some of the issues and solutions. A few key multicast routing protocols are used as illustrations.

There are four classes of multicast routing protocols differentiated by how they operate on the tree of routes through the network. *Sparse-mode* multicast routing protocols rely on individual nodes to request to join the distribution tree for a multicast group—this is called the *pull principle* since the recipients pull the data. In *dense-mode* multicast routing the *push principle* is used to push packets to all corners of the network. It relies on the routers pruning themselves from the distribution tree if they decide they are not interested in a particular multicast group. The link state protocols such as OSPF and IS-IS (see Sections 5.5 and 5.6) can be extended to carry multicast information which is advertised to build a distribution tree. Finally, interdomain routing protocols can also carry multicast information.

This chapter focuses on three multicast routing protocols. Protocol-Independent Multicast-Sparse-Mode (PIM-SM) is a popular sparse-mode routing protocol. Multicast OSPF (MOSPF) is a set of extensions to OSPF to provide support for multicast groups within the link state routing protocol. Distance Vector Multicast Routing Protocol (DVMRP) is a dense-mode multicast routing protocol used to provide most of the multicast routing across the Internet.

It is worth noting that many multicast routing protocols are still under development, and those that have reached RFC status are classed as *experimental*.

5.9.1 Multicast Routing Trees

The path that a multicast datagram follows from its source to the multiple group member destinations is called a *tree*. Some routing protocols compute a routing tree based on each source in the group; they are called *source-based multicast routing protocols*. The advantages of a source-based tree is that it is very easy to build and maintain and that routing decisions are simple. The down side is that very many routing trees have to be maintained for groups that have multiple sources—this means that source-based trees are very good for video streaming applications, but doubtful for multiparty conferencing sessions.

Other routing protocols build a single routing tree for all sources in the group. These are *shared tree multicast routing protocols* and their benefits and drawbacks are the exact converse of the source-based protocols. That is, the shared tree protocol uses a single tree to manage all data distribution, thus saving routing table space on the routers but making the routing decision and the management of the routing tree more complex. Shared trees operate by selecting a hub router (sometimes called the *rendezvous point* or the *core*) to which all datagrams for the group are sent and which is responsible for fanning the datagrams out to the destinations. The tree has two parts, therefore: a set of unicast routes from each source to the hub router, and a source-based tree from the hub router to each of the members of the group that wish to receive data. There is scope in this model for multiple sources, and for group members that send but do not receive datagrams.

Figure 5.75 shows the data paths in a shared tree multicast network. The solid arrows represent the data on its way from the source to the hub, and the dotted arrows show the data distributed from the hub. Note that there may be some unavoidable inefficiency caused by the placement of the hub node. If Router X had been chosen as the hub, there would not need to be an extra datagram exchange between the hub and Router X to deliver datagrams from Source 1 to Destination 1. On the other hand, the trade-off would have been for datagrams from Source 2 which must also be delivered to Destination 2.

The biggest challenge for a shared tree routing protocol is electing or otherwise choosing the hub node for the group. As other nodes enter and leave the

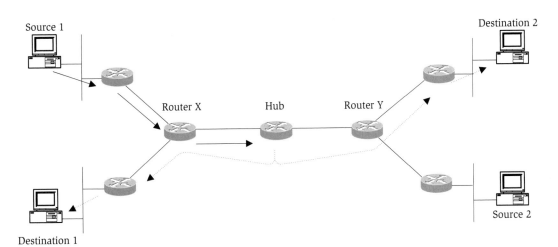

Figure 5.75 Data paths for a shared tree multicast network.

group, the optimal position of the hub may change, and as links and nodes (especially the hub node, itself) fail, the protocol must handle the selection of a new hub and notify all senders so that data is not lost.

Note that whether a routing protocol is dense-mode or sparse-mode protocol is theoretically orthogonal to whether it uses a shared tree or a source-based tree. In practice, however, the older protocols tend to be both dense-mode and source-based. See Table 5.25 for a listing of which common multicast routing protocols operate in which modes.

5.9.2 Dense-Mode Protocols

Dense-mode multicast protocols can themselves be split into two operational groups. The first operational set includes the *broadcast and prune* protocols which default to sending all multicast packets out of all interfaces of a router. The multicast distribution tree for a group is to send every packet for the group to every other router. The first datagram issued to the group address is therefore sent along every branch in the tree and reaches every router. Downstream routers check to see whether any of their attached hosts have registered (using IGMP) to receive packets for the group. If there are interested consumers, the router delivers the datagrams and everyone is happy. If there are no registered consumers of the group datagrams on the local network, the router discards the datagram and returns a routing protocol Prune message back upstream. This causes the upstream router to remove the downstream path from the tree for the group. Figure 5.76 shows how this might work.

One problem arises with this mode of pruning the distribution tree: What happens if a host changes its mind and adds itself to a group after the tree has

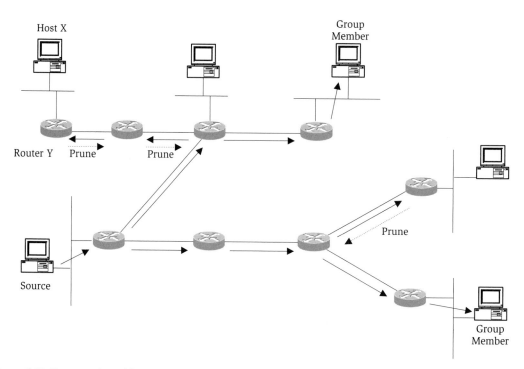

Figure 5.76 Dense-mode multicast routing protocols may use the broadcast and prune approach to building a source-based routing tree for a multicast group.

already been pruned? This question is addressed in broadcast and prune dense-mode protocols by providing a *graft* function whereby a router can request to be added back into the tree. Thus, in Figure 5.76, if Host X registers with Router Y to be added to the group, Router Y will send a Graft message router by router until a branch of the tree is reached. It is a fine point of distinction between a pruned dense-mode protocol accepting a new group member and sending a Graft message, and a sparse-mode protocol (see the next section) adding a new member to a group.

The pruned and regrafted tree can become a bit messy, so dense-mode protocols periodically revert to the default behavior. That is, they reinstate the full broadcast tree and allow it to be pruned back again. Because of this feature dense-mode protocols are favored in networks where the amount of pruning is small—that is, where the chance of having an interested receiver on each router interface is high.

The second category of dense-mode routing protocols employ group membership broadcasts or *domain-wide reports* to carry group membership information between routers. In this mode, when a host registers its interest in a group, its router broadcasts its desire to see packets for the group. This is still considered to be a dense-mode of operation because the broadcast is not focused and the resulting tree is more connected than it needs to be.

5.9.3 Sparse-Mode Protocols

Sparse-mode protocols are more suited for use in networks where group membership is widely distributed and sparsely populated. These protocols operate using a subset of the function of dense-mode protocols. The routing tree is empty by default and is filled only when individual receivers register to be part of the group. Essentially, the approach is to allow receivers to graft themselves into the routing tree when they want to receive and to prune themselves out when they are finished. Typically, dense-mode protocols use source-base trees and sparse-mode protocols use shared trees.

5.9.4 Protocol Independent Multicast Sparse-Mode (PIM-SM)

Protocol Independent Multicast Sparse-Mode (PIM-SM) and Protocol Independent Multicast Dense-Mode (PIM-DM) are a pair of multicast routing protocols that utilize the reachability and routing table information already installed in the router by the unicast routing protocols. They do not care which unicast routing protocol is used to build the routing table, and so are called "protocol independent."

PIM-SM and PIM-DM use messages from the same set and operate directly over IP using the protocol identifier 103. PIM-DM is a dense-mode routing protocol that builds a source-based tree—it is best suited to networks where the group members are packed relatively densely. PIM-SM is a sparse-mode protocol better suited to sparsely populated groups—it operates a shared tree, but since it has so much in common with PIM-DM it is able to switch over to operate with a source-based tree if it detects the need.

PIM-DM is very similar in concept to the Distance Vector Multicast Routing Protocol (DVMRP) described in Section 5.9.6, and is not described in greater detail here.

PIM-SM is documented in RFC 2362, but is being rewritten by the IETF's PIM Working Group. The new version makes no substantial changes to the protocol, although a few documentation errors are being corrected. The major difference from RFC 2362 will be in the way the protocol is described, the current RFC being a bit opaque.

PIM messages are sent as unicast when they flow between a well-known pair of PIM routers, and use the multicast address 224.0.0.13 (all PIM routers) otherwise. All PIM messages have a common 4-byte header, as shown in Figure 5.77. The remainder of each message depends on the value of the Message Type field listed in Table 5.23. The protocol version for the version of PIM described in RFC 2362 is two. The checksum is the standard IP checksum applied to the entire PIM message (with one exception—see the Register message in Table 5.23).

Table 5.23 The PIM Message Types

Message Type	Usage
0	Hello. The Hello message is sent periodically by every router on the multi-access network using the multicast address. A Designated Router is elected as the router with the numerically largest network layer (that is IP) source address. Hello retransmission ensures that router failures are detected and that a new designated router is elected if necessary.
	The body of the Hello message is built up of a series of option TLVs with 2 byte type and length fields (length is the length of the variable field only). Only one option TLV is defined in RFC 2362—the type value 2 is used for the Hold Time option, with a 2-byte value giving the number of seconds a PIM router must retain an adjacency with its neighbor if it has not received a retransmitted Hello message. The value 0xffff is used to indicate "never timeout." The default recommended value for this field is 105 seconds, representing three-and-a-half times the default retransmission time of 30 seconds.
	RFC 2362 enigmatically says, *"In general, options may be ignored; but a router must not ignore the"* [sic]. We can safely assume that this is intended to say that the Hold Time option must not be ignored.
1	Register. The Register message is used to carry multicast data packets to the Rendezvous Point (PIM-SM's name for the shared tree hub) in a unicast way.
	The body of the Register message contains 2 bits (the B-bit and the N-bit) followed by 30 bits of zero padding. After this comes the multicast data packet. Note that the checksum in the PIM header is applied only to the header and the first 32 bits of the body of the Register message. The multicast packet is not included in the checksum.
	The B-bit is the Border Bit and is left clear (zero) by a Designated Router if it knows that the source of the encapsulated multicast data packet is directly connected to it. If the source lies in a directly connected cloud, the router describes itself as a PIM Multicast Border Router (PMBR) and sets the bit to 1. PMBRs connect the PIM domain to the rest of the Internet.
	The N-bit is the Null-Register bit. It is set to 1 by a Designated Router that is sending this message with no encapsulated multicast data packet for the purpose of establishing whether it can resume sending Register messages after receiving a Register-Stop message.
2	Note that when the timer expires, the Designated Router may immediately start sending a burst of Register messages. If there are still no receivers in the group, this is a waste which can be avoided by prematurely sending a Null-Register (that is, a Register message with no encapsulated datagram) to see whether the Rendezvous Point responds with another Register-Stop.
	The body of the Register-Stop message reports the group address and the original sender's address. Since PIM-SM is protocol agnostic, these addresses are encoded in the slightly complex form shown in Figure 5.78.
3	Join/Prune. This message allows a receiver to add itself to a PIM-SM shared routing tree for a particular source in a given group. Wildcards are supported by the prefix fields shown in the address formats in Figure 5.78. This means that a receiver can easily add itself to all groups, or receive from all sources in a group.

The Join/Prune message is also used in PIM-DM to allow a receiver to add itself or prune itself to or from a source-based tree.

The format of the Join/Prune message is shown in Figure 5.79. Note that for PIM-SM running shared routing trees, the number of pruned sources in a group would always be zero.

4   Bootstrap. The Bootstrap message is used to elect a Bootstrap Router (BSR) and to distribute information about Rendezvous Points (RPs) for each group. The format of the message is a series of group addresses each followed by one or more unicast addresses of an RP.

5   Assert. The Assert message is used to resolve parallel forwarding paths which are easily detected by a router if it receives a multicast datagram traveling in what it believes is the wrong direction on its routing tree.

The Assert message is multicast to the All-PIM-Routers address and allows simple contention resolution based on the shortest path to the source (examining the SPF information available in the routing table). The metric is, therefore, carried in the Assert message.

8   Candidate-RP-Advertisement. This message is used by a router that would like to be a Rendezvous Point for one or more groups. It is unicast to the elected Bootstrap Router so that this information can be placed in the bootstrap message and sent out to all other PIM routers in the network.

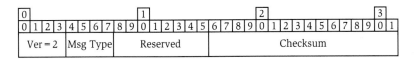

Figure 5.77 The common PIM message header.

To summarize the processing steps for PIM-SM:

- Candidate Bootstrap Routers advertise their presence using Bootstrap messages and elect a single bootstrap router (BSR).
- Candidate Rendezvous Point routers (RPs) advertise their availability to the BSR using Candidate-RP-Advertisement messages.
- The BSR selects a subset of RPs for each group and advertises them in Bootstrap messages.
- PIM-SM routers discover each other, elect a Designated Router, and maintain adjacency using Hello messages.
- A host sending to a group address multicasts its datagrams on the local network.
- The Designated Router encapsulates the multicast datagrams in Register messages that it sends to a Rendezvous Point (RP) chosen from the set on the

Bootstrap message. In practice there may be only one RP, but if there is more than one, the Designated Router is free to choose any one.

- The RP decapsulates the multicast datagrams and sends them out on the shared multicast tree.
- When the RP detects that there are no receivers left in the group, it sends a Register-Stop message to any Designated Router that sends it a Register message.
- When a receiver wants to join a shared tree it sends a Join/Prune message listing all the groups it wants to participate in and listing the senders it wants to hear from.

Figure 5.78 shows how addresses are encoded in PIM-SM. This format is necessary because PIM-SM supports many networking protocols, not just IP. The formats shown in the figure are limited to those used for IPv4.

The Join message shown in Figure 5.79 uses the source addresses shown in Figure 5.78 to indicate from which senders to a group it is prepared to receive datagrams. The S-, W-, and R-bits in the Source Address are relevant in this context. The S-bit is always set to 1 to show that PIM-SM is operating in sparse-mode (this is required for backwards compatibility with PIM-SMv1). The W-bit is set to 1 to indicate that the Join is wildcarding to include all sources in the group (this is in addition to the use of the facility to include wildcard addresses by setting the prefix mask). PIM-SM requires that Join messages sent to the rendezvous point always have the W-bit set to 1. The R-bit is set to 1 if the Join is sent to the rendezvous point, and to zero if it is sent to the source.

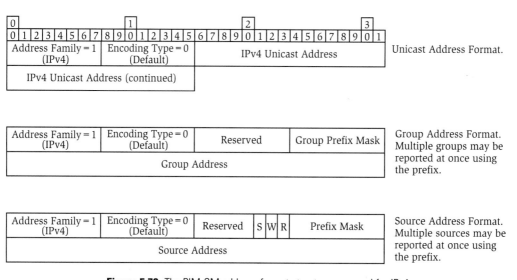

Figure 5.78 The PIM-SM address format structures as used for IPv4.

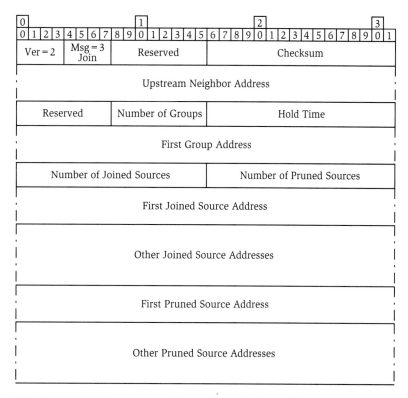

Figure 5.79 The PIM Join/Prune message lists each group being modified and shows the sources for which the upstream neighbor is being added or removed.

5.9.5 Multicast OSPF (MOSPF)

Multicast OSPF (MOSPF) is achieved with the addition of a single LSA to the standard OSPF formats. The group membership LSA (type 6) shown in Figure 5.80 is used to list the routers or networks that are members of a group. The Group ID, itself, is carried in the Link State ID field of the OSPF LSA header.

Group membership is indicated, not by repeating information about routers and networks, but by referencing the LSAs that define these resources. The reference is achieved by including the Link State type and Link State ID from the referenced LSA. There is great utility in this, not just because it reduces (slightly) the amount of traffic, but because it means that MOSPF is able to take advantage of the routing tables built for OSPF and can benefit from the withdrawal of routes, nodes, and links that are seen by OSPF.

MOSPF builds source-based trees for multicast traffic by flooding group membership to all routers. Whenever an MOSPF router is called on to forward a datagram that is addressed to the group, it knows all group destinations and

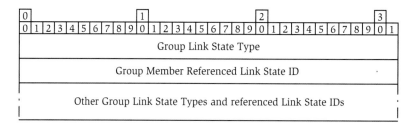

Figure 5.80 The OSPF group membership link state advertisement.

the source of the datagram. It uses this information to build an SPF tree to all destinations based at the source, finds its own place in the tree, and forwards to downstream nodes accordingly. Note that since all OSPF routers have a common view of the link state for the network, it is as easy for them to calculate routes based at other routers as it is to calculate routes for those rooted locally.

MOSPF has been shown to work in multi-area networks. In these networks, however, the way that group membership is flooded can lead to an overly dense routing tree. This means that multicast datagrams may be sent on more links than necessary, resulting in extra traffic. MOSPF could possibly benefit from a pruning mechanism as used in full dense-mode multicast routing protocols.

5.9.6 Distance Vector Multicast Routing Protocol (DVMRP)

The Distance Vector Multicast Routing Protocol (DVMRP) as first described in RFC 1075 is a dense-mode, source-based distance vector protocol. It is probably the most deployed multicast protocol through the UNIX *mrouted* program and, in reality, this program should be seen as the *de facto* standard, with the IETF standardization process struggling to keep up. To this extent, the protocol described in RFC 1075 and examined briefly here is a simple version of the full DVMRP specification.

DVMRP messages are encapsulated within IGMP packets (see Chapter 3) using the IGMP message type 0×13 and the next byte of the header showing the DVMRP packet type. There are just four DVMRP packet types, as shown in Table 5.24.

DVMRP as documented by RFC 1075 is very simple and operates as a text-book source-based tree multicast routing protocol with the addition of distance vector route advertisement to allow the calculation of preferred routes—unlike PIM-DM, DVMRP does not rely on another routing protocol to distribute and maintain a routing table. Response messages are periodically sent out by each DVMRP router to supply all routing information or to update routing information after network changes. The response message is valid only over one hop—that is, it is sent from one router to its neighbor. The routing information is managed

Table 5.24 The DVMRP Packet Types

Type	Packet
1	Response. This message carries information about routes to one or more destinations.
2	Request. This message is used to request information about routes to one or more destinations.
3	Nonmembership report. Used to notify the routing domain that a destination should be pruned from the routing tree.
4	Nonmembership cancellation. Cancels a previous Nonmembership Report. This cancellation is a graft request.

just as for any distance vector protocol, and timeouts and poisoned split horizons are used as described earlier in this chapter.

When a router is started it sends out a Request message to all of its neighbors (that is, on each of its configured DVMRP-capable interfaces) to encourage them to send Response messages with their up-to-date routing information. Note, however, that in many cases DVMRP is run over tunnels, not directly over the physical interfaces. There is no issue with this provided that the tunnels are installed as virtual interfaces on the router and configured for DVMRP support. DVMRP routers are also required to use IGMP to keep track of the group member hosts on their local networks.

RFC 1075 presents a relatively straightforward incremental algorithm for building a dense source-based tree using the routing information supplied by the Response messages. The aim is to be able to reach all parts of the network through the least cost paths without any parallel paths that would cause datagram duplication.

An edge router that receives a datagram and has no group members directly attached issues a Nonmembership report message back to the router that sent it the datagram. This prunes it from the tip of the source-based tree. If the upstream router receives a Nonmembership report message from each of its attached downstream routers, it knows it can prune itself from the tree by sending a Nonmembership report message further upstream.

If an edge router that has previously pruned itself from the tree is told through IGMP that one of its directly attached hosts wishes to join the group, it sends a Nonmembership cancellation message to the upstream router. If the upstream router is still in the tree, it grafts the edge router back in and resumes forwarding group datagrams to the edge router. If the upstream router had also pruned itself from the tree, it sends a Nonmembership cancellation message further upstream.

5.9.7 The MBONE

For a long time, the majority of Internet Service Providers did not have multicast protocols enabled on the routers in their networks. The reasons ranged from lack of support in older routers, through a natural caution about enabling unproven function without sufficient customer demand, to plain fear of the unknown. So how did multicast get going in the Internet?

Multicast routing grew up within private networks (usually academic institutions or corporate networks). These networks were experimenting with multicast traffic for audio and video streaming, and ran multicast protocols internally. It soon became an interesting challenge to join these networks together to achieve wider distribution of real-time traffic, and it was apparent to the IETF and the Internet Research Task Force (IRTF) that they should play an active part in this project. As a way to encourage this, it became a policy of the IETF to stream audio and video feeds from some of their meetings.

The connection of multicast networks was christened the Multicast Backbone (MBONE). Originally, the MBONE consisted of a multicast network superimposed on the Internet and supported by workstations that run one or many multicast routing protocols to act as multicast routers. Since the backbone itself did not support the multicast routing protocols, these workstations were connected together using virtual links (or tunnels) to form their own network, the MBONE.

If the nodes that supported the MBONE had been extracted from the whole Internet and shown just connected by their virtual links, we would have seen a fairly standard picture of a network. The core of the network exclusively ran DVMRP, but other routing protocols such as PIM and MOSPF were used in the networks at the edges both for real value and for experimentation. RFC 2715 provides some useful notes for routers that need to share multicast routing information between multicast routing protocols.

It is fair to say that Service Providers had mixed feelings about the existence of the MBONE. The virtual links between the MBONE routers could force large amounts of traffic through the real underlying links since multicast applications are often high-bandwidth audio or video streams. This situation could be made much worse when a source had to send its data halfway across the Internet to reach an MBONE router that would forward the data to a destination that might have been adjacent to the source. If an MBONE application was suddenly enabled, the Service Provider could see a dramatic increase in the amount of data on particular links in their network.

Nevertheless, the MBONE saw steady growth. In 1995 there were 901 routers participating in the MBONE spread over 20 countries. As a proportion of the 48,500 subnetworks operating in the Internet at that time, this was a very small amount, but the figures have grown consistently and in early 1999 there were 4178 routers attached to the MBONE. The focus, then as now, was on real-time multimedia streaming using the Real-time Transport Protocol (RTP) described in Chapter 7. The advent of new ways to encode audio and video streams (such as MP3) has made this concept even more popular.

Experimentation with multicast was of great benefit to Service Providers, who looked forward to offering new services to their customers (for which they could charge) and who stood to benefit from the long-term reduction in bandwidth requirements that multicast can offer. But in the shorter term, the growth of the MBONE was causing overloading of networks and was of no particular benefit to Service Providers, who found themselves playing host to a super-network over which they had no control. It was time for the Service Providers to offer multicast access.

The IETF formed the MBONE Deployment Working Group (MBONED) as a forum to coordinate the deployment and operation of multicast routing across the global Internet. Responsibility for the administration of multicast networking was restructured so that it followed the hierarchy of the Internet. This meant that the first port of call for users wanting multicast access was their ISP or enterprise network operator. These bodies, in turn, escalated the requirement to their regional Service Providers. The use of tunnels to nonlocal routers to provide multicast feeds was deprecated.

But it soon became clear that DVMRP was not a suitable core multicast routing protocol. DVMRP has many of the drawbacks of other distance vector routing protocols, such as the Routing Information Protocol described in Section 5.4. It has similar scaling and resilience concerns, and it is extremely slow to respond to changes in network topology and connectivity. Some other multicast routing protocol was required for the Internet.

But, although MOSPF and PIM work well in enterprise networks, they don't scale well beyond a few hundred routers. Each MOSPF or PIM router must store the multicast spanning tree for each other router—an impossible task as the number of routers grows. Furthermore, the time spent to recompute or redistribute these spanning trees each time a host entered or left a multicast group would be prohibitive. None of the existing protocols was good enough for the evolution of the MBONE, and in 1999 the IETF formed a new working group to develop the *Multicast Source Discovery Protocol* (MSDP).

In forming the MSDP Working Group, the IETF acknowledged that this protocol was an interim solution. The solution of choice was the *Border Gateway Multicast Protocol* (BGMP), but it was recognized that this would take longer to develop, test, and deploy. In the meantime MSDP offered a protocol that could connect networks that used shared trees without the need for interdomain shared trees. MSDP remains an Internet draft (currently on its twenty-first version), but is deployed and is replacing DVMRP. It is applicable to all shared tree protocols (such as PIM-SM and CBT) although it was specifically developed for PIM-SM. It can also be used for those multicast protocols that keep active source information at the network borders (such as MOSPF and PIM-DM).

In brief, MSDP operates by forming peering relationships between a router in each participating multicast domain. These relationships operate over TCP connections and form point-to-point information exchanges between the domains. A full mesh of such connections allows each domain to discover multicast sources in the other domains and so add them to its own source trees. Since a full mesh would be unmanageable, there is scope within MSDP for information to be passed along from one domain to another.

It was always envisaged that MSDP would have a relatively short life-span. The real solution to multicast routing in the Internet would be provided by BGMP. The Internet draft for BGMP is currently in its sixth revision and is reaching stability and it will soon be time for Service Providers to develop a migration strategy from MSDP to BGMP.

BGMP recognizes the drawbacks in the existing multicast routing protocols that make them unsuitable for deployment in the global Internet, or even across multiple provider domains. Even when the tunneling techniques of the early MBONE were replaced, the existing multicast routing protocols put undue stress on Service Providers' networks since they called on transit routers to maintain state for multicast groups over which the Service Providers had no control, some of which were managed by computers in other domains. Worse still, the Service Providers had to maintain this state information even if none of the group members were in their domain (that is, none of their customers were senders or receivers in the group).

BGMP is designed as a scalable multicast routing protocol that addresses the Service Providers' concerns and facilitates multicast across multidomain networks. BGMP uses a global root for its multicast distribution tree (just like PIM-SM), but in BGMP that root is an entire domain instead of a single router. Like the Core Based Tree protocol (CBT) described briefly in the next section, BGMP builds bidirectional shared trees, but these are trees of domains, not of routers. Thus, BGMP operates multicast at a higher level in the routing hierarchy from the previous routing protocols.

When BGMP is used as the interdomain multicast routing protocol, the domains are left to continue to use their existing multicast routing protocols such as PIM-SM. This is analogous to the role of BGP as an Exterior Gateway Protocol, and the continued use of Interior Gateway Protocols such as OSPF within unicast domains.

5.9.8 A New Multicast Architecture

The multicast architecture that has been in use for the last decade is called *Any Source Multicast* (ASM). ASM develops multicast as described in RFC 1112 (Host Extensions for IP Multicasting), and works on the principle that anyone can send to a multicast group and anyone can join the multicast group to receive. ASM has been shown to be a workable model, but it has its complexities and despite some successful deployments it has scalability concerns.

The *Single Source Multicast* (SSM) architecture takes advantage of the fact that in most multicast distributions (such as video-on-demand, Internet radio, or file

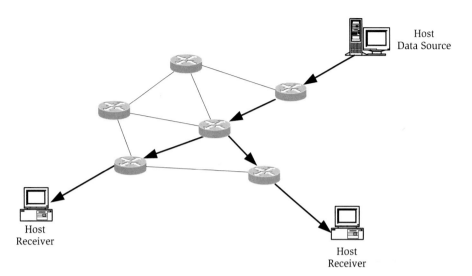

Figure 5.81 In the single source multicast model it is very easy to build the multicast tree based at
the data source by simply adding the receivers according to the shortest path from the
source.

distribution) there is only one sender in a multicast group. Any number of recipients may join or leave the group over time, but the architecture is significantly simplified by the knowledge that the distribution tree for the group has a single root.

The simplification in the multicast architecture opens the way for changes to the multicast routing protocols. The fundamental operations don't need to change since distribution trees still need to be built, but the ways in which these trees are constructed can be managed more simply. Figure 5.81 shows how much simpler an SSM system is. When a new receiver is added to the group it is simply added into the tree according to the shortest path from the source. There is no longer any requirement for a rendezvous point. One notable feature of this model is that a host cannot simply register its desire to join a group, but must also specify the group and source.

It is still the early days for the SSM architecture, but it offers some serious improvements over ASM that will attract considerable attention. The multicast address space is simplified since the group address is now specific to the context of the data source—this makes multicast groups a little like cable channels rather than actual groups. The complexity of the multicast routing process is greatly simplified, with consequent improvements in scalability and robustness. Security is enhanced because there can be only one sender in a group and the receiver's registration for a specific source and group pairing can be more easily verified.

SSM still has some questions to answer. As illustrated in Figure 3.6, the shortest paths from source to receivers may not give the best resource sharing within the network; achieving this may require some more complex routing techniques. Nevertheless, the clinching fact will be that SSM fits most of the significant applications that use multicast today and so its simplifications and benefits will be integrated into the existing multicast infrastructure.

Work is well advanced on some of the protocol features necessary to support the SSM architecture. In particular, the Internet Group Management Protocol (IGMP—see Chapter 3) has recently been extended to become IGMPv3 in RFC 3376. The changes are simple, backwards-compatible modifications to allow a host to specify the data source in which it is interested when it registers as a member of a group. The changes have been quickly adopted by implementations (for example, Windows XP includes IGMPv3).

IGMPv3 concerns itself only with the Group Membership Query and the IGMPv3 Group Membership Report. Other messages must be supported for backwards compatibility with older implementations. The Group Membership Query retains the same message number (0×11) as in previous versions of the protocol, and the message begins with the same fields as in the past, but new fields are added to the end of the message. This makes the message comprehensible to old versions of the protocol, but enhances it for more recent implementations. Figure 5.82 shows the new format of the Group Membership Query with the backwards-compatible fields shaded in gray.

The IGMPv3 Group Membership Report message has a completely new format in IGMPv3 to allow reporting on multiple groups within each report, as shown in Figure 5.83. As can be seen from the two figures, IGMPv3 allows a source address to be associated with each group, providing the level of control needed for SSM. In fact, the designers of IGMPv3 have played it safe and allowed for multiple sources to be associated with each group, giving the potential for an intermediate architecture with limited sources somewhere between ASM and SSM.

For the remaining details of the fields of the IGMPv3 messages, the reader is referred to RFC 3376.

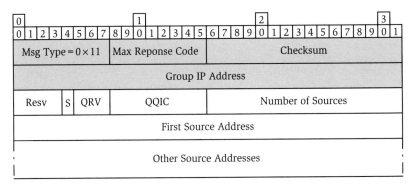

Figure 5.82 The IGMP Group Membership Query message is extended in IGMPv3.

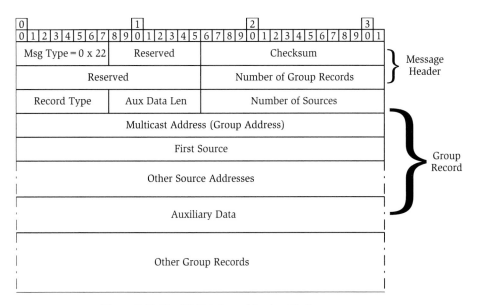

Figure 5.83 The IGMPv3 Group Membership Report message.

5.9.9 Choosing a Multicast Routing Protocol

This chapter has introduced just three of a much larger set of multicast routing protocols. Table 5.25 provides a larger list and compares the features they offer and the way they operate.

The choice between multicast routing protocols can be narrowed by the environment in which you are operating. Clearly, if you have multiple ASs you must run an interdomain protocol. If you have a large, well-connected network but sparsely populated groups, a sparse-mode protocol will prune out the traffic more quickly and result in less broadcasting of unwanted information. However, when the network grows over several hundred routers, sparse-mode protocols struggle to store the required distribution trees, and may spend most of their time updating the routing trees as hosts join and leave multicast groups.

If the groups being managed have more than a very few sources, the routing protocols that use shared trees will scale better, but if the applications involve simple point-to-multipoint streaming, then source-based trees provide a simpler solution.

On the other hand, shared tree routing has two drawbacks. As illustrated in Figure 5.75, the data paths may incur some inefficiency as datagrams traverse the same links on their way to the hub and back to group members. Also, this hub and spoke technique tends to concentrate the traffic into a single point (the hub), which may overload resources around the hub. This last point, however,

Table 5.25 A Comparison of Some Multicast Routing Protocols

Protocol	Mode	Tree Type	Domain Role
PIM-SM	Sparse	Shared	Intra- and interdomain
PIM-DM	Dense (broadcast and prune)	Source-based	Intradomain
CBT (Core Based Trees)	Sparse	Shared	Intra- and interdomain
MOSPF	Dense (domainwide report)	Source-based	Intradomain
MSDP	N/A	N/A	Interdomain
BGMP	Dense	Source-based	Interdomain
DVMRP	Dense (broadcast and prune)	Source-based	Intra- and interdomain

cuts both ways—as was discussed in Chapter 3, one of the decision points in multicast routing is whether to send the datagrams over the shortest routes or the routes with the most shared links since the latter can reduce the total amount of traffic in the network. In some circumstances, shared trees can make very efficient use of links and reduce the amount of traffic in the network even with the inefficiencies that they may include.

Perhaps the biggest concern with the shared tree protocols is the fact that a central hub presents the problem of a single point of failure. If the hub node or a nearby link fails, the network needs to elect a new hub and to redirect traffic to that hub. This process may take some time, and during that time traffic is still trying to reach the old hub and is probably being discarded.

An important distinction between the protocols is whether they are driven by data or by control events. Data events occur when multicast datagrams arrive at a router, and include the Prune messages sent by dense-mode protocols. Control events are triggered by new hosts subscribing to a group, or the manual configuration of a router, and include dense-mode Graft messages or the broadcast of group membership information in MOSPF. Dense-mode protocols may be reasonable for use within enterprise networks where the traffic has its source and destination within the single network, but the protocols are not yet sufficiently proven for an ISP to consider operating a dense-mode protocol.

Some of the other protocols have specific concerns or benefits as follows:

- The Core Based Trees protocol (CBT) is an experimental IETF standard. It is a sparse-mode protocol that operates by sending multicast group Join messages toward the core of the network and ultimately to a core router. In this way, CBT establishes a multicast tree passing through the core router. In contrast to PIM-SM, the multicast trees in CBT are bidirectional—that is, packets may flow up and down the trees. CBT is, however, extremely sensitive to the placement of the core router and so is unlikely to become a widely deployed multicast routing protocol. Within restricted domains, however, CBT can be very efficient and should scale much better than the flood-and-prune dense-mode protocols. Nevertheless, CBT has seen very little development and is unlikely to take off.

- Where OSPF is already deployed, the increment to MOSPF is relatively small, and so MOSPF may turn out to be the best choice regardless of other concerns.

- The Multicast Source Discovery Protocol (MSDP) is not a multicast routing protocol. Nevertheless, it is currently important in the MBONE as a scalable way of connecting together multicast domains and allowing them to build source trees that include sources in other domains. This protocol was developed to provide a short-term replacement to DVMRP in the global Internet until the new BGMP is developed and deployed.

- Multiprotocol BGP (MBGP) was not specifically developed as a multicast solution. It should not be confused with the Border Gateway Multicast Protocol (BGMP). As described in Section 5.8.3, MBGP facilitates communication of additional protocol information such as that needed for Multiprotocol Label Switching (MPLS) or for Virtual Private Networks (VPNs). However, MBGP also can be used to carry the details of multicast IP routes. Specifically, MBGP enables multicast routing policy across the Internet by connecting multicast networks within and between BGP autonomous systems. Thus, MBGP is not really a multicast routing protocol, but it is a means to distribute multicast routing information on behalf of (for example) PIM, and is used widely for interdomain multicast routing.

- The Border Gateway Multicast Protocol (BGMP), however, is a real interdomain multicast protocol designed to address the issues and concerns with previous multicast protocols. Although BGMP is still only an Internet draft, it is slated to become the interdomain multicast routing protocol for the global Internet.

- Although DVMRP has seen quite a bit of action in the MBONE, it is now being phased out in favor of MSDP and eventually BGMP. It was never suitable for extensive deployment in core networks because it has similar scaling and resilience concerns to RIP (see Section 5.4) and this makes it inappropriate for use in large or complex networks.

There are many factors influencing the choice of a multicast routing protocol and the whole area is still very immature. Ultimately, the choice of protocol may depend on the availability of protocol implementations and the amount of deployment experience that has been gathered. PIM-SM is reasonably widely available, and MOSPF has a fair number of implementations. The other protocols are less well deployed.

5.10 Other Routing Protocols

There are more routing protocols than you can shake a stick at. Some are historic, most are experimental, and a few were mistakes. This section aims to do nothing more than recognize the existence of some of these protocols and point the interested reader in the right direction for more information.

5.10.1 Inter-Gateway Routing Protocol (IGRP) and Enhanced Inter-Gateway Routing Protocol (EIGRP)

The Inter-Gateway Routing Protocol (IGRP) is a proprietary distance vector IGP developed by Cisco to route IP and non-IP traffic. IGRP was designed to remove many of the deficiencies in the first version of RIP and to be sufficiently flexible to route traffic for any network protocol. Notably, IGRP operates over IP as protocol number 9 without utilizing UDP as a transport protocol, and can support the concept of *process domains*, which are similar to areas, and is also sensitive to the existence of external autonomous systems.

IGRP uses a tightly packed, "efficient" packet format to distribute routing information and extends the per-destination information to include not just a hop-count (metric) but also delay, bandwidth, reliability, and load information. This is a significant step from a simple distance vector protocol toward a fully fledged traffic engineering routing protocol, and Cisco uses IGRP to manage load balancing across parallel paths that do not have the same cost. IGRP is, however, not a classless routing protocol (that is, it does not support aggregation) and does not include security protection.

As RIP evolved into RIPv2, so IGRP was extended and improved to produce the Enhanced Inter-Gateway Routing Protocol (EIGRP). EIGRP has full support for CIDR, and includes security and authentication measures such as MD5.

Another big change in EIGRP is the way paths are computed and distributed. EIGRP attempts to fit in between the standard distance vector model where best paths are progressively calculated within the network and forwarded between routers, and the link state approach where each router is responsible for the full path computation. The former technique leads to slow convergence and is prone to routing loops, and the latter requires significant storage and processing capabilities on routers. EIGRP performs *diffusing computations* on each router and forwards the results—this is claimed to significantly reduce convergence times and guarantee that the network remains loop free.

The best source for information on IGRP and EIGRP is Cisco. *Routing TCP/IP—Volume 1*, written by Jeff Doyle and published by Cisco Press, is a good starting point.

5.10.2 ES-IS

The OSI link state IGP IS-IS is described in some detail in Section 5.6. It provides routing function between routers (intermediate systems) in a network that may use one or more network layer protocols including IP.

In unicast IP networks, routing information is exchanged between hosts and routers using ICMP (see Chapter 2), and this protocol is used even when the IGP is IS-IS. However, ISO has defined its own protocol to run between hosts (end systems) and routers, called ES-IS. ES-IS is documented in the ISO document ISO N4053 which is reproduced in RFC 995.

Since ES-IS is not used for IP, we will spend no more time on it.

5.10.3 Interdomain Routing Protocol (IDRP)

The Interdomain Routing Protocol is an ISO standard built on BGP. It addresses the need for an EGP within the OSI protocol stack by supporting flexibility of address formats and scalability of administrative domains (that is, autonomous systems). When RFC 1476 was written in July 1993 to document IDRP, the expectation was that IDRP would replace BGP as the Internet's EGP, but BGP-4 (March 1995) seems to be holding on. Nevertheless, a key RFC (RFC 1863) that describes how OSPF interacts with BGP was written with two threads to describe both BGP and IDRP integration with OSPF.

IDRP was the initial favorite EGP of the designers of IPv6 because it had sufficient flexibility to handle the larger addresses needed by IPv6. However, the multiprotocol extensions added to BGP-4 (described in Section 5.8) mean that BGP can now also support IPv6 and IDRP is losing favor.

5.10.4 Internet Route Access Protocol

The Internet Route Access Protocol (RAP, not IRAP) is a distance vector protocol documented in RFC 1476. RAP is an experimental protocol aimed at spanning the entirety of the routing space from local networks to Service Provider backbones with one single distance vector protocol that doesn't recognize interior or exterior systems, except as a product of policy.

RAP rightly asserts that link state databases will not scale well enough to meet these targets and goes on to claim that a distance vector approach is the only viable solution. The fate of RAP cannot have been helped by the fact that it uses IPv7 (sic), an experimental new IP version defined in RFC 1475, but not taken very seriously by the Internet community.

5.10.5 Hot Standby Router Protocol (HSRP) and Virtual Router Redundancy Protocol (VRRP)

Cisco's Hot Standby Router Protocol (HSRP) is documented in RFC 2281. This RFC does not represent the product of an IETF Working Group, but is presented so that the rest of the Internet community can see how this protocol works and possibly implement it.

HSRP is run between routers on a subnetwork to create the impression of a single virtual router to which the hosts send their packets for forwarding. The routers negotiate their roles to act as primary forwarder or for load sharing, and if one router fails the others take over without the hosts realizing that anything has happened—they remain attached to the single virtual router.

HSRP is an IP protocol that operates using UDP as its transport protocol. Most of the protocol is concerned with how the routers form a group to represent the virtual router, and how they negotiate their roles within the group. A host or another router communicating with the virtual router uses a single IP address and MAC address to reach the virtual router. This means that all routers in the group must listen to the same MAC address (that is, it is a group address), and that each router in the group, as well as having its own IP address (for management and for HSRP communications), must also be able to represent itself as the IP address of the virtual router. This is illustrated in Figure 5.84.

Note that HSRP may be covered by a U.S. patent, but that Cisco will grant license on "reasonable, nondiscriminatory terms."

Like HSRP, the Virtual Router Redundancy Protocol (VRRP) is designed to manage multiple routers that present themselves to a local network as a single virtual router to achieve high availability and tolerance to router faults. VRRP, documented in RFC 2338, can be seen as an attempt to define an "open" protocol

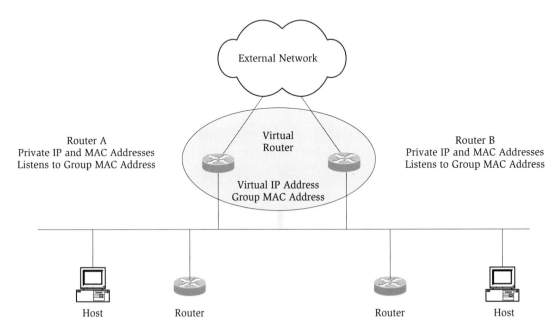

Figure 5.84 A virtual router is constructed from two or more routers using a group MAC address and masquerades as a single router using a common IP address.

freely available to the entire Internet community in the face of the proprietary solution offered by Cisco's HSRP and the similar IP Standby Protocol from DEC.

VRRP is conceptually similar to HSRP, but the routers that form part of the virtual router retain their unique identities. Thus, a host communicates with (or believes it communicates with) one of the members of the virtual router, and the routers handle the process of managing their MAC address advertisements so that the packets are sent to whichever router is currently the operational master within the virtual router grouping. This allows hosts to use any of the virtual router IP addresses on the LAN as the default first hop router. This makes it possible to provide high availability (that is, protection against failure) for default paths on hosts connected to the LAN, without requiring configuration of dynamic routing or router discovery protocols on every end-host.

5.10.6 Historic Protocols

Lest we forget those routing protocols that went before us to blaze a trail, this final section is devoted to their memory.

- Gateway to Gateway Protocol (GGP, RFC 823) was a distance vector IGP that was run in the ARPANET in the early days of the Internet.
- Exterior Gateway Protocol (EGP, RFC 827 and RFC 904), the Internet's first exterior gateway protocol, used the same message formats as GGP and was a distance vector protocol. The experience with EGP, which operationally forced autonomous systems to be arranged in a hierarchy to prevent loops, led the drive to develop BGP.
- Border Gateway Protocol (BGPv1, RFC 1105; BGPv2, RFC 1163; BGPv3, RFC 1267) had three versions before the current, widely deployed BGPv4. The process of protocol development through discussion, deployment, and evolution may look messy, but the gradual change has led to a protocol that is not over-burdened with unnecessary features. A report (RFC 1265, BGP Protocol Analysis) gives some insight into this evolution.
- Interdomain Policy Routing (IDPR, RFC 1479—not to be confused with IDRP) was an attempt to produce a link state exterior gateway protocol. For a while it looked as though IDPR was in head-to-head competition with BGP and might displace it as the Internet's EGP. IDPR has great flexibility and offers some very rich policy-based control of exactly the sort that Service Providers might want to apply to their routers to control and regulate the traffic flowing between autonomous systems. This flexibility, however, was IDPR's undoing since it made the protocol far too complex. Add to this the fact that ISPs were not ready to trust the wholesale management of their network policy to a routing protocol (preferring manual control through an OSS), and IDPR stood no real chance against BGP.
- The Hello Protocol (RFC 891) was a distance vector IGP that used as its metric measured delay on the data paths, preferring the quickest path rather than

the shortest path. This protocol saw some significant early deployment in the National Science Foundation's network (NFSNET) before it was replaced by an early version of IS-IS.

5.11 Further Reading

Routing Frameworks and Overviews

Routing TCP/IP—Volume 1, by Jeff Doyle (1998). Cisco Press. This book provides a thorough and easy-to-read introduction to all manner of routing issues. It usefully covers the differences between the modes of route distribution and explains how many of the routing protocols work. Notably, this book includes a description of IGRP and EIGRP, two of Cisco's own IP routing protocols.

Interconnections: Bridges and Routers, by Radia Perlman (1999). Addison-Wesley. Generally regarded as the cornerstone of routing texts, this book provides excellent instruction on routing as a problem to be solved and describes the different solutions.

Routing in Communications Networks, edited by Martha Steenstrup (1995). Prentice-Hall. This is a useful collection of papers on routing protocols and techniques written by experts in the field, many of whom played pivotal roles in the development of the foremost Internet routing protocols.

Algorithms, by Robert Sedgewick (1988). Addison-Wesley. A handy volume that explained many important algorithms in use in computing today (including Dijkstra's algorithm and the Patricia tree), this book has now been replaced by several series of larger volumes that both explain the algorithms and give working examples in C, C++, or Java.

RFC 1812—Requirements for IP Version 4 Routers
RFC 2236—Internet Group Management Protocol, Version 2
RFC 2519—A Framework for Interdomain Route Aggregation

Distance Vector Routing Protocols

RFC 1058—Routing Information Protocol
RFC 1721—RIP Version 2 Protocol Analysis
RFC 1722—RIP Version 2 Protocol Applicability Statement
RFC 1723—RIP Version 2

Note that RFC 1058 which defines the Routing Information Protocol (a distance vector protocol) also provides a good introduction to distance vector routing.

Link State Protocols

OSPF—Anatomy of an Internet Routing Protocol, by John Moy (1998). Addison-Wesley. This is the definitive work on OSPF written by the man who authored the OSPF RFCs.

IS-IS and OSPF: A Comparative Anatomy is an excellent presentation by Dave Katz available on the Juniper Networks web site at http://www.juniper.net.

RFC 905—ISO Transport Protocol Specification (ISO DP 8073). This RFC includes a statement of Fletcher's checksum algorithm.
RFC 2328—OSPF Version 2
RFC 2370—The OSPF Opaque LSA Option
RFC 2740—OSPF for IPv6
RFC 3101—The OSPF Not-So-Stubby Area (NSSA) Option
RFC 3137—OSPF Stub Router Advertisement
RFC 1142—OSI IS-IS Intradomain Routing Protocol
RFC 1195—Use of OSI IS-IS for Routing in TCP/IP and Dual Environments
RFC 3358—Optional Checksums in Intermediate System to Intermediate System

The Internet Draft, draft-thorup-ospf-harmful, presents a discussion of some circumstances under which multiple areas might be considered to worsen rather than improve the scalability of an IGP.

Path Vector Protocols

BGP4—Inter-domain Routing in the Internet, by John Stewart (1998). Addison-Wesley. This handy little book covers BGP-4 admirably and extensively in just 115 pages.

RFC 1771—A Border Gateway Protocol 4 (BGP-4)
RFC 1863—A BGP/IDRP Route Server Alternative to a Full Mesh Routing
RFC 1997—BGP Communities Attribute
RFC 2283—Multiprotocol Extensions for BGP-4
RFC 2796—BGP Route Reflection—An Alternative to Full Mesh IBGP
RFC 2858—Multiprotocol Extensions for BGP-4
RFC 2918—Route Refresh Capability for BGP-4
RFC 3107—Carrying Label Information in BGP-4
RFC 3392—Capabilities Advertisement with BGP-4

Multicast Protocols

RFC 1075—Distance Vector Multicast Routing Protocol
RFC 1112—Host Extensions for IP Multicasting
RFC 1584—Multicast Extensions to OSPF

RFC 2189—Core Based Trees (CBT version 2) Multicast Routing

RFC 2236—Internet Group Management Protocol, Version 2

RFC 2362—Protocol Independent Multicast-Sparse Mode (PIM-SM): Protocol Specification

RFC 2715—Interoperability Rules for Multicast Routing Protocols

RFC 3376—Internet Group Management Protocol, Version 3

Two key protocols are still in draft form: draft-ietf-msdp-spec documents the Multicast Source Discovery Protocol (MSDP) and draft-ietf-bgmp-spec describes the Border Gateway Multicast Protocol (BGMP).

More information on the experience of deploying multicast routing protocols can be found on the web site of the IETF's Multicast Backbone Deployment working group at http://www.ietf.org/html.charters/mboned-charter.html.

Chapter 6

IP Service Management

We do not live in an egalitarian society and it is, therefore, no surprise that with finite limits on the availability of Internet resources such as processing power and bandwidth, there is a desire to offer grades of service within the Internet. For example, a bronze standard of service might be the cheapest for a user, simply promising "best-effort" data delivery—the data may arrive, or it may not, and if it does, it may take some time. Silver and gold service levels might make increasing pledges as to the timeliness and quality of data delivery. The platinum service might guarantee the user reliable and instant delivery of any amount of data.

To apply levels of service to the traffic flows passing through a router, it is necessary to classify or categorize the packets so that they can be given different treatments and get preferential access to the resources within the router. This chapter examines some popular mechanisms for categorizing packets, for describing flows, and for reserving resources. Although packet categorization can be implemented differently in each router, it is important for the provision of services within a network that there is a common understanding of the service level applied to the packets within a flow. This is achieved by *Differentiated Services* (DiffServ), which allows individual packets to be labeled according to the service the originator has contracted. *Integrated Services* (IntServ) provides a standardized way to describe packet flows in terms of the amount of traffic that will be generated and the resources needed to support them. The *Resource Reservation Protocol* (RSVP) is a signaling protocol designed to install reserved resources at routers to support packet flows.

In considering how to achieve grades of service within an IP host or router it is helpful to examine a simplified view of the internal organization of such a device. Figure 6.1 shows a router with just two interfaces. Packets are received from the interfaces and moved to the Inwards Holding Area where they are held in buffers until they can be routed. This is an important function because the rate of arrival of packets may be faster than the momentary rate of packet routing—in other words, although the routing component may be able to handle packets at the same aggregate rate as the sum of the line speeds, it is possible that two packets will arrive at the same time. After each packet has been routed, it is

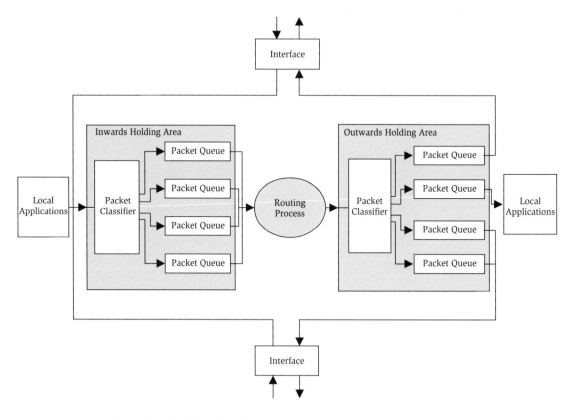

Figure 6.1 Simplified view of the internals of a router showing packet queues.

moved to an Outwards Holding Area and stored in buffers until it can be sent
on the outgoing interface.

These holding areas offer the opportunity for prioritizing traffic. Instead of
implementing each as a simple first-in first-out (FIFO) queue, they can be constructed as a series (or queue) of queues—the packets pass through a packet
classifier which determines their priority and queues them accordingly.

The queues in the holding areas obviously use up system resources (memory)
to store the packets and it is possible that the queues will become full when
there are no more resources available. The same categorization of packets can
be used to determine what should happen then. The simple approach says that
when a packet can't be queued it should simply be dropped (recall that this is
acceptable in IP), but with prioritized queues it is also possible to discard packets
from low-priority queues to make room for more important packets. A balance
can also be implemented that favors discarding packets from the Inwards Holding
Area before discarding from the Outwards Holding Area so that work that has
been done to route a received packet is less likely to be wasted.

The queues in the holding areas can also be enhanced by limiting the amount of the total system resources that they can consume. This effectively places upper thresholds on the queue sizes so that no one queue can use more than its share, which is particularly useful if the queues are implemented per interface since it handles the case in which an outgoing interface becomes stuck or runs slowly. This introduces the concept of an upper limit to the amount of resources that a queue can consume, and it is also possible to dedicate resources to a queue—that is, to pre-allocate resources for the exclusive use by a queue so that the total system resources are shared out between the queues. With careful determination of the levels of pre-allocation it is possible to guarantee particular service levels to flows within the network.

6.1 Choosing How to Manage Services

The traditional operation model of IP networks was based on *best-effort* service delivery. No guarantees were made about the quality of service provided to applications or network users, and each packet was treated as a separate object and forwarded within the network with no precedence or priority over other packets. Additionally, a fundamental design consideration of IP and the Internet was to make simplicity more important than anything else.

But the Internet was not conceived for the sophisticated real-time exchange of data for applications that are sensitive not only to the quality of the delivered data, but also to the timeliness and smoothness of that delivery. New applications have left background, bulk data transfer far behind and make more sophisticated demands on the quality of service delivered by the network.

Quality of service is a concept familiar in the telecommunications industry. Developed principally to carry voice traffic, the modern telecommunications network is sensitive to the aspects of noise, distortion, loss, delay, and jitter that make the human voice unintelligible or unacceptably hard to decipher. Nevertheless, the industry is dominated by proprietary protocols notwithstanding the existence of standardized solutions and the regulatory requirements to converge on interoperable approaches. Attempts to manage services in IP networks, therefore, are able to draw on plenty of experience and concepts, but no clear operational solution.

Further, some key differences exist between the structure of IP networks and telecommunications networks. Perhaps most obvious among these differences is the way that telecommunications networks are connection-oriented or virtual-circuit-based so that traffic for a given flow reliably follows the same path through the network. IP traffic is, of course, routed on a packet-by-packet basis. Other differences lie in the decentralized management structure of IP networks, and emphasis in IP networks on the management of elements (that is nodes, links, etc.) and not of data flows.

It is important in this light to examine what needs to be managed in order to provide service management and to attempt to address only those issues that are relevant to an IP framework. The first point to note is that in an IP network the distribution framework that is being managed (that is, the network elements that forward IP traffic) is identical to the management framework. In other words, the IP network is the tool that is used to manage the IP network. This raises several questions about the effect of service management activities on the services being managed. For example, a service management process that relied on regular and detailed distribution of statistical information to a central management point would significantly increase the amount of network traffic and would reduce the ability to provide the highest levels of throughput for applications. Thus, one of the criteria for service management in an IP network is to retain a high level of distributed function with individual network elements responsible for monitoring and maintaining service levels. This distributed model only becomes more important when we consider that IP networks are typically large (in terms of the number of network elements and the connectivity of the network).

Early attempts at service management have focused on traffic prioritization (see the ToS field in the IP header) and on policing the traffic flows at the edge of the network or on entry to administrative domains. This is not really service management so much as a precautionary administrative policy designed to reduce the chances of failing to meet service level agreements. It doesn't address any of the questions of guaranteeing service levels or of taking specific action within the network to ensure quality of service. Only by providing mechanisms to quantify and qualify both requested service and actual traffic is it possible to manage the traffic flows so that quality of service is provided.

In fact, an important requirement of IP service management is that any process that is applied should extend across management domains. This means that it should be possible for an application in one network to specify its quality of service requirements and have them applied across the end-to-end path to the destination even if that path crosses multiple networks. It is not enough to meet the service requirements in one network: they must be communicated and met along the whole path. This consideration opens up many issues related to charging between Service Providers and the ultimate billing to the end user, because the provision of a specific quality of service is most definitely a chargeable feature. In a competitive world, Service Providers will vie with each other to provide service management features and traffic quality at different price points, and will want to pass on the costs. The bottom line is that it must be possible to track service requests as they cross administrative boundaries. Techniques to measure the services actually provided are a follow-up requirement for both the end user and for Service Providers that are interconnected.

It is only a short step from these requirements to the desire to be able to route traffic according to the availability and real, financial cost of services. This provides further input to constraint-based path computation described in the previous chapter.

Not all of these issues are handled well by the service management techniques described in this chapter. As initial attempts to address the challenges, they focus largely on the classification of traffic and services, and techniques to make service requests. Some of these considerations do not begin to be properly handled until we look at traffic engineering concepts introduced in Chapter 8.

6.2 Differentiated Services

Differentiated Services (DiffServ) is an approach to classifying packets within the network so that they may be handled differently by prioritizing those that belong to "more important" data flows and, when congestion arises, discarding first those packets that belong to the "least important" flows. The different ways data is treated within a DiffServ network are called *policies*. For different policies to be applied to traffic it is necessary to have some way to differentiate the packets. DiffServ re-uses the Type of Service (ToS) byte in the IP header to flag packets as belonging to different classes which may then be subjected to different policies. The assignment of packets to different classes in DiffServ is sometimes referred to as *coloring*.

The policies applied to packets of different colors is not standardized. It is seen as a network implementation or configuration issue to ensure that the meaning of a particular color is interpreted uniformly across the network. DiffServ simply provides a standard way of flagging the packets as having different colors.

6.2.1 Coloring Packets in DiffServ

The Type of Service (ToS) interpretation of the ToS field in the IP packet header described in Chapter 2 has been made obsolete and redefined by the IETF for DiffServ. In its new guise it is known as the Differentiated Services Code Point (DSCP), but it occupies the same space within the IP header and is still often referred to as the ToS field. Old network nodes that used the ToS field cannot interbreed successfully with nodes that use the DSCP since the meaning of the bits may clash or be confused. In particular, the bits in the ToS field had very specific meanings whereas those in the DSCP simply allow the definition of 64 different colors which may be applied to packets. However, some consideration is given to preserving the effect of the precedence bits of the ToS field. The precedence bits are the most significant 3 bits in the ToS field, and DiffServ-capable nodes are encouraged to assign their interpretation of DSCPs to meet the general requirements of these queuing precedences. Figure 6.2 reprises the IPv4 message header and shows the 6 bits designated to identify the DSCP.

As previously stated, the meanings of the DSCP values are not standardized, but are open for configuration within a network. Specifically, this does not mean that a packet with DSCP set to 1 is by definition more or less important than a packet with DSCP 63. The DSCP of zero is reserved to mean that no color is applied to the packet and that traffic should be forwarded as "best-effort," but how this is handled with respect to other packets that are colored remains an

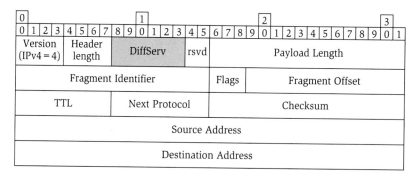

Figure 6.2 The IPV4 message header showing the Differentiated Services Code Point.

issue for configuration within the network. In fact, the interpretation of the DSCP at each node can be varied according to the source and destination of the packets, or other fields of the IP header such as the protocol. The rule that governs how packets are handled within a DiffServ network is called the Per-Hop Behavior (PHB).

The encoding of the DSCP field in the IP header is defined in RFC 2474. This RFC also describes the backwards compatibility with the precedence field of the ToS byte so that PHBs are defined to support the general properties controlled by IP precedence. This process creates PHBs (one for each combination of the top 3 bits) of the form bbb000 to match the precedence behaviors and leaves the other DSCP values open where each *b* may take the value zero or 1. However, it further restricts the meaning of the DSCP values according to Table 6.1. The RFC clearly states that care should be taken before applying any further restrictions to the meaning of DSCP values unless very clear and necessary uses are identified, since otherwise the restricted set of values will quickly be depleted.

Table 6.1 DSCP Restricted Definitions

DSCP Bit Settings	Meaning
000000	Best effort
bbb000	Conforms to the requirements of Type of Service queuing precedence
bbbbb0	Available for standardization
bbbb11	For experimental of local network usage
bbbb01	For experimental of local network usage, but may be taken for standardization

Table 6.2 DSCP Values for Assured Forwarding per Hop Behaviors

	AF Class 1	AF Class 2	AF Class 3	AF Class 4
Low Drop Precedence	001010	010010	011010	100010
Medium Drop Precedence	001100	010100	011100	100100
High Drop Precedence	001110	010110	011110	100110

The Internet Assigned Numbers Authority (IANA) is responsible for managing the allocation of DSCP values. In addition to the value for best effort, and the seven values that match the ToS queuing precedence, a further thirteen values are defined. Twelve of the values are used to represent the Assured Forwarding (AF) PHBs that are defined by RFC 2597. Four AF classes are defined, and within each class there are three drop precedences defined. Each class groups packets for common treatment and sharing of resources and the drop precedence (low, medium, or high) indicates the likelihood of dropping a packet when congestion occurs. An AF PHB is indicated by a 2-digit number showing its class and its drop precedence so that the AF PHB from class 2 with low drop precedence is represented as AF21. The AF PHBs are encoded in the DSCP as shown in Table 6.2.

Each router allocates a configurable set of resources (buffering, queuing space, etc.) to handle the packets from each class. Resources belonging to one class may not be used for packets from another class, except that it is permissible to borrow unused resources from another class so long as they are immediately released should that class need them. The drop precedence is applied only within a class, so that packets from one class may not be dropped simply because another class is congested.

The thirteenth standardized DSCP value (101110) is defined in RFC 3246 (which replaces RFC 2598) to represent an Expedited Forwarding (EF) PHB. The intention is that EF packets should be handled at least at a configured rate regardless of the amount of non-EF traffic in the system. That is, packets carrying the EF DSCP should be prioritized over other traffic at least until the configured service rate has been delivered. There are, however, two issues with this requirement. First, packets cannot be serviced faster than they arrive, meaning that a router cannot deliver the service rate if it does not receive the data quickly enough. Second, the time period over which the rate is measured and the act of measuring the rate itself will affect the apparent rate. RFC 3246 presents formal equations to define the behavior of a router that supports EF traffic—the bottom line is simply that when an EF packet arrives it should be given priority over other traffic unless the required rate has already been delivered.

6.2.2 DiffServ Functional Model

The DiffServ functional model is based on the packet classification shown in Figure 6.1. However, some details are added to help provide and distinguish between different qualities of service. Packet classification function can now be split into two stages. In the first stage (sometimes called *traffic conditioning*) traffic is assigned to a particular DiffServ class by setting the DSCP on the packets—this will most likely be done based on customer or application requirements and is performed when the traffic enters the network. The second stage is more akin to that shown in Figure 6.1, and involves the ordering and classifying of received packets based on the DSCP values they carry.

The required quality of service is maintained within a network by managing and avoiding congestion. Congestion is managed by assigning into queues the packets classified on receipt at a node. The queues can be scheduled for processing according to a priority-based or throughput-based algorithm, and limits on the queue sizes can also serve as a check on the amount of resources used by a traffic flow. Congestion can be avoided, in part, by preemptively discarding (*dropping*) packets before congestion is reached. The heuristics for avoiding congestion may be complex if they attempt to gather information from the network, or may be simple if applied to a single node, but in any case the algorithm for picking which packets should be dropped first and which should be protected is based on the DSCP values in the packets.

Reclassification of traffic may be beneficial in the core of networks where traffic is aggregated or when one Service Provider utilizes another's network. The reclassification process is similar to that originally applied at the edge of the network, and new DSCP values are assigned for the aggregated traffic flows. Note, however, that it is usually important to restore the original DSCP value to each packet as it exits the aggregated flow. Since it is impossible to restore the original classification of traffic if the DSCP is simply changed (how would we know the original value?), reclassification is best achieved by using IP tunneling (see Section 15.1), where a new IP header with a new DSCP value is used to encapsulate each end-to-end packet. When the packet emerges from the tunnel, the encapsulating IP header is removed to reveal the original IP header, complete with DSCP value.

At various points in the network it may be useful to monitor and police traffic flows. Levels of service are easiest to maintain when the characteristics of traffic flows are well understood, and it may be possible to use information fed back from monitoring stations to tune the PHB at nodes in the network to improve the quality of service delivered. The customers, too, are interested in monitoring the performance of the network to be certain that they are getting what they pay for—the wise Service Provider will also keep a careful watch on the actual service that is delivered and will take remedial action before a customer gets upset. But the flip side of this is that performance and tuning in the network may be based on commitments to upper bounds on traffic generation—no one traffic source should swamp the network. Traffic policing can ensure that no customer or application exceeds its agreements and may work with the traffic conditioning components to downgrade or discard excess traffic.

6.2.3 Choosing to Use DiffServ

The motivation for using DiffServ is twofold. It provides a method of grading traffic so that applications that require more reliable, smooth, or expeditious delivery of their data can achieve this. At the same time, it allows Service Providers to offer different classes of service (at different prices), thereby differentiating their customers.

As with all similar schemes, the *prisoner's dilemma* applies and it is important to avoid a situation in which all data sources simply classify their packets as the most important with the lowest drop precedence. In this respect, the close tie between policy and classification of traffic is important, and charging by Service Providers based on the DSCP values assigned is a reasonable way to control the choice of PHB requested for each packet.

DiffServ is most meaningful when all nodes in the domain support PHB functions, although it is not unreasonable to have some nodes simply apply best effort forwarding of all traffic while others fully utilize the DSCPs (but note that this may result in different behaviors on different paths through the network). More important is the need to keep PHB consistent through the network—that is, to maintain a common interpretation of DSCPs on each node in the network.

There are some concerns with scalability issues when DiffServ is applied in large Service Provider networks because of the sheer number of flows that traverse the network. Attention to this issue has recently focused on Multiprotocol Label Switching (MPLS) traffic engineering (see Chapter 9), and two RFCs (RFC 2430 and RFC 3270) provide a framework and implementation details to support DiffServ in MPLS networks.

6.3 Integrated Services

Integrated Services (IntServ) provides a series of standardized ways to classify traffic flows and network resources focused on the capabilities and common structure of IP packet routers. The purpose of this function is to allow applications to choose between multiple well-characterized delivery levels so that they can quantify and predict the level of service their traffic will receive. This is particularly useful to facilitate delivery of real-time services such as voice and video over the Internet. For these services, it is not enough to simply prioritize or color traffic as in Differentiated Services. It is necessary to make quality of service guarantees, and to support these pledges it is necessary for routers to reserve buffers and queuing space to ensure timely forwarding of packets.

To allow routers to prepare themselves to support the traffic at the required level of service, the requirements of data flows must be characterized and exchanged. The end points of a data flow need a way to describe the data they will send and a way to represent the performance they need from the network.

Transit nodes can then reserve resources (buffers, queue space, etc.) to guarantee that the data delivery will be timely and smooth.

IntServ provides a way to describe and encode parameters that describe data flows and quality of service requirements. It does not provide any means of exchanging these encodings between routers—the Resource Reservation Protocol (RSVP) described in Section 6.4 is a special protocol developed to facilitate resource reservation using IntServ parameters to describe data flows.

6.3.1 Describing Traffic Flows

IntServ uses a model described in RFC 1633. The internals of the router shown in Figure 6.1 are enhanced to include an *admission control* component which is responsible for determining whether a new data flow can be supported by a router and for allocating or assigning the resources necessary to support the flow. Admission control uses an algorithm at each node on the data path to map a description of the flow and quality of service requirements to actual resources within the node—it is clearly important that the interpretation of the parameters that describe those requirements are interpreted in the same way on all nodes in the network.

Admission control should not be confused with the closely related concepts of traffic policing (which is done at the edge of the network to ensure that the data flow conforms to the description that was originally given) and policy control (which polices whether a particular application on a given node is allowed to request reservations of a certain type to support its data flows, and validates whether the application is who it says it is). The admission control component on each node is linked by the signaling protocol, which is used to exchange the parameters that describe the data flow. But what information needs to be exchanged?

A lot of research has gone into the best ways to classify flows and their requirements. Some balance must be reached between the following constraints:

- The availability of network resources (bandwidth, buffers, etc.)
- The imperfections in the network (delays, corruption, packet loss, etc.)
- The amount, type, and rate of data generated by the sending application
- The tolerance of the receiving application to glitches in the transmitted data

The most popular solution, used by IntServ, is the *token bucket*. A token bucket is quantified by a data dispersal rate (r) and a data storage capacity— the bucket size (b). A token bucket can be viewed as a bucket with a hole in the bottom, as shown in Figure 6.3. The size of the hole governs the rate at which data can leave the bucket, and the bucket size says how much data can be stored. If the bucket becomes overfull because the rate of arrival of data is greater than the rate of dispersal for a prolonged period of time, then data will be lost. A very small bucket would not handle the case in which bursts of data arrive faster than they can be dispersed even when the average arrival rate is lower than the dispersal rate.

A flow's level of service is characterized at each node in a network by a bandwidth (or data rate) R and a buffer size B. R represents the share of the link's bandwidth to which the flow is entitled, and B represents the buffer space within the node that the flow may utilize.

Other parameters that are useful to characterize the flow include the peak data rate (p), the minimum policed unit (m), and the maximum packet size (M). The peak rate is the maximum rate at which the source may inject traffic into the network—this is the upper bound for the rate of arrival of data shown in Figure 6.3. Over a time period (T) the maximum amount of data sent approximates to pT and is always bounded by $M+pT$. Although it may at first seem perverse, the token bucket rate for a flow and the peak data rate are governed by the rule $p > r$; there is no point in having a dispersal rate greater than the maximum arrival rate.

The maximum packet size must be smaller than or equal to the MTU size of the links over which the flow is routed. The minimum policed unit is used to indicate the degree of rounding that will be applied when the rate of arrival of data is policed for conformance to other parameters. All packets of size less than m will be counted as being of size m, but packets of size greater than or equal to m will have their full size counted. m must be less than or equal to M.

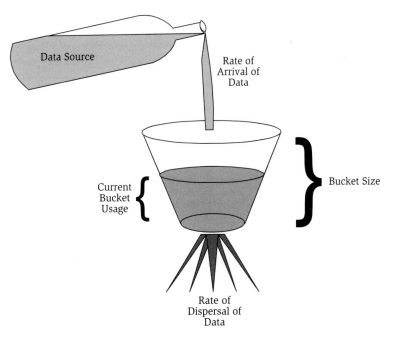

Figure 6.3 The token bucket characterization of a data flow.

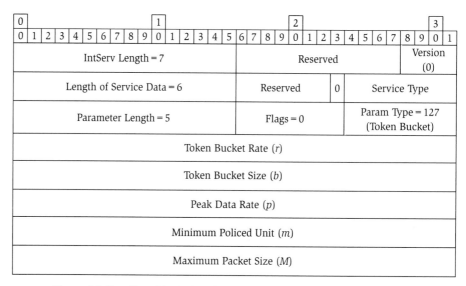

Figure 6.4 Encoding of the IntServ Controlled Load parameters as used by RSVP.

6.3.2 Controlled Load

The controlled load service is defined using the definitions of a token bucket and the other basic flow parameters described in the preceding section. The controlled load service provides the client data flow with a quality of service closely approximating that which the same flow would receive from an otherwise unloaded network. It uses admission control to ensure that this service is delivered even when the network element is overloaded—in other words, it reserves the resources required to maintain the service.

To provide the controlled load service, the flow must be characterized to the network and the network must be requested to make whatever reservations it needs to make to ensure that the service is delivered. Figure 6.4 shows how the service parameters are encoded in RSVP. When the flow is characterized (on a Path message) the service type field is set to 1, and when the reservation is requested (on a Resv message) the service type field is set to 5 to indicate controlled load.

The data rates are presented in bytes per second using IEEE floating point numbers. The byte counts are 32-bit integers.

6.3.3 Guaranteed Service

The guaranteed service sets a time limit for the delivery of all datagrams in the flow and guarantees that datagrams will arrive within this time period and will not be discarded owing to queue overflows on any transit node. This guarantee is made provided that the flow's traffic stays within its specified traffic parameters. This level of service is designed for use by applications that need firm guarantees of service delivery and is particularly useful for applications that have hard real-time requirements.

The guaranteed service controls the maximal queuing delay, but does not attempt to reduce the jitter (that is, the difference between the minimal and maximal datagram delays). Since the delay bound takes the form of a guarantee, it must be large enough to cover cases of long queuing delays even if they are extremely rare. It would be usual to find that the actual delay for most datagrams in a flow is much lower than the guaranteed delay.

The definition of the guaranteed service relies on the result that the fluid delay of a flow obeying a token bucket (with rate r and bucket size b) and being served by a line with bandwidth R is bounded by b/R as long as R is no less than r. Guaranteed service with a service rate R, where now R is a share of the available bandwidth rather than the full bandwidth of a dedicated line, approximates to this behavior and is useful for managing multiple services on a single link. To guarantee the service level across the network, each node must ensure that the delay imposed on a packet is no more than $b/R + C/R + D$ where C and D are small, per-node error terms defined in Section 6.3.4.

Figure 6.5 shows how the flow parameters are encoded for the use of the guaranteed service when reservations are requested in RSVP. A token bucket is encoded to describe the flow and two additional parameters are used to enable the

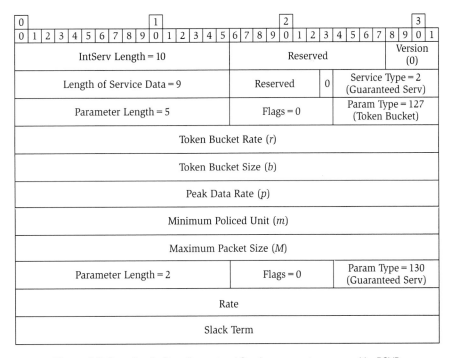

Figure 6.5 Encoding IntServ Guaranteed Service parameters as used by RSVP.

guaranteed service. The guaranteed service rate (R) increases the token bucket rate (r) to reduce queuing delays such that $r \leq R \leq p$. Effectively, it makes the hole in the bottom of the bucket a bit larger so that the build-up of data in the bucket is reduced.

The slack (S) signifies the difference between the desired delay for the flow (s) and the delay obtained by using the rate R, so $S > 0$ indicates the comfort margin. This slack term can be utilized by a router to reduce its resource reservation for this flow if it feels confident that it can always meet the requirements—that is, it can make a smaller reservation and eat into the slack.

6.3.4 Reporting Capabilities

To ensure that Integrated Services function correctly, it is useful for end nodes to be able to collect information about the capabilities and available resources on the path between them. What bandwidth is available? What is the maximum MTU size supported? What IntServ capabilities are supported?

In RSVP, this information is built up in an Adspec object (shown in Figure 6.6), which is initiated by the data sender and updated by each RSVP-capable node along the path. The Adspec object is originally built to contain the global parameters (type 1). Then, if the sender supports the guaranteed service, there is a set of service parameters of type 2. Finally, if the sender supports the controlled load service there is a set of service parameters of type 5. The IntServ length encompasses the full sequence of service parameters.

As the object progresses through the network, the reported parameters are updated, giving the *composed* parameters for the path. This serves to reduce the capabilities reported as the object progresses. For example, if one node has lower bandwidth capabilities on a link it will reduce the advertised bandwidth in the object it forwards. In this way, when the Adspec object reaches the far end of the path, it reports the best available capabilities along the path.

If some node recognizes but cannot support either the guaranteed service or the controlled load service and the service parameters are present in an Adspec, it sets the Break Bit (shown as B in Figure 6.6) and does not update the parameters for the service type.

The global parameters recorded are straightforward. They report the number of IntServ-capable hops traversed, the greatest bandwidth available (as an IEEE floating point number of bytes per second), the minimum end-to-end path latency (measured in microseconds), and the greatest supported MTU (in bytes). To support the guaranteed service, it is necessary to collect more information than just the global parameters. Two error terms are defined:

- The error term C is rate-dependent and represents the delay a datagram in the flow might experience due to the rate parameters of the flow—for example, time taken serializing a datagram broken up into ATM cells.
- The error term D is rate-independent and represents the worst case non-rate-based transit time variation. The D term is generally determined or set for

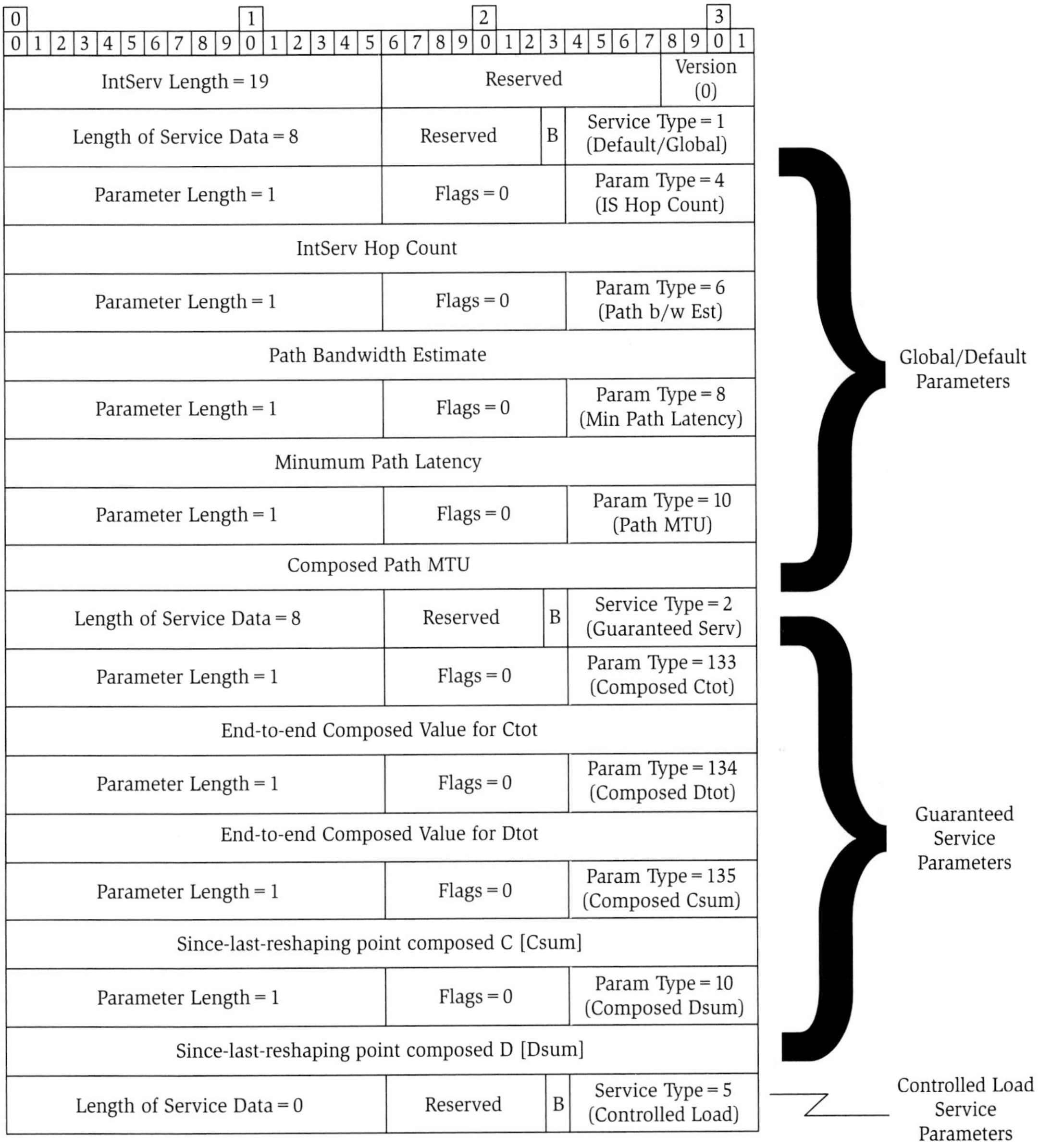

```
 0                     1                       2                       3
 0 1 2 3 4 5 6 7 8 9 0 1 2 3 4 5 6 7 8 9 0 1 2 3 4 5 6 7 8 9 0 1
```

IntServ Length = 19	Reserved	Version (0)
Length of Service Data = 8	Reserved · B	Service Type = 1 (Default/Global)
Parameter Length = 1	Flags = 0	Param Type = 4 (IS Hop Count)
IntServ Hop Count		
Parameter Length = 1	Flags = 0	Param Type = 6 (Path b/w Est)
Path Bandwidth Estimate		
Parameter Length = 1	Flags = 0	Param Type = 8 (Min Path Latency)
Minumum Path Latency		
Parameter Length = 1	Flags = 0	Param Type = 10 (Path MTU)
Composed Path MTU		
Length of Service Data = 8	Reserved · B	Service Type = 2 (Guaranteed Serv)
Parameter Length = 1	Flags = 0	Param Type = 133 (Composed Ctot)
End-to-end Composed Value for Ctot		
Parameter Length = 1	Flags = 0	Param Type = 134 (Composed Dtot)
End-to-end Composed Value for Dtot		
Parameter Length = 1	Flags = 0	Param Type = 135 (Composed Csum)
Since-last-reshaping point composed C [Csum]		
Parameter Length = 1	Flags = 0	Param Type = 10 (Composed Dsum)
Since-last-reshaping point composed D [Dsum]		
Length of Service Data = 0	Reserved · B	Service Type = 5 (Controlled Load)

Global/Default Parameters

Guaranteed Service Parameters

Controlled Load Service Parameters

Figure 6.6 Encoding of the IntServ parameters as used to collect capabilities information by RSVP.

an individual node at boot or configuration time. For example, in a device or transport mechanism where processing or bandwidth is allocated to a specific timeslot, some part of the per-flow delay may be determined by the maximum amount of time a flow's data might have to wait for a slot.

The terms C and D are accumulated across the path and expressed as totals (*Ctot* and *Dtot*) in bytes and microseconds, respectively. Further, because traffic may be reshaped within the network, partial sums (*Csum* and *Dsum*) of the error terms C and D along the path since the last point at which the traffic was reshaped are also reported. Knowing these four delay terms, a node may calculate how much bufferage is needed to ensure that no bytes will be lost.

Support of the controlled load service does not require any additional information, but it is still useful to know whether any nodes on the path do not support the service. For this reason, a "null" service parameter is inserted in the Adspec object so that the Break Bit may be recorded.

6.3.5 Choosing to Use IntServ

IntServ is sometimes described as an "all or nothing" model. To guarantee a particular quality of service across the network, all nodes on the data path must support IntServ and whichever signaling protocol is used to distribute the requirements. It may be determined, however, that this level of guarantee is not absolutely necessary and that the improvement in service generated by using resource reservations on some nodes within the network may be helpful. Protocols such as RSVP recognize this and allow for data paths that traverse both RSVP-capable and RSVP-incapable nodes.

The focus of IntServ is real-time data traffic. It is not a requirement for data exchanges that are not time-dependent, and such flows are better handled by DiffServ where there is no overhead of another signaling protocol and no need for complex resource reservations at each node. However, if real-time quality of service is required, IntServ provides a formal and simple mechanism to describe the flows and requirements.

Some people, especially those with an ATM background, consider the simplicity of IntServ's description of quality of service to be a significant drawback. Compared with the detailed qualification of flows and behavior available in ATM, IntServ appears to offer a crude way of characterizing traffic. However, IntServ (which is specifically designed for packet routers, not cell switches) has proved useful in the Internet where it is used in conjunction with RSVP to support voice over IP, and its very simplicity has brought it as many supporters as detractors. For the ATM purists, RFC 2381 addresses how IntServ parameters may be mapped to ATM QoS parameters.

The alternative to using IntServ is to not use it. There are some strong alternative viewpoints.

- The first suggests that limitations on bandwidth are likely to apply most significantly at the edges of the Internet. This implies that if an application is able to find a local link of sufficient bandwidth to support its functions, there will always be sufficient bandwidth within the Internet to transfer its data. Although this may be an ideal toward which Service Providers strive within their own networks, it is rarely the case that end-to-end data transfer across the Internet is limited only by the capacity of the first and last links. With the development of bandwidth-greedy applications, there is a continual conflict between bandwidth demand and availability. Besides, quality of service for real-time applications is not simply an issue of the availability of unlimited bandwidth, but is a function of the delays and variations introduced within the network.

- Another viewpoint holds that simple priority schemes such as DiffServ provide sufficient grading of service to facilitate real-time applications. This may be true when only a proportion of the traffic within the network requires real-time quality of service, in which case simply giving higher priority to real-time traffic can ensure that it is handled promptly and gets the resources it needs. However, as the percentage of high-priority traffic increases, the priority scheme becomes unable to handle the requirements adequately and all high-priority data flows are equally degraded. There is no way to announce that links are over their capacity or to prevent new flows.

- Yet another view is that it is the responsibility of the application and its IP transport protocol to handle the vagaries of the network. Adaptive real-time protocols for distributing data have been developed (see the Real-Time Transport Protocol in Chapter 7) and provide mechanisms to smooth and buffer data that is delayed or interrupted. But although these approaches may "heal" the data flows they can still provide interruptions that the human user is unwilling or unable to accept—readers who have tried to have meaningful conversations over a satellite telephone will know how even a predictable delay of one or two seconds can disrupt dialog.

6.3.6 Choosing a Service Type

Having decided to use IntServ, an application must choose which service to utilize. The Controlled Load is the simplest service, defining and adhering to a simple token bucket, and should be used wherever the greater control of the Guaranteed Service is not required. The Guaranteed Service is less than trivial to use, but provides firm guarantees of service delivery and is particularly useful for applications that have hard real-time requirements and require guaranteed service.

Note that some applications reduce the controlled load token bucket to its simplest form by setting the bucket rate and peak data rate to be equal at the bandwidth required for the service, setting the minimum policed unit to be equal to the maximum packet size, and setting the bucket size to an arbitrarily large multiple of the maximum packet size. Generalized Multiprotocol Label Switching (GMPLS, see Chapter 10) formalizes this by making bandwidth-only reservations using the controlled load service fields but ignoring all fields except the peak data rate, which identifies the bandwidth required.

Over time, other IntServ services have been defined for specific uses. The Null Service has been defined to allow the use of RSVP and RSVP-TE in MPLS (see Chapter 9) by applications that are unable or unwilling to specify the resources they require from the network. This is particularly useful for mixing DiffServ and IntServ within a single network.

6.3.7 Choosing Between IntServ and DiffServ

DiffServ is intrinsically more scalable than IntServ because it has a limited number of classifications—each flow must be assigned to one of 64 DiffServ PHBs, whereas in IntServ each individual flow has its own reservations and characteristics. On the other hand, DiffServ is less precise and requires coordinated configuration of all participating routers—IntServ may be combined with a signaling protocol such as RSVP to allow the PHB for a flow to be dynamically selected and set through the network. Furthermore, IntServ gives finer control of the real-time qualities of traffic delivery.

Some consideration should be given to implementing both IntServ and DiffServ within the same network. This can be done "side-by-side," with all IntServ traffic assigned to a single DSCP or by running IntServ over DiffServ. In the latter case, all traffic is classified and assigned a DSCP, and then whole DSCP classes or individual flows within a DSCP value can have their resources managed using IntServ.

6.4   Reserving Resources Using RSVP

RFC 2205 defines the Resource Reservation Protocol with the rather improbable acronym RSVP. This protocol is a signaling protocol for use in networks that support IntServ flow descriptions. The protocol is designed to allow data sources to characterize to the network the traffic they will generate, and to allow the data sinks to request that the nodes along the data path make provisions to ensure that the traffic can be delivered smoothly and without packets being dropped because of lack of queuing resources.

RSVP is intrinsically a simple signaling protocol but is complicated by its flexible support of merged and multicast flows. Complexity is also introduced by the fact that the protocol is intended to allocate resources along the path followed by the data within the network (that is, the forwarding path selected by the routers in the network) and that this path can change over time as the connectivity of the network changes.

RSVP bears close examination not simply for its value for making resource reservations in an IntServ-enabled IP packet forwarding network. The protocol also forms the basis of the signaling protocol used both for MPLS (Chapter 9) and GMPLS (Chapter 10) and so is very important in the next-generation networks that are now being built.

In addition to developing RSVP as a protocol, the IETF also worked on a common API to allow implementations to make use of RSVP in a standardized way. This meant that application programmers wanting to use RSVP from their applications could be independent of the implementation of RSVP and make use of a well-known API that provided a set of standard services. The IETF, however, "does not do" interfaces and work on the RSVP API (RAPI) was off-loaded in 1998 to The Open Group, an implementers' consortium, from where it was used more as a guide than as a rigid standard.

6.4.1 Choosing to Reserve Resources

As described in Section 6.3, IntServ can be used to describe a traffic flow, and to indicate the behavior of network nodes if they are to guarantee the provision of services to carry the flow across the network. This behavior can be met only if the nodes reserve some of their resources for the flow.

The precise nature of resource reservation depends on the implementation of the packet forwarding engine within the routers. Some may make dedicated reservations of buffers to individual microflows. Others may use statistical assignment to make sure that resources will not be over-stretched, provided that all data sources conform to the parameters of the flows they have described. Whatever the implementation, the fact that the network nodes have agreed to make reservations is a guarantee that the required quality of service will be met and that traffic will be delivered in the way necessary for the proper functioning of the applications within the constraints of the network.

Several well-known applications, such as Microsoft's NetMeeting, include the ability to use RSVP to improve the quality of voice and video services they deliver. In general, Voice over IP for IP telephony or for simple point-to-point exchanges is a prime user of RSVP since the human ear can tolerate only a small amount of distortion or short gaps in the transmitted signal.

6.4.2 RSVP Message Flows for Resource Reservation

The steps to resource reservation in RSVP are path establishment and resource allocation. RSVP uses the Path message to establish a path from the source to the destination, and a Resv message to reserve the resources along the path. The source of the RSVP flow (the *ingress*) sends a Path message targeted at the destination of the flow (the *egress*), and this message is passed from node to node through the network until it reaches the egress. The Path message is routed in the same way that IP traffic would be routed—the IP traffic would be addressed to the egress node, and by addressing the Path message in the same way, RSVP ensures that the reservations will be made using the same path and hops that will be used by the IP traffic.

The Path message carries a specification of the traffic that will constitute the flow (the traffic specification or *TSpec*). It should be noted, however, that the traffic may already be flowing before the Path message is sent. That is, an RSVP-capable network also supports best effort traffic delivery and resource reservation may be applied at any stage to improve the likelihood of traffic delivery meeting required quality standards.

Each node that processes the Path message establishes control state for the message, verifies that it is happy to attempt to deliver the requested service (for example, checking the authenticity of the message sender), and builds a Path message to send on toward the egress. The Path messages can collect information about the availability of resources along the path they traverse. The ingress advertises (in the *Adspec*) its capabilities, and each node along the way can modify the reported capabilities to a subset of the original Adspec so that by the time the Path reaches the egress the message contains a common subset of the capabilities of all routers on the path.

The egress computes what resources will need to be reserved in the network. These resources must satisfy the demands of the traffic that will be sent, as described by the TSpec, and must fit within the available resources reported by the Adspec. The egress responds to the Path message with a Resv message that requests the reservation of the computed resources by including an *RSpec*. The Resv is passed hop-by-hop back along the path traversed by the Path message and at each hop resources are reserved as requested. When the Resv reaches the ingress and has completed its resource allocations, the RSVP flow is fully provisioned.

In general, RSVP implementations follow the model described in RFC 2205. Control state is maintained separately for Path and Resv flows with only a loose coupling between them. This is not necessarily intuitive but it allows for advanced functions (described in Sections 6.4.6 and 6.4.7) where there may not be a one-to-one correspondence between Path messages and resource reservations, or where the Path may be rerouted while the reservation on the old path is still in place.

Figure 6.7 shows the basic RSVP message flows. At step 1 the application at the ingress quantifies the traffic flow that it is going to send to an application of Host D and requests reservations from the network. Host A builds and sends a Path message addressed to Host D and this is routed to Router B. Router B (step 2) creates Path state and sends its own Path message toward Host D. When the Path message reaches Host D (step 3), it also creates its path state, but recognizes that it is the destination of the flow and so delivers the resource request to the target application identified by a destination port ID contained in the Path message. The target application converts the Path message, with its description of the traffic and the capabilities of the routers along the path, into a request for resource reservation. This request is passed to the RSVP component, which creates Resv state, reserves the requested resources on the local node, and sends a Resv message (step 4). The Resv message is not addressed to the ingress node, but is addressed hop-by-hop back along the path the Path message traversed. This ensures that the resources are reserved along the path that traffic will follow (that is, along the path the Path message traversed) rather than along the shortest return path. Thus, at Router C (step 5), once the Resv state has been created and the resources reserved, a new Resv is sent out to Router B even if there is a direct route from Router C to Host A. When the Resv reaches Host A (step 6), the resources are reserved and an indication is delivered to the application to let it know that the reservations are in place.

Figure 6.7 also shows the ResvConf message sent by the ingress to the egress to confirm that the resources have been reserved. The ResvConf is sent hop-by-hop along the path of flow (steps 7 and 8) to the egress if, and only if, the egress requested confirmation when it sent the Resv (step 4). When the ResvConf reaches the egress (step 9) it knows that the reservation was successful; this may simplify processing at the egress, which can wait for a ResvConf or a ResvErr (see Section 6.4.5) to confirm or deny successful flow establishment.

When the ingress application no longer needs the reservations in place because it is stopping its transmission of traffic, it tears them down by sending a PathTear message. The PathTear is a one-shot message that traverses the path hop-by-hop (it is not addressed and routed to the egress) and lets each router know that it can release its Path and Resv state as well as any reserved resources. This is shown in Figure 6.7 at steps 10, 11, and 12.

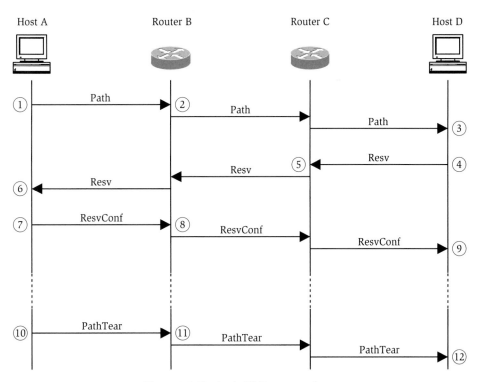

Figure 6.7 The basic RSVP message flows.

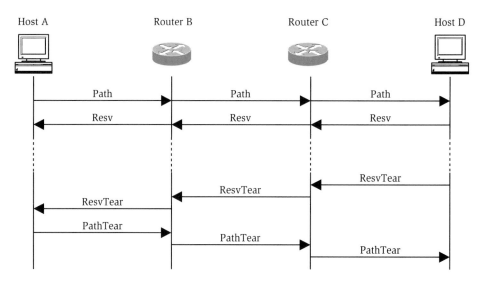

Figure 6.8 The RSVP ResvTear message flow.

Alternatively, the egress may determine that it can no longer support the reservations that are in place and can ask for them to be torn down. It may send a ResvTear message back toward the ingress along the path of the flow. Each router that receives a ResvTear releases the resources it has reserved for the flow and cleans up its Resv state before sending a ResvTear on toward the ingress. The Path state is, however still left in place since that refers to the request from the ingress. When the ResvTear reaches the ingress it may decide that the flow can no longer be supported with resource reservations and will send a PathTear, as shown in Figure 6.8. Alternatively, the ingress may modify the description of the traffic and send a new Path message to which the egress may respond with a new Resv. Finally, the ingress may decide to do nothing, leaving its current request in place and hoping that the egress will have a change of heart and will assign new resources. In any event, after a ResvTear the traffic may continue to flow and be delivered in a best effort manner.

6.4.3 Sessions and Flows

The concepts of *sessions* and *flows* are important in RSVP, but are often confused. A session is defined by the triplet {destination address, destination port, payload protocol}. This information provides the basic categorization of packets that are going to the same destination application and can be handled within the network in the same way. Sessions are identified in RSVP by the Session Object carried on Path and Resv messages, but note that the IP packet that carries a Path message is also addressed to the destination IP address (that is, the egress end of the session).

A session, however, does not identify the data flow since this depends on the source. A flow is characterized by the pair {source address, source port} in conjunction with the session identifier. This construct allows multiple flows within a single session. This facility can be used for multiple flows from a single source or for merging flows from multiple sources (see Section 6.4.7). Flows are identified on Path messages by the Sender Template Object and on Resv messages by Filter Spec Objects.

Both the destination and the source ports may be assigned the value zero. This is most useful when the payload protocol does not use ports to distinguish flows. Note that it is considered an error to have two sessions with the same destination address and payload protocol, one with a zero destination port and one with a nonzero destination port. If the destination port is zero, the source port for all the flows on the session must also be zero, providing a consistency check for payload protocols that do not support the use of ports. It is also considered an error to have one flow on a session with source port zero and another with a nonzero source port.

6.4.4 Requesting, Discovering, and Reserving Resources

Each Path message carries a Sender TSpec, which defines the traffic characteristics of the data flow the sender will generate. The TSpec may be used by a *traffic control* component at transit routers to prevent propagation of Path messages that would lead to reservation requests that would be doomed to fail. A transit router may decide to fail a Path by sending a PathErr (see Section 6.4.5), may use the TSpec as input to the routing process—especially where equal cost paths exist—or may note the problem but still forward the Path message, hoping that the issue will have been resolved by the time the Resv is processed. The contents of the Sender TSpec are described in Section 6.3. They characterize the flow as a token bucket with peak data rate, maximum packet size, and minimum policed unit.

As the Path message progresses across the network it may also collect information about the available resources on the nodes and links traversed and the IntServ capabilities of the transit nodes. The Adspec object is optional, but if present is updated by each node so that by the time the Path message reaches the egress node it contains a view of the delays and constraints that will be applied to data as it traverses the path. This helps the egress node decide what resources the network will need to reserve to support the flow described in the TSpec. Of course, by the time the Resv message is processed within the network the reported Adspec may be out of date, but subsequent Path messages for the same flow may be used to update the Adspec, causing modifications to the reservation request on further Resv messages.

The Resv message makes a request to the network to reserve resources for the flow. The FlowSpec object describes the token bucket that must be implemented by nodes within the network to support the flow described by the TSpec given the capabilities reported by the TSpec.

The format of the contents of the TSpec, Adspec, and FlowSpec for RSVP are described in Section 6.3.

6.4.5 Error Handling

RSVP has two messages for reporting errors. The PathErr message flows from downstream to upstream (the reverse direction from the Path message), and reports issues related to Path state. The ResvErr message reports issues with Resv state or resource reservation and flows from upstream to downstream. So the PathErr is sent back to the sender of a Path message, and the ResvErr is sent back to the sender of a Resv message.

Error messages carry session and flow identifiers reflected from the Path or Resv message and also include an Error Spec Object. The error is specified using an error code to categorize the problem and an error value to identify the exact issue within the category.

The PathErr message flow is shown in Figure 6.9. There are relatively few reasons why Router C might decide to reject the Path request (step 2), but the router might apply policy to the request, might not be able to support the requested flow, or might find that the session clashes with an existing session (one has destination port zero and the other nonzero). It is also possible that Router C does not recognize one of the objects on the Path message and needs to reject the message—this allows for forwards compatibility with new message

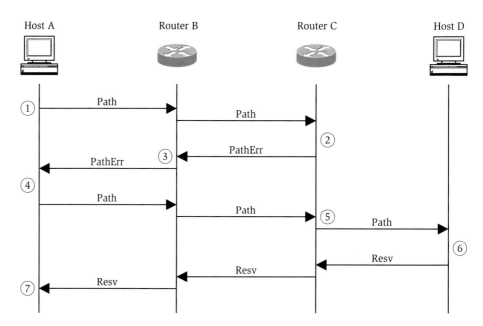

Figure 6.9 Example message flow showing the RSVP PathErr message.

objects introduced in the future. The PathErr message is returned hop-by-hop toward the ingress. Router B (step 3) examines the error code and value and determines whether it can resolve the issue by modifying the Path message it sends. If it cannot, it forwards the PathErr on toward the ingress and does not remove its own Path state.

When the PathErr reaches the ingress node (step 4) it has three options. It may give up on the whole idea and send a PathTear to remove the state from the network, it may resend the Path message as it is in the hope that the issue in the network will resolve itself (possibly through management intervention), or it may modify the Path message to address the problem. When the new Path reaches Router C (step 5) it will either reject it again with a PathErr or it will accept the message and forward it, leading to the establishment of the RSVP reservation.

PathErr may also be used after an RSVP flow has been established. The most common use is to report that a reservation has been administratively preempted.

The ResvErr message is used to reject a Resv message or to indicate that there is a problem with resources that have already been reserved. The flow of a ResvErr does not affect Path state, but it does cause the removal of Resv state and frees up any resources that have been reserved. Figure 6.10 shows an example message flow including a ResvErr message.

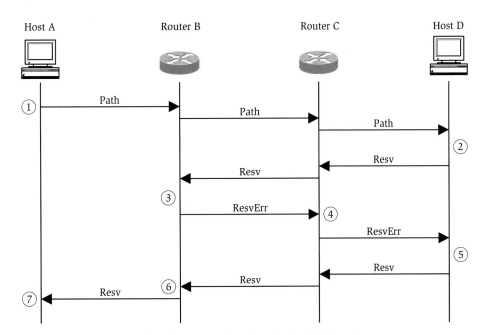

Figure 6.10 Example message flow showing the RSVP ResvErr message.

When the Resv reaches Router B it determines that it cannot accept the message (step 3). The reason may be policy or formatting of the message, as with the Path/PathErr message, or the rejection may happen because the Resv asks for resources that are not available—note that Router B's resources may have been allocated to other RSVP flows after the Adspec was added to the Path message. Some errors can be handled by transit nodes (Router C at step 4), which might issue a new Resv, but usually ResvErr messages are propagated all the way to the egress, removing Resv state and freeing resources as they go.

When an egress (Host D at step 5) receives a ResvErr it has four options. It may reissue the original Resv in the hope that the problem in the network will be resolved, or it may give up and send a PathErr back to the ingress to let it know that all is not well. However, two options exist for making constructive changes to the resource request on the Resv message that may allow the RSVP flow to be established. First, the egress may simply modify the resource request in the light of the error received—this is shown in Figure 6.10 where the new Resv reaches Router B (step 6) and is accepted and forwarded to the ingress. The second constructive change can arise if the Path message is retried by the ingress—as it traverses the network it will pick up new Adspec values that reflect the currently available resources and this will allow the egress to make a better choice of resource request for the Resv.

In practice, there may be some overlap in the procedures for handling a ResvErr at the egress. The egress will usually send a PathErr and retry the old Resv with any updates it can determine and modify its behavior if it receives a new Path message.

6.4.6 Adapting to Changes in the Network

As suggested in the preceding section, RSVP handles problems during the establishment of an RSVP flow by resending its Path and Resv messages periodically. This feature is even more important in the context of changes to the topology and routes of a network.

The initial Path message is propagated through the network according to the forwarding tables installed at the ingress and transit nodes. At each RSVP router, the Path is packaged into an IP header, addressed to the egress/destination host, and forwarded to the next router. The Resv is returned hop-by-hop along the path of the Path without any routing between nodes. The reservations are, therefore, made along the path that the Path message followed, which will be the path that IP data also traverses.

But what would happen if there were a change in the network so that IP data followed a new route? The reservations would remain on the old path, but the data would flow through other routers where no reservations had been made. This serious issue is resolved by having each node retransmit (*refresh*) its Path message periodically—each message is subject to the routing process and will be passed to the new next hop and so onward to the same egress. The Resv is now sent back hop-by-hop along the new path, and reservations are made along the new path to support the data flow that is using it.

Of course, the process described would leave unused resources allocated on the old path, which is not good because those resources could not be used to support other flows. This problem is countered by having the nodes on the old path timeout when they do not receive a Path after a period (generally 5 1/4 times the retransmission period to allow for occasional packet loss). When a node times out, it knows that there is some problem with the upstream node—maybe the link from the upstream node is broken, or perhaps the ingress has simply lost interest in the reservation, or the Path could have been routed another way. When a node stops receiving Path messages it stops forwarding Path and Resv messages and removes the Path state associated with the flow.

Resv messages are similarly refreshed. This provides for survival of packet loss and guarantees cleanup of the Resv state and the allocated resources in the event of a network failure or a change in the Path.

Message refresh processing and rerouting is illustrated in Figure 6.11. Step 1 shows normal Path and Resv exchange from Host A to Host F through Routers C and E (the shortest path). Step 2 indicates refresh processing as Path and Resv messages are resent between the routers, but Host A now routes the Path message to Router B and so through Router D to Router E. Router E (step 4) is a *merge point* for the old and new flows and sends the new Path message on to the egress (Host F) resulting in a new Resv from Host F (steps 5 and 6). Note that the merge point (Router E) may decide to handle the merging of the flows itself by sending a Resv back to Router D without sending a Path on to the destination, Host F.

Router E can now make a reservation on the interface from Router D and send a Resv to Router D. The Resv follows its new path back to Host A through Router B (step 7) and all reservations are now in place on the new path. Note that data is already flowing along the new path and was as soon as the change in the routing table took effect—this was before the Path refresh was sent on the new route. This means that for a while the data was flowing down a path for which it had no specific reservation, highlighting the fact that RSVP is a best-effort reservation process.

Step 8 indicates the refresh process on the new path and on the fragments of the old path that are still in place. Each node sends a Path and a Resv to its neighbor, with the exception that Host A sends a Path only to Router B.

After a while, Router C notices that it has not seen a Path message from Host A (step 9). It may simply remove state and allow the state to timeout downstream or, as in this case, it may send a PathTear to clean up. When the merge point, Router E, receives the PathTear (step 10) it must not propagate it to the egress as this would remove the reservation for the whole flow. Instead, it removes the reservation on the interface (from Router C) on which the PathTear was received and notices that it still has an incoming flow (from router D) so does not forward the message.

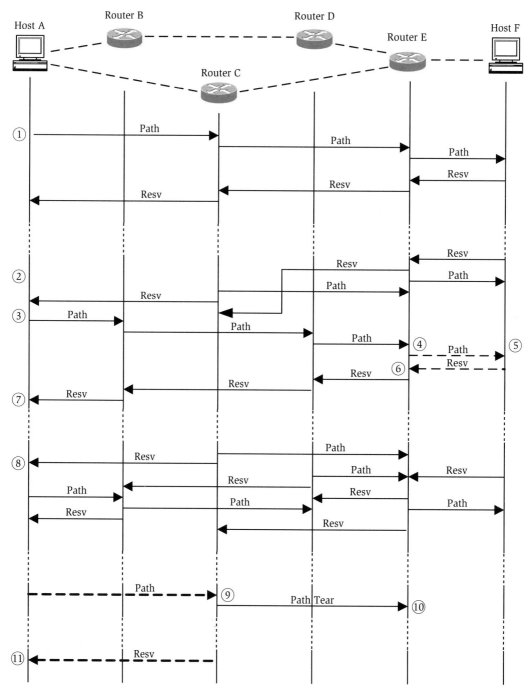

Figure 6.11 Message refresh processing and rerouting in an RSVP network.

At step 11, Host A notices that it hasn't received a Resv from Router C and cleans up any remaining resources.

Because the state messages (Path and Resv) must be periodically resent to keep the RSVP state active, RSVP is known as a *soft state* protocol. The protocol overheads of a soft state have been the cause of many heated debates within the IETF. The concern is that the number of flows in a network may reach a point at which all of the bandwidth on a link, or all of the processing power of a router, will be used up sending Path and Resv refresh messages, leaving no capacity for data forwarding. Several solutions to reduce the impact of refresh processing have been developed and are covered in a separate RFC (RFC 2961) and are described in Section 6.4.12.

Even when RSVP messages are being refreshed, there is some risk that during network overload RSVP packets will be dropped too often, resulting in the soft state timing out. For this reason, routers are recommended to give priority to IP packets that indicate that they are carrying RSVP messages.

6.4.7 Merging Flows

The preceding sections have alluded to merging flows in two contexts. First, when distinguishing between sessions and flows, the use of RSVP to reserve resources for multipoint-to-point flows was mentioned. Second, the discussion of adapting to changes in the network introduced the concept of a merge point where the old and new paths combined.

RSVP is structured to handle merging of flows within a session so that resources are not double allocated. Figure 6.12 illustrates flow merging in a very simple network to support a multipoint-to-point session from Hosts A and B to Host D. There are two flows: A to D and B to D, with a single session carrying one payload protocol for both flows and terminating at the same port on Host D.

In the example, Host A starts with the usual Path/Resv exchange (step 1). A ResvConf is sent to confirm that the reservation has been installed. Some time later (step 2) Host B wants to join in and sends its own Path message. When this second Path reaches Router C (step 3) it sees that although the flows are different (distinct source addresses) the session is the same (identical destination address, destination port, and payload protocol), so it is acceptable to merge the flows. However, merging the reservations for the flows is the responsibility of the egress host and not the merge point, so Router C forwards a Path message for the new flow.

When the new Path message reaches the egress (Host D at step 4) it may choose to merge the reservations on the shared links—in this case, for the link between Router C and Host D. It looks at the Sender TSpec from the two Path messages and computes the reservations that must be made to accommodate both flows. The reservation requests are made on a single Resv that applies to the whole session, and may be expressed as a single reservation for both flows or as a reservation for each flow.

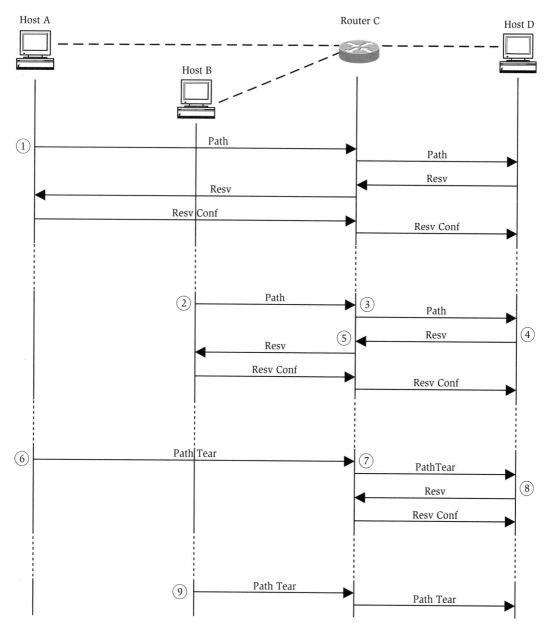

Figure 6.12 A simple example of flow merging in an RSVP network.

When the Resv message reaches Router C (step 5) it splits the reservation for the two separate upstream branches. In this simple case the existing branch from Host A does not need to be modified and Router C simply sends a Resv to Host B indicating the reservation that applies to the link from Host B to Router C. This process may be as simple as removing the reference to the flow from Host A and forwarding the Resv, but more likely it involves some recomputation.

The computation of shared resources may be nontrivial since the requirements may not lead to a simple summation of the resources for the two flows. In particular, some applications such as Voice over IP conference calling do not call for each flow to be active at the same time, in which case the reservation for merged flows is no different from that for a single flow.

Figure 6.12 also shows the removal of flows from a merged situation. At step 6, Host A withdraws from the multipoint-to-point flow and sends PathTear. Router C (step 7) forwards the PathTear, but it must be careful to remove only the state associated with the flow that is removed—in this case, it does not remove any Resv state nor release any resources because they are still associated with the active Path state from Host B. When the egress (Host D at step 8) gets the PathTear it can recompute the reservation requirements; it may do this from its records of Path state or it may wait until it sees a Path refresh for the active flow. In any case, the result is a new Resv with potentially reduced resource requirements. In the simple case, this Resv is not forwarded by Router C since it simply reduces the resource requirements to those needed (and already in place) on the link from Host B to Router C. Finally (step 9), when Host B sends PathTear, all of the remaining state and resources are released.

RSVP defines three *styles* for resource reservation. These are used by the egress to indicate how resources may be shared between flows (that is, data on the same session from different senders). Two qualities are defined: the ability to share resources and the precision of specification of flow (that is, the sender). The correlation of these qualities defines three styles, as shown in Figure 6.13. A Style Object is included in a Resv to let the upstream nodes know how to interpret the list of FlowSpecs Objects and FilterSpec Objects it carries (indicating resource requests and associated flows—annoyingly, the FlowSpec describes

		Resource Sharing	
		No Sharing	Sharing Allowed
Sender Specification	Explicit	Fixed Filter Style (FF)	Shared Explicit Style (SE)
	Wildcard	Not Defined	Wildcard Filter Style (WF)

Figure 6.13 RSVP styles are defined by the type of resource sharing and how the flows are identified.

the aggregate data flow resources and not the individual flows which are found in FilterSpecs). This becomes more obvious in conjunction with the message formats shown in Section 6.4.9.

6.4.8 Multicast Resource Sharing

The resource sharing considered in the previous section handles the case of multipoint-to-point flows in which the flows share downstream legs and optimize resource allocations on these downstream legs in the knowledge that the data sources are in some way synchronized and will not flood those legs. RSVP also supports multicast flows (that is, point-to-multipoint) in which a flow has a single upstream leg that branches as it proceeds downstream as shown in Figure 6.14.

Resource sharing in the multicast case is more intuitive since there is only one traffic source and the resources required to support the traffic are independent of the branches that may occur downstream. However, as the Path message is forwarded from node to node it is copied and sent out on many different legs. Each time it is forked, we can expect to see a distinct Resv message flow in the opposite direction. Each Resv flows back upstream to the ingress and carries a request to reserve resources. Clearly, we do not want to reserve resources for each Resv, and some form of merging of Resv messages must be achieved. On the other hand, some of the egress nodes may require different reservations, so the merging of reservations at upstream nodes may not be trivial.

RSVP uses the same mechanisms for resource sharing in multicast sessions. That is, Resv messages use styles to indicate how they apply to one or more flows or sessions. Beyond this, it is the responsibility of *split points* to merge the requirements received on Resv messages from downstream and to send a single, unified Resv upstream. It is possible that the first Resv received and propagated will ask for sufficient resources, in which case the split point does not need to send any subsequent Resv messages upstream. On the other

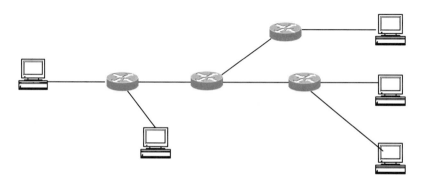

Figure 6.14 An RSVP multicast session.

hand, if a Resv received from downstream after the first Resv has been propagated upstream demands increased resources, the split point must send a new, modified Resv upstream.

Note that a split point must not wait to receive a Resv from all downstream end points before sending one upstream because it cannot know how many to expect and which end points will respond.

A split point that is responsible for merging Resvs must also manage the distribution of ResvConf messages to downstream nodes that have asked for them since these messages will not be generated by the ingress after the first reservation has been installed.

6.4.9 RSVP Messages and Formats

Formal definitions of the messages in RSVP can be found in RFC 2205. The notation used is called *Backus-Naur Form* (BNF), which is described in the Preface to this book. It is a list of mandatory and optional objects. Each object is denoted by angle brackets " < object > " and optional objects or sequences are contained in square brackets "[< optional object >]." Sequences of objects are sometimes displayed as a single composite object which is defined later. Choices between objects are denoted by a vertical bar " < object one > | < object 2 > ."

Note that the ordering of objects within a message is strongly recommended, but is not mandatory (except that the members of composite objects must be kept together) and an implementation should be prepared to receive objects in any order while generating them in the order listed here.

Figure 6.15 shows the formal definition of the Path message. The sequence of objects, Sender Template, Sender Tspec, and Adspec is referred to as the *Sender Descriptor*. This becomes relevant in the context of Resv messages which may carry information relevant to more than one Sender Descriptor.

Figure 6.16 shows the formal definition of a Resv message. The Flow Descriptor List (expanded in Figures 6.17 through 6.19) is a composite sequence of objects

```
< Path Message > ::=          < Common Header >
                              [ < INTEGRITY > ]
                              < SESSION >
                              < RSVP_HOP >
                              < TIME_VALUES >
                              [ < POLICY_DATA > ]
                              < sender descriptor >
< sender descriptor > ::=     < SENDER_TEMPLATE >
                              < SENDER_TSPEC >
                              [ < ADSPEC > ]
```

Figure 6.15 Formal definition of the RSVP Path message.

```
< Resv Message > ::=        < Common Header >
                            [ < INTEGRITY > ]
                            < SESSION >
                            < RSVP_HOP >
                            < TIME_VALUES >
                            [ < RESV_CONFIRM > ]
                            [ < SCOPE > ]
                            [ < POLICY_DATA > ]
                            < STYLE >
                            < flow descriptor list >
```

Figure 6.16 Formal definition of the RSVP Resv message.

```
< flow descriptor list > ::=        < WF flow descriptor >
< WF flow descriptor > ::=          < FLOWSPEC >
```

Figure 6.17 Formal definition of the RSVP WF Flow Descriptor List used on RSVP Resv messages.

```
< flow descriptor list > ::=        < FF flow descriptor >
                                    [ < flow descriptor list > ]
< FF flow descriptor > ::=          < FLOWSPEC >
                                    < filter spec list >
< filter spec list > ::=            < FILTER_SPEC >
                                    [ < filter spec list > ]
```

Figure 6.18 Formal definition of the RSVP FF Flow Descriptor List used on RSVP Resv messages.

```
< flow descriptor list > ::=        < SE flow descriptor >
< SE flow descriptor > ::=          < FLOWSPEC >
                                    < filter spec list >
< filter spec list > ::=            < FILTER_SPEC >
                                    [ < filter spec list > ]
```

Figure 6.19 Formal definition of the RSVP SE Flow Descriptor List used on RSVP Resv messages.

```
< PathTear Message > ::=      < Common Header >
                              [ < INTEGRITY > ]
                              < SESSION >
                              < RSVP_HOP >
                              [ < sender descriptor > ]
```

Figure 6.20 Formal definition of the RSVP PathTear message.

that allows a single Resv message to describe reservations for multiple Sender Descriptors requested on Path messages. The type of flow descriptor list that is used depends on the Style Object, which indicates the style of resource sharing. As described in Section 6.4.7, there are three styles: Wildcard-Filter (WF), which applies to all flows on the session; Fixed-Filter (FF), which applies a single reservation to a specific list of flows; and Shared-Explicit (SE), which applies different reservations to different lists of flows on the same session.

The FF Flow Descriptor is, itself, a composite object containing the FilterSpec and label objects and optionally a Record Route object. Notice that this definition of FF Flow Descriptor aligns with the definition of the Sender Descriptor.

The last element of the FF Flow Descriptor is recursive, allowing a list of sub-lists where each sublist starts with a FlowSpec. It also allows the sublist to be just an FF Flow Descriptor—in this case the FlowSpec is assumed to be identical to the most recent one seen in the message.

This rather complex notation facilitates a rather complex real-world situation in which merged flows or parallel flows share resources. Note that the notation used in the preceding figures differs slightly from that presented in RFC 2205 in an attempt at greater clarity.

Compound objects are also used for the Shared Explicit case, as shown in Figure 6.19, but note that here only one FlowSpec object may be present. The subsequent SE Filter Specifications match Sender Descriptors and all use the one FlowSpec. Again, a variation on the notation of RFC 2205 is used here for clarity.

Figure 6.20 shows the message format for a PathTear message. The PathTear is modeled on the path message. The sender descriptor is, however, optional since it is not always necessary to identify the sender when tearing down a flow; the RSVP Hop Object identifies the upstream node, and this is usually enough to clarify the Path state that is being removed. In cases of shared resources in which only one flow from a session is being removed, the sender descriptor must be present to disambiguate the flows.

The ResvTear message shown in Figure 6.21 is modeled on the Resv. Unlike the Path/PathTear relationship, the flow descriptor is mandatory and identifies exactly which resource reservations are being torn.

The PathErr and ResvErr messages shown in Figure 6.22 and 6.23 are based, respectively, on the Path and Resv messages to which they respond. That is, even though a PathErr message flows from downstream to upstream, it still is modeled to look like a Path message. As with the PathTear and ResvTear, the sender descriptor is optional on a PathErr but the flow descriptor is mandatory on a ResvErr. Both messages carry the Error Spec Object to indicate the reported problem.

There has been some contention about the presence, or rather absence, of an RSVP Hop Object on a PathErr message. Its presence would certainly have been possible since the message is generated in response to a Path message, and including it would have made implementation easier, but it is not strictly

```
< ResvTear Message > ::=      < Common Header >
                              [ < INTEGRITY > ]
                              < SESSION >
                              < RSVP_HOP >
                              [ < SCOPE > ]
                              < STYLE >
                              < flow descriptor list >
```

Figure 6.21 Formal definition of the RSVP ResvTear message.

```
< PathErr Message > ::=       < Common Header >
                              [ < INTEGRITY > ]
                              < SESSION >
                              < ERROR_SPEC >
                              [ < POLICY_DATA > ]
                              [ < sender descriptor > ]
```

Figure 6.22 Formal definition of the RSVP PathErr message.

```
< ResvErr Message > ::=       < Common Header >
                              [ < INTEGRITY > ]
                              < SESSION >
                              < RSVP_HOP >
                              < ERROR_SPEC >
                              [ < SCOPE > ]
                              [ < POLICY_DATA > ]
                              < STYLE >
                              < flow descriptor >
```

Figure 6.23 Formal definition of the RSVP ResvErr message.

```
< ResvConf Message > ::=        < Common Header >
                                [ < INTEGRITY > ]
                                < SESSION >
                                < ERROR_SPEC >
                                < RESV_CONFIRM >
                                < STYLE >
                                < flow descriptor list >
```

Figure 6.24 Formal definition of the RSVP ResvConf message.

necessary since the PathErr should be received through the interface out of which the Path was originally sent. This debate becomes interesting when a Path is sent out of one interface and then (after a change to the routing table) out of another interface—when a PathErr is received it is important to work out whether it applies to the old or the new path.

The ResvConf message shown in Figure 6.24 confirms a specific reservation and so is modeled on the Resv message. The message contains an Error Spec Object, not to report errors, but to report the source of the ResvConf, which might not be the ingress node in the case of merged flows.

As can be seen from Figures 6.15 through 6.24, all RSVP messages begin with a common header—this is shown in Figure 6.25. The header identifies the version of RSVP (currently one) and has a flags field for future use. The message type field identifies the RSVP message using values from Table 6.3. The Checksum and Length fields are applied to the whole message, including all fields of the header, with the length specified in bytes. The Checksum is computed as a standard one's complement of the one's complement sum of the message, with the checksum field replaced by zero for the purpose of computing the checksum. If the Checksum field is transmitted containing a zero value, no checksum was transmitted.

Table 6.3 RSVP Message Types

Message Type Value	Message
1	Path
2	Resv
3	PathErr
4	ResvErr
5	PathTear
6	ResvTear
7	ResvConf

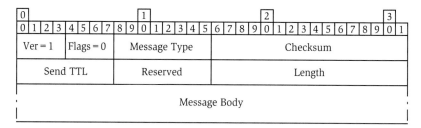

Figure 6.25 Each RSVP message has a common message header.

The Send TTL field in the message header is used to restrict the number of RSVP hops on a path. Since RSVP messages are intercepted at each RSVP-capable router, the normal IP TTL mechanism can be used only to restrict the number of IP hops between RSVP capable routers. To restrict the absolute length of the RSVP path and to provide some protection against looping, there is a TTL field in the RSVP header. The RSVP and IP TTL fields also can be used to detect the presence of non-RSVP hops since the two fields will remain in step only if each hop processes both fields.

6.4.10 RSVP Objects and Formats

As already described, RSVP messages are constructed from a common header followed by a series of message objects. All messages object have a common format, shown in Figure 6.26. The objects can be described as LTV (Length-Type-Value) constructs since they begin with a length field that gives the size in bytes of the entire object, followed by indicators of the type of object. The type indicator divides the objects into classes (primary types) indicated by the Class Number (C-Num) and subtypes indicated by the Class Type (C-Type). For example, the Session Object has a C-Num of 1, but since it contains an IP address that may be an IPv4 or an IPv6 address, two C-Types are defined.

Although the C-Num value can be treated as a unique integer identifying the class of object, the top 2 bits are overloaded to tell a message recipient how to handle the message if it does not recognize or support an object carried on the message. If the most significant bit is clear, the object must be handled or

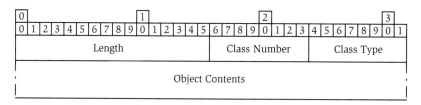

Figure 6.26 All RSVP message objects have a common format.

Table 6.4 The Top Bits of the RSVP Object Class Numbers Direct the Processing if the Object Is Unrecognized or Unsupported by the Receiver of a Message

C-Num Bit Setting	Processing of Unrecognized or Unsupported Object
0bbbbbbb	Reject entire message
10bbbbbb	Ignore object and do not propagate
11bbbbbb	Ignore object, but propagate unchanged

the entire message must be rejected. If the top bit is set, unrecognized objects may be ignored and must be propagated or removed from derivative messages according to the setting of the next most significant bit. These bit settings are shown in Table 6.4. Since this is the first version of RSVP, all objects are mandatory and have the top bit of their C-Num clear. Future extensions, such as those for RSVP-TE described in Chapter 9, may set the top bit to differentiate function when interoperating with older implementations of the base RSVP specification.

Note that it is not valid to consider a Session object with a C-Num that has the top bit set (that is with C-Num $129 = 0 \times 81$). That would be an entirely different C-Num and so would indicate a different object.

All RSVP objects are a multiple of 4 bytes in length. Where necessary, this is achieved using explicit padding. This means that during message parsing each object starts on a 4-byte boundary.

The Session Object shown in Figure 6.27 is used to define the session to which the flow belongs. A session is defined by the destination address (IPv4 or IPv6), the destination port, and the payload protocol, so all these are carried in this object. The C-Type is used to identify whether an IPv4 or IPv6 address is used. The port number may be set to zero to indicate a session that encompasses flows to all ports on the destination node. The protocol identifier is the IP Protocol identifier value that indicates the protocol carried by the IP data flow (see Section 2.2).

The other field, the Flags field, has one defined bit for use on Path messages only; if the value 0×01 is set, then the originator of the Path is unable to provide edge-based policing that the actual traffic flow falls within the parameters set in the Sender Tspec. The flag is propagated through the network until some node is able to take responsibility for policing the traffic.

The Class Number 3 is used to identify the RSVP Hop object shown in Figure 6.28. (Note, C-Num 2 is mysteriously undefined!) The object identifies the interface through which this message was sent using an IPv4 or IPv6 address. That is, on a Path message, the address identifies the downstream interface of the upstream node, while on a Resv the address indicates the

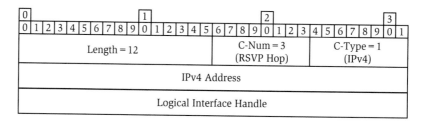

0										1										2										3	
0	1	2	3	4	5	6	7	8	9	0	1	2	3	4	5	6	7	8	9	0	1	2	3	4	5	6	7	8	9	0	1

Length = 12	C-Num = 1 (Session)	C-Type = 1 (IPv4)
IPv4 Address		

Protocol ID	Flags	Destination Port

Length = 24	C-Num = 1 (Session)	C-Type = 2 (IPv6)
IPv6 Address		
IPv6 Address (continued)		
IPv6 Address (continued)		
IPv6 Address (continued)		

Protocol ID	Flags	Destination Port

Figure 6.27 The RSVP Session Object has an IPv4 and an IPv6 type.

0										1										2										3	
0	1	2	3	4	5	6	7	8	9	0	1	2	3	4	5	6	7	8	9	0	1	2	3	4	5	6	7	8	9	0	1

Length = 12	C-Num = 3 (RSVP Hop)	C-Type = 1 (IPv4)
IPv4 Address		
Logical Interface Handle		

Length = 24	C-Num = 3 (RSVP Hop)	C-Type = 2 (IPv6)
IPv6 Address		
IPv6 Address (continued)		
IPv6 Address (continued)		
IPv6 Address (continued)		
Logical Interface Handle		

Figure 6.28 The RSVP Hop Object has an IPv4 and an IPv6 type.

upstream interface of the downstream node. The RSVP Hop Object is sometimes referred to as the PHOP (Previous Hop) when it is carried on a message that flows from upstream to downstream (as a Path) and as the NHOP (Next Hop) when it is on a message that flows from downstream to upstream (as a Resv).

The RSVP Hop also contains a Logical Interface Handle (LIH). This value is supplied by the upstream node on the Path message and is reflected back unchanged on the Resv. It can be used by the upstream node as a quick index to the interface without the need to look up any IP addresses (perhaps containing an interface index, or even a pointer to a control block). The fact that the IP address in the RSVP Hop changes but the LIH is returned unchanged, has led to innumerable implementation bugs.

The Time Values Object shown in Figure 6.29 has C-Num 5. It carries just one piece of information: the interval between refresh messages sent to refresh state, measured in milliseconds. This object is included in all Path messages and indicates how frequently the Path message will be refreshed. Similarly, the object is present on Resv messages and indicates how often the Resv will be refreshed.

In fact, refreshes are not sent precisely according to the refresh interval. It is a curious fact that messages sent periodically by independent nodes in a network can tend to become synchronized or clustered. If there are very many RSVP flows, this clustering of refresh messages may lead to contention for processing or network resources with a consequent disruption to control or even data traffic. RSVP disrupts this synchronization effect by randomly *jittering* the refresh intervals—RFC 2205 recommends that the actual refresh interval between refresh messages be picked randomly for each retransmission from the range half to one-and-a-half times the signaled refresh period. Note that the signaled refresh period is not updated for each refresh.

The refresh period is signaled to allow the receiver of the message to know when to expect to receive a refresh. This is important in determining when the soft state should timeout if no refresh is received. Clearly, the largest interval between two consecutive refreshes will be one-and-a-half times the signaled refresh period. If there is some possibility of losing packets but still continuing to support the flow, this number must be multiplied by the

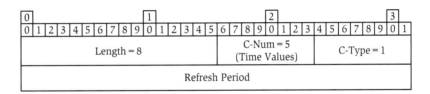

Figure 6.29 The RSVP Time Values Object.

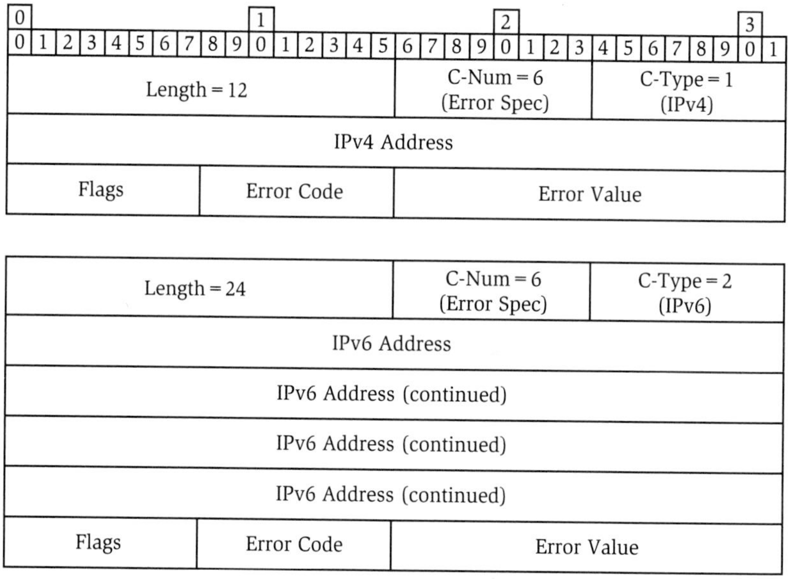

Figure 6.30 The RSVP Error Spec Object has an IPv4 and an IPv6 type.

number of refreshes that will actually be sent. This gives a formula for a state timeout (T) as follows:

$$T=K*1.5*R$$

where R is the signaled refresh period and K is the number of retransmissions (that is, we are prepared to lose K-1 refresh attempts). To this, add a little time for processing at the send and receive ends and for network propagation (say half of the maximum refresh interval) and the formula becomes

$$(K+0.5)*1.5*R$$

For general use, the value $K=3$ is suggested in RFC 2205, although this might need to be varied for very unreliable networks. Turning the handle on this gives the state timeout period of 5 1/4 R mentioned in Section 6.4.6.

Class Number 6 is used for the Error Spec Object carried on PathErr, ResvErr, and ResvConf messages and shown in Figure 6.30. Two C-Types are defined to indicate IPv4 or IPv6 addressing. The object reports the address of the node on which the error was first detected (or in the case of a ResvConf, the node that originated the message), an error code to describe or classify the error, and an error value to precisely specify the error—values for the error code and error value are listed in Table 6.5.

Table 6.5 RSVP Error Codes and Values

Code	Value	Meaning
0	0	Confirmation (used on ResvConf messages only)
1		Admission Control failure reported on ResvErr messages when the requested resources are unavailable. The first 4 bits of the error value are *ssur* where:
		ss=00: the remaining 12 bits contain an error value listed below
		ss=10: the remaining 12 bits contain an organization-specific value unknown to RSVP
		ss=11: the remaining 12 bits contain a value specific to a service, unknown to RSVP
		u=0 means that RSVP must remove local Resv state and forward the message
		u=1 means that the message is information and that RSVP may forward the message without removing local Resv state.
		The *r* bit is reserved and should be zero.
	1	Delay bound cannot be met.
	2	Requested bandwidth unavailable.
	3	MTU in FlowSpec larger than interface MTU.
2		Policy Control failures (defined in RFC 2750) appear on PathErr or ResvErr messages to show that the corresponding Path or Resv was rejected for administrative reasons such as authentication or permissions to request the reservation.
3	0	A Resv message was received but the receiver could not correlate it to any Path state for the corresponding session. This is used only on a ResvErr.
4	0	A Resv message was received and, although the receiver has Path state for the corresponding session, it cannot correlate some flow descriptor on the Resv to a sender template on a Path that it has previously sent. This is used only on a ResvErr.
5		The reservation style conflicts with style(s) of existing reservation state on the session. The error value holds the low-order 16 bits of the Option Vector of the existing style (that is, from the Style Object of a previous Resv). This is used only on a ResvErr.
6	0	The reservation style on a Resv is unknown. This is used only on a ResvErr.
7	0	Messages for the same destination address and protocol have appeared, one with a zero destination port and one with a nonzero destination port. This error would normally be used on a PathErr to reflect a problem with Path messages.
8	0	Path messages for the same session have the sender port set to zero and nonzero.
12		A previous reservation has been administratively preempted. The top 4 bits of the error value are as defined for error code 1. No RSVP-specific error values are defined.
13		An unknown object was received in a Path or Resv message and the high-order bits of the C-Num indicate that such an event should cause the entire message to be rejected. The error value shows the C-Num and C-Type of the unknown object. This Error Code may appear in a PathErr or ResvErr message.

Table 6.5 *Continued*

Code	Value	Meaning
14		An object with a known C-Num but an unknown C-Type was received in a Path or Resv message. The error value shows the C-Num and C-Type of the unknown object. This Error Code may appear in a PathErr or ResvErr message.
20		Reserved for use on the API between applications and RSVP.
21		The format or contents of the traffic parameters (TSpec, Adspec, or FlowSpec) could not be processed. The top 4 bits of the error value are broken up as *ssrr* where *ss* is as defined as for error code one and *rr* is reserved and set to zero. The remaining bits have the values set out below when $ss = 00$.
	1	Cannot merge two incompatible service requests.
	2	Can provide neither the requested service nor an acceptable replacement.
	3	The FlowSpec contains a malformed or unreasonable request.
	4	The TSpec contains a malformed or unreasonable request.
	5	The Adspec contains a malformed or unreasonable request.
22		A system error occurred while processing the traffic parameters (TSpec, Adspec, and FlowSpec). The error value is system specific and unknown to RSVP.
23		A system error occurred in the RSVP implementation. The error value is system-specific and unknown to RSVP.

The Error Spec Object also carries a Flags field. Currently just one flag value is defined for use on the wire and this is valid only on ResvErr messages. 0×01 indicates that a reservation is still in place at the failure point.

Malformed messages are not generally reported to end systems in a PathErr or ResvErr and are simply logged locally, or reported through network management mechanisms. The only message formatting errors that are reported to end systems are those that may reflect version mismatches such as unknown object C-Nums or C-Types. This choice is made because the report of a formatting error cannot be dynamically corrected by the node that caused the error, but a node that sends an unsupported object may be able to fall back to a mode of operation that does not require the object.

The RSVP Scope Object shown in Figure 6.31 is carried on Resv, ResvErr, and ResvTear messages. It contains a list of addresses of senders (that is, flow sources) to which the message applies. This is useful to prevent message loops in multicast networks using the Wildcard Filter reservation style, but is otherwise not used. All addresses carried in a single Scope Object are of the same type. The type is indicated by the C-Type field (set to 1 for IPv4 and 2 for IPv6). Since only one Scope Object may be present on a Resv, scoped Resv messages can apply to sources with one address type only.

Table 6.6 The Bit Settings in the Options
Vector of the RSVP Style Object

Bottom Five Bits	Meaning
00bbb	Reserved
01bbb	Distinct reservations
10bbb	Shared reservations
11bbb	Reserved
bb000	Reserved
bb001	Wildcard
bb010	Explicit
bb011–bb111	Reserved
10001	Wildcard Filter (WF)
01010	Fixed Filter (FF)
10010	Shared Explicit (SE)

The Style Object encodes the reservation style discussed in Section 6.4.7. As shown in Figure 6.32, the object contains a Flags field (currently no flags are defined) and an option vector. The option vector encodes the two style components (type of resource sharing, and flows identification) shown in Figure 6.13. Only the least significant 5 bits of the vector are used, as shown in Table 6.6.

The Style Object is mandatory on Resv, ResvTear, and ResvErr messages but not included on Path, PathTear, PathErr, or ResvConf messages (causing Frank Sinatra, Bing Crosby, and Dean Martin to sing, "You either have or you haven't got style").

Figure 6.33 shows the FilterSpec Object carried on Resv, ResvTear, ResvErr, and ResvConf messages to identify senders (flow sources). FilterSpecs with C-Num 10 are identical to Sender Template Objects with C-Num 11 that are present on Path, PathTear, and PathErr messages, where they serve the same purpose. The objects carry one of three C-Types according to the address formats in use, and in addition to the address of the source node, they contain a source port or an IPv6 flow label to indicate the port of flow label used by the application that is sending data. If the source port is zero, the Path message and corresponding reservation request apply to all flows on the session (that is to the same destination and destination port, carrying the same payload protocol) from the indicated address.

The Resv Confirm Object shown in Figure 6.34 is included on Resv messages to request that a ResvConf is returned to confirm the reservations. The address

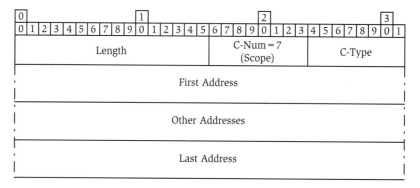

Figure 6.31 The RSVP Scope Object is a list of addresses of the same type.

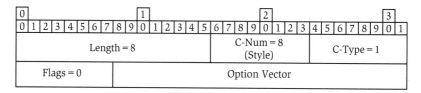

Figure 6.32 The RSVP Style Object.

specified may be IPv4 or IPv6 according to the C-Type, and indicates the destination to which the ResvConf should be sent. This targeting of a ResvConf is apparently in contradiction to the statement made in Section 6.4.2 that ResvConf messages are forwarded hop-by-hop along the RSVP path, but it simply allows a node that is not the egress to request a ResvConf from the ingress and know when the message is received that it should not forward it further downstream.

The Resv Confirm Object is returned unchanged in the ResvConf message to provide correlation.

The FlowSpec (C-Num 9), Sender TSpec (C-Num 12), and Adspec (C-Num 13) objects use C-Type 2 to indicate that they carry IntServ information describing the traffic flow. The format of the contents of these objects is described in Section 6.3 and defined in RFC 2210.

The Integrity Object (C-Num 4) is used to protect against message spoofing that could lead to theft of resources or denial of service to legitimate users. The use and contents of the Integrity object are described in RFC 2747 to include a 48-bit key, a sequence number, and a message digest (such as one produced using the MD5 algorithm). Note that IPsec (see Chapter 14) was considered as an alternative to embedding integrity information within RSVP messages, but was rejected because IPsec relies on a clear indication of source and destination

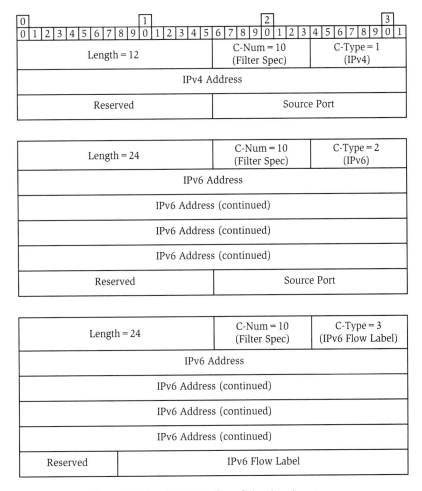

Figure 6.33 The RSVP FilterSpec Object has three types.

points, which is obscured by the addressing model used in RSVP. In addition, RSVP neighbors may be separated by multiple routers which are not RSVP capable and this may confuse the application of IPsec. On the other hand, if the network is simple, IPsec may be used following the rules of RFC 2207 so that the source and destination port fields are replaced by IPsec Security Parameter Indexes. RFC 2747 also defines Integrity Challenge and Integrity Response messages to help a node verify that its peer is legitimate.

A final RSVP object, the Policy Object (C-Num 14), is described in RFC 2205 as "for further study." A slew of RFCs provide input to the problem of managing admission control policy—that is, the question of administering which nodes are allowed to request what reservations under what circumstances. This feature first requires that applications and users are properly identified using

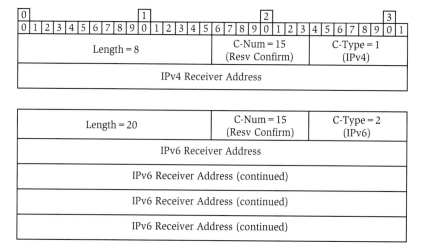

Figure 6.34 The RSVP Resv Confirm Object has two types.

the integrity procedures just discussed, and then needs the exchange of policy information between the applications and policy control elements that police reservation requests within the network. RSVP passes the contents of Policy Objects from node to node transparently and simply delivers them to policy control components on the routers.

RFC 2750 proposes a format for the Policy Object to contain a list of RSVP-like objects relating to the reservation request and a series of policy elements to identify the permissions possessed by the application requesting the service and including the identity of the application.

6.4.11 Choosing a Transport Protocol

RSVP is designed to operate over raw IP. The protocol includes sufficient mechanisms to tolerate lost packets and to detect corruption—it needs none of the services provided by an IP transport protocol (see Chapter 7). RSVP messages are encapsulated in IP packets using the protocol field value 46 ($0 \times 2E$). Because Path messages are subject to normal routing and may be forwarded through parts of the network that are not RSVP capable, the IP packets that carry them use the source IP address of the node that is the source of the RSVP flow, and the destination IP address of the node that is the destination of the RSVP flow. This creates an issue because intervening RSVP-capable routers need to act on RSVP messages and would not normally see them since the messages would be forwarded according to the destination IP address. To circumvent this problem, the Router Alert IP option is used. This process is also applied to PathTear messages, but all other messages are addressed hop-by-hop (that is, they carry the IP addresses of adjacent RSVP-capable routers).

Since some host systems (especially older ones) do not provide access to raw IP, RSVP is also specified to operate over UDP. UDP is a lightweight transport protocol (see Chapter 7) that is commonly available on host systems. A source host that does not have access to raw IP may send its RSVP messages encapsulated in UDP addresses to the next hop RSVP-capable router using port 1698. The first router that is RSVP-capable and has access to raw IP (likely to be the first router) is required to convert the RSVP exchange to raw IP for forwarding into the network.

At the egress from the network, a router may need to convert back to UDP encapsulation before it delivers RSVP messages to a host. RFC 2205 suggests that a router will learn when this is necessary by the receipt of UDP encapsulated messages from that host, but this has an obvious flaw since someone has to receive the first Path message. The net result is that routers must be configured with the capabilities of their adjacent hosts. Most hosts these days provide access to raw IP so that RSVP implementations do not need to use UDP.

6.4.12 RSVP Refresh Reduction

As mentioned earlier, one of the consequences of RSVP being a soft state protocol is that messages must be periodically exchanged to keep the state active and the reservations in place. One concern with this is that considerable bandwidth and processing capabilities may be used up in simply keeping state active, reducing the capability to establish new state promptly and even, perhaps, affecting the ability to forward data. Refresh reduction is based not on removing the requirement to refresh RSVP state, nor on changing the interval between refreshes. Instead, the focus is on reducing the amount of processing required by both the sender and the receiver of a state refresh message and minimizing the number of bytes that must be sent between the nodes.

RFC 2961 describes a small set of extensions to RSVP to facilitate refresh reduction. These extensions arise from heated debates within the IETF, both about the need for any changes and about the best way to address the issue. In the end, three procedures were standardized: the first and second are independent (although they may be used together), but the third builds on the second.

All three extensions are treated as a single functional block and are used between a pair of RSVP routers only if both support them. This support is signaled in a new flag setting in the Flags field in the Session Object. 0×01 is used to indicate support of all the refresh reduction extensions. Indicating support of the extensions does not mean that an RSVP router needs to use all or any of them in messages that it sends, but it must be able to process all of them if it receives them.

The first extension allows multiple RSVP messages to be packaged together as a *bundle* within a single IP message. A new RSVP message type, 12, indicates a Bundle message. A Bundle message is built of an RSVP message header followed by one or more RSVP messages. The number of bundled RSVP messages is not indicated, but the length of the Bundle message itself indicates whether there is more data, and hence another message, when processing of one bundled

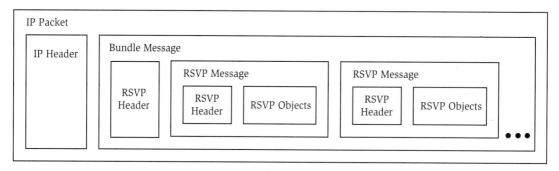

Figure 6.35 The Bundle message encapsulates one or more RSVP messages in a single IP message using an additional RSVP message header.

message has completed. The main advantages of message bundling are a small reduction in the number of bytes transmitted between RSVP routers, and a reduction in processing, especially through the IP stack—a clutch of refresh messages may be collected together into a single bundle and sent at the same time. The format of a Bundle message is shown in Figure 6.35.

When an RSVP node receives a Path or a Resv message it needs to distinguish three cases. The message may be for a new flow, it may be a change to an existing flow (for example, modifying the bandwidth required for a flow), or it may be a refresh. New flows are easily distinguished because there is no matching stored Path or Resv state. Modification requests can be distinguished from state refresh messages because they contain changes in one or more of the parameters when compared with the previous message received. This means that each time a refresh message is received, an RSVP router must compare it fully with the previous message—since the order of objects in a message may vary without affecting the meaning, the receiver cannot simply compare the whole message as a block of memory, but must compare the objects one by one. This introduces a considerable overhead in processing, which is addressed in the refresh reduction extensions by placing a message identifier on each message. The Message Identifier Object, shown in Figure 6.36, includes a monotonic increasing message identifier

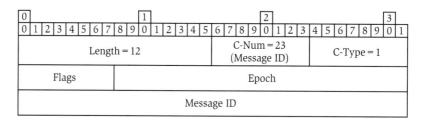

Figure 6.36 The RSVP Message ID Object.

```
< Path Message > ::=              < Common Header >
                                  [ < INTEGRITY > ]
                                  [[ < MESSAGE_ID_ACK >  < MESSAGE_ID_NACK > ] . . . ]
                                  [ < MESSAGE_ID > ]
                                  < SESSION >
                                  < RSVP_HOP >
                                  < TIME_VALUES >
                                  [ < POLICY_DATA > ]
                                  < sender descriptor >
```

Figure 6.37 Formal definition of the RSVP Path message for refresh reduction showing the optional inclusion of Message ID and Message ID Acknowledgement Objects.

number and an *epoch* that is used to disambiguate different instances of an adjacent node so that there is no confusion about the reuse of message ID values if a node is restarted. The epoch can be a random number or a function of real time.

If the message identifier on a message is identical to that previously received, no further checking is required: the message is a refresh. If the message identifier is lower than that previously received, the message is an old message that has been delayed in the network and can be ignored. If the message number is greater than that previously received, the message must be examined more closely and may be a refresh or a modification. The Message Identifier Object may be carried on every RSVP message. It serves both the purpose of ensuring acknowledged delivery of messages and of flagging Path and Resv messages as refreshes, as shown in Figures 6.38 and 6.39.

Message identifiers uniquely identify individual messages and make it possible to formally acknowledge the receipt of a message. The Message Identifier Object contains a flag (0×01) that requests the receiver to acknowledge receipt. This acknowledgment is carried in a Message Ack Object, as shown in Figure 6.39. The object contains the message identifier of the acknowledged message and may be carried one at a time or as a series in any message that flows in the opposite direction, as indicated for Path and Resv messages in Figures 6.37 and 6.38.

If there is no message being sent in the opposite direction, the receiver must still acknowledge the received message identifier as soon as possible. It can do this by sending an Acknowledgement message that simply carries the acknowledged message identifiers, as shown in Figure 6.40.

The sender of a message carrying a message identifier that has requested acknowledgment retransmits the message periodically until it is acknowledged or until it decides that there is a problem with the link or with the receiving node. Retransmission is relatively frequent (roughly every half a second), so it

```
< Resv Message > ::=        < Common Header >
                            [ < INTEGRITY > ]
                            [[ < MESSAGE_ID_ACK > < MESSAGE_ID_NACK > ] ... ]
                            [ < MESSAGE_ID > ]
                            < SESSION >
                            < RSVP_HOP >
                            < TIME_VALUES >
                            [ < RESV_CONFIRM > ]
                            [ < SCOPE > ]
                            [ < POLICY_DATA > ]
                            < STYLE >
                            < flow descriptor list >
```

Figure 6.38 Formal definition of the RSVP Resv message for refresh reduction showing the optional inclusion of Message ID and Message ID Acknowledgement Objects.

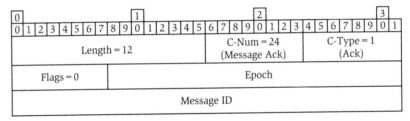

Figure 6.39 The RSVP Message Ack Object.

```
< Ack Message > ::=         < Common Header >
                            [ < INTEGRITY > ]
                            < MESSAGE_ID_ACK > < MESSAGE_ID_NACK >
                            [[ < MESSAGE_ID_ACK > < MESSAGE_ID_NACK > ] ... ]
```

Figure 6.40 Formal definition of the RSVP Ack message.

is important not to swamp the system with retransmissions. RFC 2961 suggests that the sender should apply an exponential back-off, doubling the time between retransmissions at each attempt. It also suggests that a message should be transmitted a maximum of three times even if it is not acknowledged (that is, one transmission and two retransmissions).

```
< Srefresh Message > ::=          < Common Header >
                                  [ < INTEGRITY > ]
                                  [[ < MESSAGE_ID_ACK > | < MESSAGE_ID_NACK > ] ... ]
                                  [ < MESSAGE_ID > ]
                                  < srefresh list > | < source srefresh list >
< srefresh list > ::=             < MESSAGE_ID LIST > | < MESSAGE_ID MCAST_LIST >
                                  [ < srefresh list > ]
< source srefresh list > ::=      < MESSAGE_ID SRC_LIST >
                                  [ < source srefresh list > ]
```

Figure 6.41 Formal definition of the RSVP Srefresh message.

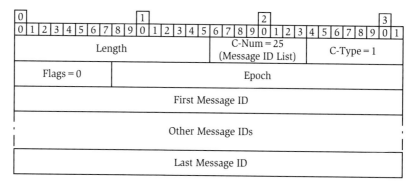

Figure 6.42 The RSVP Message ID List Object used in the Srefresh message.

The third extension for refresh reduction recognizes that once a message identifier has been assigned to a state message, it is not necessary to retransmit the whole message—only the message identifier needs to be sent to keep the state alive. The Summary Refresh (Srefresh) message shown in Figure 6.41 is used to send a list of message identifiers in this fashion. The Srefresh message itself does not carry a Message Identifier in its own right, but each of the identifiers that it does carry can be accepted or rejected, although usually no specific acknowledgement is requested, so only rejections are sent. A rejection uses the Message Nack object, which has C-Type of 2 but is otherwise identical to a Message Ack object. The Message Nack allows some message identifiers out of the set on the Srefresh to be rejected without rejecting all of them. The rejection is necessary if the receiver does not match the message identifier against a stored value—it cannot use the Srefresh to establish new state since the message does not carry the full Path or Resv information.

Message Nack Objects can be carried within the other messages such as the Path and Resv messages shown in Figures 6.37 and 6.38. Alternatively, the

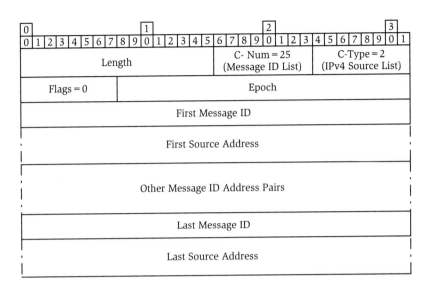

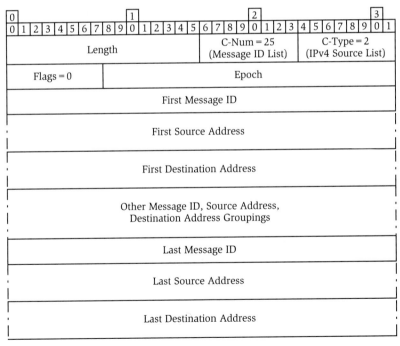

Figure 6.43 The RSVP Source Message ID List and Message ID Multicast List Objects.

Acknowledgement message shown in Figure 6.40 may be used. If the Srefresh is received and accepted, a single Message Ack carrying the message ID of the Srefresh message acknowledges all of the message IDs carried in the Srefresh list. If one or more message IDs in the Srefresh list is rejected, the message itself must still be acknowledged and Message Nacks must be used to reject each unacceptable message ID. There is no need to acknowledge individual message IDs from within the srefresh list.

The basic Srefresh contains a Message ID List, as shown in Figure 6.42. The object lists a series of message IDs for state that is being refreshed, but recognizes that the epoch value does not need to repeated for each message ID.

The Srefresh message is complicated considerably by multicast issues. It is possible that a downstream node will receive a refresh of Path state from multiple upstream interfaces and care must be taken to send the acknowledgments to the right place and only as frequently as is actually required. The Source Message List and Message ID Multicast List Objects shown in Figure 6.43 allow a single Srefresh message to refresh state with reference to source and destination addresses—the addresses shown may be IPv4 or IPv6 depending on the C-Type of the object (2 or 3 for Message List, 4 or 5 for Message ID Multicast List). Note that this format is considerably suboptimal since the addresses must be reproduced for each message ID.

All three refresh reduction procedures can be combined with Acknowledgement and Srefresh messages being bundled along with other messages.

6.4.13 Choosing to Use Refresh Reduction

The choice to use RSVP refresh reduction is not straightforward. Before it can be used at all, the protocol extensions must be supported by the RSVP nodes at each end of a link and flagged in the common message header (flag value 0×01) of all messages, and this may restrict the choice since not all implementations include support for refresh reduction.

Consideration should then be given to the value of each of the three refresh mechanisms. Although, strictly speaking, the setting of the refresh reduction-capable flag in the common message header means that a node fully supports all the mechanisms, it does not actually need to actively use them. The only requirements are that it should be able to receive and correctly process refresh reduction messages and objects that it receives. This means that in implementations that are suitably configurable the precise refresh reduction operations can be selected individually. Further, in networks that will be made up of only a single vendor's routers, a choice can be made to partially implement refresh reduction.

The basic requirement for two of the options is that Message IDs are supported, that is that Path and Resv messages and their refreshes carry Message IDs. A sender may choose whether to use a new Message ID on each refresh message, a receiver may choose whether to take advantage of the Message ID to expedite refresh processing, and a sender may opt to use the Summary Refresh message or to simply retransmit full refresh messages. These choices depend on backwards compatibility (existing implementations will check for refreshes by examining each field of a received object), implementation complexity (some implementations find it hard to know whether they are sending a refresh message or one that modifies the previous request, and the summary refresh processing is a considerable amount of new code), and the number of flows between a pair of RSVP neighbors (it may not be necessary to use summary refresh if there are only a few tens of flows).

The value of bundle messages remains debatable. On an ordinary Ethernet link carrying IPv4 packets, the saving from bundling two RSVP messages together is just 26 bytes (Ethernet header 14 bytes plus IP header 20 bytes, less 8 bytes for the RSVP Bundle message header). When RSVP messages are of the order of 100 bytes each, this saving is only around 10 percent. On the other hand, when small messages such as Acknowledgements and Resv Confirms are being sent the savings may be better.

But message bundling requires that the sender has two messages ready to be sent at the same time. The implementation of this may be hard to achieve since it is not advisable to hold on to one message in the hope that another will need to be sent soon. Similarly, it may damage the randomization of state refresh periods to deliberately bunch refreshes into a single Bundle message. Bundling may, however, be of advantage in systems that are able to recognize that there is a queue of messages waiting to be sent and can then collect those messages into a single bundle, and on routers where there is a considerable overhead associated with sending or receiving an IP packet.

6.4.14 Aggregation of RSVP Flows

Aggregation of traffic flows improves scalability within the network since individual nodes need to maintain a smaller number of queues and distinct resources to manage the same amount of traffic. RSVP and IntServ in general maintain reservations for separate micro-flows through the network, and this gives rise to concerns about scalability not just during refresh processing but also on the data path.

Some research has been done into combining DiffServ and IntServ reservations to aggregate traffic and to allow multiple flows of a similar type to be managed together with a single reservation. For example, all flows with the same DiffServ DSCP could be grouped together and handled using the same IntServ reservation (managed though RSVP) with the resources allocated being the sum of the component parts. These ideas are developed further in RFC 3175.

6.5   Further Reading

Internet QoS: Architectures and Mechanisms for Quality of Service, by Zheng Wang (2001). Morgan Kaufmann. This provides excellent coverage of all the important, implementable models for providing service differentiation in the Internet.

Inside the Internet's Reservation Protocol: Foundations for Quality of Service, by David Durham and Raj Yavatkar (1999). John Wiley & Sons. This book was written by two Intel engineers with in-depth experience of developing the RSVP standards and one of the first RSVP implementations.

Developing IP-Based Services, by Monique Morrow and Kateel Vijayananda (2003). Morgan Kaufmann. This source provides a brief overview of IP Quality of Service from the perspective of Service Providers and equipment vendors.

Differentiated Services was first proposed as an architecture and then developed by the definition of specific uses. Some key RFCs for Differentiated Services are:

RFC 2430—A Provider Architecture for Differentiated Services and Traffic Engineering
RFC 2597—Assured Forwarding PHB Group
RFC 3246—An Expedited Forwarding PHB
RFC 3270—Multiprotocol Label Switching (MPLS) Support of Differentiated Services

Integrated Services was developed as a framework by the IETF and has since been worked on by many Working Groups as they have seen the need to incorporate the features into their work. Some key RFCs for Integrated Services are:

RFC 1633—Integrated Services in the Internet Architecture: An Overview
RFC 2210—The Use of RSVP with IETF Integrated Services
RFC 2211—Specification of the Controlled-Load Network Element Service
RFC 2212—Specification of Guaranteed Quality of Service
RFC 2215—General Characterization Parameters for Integrated Service Network Elements
RFC 2381—Interoperation of Controlled-Load and Guaranteed Service with ATM
RFC 2688—Integrated Services Mappings for Low Speed Networks
RFC 2815—Integrated Service Mappings on IEEE 802 Networks
RFC 2997—Specification of the Null Service Type
RFC 2998—A Framework for Integrated Services Operation over DiffServ Networks

RSVP was developed within the IETF by the RSVP Working Group. The RSVP Working Group has been closed down because all development work has been completed. However, the new uses of RSVP for MPLS and GMPLS can be seen in the MPLS and CCAMP Working Groups. Some key RFCs for RSVP are:

RFC 2205—Resource ReSerVation Protocol (RSVP)—Version 1 Functional Specification
RFC 2207—RSVP Extensions for IPsec Data Flows
RFC 2210—The Use of RSVP with IETF Integrated Services
RFC 2747—RSVP Cryptographic Authentication
RFC 2750—RSVP Extensions for Policy Control

RFC 2961—RSVP Refresh Overhead Reduction Extensions
RFC 3175—Aggregation of RSVP for IPv4 and IPv6 Reservations

The RSVP API (RAPI) is published by The Open Group as *The Resource Reservation Setup Protocol API (RAPI)*, document number c809. It can be seen at their web site in HTML or PDF format at http://www.opengroup.org/products/publications/catalog/c809.htm.

The Service Management Research Group of the Internet Research Task Force (IRTF) has published their findings on the use of quality of service in IP networks in:

RFC 3387—Considerations from the Service Management Research Group (SMRG) on Quality of Service (QoS) in the IP Network

Chapter 7

Transport Over IP

The Internet Protocol family includes three transport protocols: the User Datagram Protocol (UDP), the Transmission Control Protocol (TCP), and a recent addition called the Stream Control Transmission Protocol (SCTP). Transport protocols play an important role in the IP suite, where they provide data delivery services for most application protocols and for a large number of control protocols. This chapter introduces some of the concepts of transport before describing each of the three transport protocols.

A final section of this chapter details RTP, a transport protocol for real-time applications. RTP is a somewhat special transport protocol because it is usually run both as a transport service provider for applications and as a user of other transport protocols.

7.1   What Is a Transport Protocol?

The transport layer acts as a common service provision layer between its users, the applications, and the underlying network. Network layers can have vastly differing characteristics in terms of reliability, throughput, and quality of traffic delivery, and if applications ran directly over network protocols they would each need to be implemented to handle these varied behaviors. This would be hard for the designers of applications protocols and for application implementers—each would need to reinvent the same wheel. The transport layer addresses this by bringing the service level up to a common standard and allowing the application to make assumptions about the transport of any data it sends.

A transport protocol is a set of rules for the exchange of control messages and data between participating nodes. Transport protocols run end-to-end (that is, between the nodes on which the applications reside) but network protocols involve strictly point-to-point exchanges. Figure 7.1 illustrates this point.

The Internet family has three key transport protocols, each designed to offer a different level of service to the application. An application protocol chooses which transport protocol to use based on the level of its specific requirements—it may choose to use a protocol that provides a higher level of function than it

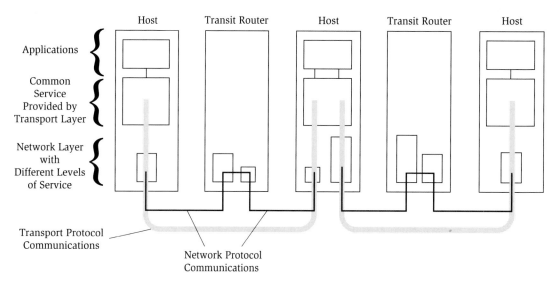

Applications

Common
Service
Provided by
Transport Layer

Network Layer
with
Different Levels
of Service

Transport Protocol
Communications

Network Protocol
Communications

Figure 7.1 Transport protocols offer a common level of service and run end-to-end.

needs, but this is generally considered wasteful since the higher level of function requires greater overhead in implementation and network resource usage.

Note that there is no requirement for an application protocol to use a transport protocol. It is free to decide to build the function it needs on top of common network services such as IP and include in its own processing whatever features it needs to ensure that it survives any issues the network may throw at it.

The three transport protocols are the User Datagram Service, the Transmission Control Protocol, and the Stream Control Transmission Protocol. Discussion of these protocols forms the bulk of this chapter, but first it is worth covering some basic concepts in the world of a transport protocol.

7.1.1 Choosing to Use a Transport Protocol

As described in the preceding section, the level of service provided by a network (the physical layer, data-link layer, and the network protocol) is varied and may not be high enough to be of good use to an application. Some of the issues are as follows:

- Networks typically provide little or no error detection. Data may be corrupted, delivered out of order, or lost completely within the network without any indication being passed to the consumer. Even failures of physical network connections may go unreported, with the network layer happily accepting data from its user and dropping it into the void.

- Even when a network protocol does detect an error, it makes no attempt to correct it, for example, by retransmitting a packet. Detected errors are simply a cause to drop the errored packet.
- Communications within the network are managed in a point-to-point, connectionless manner. There is no end-to-end connectivity and so no easy regulation or management of data flows.
- There is no handshaking of end-point capabilities, no verification of data delivery, no flow control of data, and not even any verification that the other end of a connection exists.

These issues are addressed at various levels by transport protocols, but each function comes at a cost. The price is paid in complexity of implementation and traffic overhead that reduces the capacity for data transport. If an application really does not need these services it should not use a transport protocol. If an application needs only some of the services, it should choose a transport protocol that provides the best fit to its requirements from those described in the remainder of this chapter. It is sensible for an application to use a transport protocol if it needs these services because it can utilize existing, tested, and proven protocols and code.

Some applications choose not to use a transport protocol even though they do actually need some of the services that such a protocol would provide. The reasons are varied and range from pig-headed protocol designers who believe that they can invent a rounder wheel than their predecessors could, to legitimate concerns about the overhead imposed by a transport protocol when only a few specific services are needed. One other reason for not using a transport protocol arises when an application is planned to run on a switch or router that might not have the transport protocol readily available—this was a serious concern in the early days of the Internet when TCP, for example, was not a standard part of every operating system.

7.1.2 Ports and Addresses

Transport protocols deliver data between well-defined end points. The main identifier of an end point is an IP address—it defines the nodes from which data is sent and to which it is delivered. But an IP address does not provide sufficient granularity for delivery of data between applications because multiple applications may run on a single node. What is worse, multiple applications of the same type may run on a single node, so we cannot even simply peek inside the IP payload to discover what is being carried and deduce to where it should be delivered.

The problem of identifying source and destination points is solved by defining *ports* on each node. A port is a 16-bit number that qualifies an individual IP address. Thus, there can be 65,535 ports for each IP address. Applications bind to specific ports and transport connections between applications are made between {source IP address, source port} and {destination IP address, destination port} pairs and are uniquely identified by those coordinates. These address–port pairings are usually expressed using a colon as a separator: 192.168.254.14:80 is port 80 on the node identified by the IP address 192.168.254.14.

When discussing addresses and ports it is conventional to construct some form of analogy, metaphor, or as a last resort, simile. One way to look at this schema is by comparing the IP address to the postal address of an apartment building. The port represents the numbered mailbox that is owned by Mr. Application. Different people can be reached at different mailboxes even if they are all called by the same name, Mr. Application. Any individual recipient can choose to have all his mail delivered to one mailbox or can utilize multiple mailboxes.

When a sender wants to transfer data to a remote receiver he prepares it (writes a letter) and passes it to the transport protocol to send. The transport protocol puts the letter into an envelope (or a series of envelopes if it is a long letter), addresses the envelope, writes a return address on the top left-hand corner and gives it to the postman (the IP delivery system). Receivers can use the return address to respond to the right mailbox at the sender's address. This is illustrated in Figure 7.2.

One issue with this is the determination of the destination address and port number. How do you know how to address your letter? This is a distinct problem that IP faces when it needs to know how to deliver your letter to a specific IP address. The determination of IP addresses using host names or Universal

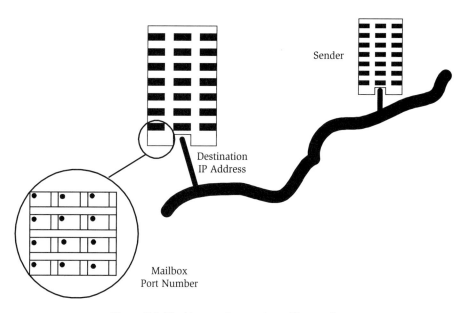

Figure 7.2 IP address and ports: the mailbox analogy.

Resource Locators (URLs) is within the realm of application-level protocols discussed in Chapter 12. We can assume that the sender either knows the destination IP address or else uses some utility (akin to an address book) to map from a known name to the destination address. But how do we know which ports to use?

Well-known applications have well-known port numbers. This makes life simple. If, for example, you want to contact the HTTP server at a given node, you use port 80. In fact, if you want to contact the HTTP server at *any* node you use port 80 (although note that there are some security considerations with this choice of port on an HTTP server). But how do I know which port to target? And suppose I am writing an application: How do I know which port to listen on? I know where I live, but which is my mailbox?

The Internet Assigned Numbers Authority (IANA) is the single central body that assigns and tracks port numbers. They have divided the 65,535 numbers into three ranges.

The *well-known ports* are ports 1 through 1023. These are assigned for use by server applications. By tradition, these are applications that need to run with restricted privileges and these ports may be accessed only by securely managed applications—so that, for example, on a UNIX system only an application running with root privileges may use one of these ports.

The *registered ports* are in the range 1024 to 49,151. These ports have well-defined uses assigned by IANA. They are mainly used for server applications since the usual requirement is for a client to contact a server to start a conversation, but in some cases client applications are also assigned port numbers so that the server may contact the client. Lots of these port numbers have not been assigned yet, but a surprisingly large number have.

The *dynamic* or *private ports* are the final set of port numbers, 49,152 to 65,535. These ports, sometimes called ephemeral ports, are assigned by the local system on an as-needed basis and are freed up when they are no longer needed. These ports are never used as a destination address when a conversation is started, but may be used by the initiator as his return address. This allows a client application to start many parallel conversations with a single server application, which is useful if, for example, you like to have several Web browser windows open to the same site at the same time.

There is a slight deviation to these clear rules. Some network managers choose to obfuscate their networks, perhaps as protection against hackers, by mixing their port IDs around. So, for example, the email POP3 server might be accessed through port 999 instead of port 110 so that only those clients who know in advance how to reach the POP3 server will be able to do so.

7.1.3 Reliable Delivery

Some letters we mail and trust that they will probably arrive. We accept the small probability of delivery failure and choose to ignore it—at worst Granny will assume that she didn't get a birthday card from you because you always were a lazy good-for-nothing. Other letters, such as tax refunds, we consider more important and when we don't receive them in a timely manner we poll the tax man to find out what has happened. Some exchanges, such as sending final manuscripts to our editors, make us so jittery that we use tracked delivery services that "guarantee" delivery.

And so it is with data transfer. Some transport mechanisms provide no indication of whether the data has been delivered, some will allow you to discover that something has gone wrong, and others make guarantees about delivery. In practice, of course, all the guarantees reduce to "We will deliver your letter or let you know that we failed," but even this can be a great help to the letter writer.

7.1.4 Connection-Oriented Transport

When a transport service requires the end points to acknowledge each other's existence, negotiate terms for communication, and maintain state information to make data exchange possible, the connection is known as *connection-oriented*. That is, a specific end-to-end connection is established between the end points and data is then transferred. When the data transfer is complete, the connection is torn down.

At this point it is useful to switch from a metaphor to a simile. A connection-oriented transport system is like a telephone network. When you want to place a phone call you need to know the receiver's number and extension. The receiver may have as many phones on his desk as he chooses and might reserve some for specific uses (the red phone is the line to Moscow).

Connection-oriented transport has many advantages. It is easier to communicate with someone if you first establish his presence (he answers the phone), you verify that you're talking to the right person ("Hello, is that Mr. Application?"), and you check that he speaks the same language as you. Beyond that, you can apply all sorts of error correction mechanisms ranging from, "Sorry, I didn't catch that," through, "No, I think you may have misunderstood me, I actually said...," to the incantation so popular among cell phone users, "Hello? Hello? I think I've lost you. Are you still there?"

There are also some disadvantages to connection-oriented transport. In general, it requires heavier-weight protocols, and these need more sophisticated implementations to manage and store connection state. Connection-oriented transport protocols also tend to divert a proportion of network bandwidth to manage the connection instead of transmitting data.

7.1.5 Datagrams

Some transport protocols are based on datagram services. These are much more akin to letter writing, but the delivery is as quick as a phone call. Applications that use datagram transport services are able to leverage rapid transfer of data without connection setup and with no need to maintain connections. On the other hand, datagram services are not reliable, so the applications risk out of order or failed delivery of their messages. Applications that use datagram transport services either must not care too much about their data or must take precautions at an application level to keep track of what is going on. Datagrams operate as a *connectionless* transport service.

7.2 User Datagram Protocol (UDP)

The User Datagram Protocol (UDP) appears at first glance to be a marketing ploy by a software house that wanted to sell another communications protocol product! UDP does not provide a connection-oriented service. There is no error detection or recovery, no flow control, and no way to determine whether the application at the other end has received the data sent or even if the intended receiver exists at all. So does UDP do anything at all or is it vapor?

The answer, of course, is that UDP provides a very useful, but simple service. It provides targeted delivery within a node identified by an IP address. If a UDP application is an individual, as in the analogy of Section 7.1.2, UDP allows data to be targeted at the user's mailbox and, hence, delivered to the user without any need to examine the contents of the data. That is, UDP identifies the target port as well as the target address.

In fact, UDP supplies several basic functions above the services of raw IP.

- Destination port identification allows data to be delivered directly to the application.
- Source port identification enables the receiver to quickly determine the sending application and respond directly to that application.
- Data integrity verification occurs through a checksum. This does not allow repair or analysis of corrupt data, but does allow damaged packets to be discarded.
- UDP provides data reassembly. IP datagrams may be segmented as they pass through the network, each being broken into a series of smaller packets to fit within the Maximum Transmission Unit (MTU—see Section 1.5) of the network segment that must be traversed. UDP reassembles the IP packets so that it delivers whole UDP datagrams at the destination.

7.2.1 UDP Message Format

Each UDP message begins with a header and is followed by the UDP data payload, as shown in Figure 7.3. UDP messages are sent as the payload of one or more IP packets using the protocol identifier value of 17. If the UDP message is broken up into multiple IP packets, the whole UDP message is simply chopped up to fit, as shown in the figure. The UDP header is not repeated.

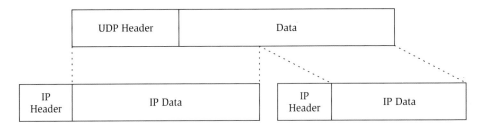

Figure 7.3 A UDP message is carried within one or more IP datagrams.

0										1										2										3	
0	1	2	3	4	5	6	7	8	9	0	1	2	3	4	5	6	7	8	9	0	1	2	3	4	5	6	7	8	9	0	1
Source Port																Destination Port															
UDP Datagram Length																UDP Checksum															

Figure 7.4 The UDP message header.

The UDP header is very simple, containing just four fields, as shown in Figure 7.4. The Source and Destination Ports are 16-bit port identifiers assigned as described in Section 7.1.2. *Source* always applies to the sender of the message and *destination* to the intended receiver, so when a response is sent, the roles of source and destination are reversed. The Datagram Length gives the length of the entire UDP datagram, including the header itself. Since the length field is only 16 bits, there is a practical limit to the size of a UDP message of 65,535 bytes: that is, 65,527 bytes of data. The checksum provides a way of verifying the sanity and completeness of the delivered data and is discussed further in the next section.

7.2.2 Choosing to Use the UDP Checksum

The UDP checksum is provided to verify the integrity of the delivered UDP datagram. This may be desirable when the network layer does not provide such a service, but is of debatable value on some networks, such as Ethernets where network frames are treated to Cyclic Redundancy Check (CRC) processing to ensure that they are delivered correctly.

In general, the UDP processes cannot know for certain which network technologies will be used to deliver the data. Even when there is a series of reliable Ethernet connections from source to destination, UDP cannot know for certain that the IP traffic will not be routed along another path that includes unreliable links. For this reason, the use of the UDP checksum is strongly recommended in all circumstances.

The choice not to use the checksum can be made by the sender—the Checksum field is simply filled with zero. Alternatively, even if the sender uses a checksum, the receiver may choose to ignore the fact and not verify it—this second option is, however, strictly forbidden by the guidelines for implementing Internet hosts (RFC 1122)—if a sender uses the checksum, the receiver must verify it.

The decision not to use a checksum in UDP was usually made on performance grounds since the checksum algorithm performs a calculation on every byte of data. In practice, modern chip speeds are such that calculating a checksum is rarely now seen as a constraint. Where it is an issue, specialized chips for performing checksum processing are available.

Unlike many protocols which compute checksums only on the message itself, UDP adds a piece of untransmitted data, a *pseudomessage header*, to the front of the message before calculating the checksum on the combination of the pseudoheader and the message, as shown in Figure 7.5. The checksum field itself is set to zero, the pseudoheader is filled in, and the checksum is calculated. The result is placed in the checksum field, the pseudoheader is discarded, and the datagram is sent. The use of the pseudoheader helps to verify that the headers of the IP packets carrying the UDP datagrams have not themselves been corrupted.

UDP receive processes must also construct pseudoheaders to verify the checksum. They save the received checksum value, insert zero in the checksum field, calculate the checksum, and compare the new value with the stored, received value. A match signifies a valid datagram, and a mismatch should

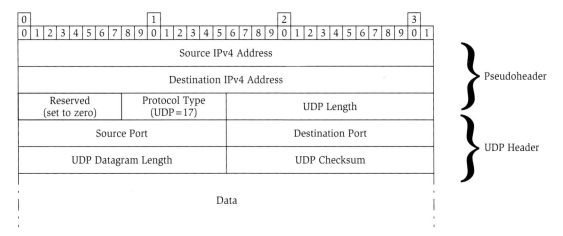

Figure 7.5 A UDP datagram with the pseudoheader for checksum processing.

result in the received datagram being discarded. In UDP there is no way for such discards to be reported to the sender—reporting them to the receiver may not be helpful since there is no way to know who the intended receiver of a corrupt datagram actually is because it may be the destination port and address that have been garbled. It is the responsibility of the application-level protocols to verify that data has actually been delivered (if they are concerned).

If IPv6 is used to transport the UDP datagram the pseudoheader is constructed using IPv6 addresses. Note that if IPv6 is used the use of the checksum is mandatory according to the IPv6 specification, RFC 2460.

The UDP checksum uses the standard checksum algorithm described in Chapter 2. That is, the checksum is the 16-bit one's complement of the one's complement sum of the entire message. The message is padded with a zero-filled byte at the end (if necessary) to bring it up to a multiple of 2 bytes in length. This additional byte is not transmitted and not added to the length of the datagram. Note that if the result of the checksum calculation is zero, the checksum field is filled with ones (0xff) to distinguish it from the value of zero, which indicates no checksum in use—all ones is equivalent to all zeros in one's complement arithmetic.

7.2.3 Choosing Between Raw IP and UDP

An application chooses to use UDP specifically to leverage one or more of the functions described at the start of Section 7.2. If any of the functions is required, there is a direct choice between incorporating the function into the application-layer protocol or utilizing UDP. Since each application might need to add the same function, it makes sense to share the code and services of a UDP implementation. This is particularly the case in applications such as TFTP and BOOTP (see Chapter 12) which are often implemented on diskless network devices and used as part of their start-up processing. In these cases, the code is burned onto a chip in the device, and the less code that is required, the better.

Additionally, by using ports, UDP is able to support very many services and applications at the same time. Raw IP has only the *Next Protocol* field to identify the payload and thereby the recipient. This field is just 1 byte long, so only 255 payload protocols can be defined. The IETF and IANA are justifiably nervous about running out of protocol identifiers and prefer new protocols to use UDP with a well-known or registered port number (there are 65,535 ports available with 1023 being managed as well-known ports and a further 48,128 available as registered ports) to distinguish applications.

7.2.4 Protocols That Use UDP

Common bootstrap protocols such as BOOTP and TFTP use UDP as their transport because it is simple and provides common services, avoiding the need to incorporate them into the application protocols.

Other applications use UDP because they are essentially datagram service users and require just the basic delivery and checksum function. An example of such a protocol is the Network Time Protocol (NTP). Some protocols need to move large amounts of data and are looking for a transport mechanism that has very low overhead. This is the reason Network File System (NFS) applications run over UDP.

The Link Management Protocol (LMP, see Chapter 10) was originally specified to run over raw IP. It is a simple point-to-point protocol that includes its own error detection and correction mechanisms. There are no transport services that LMP requires from the lower layers, but LMP has been moved to run over UDP to preserve the scarce IP protocol identifiers.

Lastly, because UDP is not connection-oriented, it can easily support multicast and broadcast traffic. This makes it popular for discovery mechanisms, such as that of the Label Distribution Protocol (LDP, see Chapter 9).

7.2.5 UDP Lite

UDP Lite is not a sugar-free drink, but is intended as an ultra-lightweight version of UDP. It is in the early stages of development within the IETF and currently merits only a brief discussion.

Some applications such as codecs for voice and video are designed to handle errors in their data streams better than they handle entire dropped packets. Since there are some link technologies (such as radio frequency links) that can partially damage data but still deliver the packets, it is desirable to investigate ways of persuading UDP to not discard damaged packets based on checksum calculations but to deliver them. Furthermore, since checksum calculation takes up valuable CPU cycles, any reduction in processing is advantageous.

The checksum could be left out altogether, but it is highly desirable to protect the addressing information of the packet, and it is, in any case, mandated in UDP for IPv6 (see the IPv6 specification, RFC 2460).

UDP Lite offers a protocol that applies the checksum to part of the packet only. The protected part of the packet is called the *sensitive* part and should include at least the addressing information, but does not need to include the data. Errors detected by the checksum still cause the packet to be discarded by the transport protocol, but errors in the insensitive part of the packet that is not protected by the checksum are not noticed by UDP Lite. The default behavior is that the whole packet is treated as sensitive, making UDP Lite behave exactly as UDP.

The UDP Lite message header is shown in Figure 7.6. The Length field from UDP is replaced with a Checksum Coverage field to indicate the number of bytes in the UDP header that should be included in the checksum. A value of zero indicates that all bytes should be included. A value equal to the packet length provides for backwards compatibility with UDP. The actual packet length can be derived from the IP packet length. UDP checksum calculations use the same algorithm and pseudoheader as UDP.

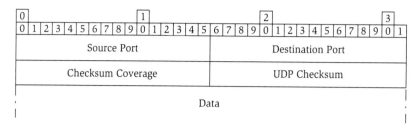

Figure 7.6 The UDP Lite message header.

For more information on UDP Lite refer to the IETF's Transport Area Working Group.

7.3 Transmission Control Protocol (TCP)

It is possible that the Transmission Control Protocol (TCP) is single-handedly responsible for the greatest volume of written material about any networking protocol. This certainly reflects TCP's importance in the Internet, where it is by far the most used transport protocol. At the same time, a large quantity of text can sometimes serve only to obfuscate what is really a very simple protocol.

One of the main issues with the presentation of TCP is a confusion between the protocol itself and specific implementations. Indeed, many detailed texts on TCP spend most of their time explaining how and why a specific implementation is constructed, and examining *sockets*, the conventional API to TCP.

7.3.1 Making IP Connection Oriented

TCP is a connection-oriented protocol. Before data can be transferred, a connection must be established between {source IP address, source port} and {destination IP address, destination port}. Connection establishment ensures that applications are present at both sender and receiver (connections are usually established from client to server) and negotiates capabilities for use on the connection.

TCP is a reliable transport protocol. This means that it makes certain guarantees to detect and correct errors, and promises that it will either deliver the data for the application or notify the application that there was a problem. When data exchange on the connection is complete it is torn down to free up system resources for other applications.

7.3.2 TCP Messages

TCP uses a single message for all signaling and data transfer and sends it in an IP datagram using the protocol identifier value 6. Control requests are flagged

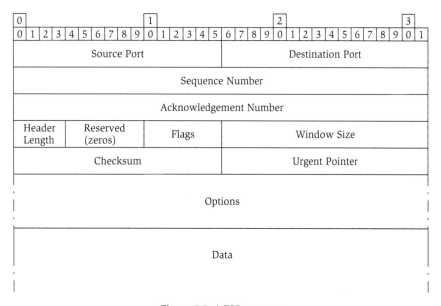

Figure 7.7 A TCP message.

on messages by the use of Flag bits that indicate which operations are in progress. Control details and negotiation of parameters are managed through TCP options in the TCP message header. Control and data may be present on the same message or may use distinct messages. For example, it would be usual to establish a TCP connection using messages that carry no data but do carry TCP options, and most data transfer will not include any control requests. But it is not uncommon to send the last data message together with a request to close the TCP connection, thus mixing control and data information on one message. The format of a TCP message is shown in Figure 7.7.

7.3.3 Connection Establishment

TCP connections are established and maintained on demand from applications and are kept active (barring network failure) until the applications explicitly release them.

The interface most commonly used by applications to request TCP connections and to send and receive data is the sockets API. It is important to note that the sockets API is not part of the TCP specification and is simply a method for applications to access the services provided by TCP. Nevertheless, the sockets API has become close to ubiquitous, allowing applications to be implemented above a standard programming interface that gives access to TCP on nearly all platforms, and in particular on standard operating systems that include a packaged version of TCP.

In order for a TCP connection to be established, the receiver must be listening—if you make a phone call, the other party needs to be in to answer. An application (typically a server application) goes into listen (or passive receive) mode by issuing a Listen request to sockets or some similar API. This is a local implementation matter and does not involve a protocol exchange. The parameters for a Listen may range from a general "all ports" Listen, through the normal Listen on a specific port and address pairing, to a request that accepts incoming calls only on a particular port when the requests come from a given source address and port.

When an application wishes to establish a TCP connection to a server that is in listen mode it makes a request through its programming API (such as sockets) specifying the destination IP address and destination port. It may also specify a source port, although it will usually leave this choice to the TCP implementation. At the same time, the application may make requests to control the behavior of the connection that will be reflected in TCP options or in specific behavior on the connection.

TCP initiates the connection by sending a TCP connection establishment message carrying the Synchronize flag set. If the source application does not require a specific source port, the TCP implementation allocates an unused one from the range 49,152 to 65,535. The receiving TCP implementation checks that there is an application listening on the specified port and replies with a message that both acknowledges the received request by setting the Acknowledge flag, and requests that the connection be opened in the reverse direction by setting the Synchronize flag bit. When it receives this message, the initiator responds by sending an acknowledgement (setting the Acknowledge flag). At this point the TCP connection is open and data can be sent in both directions: TCP implementations would usually report this to their applications.

The message exchange described in the preceding paragraph is shown in Figure 7.8. At step 1 the server application issues a passive Open or Listen to the TCP Stack. Some time later (step 2) the client application attempts to open a connection to the server—the client TCP Stack sends a TCP message carrying the Synchronize flag and sets the Sequence Number field to indicate the identifier of the first byte of data that it will send. When the message containing the Synchronize is received by the server (step 3) it may issue an indication to its application and then responds with a TCP message carrying the Acknowledge and Synchronize flags. The Acknowledgement Number in this message has the same value as the received Sequence Number, indicating that the client can start sending data from this sequence number. The server fills in the Sequence Number in the message it sends to indicate the identifier of the first byte that it will send. When the Acknowledge/Synchronize reaches the client (step 4) the TCP Stack reports to the application that the connection is open and

Table 7.1 The TCP Flags Bits

Hex	Flags	Name	Meaning
0×01	000001	Finish	Used to close the TCP connection when all data has been transferred. See Section 7.3.7 for more details.
0×02	000010	Synchronize	Used during connection establishment to indicate that a connection is being established and to synchronize the sequence numbers in use by each end point so that they can know what data to expect to receive next. The synchronize can be used to resynchronize a connection that has gone awry, but this is rarely if ever done.
0×04	000100	Reset	The Reset bit is used to reject a received connection request or to precipitously abort an existing connection.
0×08	001000	Push	This flag is used to indicate "end of record" on a sequence of data segments. It is often derived from a flushed write at the sender's API, indicating that the sending TCP stack should not hold on to the last fragment of data waiting to fill an MTU, but should send it immediately. At the receiver, the Push bit indicates that the receive buffer should be flushed to the application, often with some indication that the sender has finished sending.
0×10	010000	Acknowledgement	Used to show acknowledgement of a previously received TCP message. Operationally, all messages except for the initial setup request, midflow synchronizations, and a connection abort reset message carry this bit set.
0×20	100000	Urgent	Used to indicate that the TCP message carries urgent data that should be expedited through the system if possible. This bit is used in conjunction with the Urgent Pointer field in the TCP header, as described in Section 7.3.6.

sends a message acknowledging the server's sequence number. The server TCP Stack reports the connection open to the server application and both end points are ready to send data.

Table 7.1 shows the interpretation of the Flags bits within the TCP message header. Note that multiple flags bits may be set on a single message, but that some combinations (for example, Reset and Synchronize) would be ambiguous.

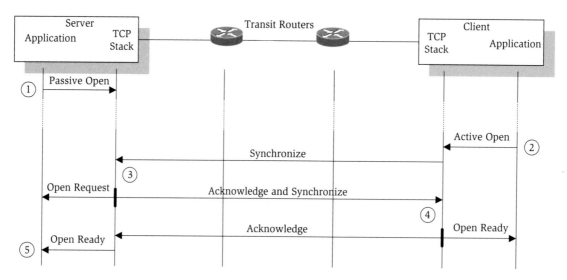

Figure 7.8 Message flow during TCP connection establishment.

7.3.4 Data Transfer

Data transfer in TCP is handled by placing a block of data in a TCP message immediately after the header. This data message is often referred to as a *segment* because it carries a segment of the total application data transfer. Many APIs to TCP allow an application to send a stream of data as a series of buffers that are held by the TCP implementation until they can be chopped up or glued together into segments and sent. The API guarantees to deliver the data or to notify the application of the failure.

The size of a TCP segment at the source node is determined by the MTU of the local link. The TCP message is sized to fit within an IP message within a single MTU. As the message is forwarded across the network, however, the MTU size on some component link may be smaller and may result in the TCP message being segmented into smaller IP packets, as shown in Figure 7.9. If this happens, it is the responsibility of the destination TCP stack to collect the IP fragments and reassemble them into the original TCP message before making the data available to the application. Note that TCP cannot simply present the data from the IP fragments to the application as they arrive because the packets may arrive out of order and, more significantly, the TCP checksum must be applied to the whole TCP message.

Fragmentation of TCP packets into smaller IP packets may be very inefficient. In the worst case, a new IP packet would be needed to carry 1 byte of overflow data. Although such an extreme situation is unlikely, implementations may desire to avoid the problem by understanding the lowest common denominator MTU size on the intervening links in the TCP connection—a TCP option

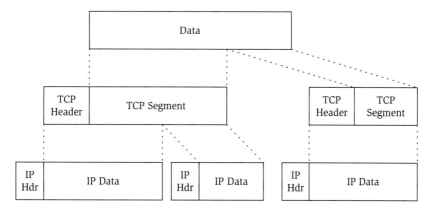

Figure 7.9 Data is carried in TCP segments which may be fragmented into multiple IP packets as they traverse the network.

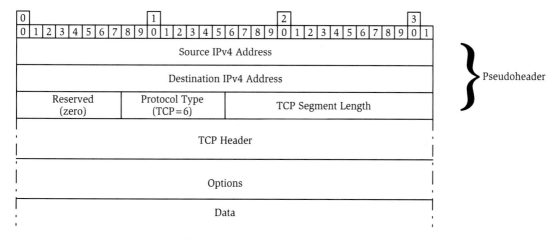

Figure 7.10 A TCP message with the pseudoheader for checksum processing.

exists to collect this information and make it available to the sender so that the TCP segments sent by the source will fit in a single IP packet and MTU across the whole network. As an alternative, the sending TCP stack may request no segmentation within the IP network, but this probably will not help because it will simply prevent the transfer of data.

The sending TCP stack may set the Push flag in any TCP message, regardless of whether or not the message carries data. This flag is somewhat analogous to an end of record marker and indicates to the receiver that all data received up to this point should be flushed to the application. In practice, this flag is often set on every segment by the sender, and receivers flush all data to their applications regardless of the setting of the flag.

TCP data exchange is protected by checksum and explicitly acknowledged to confirm delivery. If the data is rejected or not acknowledged, the sender can retransmit it to reattempt delivery.

The TCP checksum uses the IP CRC checksum as described in Chapter 2. It applies to the whole TCP message with a pseudoheader prefixed just as in UDP. This pseudoheader, shown in Figure 7.10, provides an additional check that the packet has been delivered to the correct address and is on a real connection.

7.3.5 Acknowledgements and Flow Control

Acknowledgement of data relies on a sequence number associated with the transmitted data. TCP essentially counts all transmitted bytes and acknowledges them. This allows a receiver to acknowledge all, part, or none of a received segment according to its ability to save the data ready for its application. The Sequence Number field is encoded as a 32-bit number in the TCP header, so must wrap every 4 gigabytes. When a receiver acknowledges data it places the sequence number of the next byte that it is prepared to receive in the Acknowledgement Number field of the TCP header of the next message it sends. If there is a regular two-way exchange of data, the acknowledgment can be placed on the next reverse-direction data message. If there is no data waiting to be sent in the opposite direction, the receiver may choose to send an empty TCP message just to acknowledge the data. Figure 7.11 shows transmission and acknowledgment of data on a TCP connection.

In Figure 7.11 the application on the server requests that 6500 bytes be transmitted to the client (step 1). The server TCP stack breaks the data into 1000-byte segments and starts to send them—the first segment has Sequence Number 1 and the data length can be deduced from the length of the TCP message by subtracting the length of the TCP header. The receiver secures the received data and sends an acknowledgement by setting the Acknowledgement Number to the next expected byte, 1001 (step 2).

The receiving TCP stack is configured to deliver data in 2000-byte blocks, so when it receives the second segment (step 3) it acknowledges it and passes data to its application. The third segment (bytes 2001 to 3000) gets lost in the network (step 4), and the next segment to arrive at the receiver carries the Sequence Number 3001. The receiver (step 5) notices that there is missing data and cannot acknowledge the new message. Instead, it stores the received data and sends an acknowledgement carrying the Acknowledgement Number 2001—that is, it re-acknowledges the in-order data it has seen and asks to see byte 2001 next.

Allowing for some transmission delay in the network, the sender is still processing regular acknowledgements and sending data (step 6), but eventually it receives what appears to be a duplicate acknowledgement (step 7). At this point an implementation decision is required to decide what to do—in this example, the sender immediately stops sending and waits to see whether it will receive an acknowledgement for the missing data (the IP datagram carrying bytes 2001

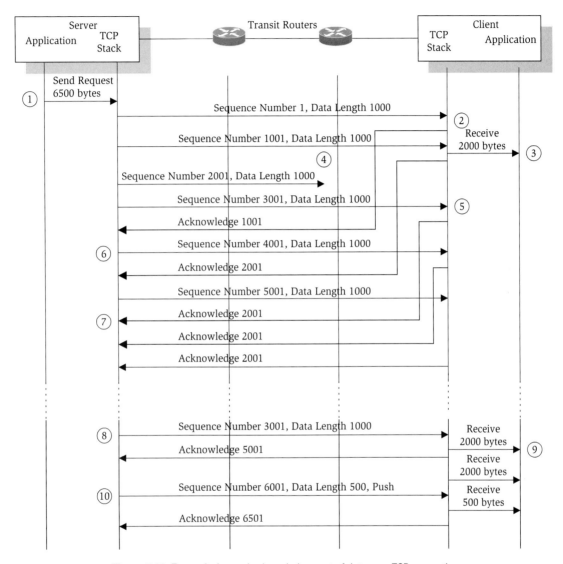

Figure 7.11 Transmission and acknowledgement of data on a TCP connection.

to 3000 might just have gotten delivered out of order). The retransmission policy could cause the sender to immediately retransmit the unacknowledged data, but in this case the sender waits for a configurable time before retransmitting (step 8). The receiver is immediately able to acknowledge all the way up to byte 6001 because it has secured the out-of-order data and can also continue delivering data to its application (step 9). The sender transmits the last 500 bytes and sets the Push bit to indicate that this is all it has to send (step 10). The Push bit is used by the receiver to tell it to deliver the remaining data to its application without waiting to build up a 2000-byte block.

In this example, the sending TCP stack stops sending data when it becomes suspicious that the receiver might not have received one of the segments, but it need not do this. It could continue sending data, but that might lead to the receiving TCP stack becoming swamped with data that it cannot deliver to its application and must store. The receiver could choose to throw away excess data and force the sender to retransmit, but ideally it needs a way to apply back-pressure on the sender to slow the sender down. It may even need to do this in normal operation if the sender is transmitting data faster than the receiver can deliver it to its application.

The receiver uses the Window Size field to control the amount of data beyond the last acknowledged byte that the sender may transmit. The Window Size effectively grants the sender permission to send a certain number more bytes. Figure 7.12 gives a diagrammatic representation of the use of the Window Size. Send and receive applications are shown with a send and receive buffer, respectively. The send application places data in the send buffer for the sending TCP stack to transmit to the receiving TCP stack. The receiving TCP stack places the data in the receive buffer from where the receiving application can retrieve it. For simplicity, Figure 7.12 shows only the use of the Window Size and does not show acknowledgements. Note that the Window Size is only a 16-bit field, which serves to significantly limit the flow of data on a fast system. See Section 7.3.9 for a description of the Window Scaling TCP option that addresses this issue.

In the example, the receiver initially issues a window the size of its receive buffer (step 1). As data arrives in the send buffer, the sender starts to send it in blocks according to the MTU size. This depletes the send buffer and starts to fill up the receive buffer (step 2). As the data builds up in the receive buffer, the receiver reduces the size of the receive window so that the sender will not flood it with more data than it can store (step 3). The sender continues to receive more data from its application (step 4) and send it across the TCP connection. The receiver starts to deliver data to its application from the receive buffer (step 5) and refreshes the current window size. The sender transmits a smaller than usual segment, using up the entire window size granted by the receiver (step 6). Since the receive buffer is now entirely full, the receiver sends a TCP message with a zero window size (step 7) and the sender must stop sending even though it continues to receive data from its application until its send buffer is full (step 8).

Eventually, the receiving application starts to read data from the receive buffer (step 9) and this allows the receiving TCP stack to reopen the window (step 10), and so the transfer of data continues.

It is important to note the interaction between Acknowledgement Numbers and Window Size. The acknowledgement of a TCP segment says nothing about whether more data can be sent. It simply states that all data up to the indicated byte has been received and secured. The Window Size says how many more bytes

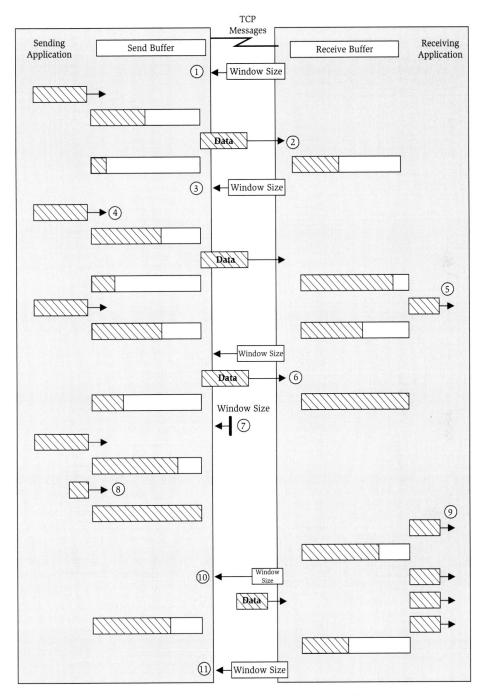

Figure 7.12 The TCP Window Size is used to prevent the sender from flooding the receiver.

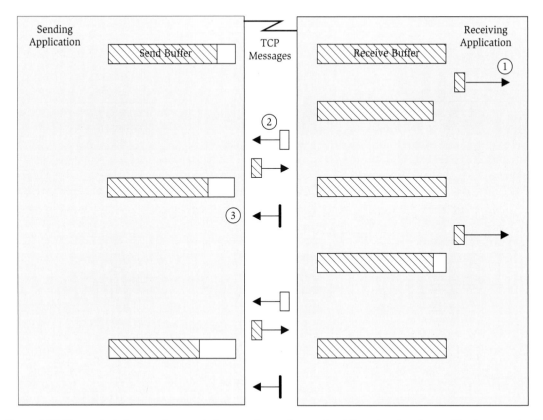

Figure 7.13 The send window may be repeatedly opened a small amount and then closed again, resulting in poor network usage.

after the last acknowledged byte may be transmitted. In some circumstances the receiver may choose to shut the send window even though it has previously said that it could receive data. In this case, the sender may already have transmitted data outside of the window—it is up to the receiver whether to accept this data or to drop it, and the sender should be prepared to retransmit the data if it is not acknowledged.

Figure 7.13 illustrates a degenerative condition in which the receive buffer is full and the data is read by the receiving application in very small chunks (step 1). The result is a stop-start transfer of data as the window is repeatedly opened a little (step 2) and closed again (step 3)—this is not an efficient use of the network. If many applications get into this state it can affect the ability of other applications to transfer data at all since the send buffers may all be taken up with data that is queued to be sent, and the network traffic may be so busy exchanging small acknowledgements, and tiny amounts of data, that network bandwidth is not available for other applications.

A similar condition can arise on an otherwise perfectly well-behaved TCP connection if the sender presents data only a few bytes at a time and these bytes are immediately picked up by the TCP stack and sent to the receiver. These problems are addressed by the *Nagel algorithm*, which requires the sender to wait until either it has a full-size segment to send (and is allowed to send it) or it has received an acknowledgement for all of the data it has previously sent. Although this algorithm doesn't completely eradicate the issues described in the preceding paragraph, it helps to slow down the exchange of small segments and lets them build up into larger pieces.

7.3.6 Urgent Data

TCP allows a sender to flag a TCP segment as urgent by setting the Urgent bit in the Flags field in the TCP header. This is useful for a sender to present data that can overtake any bytes queued in the send and receive buffers and be presented directly to the receiving application. For example, in Telnet the interrupt key sequence may be pressed and sent to overtake all other traffic and enable the receiver to abandon whatever it is doing with the received data.

If the Urgent flag is set, at least the first byte of data in the segment must be treated as urgent. The Urgent Pointer in the TCP header indicates the end of the urgent data relative to the Sequence Number (that is the first byte) carried in the TCP header. Thus, an Urgent Pointer value of zero indicates that exactly 1 byte (the first byte in the segment) is urgent. This allows part or all of the TCP segment to be urgent. What is more, if the Urgent Pointer indicates a value greater than the size of the current TCP segment, then the first bytes of the next segment must also be treated as urgent data.

Regrettably, some early and influential implementations of TCP misinterpreted the specification. Since the whole point of a protocol is to interoperate with other implementations, and given the extent of deployment of these discrepancies, it is important to understand them and to implement around them. Some implementations, for example BSD, use the Urgent Pointer to indicate the first byte of nonurgent data rather than the last byte of urgent data (the offset has been assumed to be a count of the number of bytes of urgent data rather than a zero-based offset from the sequence number of the first byte). Other implementations determine that the whole of any segment carrying the Urgent flag should be treated as urgent, and that a segment not carrying the flag should not be considered urgent. Some applications simply don't support urgent data at all—they never set the Urgent flag and treat all received data with the same priority.

To implement support for urgent data correctly and to ensure interoperability, a TCP stack should:

- Never mix urgent and nonurgent data in a single segment.
- Set the Urgent flag on every segment that carries urgent data.

- Treat the whole of any segment carrying the Urgent flag as urgent regardless of the value of the Urgent Pointer.
- Consider any segment that does not carry the Urgent flag as nonurgent regardless of the value of the Urgent Pointer.

7.3.7 Closing the Connection

When an application has finished using a TCP connection it will ask the TCP stack to close it. Just as the connection establishment required a three-way handshake, so connection teardown uses a three-way exchange.

When one end of the connection knows it has finished with the connection, it sends a TCP message with the Finish flag set. This message may itself carry data (the last data to be sent in this direction on the connection) or may be empty. The message may also acknowledge received data. If the other end point is ready to close the connection, it sends a message carrying the Acknowledge flag to show that it received the Finish flag and it also sets the Finish flag. This exchange is illustrated in Figure 7.14.

To distinguish the acknowledgement of the Finish flag from an acknowledgement of the previous data sent, an empty TCP segment carrying the Finish flag must increment the Sequence Number by one, as if it were carrying 1 byte of additional data. (Some implementations choose to put 1 byte of data into the segment, although this is not necessary.) The acknowledgement of the Finish flag increments the Acknowledge number to show that the segment carrying the flag has been received.

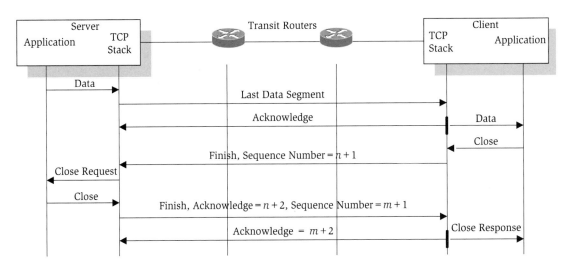

Figure 7.14 Immediate TCP connection closure.

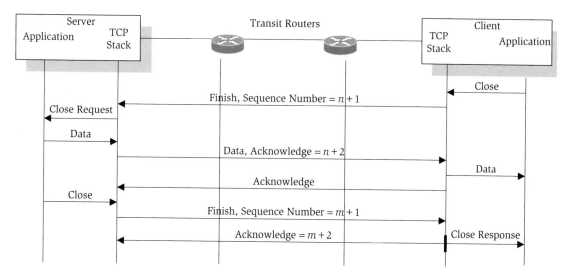

Figure 7.15 Staggered TCP connection closure.

TCP connection closure may be initiated by either end of the connection, regardless of which end initiated it, although it is usually the client that is responsible for starting the teardown. It is also not a requirement for the end point that receives a Finish flag to respond with its own Finish flag immediately. Instead, it may continue to send data for as long as it wants. Note, however, that as soon as an end point has sent the Finish flag it can only receive data, and can no longer send anything except empty segments to acknowledge data that it receives. Figure 7.15 shows the message exchange for this staggered shutdown.

There are other, less graceful, ways of closing a TCP connection. If something goes wrong, either end may send a TCP message carrying the Reset bit—this immediately terminates the connection in both directions and does not require acknowledgement. An even more extreme way for an end point to end a TCP connection is to simply stop using it—no more data is sent and no more acknowledgements are made. This last choice may be ungainly, but it simply mimics a broken link in the network (or more precisely, broken IP connectivity). It will likely result in all sorts of additional traffic as the other end of the connection first continues to send data, and then retries the data for a while. Eventually the remote end will give up (based on some timer or transmission retry count) and will itself close the connection.

7.3.8 Implementing TCP

Successful implementations of TCP require certain behavioral characteristics to optimize the protocol and to avoid issues with the way the protocol may operate.

Although these behaviors are not really part of the protocol specification, they are fundamental to the way the protocol works, and so some of them are covered here briefly. They are typically specified by the IETF in informational RFCs.

Timers are essential to smooth operation of TCP. They may be used to trigger retransmission of unacknowledged data and to resend acknowledgements or window reopenings if there is no associated data to be acknowledged and no new data is received.

Timers may also be used to close down idle connections. This can be important on a server when the client may have simply dropped the connection or when the client end point is no longer reachable through IP. If the server has data to send it will notice that the client is not responding, but if the server is waiting for further instructions from the client it will wait forever without some timer to close the connection down. Such processing may be particularly valuable if system resources (processes and buffers) are assigned to the broken connection. In some implementations it is up to the application to run this sort of timer or even to run its own keep-alive exchange to monitor the connection—in others, the TCP connection will timeout after a long period of inactivity.

Since there is no easy way to determine that an idle connection has actually failed, some TCP implementations offer a keep-alive mechanism of their own. This mechanism is achieved by one end of the connection sending an empty TCP segment with the Sequence Number set to one less than the last actual byte of data sent. This forces the receiver to resend an acknowledgement indicating that all of the data has actually been received.

The whole issue of sequence numbers may need some attention. Since a TCP connection may be short-lived, but reestablished rapidly after teardown, it is possible that an old message carrying an acknowledgement will arrive and be assumed to belong to the new connection. Although the random assignment of client port number can help to address this issue, there are still concerns when the client port is specified by the application. To resolve this problem the sequence number for the first data byte on a new connection could be set to run on from the last value used for the last byte of data the last time the connection was used. But this would require the implementation to store state for connections even after they have been closed, so the preferred solution is to randomly seed the sequence number for each new connection. This has the added advantage of making life a little harder for anyone attempting to breach the security of TCP.

Sequence numbers wrap at 4 billion (they are held in a 32-bit number) and that is not such a large number these days. TCP implementations must handle this carefully to recognize in-order and out-of-order acknowledgements over the wrapping boundary. In general, the number A is assumed to be less than the number B only if the following applies:

$$\text{if } ((A < B \text{ \&\& } B - A < 0 \times 7\text{fffff}) \text{ || } (A > B \text{ \&\& } A - B > 0 \times 7\text{fffff}))$$

Using this formula, a receiver can determine whether a newly received sequence number is an old retransmission (which can be dropped) or an out-of-order receipt of new data (which should be stored). In either case, however, the receiver should send an acknowledgement of the last correctly received data so that the sender is aware of what is going on.

In the examples shown in the previous section both sender and receiver have data buffers to store data on its way from or to the applications. It is usual for TCP implementations to provide such a service so that the applications can handle data at their own speed. At the sender it may be necessary for the TCP stack to have the ability to apply back-pressure to the application so that the whole of the system's resources don't end up on a TCP send queue. At the receiver, there will need to be a mechanism to report or post data to the application. As described, the size of the buffer may be used to set the Window Size by a receiver—this can lead to the sender transmitting a large amount of data very quickly, which could be a bad idea if the links between client and server are actually far slower than the end points themselves (for example, consider file transfer or web browsing over a dial-up link). What would happen is that the first segments would be delivered, but many more would be dropped by IP in the resultant network congestion. To avoid the resulting bursty behavior (sender sends too many segments, transmission throttles back for retries, everything catches up, and sender again sends too many segments), a process known as *slow start* is used followed by the management of the flow using a sender's *congestion window*. Congestion avoidance and management algorithms were developed mainly by Van Jacobson in the late 1980s.

The congestion window is a sliding window maintained completely by the sender. The sender sends until the window is empty and then must wait for acknowledgements before sending more data. The slow start process initially sets the window to be quite small (opinions vary as to how small—RFC 2581 suggests that it should not be greater than one segment in size, while RFC 2414 suggests use of up to four segments), and increases the size of the window gradually (by the size of one segment) each time a TCP message is received that acknowledges new data. An alternative scheme uses the round-trip time (measured using a TCP option—see Section 7.3.9) and increases the congestion window by the size of one segment for every round-trip interval that passes. Some slow start schemes prefer a logarithmic increase in the window size since this gives an upper threshold and eases the size of the congestion window asymptotically toward the threshold. The congestion window can continue to increase indefinitely unless congestion is observed or a locally-defined threshold is reached.

Note that TCP does not provide any mechanism for detecting network congestion, although the continued need to retransmit data because it has not been acknowledged, should be taken as an indication. Many TCP implementations watch for the ICMP Source Quench message (see Chapter 2) to discover whether traffic that they are sending is causing congestion.

If congestion is detected, the sending TCP stack needs to back off and send somewhat less data. It does this by reducing the congestion window—at the same time, it learns from its mistake and reduces the upper threshold to which the congestion window may grow. The upper threshold could be raised again (carefully!) if the congestion window has been operating at its maximum without any problems for a reasonable period of time.

The Sockets Interface

The sockets interface is regarded by many to be an integral part of a TCP implementation, but it is not part of the protocol and is not even defined by the IETF. As an API, sockets has immense value because it allows application writers access to TCP in a standardized way without having to worry about who implemented their TCP stack, or on which platform they are running. Nevertheless, the sockets API deviates slightly from one implementation to another, with the result that unless an application is to be run on a single well-known platform, it is usually constrained to a subset of the API to ensure that it can be ported.

The best place to start with the definition of the sockets API is with the user documentation of an established UNIX operating system such as BSD or Linux. Other common operating systems such as Windows may also contain good references.

7.3.9 TCP Options

TCP options allow additional control information to be exchanged by connection end points. The information is positioned between the normal TCP header and the data segment, but is considered as part of the header.

TCP options are encoded as type-length-variable (TLV) sequences, as shown in Figure 7.16. Each element in the sequence comprises a single byte to indicate which option is being signaled, a single byte to give the full length of the option (including the type and the length field), and then a series of bytes comprising the option data that are interpreted according to the specific option being passed. The option data is built of complete bytes, and the sequence of options is padded to a 4-byte (32-bit) boundary with zero bytes. It is important that the padding bytes are zeros since the receiver will parse through the options until the full length of the TCP header has been reached—a zero option type can be taken to indicate that the sequence of options has been completed.

Figure 7.17 shows the encoding of some of the more commonly used TCP options. Note that the option types zero and 1 have special interpretation. As described in the preceding paragraph, option type zero indicates that the end of the option list has been reached—a receiver finding an option type of zero can

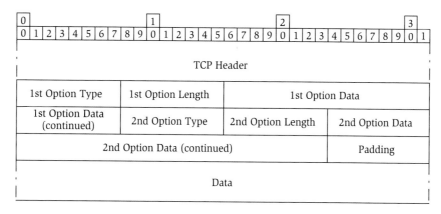

Figure 7.16 TCP options are encoded as a sequence of TLVs padded to a 4-byte boundary.

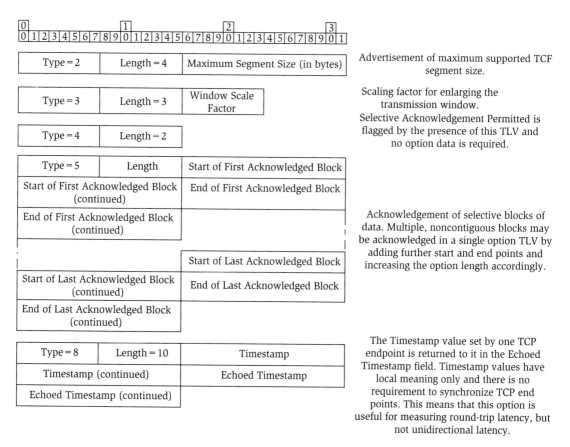

Figure 7.17 Some of the more common TCP options.

complete its processing of the TCP header. Option type 1 is used to provide padding within a sequence of options—this might be used if an implementation needs to start the following option on a 4-byte boundary, or if it wants to remove an option from a buffer without shuffling all of the data to close the gap. For an option of type 1, the option length field is still valid, but the option data should be ignored.

Option 2 carries the maximum segment size. It is sometimes used by the receiver to notify the sender of the largest TCP segment that it can receive. This is useful to reduce the likelihood of IP fragmentation within the network, but is actually rarely used; most implementations simply restrict their segment size to their own MTU size. Note that the actual MTU size for a TCP connection can be probed by sending an IP message of the suspected maximum size with the "don't fragment" flag set and seeing if it is rejected using ICMP by any intermediate router.

Option 3 manages window scaling. It is used to allow the receive window to be increased above the normal limitations of the 16-bit field. The window scale factor is simply a two's power multiplier to be applied to the Window Size field. Thus, a Window Size field with value 64,000 (0xFA00) and a window scaling factor of 3 results in an actual window size of 512,000 (0×7D000, that is 0xFA00 left-shifted three times). The window scaling option may be present only if the Synchronize flag is set—the window size scaling factor is set once for each direction during connection establishment and is not modified thereafter. Note that care must be taken in providing interoperation between two end points, one of which supports window scaling and one of which does not, or one direction may end up with a spectacularly small window size. This is handled by insisting that both ends use the option if they support it—they can keep their window size as small as they want by using a scaling factor of zero.

Option 4 is used during connection setup to show that option 5 may be used.

Option 5 is a performance optimization that allows out-of-order segments to be selectively acknowledged by specifying the start and end points of each acknowledged block of data.

Option 8, the timestamp option, is used to measure the round-trip time on the connection. This has uses both in measuring the performance of the connection and also in scaling the congestion window. On systems with small segments, concern is sometimes expressed about the impact of this option eating 10 bytes out of each segment that is sent, but it has its uses in the development cycle as part of a test tool or for modeling network performance.

7.3.10 Choosing Between UDP and TCP

The choice between TCP and UDP is simple. If the application wants to use reliable transport services it should use TCP. If it needs only managed delivery to a specific port, it should use UDP.

There are, in fact, some ambiguities in this choice for applications that want only a lightweight reliable service. For example, an application might want notification of lost messages but not actually care enough to have a transport protocol attempt to redeliver the missing data. For such applications the choice is between using TCP and attempting to reduce the overhead by using as few options as possible (perhaps controlling the behavior of the local TCP implementation through runtime parameters at the sockets API), and using UDP with additional application-level protocol exchanges to provide the level of service that is required.

In the end, the fact that TCP is implemented and readily available on most platforms usually counts for a lot, and the savings in protocol design and application implementation usually means that TCP is chosen whenever there is any doubt.

7.3.11 Protocols That Use TCP

Many application protocols associated with bulk transfer of data use TCP. These include the File Transfer Protocol (FTP), the Hypertext Transfer Protocol (HTTP), and email protocols such as the Simple Mail Transfer Protocol (SMTP) and the Post Office Protocol (POP3).

Telnet is an interesting example of a protocol that commonly transfers small amounts of data but still uses TCP. The command–response nature of Telnet and its immediate visibility to a human user is such that it is essential to ensure that messages are delivered correctly.

TCP is also used by control and routing protocols to transport their data. The Border Gateway Protocol (BGP-4) and the Label Distribution Protocol (LDP) are good examples. The use of TCP makes sense for them because they establish clear and long-lived associations with "adjacent" nodes over which they need to keep exchanging information. Using TCP means that these protocols do not need to include methods to track the data that is exchanged—they are heavily dependent on the reliability of TCP. On the other hand, many control and routing protocols that use TCP need to include their own keep-alive mechanisms to ensure that the TCP connection is still active and to detect connection failures in a timely manner.

7.4 Stream Control Transmission Protocol (SCTP)

TCP is a well-established, proven transport protocol that is used by a substantial number of application protocols. So why invent another transport protocol? As can be seen by the number of RFCs that apply to TCP, it has been necessary to make small tweaks to the protocol over the years as the Internet has evolved and as the requirements on a transport protocol have become clearer. A new class of control protocols has recently started to be used within the Internet to signal Packet Switched Telephone Network (PSTN) connections, and these protocols place a high level of requirements on their transport service provider. Rather than developing still more modifications to TCP, the opportunity was taken to invent a new transport protocol, the Stream Control Transmission Protocol (SCTP). SCTP is defined in RFC 2960.

Although SCTP was designed specifically to meet the transport requirements of PSTN signaling messages over IP networks, it is available as a transport protocol for any application or control protocol. The main features of SCTP are as follows. Many of these will be familiar to those who understand the services provided by TCP.

- SCTP is a reliable connection-oriented transport protocol.
- It operates over a connectionless network protocol such as IP.
- It provides acknowledged, error-free, nonduplicated transfer of user data.
- It can be supplied and can deliver data in large blocks.
- It fragments data to fit within the MTU size.
- It includes sender pacing and congestion avoidance schemes.

In addition, SCTP provides some new, unique features. SCTP facilitates the establishment and maintenance of multiple *streams* between the same pair of end points. This is equivalent to having multiple conversations between two people at the same time on the same phone call, but actually allows for an extra level of hierarchy in the address scheme. To revert to the postal analogy, this is like having a whole family served by a single mailbox with different mail exchanges (streams) going on to different family members. Messages within the SCTP connection may be delivered in strict order of arrival across all streams or may be separated into individual streams for delivery—in either case, SCTP ensures in-order delivery within each stream.

Some moderate performance enhancements are included to allow multiple SCTP messages to be bundled into a single SCTP packet for transmission. This reduces the network overhead of the IP header for small SCTP messages and, more importantly, reduces the processing overhead associated with sending and receiving each SCTP packet.

SCTP also includes some improved network-level fault tolerance through the concept of multihoming. At either or both ends of an SCTP association multiple addresses may be used so that the association can be dynamically moved from one point of attachment to another. This allows distinct routes to be engineered through the network for the different addresses and allows the SCTP association to be redirected around network outages without the need to tear it down and reestablish it. Figure 7.18 shows how an SCTP association is formed to support multiple streams across an IP network using multihoming.

Finally, SCTP also includes some additional security features to provide resistance to flooding and masquerade attacks.

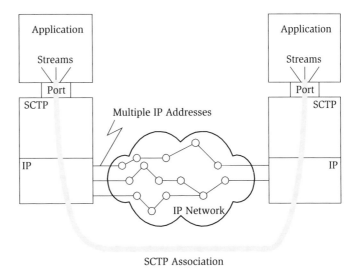

SCTP Association

Figure 7.18 An SCTP Association carries multiple streams between a pair of ports on end points that may be identified by multiple IP addresses.

7.4.1 SCTP Message Formats

SCTP communicates end-to-end using SCTP packets that are sent within IP datagrams using the protocol identifier value of 132. Each SCTP packet contains a single SCTP header and one or more SCTP *chunks*. The SCTP header identifies the SCTP association and contains security and verification details. Each chunk may be a control message applicable to the association or one of the streams that run through it, or may be data being exchanged on one of the streams. Figure 7.19 shows how an SCTP packet is constructed.

Just as in UDP and TCP, the primary identifiers in the SCTP header (shown in Figure 7.20) are the source and destination port numbers. Port numbers for SCTP are managed from the same space as they are for the other IP transport protocols and are administered by IANA. This means that an application can be run over any transport protocol without needing to change its port number. The header also includes a Verification Tag assigned during association establishment. The sender of an SCTP packet inserts the receiver's tag as a form of protection

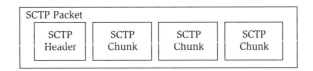

Figure 7.19 An SCTP packet contains a single header and one or more SCTP chunks.

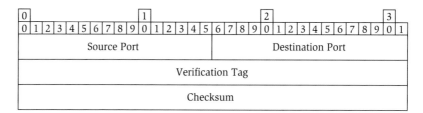

Figure 7.20 The SCTP message header.

Figure 7.21 SCTP chunks have a common format.

against old SCTP packets being delivered very late and also to help protect the association from security attacks.

The final field in the SCTP header is a 32-bit checksum field. Unlike TCP and UDP, SCTP does not use the standard IP checksum, but instead uses the Adler 32-bit checksum. This checksum is somewhat of an improvement over the 16-bit Fletcher checksum (see Section 5.6.2), allowing fewer corruptions to be missed. Note that SCTP does not use a pseudoheader since the inclusion of the verification tag provides some protection against misdelivery, but also because the multihoming nature of SCTP means that it would not be so simple to pick the correct IP addresses to use in the pseudoheader. The Adler 32-bit checksum is described in RFC 1950.

Note that the SCTP header does not include a length field. The length of the whole packet can be deduced from the size of the reassembled IP fragments.

Each SCTP chunk has a common format, as shown in Figure 7.21. It begins with a type identifier to indicate how the chunk should be interpreted, a set of flags that have distinct meanings according to the chunk type, and a length indicator that shows the length of the entire chunk, including the type, flags, and length fields. Each chunk must start on a 4-byte boundary, so it may be necessary to insert padding between chunks, but the chunk length still reflects the actual length of a chunk without the padding.

After this chunk common header, the contents of the chunk are interpreted according to the chunk type. Most chunk data are built up from a type-dependent header followed by a sequence of chunk parameters. Each chunk parameter is encoded as a type-length-variable (TLV) with 2 bytes assigned to the type and 2 bytes to the length, which is calculated to include the type and length fields. As with chunks, the chunk parameters must start on 4-byte boundaries, and

Table 7.2 The SCTP Chunk Types

Chunk Type	Chunk Usage
0	Payload Data
1	Association Initiation
2	Initiation Acknowledgement
3	Selective Acknowledgement
4	Heartbeat Request
5	Heartbeat Acknowledgement
6	Abort
7	Shutdown Request
8	Shutdown Acknowledgement
9	Operation Error Notification
10	State Cookie Echo
11	State Cookie Echo Acknowledgement
12	Explicit Congestion Notification Echo
13	Congestion Window Reduced
14	Shutdown Complete
15 to 255	Reserved by IETF

so padding may need to be inserted between chunk parameters—this padding is not included in the parameter length.

Note that chunks within a single SCTP packet all apply to the same association, but may refer to different streams. It is important that some sense of order be preserved when processing chunks from the same packet—any chunk that applies to the whole association must be processed in order, and chunks for an individual stream must also be kept in sequence.

Table 7.2 lists the defined SCTP chunk types. Note that each chunk is effectively a control message in its own right.

7.4.2 Association Establishment and Management

Figure 7.22 shows some sample chunk exchanges in the life of an SCTP association. In SCTP the end points are perceived as peers rather than as client and server. This is a semantic nicety that allows applications to have less of a master–slave relationship, but does not alter the fact that one end must initiate the association.

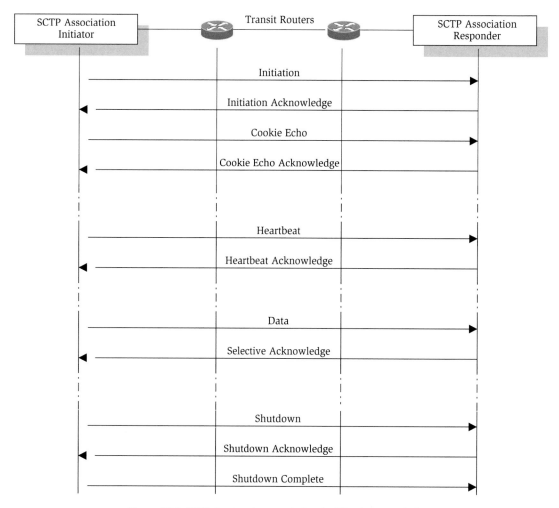

Figure 7.22 SCTP chunk exchanges during the life of an association.

Association establishment is initiated when one SCTP peer sends a packet containing an Association Initiation chunk, shown in Figure 7.23. This chunk carries several common fields to negotiate the terms of the association and a series of optional parameters encoded as chunk parameters. The common fields are listed in Table 7.3. The optional parameters carried in an Association Initiation chunk are listed in Table 7.4.

The remote end point responds to an Association Initiation chunk with an Initiation Acknowledgement chunk, shown in Figure 7.24. This chunk accepts the association and supplies the negotiated values and reverse direction parameters for management of the association. The same common fields are present

Table 7.3 Common Fields in an SCTP Association Initiation Chunk

Association Initiation Chunk Field	Use
Initiate Tag	This 32-bit tag is exchanged during association initialization and is placed on every message that applies to the session. It is used to help prevent security breaches and to validate that individual packets apply to this instance of the association. The tag must not have value zero.
Advertised Receiver Window Credit	The initial size of the receiver window—that is, the number of bytes that the sender may send. This value may be modified by Selective Acknowledgement chunks.
Number of Outbound Streams	Defines the maximum number of outbound streams the sender of this chunk wants to create in this association. A value of zero must not be used.
Number of Inbound Streams	Defines the maximum number of inbound streams the sender of this chunk is willing to allow the receiver to create in this association. A value of zero must not be used.
Initial Transmission Sequence Number (TSN)	The initial TSN is the sequence number that identifies the first byte of data that will be sent on the association. Any number in the range 0 to 4,294,967,295 is acceptable. Some implementations randomize this value and set it to the value of the Initiate Tag field.

Table 7.4 Optional Parameters in an SCTP Association Initiation Chunk

Parameter Type	Parameter Name	Use
5	IPv4 Address	One of the IPv4 addresses that may be used to identify the sender's end of the association. Multiple IPv4 and IPv6 addresses may be present. If no addresses are present, the SCTP application should use the address from the IP datagram that delivered the SCTP packet.
6	IPv6 Address	One of the IPv6 addresses that may be used to identify the sender's end of the association. Multiple IPv4 and IPv6 addresses may be present. If no addresses are present, the SCTP application should use the address from the IP datagram that delivered the SCTP packet.
9	Cookie Preservative	A value in milliseconds by which the sender is suggesting that the cookie timeout value be increased to prevent the cookie expiring again (as it has just done) during association establishment.
11	Host Name Address	A single host name that may be used to identify the sender's end of the association. The host name may not be present along with any IPv4 or IPv6 addresses, and only one host name may be used.
12	Supported Address Types	The address types that the sender supports and from which the receiver may choose addresses for its end of the association. If this parameter is absent, the sender supports all address types.

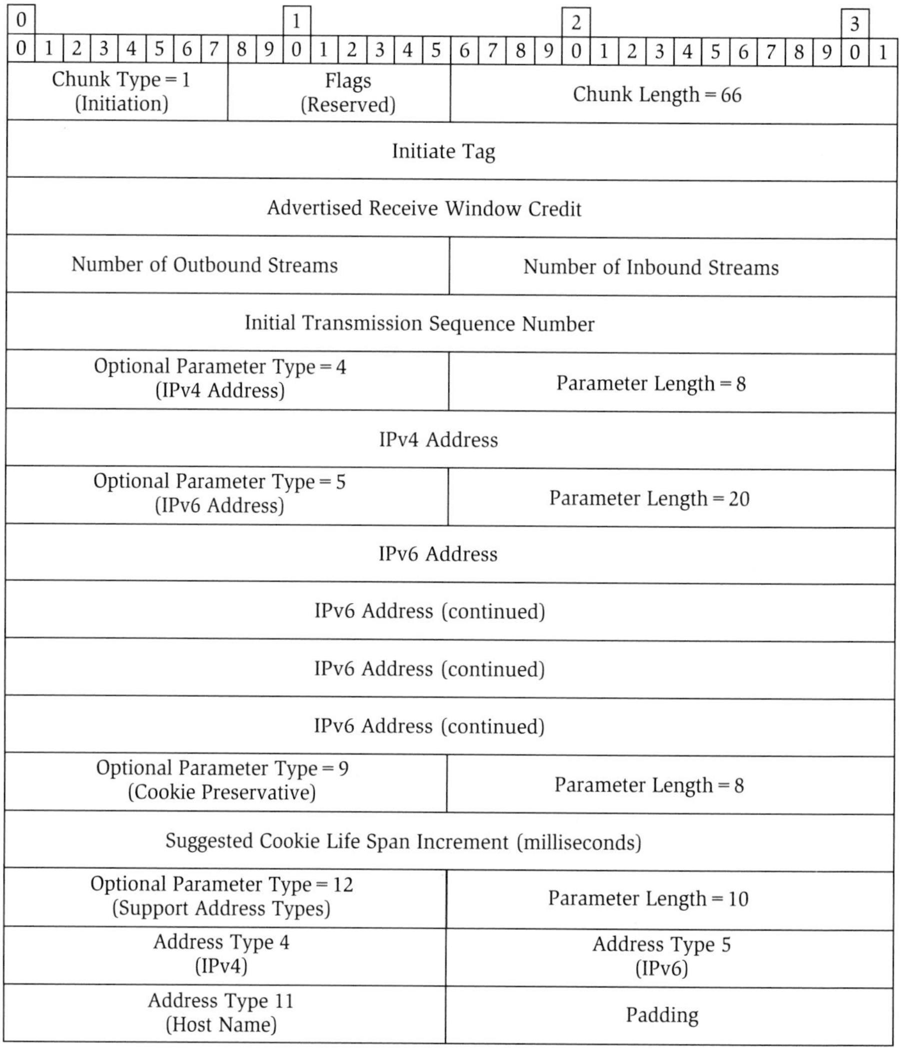

0										1										2										3	
0	1	2	3	4	5	6	7	8	9	0	1	2	3	4	5	6	7	8	9	0	1	2	3	4	5	6	7	8	9	0	1

Chunk Type = 1 (Initiation)	Flags (Reserved)	Chunk Length = 66
Initiate Tag		
Advertised Receive Window Credit		
Number of Outbound Streams		Number of Inbound Streams
Initial Transmission Sequence Number		
Optional Parameter Type = 4 (IPv4 Address)		Parameter Length = 8
IPv4 Address		
Optional Parameter Type = 5 (IPv6 Address)		Parameter Length = 20
IPv6 Address		
IPv6 Address (continued)		
IPv6 Address (continued)		
IPv6 Address (continued)		
Optional Parameter Type = 9 (Cookie Preservative)		Parameter Length = 8
Suggested Cookie Life Span Increment (milliseconds)		
Optional Parameter Type = 12 (Support Address Types)		Parameter Length = 10
Address Type 4 (IPv4)		Address Type 5 (IPv6)
Address Type 11 (Host Name)		Padding

Figure 7.23 The SCTP Association Initiation chunk.

that were used on the Association Initiation chunk. Some of the same optional parameters may also be present: the IPv4 Address, IPv6 Address, and Host Name Address parameters may all be included. Additionally, the Initiation Acknowledgement chunk must include the State Cookie parameter (type 7). The State Cookie is used to authenticate and correlate the Initiation Acknowledgement chunk with the third stage of the four-way association establishment handshake, the State Cookie Echo chunk. The State Cookie contains all of the

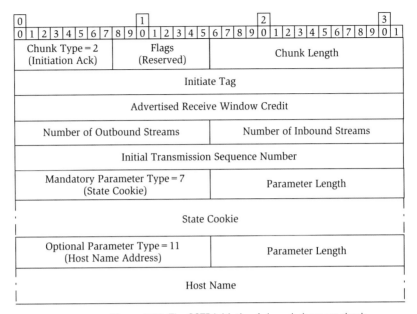

Figure 7.24 The SCTP Initiation Acknowledgement chunk.

information the responder needs to coordinate between the SCTP chunks, and additionally includes a Message Authentication Code (MAC) to provide additional security. When a responder builds a State Cookie and sends it in an Initiation Acknowledgement chunk, it starts a timer to protect itself from leaving around half-open associations. The State Cookie may, therefore, timeout during association establishment. If the sender detects this, it can try to reestablish the association and may present a Cookie Preservative parameter to suggest an amount by which the receiver should increment its timer so that the association will be correctly established.

The Initiation Acknowledgement chunk may also contain an Unrecognized Parameter (type 8), which allows the responder to return any parameters that were seen on the Association Initiation chunk that it does not support. Note that the Association Initiation and the Initiation Acknowledgement chunks may be quite large because of the presence of a potentially large number of addresses and the size of a State Cookie.

If the initiator is happy with the parameters on the Initiation Acknowledgement chunk, it echoes the responder's State Cookie back to it using a State Cookie Echo chunk, which contains just the cookie as received on the Initiation Acknowledgement chunk. As a final handshake, the responder acknowledges the State Cookie Echo chunk with a State Cookie Echo Acknowledgement chunk that contains no data or parameters. At this point the association is up and ready to carry data in both directions.

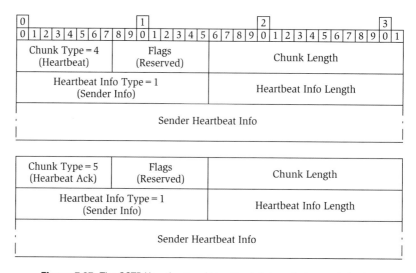

Figure 7.25 The SCTP Heartbeat and Heartbeat Acknowledgement chunks.

Once an association is open, the SCTP implementation may probe it periodically to check that it is still established and active. It does this using the Heartbeat and Heartbeat Acknowledgement chunks shown in Figure 7.25. The Heartbeat chunk contains Sender Heartbeat Information, which is in any format that the sender may choose and is transparent to every node apart from the sender. The information would normally include a timestamp in local format and probably the source and destination addresses used for the SCTP packet that contains the chunk. When a receiver gets a Heartbeat chunk it turns it around as a Heartbeat Acknowledgement chunk and copies the sender information back to the sender. A receiver should send the SCTP packet that contains the Heartbeat Acknowledgement as soon as it can and should not wait for the packet to be filled with other chunks.

An active association can carry data for any of the streams that thread it. The process of data transfer is described further in Section 7.4.3.

Orderly association closure requires a three-way handshake in SCTP. The Shutdown Request chunk is used to begin the process. It contains the sequence number of the last received contiguous byte of data on the association. Note that although acknowledgement of noncontiguous data is allowed (see Section 7.4.3), this facility is not available on association shutdown. Either end point may initiate shutdown and, just as in TCP, the shutdown may be staggered, with the end that begins the shutdown sending no further data but the other end able to continue to send. Eventually, when the remote end has finished sending data, it responds with a Shutdown Acknowledgement chunk and the end that started the shutdown confirms this step with a Shutdown Complete chunk. At this

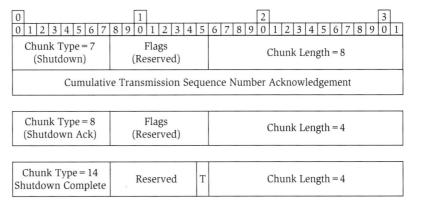

Figure 7.26 The Shutdown Request, Shutdown Acknowledgement, and Shutdown Complete chunks used in graceful association termination in SCTP.

point the association is closed. Figure 7.26 shows the three chunks used in the shutdown sequence.

There is one flag on the Shutdown Complete chunk. The T-flag is used (set to zero) to indicate that the sender of the message found and destroyed a Transmission Control Block (TCB) associated with this association—in other words, that this was a normal shutdown and that state matching the received Shutdown Acknowledgement chunk was found. If the state couldn't be found, the Shutdown Complete chunk should still be sent to help the far end of the (nonexistent) association to clean up—in this case the T-flag should be set to 1.

Two other important SCTP chunks exist. The Abort chunk is used to preemptively abort an association if any error is detected during establishment or even during normal processing. The Abort chunk may contain one or more Cause parameters giving the reason for the chunk and passing associated data. In the same way, a nonfatal error observed during the life of an association can be reported using Cause parameters on an Operation error chunk. Note that an SCTP peer that receives what it considers to be a badly encoded Abort or Operation Error chunk must silently discard the chunk and must not respond with its own Abort or Operation Error chunk since to do so risks a tight loop of message exchanges.

Table 7.5 lists the cause codes defined for Cause parameters carried in Abort or Operation Error chunks. Along with each cause code is listed the additional information passed in the Cause parameter.

Figure 7.27 shows the Abort and Operation Error chunks with their payloads of Cause Parameters. The Abort chunk carries the T-flag with the same meaning as on the Shutdown Complete chunk.

Table 7.5 SCTP Cause Codes and Additional Information

Cause	Meaning	Additional Information
1	Invalid Stream Identifier	The value of the invalid stream identifier was received in a data chunk.
2	Missing Mandatory Parameter	This is a count of missing mandatory parameters and the parameter type number of each missing parameter.
3	Stale Cookie Error	A cookie has been received in a State Cookie Echo chunk but the cookie has expired by the number of microseconds indicated. Note that this value is in microseconds even though the Suggested Cookie Life Span Increment given by the Cookie Preservative chunk is in milliseconds.
4	Out of Resource	No data is passed when this error is reported.
5	Unresolvable Address	The complete unresolvable address is passed encoded as an SCTP parameter so that its type and length can be seen.
6	Unrecognized Chunk Type	This error returns the chunk type, flags, and length of the unrecognized chunk.
7	Invalid Mandatory Parameter	This error is returned when one of the mandatory parameters on an Association Initiate or Initiate Acknowledgement chunk is set to an invalid value. No data is returned with this error, so it is not possible for the sender to determine which parameter is at fault.
8	Unrecognized Parameters	This error returns the full SCTP parameter that is unrecognized.
9	No User Data	A data chunk (see below) was received with a valid TSN but no data was present. This error returns the TSN that was received.
10	Cookie Received While Shutting Down	No data is passed when this error is reported.

7.4.3 Data Transfer

Data transfer in SCTP is managed, as in TCP, as a single sequenced and numbered flow of bytes on the association. That is, each data chunk contains a Transmission Sequence Number (TSN) that identifies the first byte in the context of the association. The amount of data is indicated by subtracting the Data chunk parameters from the Data chunk length.

One of the most important features of SCTP is that it can multiplex more than one data stream onto the same association. It does this by identifying the data stream to which the data applies through a 16-bit field in the Data chunk parameters, as shown in Figure 7.28. Additionally, a stream sequence number encodes a message number from the sending application so that the data chunks can be reassembled by the receiving application. Finally, a payload protocol identifier is included to help applications that multiplex data from several protocols through the same association.

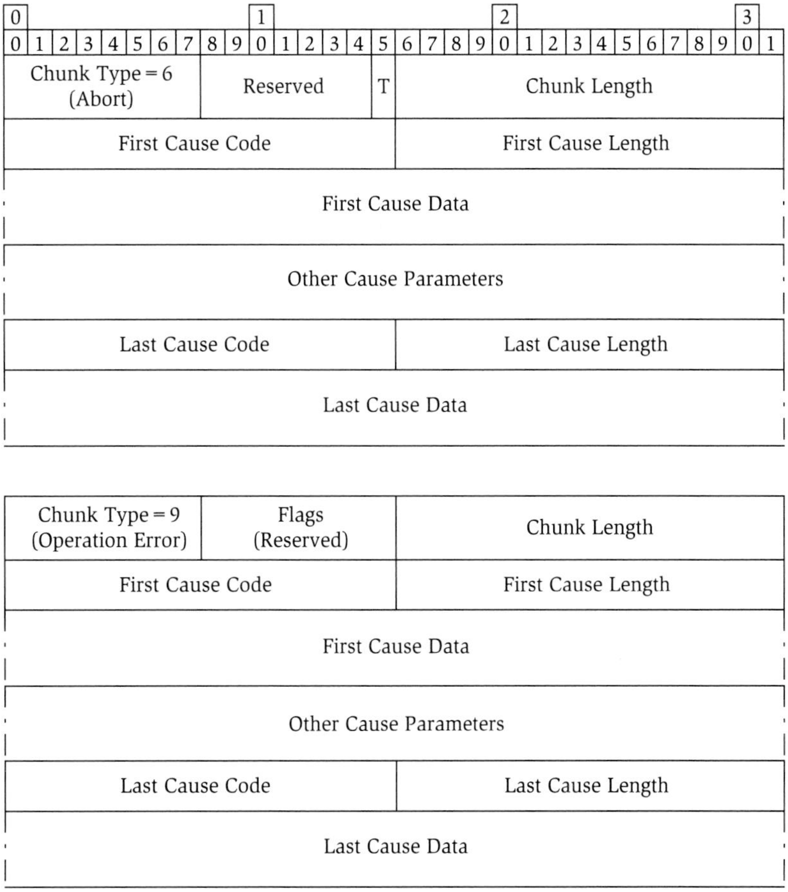

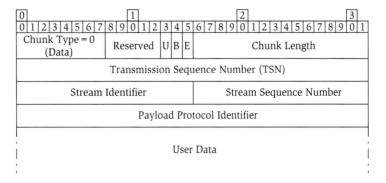

Figure 7.27 The SCTP Abort and Operation Error chunks.

Figure 7.28 The SCTP Data chunk.

Data delivery in SCTP is closely tied to the concept of user data messages. That is, the application delivers data to the SCTP service in discrete lumps (of arbitrary size) and these are transferred by SCTP (which may need to segment them to send them), reassembled, and delivered whole to the application at the remote end. User data messages are given sequence numbers by the application within the context of the stream on which they flow, and SCTP undertakes not only to reassemble the data chunks so that the right data is placed in the right message, but also to deliver the messages in order.

Three SCTP Chunk Flags are used on the Data chunk to help manage this. The B-flag indicates that the data chunk comes from the beginning of a user message. The E-flag indicates that this is the end of a user data message. The B- and E-flags may both be set on a data chunk if the chunk represents the entirety of the user data message. The third flag, the U-flag, indicates that the chunk contains all or part of an unordered data message. Unordered messages do not have valid Stream Sequence Numbers and should be delivered on the stream as soon as they have been reassembled—this makes them behave a little like the receive side of urgent data in TCP.

Figure 7.29 shows how data may be multiplexed from two streams onto a single SCTP association and then demultiplexed for delivery. Note that for simplicity in this example, no acknowledgments of the data are shown. Also for

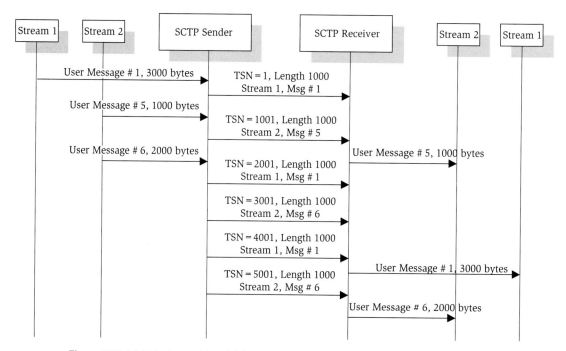

Figure 7.29 Multiplexing and demultiplexing of user data streams on a single SCTP association.

simplicity the SCTP packets shown in Figure 7.29 carry just one Data chunk each—there is no reason, except perhaps for the maximum size of the MTU, for a single packet not to carry multiple Data chunks. If a packet carries more than one Data chunk, each is encoded just as it would be if it were the only chunk in the packet. In particular, the TSN of one chunk follows on from the last byte of the previous chunk.

Acknowledgements in SCTP utilize the understanding of selective acknowledgment gained over the years using TCP. A Selective Acknowledgement chunk in SCTP acknowledges up to a specific TSN (the Cumulative TSN Acknowledgement), indicating that all bytes up to and including that TSN have been successfully received. Note that this is different from TCP, in which the Acknowledgement Number indicates the next expected Sequence Number. It is not necessary to issue multiple Selective Acknowledgement chunks for each stream; a single Selective Acknowledgement chunk can serve the needs of the whole association.

At the same time, the Selective Acknowledgement chunk can indicate blocks of data after the Cumulative TSN Acknowledgement value that have been received, and can acknowledge them selectively. It does this using the perversely named *gap acknowledgement blocks*, which indicate the start and end offsets from the Cumulative TSN Acknowledgement value of each block of received—not missing—data. Consider the sequence of bytes shown in Figure 7.30. All bytes on a shaded background have been successfully received, but those not shaded are missing. In this case, the Selective Acknowledgement chunk should report a Cumulative TSN Acknowledgement of 37 with two gap acknowledgement blocks: {4, 11} and {15, 20}.

The Selective Acknowledgement chunk shown in Figure 7.31 contains the Cumulative TSN as described in the preceding paragraph. It also sets the receiver window just as in TCP, but learning from the lessons of window scaling in TCP, the Receiver Window is a full 32 bits so that scaling is not needed. The next portion of the chunk is used to indicate gap acknowledgement blocks and is preceded by a count of blocks—an implementation that does not support selective

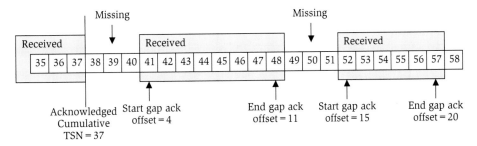

Figure 7.30 SCTP Selective Acknowledgements can acknowledge blocks of data beyond the acknowledged Cumulative Transmission Sequence Number.

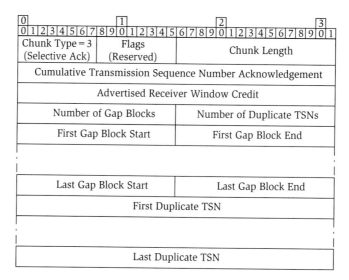

Figure 7.31 The SCTP Selective Acknowledgement chunk.

acknowledgement or which is lucky enough to receive its data in perfect order sets the gap block count to zero and does not supply any start or end offsets.

Also included in the Selective Acknowledgement chunk is a series of duplicate TSNs. Each time a receiver gets a duplicate TSN it lists it in the next Selective Acknowledgement chunk so that the sender knows that its data is being echoed or it is retransmitting too fast. There are a few points to note:

- Only the TSN indicated in the Data chunk is included. It is not the intention that every duplicate byte be listed.
- If a TSN is received multiple times, it should appear in the list multiple times. Only the first receipt is not included.
- Each time a Selective Acknowledgement chunk is sent the counts are reset, and only new duplicates are reported on the next Selective Acknowledgement chunk.
- If no duplicates have been received, the Number of duplicate TSNs is set to zero and no duplicates are included in the chunk.

7.4.4 SCTP Implementation

RFC 2960 does not simply define SCTP as a protocol. It also gives many details on how the protocol should, and in some cases must, be implemented. These details cover the use of timers, retransmission algorithms, flow control and congestion windows, and so forth. The RFC even includes state machines to ensure that there is no mistake in the behavior of an implementation. Lacking the weight of reference material and sample implementations that TCP has, new SCTP implementations should pay close attention to the text in the RFC.

Although the IETF does not normally specify interfaces, it has published a Working Group draft that documents extensions to the sockets API to make the full features of SCTP available to applications in a standardized way. This draft is making its way toward being an RFC, and it describes a mapping of SCTP into a sockets API to provide compatibility for existing TCP applications, access to the new features of SCTP, and a consolidated error and event notification scheme. Implementations of SCTP should aim to provide the sockets interface to make themselves fully useable by existing TCP-based applications.

7.4.5 Choosing Between TCP and SCTP

As yet, SCTP is not a commonly used transport protocol. Perhaps the greatest gating factor to its adoption is simply its lack of availability—TCP is built into most common operating systems as standard, but SCTP is relatively rare. Add to this a natural conservatism among protocol engineers, who would rather stick with the established and proven technology of TCP, whatever its issues, than go out on a limb with a new implementation of a new protocol.

For an existing application to move to using SCTP, both end points must contain an implementation of SCTP and the applications at each end must be migrated to use the new protocol. Given the size of the installed base of applications, this is unlikely to progress quickly. There is no easy way for an application to know whether a remote application with which it wants to communicate supports SCTP, so unless it is specifically configured it will fall back on TCP. The first deployments of SCTP in support of existing applications are likely to be in private networks where it is easier to manage which applications use which transport protocol. It is certainly true that the recent work to enhance the sockets API to allow applications to make use of the features of SCTP will make the process easier.

Nevertheless, SCTP has some distinct advantages and is growing in popularity. New control and application protocols that are developed are free to choose between TCP and SCTP without the weight of history. Since the new protocols require new development and installation, it is less painful for them to also require a new transport protocol, so if the new applications require or can make sensible use of the additional features offered by SCTP they are free to choose it.

7.4.6 Protocols That Use SCTP

IANA lists very few protocols as having registered ports specifically for use with SCTP. However, there is nothing to prevent an application or control protocol that has a registered port number for TCP being successfully run over SCTP. This is increasingly what is happening with some implementations of PSTN protocols such as SIP and MTP2.

7.5   The Real-Time Transport Protocol (RTP)

The Real-Time Transport Protocol (RTP) is a transport protocol in the sense that it provides transport services for its applications for the delivery of end-to-end data across the Internet. On the other hand, as a protocol it is remarkably light-weight, comprising just a single message (the data message) and being so short of features of its own that it must actually run over another transport protocol to achieve the level of function normally expected by an application. RTP should be considered as a top-up transport protocol.

RTP is usually used on top of UDP, although it could actually be run over any other transport protocol from any protocol suite. Since RTP is intended to help manage data delivery for real-time applications (such as video and voice), it is desirable to keep the protocol overheads to a minimum, and UDP is best placed to do that. Of course, RTP could have been designed as a full transport protocol with the features of UDP and capable of standing on its own. There were two reasons not to do this. First, UDP already existed and was readily available—why reinvent or reimplement the same function? Second, to have made RTP a stand-alone and not a top-up protocol would have limited the options for its deployment over other transport protocols and would have lost the ability to build services suitable to different applications.

RTP is accompanied by a management protocol called the Real-Time Transport Control Protocol (RTCP). It should be emphasized that RTCP is not a signaling protocol—it is not used to set up or manage connections, and it is not used to directly control the way data is exchanged by RTP. However, RTCP does allow end points to exchange information about the behavior of data flows between them, and this can be very useful to real-time applications that must act to ensure that the traffic meets the demanding quality of service requirements of voice and video applications. The information exchanged by RTCP may, there-fore, be used by RTP applications to change how they present data to RTP and how it is sent over the network.

Since RTP runs over other transport protocols it does not have a registered IP protocol identifier, but it does have registered server port numbers (5004 for RTP and 5005 for RTCP). Although RTP and RTCP are really client–server proto-cols, these registered port numbers give all nodes ports on which to passively listen for traffic. Source port numbers are taken from the dynamic ports range and must be allocated with RTP using an even port number and RTCP using a port number one greater in value.

The International Telecommunications Union (ITU) standard H.323 mandates the use of RTP, and it is used in products such as Microsoft's NetMeeting.

7.5.1 Managing Data

The primary purpose of RTP is to monitor, and, hence, maintain, the quality of data traffic for real-time applications. The requirements vary somewhat according

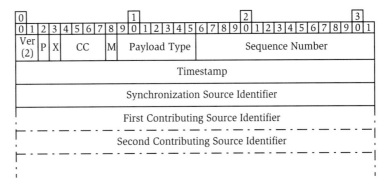

Figure 7.32 The RTP header is at least 12-bytes long.

to application but are not limited simply to timely delivery of in-order, uncorrupted data. It is also important to manage the rate of delivery of data to avoid *jitter*, the distortions of media streams caused by data arriving in bursts with gaps in between.

For this reason, the most important field in the RTP header shown in Figure 7.32 is the timestamp field. The timestamp is a 32-bit integer and contains the timestamp of the generation of the first byte of payload data. The stamp itself is in local format and does not need to be understood by the remote end point. It must, however, be monotonically increasing (that is, the timestamp on one packet is always the same as or greater than that on the previous packet—within the scope of wrapping the 32-bit integer) and must provide sufficient granularity for the application to determine and resolve jitter issues. For example, audio applications would probably implement a clock that incremented by one for each audio sampling period.

The other fields in the header are as follows. A 2-bit field indicates the version number of the protocol. Currently, version two is in use. This is followed by a single bit that indicates whether the packet concludes with 1 or more bytes of padding that are included in the packet length but do not form part of the packet data. If this is the case, the last byte of the packet is a count of the number of bytes of padding (that is, preceding and including the count) that should be ignored. It may be necessary to pad an RTP packet up to a particular block size if multiple packets are concatenated in a single lower-layer protocol packet, or if the data must be presented in well-known units to an encryption algorithm.

The next bit is the X-flag and indicates whether the header contains any private extensions (see below). The Contributing Source Identifier Count (CC) is a count of the number of Contributing Source Identifiers appended to the header and is important in defining the length of the header.

The use of the M-flag is dependent on the value of the Payload Type that follows it. It is most commonly used to help manage the data by providing synchronization events such as end of frame markers. This can allow the receiving application to reset itself without needing to parse the payload.

The Payload Type defines the use to which the data is put, and so controls how the RTP header is used and what RTCP messages should be sent. The current list of registered Payload Types is shown in Table 7.6. Since the M-flag and the Payload Type field of RTP overlap with the Message Type field of RTCP, the Payload Type is chosen from a distinct set to make processing simpler. RTCP message types run from 200 to 204, so RTP message types 72 through 76 are reserved. Most of the older payloads are discussed in RFC 1890.

The Sequence Number is simply a 16-bit packet count that increments for each packet sent and wraps back to zero. This is used to help detect packet loss. The first number used should be chosen at random to help protect against clashes with previous uses of the same ports.

The Synchronization Source Identifier (SSRC) is a random 32-bit identifier that identifies the source of the data within an RTP session. Since multiple nodes may participate in an RTP session (two-way traffic, multicast distribution, and so forth) it is necessary that the SSRC be unique across the session to guarantee identification of individual sources. Random generation of SSRCs is almost, but not quite, sufficient to make this guarantee, and there remains a slight possibility of two nodes picking the same values. SSRC contention is resolved by both sources dropping out of the session and picking new random SSRC values. This process also helps detect data that is sent in a loop.

Contributing Source Identifiers (CSRCs) identify multiple data sources that have been combined to form a single stream. This may be useful when separate applications generate data for the same RTP session (for example, audio and video) and the multiple streams are merged into a single stream. In such cases, the SSRC identifies the *mixer*, that is the application that merges the streams, and the CSRCs identify the individual source applications.

It is also possible for mixers to merge data streams from disjoint nodes. For example, in an audio conference, the mixer acts as a clearing house for all source voice streams, merges them, and sends them out to all of the listeners. The SSRC identifies the mixer and the CSRC identifies the speaker.

RTP headers may be extended to carry information specific to the payload. The presence of a header extension is indicated by setting the X-flag to 1. The format of the extension is dependent on the payload type, but the extension is itself identified by a type (to allow multiple different extensions for a given payload type). An Extension Length field indicates the length of the extension in 32-bit words, not including the identifier or length fields. This is illustrated in Figure 7.33.

Table 7.6 Registered RTP Payload Types

Payload Type	Name	Clock Rate (Hz)	Usage
0	PCMU	8000	Audio
1	1016	8000	Audio
2	G721	8000	Audio
3	GSM	8000	Audio
4	G723	8000	Audio
5	DVI4	8000	Audio
6	DVI4	16000	Audio
7	LPC	8000	Audio
8	PCMA	8000	Audio
9	G722	8000	Audio
10	L16	44100	Audio
11	L16 (2 channel)	44100	Audio
12	QCELP	8000	Audio
13	CN	8000	Audio
14	MPA	90000	Audio
15	G728	8000	Audio
16	DVI4	11025	Audio
17	DVI4	22050	Audio
18	G729	8000	Audio
25	CellB	90000	Video
26	JPEG	90000	Video
28	nv	90000	Video
31	H261	90000	Video
32	MPV	90000	Video
33	MP2T	90000	Audio/Video
34	H263	90000	Video
Dynamic	GSM-HR	8000	Audio
Dynamic	GSM-EFR	8000	Audio
Dynamic	L8	variable	Audio
Dynamic	RED	variable	Audio

Table 7.6 *Continued*

Payload Type	Name	Clock Rate (Hz)	Usage
Dynamic	VDVI	variable	Audio
Dynamic	BT656	90000	Video
Dynamic	H263–1998	90000	Video
Dynamic	MPIS	90000	Video
Dynamic	MP2P	90000	Video
Dynamic	BMPEG	90000	Video

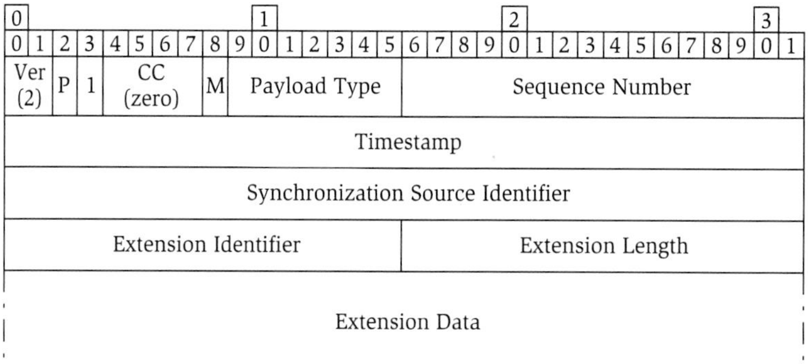

Figure 7.33 An RTP header with no Contributing Source Identifiers, but with a header extension.

7.5.2 Control Considerations

The Real-Time Control Protocol (RTCP) has three purposes.

- It allows participants in an RTP session to register their presence and to leave the session gracefully.
- It is used to monitor RTP data traffic and to feed back information about the quality of service being delivered.
- It can carry application-specific information.

There are five RTCP packet types, which are described in the following paragraphs.

The Sender Descriptor (SDES) packet is sent by an application when it joins an RTP session. The SDES gives the SSRC of the application and supplies additional information such as the host name or the geographical address of the node in Source Description Items. Figure 7.34 shows how the SDES packet is

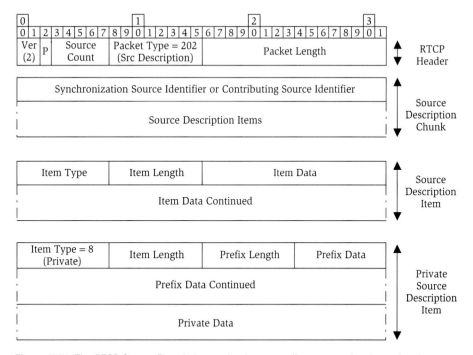

Figure 7.34 The RTCP Source Description packet has a smaller common header and at least one Source Description chunk built up from a sequence of source description items.

built of a common RTCP header followed by a series of Source Description Chunks. The header includes a version number (two is the current version), the P-flag to indicate whether the packet is terminated with padding, a count of the number of Source Description Chunks present, a packet type field, and a packet length, which includes the header fields and is represented as a count of 32-bit words in the packet, *minus one*. This peculiarity in the length field is intended to protect against scanning buffers built up of concatenated RTP packets where there is some corruption and the length field contains zero—in practice, it means that the length field counts the number of 32-bit words that follow the length field.

The Source Description Chunk describes an individual source. It begins with the SSRC of the participant in the session and contains one or more Source Description items. Each Source Description Item has an item type, an item length and item data. Table 7.7 lists the defined item types and gives their purpose. The length of each chunk is given in bytes and does not include the item type or item length fields. Individual items are not padded to reach any special byte boundaries, and text strings are not null terminated. However, each chunk begins on a 4-byte boundary, so there may be null padding at the end of

Table 7.7 The RTCP Source Description Items

Item	Contents
0	End of list marker. Length should be zero and data is ignored
1	Persistent transport name (canonical name) of the form "user@host" or "host" where host is either the fully qualified domain name of the host or is the IP address of the host on one of its interfaces presented in dotted notation
2	User name
3	User's email address
4	User's phone number
5	User's geographical location (address)
6	Application name
7	Free-form notes about the source
8	Additional private data. As shown in Figure 7.34, this is comprised of prefix and private data

a chunk. Since the Source Description Chunk does not include a length field or a count of the number of items in the chunk, the chunk is ended with a special item of type zero with a length field of zero.

A mixer, that is a node that merges RTP streams from multiple sources, sends an SDES packet for itself and includes Sender Descriptor Chunks for each of its contributing participants. If there are more than 31 chunks (governed by the size of the Source Count field) the mixer simply sends multiple SDES packets. Similarly, if a new participant joins the session through the mixer, the mixer just sends another SDES.

When an application leaves the session, it sends a BYE packet if it is well behaved. This lets other participants know that it has gone and allows them to free up resources associated with the participant. Similarly, if an application notices a clash in SSRC values between its own SSRC and that of another participant, it sends a BYE packet and immediately selects a new SSRC value and sends a new SDES.

The BYE packet, shown in Figure 7.35, also begins with the standard RTCP header. Like the SDES, the BYE allows for multiple participants to be referenced in one packet; this is useful if a mixer leaves the session. Additionally, the BYE packet includes information encoded as a printable text string about why the participants have left. Only one reason is allowed for all participants identified on a single BYE packet. If no reason is included, the reason length is set to zero.

Traffic monitoring is achieved using the Sender Report (SR) and Receiver Report (RR), shown in Figures 7.36 and 7.37. Periodically, every source of data on the RTP session sends a Sender Report to show the number of bytes and

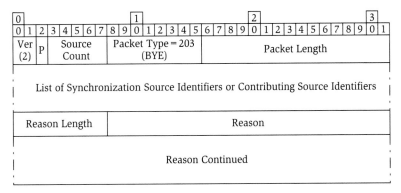

Figure 7.35 The RTCP BYE packet can report on multiple sources leaving the session.

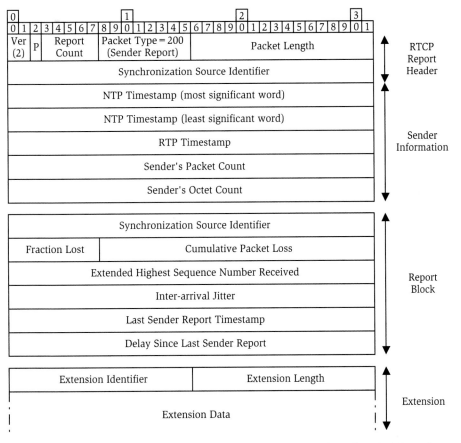

Figure 7.36 The RTCP Sender Report packet has a common header, a mandatory piece of sender information, and at least one report block. It may be followed by a profile-specific extension.

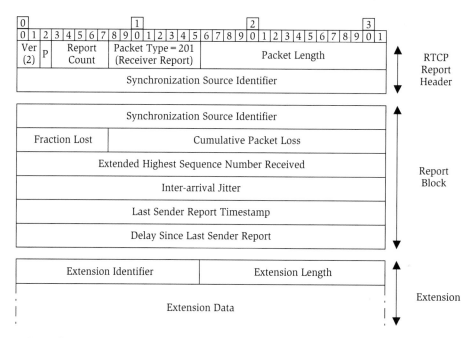

Figure 7.37 The RTCP Receiver Report packet has a common header and at least one report block. It may be followed by a profile-specific extension. It does not carry any sender information.

packets it has sent. It includes an NTP timestamp to correlate the SR across the whole network, and also shows the RTP time at which the packet was generated (using the same clock that is used to generate the timestamps on the RTP packets).

Each SR also includes a Report block for each participant (again allowing for multiple participants on a single SR if the sending node is a mixer). The Report Block quantifies the quality of data received by the sender—which makes sense in the case of bidirectional traffic.

When it receives an SR, a participant responds with a Receiver Report. The RR is similar to an SR in that it contains an SSRC to identify the receiver and a Report Block to describe the received data. The Sender Information is, however, omitted.

Both SRs and RRs may include extensions with interpretation left up to the applications.

A final RTCP packet is defined to allow applications to use RTCP to transfer their own control information. The Application packet shown in Figure 7.38 begins with a standard RTCP header and the SSRC of the sender. This is followed by a 4-byte field that identifies the packet usage in printable text, and application data that is interpreted according to the application.

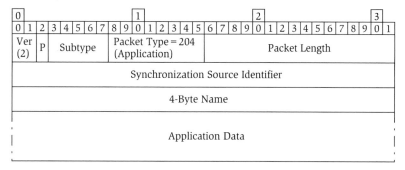

Figure 7.38 RTCP defines the Application packet for private use by an application.

7.5.3 Choosing a Transport for RTP

As mentioned before, RTP is a supplementary transport protocol that needs to run over some other transport protocol to provide the correct level of integrity and delivery. Any transport protocol would do, but in the context of the Internet the choice is between UDP, TCP, and SCTP.

RTP traffic does not require 100 percent reliability. In fact, it is acceptable to lose the odd voice sample and it is only when losses get reasonably high that the listener will notice the degradation. Furthermore, a protocol that attempts 100 percent packet delivery will back off while doing retires—this would be wholly unacceptable to a real-time application. Other back-off mechanisms for flow control and pacing are also ill-suited to real-time applications.

All this makes TCP and SCTP pretty poor choices to underlie RTP. Add to these issues the signaling overhead of TCP and SCTP and the additional cost of maintaining connections and there is really no choice but to use the lighter-weight choice of UDP.

If any further evidence was needed, it should be recalled that RTP is capable of being used by multicast applications. TCP would require a full mesh of end-to-end connections, but UDP is capable of working with IP multicast (see Chapter 3) to address these needs.

7.5.4 Choosing to Use RTP

RTP offers real-time applications ways of monitoring quality of service so that they can take action to deliver the level of function their users need.

There are, however, some issues with RTP and RTCP. The principle concern with RTP is the amount of control information that is transmitted in each data packet. This is illustrated in Figure 7.39, which shows the best case where a total of 40 bytes of overhead are sent before each piece of data. If the data is made up of audio samples, which are typically 16 bytes each, this means that more than 70 percent of the bandwidth is being used for control information.

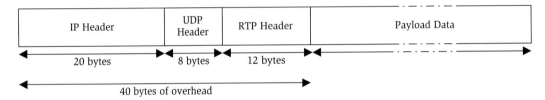

IP Header	UDP Header	RTP Header	Payload Data

| 20 bytes | 8 bytes | 12 bytes |

40 bytes of overhead

Figure 7.39 RTP over UDP and IP imposes at least a 40-byte overhead in IPv4.

But the worst case is far worse. The IP header might have a few extra bytes for IP options, and the RTP header might include one or more CSRCs. Then security might be adding to the header size, and the IP addresses might use IPv6. Further, there may be considerable overhead from the lower-layer network protocols such as ATM or Ethernet—in fact, the overhead can be so large that several ATM cells are needed to send the header information before any data is actually sent. All this can add up to very poor use of the network bandwidth and, since the whole point of RTP is to enhance the quality of traffic for real-time applications, it is reasonable to wonder whether things might not be better if RTP was abandoned and some other method was used.

The features of RTP (together with RTCP) are still sufficiently important that RTP is used extensively. Header compression techniques are used to reduce the amount of IP, UDP, and RTP information sent in each packet, thus improving the available bandwidth for data. See Chapter 15 for a discussion of header compression.

RTP scales well as the number of participants in the session increases, but RTCP traffic increases exponentially as each participant exchanges control and monitoring information with all other participants. Obviously, this can affect the bandwidth available for data throughput.

To get around this issue, the Sender Reports can be sent out less frequently and the responding Receiver Reports can be delayed a small amount. These delays can be randomized to avoid bunching of traffic, and can be factored according to the number of participants in the session.

More sophisticated schemes can favor Sender Reports from active senders (that is, those that are currently sending RTP packets), giving them immediate Receiver Reports, and delay the Receiver Reports from silent participants. Similarly, silent participants can send Sender Reports less frequently.

7.6 Further Reading

There are numerous books that cover some or all of the common IP transport protocols at a variety of levels ranging from brief overview to thorough in-depth analysis of an individual implementation.

Internetworking with TCP/IP, Vol. 1, by Douglas Comer (1996). Prentice-Hall. This is often considered the ultimate reference for TCP/IP.

TCP/IP Illustrated, Vol. 1, by Richard Stevens (1994), and *TCP/IP Illustrated, Vol. 2,* by Gary Wright and Richard Stevens (1995). Addison-Wesley. These volumes give, respectively a, thorough explanation of TCP and how to implement it, and a detailed, line-by-line explanation of a sample implementation.

TCP/IP Clearly Explained, by Peter Loshin (1999). Academic Press. This has useful chapters on TCP and UDP.

The Design and Implementation of the 4.3 BSD UNIX Operating System, by Leffler, McKusick, Karels, and Quarterman (1989). Addison-Wesley. This gives a useful overview of UDP, TCP, and sockets within the context of an operating system implementation.

Stream Control Transmission Protocol (SCTP): A Reference Guide, by Stewart, Xie, and Allman (2001). Addison-Wesley. The definitive guide to SCTP, written by two of the principal designers of the protocol.

IP Telephony, by Bill Douskalis (2000). Prentice-Hall. This provides an overview of RTP and RTCP together with plenty of technical details about how the protocols can be used to carry voice traffic in the Internet.

The IETF has published multiple RFCs covering the material in this chapter. They can be found through the IETF's web site at www.ietf.org. New work on IP transport protocols is split between two key Working Groups: the Transport Area Working Group (http://www.ietf.org/html.charters/tsvwg-charter.html) and the Signaling Transport Working Group (http://www.ietf.org/html.charters/sigtran-charter.html). Some key RFCs are:

UDP

RFC 768—User Datagram Protocol

TCP

RFC 793—Transmission Control Protocol
RFC 1122—Requirements for Internet Hosts
RFC 1323—TCP Extensions for High Performance
RFC 2018—TCP Selective Acknowledgement Options
RFC 2414—Increasing TCP's Initial Window
RFC 2525—Known TCP Implementation Problems
RFC 2581—TCP Congestion Control

SCTP

RFC 1950—ZLIB Compressed Data Format Specification version 3.3 (contains the definition of the Adler checksum algorithm)
RFC 2960—Stream Control Transmission Protocol
RFC 3257—SCTP Applicability Statement

RTP

RFC 1889—RTP: A Transport Protocol for Real-Time Applications
RFC 1890—RTP Profile for Audio and Video Conferences with Minimal Control

Chapter 8

Traffic Engineering

This chapter introduces the concept of traffic engineering (TE) as applied to IP traffic in the Internet. Traffic engineering has long been a familiar concept to town planners and road safety engineers—they are concerned with how to get the best flows of vehicles through congested streets with the minimum number of accidents. A road planner is concerned about the effects of road junctions, merging traffic flows, and sudden turns. When they build a new road will a single lane street be sufficient or do they need an eight-lane highway? What are the optimum speed limits they should set, and how should they coordinate traffic light phasing? Can they prioritize certain traffic (buses, high-occupancy vehicles, or emergency services) without causing additional disruption to the lower-priority traffic.

Most of these concepts apply within packet switched networks. A data packet is equivalent to an individual car, the links (cables, fibers, etc.) can be compared with roads, and the junctions are the switches and routers within the network. Just as vehicular traffic congestion causes delays and accidents, so data traffic congestion results in slow delivery times and lost packets.

This chapter examines some of the concepts used to manage the traffic within an IP network to make better use of the available resources, and looks at the extensions to the IGP routing protocols that are being developed within the IETF to make available information about the capabilities of, and stresses on, the network.

8.1   What Is IP Traffic Engineering?

The Internet is a collection of nodes and links with the purpose of delivering IP datagrams from a source host to a destination host. The source does not, in general, care how the data is delivered so long as it arrives in a timely and reliable way. The routing protocols discussed in Chapter 5 are based on *shortest path first* (SPF) routing, in which each datagram is routed on the shortest path between the source and the destination.

In an otherwise unused network, SPF routing is ideal: datagrams are delivered expeditiously with the least use of network resources. However, as network traffic increases it may be the case that a link or router is saturated and cannot handle all of the traffic that it receives. When this happens, data will be lost either in a random way through data collisions, or through an organized scheme within routers. Chapter 6 presented ways to prioritize traffic so that the low-priority datagrams are dropped and the higher-priority traffic is successfully delivered. The chapter went on to discuss ways to quantify and measure service requirements so that resources may be reserved ahead of time for handling specific flows. This ensures that the services are successfully delivered, and that an application may calibrate its expectations of reliable delivery of its data. Chapter 7 introduced mechanisms for congestion detection within transport protocols and means to regulate the rate at which traffic is presented to the network so as to increase the chance of error-free delivery.

All these techniques are good ways to increase the reliability of traffic delivery within an SPF routing system, but they do not increase the amount of traffic the network can handle. Consider the network shown in Figure 8.1. In this network traffic from Hosts U, V, and W is routed across the network to Host X, Y, and Z. Using SPF routing, traffic tends to converge on the link between Routers F and G. This is fine until the link or the routers become overloaded, at which time data is dropped. But what about the other links in the network? Surely they could be used to reduce the burden on the congested resources. For example, if traffic between Hosts U and X was sent through Routers B, C, and D, the datagrams would take a slightly longer path but would avoid the congested link.

Traffic Engineering is all about discovering what other paths and links are available in the network, what the current traffic usage is within the network, and directing traffic to routes other than the shortest so that optimal use is made of the resource in the network. This is achieved by a combination of extensions to the existing IGP routing protocols, traffic monitoring tools, and traffic routing techniques, respectively. The remaining sections in this chapter examine these mechanisms.

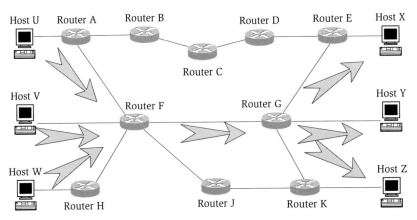

Figure 8.1 Shortest path first routing may result in unnecessarily congested links and nodes.

8.2   Equal Cost Multipath (ECMP)

In Figure 8.1 the route from Host V to Host Z is shown as VFGKZ, but it should be noted that the route VFJKZ is the same length and so the same cost as the chosen path. When the routing protocol discovers it has two equally short paths it selects one by some arbitrary process—usually selecting the first one discovered.

However, *equal cost multipath* (ECMP) routes offer a simple way to share the network load by distributing traffic onto other paths. Sophisticated systems may examine the load on the system and route traffic accordingly. For example, Router F knows that the link to Router G is already congested and so can select the alternative equal cost path through Router J. The level of knowledge required within Router F to perform this decision is limited to it measuring its own rate of traffic forwarding, so making the decision is quite achievable. However, if the congested link is actually between Routers G and K, it may be harder for Router F to decide to use the alternative path.

Router F can nevertheless take advantage of the equal cost paths if it simply load balances traffic across the two paths. The obvious technique is to alternate datagrams between the two paths, or to apply some other statistical technique to place datagrams onto the paths. This is a satisfactory approach from the point of view of the network, but may not be appreciated by the applications running on the hosts, since it can break a traffic flow datagram by datagram between the two paths. One path with a slightly higher latency than the other could lead to every datagram arriving out of order, with the result that some applications will be unable to successfully transfer data. Not clever!

ECMP is therefore typically applied only to entire flows or sets of flows. A flow in this respect may be characterized by destination address, source address, transport level ports, payload protocol, DiffServ colors, or any combination of these. For example, traffic from Host V to Host Z could be routed through Router G while traffic from Host W to Host Z could be sent through Router J.

This type of load balancing is a local decision made at a router within the network (in this case Router F). Such behavior is typically under the close control of a network operations manager and is not left as an open choice for the router.

8.3   Modifying Path Costs

Figure 8.2 repeats the network from Figure 8.1 but shows costs assigned to each of the links. Four of the links (AF, FG, GE, and GK) have abstract values assigned (a, b, c, and d, respectively) and all of the other links have a cost of 1. Link costs can typically be assigned under operator control as per-link configuration parameters on a router.

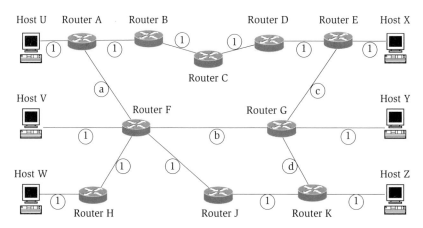

Figure 8.2 Modifying link costs may facilitate load distribution within a network.

If the link costs a, b, and c are all set to 1, we have the network in Figure 8.1 and all traffic tends toward the link FG. This can be modified by giving b, the cost of the link FG, a value of 7—this makes FG much less attractive and traffic from Host U to Host X will be routed through Routers B, C, and D (total cost 6) rather than through Routers F and G (total cost 11). Similarly, traffic from Host W to Host Z will be routed through Router J (total cost 5) rather than through Router G (total cost 11). Unfortunately, with this assignment of costs the path VFABCDEGY costs only 8 and is therefore preferable to VFGY which costs 9, and the path VFJKGY costs only 5 and so is chosen to carry the data. This has eased the problem, but has moved some of the congestion to Router J.

Further tweaking of the link cost by setting a=2, c=2, and d=10 achieves the desired result, sending traffic along the paths UABCDEX (cost 6), VFGY (cost 9), and WHFJKZ (cost 5), which are the cheapest available. This all looks very good until we consider traffic flowing from Host W to Host X. Do we really want this to take the path WHFABCDEX (cost 9) in preference to the much shorter WHFGEX (cost 12)? Perhaps we should increase the value of cost a to 6; that would do the trick, but what about traffic from Host U to Host Y? This is now going to prefer UABCDEGY (cost 8) over the path UAFGY (cost 15), which we might rather it took.

It can be seen from this simple example that using link costs to manage traffic flow is far from trivial. It must always be done only after careful planning and the effects on the network must be monitored diligently. Wherever possible, such solutions should be modeled using network planning tools before they are used to carry live traffic, since the consequences of misconfiguration may be worse than the original congestion.

8.4 Routing IP Flows

As described in Section 8.2, equal cost paths may be selected by a router for different flows to help balance the load within the network. But suppose that some observer of the network (an operator or an application program) determines that there is a longer, more expensive, underused path that is suitable for the traffic: Can the data be sent down that path without having to modify path costs as described in the previous section? If this could be achieved, network congestion could be avoided (the drivers could download new routes from their GPS navigation systems and find a way around the traffic jams).

Section 2.5 introduced the concept of source routing. In this mode each datagram contains a list of IP addresses of the links or nodes it must pass through, in order, on the way to its destination. SPF routing is performed at each stage on the next address in the list so that the datagram may be sent along a path under the control of the source application. This is ideal because it gives complete control to the sender, allowing it to choose whether to use the shortest (lowest cost) path (which may be congested) or some other more expensive path that would otherwise not be chosen by the network.

But, notwithstanding the limitations of IP source routing described in Section 2.5, source routing is also not ideal because it forces the hosts to make routing decisions. This is both too much function to place in a host and too much responsibility. Proper choice of routes requires detailed analysis of traffic flows and available resources (see Section 8.8), and this requires a sophisticated application. At the same time, if each individual traffic source makes uncoordinated routing decisions based on the same network data, the result may be the sudden and simultaneous transferal of all traffic from one over-used link to another (formerly underused) link in a way that may cause even more serious congestion. (Compare this with the rush hour traffic that responds to a radio traffic report by diverting en masse from the slightly congested freeway to the single-lane country road.)

A better model, therefore, might have paths selected in coordination with a centralized traffic control station. This sort of model is applied very successfully in vehicular traffic engineering when a city or motorway network is controlled through an operational headquarters that can control speed limits, traffic lights, diversions, and lane assignments. An individual host may, however, find that the overhead of soliciting a path for its traffic is unacceptably high given the small amount of data it wants to send.

On the other hand, significant traffic management can usefully be performed within the core of the network where the traffic volumes are greater. Here individual flows from host to host can be bundled together and treated in the same way for forwarding down routes that are not necessarily the shortest. The easiest way to handle this is through a process known as *tunneling*. A tunnel is a well-defined path from one point in the network to another, and flows may be injected into the tunnel at one end to emerge at the other end, as shown in Figure 8.3.

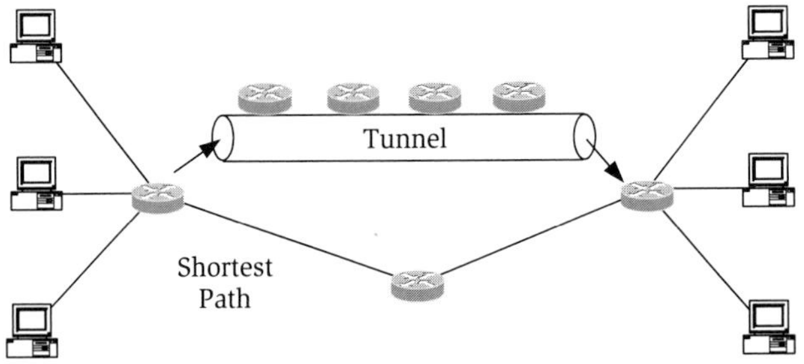

Figure 8.3 A tunnel carries a collection of flows from one point in the network to another by a path that may not be the shortest.

Tunnels may run from one edge of the network to another, or may be used to bypass an area of congestion. The simplest way to achieve a tunnel is to impose a source route on each datagram that enters the tunnel. In this way the router at the head end of the tunnel determines the path of the datagram until it reaches the end of the tunnel. Other, more sophisticated, IP tunneling techniques are described in Section 15.1. Note that tunnels may themselves be routed through other tunnels, providing a hierarchy or nesting of tunnels.

Tunneling may also be achieved at a level below IP in the network. A good example of this is described for Multiprotocol Label Switching (MPLS) in Section 9.5. When sub-IP tunnels are established, they may be defined to the network as *virtual links*, which are logical point-to-point connections between routers that are not actually physically connected, as described in Chapter 5. These virtual links may be assigned costs and can be advertised through the routing protocols just as physical links are, resulting in traffic being routed down the tunnels rather than across the physical links.

8.5 Service-Based Routing

The choice of an ECMP route may be based on other dynamic factore such as the DiffServ color of the datagrams. Similarly, source routing and tunneling may be determined by examination of the datagrams to select which should take which routes.

An important option is the ability to select a route that meets the required network characteristics of a traffic flow. For example, a stream of IP datagrams carrying voice traffic requires a reliable link with relatively low variation in delivery rates. On the other hand, a file server does not need these qualities but does demand high bandwidth. Different links within the network have different characteristics and it will often be the case that the shortest path does not meet the needs of a particular flow. The datagrams in a flow can be flagged using DiffServ to indicate their requirements, and the flow can be qualified for its desired quality of service using IntServ.

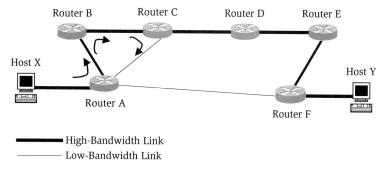

Figure 8.4 Hop-by-hop routing on choices other than shortest path first risks causing routing loops if some router in the network still uses only shortest path first routing.

The routers in a network can select a path through the network that is the least cost given the quality of service limitations of the flow if the routers can obtain a view of the network that tells them not just the topology and the cost of each link, but also lets them know the link capabilities. On a per-datagram basis, routing decisions can be made hop-by-hop, resulting in the datagrams being routed on links that meet the needs of the service but are not necessarily the shortest paths through the network. The problem with this system of *constraint-based routing* is that it requires that all routers in the network make routing decisions on the same basis—if one of the routers uses conventional SPF routing, a routing loop may occur, as shown in Figure 8.4, where Routers A and B select high-bandwidth links but Router C picks the shortest path.

Service-based routing, therefore, requires either a network of homogeneous routers or a tunneling approach.

8.6   Choosing Offline or Dynamic Traffic Engineering

Various comments in the previous sections have indicated the problems with making traffic engineering routing decisions dynamically within the network. Among these concerns are problems caused by routers that do not share the same routing paradigms as the rest of the network—they may place traffic using different rules and this unpredictability may cause links to be overloaded. Conversely, the simultaneous application by multiple routers of the same routing and traffic balancing rules may result in decisions to move lots of traffic from several slightly overused links to a single underused link, making the one link severely congested. These difficulties arise to a lesser extent if the traffic engineering routing decisions are made only by the data sources or by TE tunnel head-end routers within the network, but even then the reactivity of a single network node to changes within the network is limited by the node's view of the network.

A more controlled approach favored by many network operators is *offline traffic engineering*. In this mode of operation, all decisions about how to route traffic are made by one (or a few) centralized servers. Such servers can keep a coordinated view of the network and react to changes in traffic loads. They can supply source routes to hosts, tunneling information to selected routers, or constraint-based routing instructions to all routers in the network. These instructions from the traffic engineering server can be applied to new flows or to existing flows, making it possible for the traffic to be dynamically redistributed within the network.

One key advantage of offline traffic engineering is that more time can be taken to perform complex calculations and modeling before the new flow paradigms are applied within the live network. This reduces the chance of a major mistake—it is better to have traffic continue to flow with some congestion than it is to bring complete gridlock to the network.

Offline traffic engineering is best suited to a tunneling model. This may use IP tunnels as described in the previous sections, or lower-layer tunneling using MPLS or layer two tunnels.

8.7   Discovering Network Utilization

Essential to successful traffic engineering is an understanding of current network utilization. Individual routers can, of course, maintain a good picture of how much traffic they send and receive on each link, and they can use this information to influence their own routing decisions. However, for system-wide traffic engineering, a network-wide view of resource utilization is needed.

Various applications exist to collect and consolidate network usage information. At a basic level, applications can use SNMP or similar network management protocols (see Chapter 13) to read statistics from each of the routers—standard Management Information Base (MIB) data collects counters of the number of datagrams and bytes sent and received on each interface of a router and also gives the number of packets discarded because of congestion. An application can periodically poll each router and convert the returned information into a view of usage across the whole network.

Although this technique gives a good impression of which links are over-used and which underused, it doesn't help determine which flows need to be redistributed to ease any congestion. All that is known is an absolute measure of traffic load where we need to see the traffic broken down by flow.

Several different tools have been designed to help analyze traffic flows within IP networks. Some of these are used to identify hot spots with a view to provisioning additional links and routers, and others provide billing and accounting information. Some of the applications can also be used to collect and aggregate information for use by traffic engineering servers.

NetFlow is Cisco's answer to collecting and analyzing network traffic usage information. Now supported by many tools and router vendors, *NetFlow* is based on the collection of information at key points within the network, and particularly around the edges. Data is formatted into well-known record formats so that it can be exchanged between collection points and analysis tools in an easily understood way. *NetFlow* also addresses the problem that a detailed and up-to-date record of data flows at every router requires a very large amount of information. If this information is regularly transmitted through the network it will account for a significant proportion of the total data within the network and may itself contribute to congestion. *NetFlow* includes aggregation points (*NetFlow* collectors) that can be placed within the network to take responsibility for local TE decisions and to consolidate the information from a subset of the network before forwarding it to a central site where network-wide analysis can be performed.

An alternative to *NetFlow* is offered by *sFlow*. sFlow.org is an international, multivendor, and end-user forum that promotes a different mode of network sampling technology, but can similarly be used to monitor and manage traffic in IP networks. *ntop* is an open source network traffic probe that utilizes *sFlow* and can be used to show the network usage, capture packets, and perform traffic analysis. *ntop* performs much of the same function as *NetFlow* and can be integrated to act as a *NetFlow* collector.

8.7.1 Explicit Congestion Notification

RFC 2481 describes an experimental method for notifying transport level protocols when congestion is experienced within the network. When this happens, the transport protocols may throttle back the rate at which they send datagrams and so help to reduce the congestion in the network.

Explicit Congestion Notification (ECN) requires two additional flags within the IP header. The first is the ECN-Capable Transport (ECT) bit, which is set by the data sender to indicate that the end points of the transport protocol are ECN-capable—this means that if congestion is notified for this data flow, the transport protocol will be able to do something about it. The second bit is the Congestion Encountered (CE) bit, which is set by a router to indicate to the end nodes that congestion has occurred.

Notice that there is a dichotomy here since before congestion occurs there is no congestion, and when it occurs packets are dropped, preventing the CE bit from being delivered. In fact, what is used is an adaptation of the Random Early Detection (RED) mechanism for active queue management to detect incipient congestion (see RFC 2309). In its basic form, RED is designed to drop packets before congestion occurs in an attempt to keep the queues at manageable levels, but in an ECN system these packets are not dropped, but are forwarded with the CE bit set.

The ECN bits are carried in the IP header in bits 6 and 7 (ECT and CE, respectively) of the Type of Service (ToS) byte. This is only a relatively safe thing to do because of the various ways that the byte has been used (or not used) over time. Where the ToS byte is unused or is used for DiffServ these bits were previously reserved and unused, so their allocation for ECN processing is without problems.

The mechanism by which transport protocols throttle back on the data they send is not important to the functioning of ECN. It is best if the regulation is passive (for example, by not sending sliding window acknowledgments) since active methods (such as sending quiescent messages) may suffer from messages being discarded owing to the network congestion.

Note that ECN for IP is not to be confused with similar schemes in data-link layer protocols such as Frame Relay and ATM. These protocols have indicators (the FECN and EFCI flags, respectively) that show when congestion has been reached, but do not take into account average queue sizes. This means that these protocols may be expected to show congestion on bursty traffic, and throttling back on transport or application protocols as a result may be over-zealous.

8.8 Routing Extensions for Traffic Engineering

There is one other requirement for successful traffic engineering: the application making TE decisions must have a clear view of the topology and capabilities of the links within the network. Within a small, static network this information can be configured at a TE server, but this approach does not serve the needs of distributed TE systems nor does it handle large and dynamic networks.

IGP routing exchanges (described in Chapter 5) already provide a successful means of determining connectivity within the network, so it is natural to consider extending them to distribute additional information about the links they recognize. For example, it would be a simple matter for each link state advertisement in OSPF to also include as part of the state the total bandwidth that the link is capable of supporting. This small amount of additional information would be hugely useful to a TE system since in conjunction with a traffic flow monitoring process it can help distinguish which links are underused and which are congested. But even without traffic monitoring, the knowledge of the capabilities of the links in a network can help the TE system place traffic optimally.

Additional information such as the amount of bandwidth currently on the link and the way in which bandwidth can be reserved can only further enhance the ability of a TE system to manage the network. The remainder of this section examines extensions to OSPF and IS-IS in support of traffic engineering. If the information gathered and reported in the two protocols looks similar, that is because the two sets of extensions were derived in parallel within the IETF where, at the time of writing, the OSPF extensions have been published as RFC 3630, and the IS-IS extensions are about to be published as an RFC.

8.8.1 OSPF-TE

OSPF includes the concept of opaque Link State Advertisements (LSAs). These allow routers to share private or proprietary information across the network in an interoperable way. Routers that do not understand the opaque LSAs are not required to examine them nor to use them in their path calculations, but they are required to store them and to forward them. This provides a neat way of adding function to a network in a backwards-compatible way, and it is used to add TE information to OSPF so that TE-aware routers can distribute and act on TE information in cooperation with older routers that continue to implement standard OSPF.

The standard format of the OSPF opaque LSA is shown in Figure 8.5. LSAs may be flooded in a variety of ways, and for TE the flooding is limited to an area by setting the LSA Type to the value 10, as described in Chapter 5. The LSA Identifier is a 32-bit quantity which is split into an 8-bit type (set to 1 to indicate a TE LSA) and 24 bits of type-specific data used in the TE LSA as an LSA instance identifier.

The body of the opaque LSA is constructed from type-length-variable (TLV) constructs. These form a sequence but may also be nested so that the length of one top-level TLV covers the entirety of a series of sub-TLVs. All of the sub-TLVs are found in the variable of the top-level TLV. The format of a TE LSA TLV is shown in Figure 8.6; the type and length are 2 bytes each and the length field indicates a count of bytes that follow in the variable field. Table 8.1 shows the TLVs that are defined for inclusion in the TE LSA. There are two top-level TLVs (Router address and Link information), and the Link information TLV may contain a number of sub-TLVs to supply information about the given link.

Figure 8.7 shows how IEEE floating points are carried in TE LSAs. The S-bit gives the sign, the exponent is base 2 in "excess 127" notation; and the fraction is

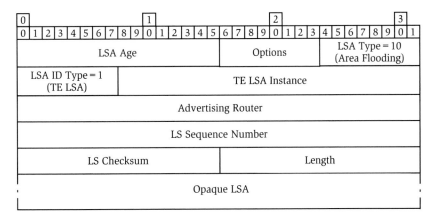

Figure 8.5 The standard OSPF opaque LSA header used for the TE LSA.

Table 8.1 Type Values for Top-Level and Sublevel TLVs within the TE LSA

Top-Level TLV	Sublevel TLV	Length	Meaning
1		4	Router address. A link-independent, reachable address of the reporting router. For example, a loopback address.
2		varies	Link TLV. Sub-TLVs follow. Length varies according to the total sub-TLVs present.
	1	1	Link type. A single byte showing that the link is point-to-point (1) or multi-access (2).
	2	4	Link ID. Perhaps a misnomer, this TLV provides the Router ID of the router at the other end of the link for point-to-point links and the interface address of the designated router for multi-access links.
	3	4n	Local interface IP address. One or more IPv4 addresses may be present in this sub-TLV. Each is the address of an interface that corresponds to this link.
	4	4n	Remote interface IP address. One or more IPv4 addresses that identify the remote interfaces corresponding to this point-to-point link. On a multicast link this variable may be set to 0.0.0.0 or the sub-TLV may be omitted.
	5	4	Traffic engineering metric. A 4-digit metric for use in traffic engineering path computation. This metric may be different from the standard OSPF link metric, allowing different weights to be assigned for normal and TE traffic.
	6	4	Maximum bandwidth. The link capacity. That is, the maximum amount of bandwidth that can be used by traffic on this link in this direction (from the router originating the LSA). This value is expressed in bytes per second using the IEEE floating point notation shown in Figure 8.7.
	7	4	Maximum reservable bandwidth. The largest amount of bandwidth that may be reserved on this link in this direction. This value may be greater than the maximum bandwidth if over-subscription is supported, or smaller if some bandwidth is always held back for non-TE best-effort traffic. The default value is the same as the maximum bandwidth. This value is also expressed in bytes per second using the IEEE floating point notation shown in Figure 8.7.
	8	32	Unreserved bandwidth. A series of eight floating point numbers giving the amounts of bandwidth that can still be reserved at each of the priority levels zero through seven (in that order). This construct allows for preemptable bandwidth and segmentation of the available bandwidth by priority.
	9	4	Administrative group. The bit-sensitive administrative groups or resource colors to which this link belongs.

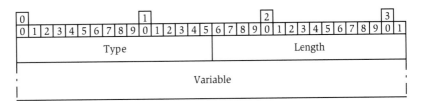

Figure 8.6 The standard format of TLVs within the TE LSA.

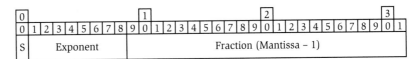

Figure 8.7 Representation of IEEE floating point numbers in TE LSAs.

the mantissa minus 1 with an implicit binary point in front of it. In this way, the number represented is

$$(-1)^{**}(S) * 2^{**}(Exponent - 127) * (1 + Fraction)$$

8.8.2 IS-IS TE

The traffic engineering extensions for IS-IS are needed to carry exactly the same information as the extensions previously described for OSPF.

IS-IS Link State Protocol Data Units (LSPs) are composed of a series of TLVs. For IS-IS TE two new TLVs are defined: the Extended IS Reachability TLV with type value 22, and the Traffic Engineering Router ID TLV with type value 134. A new concept is also introduced to IS-IS LSP encoding—sub-TLVs are used to allow multiple pieces of information to be packaged within one TLV. Figure 8.8 shows the format of the new Extended IS Reachability TLV and Table 8.2 lists the sub-TLVs that have been defined.

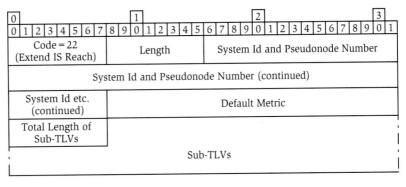

Figure 8.8 The IS-IS Extended IS Reachability TLV.

Table 8.2 Extended IS Reachability Sub-TLVs

Sub-TLV Code	Length	Meaning
3	4	Administrative group (color). As described for OSPF-TE.
6	4	IPv4 interface address. As described for OSPF-TE local interface IP address. Multiple addresses may be conveyed by including multiple instances of this sub-TLV.
8	4	IPv4 neighbor address. As described for OSPF-TE remote interface IP address. Multiple addresses may be conveyed by including multiple instances of this sub-TLV.
9	4	Maximum link bandwidth. As for OSPF-TE.
10	4	Reservable link bandwidth. As for OSPF-TE.
11	32	Unreserved bandwidth. As for OSPF-TE.
18	3	TE Default metric. As for OSPF-TE but note that only 3 bytes are used to encode metrics in IS-IS.

The new Traffic Engineering Router ID TLV is shown in Figure 8.9. It is used to carry the router ID of the router that originated the LSP. This can be used in traffic engineering to guarantee the availability of a single, stable address (for example, the loopback address) that is always reachable regardless of the state of the node's interfaces. This corresponds to the OSPF-TE Router Address TLV.

The IS-IS TE Internet Draft additionally takes the opportunity to look at some problems with the existing IS-IS specification as applied to IP networks. It introduces a further TLV, the Extended IP Reachability TLV, with type value 135 shown in Figure 8.10. The main piece of new information is the U-bit, which is used to determine the looping of routing information between level one and level two routing. The base IS-IS specification (RFC 1195) handles the problem by only allowing prefixes to be advertised upwards within the hierarchy, but the U-bit (the up/down bit) can improve the process by flagging whether the prefix has ever been advertised down through the hierarchy (set to 1). Prefixes that have the up/down bit set to 1 may only be advertised

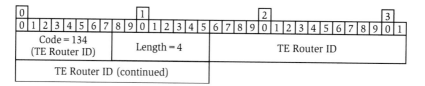

Figure 8.9 The IS-IS Traffic Engineering Router ID TLV.

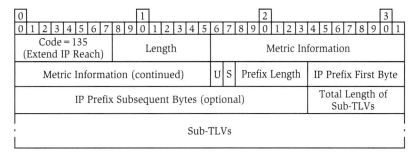

Figure 8.10 The IS-IS Extended IP Reachability TLV.

down the hierarchy to lower levels and may never be advertised back into higher levels.

The S-bit indicates whether there are any sub-TLVs present. If the bit is clear (zero) neither the sub-TLV length field nor the sub-TLVs themselves are present. This construction is put in place for future extensibility, although no sub-TLVs have been defined so far. The prefix length may take any value from zero to 32, and it governs the number of bytes of prefix information that are present—only the number of bytes needed to carry the length of prefix are actually used.

8.9   Choosing to Use Traffic Engineering

Traffic engineering maximizes the performance of existing network connections, allowing more traffic to be carried. This increases revenues from deployed equipment, and an increase in revenue without an increase in expenditure should imply increased profits. Further, maximizing the performance of the existing infrastructure delays the point at which more money has to be spent to add links and nodes to the network.

Of course, if the network is massively over-provisioned there is nothing the operator needs to do other than possibly monitor the most congested links to check that traffic is well within the safe parameters. A network provider who considers himself lucky in this situation should appreciate that although he is able to satisfy his customers' Service Level Agreements (SLAs) he is not generating as much revenue from his network as he could. More traffic means higher revenues.

Traffic engineering is a tool for operators of well-used networks who need to move the traffic around to take the pressure off congested links without compromising the SLAs they are contracted to meet. Path computation engines can run offline or can be dynamic, as already described. Path computation can be a single shot for each flow (that is, the route is computed when the flow is first established) or can be adaptive, adjusting the routes of the flows in the network according to the pressures of traffic.

Additionally, the rules for computing paths can be based on a variety of constraints above and beyond the volume of the flows and the available bandwidth on the links. Constraints can cover priority, quality of service, reliability, and security. Other constraints can be used to ensure that flows include or exclude specific resources (such as links that are known to be vulnerable, or paths that are used to provide diverse backup routes), nodes, or groups of resources known as *Shared Risk Link Groups* (SRLGs) that share the same risk of failure.

The greater the complexity of the traffic engineering scheme that is applied, the more sophisticated are the features that can be sold to customers and the more flexible are the management options for the network provider. At the same time, increased complexity demands more detailed and reliable collection of network statistics as well as increased processing resource. The trade-off between cost and benefit will be met at a different level for each network, and it should be borne in mind that with increased complexity may come a greater risk of a mistake that could cause severe perturbations within the network.

8.9.1 Limitations of IP Traffic Engineering

There are some distinct limitations to the way traffic engineering can be performed using IP. If forwarding rules are modified, then the routers in the network need to be kept synchronized and must all operate with the same level of function, or loops and increased congestion may result. On the other hand, IP source routing is limited both by the size of the route that may be specified (just nine hops) and the fact that not all routers support IP source routing in a consistent way (or at all).

Other IP tunneling techniques may help to direct traffic around hot spots and do have some efficacy, especially as they allow data flows to be grouped together and handled in the same way. But even these tunneling techniques really need some form of source routing to route them through the network. Clearly, some other form of tunneling is really needed.

8.9.2 Future Developments in Traffic Engineering

Traffic engineering is increasingly utilizing Multiprotocol Label Switching (MPLS) to meet its tunneling needs. MPLS (described in Chapter 9) provides data tunnels through the network that can be placed according to explicit routes calculated offline or online and modified in real time. These tunnels rely on IP routing information gathered through the TE extensions to the IGPs for computation of their paths and distribution of tunnel forwarding information, but do not use the IP addresses of the datagrams to actually forward the data within the tunnels. This gives the best of both worlds because all the information from the IP world can be used to determine paths to forward IP data, but the issues with IP forwarding can be overcome by using non-IP forwarding techniques.

Note that preexisting layer two forwarding protocols such as Frame Relay and ATM have offered the same sort of tunneling as MPLS for some time. MPLS just brings them together under one generic protocol umbrella for ease of management and the construction of heterogeneous networks.

8.10 Further Reading

A search of online bookstores for works on traffic engineering uncovers a vast number of texts on the management of vehicular traffic through congested road networks. Interesting though this topic is, it is only somewhat relevant (perhaps more relevant than one would immediately realize, but still not very pertinent), and there are very few up-to-date books on the application of traffic management to IP networks—perhaps this is a fertile field for a budding author.

Dynamic Routing in Telecommunication Networks, by Gerald Ash (1997). McGraw-Hill. This is an implementation- and practice-based guide to the tools and techniques required to design, operate, and manage dynamic routing networks.

MPLS Network Management—MIBs, Tools and Techniques, by Thomas Nadeau (2003). Morgan Kaufmann. A good introduction to traffic engineering, albeit with an MPLS slant, this also has an overview of the *NetFlow* data collection and distribution techniques.

Traffic Engineering with MPLS, by Eric Osborne and Ajay Sinha (2002). Cisco Press. This book is a hands-on guide to the use of Cisco routers to provide traffic engineered services in an MPLS network. It gives a good introduction to the concepts of traffic engineering.

NetFlow is described on Cisco's web site at http://www.cisco.com. A description of *sFlow* can be found at http://www.sFlow.org. Information on the *ntop* application can be found at http://www.ntop.org.

Various RFCs and Internet Drafts provide a background to Traffic Engineering and introduce the specific protocol extensions. The following Internet Drafts are likely, in the fullness of time, to become RFCs in their own right.

General Traffic Engineering Material

RFC 2309—Recommendations on Queue Management and Congestion Avoidance in the Internet

RFC 2430—A Provider Architecture for Differentiated Services and Traffic Engineering (PASTE)

RFC 2481—A Proposal to add Explicit Congestion Notification (ECN) to IP

RFC 3272—Overview and Principles of Internet Traffic Engineering

draft-ietf-tewg-measure—A Framework for Internet Traffic Engineering Measurement

Routing Protocol Extensions for Traffic Engineering

RFC 1195—Use of OSI IS-IS for routing in TCP/IP and dual environments

RFC 2328—OSPF Version 2

RFC 2370—The OSPF Opaque LSA Option

RFC 2966—Domain-wide Prefix Distribution with Two-Level IS-IS

RFC 3273—Overview and Principles of Internet Traffic Engineering

RFC 3630—Traffic Engineering Extensions to OSPF Version 2

draft-ietf-isis-traffic—IS-IS extensions for Traffic Engineering

draft-srisuresh-ospf-te—OSPF-xTE: An experimental extension to OSPF for Traffic
Engineering

Futures of Traffic Engineering

RFC 2702—Requirements for Traffic Engineering Over MPLS

RFC 3210—Applicability Statement for Extensions to RSVP for LSP-Tunnels

RFC 3346—Applicability Statement for Traffic Engineering with MPLS

Chapter 9
Multiprotocol Label Switching (MPLS)

Multiprotocol Label Switching (MPLS) has its roots in several IP packet switching technologies that were under development in the early- and mid-1990s. In 1996 the IETF started to pull the threads together, and in 1997 the MPLS Working Group was formed to standardize protocols and approaches for MPLS.

MPLS defines ways to switch data through a network by looking up a short label or tag carried in each data packet. Each node extracts the label from the packet, looks it up in a table to determine the next hop over which to send the packet, and substitutes a new label in the packet. This process does not need to be aware of the protocol contained in the packets, nor does it care what the underlying transport mechanism is on each hop—it is truly multiprotocol.

Some process is needed to populate the look-up tables at each MPLS node. As well as the obvious possibility for manual configuration, several protocols have been developed to distribute labels and construct the look-up tables. Some of these protocols have been adapted from their previous uses, and a couple of new protocols have been invented. These protocols have been developed by the IETF to give a full suite of routing and signaling protocols for MPLS. In all cases the control protocols utilize IP, but this has no bearing on whether the data switched through an MPLS network is IP traffic or not. For the sake of clarity, the remainder of this chapter will assume that the payload is IP data.

Note that the reason that MPLS is of interest to the IETF is not that IP traffic can be switched through an MPLS network. This is undoubtedly interesting to the participants in the IETF, but the means of carrying IP traffic across networks are of only marginal concern to the IETF itself. The key reason for the IETF's involvement in MPLS is the fact that the control protocols are based on IP technology.

This chapter begins with a general description of label switching, contrasting it with packet routing. It moves on to examine MPLS in detail and to introduce some of the important concepts. Next comes an examination of the role of a signaling protocol in MPLS, and that is followed by a detailed description of the Label Distribution Protocol (LDP), one of the most important MPLS protocols.

The chapter continues to describe the importance of traffic engineering (TE) in MPLS, and looks in depth at two MPLE-TE signaling protocols: Constraint-Based LSP Setup using LDP (CR-LDP), and Extensions to RSVP for LSP Tunnels

(RSVP-TE). Final sections of the chapter examine how MPLS can be used to help prioritize traffic within a network, and how extensions to the Border Gateway Protocol (BGP-4) routing protocol can be used to make MPLS part of the infrastructure that supports Virtual Private Networks (VPNs).

In recent years, MPLS has been extended as a technique for managing networks that are not packet based. Generalized MPLS (GMPLS) is a set of protocols used to control optical and time division multiplexed networks. It is the subject of Chapter 10.

9.1 Label Switching

IP packet switching is the process of forwarding data packets within the network, based on some tag or *label* associated with each packet. In some senses, traditional IP routing (described in Chapter 5) is a form of packet switching—each packet carries a destination IP address which can be used to determine the next hop in the path toward the destination by performing a look-up in the routing table. There are, however, many limitations to routing, and label switching has been developed to address some of them. The following list identifies some of the major issues with routing.

- **Flexibility of routing**: It is not always desirable to route all data for the same destination along the same path. For example, low-priority data may be sent on a longer path to keep the shortest path clear for higher-priority traffic. Most routing techniques tend to converge traffic onto the shortest path or to use multiple labels (such as IP address and color in DiffServ) to segregate packets.
- **Integration with established technologies**: ATM and Frame Relay are label switching technologies. Neither is IP based, but both are extensively deployed. A formalized approach to IP label switching allows IP traffic to be carried over ATM and Frame Relay networks without complex discovery or mapping functions.
- **Scalability**: When all nodes in the network are data switches they can also be given IP routing capabilities. This does not mean that they route data packets—those are switched. However, the switches can use routing to exchange control information and to establish switched circuits along which to forward data. Making all the nodes in the network capable of IP routing reduces the connectivity requirements at the edges: Instead of each edge node needing to maintain connectivity with each other edge node, it simply maintains connectivity to its physically adjacent router(s). The number of connections at the edges of the network drops from $n(n -1)/2$ to n, where n is the number of edge nodes.
- **Administrative stability**: An issue often raised with IP routing is the large size of the routing tables that must be supported, in particular in the core networks. At the same time, changes in network topology cause routing updates and

require the recalculation of routes on all participating routers. One way to reduce the impact of this is to segment the network on administrative boundaries and reduce the amount of routing information that is leaked across these boundaries. MPLS offers some help in this respect, with edge networks not concerned with the route taken across the core network, and the core network using MPLS to provide edge-to-edge connections through virtual private wire services.

- **Additional services**: Some of the traditional problems associated with Virtual Private Networks (VPNs) are simply addressed using label switching. Where IP addresses from private address spaces needed to be mapped or hidden from the core IP network, labels can be superimposed and used across the whole MPLS network.
- **Extensibility into new technologies**: Although it wasn't part of the initial motivation for MPLS, the process of labeling data flows has become a useful concept in new technologies, offering the possibility of dynamic provisioning in Time Division Multiplexed (TDM) and optical networks. See Chapter 10 on GMPLS for more details.

Since the advent of MPLS, various hardware approaches to IP routing have been developed. Some of these dilute the motivations for packet switching described above, but the drive for and value of MPLS remains.

9.1.1 Choosing between Routing and Switching

Packet switching offers a new paradigm for data forwarding in the network. Instead of forwarding each packet based on the network layer address and information distributed by routing protocols, the nodes in the network can use labels carried on the packets and label switching information distributed by new protocols or extensions to the existing protocols.

Some of the motivations for label switching are outlined in the preceding section. No single issue is generally regarded as an absolute reason to select a switching technology, but the combination of traffic engineering and the ease of provision of services such as VPNs is encouraging Service Providers and enterprises to migrate their networks to use label switching.

It should also be noted that most switching-capable network elements are capable of forwarding IP packets based on routing information without applying a label to them. In particular, the control protocols used to manage the switching network are IP-based and rely on IP forwarding. This means that the choice between routing and switching is not a stark one, but allows a degree of flexibility. Correctly configured, a node will apply switching techniques to labeled packets and routing techniques to unlabeled packets; it will send labeled packets to other switching-capable nodes and unlabeled packets to nodes that cannot perform switching. However, it is often the case that label switches are optimized for label switching and may display poorer performance when forwarding based on

IP routing. Some devices, on the other hand, include all of the best features of routers and label switches. For these devices, the choice between switching and routing really depends on the services being provided.

9.2 MPLS Fundamentals

Label Switching relies on associating a small, fixed format label with each data packet so that it can be forwarded in the network. This means that each packet, frame or cell must carry some identifier that tells network nodes how to forward it. At each hop across the network the packet is forwarded based on the value of the incoming label and dispatched onwards with a new label value.

9.2.1 Labeling Packets

In an MPLS network, packets are labeled by the insertion of an additional piece of information called the *shim header*. It is found between the network headers and the IP header as shown in Figure 9.1.

The shim header carries a 20-bit label. The other fields are listed here and shown in Figure 9.2.

- Three "Experimental" bits are used for grading services (see Section 9.2.4).
- One bit indicates that this label is the last in a stack of labels (see Section 9.2.5).
- Eight bits carry the Time to Live (TTL). The TTL is copied from the IP header when a packet is labeled and is treated in the same way (that is, decremented on a hop-by-hop basis) as the labeled packet is forwarded across the network.

---

shim\'shim*n* [origin unknown]: a thin often tapered piece of material (such as wood, or stone) used to fill a space between things (as for support, leveling, or adjustment of fit).

Network Header	Shim Header	IP Header	Data

Figure 9.1 The shim header is inserted between the network protocol header and the IP header.

Label (20 bits)	Exp (3 bits)	Stack (1 bit)	TTL (8 bits)

Figure 9.2 The shim header carries a 20-bit label.

9.2.2 Label Swapping and the Label Switched Path (LSP)

The path that a data packet follows through the network is defined by the transition in label values. Since the mapping at each node is constant, the path is uniquely determined by the label value at the first node. Such a path is called a *Label Switched Path* (LSP). Each node in an MPLS network maintains a look-up table that allows it to determine the next hop in the LSP. The table is known as the *Label Forwarding Information Base* (LFIB) and maps {incoming interface, incoming label} to {outgoing interface, outgoing label}. This is all the information necessary to forward labeled packets.

Note that once the LFIB has been populated there is no freedom of choice of label values. The process of populating the LFIB is controlled through configuration or through the label distribution protocols described later in this chapter. In general, the choice of label values to put in the LFIB is governed only by consideration of which labels are already in use, and the capabilities of the hardware/software that will be switching packets based on label values.

Figure 9.3 illustrates two LSPs carrying data from IP Host A to Hosts B and C. The MPLS network is made up of four *Label Switching Routers* (LSRs) that forward the packets. Host A sends normal IP packets to LSR V using its default route. LSR V is an ingress LSR and classifies the packets based on the final destination, assigns them to an LSP, and labels them. Those packets targeted at Host B are assigned to the upper LSP and are labeled 15; those for Host C are assigned to

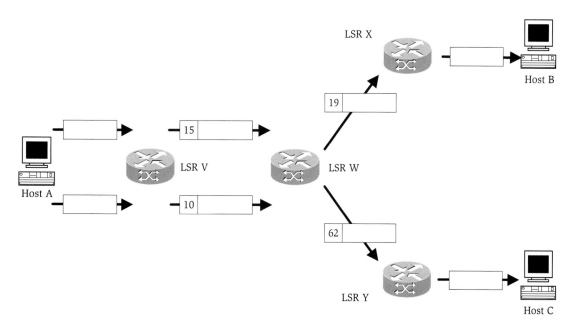

Figure 9.3 Label Switched Paths.

Table 9.1 The LFIB at LSR W

Incoming Interface	Incoming Label	Outgoing Interface	Outgoing Label
From LSR V	15	To LSR X	19
From LSR V	10	To LSR Y	62

the lower LSP and are labeled 10. Once labeled, the packets are forwarded out of the appropriate interface toward LSR W.

At LSR W each labeled packet is examined to determine the incoming interface and incoming label. These are looked up in the LFIB (see Table 9.1) to determine the outgoing label and outgoing interface. The label values are swapped (incoming replaced with outgoing) and the packets are forwarded out of the designated interfaces. In the figure, packets labeled 15 are forwarded out of the interface to LSR X carrying the new label 19; packets labeled 10 are forwarded out of the interface to LSR Y carrying the new label 62.

LSR X and LSR Y are egress LSRs. They also perform a look-up into their LFIBs, but the entries indicate that they should remove the shim header and forward the packet as normal. This forwarding may be through the normal IP routing table, but can be optimized by the LFIB indicating the outgoing interface so that no routing look-up is required. So, in the figure, if LSR V associates all packets for Host B with the upper LSP and labels them with the value 15, they will be successfully forwarded through the network and delivered to Host B.

9.2.3 Inferred Labels in Switching Networks

Figure 9.1 shows how a shim header is inserted between a network layer header and the IP header. This might be used, for example, where the LSRs are connected by Ethernet links. If the network connectivity is provided by a switching technology, such as Asynchronous Transfer Mode (ATM) or Frame Relay, the MPLS label is carried in the network layer protocol fields. The Virtual Path Identifier and Virtual Circuit Identifier (VPI and VCI) are used for ATM, and the Data Link Connection Identifier (DLCI) is used for Frame Relay. This means that the shim header is needed only if the other fields need to be passed, or if label stacking is used (see Section 9.3).

In an ATM network, the whole MPLS packet is presented as an ATM Adaption Layer 5 (AAL5) Protocol Data Unit (PDU) and is then segmented into ATM cells. Each cell is labeled with a VPI/VCI that is equivalent to the MPLS label (see Figure 9.4). The cells are forwarded through the ATM network and reassembled at the end to reform the MPLS packet.

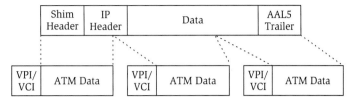

Figure 9.4 MPLS in an ATM network.

9.2.4 Mapping Data to an LSP

One of the key functions of the first LSR in an MPLS network is to determine with which LSP to associate the data packets. In the simplest case this decision is based on the destination of the data packets and can be achieved through a look-up mechanism just like that used for IP routing. In fact, the ingress point of an LSP can be installed as an IP interface so that the normal routing procedures can be used unmodified and packets can be routed onto an LSP. The ingress LSR is responsible for imposing a label on the packets so that they will follow the correct path through the network.

As with Differentiated Services (see Chapter 6), it is often desirable to prioritize data in the network. This allows different traffic flows between hosts to be treated in different ways. In particular, it allows packets on the same LSP to be handled differently.

The Experimental bits in the MPLS shim header allow eight classes of service to be defined within an LSP. The value of these bits can be used to indicate relative priority in processing and in the use of LSR resources. For example, an LSR could choose to maintain eight input queues according to the value of the Experimental bits—the higher-priority queues would always be drained first, and in the event of resource shortage, packets from the lower-priority queues would be discarded first. At the same time, it is possible to associate classes of service with whole LSPs. In this case, where multiple LSPs transit a single LSR, the LSR can choose to prioritize processing and resources according to the class of service of each LSP.

The set of all packets that are forwarded in the same way is called a Forwarding Equivalence Class (FEC). A FEC is described by the parameters that are used to identify the packets that constitute it. In its simplest form, a FEC is a single IP address—all packets addressed to a particular node may be forwarded in the same way through the network. The FEC may be opened up as a subnetwork address such as 172.19.23.96/28, so that all matching addresses are forwarded together. In more advanced applications, the identity of a FEC may include the class of service of the packets, the VPN identified with the traffic, the source address, and even the application.

With this interpretation, the job of the ingress LSR is to identify the FEC to which each packet belongs and to use this to determine the LSP and first label so that it can forward the packet through the MPLS network. Many LSR implementations include a FEC to Next Hop Label Forwarding Entry (FTN) mapping table to help with this resolution.

Just as IP routes converge toward their destination, so the paths taken by MPLS packets may converge. It is possible to maintain distinct LSPs from ingress to egress, but this is not necessary and may be wasteful of network resources and processing power. Instead, LSPs can merge at transit nodes so that packets from the same FEC are grouped together onto the same LSP.

In Figure 9.5, Hosts A and B are sending packets to Host C. Ingress LSRs V and W label the packets (12 and 27, respectively) and forward them to LSR X. LSR X maps both sets of packets to the same outgoing label (71) and forwards them to LSR Y as shown by the LFIB in Table 9.2.

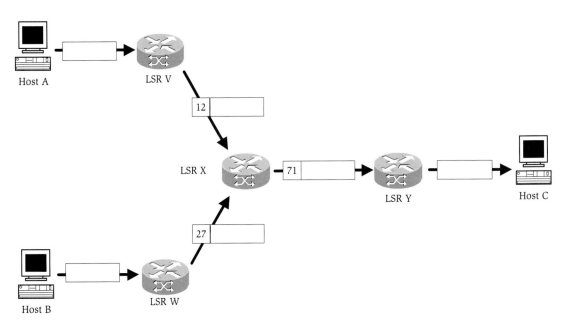

Figure 9.5 LSP merging.

Table 9.2 The LFIB at LSR X

Incoming Interface	Incoming Label	Outgoing Interface	Outgoing Label
From LSR V	12	To LSR Y	71
From LSR W	27	To LSR Y	71

9.2.5 Hierarchies and Tunnels

MPLS allows for LSPs to be nested or tunneled. This mechanism is useful for allowing many LSPs to be treated in the same way in the core of the network while preserving their individuality at the edges. Doing this enhances the scalability of LSRs in the core of the network and significantly improves the manageability of connections across the network.

Tunnels like the one between LSR W and LSR Z in Figure 9.6 may conveniently be presented to the routing protocol as virtual routing adjacencies or *Forwarding Adjacencies* (FAs). This allows other LSPs to be tunneled through these trunk LSPs as though they were simply stepping from one LSR to the next (that is, from LSR W to LSR Z). There are many ways to achieve this, but a convenient one is to install the tunnel LSP as an interface at LSR W and to treat it as a virtual link between LSR W and LSR Z. Appropriate care must be taken to set the cost of this link correctly—it should be assigned a cost that is cheaper than taking the hop-by-hop route W-X-Y-Z, but not so cheap that a shorter route is excluded.

When MPLS packets are received at LSR Z in Figure 9.6, some identification is required so that LSR Z can easily determine the correct next label value and outgoing interface. It would be possible to match each packet against a FEC and so determine the correct LSP to use, but this would actually be a concatenation of LSPs—we require a way of stripping off the outer tunnel at Z, to be left with the inner LSP. This is achieved using a *label stack* on each packet. When each packet enters the tunnel at LSR W the label is replaced as usual, but an

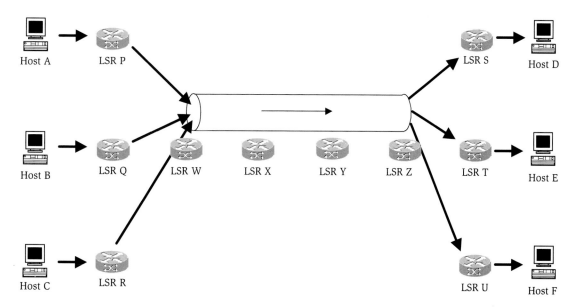

Figure 9.6 An LSP Tunnel carrying multiple LSPs.

additional label is *imposed* on the packet. That is, a further label is pushed onto the label stack. This top-most label is used to forward the packet from LSR W to LSR Z. At LSR Z, the top label is popped from the stack, revealing the label of the tunneled LSP.

A label stack is achieved simply by adding additional shim headers to the data packet as shown in Figure 9.7. The first shim header encountered represents the topmost label (the one that is being actively used to forward the packet). The last shim header has the Stack bit set to indicate that it is the bottom of the stack.

Figure 9.8 illustrates how label stacks are used in the network shown in Figure 9.6. LSR P takes traffic from Host A targeted at Host D and imposes a label (5). Similarly, traffic from Host C to Host E is handled at LSR R where a label (8) is imposed. At LSR W, both LSPs undergo label swapping (5 to 3, and 8 to 7) and are tunneled into a new LSP where an additional label (9) is pushed onto the stack. Forwarding along the path W-X-Y-Z is as described

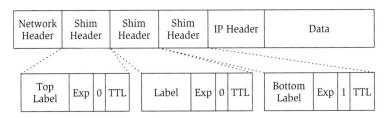

Figure 9.7 The label stack.

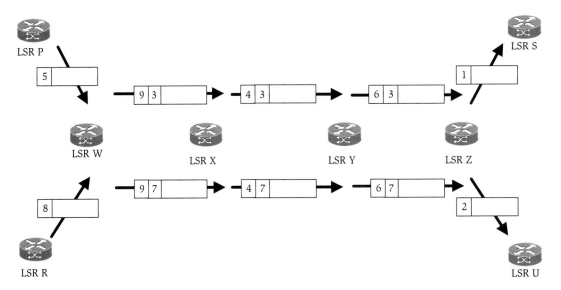

Figure 9.8 Label stacks in use.

Table 9.3 LFIBs at LSR W, LSR X, and LSR Z for LSP Tunnels

LSR W

Incoming Interface	Incoming Label	Action	Outgoing Interface	Outgoing Labels
From LSR P	5	Swap and Push	To LSR X	9, 3
From LSR R	8	Swap and Push	To LSR X	9, 7

LSR X

Incoming Interface	Incoming Label	Action	Outgoing Interface	Outgoing Label
From LSR W	9	Swap	To LSR Y	4

LSR Z

Incoming Interface	Incoming Label	Action	Outgoing Interface	Outgoing Label
From LSR Y	6	Pop	N/A	N/A
From Tunnel	3	Swap	To LSR S	1
From Tunnel	7	Swap	To LSR U	2

before—the top label on the stack is swapped and the packet is forwarded. Note that the labels lower down the stack are not examined or processed. At LSR Z, the label that defines the tunnel is popped from the stack, and traffic is forwarded using the next label on the stack.

The actions needed for tunneling can be encoded in the LFIB by using an additional column. This is illustrated in Table 9.3.

The LFIB in Table 9.3 shows how the processing at the tunnel egress (LSR Z) is a bit clumsy. First, a look-up in the LFIB is made for the received label (6), and then a second look-up must be made to process the labels of the tunneled LSPs (3 and 7) to determine how to forward the packets. The second look-up may be hard to perform in hardware implementations and is not actually required if the previous node performs *Penultimate Hop Popping* (PHP).

PHP is a process in which the top label is popped from the stack one hop before the end of the tunnel. The packet is forwarded and the next LSR (the real end of the tunnel) processes the tunneled LSP. Figure 9.9 shows how PHP might be used in the network shown in Figure 9.8. LSR Y performs Penultimate Hop Popping by stripping the top label (4) from the received packets, and forwarding the packets. Table 9.4 shows the LFIBs at LSR Y and LSR Z when PHP is used.

Table 9.4 LFIBs at LSR Y and LSR Z for Previous Hop Popping

LSR Y

Incoming Interface	Incoming Label	Action	Outgoing Interface	Outgoing Label
From LSR X	4	Pop	To LSR Z	N/A

LSR Z

Incoming Interface	Incoming Label	Action	Outgoing Interface	Outgoing Label
From LSR Y	3	Swap	To LSR S	1
From LSR Y	7	Swap	To LSR U	2

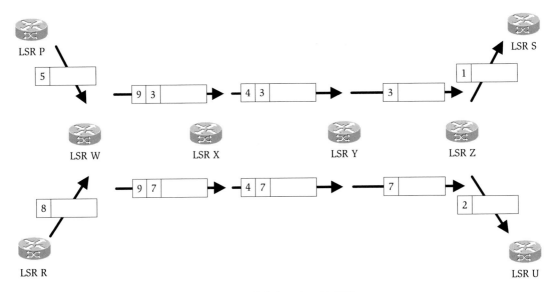

Figure 9.9 Label stacks with PHP.

9.2.6 Choosing MPLS Over Other Switching Technologies

MPLS was not the first label switching technology to be defined. Toshiba derived one of the earliest IP-controlled switching technologies when they introduced the Cell Switching Router (CSR) that used the Flow Attribute Notification Protocol (FANP) to distribute the information with which to populate forwarding tables. Ipsilon invented IP Switching in which ATM hardware was programmed with switching instructions according to the required forwarding paths distributed using the Ipsilon Flow Management Protocol (IFMP). Tag switching, propounded by Cisco, was not limited to ATM switches, but was a more generalized approach to label switching in which label information was distributed using the Tag

Distribution Protocol (TDP). Aggregate Route-Based IP Switching (ARIS), supported by IBM, was a control-based switching technology like TDP; although it was also general in its applicability, it was most keenly focused on ATM hardware.

All four of the switching technologies listed in the preceding paragraph are described in the past tense. Each had its strengths and weaknesses, but, apart from legacy equipment, they have been deprecated by MPLS, which was developed by the Internet community by taking the best features from all of the previous work and adding to them as required. In practice, there is now no choice between switching technologies: only MPLS is available.

9.3 Signaling Protocols

All approaches to label switching have used a control protocol to distribute label information between the nodes in the network. Such protocols are called *signaling protocols*.

9.3.1 What Does a Signaling Protocol Do?

Before an LSP can be used, the LFIBs must be populated at each LSR along the path. The tables could be managed manually, perhaps using a command line interface on each LSR to configure the mappings. This is clearly a long process requiring coordination between LSRs to ensure that all the mappings match up. In a large network it would be almost impossible to manage. Centralized management is an improvement. The label mappings can be calculated in one place and distributed to the LSRs using network management (such as SNMP). Although this approach is much better than manual management of the individual LSRs, it still does not scale well. Dynamic label distribution places the intelligence for populating the LFIBs into the network itself. Signaling protocols called *label distribution protocols* are used to exchange label information to set up LSPs.

The IETF has deliberately avoided mandating a single label distribution protocol for use with MPLS. This allows different protocols to be used to suit the requirements of different operating environments. Several label distribution protocols have been developed by the IETF and they are described in subsequent chapters. In all cases, labels are allocated by the downstream LSR (with respect to the data flow) and are advertised to the upstream LSR. Thus, in Figure 9.9, LSR W is responsible for choosing the label (8) for the LSP that comes from LSR R, and LSR W must advertise that label to LSR R using a signaling protocol.

9.3.2 Choosing an IP-Based Control Plane

All of the control plane protocols described in the remainder of this chapter utilize IP as the underlying network protocol. Some run over transport protocols (TCP or UDP) and others use raw IP, but each assumes the availability of IP forwarding. The motivation for this has come partly from the fact that the predominant deployed data and routing networks utilize and carry IP; it made a lot of sense to build on top of existing routing and forwarding technology and not reinvent the wheel. At the same time, the IETF, which has been largely responsible for the development of MPLS, is specifically limited to consideration of the Internet, and that has come to mean that there must be some strong link to IP.

Some consideration has been given to extending Peer Network to Network Interconnect (PNNI) for use in MPLS. It is designed for use in ATM networks in which the forwarding paradigm is essentially label switching. It has been deployed successfully for many years and has highly flexible ways of characterizing data flows through Quality of Service (QoS) parameters. For these reasons, PNNI remains a popular choice in ATM networks, but it does not use an IP infrastructure, which makes it hard to use across network technologies, and it is more difficult to integrate with the common routing protocols used for IP, so its use and applicability to MPLS is limited.

9.3.3 Routing-Based Label Distribution

In routing-based label distribution, labels are allocated and advertised to match the routes in the local routing table. This mode of operation is usually referred to as *downstream unsolicited* label distribution. Each LSR examines its routing table and, for each onwards route, it advertises a FEC and a label on each other interface. Thus, in Figure 9.10, LSR G has a route to 172.19.23.4/30. It advertises

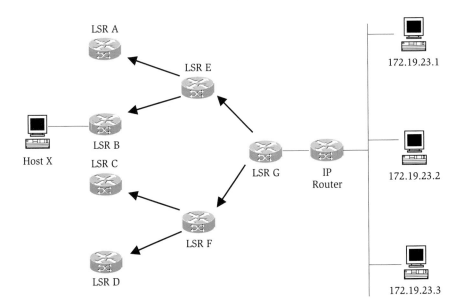

Figure 9.10 Downstream unsolicited label distribution.

a label for this FEC to LSR E and LSR F so that they know how to label and forward traffic. In turn, LSR E and LSR F distribute labels for the FEC to their upstream neighbors and LSP connectivity is made to Host X.

Downstream unsolicited label distribution is a good solution to ensure that all data can be forwarded immediately using an LSP. However, it uses a lot of network resources, since labels are distributed for all routes regardless of whether anyone actually wants to send any data. Furthermore, each LSR will advertise a label for each route to each of its neighbors even when that would not be an optimal way to set up an LSP—for example, in Figure 9.10, if LSR C is also connected to LSR D and LSR E it will advertise a label for the route it has through LSR F. This means that LSR D and LSR E must parse received advertisements and discard those that are suboptimal.

9.3.4 On-Demand Label Distribution

On-demand label distribution addresses many of the issues of unsolicited label distribution, at the price of LSPs not necessarily being preestablished. In this mode, the upstream node makes an explicit request to a downstream node for a label to use for a particular FEC. The downstream node may answer immediately or may forward the request further downstream.

The trigger for on-demand label distribution can vary depending on the network. It may be caused by a threshold based on IP traffic flow, so that when a certain number of packets to a particular destination are seen within a particular time frame, a request is made to set up an LSP. Alternatively, it could be triggered by the arrival of a new route in the local routing table. The request for a label is usually directed according to the local routing table. It is possible to run downstream unsolicited and on-demand label distribution within the same network.

9.3.5 Traffic Engineering

Traffic engineering is the process in which data is routed through the network according to a management view of the availability of resources, and the current and expected traffic loads (see Chapter 8). The class of service and the required quality of service can be factored into this process.

Traffic engineering may be an offline process in which data is collected from across the whole network and processed to derive optimal routes for traffic. Alternatively, it may be a dynamic operation in which each new traffic flow is routed according to the current network usage. Traffic engineering may also be performed on a flow-by-flow basis by direct user intervention, allowing an operator to monitor the network and redirect traffic around hot-spots or network outages. In this way, traffic engineering helps the network provider make the best use of available resources to meet service level agreements, to spread the load over the layer 2 links, and to allow some links to be reserved for certain classes of traffic or for particular customers.

One of the key uses of MPLS is to facilitate improved traffic engineering in Service Provider networks. On-demand label distribution is used, but the requests for labels are routed using more complex constraints. For example, the label request could ask for a label to reach a specific FEC, but also ask that only links with at least 10 gigabits of bandwidth be used. If the path is computed offline or at the initial node, it can be signaled as an *explicit route* by the signaling protocol as part of the process of establishing the LSP.

The common constraints to LSP setup in a traffic engineered network include available bandwidth, quality and reliability of links, and specific routes. These constraints are discussed in greater detail later in this chapter.

9.3.6 Choosing to Use a Signaling Protocol

A signaling protocol is not the only way to set up LSPs through a network. Each LSP requires that an entry be made in the LFIB at each node along the path, and such entries can be made manually. That is, an operator can go to a management interface on each node such as a command line interface (CLI) and configure the entries into the LFIB. This process would usually be made more useable by allowing remote attachment to the nodes, perhaps using Telnet to operate the CLI, or by running a remote management protocol such as SNMP.

The manual approach to configuring LSPs makes them like permanent virtual circuits (PVCs). That is, they are provisioned as the direct response to operator requests, survive on the nodes through node reboots, and are not reactive to network failures. PVCs have an established place in connection-oriented networks and have the great benefit of predictability. They are preferred by some operators because they allow complete control of network resources.

However, management of PVCs in a large network with many thousands of flows takes time and effort. As the complexity of the network grows, more effort is needed to safely provision a new LSP and deprovisioning resources becomes a task for the courageous because of the risk of accidentally affecting other LSPs. So, inevitably, management tools are used to help coordinate the LSPs in the network, to compute the route of the next LSP, and to provision the resources.

Signaling protocols can help in two ways. They reduce the number of interactions between management and the network when a new LSP is required. Instead of sending a message to each of the nodes on the LSP, a single management request can be sent to the head end or ingress of the LSP and the signaling protocol can take over, setting up the LSP automatically. At the same time, the signaling protocols can be closely tied to the routing and resource advertisement protocols in the network so that the intelligence used to route LSPs can be placed within the network. This last point makes a signaled approach more flexible, more able to react to the most recent state of the network, and even allows LSPs to be dynamically routed around network problems as they occur.

9.4   Label Distribution Protocol (LDP)

The Label Distribution Protocol (LDP) is one of the fundamental approaches to distributing labels between LSRs. It was worked on by the IETF's MPLS Working Group through the late 1990s, drawing ideas from TDP and ARIS, and was published as an RFC in January 2001.

LDP can be used to distribute labels that can be used for traffic that matches a FEC according to specific requests for such a label, or in an unsolicited manner as new routes become available. These two distinct approaches provide significantly different network characteristics and each has its own benefits and disadvantages.

As a protocol, the activities of LDP can be separated into four categories.

1. Discovery of LDP-capable LSRs that are "adjacent"—that is, recognition by the nodes that are connected by a logical or physical link that they both support LDP.
2. Establishment of a control conversation between adjacent LSRs, and negotiation of capabilities and options.
3. Advertisement of labels.
4. Withdrawal of labels.

LDP exchanges messages between LDP-capable LSRs packaged in Protocol Data Units (PDUs). Each LDP PDU begins with a header that indicates the length of the whole PDU and is followed by one or more messages from one LSR to the same partner LSR. Each message is itself made up of a header that indicates the length of the message followed by the contents of the message. The message contents are built from TLV (type-length-variable) component objects so that as the message is read byte by byte there is first an identifier of the object type, then an indication of the length of the object, and then the contents of the object. TLVs may be nested so that the variable of one TLV is a series of sub-TLVs. In LDP, all lengths exclude any fields up to and including the length field itself so that, for example, the TLV length indicates the length of the variable and does not include the type field or the length field itself. Figure 9.11 gives an overview of an LDP PDU.

Building LDP messages from TLVs and packaging them in a PDU has made LDP highly extensible, allowing new features and functions to be supported easily and in a backwards compatible way, and making it possible to devise new protocol uses such as CR-LDP (see Section 9.6).

The PDU header identifies the version of LDP that is being used and gives the length of the entire PDU (excluding the version and PDU length fields) in bytes. The context of the PDU is established by a 16-bit field that identifies the LSR in a unique way across the network and by a Label Space Identifier. The LSR Identifier must be unique across the network and, since IP routing protocols are

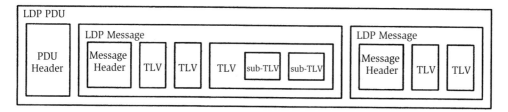

Figure 9.11 Overview of the LDP PDU.

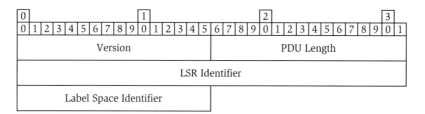

Figure 9.12 The LDP PDU header.

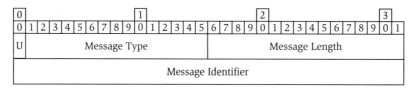

Figure 9.13 The LDP message header.

assumed to be in use, is defined as the Router ID of the LSR. The format of the LDP PDU header is shown in Figure 9.12.

The format of a standard LDP message header is shown in Figure 9.13. The first bit (the U-bit) indicates the required behavior of the recipient if it does not recognize or cannot process the type of message indicated by the Message Type field. In the current core specification of LDP (RFC 3036) all messages use the value of zero in this bit to indicate that the receiver must send an error response under these circumstances; a value of one would indicate that the receiver could ignore the unknown or unsupported message. The message length indicates the length of the entire message excluding the U-bit, Message Type, and Message Length fields.

The message header also includes a Message Identifier. This is used to correlate protocol responses and subsequent messages related to this message. The Message Identifier needs to be kept unique for some time after the message is sent, certainly until the associated processing and message exchanges have

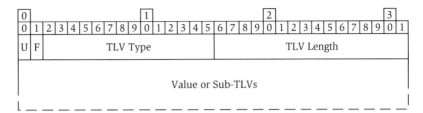

Figure 9.14 The LDP TLV common format.

completed. Some implementations maintain an incrementing counter to identify messages, but others use pointer values (that is, memory addresses) to facilitate quick correlation.

The message header is followed by a series of zero or more TLVs. Some of these are mandatory on a given message and others are optional. LDP specifies that mandatory TLVs must be present first, before any optional TLVs. Even the TLV has a common format in LDP, as shown in Figure 9.14. The first 2 bits of the TLV describe how the TLV should be handled by the receiver if it does not recognize or cannot process the TLV. If the first bit (the U-bit) is set to zero the receiver must reject the whole message and send an error if the TLV is unknown or cannot be handled. If the U-bit is set to 1 and the second bit (the F-bit) is also set to 1, the receiver must forward the unknown TLV if it forwards the message. The TLV length gives the length of the TLV (including any sub-TLVs) but excluding the U-bit, F-bit, TLV Type, and TLV Length fields.

TLVs may include fields that are designated as *reserved*. Reserved fields should be set to zero when an LSR sends a message and should be ignored when an LSR receives a message. This allows the protocol to be extended through the use of currently unused bits and bytes within TLVs without causing any backwards-compatibility issues.

9.4.1 Peers, Entities, and Sessions

Two LSRs that use LDP to advertise labels to each other are referred to as *LDP peers*. An LSR introduces itself to its peers by multicasting an LDP Hello message using UDP. It periodically sends to the group address "all routers on this subnet" and targets a well-known UDP port reserved for LDP discovery (port 646 has been assigned by the Internet Assigned Numbers Authority, IANA). See Section 9.4.9 for an explanation of the choice of transport protocols in LDP. Figure 9.15 shows the format of an LDP Hello message.

When an LSR receives a Hello message it knows that a new peer has come on line or that an existing peer has sent another Hello message. The receiver keeps track of its peers by running a *Hold Timer* for each one, as identified by the LSR identifier in the PDU header. If the Hello is from an existing peer, the receiver restarts the hold timer using the value supplied in the Hello message.

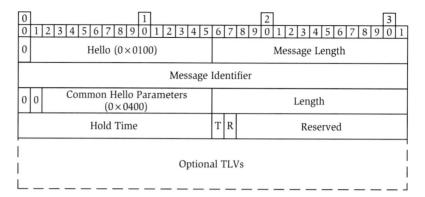

Figure 9.15 The LDP Hello message.

If the Hello is from a new peer, the receiver creates a *Hello Adjacency* with its peer and starts a hold timer using the value supplied in the Hello message.

If an LSR does not receive a new Hello message from a peer for which it is maintaining a Hello Adjacency before the hold timer expires, it declares the adjacency down and assumes that connectivity with the peer has been lost. For that reason, the sender of a Hello message is recommended to resend the Hello at least every third of the value of the Hold Time that it advertises in the Hello message.

If the receiving peer is not willing to accept the message, it simply ignores it. Reasons for ignoring a Hello message might include LDP not being configured on the interface, or the receiver having reached a maximum threshold for the number of peers that it can support. Optional TLVs can be included at the discretion of the sender and supply additional information for use in managing the connection between the peers.

Although Hello messages are usually multicast, the UDP packets that carry the Hello messages can also be targeted at specific recipients. This is indicated by setting the T-bit in the Hello message, and an LSR can request that it receives targeted Hellos in response by setting the R-bit. An LSR receiving a targeted Hello will accept it if that LSR has been configured to accept all targeted Hellos or if it has been configured to send a targeted Hello to the originator of the message. Targeted Hellos have the advantage of reducing the LDP connectivity in a highly connected network at the expense of increased configuration. Alternatively, targeted Hellos can be used to set up Hello adjacencies between LSRs that are not on the same subnetwork, but that are connected, for example, by an MPLS tunnel. Figure 9.16 shows how this might work: LSR X and LSR A can exchange normal, untargeted Hellos. Similarly, LSRs D, Y, and Z can use multicast Hellos to discover each other and set up adjacencies. However, in the core cloud there may be an MPLS tunnel from LSR A to LSR D. This tunnel (perhaps established for traffic engineering—see Section 9.5) will be used to forward packets across the cloud and it forms a virtual adjacency between LSR A and LSR D. These two LSRs can use targeted Hellos to set up a remote Hello adjacency.

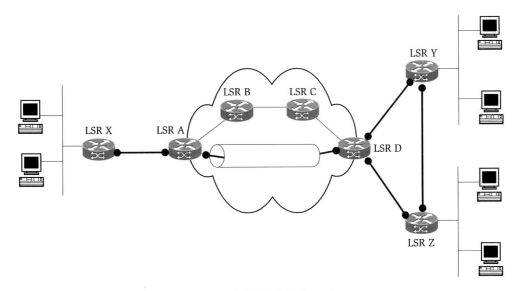

Figure 9.16 LDP Hello Adjacencies.

Note that Hello messages are not responded to *per se*. However, an LSR that is configured to receive multicast Hellos will also be sending them, so both nodes will have a view of the Hello adjacency. Similarly, two nodes that are configured to send targeted Hellos to each other will each maintain a Hello adjacency. A node that is configured to accept all targeted Hellos must act as though it had been configured to send a targeted Hello to the originator, effectively responding with a Hello and making this mode of operation asymmetric.

Hello messages from one peer may identify different label spaces in the PDU header. Each time a Hello message is received for a new label space, the receiving LSR establishes an *LDP session* with the peer over which to manage and exchange labels from the label space. Although LDP sessions are run between peers, some implementations and the LDP MIB refer to the logical end points of LDP sessions as entities. This allows the concept of multiple instances of the LDP code running in an LSR and makes more concrete the separate states that exist for each session.

An LDP session is a protocol conversation between LDP peers that is used to manage and exchange information about a single pair of label spaces, one at each peer. LDP assumes reliable transfer of its protocol message within a session, so sessions are run over TCP. TCP connections are set up between the peer LSRs using the well-known LDP port number 646, as for UDP carrying the Hello message. The IP address used for the TCP connection defaults to the LSR ID carried in the PDU header, but may be overridden by an optional Transport Address TLV in the Hello message itself. One single TCP connection may carry no more than one LDP session between a pair of LDP peers. See Section 9.4.9 for an explanation of the choice of transport protocols in LDP.

Protocol exchange on an LDP session can be categorized in five phases.

1. Session initialization (including TCP connection establishment).
2. Session maintenance.
3. Address advertisement.
4. Label advertisement and management.
5. Error and event notification.

Session initialization begins when a new Hello message is received, as described in the preceding paragraphs. As a first step, a new TCP connection must be set up if one does not already exist between the addresses represented by the LSR identifiers in the exchanged Hello messages. Note that the LSR identifier is characterized as a Router ID, which is not necessarily an address—this fact appears to be glossed over in RFC 3036 and as a result, everyone assigns an address as the Router ID of their LDP router (or at least assigns an address for the LSR Id). Since only one TCP connection is required, it is set up by the *active* peer—the one with the "greater" LSR ID, where greater is defined by treating the LSR IDs as unsigned integers. Obviously, if the LSR IDs match there is an error and no attempt should be made to set up a connection.

Once the TCP connection is up, the active peer can initialize a new session. The *passive* peer listens for new sessions and responds. Session initialization is achieved by exchanging Session Initialization messages. Although the Session Initialization message, shown in Figure 9.17, is described as negotiating session characteristics for use on the session, there is virtually no negotiation. The

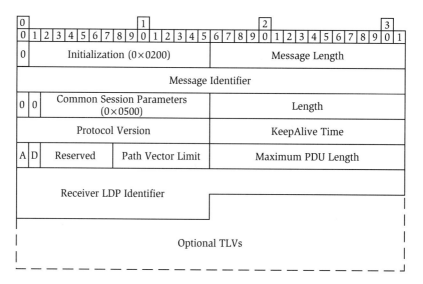

Figure 9.17 The LDP Session Initialization message.

message describes the way the message sender intends to perform and may either be accepted or rejected.

The active peer sends a Session Initialization message advertising the behavior it intends to apply to the session. It contains information such as the version of LDP to be used, the timeout that will be applied to send periodic messages to keep the session open, and the largest size of LDP PDU that it is prepared to receive. The A- and D-bits describe the label distribution mode and the use of loop detection (see Section 9.4.3). If loop detection is in use, the sending node also indicates the Path Vector Limit that it will use to detect loops—this is included for consistency checking within the network but is not otherwise used by the receiving node.

The Receiver LDP Identifier is used by the sender to indicate which label space the session is intended to control. This value is taken from the Hello message and allows the passive peer to correlate the requested session with the right internal state.

Optional parameters on session initialization are used to provide a detailed description of the label space if ATM or Frame Relay is used.

When the passive node receives a Session Initialization message it checks to see that it can handle the parameters. If it can't, it rejects the session by sending an Error Notification message (described in Section 9.4.7). An error code indicates that the session parameters were unacceptable, and the specific problem is indicated by including the received message up to the point of the bad parameter. Once a node has rejected a session it closes the TCP connection. Note that the next Hello exchange will cause the TCP connection to be reestablished and the session to be reattempted. To reduce the amount of network thrash when a pair of LDP LSRs disagree about session parameters, implementations should use an exponential back-off and not automatically attempt to set up a session on receipt of a Hello for a session that had previously failed. Since this might result in long delays in setting up adjacencies when the disagreement has been resolved by a change in configuration, the Hello message can carry an optional Configuration Sequence Number TLV—a change in the value of this TLV received from a peer indicates that some change has been made to the configuration and it is worth immediately trying to establish an adjacency.

If the passive node is happy with the received session parameters it must send a message to accept them and it must also send its own session parameters. Two separate messages are used: the passive node sends a Session Initialization message of its own containing its choices for protocol behavior on the session, and it acknowledges the received parameters by sending a KeepAlive message (see Figure 9.18). The KeepAlive message is periodically retransmitted by both peers on a session when there is no other traffic to maintain the session, or more precisely, to make it possible to detect that the session has failed. This is necessary since TCP connection failure timeouts are typically quite large. Each node advertises in the Session Initialization message the time that it is prepared to wait without receiving any message on the session before it declares the session

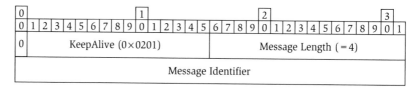

Figure 9.18 The LDP KeepAlive message.

to have failed—both peers are required to use the same value on a session and this is taken to be the smaller of the two values exchanged on the Session Initialization messages. Each node should send some message on the session so that its peer receives it within the KeepAlive period. If there is no other protocol message to be sent, a node can send a KeepAlive message. Since there is some possibility of delay in transmission and receipt of a message over TCP, the sender should make sure that it sends some message roughly every one third of the KeepAlive interval. Many implementations simply run a timer and send a KeepAlive message every one-third of the KeepAlive interval regardless of whether it has sent another message or not.

In the special case of session establishment, the first KeepAlive message is used to acknowledge the received Session Initialization message.

When the active peer receives a Session Initialization message it, too, checks that the received parameters are OK and acknowledges with a KeepAlive message. When both peers have received Session Initialization and KeepAlive messages, the session is active.

Note that the state machine for session initialization depicted in RFC 3036 is not complete. In particular, and contrary to the text of the RFC, it suggests that it would be invalid for the active peer to receive a KeepAlive message before it receives a Session Initialization message. Since implementations may have strictly followed the state machine, it would be best if all passive peers sent their Session Initialization message before sending the KeepAlive message that acknowledges the received session parameters.

Once the session has been established, but before it can be used, the peers must exchange information about the addresses that they support and use. This is done using Address messages, as described in Section 9.4.2.

Figure 9.19 shows the full sequence of messages exchanged between a pair of LDP LSRs during session establishment and to keep the session active. LSRs A and B send out Hello messages using UDP to the multicast address on their shared subnetwork. They examine the LSR IDs and discover that LSR A is the active peer and LSR B is the passive peer, so LSR sets up a TCP connection and sends the first Session Initialization message on the connection. LSR B responds with its own Session Initialization message and also sends a KeepAlive message to acknowledge receipt of LSR A's Session Initialization message. LSR A receives the Session Initialization message from LSR B and acknowledges it with a Keep-Alive message. Now the session is active and address information is exchanged

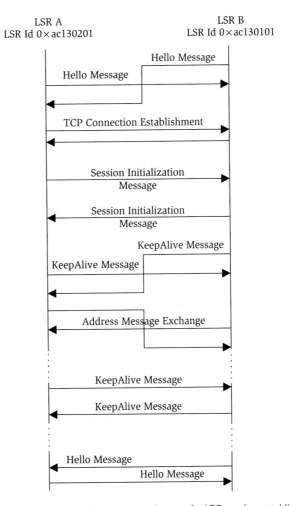

Figure 9.19 The sequence of message exchanges for LDP session establishment.

using Address messages. After a while, both peers send KeepAlive messages on the TCP connection to keep the session active. Also on a timer, both peers send Hello messages using UDP to keep the Hello Adjacency active.

9.4.2 Address Advertisement and Use

Immediately after the LDP session has been established, and before any protocol messages for label distribution are sent, the peers exchange addressing information using Address messages (see Figure 9.20). This allows an LSR to map between IP routes distributed by routing protocols and LSPs. More precisely,

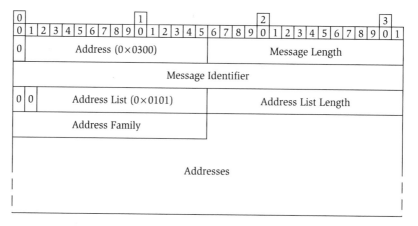

Figure 9.20 The LDP Address message.

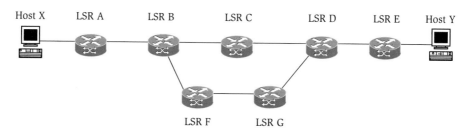

Figure 9.21 Using address information in LDP.

it enables an LSR to know all of the next hop IP addresses that correspond to a particular adjacent LDP peer.

Consider the network in Figure 9.21. LSR E will advertise the FEC for Host Y together with a label for each interface—just one advertisement to LSR D. LSR D will advertise the FEC and a label to both LSR C and LSR G. In this way, LSR B will become aware of two LSPs that it could use to send traffic to Host Y, one to LSR C, and one to LSR F. It chooses between these routes using the routing protocol to advise it of the shortest/cheapest/best route and it installs an entry in its LFIB to map the label that it advertises to LSR A for this FEC to the label advertised to it by LSR C.

This process, however, is not absolutely simple. LSRs C and F have advertised labels using their LSR Identifier to identify themselves. The routing protocol will indicate the preferred path using interface addresses. LSR B needs a way to map from the address of the interface between LSRs B and C to the LSR ID of LSR C. Only then can it work out the correct label to use. If LSRs C and F advertise all of their addresses as soon as the LDP sessions with LSR B are established, LSR B can resolve the preferred path to an LSP.

Similar issues arise when a link fails. For example, if the link between LSRs C and D fails and the failure is reported by the routing protocol, LSR B needs to discover that the link to LSR F is now the preferred path and work out which label to use.

The Address message can distribute one or more addresses belonging to a single address family (for example, IPv4 or IPv6) but cannot mix addresses from multiple families. The body of the Address List TLV contains a family identifier followed by a list of addresses. Since the format of an address within a family is wellknown, the addresses in the list are simply concatenated and the TLV length is used to determine the end of the list.

New addresses may be added at any time during the life of the session simply by sending a new Address message. Addresses may also need to be withdrawn, for example, when an interface is taken out of service. This is done by sending an Address Withdraw message, which has the identical form to the Address message shown in Figure 9.20, but carries the message identifier 0x0301. When an LDP peer receives an Address Withdraw message it must remove all entries from its LFIB that utilized the address as a next hop, and should attempt to find an alternative label on another interface to carry the traffic. This is discussed further in the following sections.

9.4.3 Distributing Labels

LDP has two modes of label distribution: Downstream on Demand and Downstream Unsolicited. In both cases the downstream node is responsible for distributing the labels, but in the first case it does so only in response to a specific request from upstream, whereas in the second case the downstream node distributes labels whenever it can.

The mode of label distribution on any session is negotiated using the A-bit in the Session Initialization message. If the A-bit is set, Downstream on Demand is requested. If the bit is clear, Downstream Unsolicited is requested. If the peers request different modes of label distribution they should resolve their differences according to RFC 3036, which says that if the session is for an ATM or Frame Relay link Downstream on Demand should be used; otherwise Downstream Unsolicited must be used. An LSR can reject a label distribution mode that it doesn't want to support by rejecting the Session Initialization as described in Section 9.4.1.

Both modes of label distribution can operate simultaneously in a single network with islands of LSRs or individual links given over to one mode or the other. Section 9.4.4 discusses how to choose between one mode and another.

Label distribution uses the same mechanism in both distribution modes. The downstream LSR sends a Label Mapping message to the upstream node to let it know that if it wants to send a packet to any address represented by a particular FEC it may do so by sending a labeled packet on a particular interface to the downstream LSR. The interface to use is indicated by the LDP session on

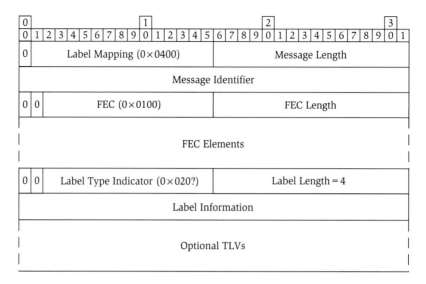

Figure 9.22 The LDP Label Mapping message.

which the Label Mapping message arrives; the FEC and the label are carried in the message as shown in Figure 9.22.

This appears to be a looser specification than for any of the LDP messages previously discussed because there are two variables being handled at once.

First, recall that a FEC is the set of packets that are all forwarded in the same way. It may, therefore, be difficult to represent the FEC through a single identifier such as an IP address prefix, and a list of such identifiers may be needed. Although it is perfectly acceptable to send multiple Label mapping messages for the component elements of a FEC, it was recognized that it was far better to place all of the elements of the FEC on a single message so the Label Mapping can carry a series of FEC elements, each encoded as a single byte to identify the element type, followed by a well-known, context-specific number of bytes to carry the element. The number of elements is scoped by the length of the FEC TLV itself. Two FEC elements are shown in Figure 9.23. Two further FEC elements are defined for special uses. The Wildcard FEC element is shown in Figure 9.29. The CR-LSP FEC element is shown in Figure 9.40.

The Prefix FEC element represents an address prefix. The address family is indicated using the standard numbers from RFC 1700 (1 for IPv4 or 2 for IPv6) and the prefix length is in bits. The prefix itself is contained in the smallest number of bytes necessary and is right-padded with zeros. A default route can be conveyed in this way by specifying a prefix length of zero and supplying no bytes to carry the prefix itself.

The Host Address FEC element represents a fully-qualified host address. The address family is indicated as before and the host address is presented, but

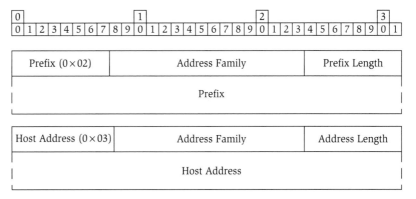

Figure 9.23 LDP FEC Elements for Label Mapping messages.

in this case, the Length field indicates the length of the address in bytes. One might wonder at the presence of the address length here since the address family defines the address length, but including the length allows nodes that do not recognize a particular address family to easily parse the message, and indeed keeps all message parsing on the same footing of type-length-variable. Similarly, there is a question as to why the Host Address FEC element is needed at all, given that the Prefix element could be supplied with a prefix length indicating the whole address—a distinction is drawn in LDP so that an LSP associated with a FEC that contains a Host Address FEC element may carry only packets destined to that host address, whereas an LSP that uses a Prefix FEC element to represent the same fully qualified address may also include other Prefix FEC elements and so carry packets for multiple destinations.

The second variable in the Label Mapping message is the label itself. As described in Section 9.3, labels may be included in shim headers or may be derived from the VPI/VCI of ATM cells or the DLCI of Frame Relay frames. Although these three formats can be encoded into TLVs of the same length, different type identifiers are required to identify the three types of labels, as shown in Figure 9.24.

If the label is a generic label for use in shim headers it is encoded as a 20-bit number in a 4-byte field so that at least the first 12 bits are zero. If the label is used for ATM, the VPI and VCI are encoded as shown as 12- and 16-bit numbers, respectively—to handle VP and VC switching, the two V bits show 00 if both the VPI and VCI are significant, 01 if only the VPI is relevant, and 10 if only the VCI should be used. Frame Relay labels may be for 10- or 23-bit DLCIs, but are always encoded as 23-bit numbers, with the distinction indicated by the Length field, which is set to 0 for 10 bit DLCIs and 2 for 23 bit DLCIs.

Figure 9.25 shows a Label Mapping message. The FEC is comprised of two elements: a 24-bit prefix and a fully qualified address specified as a 32-bit prefix. The label 54,321 has been assigned from the global label space.

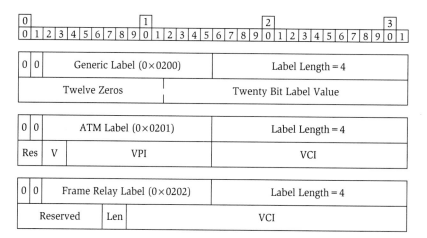

Figure 9.24 LDP label encodings.

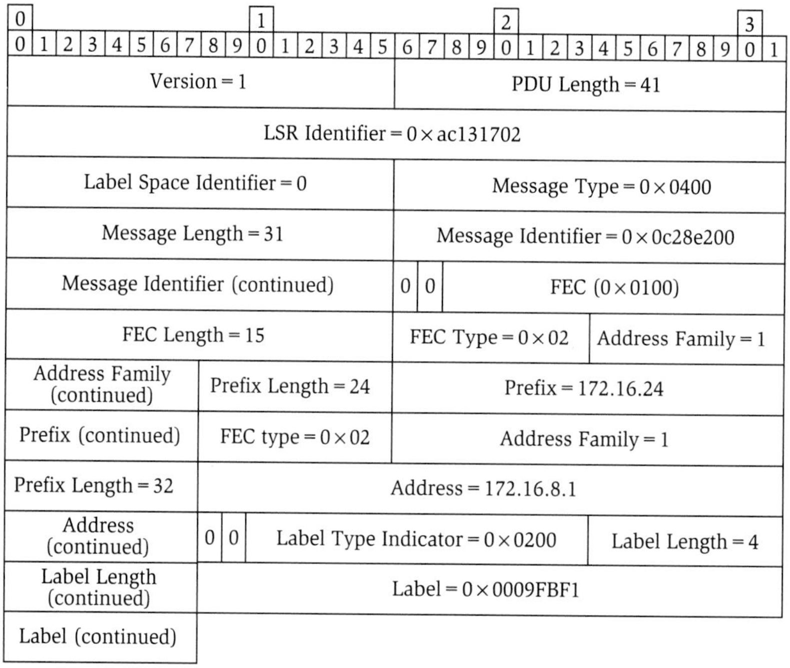

Figure 9.25 An LDP Label Mapping message.

Label Mapping messages can also carry some optional TLVs. Loop detection (discussed later in this section) makes use of the Hop Count TLV and Path Vector TLV. Label Mapping messages can be correlated to the Label Request that caused them (in Downstream on Demand label distribution) by the inclusion of the Message Identifier from the Label Request message as an optional TLV (the Label Request Message ID TLV—type 0x0600) in the Label Mapping message.

In Downstream Unsolicited mode, the downstream LSR advertises a label to each upstream LSR every time a new route is added to its routing table. This may require it to update an existing label advertisement, but more likely it will advertise a new label.

When an upstream LSR receives an unsolicited Label Mapping message it must not simply make a new entry in its LFIB because it might receive a label advertisement for the same FEC from multiple downstream LSRs (see the example in Section 9.3.3). Instead, it checks to see if there is already an entry in its FTN mapping table: if there isn't, it can create an entry, allocate local labels, advertise those labels, and populate the LFIB. On the other hand, if an entry already exists in the FTN mapping table for the received FEC, the LSR must consult the routing table to determine the preferred route and replace the outgoing interface and label in the LFIB. The addresses advertised using Address messages are important to correlate the next hop address in the routing table with the LSR advertising the new FEC/label.

In Downstream on Demand mode an upstream LSR makes a specific request for a label of one or more downstream LSRs for a specific FEC. The downstream LSRs do not advertise labels until they are requested to. The upstream LSR may be triggered to request a label by one of many factors, depending on the implementation and the use to which LDP is being put. In most cases, the decision is made based on the installation of a new route in the local routing table—this tells the LSR which way to route packets for a specific FEC and it can then ask the LSR that advertised the address that matches the routing next hop address for a label. In some cases (where it is desirable to keep the size of the LFIB small) the request is not made unless the rate of traffic flow for the FEC exceeds a threshold. Another mode of operation requests labels only for FECs that have been configured by the operator.

Triggers for label request can usually be left to the edges of the network or at least to the edges of regions within the network. When a node within the network receives a request for a label for a FEC for which it doesn't have a forward label, it can itself make a request downstream for a label.

Label requests are made in LDP using the Label Request message, as shown in Figure 9.26. The FEC is represented in the same way as on the Label Mapping message. The optional parameters can include a Hop Count TLV and a Path Vector TLV for use in loop detection, as discussed in the following paragraphs.

Label Mapping messages can be correlated to the Label Request that caused them by the inclusion of the Message Identifier from the label request message as an optional TLV (the Label Request Message ID TLV—type 0x0600) in the Label Mapping message.

Loop detection is an important part of LDP label distribution. Without loop detection it would be possible for a Label Request to be passed from one LSR to

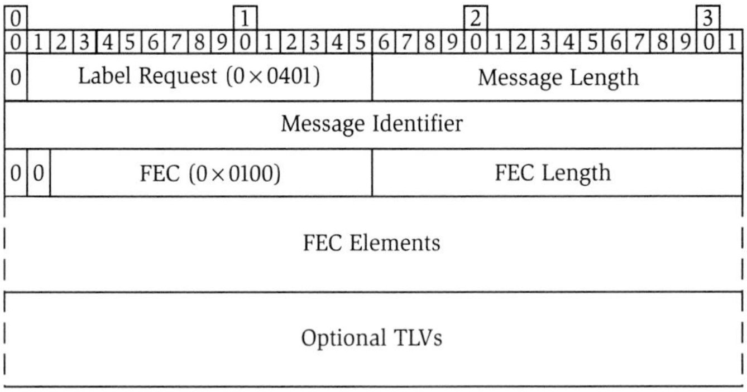

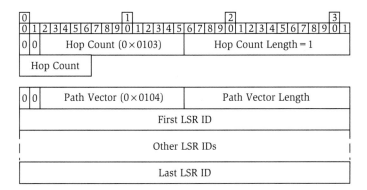

Figure 9.26 The LDP Label Request message.

Figure 9.27 The LDP Hop Count and Path Vector TLVs.

another around a loop and back to the original LSR, which might then forward it onward. Although it might seem that an adequate solution to loop detection is for an LSR to keep a record of the Label Requests that it has sent and to not reproduce them, this technique is heavy in implementation terms and is not sufficient in the case of LSRs, which cannot merge LSPs. Loop detection mechanisms can also be used to limit the scope of a label request so that it travels across a limited number of nodes.

Loop detection is a configurable option on an LSR and is negotiated on the Session Initialization message using the D-bit. Operationally, it relies on two TLVs which can be optionally included in Label Request messages. The Hop Count TLV is set to 1 by the initiator of the Label Request message, and each LSR that forwards the message increments the count by 1—if a received message carries a hop count that is greater than the configured maximum it is defined as having looped and is rejected with an Error Notification message (see Section 9.4.7).

The Path Vector TLV, if present, contains a list of LSR IDs of the LSRs through which the message has passed. Each LSR that forwards the message adds its own LSR ID to the Path Vector, and each LSR that receives a message checks to see that its LSR ID is not already present in the Path Vector. Again, if a loop is detected, the message is rejected using an Error Notification message.

Label Mapping messages may also carry the Hop Count TLV and the Path Vector TLV to detect looping messages. The Hop Count TLV and the Path Vector TLV are shown in Figure 9.27.

9.4.4 Choosing a Label Distribution Mode

A key deployment decision for LDP networks is which label distribution mode to use. There is no simple answer, and the picture can be further confused by defining operation modes in which labels advertised from downstream are always propagated upstream (*ordered control*) and in which they are only propagated on request or when the local LSR sees a good reason for it (*independent control*).

In general, both distribution modes can be used in networks where label advertisement is driven by the availability of routes. Many systems use Downstream Unsolicited distribution to advertise labels as routes become available—in this way, label advertisement models route advertisement and labels are available more or less as soon as routes are available. Other networks use Downstream on Demand distribution to request labels only when the new route reaches the edge of the network.

Note that Downstream Unsolicited label distribution with independent control may work badly in multi-area systems if the area border routers (ABRs) are configured to aggregate route information when they advertise it over the area border (see Section 5.5.6). This is because the first router to receive the advertisement may choose to advertise a FEC for the advertised aggregated route, and supply just a single label for the FEC. This means that when MPLS traffic reaches the ABR it will need to be decapsulated and examined before it can be assigned the right label to progress across the next area.

Where LSPs are required to meet specific services (such as traffic-driven LSPs, VPNs, or traffic engineering), label distribution is usually Downstream on Demand since this helps minimize the number of LSPs in the system, albeit at the expense of a small delay while the LSP is established in response to the demand. However, even this is not a golden rule, and many VPN models operate successfully using Downstream Unsolicited distribution.

Recall, however, that the label distribution mode is chosen on a per-link basis. This means that distribution modes may be mixed within a network, with islands of nodes using one mode of distribution and other islands using the other mode. A potential deployment of mixed modes would see the core of the network using Downstream Unsolicited distribution so that all core nodes had entries in their FTN mapping tables and LFIBs for all FECs, but the edge nodes exchanged labels only as demanded by traffic flows. The use of independent control at the edges of the core would ensure that labels were advertised from the core only on demand.

Downstream on Demand is also preferred when LDP is run over a native switching system such as ATM since it helps to reduce the number of labels that need to be assigned within the network.

9.4.5 Choosing a Label Retention Mode

When an upstream LSR replaces the labels in its LFIB because it has received an advertisement from a "better" downstream LSR, it can choose to retain the previous label (*Liberal Label Retention*) or to discard it (*Conservative Label Retention*). Conservative Label Retention obviously requires far less in the way of system resources; however, look again at the simple network in Figure 9.21. In this network LSR B will have an LFIB entry mapping a label from the interface with LSR A to a label on the interface with LSR C for use with the FEC of Host Y. It will also have received a label advertisement from LSR F for the same FEC but will not use it because the routing table shows that the route through LSR C is preferable. If the link between LSRs C and D fails, LSR B will notice the fact through the routing protocol and realize that the preferred route is now through LSR F. If it has discarded the label advertised by LSR F (Conservative Label Retention) it has no label to use to forward traffic to Host Y, but if it has used Liberal Label Retention it can install the label advertised by LSR F in its LFIB and continue to operate.

This distinction between label retention modes is equally applicable in Downstream Unsolicited and Downstream on Demand label distribution, but the effect of not retaining all labels is more significant in Downstream Unsolicited mode because if LSR B uses Downstream on Demand it can always issue a new Label Request message to rediscover the label advertised by LSR F.

This issue with Conservative Label Retention can be addressed in two ways. The downstream nodes can periodically re-advertise all labels—this ensures that the upstream node has the opportunity to reevaluate the best next hop for its LFIB, but is costly in terms of network usage, still leaves a window where the upstream node may be unable to forward labeled packets after a network failure, and requires that the downstream nodes be aware of the upstream node's label retention behavior. Alternatively, the upstream node may use a Label Request message to solicit a label for any of its preferred routes—this may appear to be strange in a system that is supposedly using Downstream Unsolicited label distribution, but is explicitly allowed by RFC 3036 to handle this problem. Thus, even in Downstream Unsolicited mode, Label Request messages can be sent and must be correctly handled and responded to. Note that an upstream node can tell whether a Label Mapping message is unsolicited or is a response to its Label Request message by looking for the Label Request Message ID TLV in the Label Mapping message.

9.4.6 Stopping Use of Labels

An LSR that has distributed a label for a FEC may decide that the label is no longer valid. There are many possible reasons for this, including local policy decisions to rearrange the use of labels or to reassign resources to more frequently used traffic flows. Obviously, when a link is decommissioned the labels previously advertised for the associated session with a peer are no longer valid.

The most common reason for a label to become incorrect is when the LSR is informed that it is no longer on any path for the FEC. It may discover this through the routing protocol or through LDP from the downstream LSRs.

Whenever an LSR decides that a label that it has previously advertised is no longer valid, it withdraws the advertisement by sending a Label Withdraw message. The receipt of a Label Withdraw message by one LSR may cause it to send a similar message to its upstream peers or, if liberal label retention is being used, may simply cause it to switch traffic to a different next hop.

There is good scope for network thrash when labels are withdrawn in networks in which conservative label retention is used. A trade-off is required between not immediately telling upstream nodes that traffic can no longer be forwarded (which will cause packets to be black-holed), and telling them too quickly when an alternative route is just one Label Request message exchange away.

Figure 9.28 shows a Label Withdraw message. It maps closely to a Label Mapping message, but note that the FEC can be a subset of that carried on a Label Mapping message to leave the label in place for a reduced FEC, the union of FECs from multiple Label Mapping messages to remove multiple labels at once, or a wildcard FEC to remove all advertised labels. The wildcard FEC, shown in Figure 9.29, is a single byte type identifier followed by no other data (none is required). If the wildcard FEC is used, no other FEC elements are valid on the message.

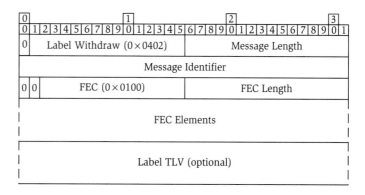

Figure 9.28 The LDP Label Withdraw message.

Figure 9.29 The LDP wildcard FEC element.

In this way, label withdrawal is really FEC withdrawal. The downstream node is saying which FECs can no longer be reached through it and asking that all associated labels that have no other use be released.

The Label Withdraw message may optionally include a Label TLV. This means that the specified label only is to be withdrawn from all uses where it matches the FECs carried in the message; other labels for those FECs are to remain in place. The most common usage of the Label TLV is with the wildcard FEC to show that the entire label is to be withdrawn from any FEC to which it is bound.

When an upstream node receives a Label Withdraw message, it must stop using the label in the way indicated by the message and must respond so that the downstream node knows that cleanup has completed. It does this using a Label Release message. This message is a direct copy of the received Label Withdraw message but carries the message type 0x0403.

Figure 9.30 shows the message exchanges in a simple network running Downstream Unsolicited label advertisement and demonstrates the use of Label Mapping, Label Withdraw, Label Release, and Label Request messages. Initially, LSR E advertises a label for a FEC by sending a Label Mapping message to LSR H (step 1). In turn, this FEC is advertised with a label by LSR H to LSRG, and so on hop-by-hop through LSR F and LSR B until it reaches LSR A. LSR E also advertises a label for the FEC by sending a Label Mapping message to LSR D (step 2). In turn, the FEC is advertised with a label by LSR D to LSR C and LSR C to LSR B.

When the advertisement reaches LSR B from LSR C (step 3), LSR B recognizes that the route through LSR C is preferable because it is shorter. Since it is using conservative label retention, LSR B discards (but does not release) the label advertised by LSR F and uses the one advertised by LSR C. It does not need to tell LSR A about this operation—the only change is in the tables on LSR B.

After some time, the link between LSR D and LSR E fails (step 4). LSR D decides to withdraw the label it had previously advertised by sending a Label Withdraw message to LSR C. LSR C responds at once (step 5) with a Label Release message and, recognizing that it has no one else to ask for a label, propagates the withdrawal by sending a Label Withdraw message to LSR B. In turn, LSR B responds at once with a Label Release message (step 6). Since LSR B has connectivity to more than one downstream node it is worth it trying to get another label from downstream before it withdraws its label from upstream. (Recall that LSR B is using conservative label retention, so it no longer has the label originally advertised by LSR F.) LSR B sends a Label Request to LSR F,

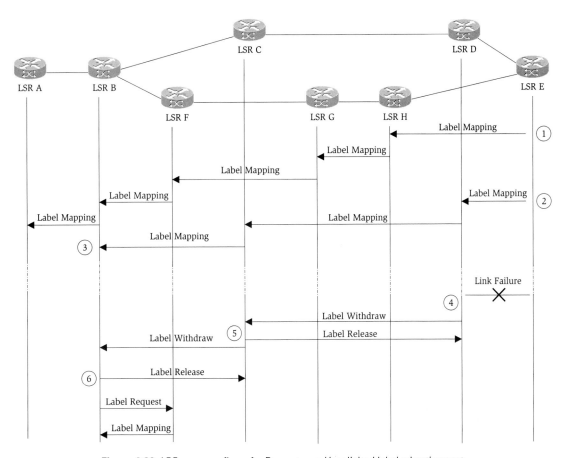

Figure 9.30 LDP message flows for Downstream Unsolicited label advertisement.

which is able to respond at once with a Label Mapping message. LSR B updates its tables and does not need to tell LSR A about any changes.

A Label Release message can also be used by an upstream LSR to show that it no longer wishes to use a label that was previously advertised to it. As with the Label Withdraw message, the unit of currency on the Label Release message is the FEC so that the upstream node is saying that it is no longer interested in reaching the specified FEC(s) and that the downstream LSR may consider the associated labels released if they are not used for any other FECs. Again, if the optional Label TLV is present it indicates that only this label as applicable to the listed FECs should be released. This message is used in Downstream on Demand mode to release a label that was previously requested and advertised, as shown in Figure 9.31.

The processing is illustrated by the steps in Figure 9.31. LSR A requests a label for a FEC by sending a Label Request message to LSR B (step 1). LSR B

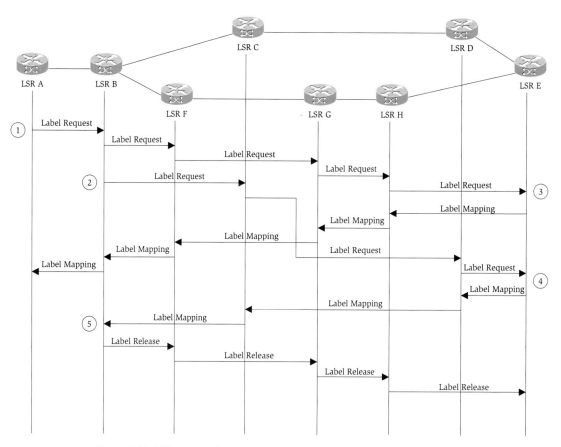

Figure 9.31 LDP message flows for Downstream on Demand label advertisement.

forwards the request to LSR F, and so onward through LSR G, LSR H, and LSR E. At the same time (step 2), LSR B also forwards the request to LSR C and onward through LSR D and LSR E.

LSR E receives the first request from LSR H and responds by allocating a label and sending a Label Mapping message to LSR H (step 3). Labels are allocated and mapped through the network by LSR H, LSR G, LSR F, and LSR B until a Label Mapping message is received back at LSR A and a full LSP is in place. LSR E also receives a Label Request message from LSR D (step 4), allocates a label, and sends a Label Mapping message back. LSR D and LSR C also allocate labels and forward Label Mapping messages.

LSR B receives a Label Mapping message from LSR C (step 5) and now has two LSPs to choose from. Since the path through LSR C is shorter, it switches traffic to that path by updating its FTN mapping table and LFIB—it does not need to tell LSR A about this. Optionally, LSR B can also clean up the labels that have been allocated on the other path by sending a Label Release message to

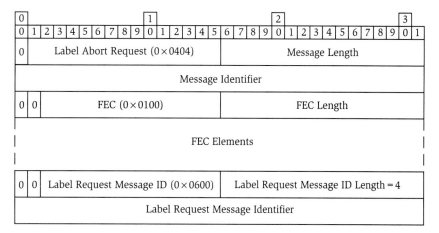

Figure 9.32 The LDP Label Abort Request message.

LSR F which may be propagated through the network, depending on the policy at each LSR and on whether there are other uses for the labels. If an upstream node decides that it no longer requires a label after it has sent a Label Request message, but *before* it receives a Label Mapping message in response, it cannot send a Label Release message since there is no label to release. Instead, it sends a Label Abort Request message to cancel its request. This message, shown in Figure 9.32, carries the FEC originally requested and the Message Identifier of the original Label Request message.

When an LSR receives a Label Abort Request message it may or may not have already sent a Label Mapping message in response to the original Label Request. If it has not sent a Label Mapping message, it responds with a Notification message (see Section 9.4.7) and may choose to forward the Label Abort Request down-stream. If it has already responded to the Label Request, it simply ignores the Label Abort Request. This means that an LSR that sends a Label Abort Request may still receive a Label Mapping message in response to the original Label Request message—it handles this by using the label as advertised, storing it in its FTN mapping table and LFIB, or by releasing it by sending a Label Release message.

9.4.7 Error Cases and Event Notification

In LDP, one LSR may need to inform another of errors or events that have occurred. For example, an LSR may want to reject parameters passed on a Session Initialization message and so prevent the establishment of an LDP session. Similarly, an LSR that receives a Label Abort Request message needs to inform the sender that the message has arrived.

Such notifications are carried in LDP using Notification messages. The Notification message (shown in Figure 9.33) includes a Status TLV which identifies

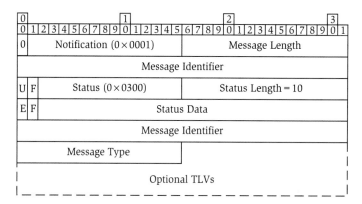

Figure 9.33 The LDP Notification message.

the error or event that is being reported by including a Status Code from the list in Table 9.5. The first two bits in the Status Code indicate how the notification should be handled by the recipient. If the E-bit is set, the notification is of a fatal error and both the sender and the recipient of the message should immediately close the LDP session—the setting of the E-bit is defined for each of the Status Code values defined in RFC 3036 and is indicated in Table 9.5. The F-bit is set at the discretion of the LSR that sends the Notification message; when the F-bit is set, the recipient of the Notification message is required to forward the message upstream or downstream along any LSP(s) or sessions associated with the original message, but when the F-bit is clear, the recipient must not forward the message.

The Status TLV also includes a Message Identifier that indicates the Message ID of a received message that caused the Notification message to be sent. Perhaps as an exercise in determination for the reader, RFC 3036 does not name the Message Identifier in the Notification message differently from the Message Identifier in the Status TLV. If there is no specific original message (for example, if the Notification is unsolicited or is in response to a bad LDP PDU) this Message Identifier is set to zero (note that this means that the Message ID value of zero may not be used to identify any message). If a nonzero Message Identifier is supplied in the Status TLV, the type of the original message is also supplied as a further cross-check for the receiver of the notification message, helping to limit confusion when Message Identifiers are reused.

Optional parameters can be carried in the Notification to help clarify the error or event being reported. The Extended Status TLV (0x0301) carries a 4-byte supplementary status code to give additional information or granularity to the main Status Code—values for the Extended Status Code are implementation specific and are not defined in RFC 3036. The Returned PDU TLV (0x0302) is used to return the whole of an errored PDU up to (and usually including) the part of the PDU that is in error—this can be particularly useful when debugging in the field or in the interop lab because it makes it very clear what is being

Table 9.5 LDP Status Codes Showing Settings of the E-bit

Status Code	E-Bit Setting	Meaning
0x00000000	0	Success
0x00000001	1	Bad LDP Identifier
0x00000002	1	Bad Protocol Version
0x00000003	1	Bad PDU Length
0x00000004	0	Unknown Message Type
0x00000005	1	Bad Message Length
0x00000006	0	Unknown TLV
0x00000007	1	Bad TLV Length
0x00000008	1	Malformed TLV Value
0x00000009	1	Hold Timer Expired
0x0000000A	1	Shutdown
0x0000000B	0	Loop Detected
0x0000000C	0	Unknown FEC
0x0000000D	0	No Route
0x0000000E	0	No Label Resources
0x0000000F	0	Label Resources/Available
0x00000010	1	Session Rejected/No Hello
0x00000011	1	Session Rejected/Parameters Advertisement Mode
0x00000012	1	Session Rejected/Parameters Max PDU Length
0x00000013	1	Session Rejected/Parameters Label Range
0x00000014	1	KeepAlive Timer Expired
0x00000015	0	Label Request Aborted
0x00000016	0	Missing Message Parameters
0x00000017	0	Unsupported Address Family
0x00000018	1	Session Rejected/Bad KeepAlive Time
0x00000019	1	Internal Error

objected to by the sender of the Notification message. The Returned Message TLV (0x0303) is similar to the Returned PDU TLV but contains only an errored message rather than the whole PDU. It would not be usual to include both the Returned PDU and Returned Message TLVs in the same Notification message.

9.4.8 Further Message Flow Examples

Figure 9.34 shows the message exchanges in LDP Downstream on Demand label distribution. LSR A determines that it needs an LSP for a FEC routed through LSR D and sends a Label Request message (step 1). LSR receives the message (step 2) and determines that it does not currently have a label for the FEC; since it is running in ordered control mode it forwards the Label Request downstream according to its routing table. LSR D is the LER for the requested FEC, so when the Label Request reaches LSR D it is able to allocate a label and send it back upstream in a Label Mapping message (step 3). At each transit node (step 4) a new label is allocated and installed in the LFIB together with the label received from downstream—the new label is advertised further upstream. When the Label Mapping message reaches the initial node (LSR A at step 5) the LSP is fully established.

Teardown is initiated by LSR A when it no longer wants the LSP. It sends a Label Release message (step 6). Each transit node releases the label and forwards the Label Release message (step 7) until the egress is reached (step 8).

Figure 9.35 shows what happens if there is a network failure event some time after a Downstream on Demand LSP has been established. The failure (step 1) is detected by the upstream node through a failure of KeepAlive message exchange or through notification by the transport protocol (step 2). The upstream node removes the labels for the LSP and sends a Notification message further

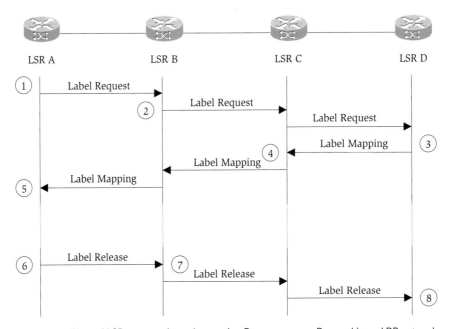

Figure 9.34 Normal LSP setup and teardown using Downstream on Demand in an LDP network.

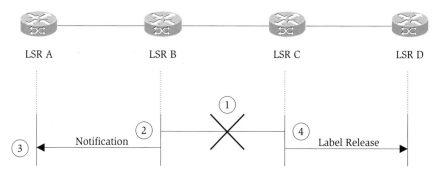

Figure 9.35 Reporting a network failure and cleaning up an LSP in a Downstream on Demand LDP network.

upstream. All upstream nodes similarly remove labels for the LSP and forward the Notification to the ingress (step 3).

Similarly, the LSR downstream of the failure is notified (step 4). It sends a Label Release downstream as though the LSP had simply been torn down. The precise choice of action at step 4 may depend on whether LSR C is using conservative or liberal label retention and whether it has advertised a label for the FEC of the LSP at some other interface. In these cases, it may choose to retain the label and not send a Label Release message.

Message flows for Downstream on Demand label distribution in LDP are common to those used by CR-LDP (see Section 9.6). Further message flow diagrams for Downstream on Demand label distribution in LDP are presented in Section 9.6.4.

Figures 9.36 and 9.37 show LSP setup, teardown, and failure for Downstream Unsolicited label advertisement. Again, ordered control is assumed. In Figure 9.36, LSR D becomes aware of a new FEC in its routing table and distributes a label by sending an unsolicited Label Mapping message. Upstream nodes (step 2) allocate a new label and install it in the LFIB together with the label received from downstream—the new label is advertised further upstream. When the Label Mapping message reaches the initial node (LSR A at step 3) the LSP is fully established.

When LSR D wishes to end the life of the LSP it cannot simply remove the label from its LFIB because data may still be flowing. It sends a Label Withdraw message upstream to indicate that it wishes to remove the label. At each step along the way (step 5) LSRs may see that they have an alternative route for the FEC and install that in place of the old label, responding with a Label Release message, or may forward the Label Withdraw upstream. If the Label Withdraw reaches the ingress (step 6), it should cease putting traffic onto the LSP, remove the label from its LFIB, and send a Label Release. Each node receiving a Label Release (steps 7 and 8) removes the label from its LFIB and forwards the message.

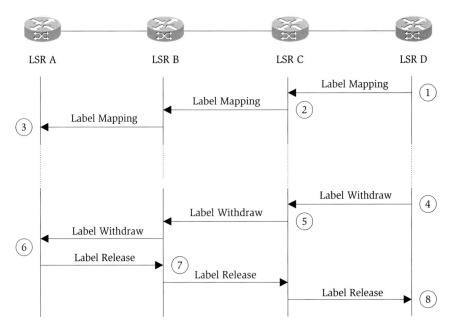

Figure 9.36 Normal LSP setup and teardown using Downstream Unsolicited label distribution in an LDP network.

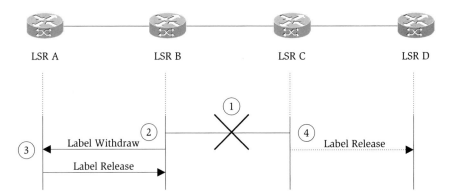

Figure 9.37 Reporting a network failure and cleaning up an LSP in a Downstream Unsolicited LDP network.

Finally, Figure 9.37 shows how an LSR upstream of a failure withdraws the label and sees to its release (steps 2 and 3). Downstream of the failure there is no requirement to release the label. The decision may be influenced by the label retention mode of the LSR and whether it has further interfaces on which to advertise a label for the FEC.

9.4.9 Choosing Transport Protocols for LDP

As described in the previous sections, LDP makes use of UDP and TCP as transport protocols. This reflects a well-thought-through decision. When LDP was being invented, it was clear that special consideration would need to be given to handling the cases in which protocol messages arrived out of order or were lost completely. It would also be necessary to implement a mechanism to stop one LSR from flooding a peer with a large number of protocol messages. Many protocols have had to address the same issues and the solutions usually result in a significant increase in the protocols' complexity. The designers of LDP decided that, rather than encumber LDP with the mechanisms to handle these issues, they would rely on a transport protocol that already addresses the problems. So they built LDP on top of TCP.

There is, however, one piece of LDP that cannot use TCP. When peers are discovering each other they cannot already have established TCP connections because that would imply that they already knew about each other. So the Hello message must be sent in some other way: UDP and raw IP were two immediate options. Raw IP had the disadvantage of requiring another IP protocol identifier to be assigned from the very limited number available, but also was a concern if LDP was to be extended to host systems which do not always have access to raw IP. Consequently, UDP was selected.

9.4.10 Surviving Network Outages

LDP function is based on TCP connections between LDP peers. If a network connection on an LSR fails, the TCP connection will be brought down, resulting in a break in the LDP session. Even if this break is very short, and the TCP connection can be reestablished at once, the LSRs must follow the procedures in RFC 3036 and consider all labels previously advertised across the link to be released. This is necessary because it is not possible to tell whether any messages relating to these labels have been lost, and because the connection might actually stay down for a long time.

This is obviously a nuisance when connections or LSRs can recover quickly, and makes it hard to implement fault tolerant systems in which the protocol processing and packet forwarding can be switched to replacement hardware when a fault is detected. In particular, it may be possible for an LSR to retain forwarding state for labeled packets during an outage of the connection or the processor/software that handles LDP. Several solutions exist.

LDP could be run over a fault tolerant implementation of TCP. This is possible, but is not normally considered since to be fault tolerant a TCP implementation must copy all data sent over a connection from one instance of the code to another (usually on another set of hardware).

LDP could be run over SCTP since that protocol is far more resilient to faults than TCP is. There is no real reason why this can't be done except that it isn't! In order that all peers in an LDP network can interoperate they have to use the same transport protocol: SCTP implementations are still rare, and so this option is not used. Besides, using SCTP is not a panacea for all network faults, and some of the issues still exist.

The IETF has produced two sets of extensions to LDP to address the issue of surviving network outages. LDP Graceful Restart allows a restarted LSR to learn about the label mappings and advertisements in which it had previously participated by receiving duplicate messages from its peers which do not remove label state when a session fails if that session was flagged as "restartable" during session initialization. Fault Tolerant LDP is a heavier approach that uses sequence numbers and acknowledgements to securely deliver LDP messages on a session so that it can span instances of the TCP connection.

In deciding which of these IETF options to implement or deploy to build a fault tolerant LDP implementation, you should consider the complexity, rate of change, and robustness of your network. In a relatively simple network in which there are not many entries in the LFIB it will be acceptable to relearn the protocol state from peers during recovery. If the network is large but stable, careful consideration is needed to examine the time needed to repopulate the protocol state—a very large number of messages may need to be sent and these have to be paced to avoid flooding the network, but new label advertisements must not be allowed to interfere with the old labels being relearned. If the network needs to be able to recover quickly without retransmitting messages, then Fault Tolerant LDP is a better option—such a choice is well suited to an implementation with dual processors when building a "carrier class" LDP network.

9.4.11 LDP Extensions

The message and TLV format of LDP means that new functions and features can be added easily, and additions have been happening almost since LDP was first published. Extensions cover network survivability, the ability to trace LSPs through a network, and MTU discovery. Many other extensions exist as proposals that have not yet been adopted by the MPLS Working Group.

When examining any extension to LDP, attention must be paid to the behavior of the extension when some nodes in the network do not support it. Most extensions are designed with backwards compatibility in mind so that use of the extension can be negotiated during session initialization. Others rely on the forwarding, untouched by an LSR, of TLVs that a node does not understand. In most cases, mixing LSRs that do and do not implement an extension to LDP will result in partial or poor support of the extension.

The most substantive extension to LDP is Constraint-Based LSP Setup Using LDP (CR-LDP). This is a set of additional TLVs that make LDP suitable for use in a traffic engineered network. See Section 9.6 for more details. The best place to look for a full list of such extensions is on the MPLS Working Group's web site.

9.5 Traffic Engineering in MPLS

Traffic engineering is discussed in general in Chapter 8 and its applicability to MPLS is briefly raised in Section 9.3.5. This section describes how MPLS can be used to achieve traffic engineering and examines the requirements on MPLS signaling protocols.

MPLS offers the ability to implement traffic engineering at a low cost in equipment and operational expenditure. Capital expenditure can be reduced because MPLS is able to supply much of the function of the traffic engineered overlay model in an integrated manner. Operational costs may be reduced by the use of automated provisioning of tunnels, proactive distribution of traffic between tunnels, and dynamic computation of optimal routes through the network. In many cases, this pushes the intelligence for operation of a traffic engineered network into the network itself and away from central management stations.

MPLS has many components that make it attractive for use in a traffic engineered network. These aspects are examined in the sections that follow. They include the following.

- MPLS has the ability to establish an LSP that follows a path other than the one offered as "preferred" by the routing protocol and forwarding algorithm.
- Resources within the network can be dynamically reserved as LSPs are established and can be dynamically updated as the needs of the LSPs change so that traffic flows can be guaranteed a level and quality of service. Routing of the LSPs can be made dependent on the resource requirements.
- Traffic can be groomed on to "parallel" LSPs. That is, multiple LSPs can be established between a pair of source and destination end points, and traffic can be distributed between the LSPs according to any number of algorithms. The "parallel" LSPs can take significantly different paths through the network.
- Network resources can be automatically managed with new LSPs set up to meet the immediate demands of the network, and with resources freed up again as old LSPs that are no longer required are released.
- The network can be managed centrally through a common set of management options and with a common underlying granularity of managed object—the LSP.
- Recovery procedures can be defined describing how traffic can be transferred to alternate LSPs in the event of a failure, and indicating how and when backup and standby LSPs should be set up and routed.

Ultimately, MPLS scores over previous traffic engineering implementations because the load-sharing and traffic grooming decisions need only be made once (at the entry point into the LSPs) rather than at each node within the network. This makes traffic propagation considerably more efficient.

Consider the gratuitously complex but miraculously symmetrical network in Figure 9.38. There are five data sources, all sending traffic to a single data

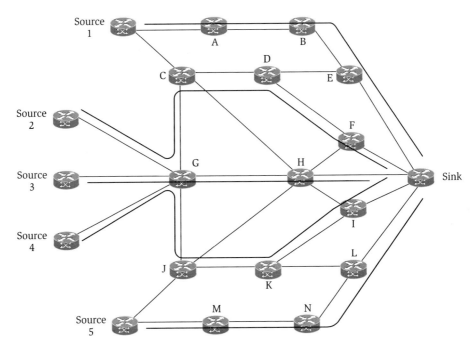

Figure 9.38 Explicit path control in an MPLS network.

sink. Left to itself, a shortest path first algorithm will serve to converge all of the traffic onto the link between node H and the sink. This might overload that link even though the network contains sufficient independent routes, as illustrated by the heavy lines in the figure.

Some diversity can be achieved by modifying the costs of key links. For example, if the link from source 5 to node J is made expensive, the SPF algorithm will choose to send traffic via node M. But this approach cannot address the whole of the problem for our network since all of the traffic from sources 2, 3, and 4 converges on node G, and so we might need to implement some form of constraint-based routing at node G to send some traffic through node C and some through node J. Even then the problems are not over because the traffic tends to converge again at node H, so we would need to increase the costs of links CH and JH or do more constraint-based routing at node H to split the traffic through nodes F and I. This all becomes very complicated and might be entirely broken if a new traffic flow were added through a new source or sink.

However, if MPLS LSPs are used, the computation of diverse paths can be performed offline and no changes to the behavior of the routing or forwarding code are needed. LSPs are simply established (manually or through the signaling of explicit paths) to follow the computed routes shown in bold and data flows without congestion.

9.5.1 Explicit Routes

MPLS LSPs can be set up using signaling protocols utilizing the existing routing protocols. This is how LDP Downstream on Demand label distribution works and is also used by MPLS traffic engineering protocols in the absence of any explicit route control.

The request to set up an LSP includes the address of the end point or egress LSR. The first LSR in the network performs a routing look-up based on the egress address and sends a signaling message to the next hop. This process is repeated LSR by LSR through the network until the egress is reached.

One of the main issues in a network is that preferred routes tend to converge. This serves to place much traffic onto a few links while other links remain relatively free of traffic. A key aim of traffic engineering is to distribute traffic across the links to ensure that the load is shared. If LSPs can be forced to follow other routes, the traffic can be made to traverse underutilized links and so take the pressure off busy links.

The fundamental facility that MPLS brings to traffic engineered networks is the ability to set up a virtual circuit switched overlay to the Internet routing model. In a manually provisioned MPLS network this is simple—the LSRs can have their FTN mapping tables and LFIBs explicitly set to send traffic down specific paths. This process can be automated through the use of a management protocol (such as SNMP) or the use of any form of remote access (such as Telnet) to configure the LSRs.

Ideally, however, MPLS signaling protocols like those discussed in Sections 9.6 and 9.7 will allow the path, the explicit route, of the LSP to be provided by the head end of the LSP, and will traverse the chosen path establishing the LSP. Explicit routes are specified as a well-ordered series of hops expressed as IP addresses, IP prefixes, or identifiers of autonomous systems. The LSP must traverse the hops in order.

Because each hop can be an expression of multiple nodes (as a prefix or as an autonomous system), the elements of an explicit route are referred to as *abstract nodes*. The LSP must traverse the abstract nodes in the order that they are specified in the explicit route, and where the abstract node defines more than one node, the LSP must traverse at least one LSR that is a member of the abstract node.

The fully specified addresses used in explicit routes give rise to some confusion. If loopback addresses are used, it is clear that the path must include the node with the specified address, but if an interface address is used, consideration must be given as to whether this refers to an incoming address or an outgoing address. Some systems prefer the interface address to indicate the outgoing interface because this does not require any routing look-up as the route is processed at a node, but others consider that a precise interpretation of the explicit route processing rules (see the following section) requires that addresses always indicate the next hop. It is important when building an MPLS network that you understand the processing rules applied to explicit routes by the various equipment vendors who supply you—many switches now support both modes of operation at the same time, but others require configuration to select the mode, and a few utilize one mode only. Failure to harmonize this aspect of explicit route processing will possibly prevent LSP setup in your network.

The abstract node hops in the explicit route may each be defined as *strict* or *loose*. If a hop is strict, no LSR may be inserted in the actual path of the LSP between LSRs that are members of the previous abstract node and those that are members of the current hop. If the hop is loose, the local routing decisions may fill in additional nodes necessary to reach an LSR that is a member of the abstract node that is the current explicit route hop. Loose and explicit hops can be explained further with reference to Figure 9.39. Suppose we want to set up an LSP from the ingress LSR to the egress LSR. The simplest explicit route we can give is a single loose hop specifying the loopback address of the egress LSR that leaves the network free to choose a route in between.

Now, suppose further that we want to include the link between LSR E and the egress because we know that it is currently underutilized. There are several options that force the route through LSR E (for example, including a hop that specifies the loopback address of LSR E), but these rely on the CSPF algorithm at LSR E not choosing to pick a route back through LSRs B and D. The best

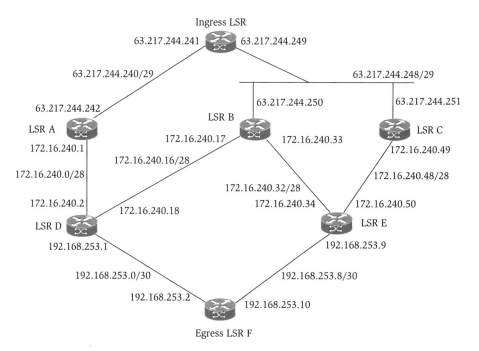

Figure 9.39 Strict and loose hops in explicit path control in an MPLS network.

option is to include an address that forces the link to be used—192.168.253.10 as a loose hop would achieve the desired result in some networks and 192.168.253.9 would be satisfactory in others. This explicit route looks like {loose (192.168.253.9), loose (egress LSR)}.

So far we have left the choice of route in the upper part of the network open and that still allows routes to be picked through LSR A and LSR D. In particular, it is possible that a path {Ingress, LSR A, LSR D, Egress, LSR E} would be chosen to reach the first hop in the explicit route given in the preceding paragraph. We need to apply more control. Suppose we would rather not use any path through LSR A, but we don't have any preference between LSRs B and C. If we include a strict abstract node hop with prefix 63.217.244.248/29 we will ensure that the path goes in the right direction, but there is still a possibility of a path through LSR B and LSR D that misses our objectives, so it is necessary to include a strict hop to LSR E.

This gives us the explicit route of {strict (63.217.244.248/29), strict LSR E,...}. Now we will definitely reach LSR E and we may simplify the remaining route to the egress as a strict hop to its loopback address, or (depending on the system) a strict hop to 192.168.253.9 or 192.168.253.10. The final explicit route is {strict (63.217.244.248/29), strict LSR E, strict (LSR F)}.

Explicit Route Processing Rules

The processing rules for MPLS explicit routes are laid out in the definitions of the IETF's two signaling protocols for traffic engineered MPLS (CR-LDP in RFC 3212 and RSVP-TE in RFC 3209) and are, fortunately, identical.

When an LSP setup request message carrying an explicit route object is received by an LSR it must follow the simple steps in the following list. These steps all follow the assumption that as the message propagates through the network, the explicit route on the message is trimmed so that only parts of the route relevant to the nodes that have not yet been reached remain in the message.

1. On receipt, the LSR must check that it is a member of the first abstract node in the explicit route. If it isn't, processing must fail.
2. If there is only one abstract node in the explicit route it must be removed. Processing continues at step 8.
3. If the LSR is also a member of the second abstract node, the first node is removed and processing continues at step 2.
4. If the LSR determines that it is topologically adjacent to (that is, only one hop away from) some node that is a member of the second abstract node, it selects the next hop, removes the first abstract node and continues at step 9.
5. The LSR attempts to find a next hop that is a member of the first abstract node and is on the route toward the second abstract node. Note that if the first abstract node is explicit (that is, not a prefix or an autonomous system) this attempt will fail, but it is at this point that the difference in processing

for interface addresses as incoming or outgoing addresses can be applied. If such a next hop is found, processing continues at step 9.

6. If the second abstract node is a loose hop, the LSR chooses any next hop toward the second abstract node, removes the first, and continues at step 9.

7. If no route has been found (which includes no route available, and second abstract node is a strict hop) the LSP setup fails.

8. There being no more explicit route present, the LSR may insert a fresh series of abstract nodes as a new explicit route toward the destination. If it does, processing continues with step 10; otherwise, the LSP setup continues but is routed on a hop-by-hop basis across the rest of the network.

9. If the selected next hop is a member of the (new) first abstract node in the explicit route, and that abstract node is not an explicit address, the LSR may insert additional abstract nodes at the head of the explicit route as a result of local path computation. The one proviso is that all inserted abstract nodes must be subsets of the first abstract node.

10. If the selected next hop is not a member of the (new) first abstract node in the explicit route (possible if the first abstract node is a loose hop) the LSR must insert a new abstract node that the next hop is a member of at the start of the explicit route. This ensures that the explicit route is accepted at the next node.

9.5.2 Reserving Resources and Constraint-Based Routing

Chapter 6 described the desirability of specifying the characteristics of traffic flows so that resources can be reserved to help to satisfy quality of service requirements and to implement *service level agreements* (SLAs). A virtual circuit-switched overlay is established using MPLS and, if specific reservation requirements are associated with each LSP, it becomes possible to reserve precisely enough resources for each flow and to guarantee SLAs based on a much more precise allocation of network capabilities. This can lead to considerable savings or, more precisely, it can allow network operators to make full use of their networks without needing to over-provision resources to play it safe with their SLAs.

The following features are necessary for MPLS to fully provide this service.

- The routing protocol must advertise the capabilities and available resources on each link. See Section 8.8 for a description of extensions to routing protocols for traffic engineering.
- The requester of a flow of LSP must indicate the characteristics of the flow (average bandwidth, peaks, quality requirements).
- The engine that computes the paths must take into account the requirements of the LSP and the availability of network resources by performing constraint-based routing.
- The MPLS signaling protocol must support setting up explicitly routed LSPs.

- The MPLS signaling protocol must be able to signal the LSP resource requirements so that the appropriate reservations can be made at each LSR along the path.
- The routing protocol must re-advertise the modified resource availabilities for each link on the LSP so that subsequent path computations at other nodes can know the current state of the network.

Even when all of the available resources have been used, it is still possible to set up a new LSP by commandeering the resources used by one or more existing LSPs. This process of LSP *preemption* needs some form of policing, otherwise the network will simply thrash with LSPs alternately replacing each other. In MPLS, preemption is achieved by using two priority values associated with each LSP. The *holding priority* indicates how hard an existing LSP will hold on to resources once it has them, and the *setup priority* says how important the setup of the new LSP is. An LSP with a greater setup priority may preempt an LSP with a lower holding priority. Obviously, network thrash will be avoided only if LSPs have holding priorities greater than or equal to their own setup priorities (and if operators show a modicum of self-discipline about their choice of priorities).

9.5.3 Grooming Traffic

In some cases there will be multiple traffic flows between a source and a sink. Perhaps there are multiple applications, some serving high-bandwidth, low-priority file transfers, and others serving low-bandwidth, rapid-response user interfaces. In these cases it is desirable to keep the flows separate as they pass through the network, allowing the high-priority traffic to overtake the larger quantity of low-priority traffic. This is the sort of behavior that DiffServ (see Section 6.2) can provide in an IP forwarding network.

In an MPLS network, the same effect can be achieved by establishing two LSPs between the same source and destination. The LSPs can follow the same route and be given different characteristics to prioritize the traffic. Alternatively, the LSPs can follow diverse paths. All that is necessary once the LSPs are established is for the source node to decide which LSP to assign each packet to based on the source application or the DiffServ packet color.

9.5.4 Managing the Network

Managing the network as a mesh of LSPs allows regulated predictability to be applied to the traffic flows. This makes it much easier to handle planned network outages in a seamless way since the LSPs can be rerouted around the resource that is going to be taken out of service to preserve traffic. At the same time, management techniques can be applied to predict future flows and control current demands so that congestion is avoided and quality of service is provided to users.

Such network management can be centralized or operated from multiple sites, all using the topology and resource information supplied by the routing protocols and establishing new LSPs as required. Such management can even be distributed to the LSRs, building an intelligent network that is capable of routing and rerouting LSPs according to the current traffic load conditions.

9.5.5 Recovery Procedures

In the event of unplanned network outages, traffic engineering with MPLS can define how data flows can be protected. Backup or protection LSPs can be presignaled using disjoint paths through the network so that when there is a failure on the primary or working LSP the data can immediately be switched to the backup path. In the same way, single LSPs called *bypass tunnels* can provide protection for a group of working LSPs, a physical link, or even a bundle of physical links.

Presignaled backup LSPs utilize network resources without carrying traffic until there is a failure. There are a host of schemes to mitigate this issue, ranging from LSPs that reserve resources only when they start to see traffic, through LSPs that support low-priority preemptable traffic until the failure occurs, to backup LSPs that are signaled only after the failure. The choice between these different protection models is complicated by the configuration of the network and the capabilities of the LSRs.

9.5.6 Choosing to Use a Constraint-Based Signaling Protocol

Traffic engineered LSPs can be configured manually. That is, the operator can precompute the path of the LSP, perhaps using a path computation engine fed by topology and availability information from the routing protocol and by traffic statistics gathered from the edges and core of the network. Having selected a path for the LSP, the operator can visit each LSR in the network to configure the LFIB and install the LSP. Finally, the operator can configure the ingress LSR through the FTN mapping table and through the routing table so that the correct traffic is placed on the LSP. How the operator achieves this will depend on the devices, but might include using Command Line Interfaces through Telnet, configuration through Management Information Bases (MIBs) using SNMP, or proprietary configuration protocols.

The manual configuration process is time-consuming and error-prone. One of the requirements of traffic engineering is that it must be able to respond quickly to changes within the network, and operator intervention is unlikely to achieve this.

A signaling protocol reduces the number of configuration steps and allows a spectrum of control from full operator selection of paths, through offline traffic engineering, to on-demand traffic engineering with intelligence within the network. The use of a software application may determine the need to establish new

LSPs or to reposition existing ones and issue a request to the ingress of the LSP. From there, the request is signaled along the path of the LSP conventionally using Downstream on Demand label distribution.

The IETF did not specify that only one signaling protocol could be used to establish constraint-based LSPs in a traffic engineered MPLS network. As a result, two protocols grew up side-by-side with similar, but not identical, features. The next three sections examine Constraint-Based LSP Setup Using LDP (CR-LDP), and Extensions to RSVP for LSP Tunnels (RSVP-TE), and make some comparisons between them.

9.6 Constraint-Based LSP Setup Using LDP (CR-LDP)

Constraint-Based LSP Setup Using LDP builds on LDP to provide a mechanism for establishing end-to-end LSPs through an MPLS network under a set of constraints. Constraints may be applied by the user or application requesting the LSP, or by provisioning and policy modules within the devices providing the LSP. CR-LDP is defined in RFC 3212.

CR-LDP supports two basic classes of constraint: explicit routes and traffic parameters. The former allows part or all of the route of the LSP to be imposed on the normal routing processes. The latter states a requirement for traffic characteristics, such as bandwidth, which must be met on whatever route is chosen for the LSP.

Additional features in CR-LDP allow priorities to be assigned to LSPs so that resource preemption schemes can be applied, LSPs to be dynamically rerouted after failure or for administrative reasons, and LSPs to be pinned or "nailed down" so that they cannot be rerouted.

9.6.1 Adding Constraints to LDP

CR-LDP operates in Downstream on Demand mode with all LSP setup requests originating at the ingress or head end of the LSP and labels being distributed from the egress. All of the necessary messages already exist in LDP and the only extensions necessary are the addition of some TLVs and a few status codes. Specifically, CR-LDP reuses the following mechanisms from LDP:

- Hello messages for discovery of other CR-LDP peers.
- Label Request message to request label advertisement from downstream nodes when setting up an LSP.
- Label Mapping message to advertise labels from downstream nodes strictly in response to Label Request messages.
- Label Release message to tear down a previously established LSP.
- Label Withdraw message to allow a downstream LSR to request that an LSP be torn down.

- Label Abort message to abort a request for LSP setup.
- Notification messages to report errors or events as for LDP, but with a few additional causes.

The loop detection mechanisms of LDP also turn out to be important and useful in CR-LDP.

In fact, CR-LDP is so similar to LDP that it is possible to run both protocols in the same network at the same time. An LSR can detect whether LDP or CR-LDP is being used by spotting the new TLVs on a message (such as the Label Request message) and can act accordingly. An LSR that supports LDP but not CR-LDP can participate in the network since the new TLVs all have the U-bit set to zero, meaning that the recipient should reject the whole message that carries the TLV using a Notification message with status code "Unknown TLV" (0x00000006) so that the sender can deduce that its neighbor is LDP-capable but cannot handle CR-LDP.

9.6.2 New TLVs

The sections that follow describe the new LDP TLVs introduced to create CR-LDP and explain how they are used to achieve the function described in Section 9.5.

Choosing a FEC in CR-LDP

Path choice decisions in LDP are taken by making routing choices based on the FEC. The same approach can be taken in CR-LDP, so that at each hop along the path a constrained routing decision is made based on the traffic requirements of the LSP and the FEC, both of which are indicated in the Label Request message received from upstream. One of the options in CR-LDP, however, is to constrain the path of the LSP by supplying an explicit route, and in most implementations this will conflict with the idea of routing based on the FEC.

To avoid any confusion, one would ideally omit the FEC from CR-LDP messages, but the definition of LDP has made it compulsory, so a new FEC element (the CR-LSP FEC element) is defined, which indicates that CR-LDP is in use and that the FEC is not relevant—this is essentially a null FEC and is shown in Figure 9.40. Note that CR-LDP does not forbid the use of FEC elements defined

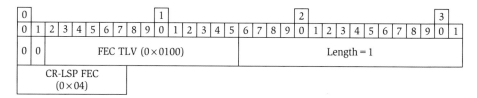

Figure 9.40 The LDP FEC TLV with a CR-LSP FEC element.

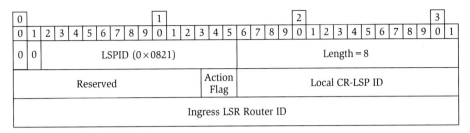

Figure 9.41 The CR-LDP LSPID TLV.

in the LDP specification even if an explicit route is used, but the interpretation of such a combination is left to the individual implementation. What is forbidden is the use of multiple FEC elements where one of them is the new CR-LSP FEC element.

Identifying the LSP

It is useful to identify an LSP in some unique way within the network. At the very least, when managing a traffic engineered MPLS network it is important to be able to distinguish the LSPs with some kind of tag so that the operator can easily see where a particular LSP is routed and can reroute it or tear it down. At the same time, when LSPs are tunneled one through another, it is convenient to be able to specify the identity of the tunnel when establishing the tunneled LSP.

The LSP identifier needs to be unique for all LSPs in the whole network. This is achieved by constructing the identifier from the router ID of the source node (that is, the head end of the LSP) and some unique number (called the *Local CR-LSP ID*) allocated by the source node. RFC 3212 suggests that a source node may use any of its IPv4 addresses as the Source Router ID. These parameters are encoded into the LSPID TLV as shown in Figure 9.41.

Note that RFC 3212 incorrectly states that the length of this TLV should be set to 4.

The Action Flag in the LSPID is used to indicate whether this is an initial LSP setup (value 0x0) or some form of change or modification to an existing LSP (value 0x1). See the section on "Rerouting and Pinning the LSP" for a description of the use of this flag.

Explicit Routes

The Explicit Route TLV shown in Figure 9.42 is no more than a vehicle for the ordered list of sub-TLVs that make up the explicit route. The sub-TLVs are called Explicit Route Hop TLVs; there are four types defined, depending on the addressing being applied for the hop. These are shown in Figure 9.42.

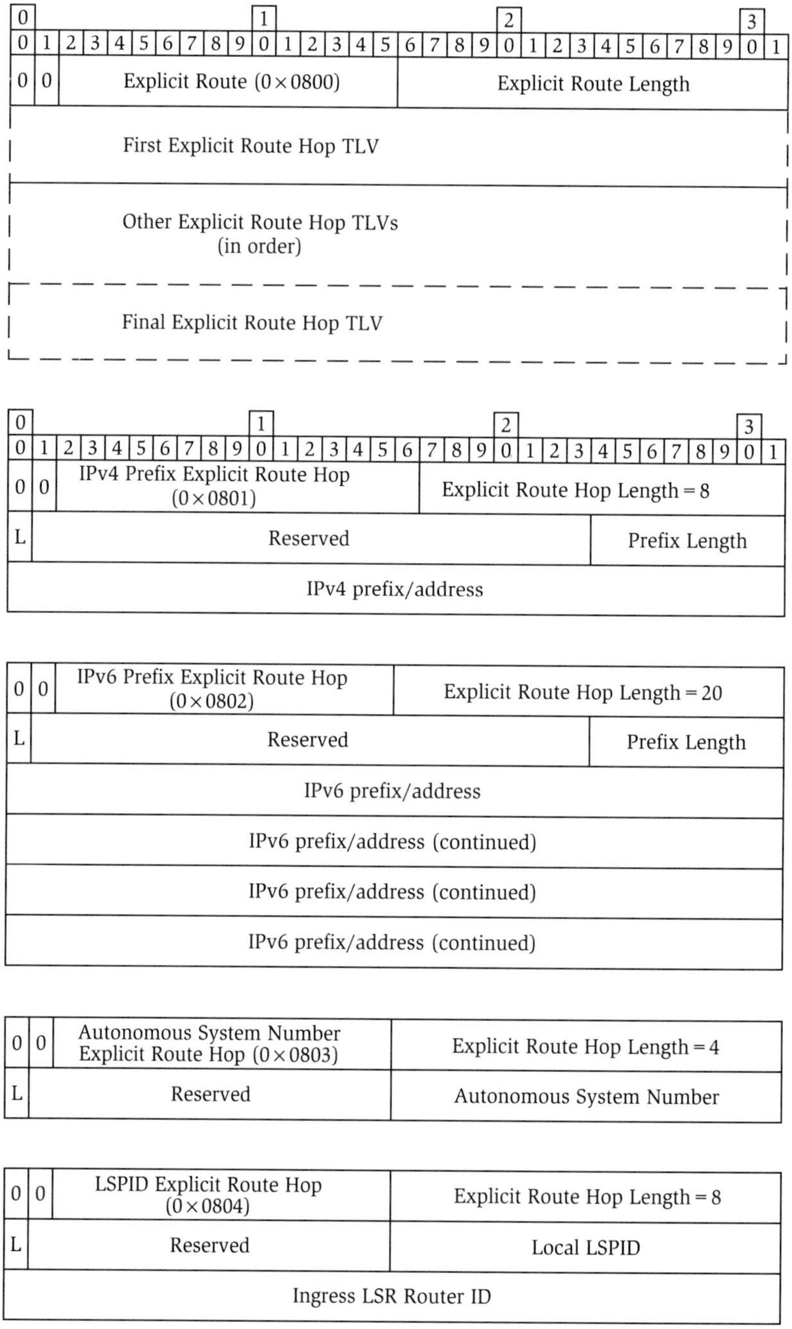

Figure 9.42 The CR-LDP Explicit Route TLV and the different Explicit Route Hop TLVs.

The format of the Explicit Route Hop TLVs is common. Each begins with the U- and F-bits set to zero, a field to indicate the type of the hop, and a length. Then follows a single bit, the L-bit, that indicates whether this hop in the explicit route should be considered as loose or strict. Setting the L-bit to 1 shows that this is a loose hop. After the L-bit there is a reserved field to pad the TLV up to a convenient byte boundary.

The IP address Explicit Route Hops (IPv4 and IPv6) combine host addresses with prefixes (compare with FECs, which use a separate type for a host address and a prefix). The prefix length is given in bits and precedes the address, which is fully specified and right-padded with zeros (again compare with FECs, which are truncated at byte boundaries).

The autonomous system number Explicit Route Hop TLV is straightforward, as is the LSPID Explicit Route Hop TLV, but note that the LSPID is composed of two pieces: the Source LSR ID identifies the LSR on which the tunnel LSP starts and is a routable commodity (that is, the previous LSRs in the path can route toward this LSR ID), and the Local LSPID identifies the LSP strictly within the context of the source LSR.

Traffic Parameters

CR-LDP allows for a basic specification of the traffic characteristics of an LSP. To those familiar with ATM this may appear to be a tiny subset of the detailed description of the required quality of service (QoS) and traffic flows that is available in that protocol. Debate continues to rage over whether this is a Good Thing or a Bad Thing since the network is made considerably more manageable and easy to understand through these simplifications, but we are left wondering exactly how to control the high function of an underlying ATM network that supports MPLS.

The available parameters are peak data rate (PDR), peak burst size (PBS), committed data rate (CDR), committed burst size (CBS), and excess burst size (EBS). They are informed by the basic Integrated Services parameters (see Chapter 6), and this is the crunch—CR-LDP was principally envisaged for carrying IP traffic (despite the M in MPLS) and so such a traffic model was considered adequate. This is not to say that there is no scope for a more detailed QoS-based set of traffic parameters, and it is within the TLV nature of CR-LDP that such traffic parameters could be defined for a private implementation or in an Internet draft.

Figure 9.43 shows the CR-LDP Traffic Parameters TLV. Each of the five traffic parameters is encoded as a 32-bit single precision IEEE floating point number, and positive infinity, should it be required, is represented using an exponent of all ones and a mantissa of all zeros. Note that the values count bytes not bits.

PDR (in bytes per second) and PBS (in bytes) are used to specify the peak data rate, that is the maximum rate at which data will be supplied to the LSP at

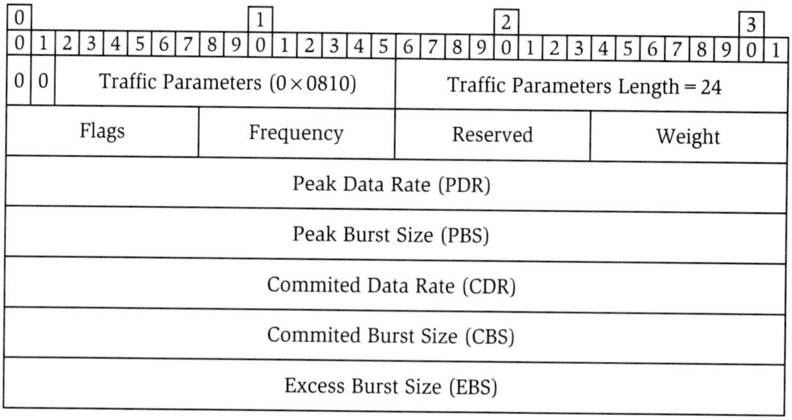
0
1
2
3
0 1 2 3 4 5 6 7 8 9 0 1 2 3 4 5 6 7 8 9 0 1 2 3 4 5 6 7 8 9 0 1
0 0
Traffic Parameters (0×0810)
Traffic Parameters Length = 24
Flags
Frequency
Reserved
Weight
Peak Data Rate (PDR)
Peak Burst Size (PBS)
Commited Data Rate (CDR)
Commited Burst Size (CBS)
Excess Burst Size (EBS)

Figure 9.43 The CR-LDP Traffic Parameters TLV.

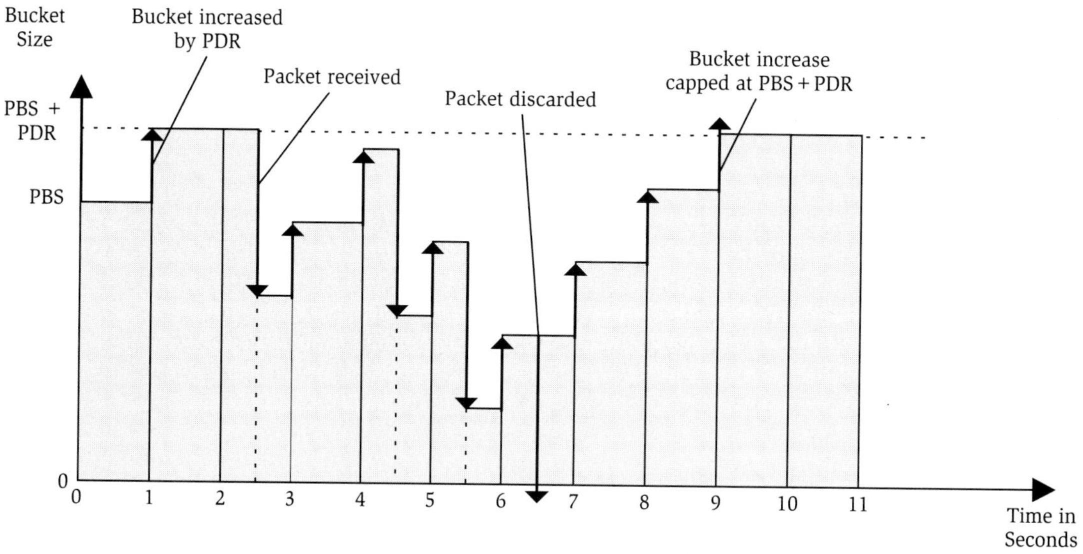
Bucket Size
Bucket increased by PDR
Packet received
Packet discarded
Bucket increase capped at PBS + PDR
PBS + PDR
PBS
0
0
1
2
3
4
5
6
7
8
9
10
11
Time in Seconds

Figure 9.44 An example of the CR-LDP formal peak token rate bucket.

the head end. A peak rate token bucket can be formally defined, allowing the peak rate to be policed so that an LSR can (but need not) discard packets that fall outside the bucket. The bucket size is initialized to the value of PBS. Every second, if the bucket size is less than the value of PBS, the bucket size is incremented by the value of PDR (that is, up to a maximum value of PBS+PDS). Every time a packet is received it is allowed if the packet size is less than or equal to the bucket size, and the bucket size is then correspondingly decremented by the size of the received packet. This is illustrated in Figure 9.44.

Note that RFC 3212 states that setting either the PBS or the PDR to positive infinity guarantees that all packets will always fall within the acceptable rate, but this is not actually true within the first second of operation if only the PDR is set to infinity.

The committed data rate of an LSP is the rate at which the MPLS network guarantees to be available to the data on the LSP. This rate is specified in terms of the other three parameters. The CDR (in bytes per second) is the data rate that the network pledges to be able to carry for the LSP, and the CBS (in bytes) is the maximum burst size that the network promises to handle. The EBS (in bytes) allows for bursts of data to exceed the committed data rate and still be guaranteed delivery. Again, a formal token bucket model can be defined for the committed data rate, but it is not a requirement that an LSR implements this model. Two buckets are defined: the committed bucket initialized to the value of CBS and the excess bucket initialized to the value of EBS. Every second the committed bucket is incremented by the value of CDR up to a maximum of the value of CBS, and the excess bucket is incremented by the value of CDR up to a maximum of the value of EBS. (Note that RFC 3212 is confused between an implementation that counts bytes in a bucket and one that counts the receipt of acceptable packets. It erroneously says that the increment each second should be by just one, which would very quickly lead to a situation in which no data could pass for a very long time.) When a packet arrives, if the size is greater than or equal to the committed bucket size, the packet is accepted and the committed bucket size is decremented by the size of the packet. If the packet size is greater than the committed bucket size, it is compared against the excess bucket size instead—if the excess bucket size is greater than or equal to the packet size, it is decremented by the size of the packet and the packet is accepted. If the packet size is greater than both the bucket sizes, the packet falls outside the committed rate and need not be forwarded. Figure 9.45 shows the committed data rate buckets in a simple example.

CDR is actually an average, and it may be important to control the sampling interval that is used to measure the rate. To indicate the frequency of the sampling, the Traffic Parameters TLV includes a Frequency field which may be set as follows:

- Very Frequent (2) requests that the available flow rate should be at least the CDR when averaged over any time period equal to or longer than the shortest time taken to receive a packet.
- Frequent (1) requests that the available flow rate should be at least the CDR when averaged over any time period equal to or longer than "a small number of shortest packet times."
- Unspecified (0) requests that the available flow rate should be at least the CDR when any (that is, some reasonable) average is applied.

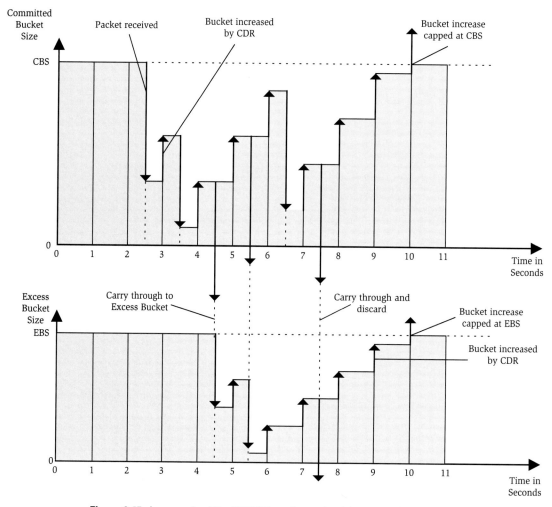

Figure 9.45 An example of the CR-LDP formal committed data rate token buckets.

It is not necessary to discard packets that exceed the committed data rate as long as resources are available to forward them. At any time there are likely to be some spare unreserved resources on an LSR and it might be regarded as unhelpful not to use these to forward traffic; further, there may be reserved resources that are underutilized. (This view of unhelpful depends upon who is providing the service and who is paying for it!) The Weight field in the Traffic Parameters TLV indicates the relative share of the unused resources that may be allocated to the LSP. Weight is specified as a number from 1 to 255 where the higher number means that the LSP has greater weight and should be assigned more of the unused bandwidth than an LSP with a lesser weight, although the precise algorithm for achieving this is not part of the CR-LDP specification. A value of zero indicates that weight is not applicable, but does not preclude spare resources being used for the LSP.

When an LSR requests an LSP to be set up it builds a Label Request message. If it wishes the LSP path to be constrained by the availability of network resources and for those resources to be reserved along the route of the LSP, it includes the traffic parameters for the flow it intends to place on the LSP. It describes the traffic it intends to generate using the PDR and PSB, and requests service from the network using the CDR, CSB, and ESB. If it is prepared to compromise on some or all of the characteristics of the flow, it sets bits in the Flags field to indicate which elements of the traffic parameters TLV may be negotiated by other LSRs in the network. Six of the eight bits have meaning— the list is shown in Table 9.6.

When an LSR receives a Label Request message that carries a Traffic Parameters TLV, it first checks the parameters for correctness and consistency (for example, that the value of PDR is less than or equal to the value of CDR) and sends back an error notification using a Notification message if there are any problems. The receiving LSR then checks to see whether it can reserve the resources necessary to meet the demands of the traffic flow. In many implementations this will require a resource reservation on the incoming and outgoing interfaces—the outgoing interface may actually be chosen as the result of a constraint-based routing decision using the explicit route and the signaled traffic parameters. If the requested flow can be satisfied, the LSR reserves the required resources and forwards the Label Request. Note that the LSR is reserving resources as the Label Request is propagated and before the label has been allocated—this ensures that the resources will remain available for the LSP and will not be stolen by another LSP that is set up through the same LSR.

Table 9.6 Interpretation of the Bits in the CR-LDP Traffic Parameters TLV Flags Field

Bit 0	Reserved (transmitted first)
Bit 1	Reserved
Bit 2	Set if the PDR field is negotiable
Bit 3	Set if the PBS field is negotiable
Bit 4	Set if the CDR field is negotiable
Bit 5	Set if the CBS field is negotiable
Bit 6	Set if the EBS field is negotiable
Bit 7	Set if the weight field is negotiable

If the necessary resources are not available but a smaller reservation can be satisfied, the LSR may configure itself for a lesser flow, provided that the traffic parameters are marked as negotiable in the received TLV. In this case, the LSR updates the traffic parameters (always to numerically lower values) before forwarding the Label Request message. If the requested traffic parameters cannot be satisfied, the LSR returns a Notification message to indicate failure.

When the end-point of the LSP turns the Label Request around as a Label Mapping message, it echoes back the traffic parameters that it received after applying any local negotiation. As the Label Mapping message is propagated through the network, the traffic parameters are not updated, so the message received at the head end of the LSP indicates the smallest set of parameters within the network and guides the ingress LER on the rate at which to apply data to the LSP. Each LSR on the LSP may update its reservations to reflect the new traffic parameters if the requirements have decreased so that it frees up any unneeded resources. If the traffic parameters that reach the ingress are unacceptably small, the LER must tear down the LSP and resignal it without the use of negotiation, or it may attempt to increase the reservation using in-place modification of the existing LSP.

Rerouting and Pinning the LSP

Strict hops within an explicit route are fixed points within an LSP, but loose hops allow some variation in the intermediate LSRs along the route. Similarly, abstract nodes that define a collection of nodes rather than a precise address of a single LSR provide for flexibility in routing. Once an LSP has been established, changes in the topology, or changes in resource availability, may mean that a better route becomes available. CR-LDP can take advantage of these changes if they occur on the flexible part of the route of the LSP by rerouting the LSP.

The rerouting procedure must take into account the fact that data is flowing and must not cause any interruption to that flow. Consider the network in Figure 9.46. At step 1, an LSP is requested from LSR A to LSR F with the explicit route {strict A, strict B, loose E, strict F}. Step 2 shows LSR B routing this LSP through LSR C—perhaps LSR X is not available at the time. The Label Request reaches LSR F (step 3) and is turned around as a Label Mapping, which makes its way back to LSR A (step 4). The LSP is not established from LSR A to LSR F through LSRs B, C, D, and E.

After some time, LSR X becomes available and the routing computation at LSR B determines that a better route within the constraints of the explicit route is via LSR X (step 5). Without making any changes to its LFIB, LSR B sends a Label Request message to LSR X, setting the LSPID to match that of the existing LSP and setting the Action flag to indicate *modify*. LSR X treats this Label Request in the usual way (step 6) and forwards it with the Action flag unchanged. LSR E sees the Action flag and recognizes that this is a change to the existing LSP, so it does not forward the Label Request, but makes the required reservations on

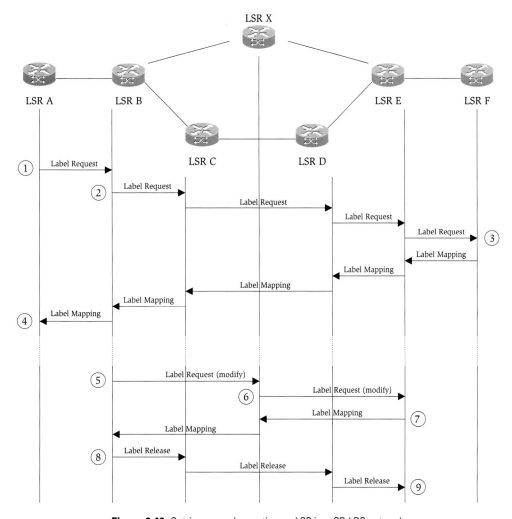

Figure 9.46 Setting up and rerouting an LSP in a CR-LDP network.

the incoming interface, allocates a new label, adds a new entry to its LFIB, does not delete the old entry from the LFIB, and returns a Label Mapping message (step 7). When the Label Mapping message arrives at LSR B it sees the Action flag in the LSPID TLV and knows that it doesn't need to forward the Label Mapping message. LSR B replaces the entry in its LFIB with the new label, at which point the data is flowing down the new route of the LSP. All that remains is to clear up the old segment of LSP, so LSR B sends a Label Release message down the old path to LSR C (step 8). When the Label Release message reaches LSR E (step 9) it notices that it has two upstream segments for the same LSPID, so it does not forward the Label Release message but simply cleans up on the old path.

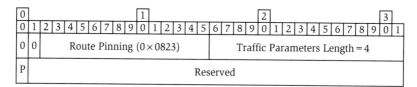

Figure 9.47 The CR-LDP Route Pinning TLV.

Sometimes it is undesirable to reroute an LSP as described in the preceding paragraph. For example, the LSP may traverse a part of the network that is subject to a high rate of change, or it may be known that the process of updating the LFIB at the point of divergence in the path (LSR B in Figure 9.46) causes an unacceptable hit to the traffic flow. In this case the LSP needs to be *pinned* to its route.

Pinning can be achieved by specifying every hop in the path as a strict hop with explicit definition. This is not always possible or desirable, so a Route Pinning TLV (Figure 9.47) is introduced on Label Request messages. If the Route Pinning TLV is present with its P-bit set to 1, the LSP that is set up may not be rerouted at a later time.

Coloring the LSP

When an LSP is requested, the network manager may wish to assign it to an administrative group so that it can be handled within the network according to the policy and admission control rules associated with that group. For example, resources on an LSR may be reserved for use by different administrative groups so that LSPs designated to carry high-priority data can be assured of available resources. Alternatively, new LSPs of another group may not be allowed to take more than 25 percent of the unused resources. A further use of administrative groups is to associate them with *resources classes* defined for each link in the network and advertised by the routing protocols. This allows the network topology to be pruned before routing decisions are made, simplifying the routing process and making it possible to classify links as stable/unstable, reserved for high priority, reserved for low bandwidth, and so forth.

Each administrative group is assigned an identifier or *color* which is signaled on the LSP using the Resource Class TLV shown in Figure 9.48. The color is specified as a 32-bit integer. It is an implementation decision both within the LSR and within the MPLS domain how the signaled resource class is interpreted.

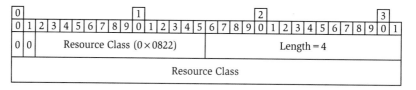

Figure 9.48 The CR-LDP Resource Class TLV.

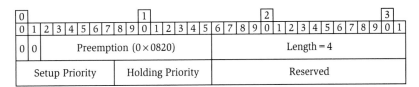

Figure 9.49 CR-LDP Preemption TLV.

LSP Priorities

CR-LDP supports preemption through the use of setup and holding priorities signaled in the Preemption TLV shown in Figure 9.49. Both priorities are encoded as 8-bit integers but are restricted to the numeric range zero to 7. Zero is the higher priority—that is, an LSP with holding priority zero cannot be preempted, but an LSP with setup priority 3 can preempt an LSP with holding priority 5. In the absence of this optional TLV, both the setup and holding priorities of a CR-LDP LSP default to 4. The setup priority of an LSP should not be greater than (that is, numerically less than) the holding priority, otherwise preemption thrash may happen, with two LSPs endlessly preempting each other.

Preemption is, of course, subject to all of the other constraints of the LSPs so that preemption will not occur unless a suitable route within the requirements of the administrative group is found.

9.6.3 New Status Codes

CR-LDP uses the LDP Notification message to indicate errors and events in the same way as in LDP. The Status TLV can carry any of the status codes defined for LDP, but the set of values that can be signaled is extended by those in Table 9.7. For clarity, all of the new status codes come from a range beginning with 0x04000000. Note that each of these new statuses reports on a single LSP only

Table 9.7 Additional Status Codes for CR-LDP

Status Code	Meaning
0x04000001	Bad Explicit Routing TLV Error
0x04000002	Bad Strict Node Error
0x04000003	Bad Loose Node Error
0x04000004	Bad Initial ER-Hop Error
0x04000005	Resource Unavailable
0x04000006	Traffic Parameters Unavailable
0x04000007	LSP Preempted
0x04000008	Modify Request Not Supported

and does not need to affect the LDP session, so the E-bit should be set to zero. All Notification messages associated with CR-LDP LSPs must be forwarded to the end points of the LSP and so should have the F-bit set to 1.

9.6.4 CR-LDP Messages

No new messages are introduced to support CR-LDP, but new rules define which TLVs are mandatory, mandatory for CR-LDP, optional for CR-LDP, or optional on any message. The category, of "mandatory for CR-LDP" can be expressed as "mandatory if the FEC TLV contains the CR-LSP FEC element or if the LSPID TLV is present in the message." Similarly, the category "optional for CR-LDP" could be expressed as "optional, but may only be present if the LSPID TLV is present." These rules are summarized for Label Request and Label Mapping messages in Table 9.8. Label Withdraw, Label Release, Label Abort,

Table 9.8 TLV Presence on CR-LDP Messages

Message	TLV	Presence
Label Request	Message ID	Mandatory
	FEC TLV	Mandatory
	LSPID TLV	Mandatory for CR-LDP
	ER-TLV	Optional for CR-LDP
	Traffic Parameters TLV	Optional for CR-LDP
	Route Pinning TLV	Optional for CR-LDP
	Resource Class TLV	Optional for CR-LDP
	Preemption TLV	Optional for CR-LDP
	Hop Count TLV	Optional
	Path Vector TLV	Optional
Label Mapping	Message ID	Mandatory
	FEC TLV	Mandatory
	Label TLV	Mandatory
	Label Request Message ID TLV	Mandatory (downstream on demand)
	LSPID TLV	Optional for CR-LDP (required if on Label Request)
	Traffic Parameters TLV	Optional for CR-LDP (required if on Label Request)
	Hop Count TLV	Optional
	Path Vector TLV	Optional

and Notification messages are unchanged for CR-LDP except to note that the LSPID TLV is an optional parameter on each of them. Discovery, session establishment, address advertisement, and KeepAlive messages are unchanged.

Figure 9.46 showed the basic message flows for CR-LDP LSP establishment. The following figures show some of the special cases. In Figure 9.50 the ingress LSR starts to set up an LSP (step 1) but some time later, and before the LSP has been fully established, it changes its mind and decides to abort the setup (step 3). The Label Request message has already reached the egress and been turned around as a Label Mapping message (step 2). In the middle of the network the Label Mapping and Label Abort messages pass each other (steps 4 and 5) so that LSR C receives the Label Abort when it has already installed the LSP and must send a Label Release to remove the LSP from downstream nodes (step 6). On the other hand, LSR B receives the Label Mapping after it has processed the Label Abort (step 7). Since the Label Mapping message indicates that it is responding to a Label Request, LRR B knows that it can simply discard the message.

Figure 9.51 shows the simple flow when an attempt to set up an LSP fails for some reason (perhaps the resources or the route are not available). The Label Request is issued by LSR A (step 1) and when it reaches LSR C (step 2) it cannot be satisfied. It is responded to with a Notification message (step 3) carrying a suitable status code and requesting that it be forwarded all of the way to the ingress of the LSR. When the Notification reaches the ingress (step 4), all record of the LSP has been removed.

Figure 9.52 shows how a CR-LDP may be torn down from the egress node. The example assumes that the LSP has been established at some time in the past. LSR D wants to stop receiving traffic on the LSP—perhaps the application that handles the traffic is going down. LSR D sends a Label Withdraw message (step 1), which is propagated through the network to the ingress (step 2). LSR A,

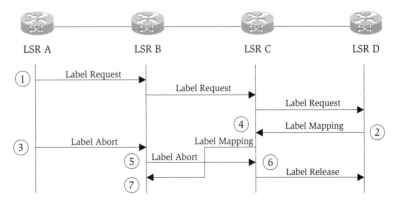

Figure 9.50 Aborting LSP setup in a Downstream on Demand LDP or CR-LDP network.

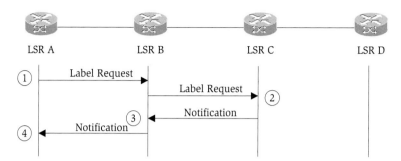

Figure 9.51 LSP setup failure and subsequent cleanup in a Downstream on Demand LDP or CR-LDP network.

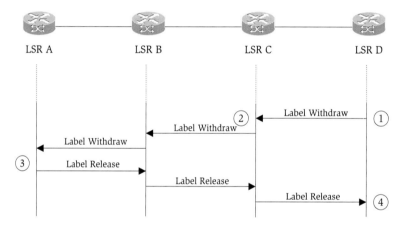

Figure 9.52 Handling a request for LSP teardown from a downstream LSR in a Downstream on Demand LDP or CR-LDP network.

the ingress, sees the Label Withdraw as a request rather than a demand, and it is a local policy decision that determines how it reacts. It may choose to ignore the request and continue sending traffic, in which case LSR D would still be able to decisively and ungracefully kill the LSP by sending a Notification message. Alternatively, as illustrated in step 3 and step 4, LSR A may cleanly finish sending data and then release the label. Nodes in the network must not remove the labels from their LFIBs until they see the Label Release message.

Figures 9.53 and 9.54 depict sample CR-LDP PDUs that might be exchanged while an LSP is being set up. As you can see, the messages are considerably longer and more complex than those used in basic LDP, but they do achieve significantly more function in terms of control and management of the network.

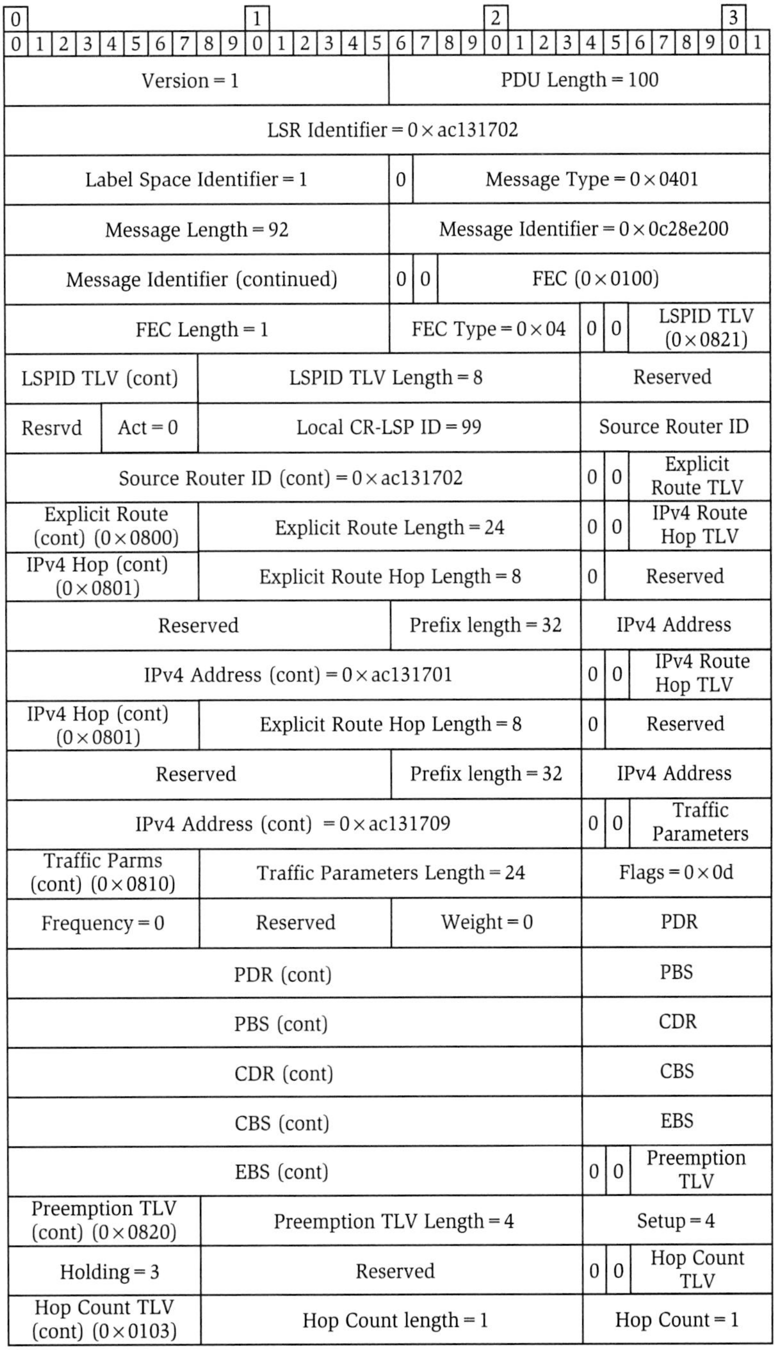

0										1										2										3	
0	1	2	3	4	5	6	7	8	9	0	1	2	3	4	5	6	7	8	9	0	1	2	3	4	5	6	7	8	9	0	1

Version = 1			PDU Length = 100		
LSR Identifier = 0 × ac131702					
Label Space Identifier = 1		0	Message Type = 0 × 0401		
Message Length = 92			Message Identifier = 0 × 0c28e200		
Message Identifier (continued)		0 0	FEC (0 × 0100)		
FEC Length = 1		FEC Type = 0 × 04	0 0	LSPID TLV (0 × 0821)	
LSPID TLV (cont)	LSPID TLV Length = 8		Reserved		
Resrvd	Act = 0	Local CR-LSP ID = 99		Source Router ID	
Source Router ID (cont) = 0 × ac131702			0 0	Explicit Route TLV	
Explicit Route (cont) (0 × 0800)	Explicit Route Length = 24		0 0	IPv4 Route Hop TLV	
IPv4 Hop (cont) (0 × 0801)	Explicit Route Hop Length = 8		0	Reserved	
Reserved		Prefix length = 32		IPv4 Address	
IPv4 Address (cont) = 0 × ac131701			0 0	IPv4 Route Hop TLV	
IPv4 Hop (cont) (0 × 0801)	Explicit Route Hop Length = 8		0	Reserved	
Reserved		Prefix length = 32		IPv4 Address	
IPv4 Address (cont) = 0 × ac131709			0 0	Traffic Parameters	
Traffic Parms (cont) (0 × 0810)	Traffic Parameters Length = 24		Flags = 0 × 0d		
Frequency = 0	Reserved	Weight = 0	PDR		
PDR (cont)			PBS		
PBS (cont)			CDR		
CDR (cont)			CBS		
CBS (cont)			EBS		
EBS (cont)		0 0	Preemption TLV		
Preemption TLV (cont) (0 × 0820)	Preemption TLV Length = 4		Setup = 4		
Holding = 3	Reserved		0 0	Hop Count TLV	
Hop Count TLV (cont) (0 × 0103)	Hop Count length = 1		Hop Count = 1		

Figure 9.53 A CR-LDP Label Request message.

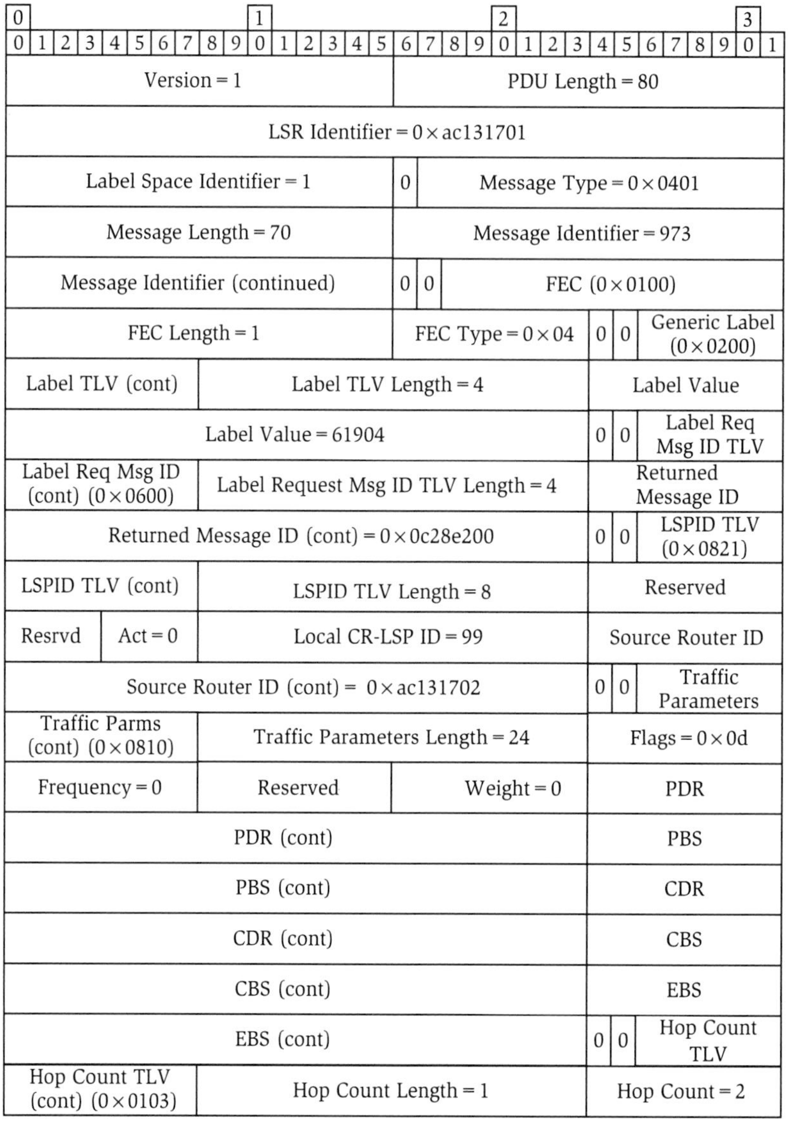

0										1										2										3	
0	1	2	3	4	5	6	7	8	9	0	1	2	3	4	5	6	7	8	9	0	1	2	3	4	5	6	7	8	9	0	1

Version = 1	PDU Length = 80
LSR Identifier = 0 × ac131701	
Label Space Identifier = 1 / 0	Message Type = 0 × 0401
Message Length = 70	Message Identifier = 973
Message Identifier (continued) / 0 0	FEC (0 × 0100)
FEC Length = 1	FEC Type = 0 × 04 / 0 0 / Generic Label (0 × 0200)
Label TLV (cont) / Label TLV Length = 4	Label Value
Label Value = 61904	0 0 / Label Req Msg ID TLV
Label Req Msg ID (cont) (0 × 0600) / Label Request Msg ID TLV Length = 4	Returned Message ID
Returned Message ID (cont) = 0 × 0c28e200	0 0 / LSPID TLV (0 × 0821)
LSPID TLV (cont) / LSPID TLV Length = 8	Reserved
Resrvd / Act = 0 / Local CR-LSP ID = 99	Source Router ID
Source Router ID (cont) = 0 × ac131702	0 0 / Traffic Parameters
Traffic Parms (cont) (0 × 0810) / Traffic Parameters Length = 24	Flags = 0 × 0d
Frequency = 0 / Reserved / Weight = 0	PDR
PDR (cont)	PBS
PBS (cont)	CDR
CDR (cont)	CBS
CBS (cont)	EBS
EBS (cont)	0 0 / Hop Count TLV
Hop Count TLV (cont) (0 × 0103) / Hop Count Length = 1	Hop Count = 2

Figure 9.54 A CR-LDP Label Mapping message.

9.7   Extensions to RSVP for LSP Tunnels (RSVP-TE)

A second protocol suitable for label distribution in traffic engineered MPLS networks is based on the Resource Reservation Protocol (RSVP) examined in Chapter 6. RSVP is suitable for extension to the MPLS world because it deals with end-to-end reservation of resources for traffic flows, a concept similar to traffic engineered MPLS. On the other hand, it does not address all of the requirements needed for MPLS (most notably label distribution and control of paths through explicit routes).

RSVP was first extended for this kind of application by Cisco when it was developing Tag Switching. Since then the IETF has published *RSVP-TE: Extensions to RSVP for LSP Tunnels* as RFC 3209.

The reader is advised to read Section 6.5 on RSVP before reading the rest of this section.

9.7.1 Reuse of RSVP Function

RSVP-TE manages to reuse RSVP fairly comprehensively. All seven of the RSVP messages find a use in RSVP-TE, although the ResvConf is less significant than it is when used for RSVP. RSVP is essentially a request/response protocol with Path messages being used to navigate a path and request resources for traffic flows, and Resv messages returning along the path to indicate what resources should be reserved. This flow of messages matches the requirements for Downstream on Demand label distribution and can be extended easily by adding information to the messages. Since RSVP messages are built from *objects*, which are basically LTV structures, this is easily achieved (recall that in RSVP, objects are presented as Length-Type-Variable triplets in which the Length field defines the length of the triplet, including the Length and Type fields).

Although RSVP contains good mechanisms for describing traffic and for specifying reservation requirements, it does not have facilities for other aspects necessary in a traffic engineered MPLS protocol. Extensions are necessary to cover the following features, which are described in more detail in the following sections.

- Label management.
- Requesting and controlling routes.
- Preempting resources.
- Maintaining connectivity between RSVP-TE LSRs.

Additionally, a big concern inherited from RSVP is the processing overhead associated with the soft state nature of the protocol. In traffic engineered MPLS, LSPs do not always need to fluctuate according to changes in the routing database; in fact, if an LSP has been set up using a strict explicit route, it doesn't need to change at all. Furthermore, there are satisfactory methods in RSVP-TE for controlled rerouting of an LSP. For these reasons and the reasons expressed in the RSVP section of this book, the techniques of refresh reduction described in Section 6.4.12 and *RSVP Refresh Overhead Reduction Extensions* (RFC 2961) are very relevant to MPLS.

One of the objectives of the designers of RSVP-TE was to allow RSVP and RSVP-TE to operate in the same networks at the same time. This has not led to any startling design choices, but has resulted in a few small quirks, which are highlighted in the following sections.

9.7.2 Distributing Labels

LSP setup is requested in RSVP-TE using Downstream on Demand label distribution by the inclusion of a Label Request Object on a Path message. It is the presence of this object that distinguishes this and all other messages on this session as RSVP-TE rather than RSVP transactions.

The requester indicates the type of label that it is interested in (general, ATM, or Frame Relay) by the C-Type of the object, and if the label is for ATM or Frame Relay the requester also indicates the range of acceptable labels as governed by the hardware capabilities and local policy. The three formats of the Label Request Object are shown in Figure 9.55. All three formats also carry a Layer Three Protocol ID to indicate to the egress of the LSP what kind of traffic it should expect to discover when it removes the shim header from the MPLS packets.

The Resv message that successfully responds to the Path message that carried a Label Request Object advertises a label using the Label Object, as shown in Figure 9.56. The label is conveyed within a 32-bit field and is right-justified and left-padded with zero bits.

9.7.3 Identifying LSPs

RSVP sessions are identified using a Session Object present on all RSVP messages, and this practice is continued in RSVP-TE. Two new C-types are introduced to distinguish the IPv4 LSP Tunnel Session and the IPv6 LSP Tunnel Session, shown in Figure 9.57.

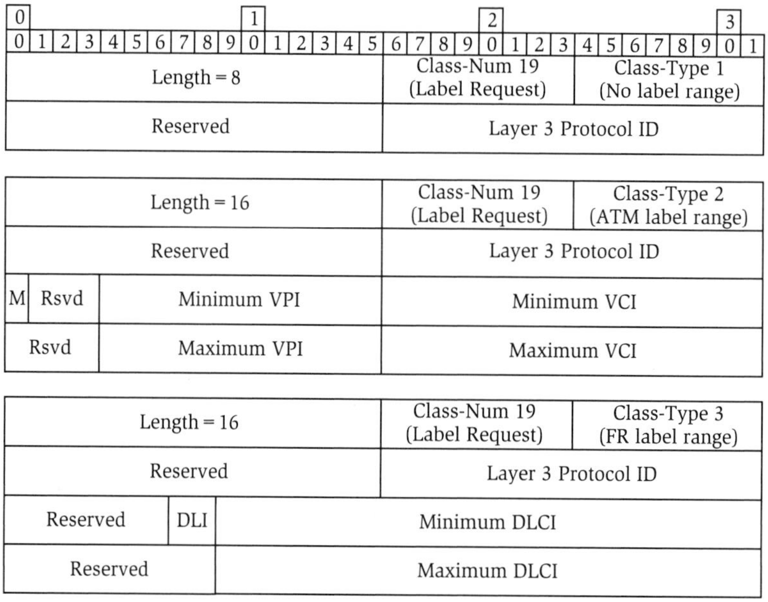

Figure 9.55 The RSVP-TE Label Request Objects.

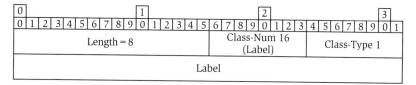

Figure 9.56 The RSVP-TE Label Object.

The destination address field is common between the RSVP and RSVP-TE Session Objects, but from there on the fields are different (although you will find some implementers and implementations so entrenched in RSVP that they refer to the new Tunnel ID field as the port ID). To ensure that there is no accidental overlap or interpretation of the Protocol ID and Flags fields from the RSVP Session Object, the Reserved field of the RSVP-TE Session Object must be set to zero. The Tunnel ID field is used to give a unique identifier to the tunnel, and the Extended Tunnel ID gives context to the name space from which the Tunnel ID was chosen—it is usually set to the source address of the tunnel.

If LSP merging is desirable, all ingresses must use the same session identifier. This means that the Tunnel ID must be known to all sources (possibly as a feature of the application that requests the tunnel, or possibly through a management protocol) and that each source must use the same Extended Tunnel ID. This last point means that for LSP merging, the Extended Tunnel ID cannot be the source address of the tunnel, and a well-known value (usually zero) must be used.

The Sender Template is used to identify traffic flows in RSVP within the context of a session. In RSVP-TE there may often be little difference between a traffic flow and a tunnel, and the RSVP-TE form of the Sender Template Object shown in Figure 9.58 includes a Source Address as in RSVP and an LSP ID to replace the Source Port. The LSP ID is unique within the context of the Source Address and in many implementations represents an *instance* of the tunnel identified by the Tunnel ID of the Session Object. This concept of tunnel instances is useful in configurations in which a series of alternative routes are configured for the same tunnel for use either as alternatives when one route fails, or in parallel to offer distribution of traffic along different paths.

As in RSVP, FilterSpecs have the same format as Sender Templates and are differentiated solely by the C-num, which is 10 for a FilterSpec.

9.7.4 Managing Routes

Explicit routes can be signaled in RSVP-TE by the inclusion of an Explicit Route Object. This object is a single header followed by a series of subobjects. Perversely, the subobjects are encoded as TLVs not LTVs, but the value of the Length field still includes the Type and Length fields. The Explicit Route Object and the Explicit Route Subobjects are shown in Figure 9.59. They are subject to the processing rules described in Section 9.5. Each subobject begins with a single-bit flag to indicate whether the hop is strict or loose. Unlike CR-LDP,

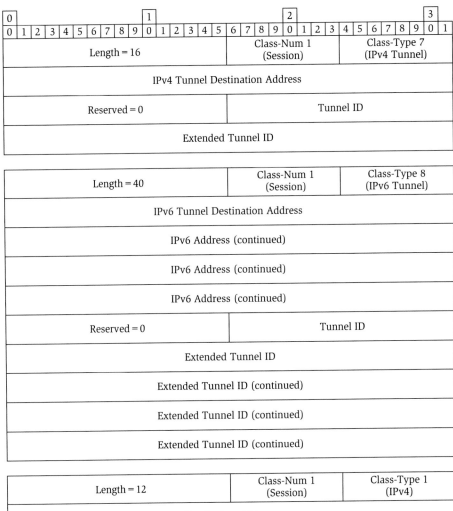

Figure 9.57 The RSVP-TE Session Objects with the RSVP IPv4 Session Object for comparison.

there is no subobject to encode an LSP ID, meaning that secondary action is required if one LSP is to be tunneled through another—for example, the outer tunnel can be installed as an IP interface, and the inner LSP can be routed through the address of the new interface.

RSVP-TE also includes a mechanism known as *route recording*. The Record Route Object may be present on Path or Resv messages and it records the hops

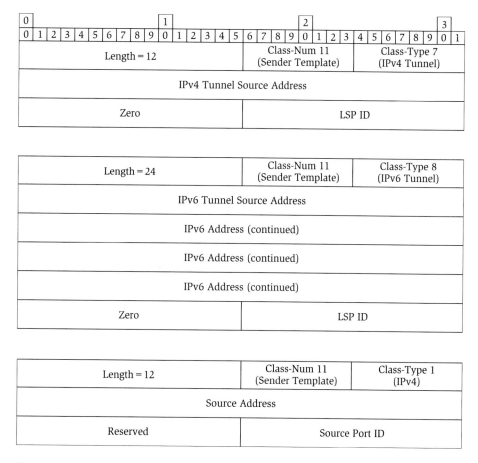

Figure 9.58 The RSVP-TE Sender Template Objects with the RSVP IPv4 Sender Template Object for comparison.

through which the message has been routed. When received at the egress or ingress, the Record Route Object gives a full picture of the path of the tunnel. At transit nodes, the Record Route Object from the Path and Resv messages must be combined to see the full route.

The rules for including the Record Route Object are simple: If the object is present on a received message, it should also be present on the message when it is forwarded. The ingress node is free to choose whether to include the Record Route Object on a Path message. The egress LSR must include the Record Route Object in the Resv it sends if it was present in the received Path message.

Each node processing the Record Route Object adds itself to the head of a list of nodes. RFC 3209 is careful to say that the address added may be "any network-reachable interface address," but conventionally the address used is the address through which the Path message was received or the address out of which the Path message was sent. When a Record Route Object is received on

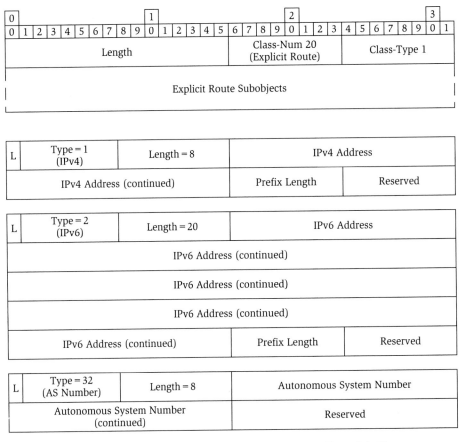

Figure 9.59 The RSVP-TE Explicit Route Object and Explicit Route Subobjects.

a Resv at the ingress node it "therefore" carries the precise sequence of addresses necessary to form a strict explicit route that follows the course of the LSP, and in this way route pinning can be achieved even if the LSP was originally set up using loose routes.

In fact, the Record Route Object, shown in Figure 9.60, is structured so that it may be converted to an Explicit Route Object with the minimum of effort. The fields are precisely aligned—note that there is no strict/loose bit in the Record Route Subobjects, and that this is consistent with the fact that any explicit route generated from a Record Route Object would have the strict/loose bits set to zero to indicate strict hops. Note that all of the hops in the Record Route Object are explicit nodes; that is, there are no prefixes and no abstract nodes—again, this is a feature of the recorded route representing every node in the path.

A Flags field (which corresponds to a reserved field in the Explicit Route subobjects) has two settings, both of which are permissible only if support for

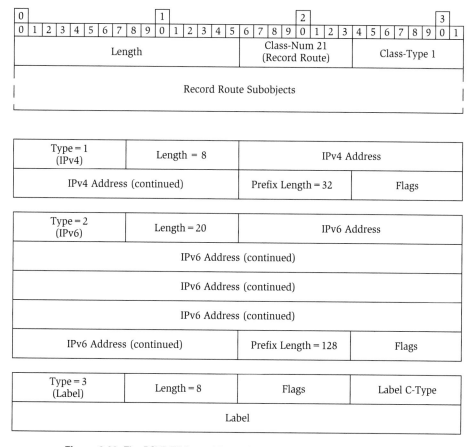

Figure 9.60 The RSVP-TE Record Route Object and Record Route Subobjects.

local protection was indicated in the Session Attributes Object (see Section 9.7.6) in the original Path message. The value 1 indicates that the link downstream of the node represented by this subobject can be protected through a local repair mechanism. The value 2 indicates that a local repair mechanism is currently in use to maintain this LSP.

A flag in the Session Attributes Object (see Section 9.7.6) is used to request that the Record Route Object will also collect information about the labels allocated at each hop. This is particularly useful for analyzing the behavior of the network and tracing data. Note that the Label Subobject breaks the formatting conventions of the other subobjects by putting the Flags field before the rest of the main value of the subobject—this is permissible because there is no Label Subobject in the Explicit Route Object. The Flags field in the Label Subobject has value 1 to indicate that the label comes from the Global Label Space and zero to show that this is a per-interface label. The Label C-Type is copied from the C-type of the corresponding Label Object (which is limited to the value 1 for RSVP-TE, but has extended use in Generalized MPLS).

It is possible that the construction of a Record Route Object will cause the Path or Resv message to grow to larger than the MTU size. In this case the Record Route is abandoned (that is, dropped from the message) and an error (PathErr or ResvErr) is sent to inform the ingress/egress of the problem.

9.7.5 Resource Requests and Reservation

FlowSpec objects are inherited from RSVP without any change. Recall that IntServ encodings are a little unusual in that the length counting the number of words in the IntServ descriptor does not include the header.

RSVP defines three reservation styles that allow for different modes of resource sharing. Two of these, Fixed Filter (FF) and Shared Explicit (SE), are supported in RSVP-TE, but the Wildcard Filter (WF) is not considered appropriate for traffic engineering since its real application is for multipoint-to-point flows in which only one sender sends at any time.

In RSVP-TE the choice of style is made by the egress node, but should be heavily influenced by the setting of the SE Style Desired bit in the Session Attributes Object (see the following section). If FF is used, a unique label and unique resource reservations are assigned to each sender (as specified in the Sender Template)—this means that there is no resource sharing and no merging of LSPs. SE style, on the other hand, allows sharing and merging, which is particularly useful in rerouting techniques such as make-before-break. Note that once SE style has been selected it is often necessary to take explicit action to prevent sharing of resources between LSPs targeted at the same egress, because the Tunnel ID may accidentally be the same for two distinct LSPs from two separate sources. This prevention is achieved by setting the Extended Tunnel ID to the IP address of the source node.

The choice between FF and SE styles is therefore governed by the function within the network. If resource sharing and LSP merging are not supported, FF must be used. Many existing MPLS implementations do not support SE style and will clear the SE Style Desired bit in the Session Attributes object as they forward the path message. This act in itself does not guarantee that the egress will not select the SE style, but may help to prevent it.

The Adspec object plays an important part in RSVP in recording what resources are available along a path to help the egress determine appropriate reservations to make. In RSVP-TE, however, Adspec adds little value.

Note that, as in RSVP, the resources in RSVP-TE are technically not reserved until the Resv message reaches a node. However, in practice, it is simple in RSVP-TE for a transit node to make a reliable guess as to the reservation requirements of an LSP, and so many implementations make a provisional resource reservation as they process the Path message. The final reservation requirements are still carried on the Resv message with the label, and may require a modification (which might fail) to what has already been reserved, but this is generally more efficient than handling resource contention when processing Resv messages.

9.7.6 Priorities, Preemption, and other Attributes

The Session Attribute Object, shown in Figure 9.61, is an optional object that contains additional qualifying details for the session and, hence, the tunnel. The setup and holding priorities necessary for preemption control are carried as values in the range zero to 7 (zero is the highest priority) and no default values have been defined to cover the case in which the Session Attribute Object is absent. Using a value of 4 as in CR-LDP is not unreasonable, but one might consider that the absence of any specified value should mean that the tunnel be treated as the lowest priority, that is, 7.

RSVP also contains a more complex priority scheme in the Preemption Priority Policy element. In practice, MPLS systems will likely use only the Session Attribute Object, but RFC 3209 explains in detail how to handle the case when both are present or when only the Preemption Priority Policy element is used.

Three bits are defined within the Flags field and are interpreted as follows.

- **0x01, Local protection desired**: This flag indicates that local repair mechanisms may be used to reroute the LSP around network faults after the LSP has been established and in violation of the explicit route.
- **0x02, Label recording desired**: This flag requests that the recorded route includes label information.
- **0x04, SE style desired**: This flag is used by the ingress node to state that it may wish to reroute the tunnel without first tearing it down. This is a request for the egress node to use the SE Style in the corresponding Resv.

The last element of the Session Attribute Object is a name. The name length gives the length in bytes, but note that the name field itself must be increased to a multiple of 4 bytes and right-padded with zeros. The name is intended to be a user-friendly printable string for diagnostics and management, but many implementations have found this a convenient place to hide additional control

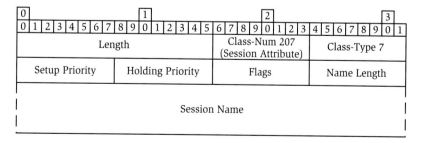

Figure 9.61 The RSVP-TE Session Attribute Object.

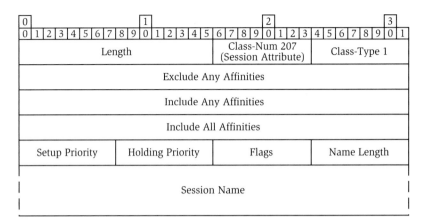

Figure 9.62 The RSVP-TE Session Attribute Object with resource affinities.

information, so don't be surprised to find strange, unprintable characters at the end of the name.

9.7.7 Coloring the LSP

RSVP-TE supports routing tunnels through the network using resource affinities. This can be used to help control free-routing when there is no explicit route present or when loose or nonexplicit hops are encountered. The individual links in the network are "colored" and the Path message is flagged with the colors that must not be used (exclude any), the colors at least one of which must be used (include any), and the colors that must be used (include all).

These three values are carried within a variant of the Session Attribute Object indicated by a different C-type value and shown in Figure 9.62. Only one Session Attribute Object may be present on a Path message.

The Exclude Any Affinities might more reasonably be known as the Exclude All Affinities since the inclusion of any of the listed affinities on a link renders the link unacceptable, but the logic says that it is the link that is excluded if any affinity matches, so the name is not wrong.

9.7.8 Detecting Errors and Maintaining Connectivity

In classic RSVP, if a network link fails, the routing protocol at both ends of the link will become aware of the problem through the failure of its Hello exchanges and will start to route packets down an alternative route (notwithstanding the fact that resources have not been reserved on that alternative route). This approach does not work for RSVP-TE because the packets are labeled and routing is not involved in their forwarding.

What is needed is for the control plane (that is, RSVP-TE signaling) to become aware of the network failure and to rapidly reroute the affected tunnels or report the failure to the ingress node. The existing methods of state refresh provide a mechanism to detect failures, but since state refresh is designed to tidy up after failure rather than to trigger recovery, the process is typically too slow. Any attempt to increase the refresh time on a per-LSP basis to be fast enough to handle errors would swamp the network with refresh messages.

This issue is combated in RSVP-TE by the introduction of a new message exchange. Each pair of adjacent LSRs exchanges Hello messages to keep the control connection between them open. It should be noted that this exchange is NOT a discovery mechanism as in LDP and CR-LDP, but is more akin to the KeepAlive processing of those protocols.

Figure 9.63 shows the new Hello message and its single mandatory object, the Hello Object. The Hello Object has 2 C-Types: the value 1 indicates a Hello Request, and the value 2 indicates a Hello Ack. Both variants of the object carry a source and destination instance number. When an LSR becomes aware of the existence of an RSVP-TE–capable neighbor through the receipt of a Path or Resv message it may start the Hello exchange.

The initiator of the Hello exchange uses a Hello Request Object and sets the source instance to some reference number (perhaps random, perhaps time-dependent) and the destination instance to zero. The receiver of such a Hello message responds with a Hello Ack Object carrying its own source instance and returning the received instance as the destination instance. The messages can now bounce back and forth, certifying that the link is active. RFC 3209 recommends that the default retransmission time for Hello messages is 5 milliseconds, and that a link should be declared down if no response is received in three-and-a-half times this interval. In practice, somewhat larger timer values are used, with the norm often being around 1 second.

If a node restarts after a failure of its software or of the link, it is required to select a new value for its source instance, allowing the following procedure to apply. If a Hello message is received with a destination identifier set to zero

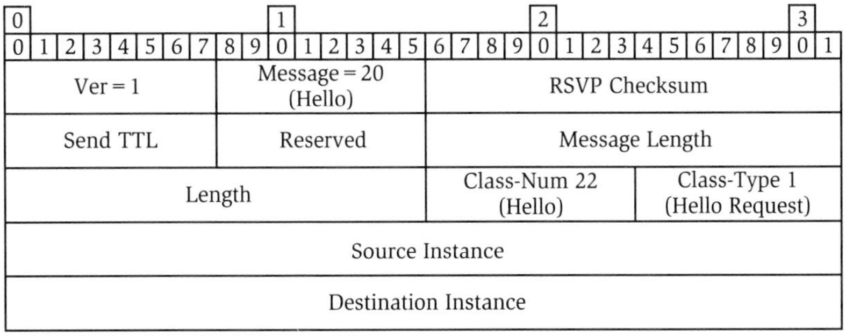

Figure 9.63 The RSVP-TE Hello message showing the Hello Request Object.

it indicates that the previous Hello message was not received. After this has happened a configurable number of times in a row the link should be declared to have failed. If the received Hello message does not reflect the correct destination identifier (that is, local source identifier) it also indicates some failure in the link. Finally, if a node detects a change in the remote instance identifier (that is, the received source identifier) it knows that the remote node has detected a link failure and has restarted.

The Hello exchange is usually (although not necessarily) stopped when the last piece of state between a pair of LSRs is removed.

9.7.9 Summary of Messages and Objects

Formal definitions of the messages in RSVP-TE can be found in RFC 3209 and, when a message is inherited direct from RSVP without modification, in RFC 2205. The notation used is called *Backus-Naur Form* (BNF) and is described in the Preface to this book. It is a list of mandatory and optional objects. Each object is denoted by angle brackets " < object > " and optional objects or sequences are contained in square brackets "[< optional object >]." Sequences of objects are sometimes displayed as a single composite object, which is defined later. Choices between objects are denoted by a vertical bar " < object one > | < object two > ."

Note that, while the ordering of objects within a message is strongly recommended, it is not mandatory (except that the members of composite objects must be kept together) and an implementation should be prepared to receive objects in any order while generating them in the order listed here.

Figure 9.64 shows the formal definition of the Path Message. The sequence of objects, Sender Template, Sender TSpec, Adspec, and Record Route are often referred to as the Sender Descriptor. This becomes relevant in the context of Resv messages, which may carry information relevant to more than one Sender Descriptor.

```
< Path Message > ::=     < Common Header >
                         [ < INTEGRITY > ]
                         < SESSION >
                         < RSVP_HOP >
                         < TIME_VALUES >
                         [ < EXPLICIT_ROUTE > ]
                         < LABEL_REQUEST >
                         < SESSION_ATTRIBUTE > ]
                         [ < POLICY_DATA > ]
                         < SENDER_TEMPLATE >
                         < SENDER_TSPEC >
                         [ < ADSPEC > ]
                         [ < RECORD_ROUTE > ]
```

Figure 9.64 Formal definition of the RSVP-TE Path message.

```
< Resv Message > ::=          < Common Header >
                              [ < INTEGRITY > ]
                              < SESSION >
                              < RSVP_HOP >
                              < TIME_VALUES >
                              [ < RESV_CONFIRM > ]
                              [ < SCOPE > ]
                              [ < POLICY_DATA > ]
                              < STYLE >
                              < flow descriptor list >
```

Figure 9.65 Formal definition of the RSVP-TE Resv message.

```
< FF flow descriptor list > ::=       < FLOWSPEC >
                                      < FF flow descriptor >
```

Figure 9.66 Formal definition of the RSVP-TE FF Flow Descriptor List used on RSVP-TE Resv messages.

```
< FF flow descriptor > ::=        < FILTER_SPEC >
                                  < LABEL >
                                  [ < RECORD_ROUTE > ]
                                  [ < FF flow descriptor list > | < FF flow descriptor > ]
```

Figure 9.67 Formal definition of the RSVP-TE FF Flow Descriptor used on RSVP-TE Resv messages.

Figure 9.65 shows the formal definition of a Resv message. The Flow Descriptor List (expanded in Figure 9.66) is a composite sequence of objects that allows a single Resv message to describe reservations for multiple Sender Descriptors requested on Path messages. Although this is less common in RSVP-TE than in RSVP, the practice is not without uses—it is often used to handle cases in which LSP tunnels merge at some LSR within the network. There are two methods of listing Flow Descriptors within RSVP-TE, depending on the Sender Selection Control field in the Style object. Only Fixed Filter and Shared Explicit styles are supported in RSVP-TE.

The FF Flow Descriptor is, itself, a composite object containing the FilterSpec and Label Objects and, optionally, a Record Route Object. It is shown in Figure 9.67. Notice that this definition of FF Flow Descriptor aligns with the definition of Sender Descriptor in the preceding paragraphs.

The last element of the FF Flow Descriptor is recursive, allowing a list of sublists where each sublist starts with a FlowSpec. It also allows the sublist to be just an FF Flow Descriptor—in this case the FlowSpec is assumed to be identical to the most recent one seen in the message.

```
< SE flow descriptor > ::=        < FLOWSPEC >
                                  < SE filter spec list >
```

Figure 9.68 Formal definition of the RSVP-TE SE Flow Descriptor List used on RSVP-TE Resv messages.

```
< SE filter spec list > ::=       < FILTER_SPEC >
                                  < LABEL >
                                  [ < RECORD_ROUTE > ]
                                  [ < SE filter spec list > ]
```

Figure 9.69 Formal definition of the RSVP-TE SE Filter Spec List used on RSVP-TE Resv messages.

```
< Hello Message > ::=             < Common Header >
                                  [ < INTEGRITY > ]
                                  < HELLO >
```

Figure 9.70 Formal definition of the RSVP-TE Hello message.

This rather complex notation facilitates a rather complex real-world situation in which multiple tunnels share resources; it is somewhat less likely in MPLS than in plain RSVP. Note that the notation used in these paragraphs differs slightly from that presented in RFC 3209 and derived from RFC 2205 (in an attempt at greater clarity).

Compound objects are also used for the Shared Explicit case, as shown in Figures 9.68 and 9.69, but note that here only one FlowSpec object may be present; the subsequent list of SE Filter Specifications matches Sender Descriptors and all use the one FlowSpec. Again, a variation on the notation of RFC 3209 is used here for clarity.

The other RSVP messages are not changed for RSVP-TE and can be found listed in Section 6.5. Obviously, when used for RSVP-TE the objects carried must be the RSVP-TE variants described in Sections 9.7.2 through 9.7.8.

The new RSVP-TE Hello message is described in Section 9.7.8 and may be formally defined by the BNF encoding in Figure 9.70.

9.7.10 Choosing a Transport Protocol

RSVP is defined to run over IP or UDP. UDP was provided as an option because many host systems did not support direct access to the IP stack and yet RSVP was seen as a host-to-host protocol.

On the other hand, RSVP-TE is intended only for MPLS, a router protocol being developed only on new equipment. It can be taken that direct access to the IP stack is available on all RSVP-TE systems and so RSVP-TE over UDP is not considered as an option (although there is nothing that would prevent it from working).

RSVP-TE uses the same protocol identifier (46, or 0x2E) as RSVP, and any differentiation that is necessary between RSVP and RSVP-TE must be made on the basis of the message objects and the sessions.

9.7.11 Security, Admission Control, and Policy Considerations

RSVP-TE is subject to the same security, admission control, and policy considerations as plain RSVP. These features can be managed using the Integrity and Policy objects defined in RSVP.

9.7.12 New Error Codes and Values

As new functions are introduced to RSVP through RSVP-TE, it becomes necessary to define new error codes and values to signal errors and events in PathErr and ResvErr messages. Table 9.9 sets out the new codes and values.

Table 9.9 New RSVP-TE Error Codes and Values

Error Code	Error Value Setting	Meaning
24		Routing problem
	1	Bad explicit route object
	2	Bad strict node
	3	Bad loose node
	4	Bad initial subobject
	5	No route available toward destination
	6	Unacceptable label value
	7	RRO indicated routing loops
	8	MPLS being negotiated, but non-RSVP-capable router in the path
	9	MPLS label allocation failure
	10	Unsupported L3PID
25		Notify Error
	1	RRO too large for MTU
	2	RRO notification
	3	Tunnel locally repaired

9.7.13 Message Flows

Set out on the following pages are sample message flows for RSVP-TE, covering the main LSP setup and teardown cases as well as a few edge conditions. Figure 9.71 shows the normal flow of messages for LSP establishment with a Path message issued by LSR A (step 1). When LSR B receives the Path message (step 2) it checks that it can satisfy the constraints in terms of resources and routes, may make a provisional resource reservation, and sends a Path message downstream. When the Path message reaches the egress (step 3) it also checks the constraints, and if all is well, reserves resources, allocates a label, and sends a Resv message back upstream. Transit nodes (step 4) allocate or confirm their resource reservations, choose an upstream label, install the received and upstream label in their LFIBs and send a Resv further upstream. When the Resv reaches the ingress node and it completes its resource reservations and adds the label to its LFIB, the LSP is established.

LSP teardown involves a simple unidirectional message flow. The ingress removes the label from its LFIB, releases the resources allocated to the LSP, and sends a PathTear message downstream. On receiving a Path Tear message, each node in the network also releases the label and resources before sending a PathTear onward. Should a PathTear message get lost, RSVP-TE relies on the soft state nature of RSVP to timeout the LSP remnants and continue to clean up in a downstream direction.

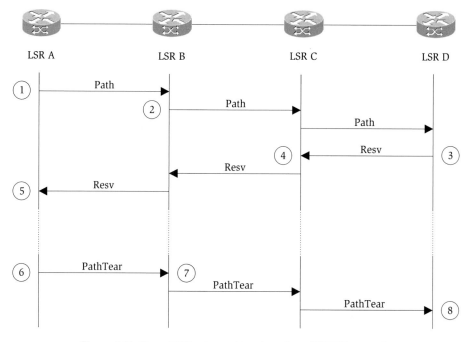

Figure 9.71 Normal LSP setup and teardown in an RSVP-TE network.

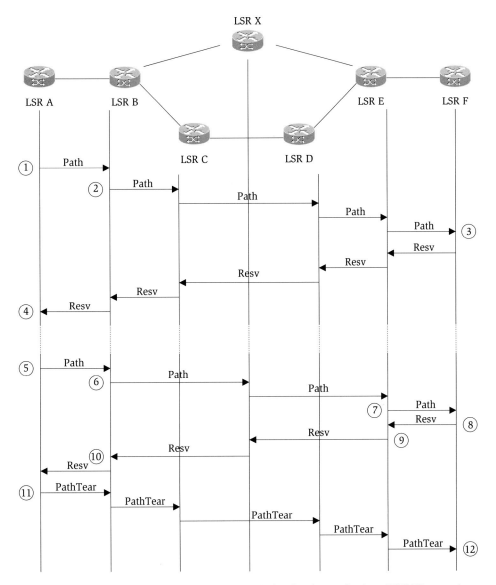

Figure 9.72 Setting up an LSP and applying make-before-break rerouting in an RSVP-TE network.

Figure 9.72 shows how an LSP can be set up and then rerouted. The process involved is called *make-before-break*, and it establishes the new path before the old one is torn down so that traffic can be transferred from one path to the other without interruption. By using the SE style, RSVP-TE is able to establish the new LSP sharing resources on common legs so that no over-provisioning is needed.

Steps 1 through 4 show an LSP being set up along the path A, B, C, D, E, F: the SE style is used. Some time later, LSR X becomes available, and since this offers a better path for the traffic, LSR A wants to reroute the LSP as A, B, X, E, F. At step 5 LSR A issues a new Path message carrying the desired explicit route through LSR X. It sets the Sender Object to exactly match the one on the original LSP (that is, the same destination, same tunnel ID, same extended tunnel ID), but it selects a new LSP ID in the Sender Template and sets the SE style desired bit in the Session Attributes object. LSR B (step 6) sends the Path message out toward LSR X and does not do anything about the old LSP. If LSR is reserving resources during Path processing, it notices that sharing is allowed. Similarly, when the paths converge at LSRs E and F resource sharing is allowed.

As the Resv progresses back across the network, labels are allocated and installed in the LFIBs. LSR F does not the same label for both old and new LSPs. LSR E allocates a new label to advertise to LSR X and installs a second mapping in its LFIB. LSR B (step 10) installs the new label from LSR X and immediately switches traffic to the new path. It uses the same label for both LSPs back to LSR A. When LSR A is satisfied that the new LSP is established, it uses a PathTear message to tear down the old one.

Figure 9.73 shows how the ingress LSR may abort an LSP setup request by sending a PathTear message before it receives a Resv. If the PathTear and Resv cross in the network (step 4), the PathTear continues to flow downstream as though a normal teardown was in progress, while an "unsolicited" Resv is received at an upstream node (step 5) and is discarded.

Figure 9.74 shows what happens when an LSP setup fails, perhaps because of resource or route unavailability. The ingress initiates LSP setup by sending a Path message (step 1). When this Path message reaches LSR C it is unable to process the message any further and returns a PathErr message indicating the problem (step 2). Neither LSR C nor the other transit nodes (LSR B) remove state. Instead, they wait for the ingress node to send PathTear (step 3) and only

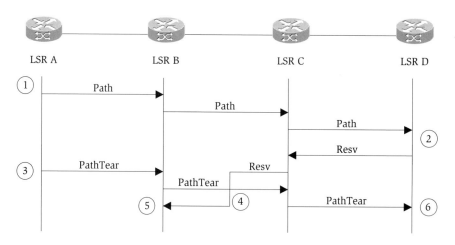

Figure 9.73 Aborting an LSP setup in an RSVP-TE network.

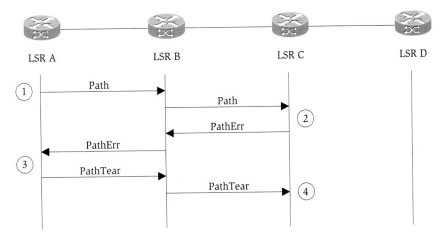

Figure 9.74 LSP setup failure and subsequent cleanup in an RSVP-TE network.

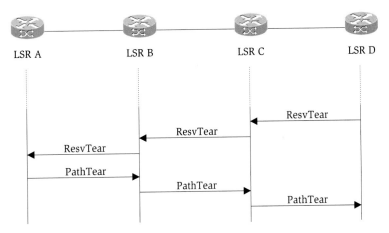

Figure 9.75 Handling a request for LSP teardown from a downstream LSR in an RSVP-TE network.

clear up Path state when they see the PathTear message (step 4). It is possible for the ingress to retry the Path message with changed constraints.

Figure 9.75 shows how an egress node may request the removal of an LSP. The ResvTear message indicates to the ingress node that the LSP is no longer appreciated and it can tear it down by sending PathTear. Alternatively, the ingress node is free to ignore the ResvTear, leaving Path refreshes to ensure that the forwarding state and reservations are still in place at transit nodes.

In fact, opinion varies about how transit nodes should support ResvTear messages. Some implementations choose to remove labels and release reserva-tions when they see a ResvTear. This approach means that traffic on the LSP

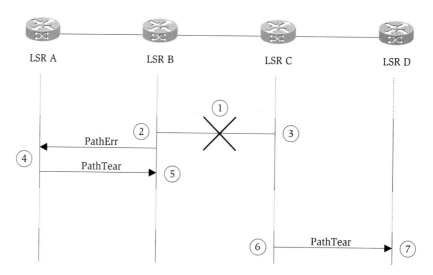

Figure 9.76 Reporting a network failure and cleaning up an LSP in an RSVP-TE network.

may be black-holed or at very best may emerge from the LSP and be forwarded as IP packets. Other implementations maintain the LSP completely until they see the PathTear message.

Finally, Figure 9.76 shows how a network failure (step 1) is handled in RSVP-TE. The failure is detected at the upstream node (step 2) and downstream node (step 3), perhaps by notification from hardware or lower-level protocols, or perhaps through the RSVP Hello protocol. The upstream node immediately reports the problem to upstream nodes by sending a PathErr message, but the downstream node is not required to do anything. The downstream node might choose to send an immediate PathTear message downstream, but this could interfere with future repair efforts and is not necessary.

When the ingress receives the PathErr message (step 4) it may make rerouting attempts and it may decide to retry along the existing route. Ultimately, however, if the LSP cannot be reestablished, the ingress sends a PathTear message to clean up the LSP. When the PathTear reaches the network break (step 5) it obviously cannot be sent any further.

The downstream part of the network is cleaned up when LSR C times out the LSP because it hasn't received a Path refresh from upstream. It sends a PathTear downstream (step 6) and the LSP is removed (step 7).

9.7.14 Sample Messages

Figures 9.77 and 9.78 depict sample RSVP-TE messages that might be exchanged while an LSP is being set up.

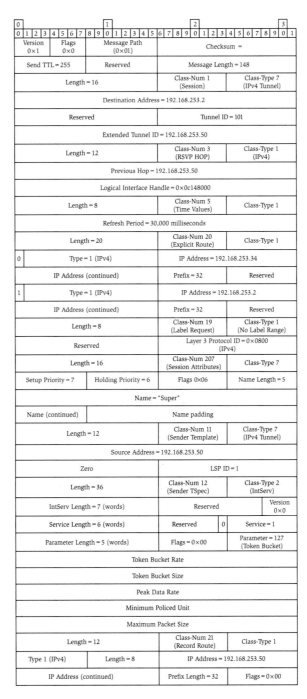

Figure 9.77 An example RSVP-TE Path message.

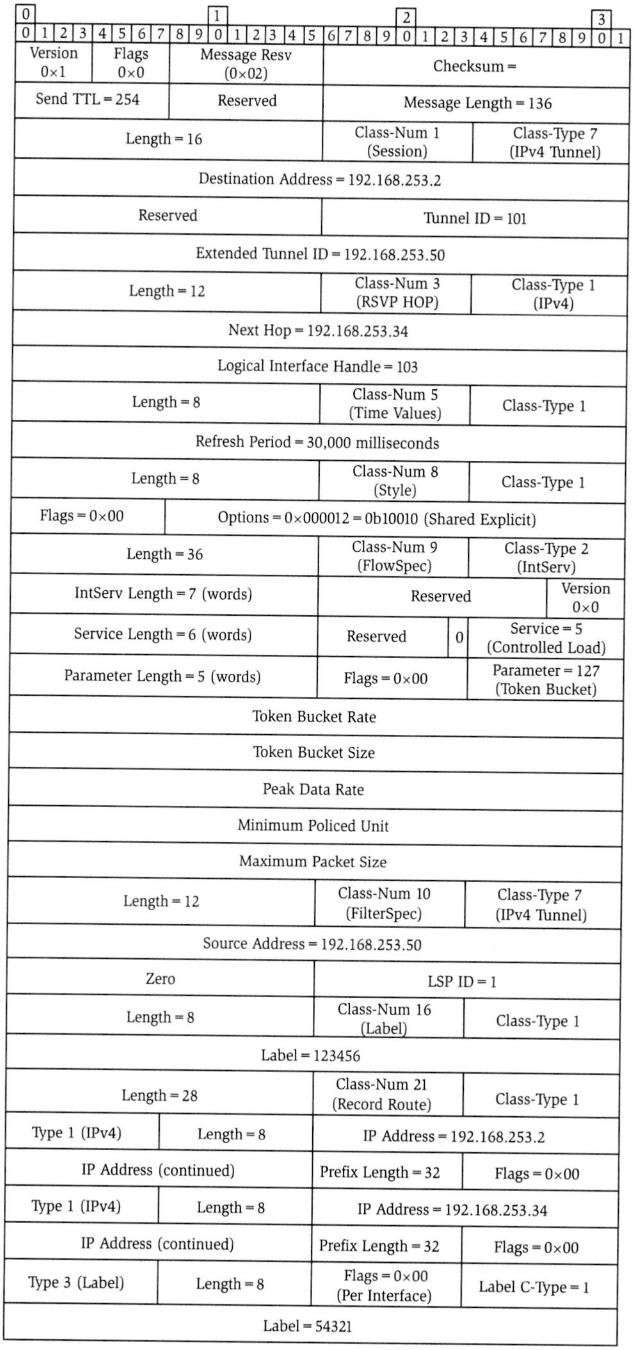

0			1			2			3	
0 1 2 3 4 5 6 7	8 9	0 1 2 3 4 5	6 7 8 9	0 1 2 3 4 5 6 7 8 9	0 1

Version 0×1	Flags 0×0	Message Resv (0×02)	Checksum =
Send TTL = 254		Reserved	Message Length = 136
Length = 16		Class-Num 1 (Session)	Class-Type 7 (IPv4 Tunnel)
Destination Address = 192.168.253.2			
Reserved		Tunnel ID = 101	
Extended Tunnel ID = 192.168.253.50			
Length = 12		Class-Num 3 (RSVP HOP)	Class-Type 1 (IPv4)
Next Hop = 192.168.253.34			
Logical Interface Handle = 103			
Length = 8		Class-Num 5 (Time Values)	Class-Type 1
Refresh Period = 30,000 milliseconds			
Length = 8		Class-Num 8 (Style)	Class-Type 1
Flags = 0×00		Options = 0×000012 = 0b10010 (Shared Explicit)	
Length = 36		Class-Num 9 (FlowSpec)	Class-Type 2 (IntServ)
IntServ Length = 7 (words)		Reserved	Version 0×0
Service Length = 6 (words)		Reserved 0	Service = 5 (Controlled Load)
Parameter Length = 5 (words)		Flags = 0×00	Parameter = 127 (Token Bucket)
Token Bucket Rate			
Token Bucket Size			
Peak Data Rate			
Minimum Policed Unit			
Maximum Packet Size			
Length = 12		Class-Num 10 (FilterSpec)	Class-Type 7 (IPv4 Tunnel)
Source Address = 192.168.253.50			
Zero		LSP ID = 1	
Length = 8		Class-Num 16 (Label)	Class-Type 1
Label = 123456			
Length = 28		Class-Num 21 (Record Route)	Class-Type 1
Type 1 (IPv4)	Length = 8	IP Address = 192.168.253.2	
IP Address (continued)		Prefix Length = 32	Flags = 0×00
Type 1 (IPv4)	Length = 8	IP Address = 192.168.253.34	
IP Address (continued)		Prefix Length = 32	Flags = 0×00
Type 3 (Label)	Length = 8	Flags = 0×00 (Per Interface)	Label C-Type = 1
Label = 54321			

Figure 9.78 An example RSVP-TE Resv message.

9.8 Choosing Between CR-LDP and RSVP-TE

As might be expected when there is more than one way of doing a job, debate rages about the correct solution. There has been a long and sometimes acrimonious discussion about whether CR-LDP or RSVP-TE is best suited to MPLS traffic engineering. The argument has been fuelled by commercial considerations with the major switch vendors pitching in on one side or the other, and regrettably, truth has not always been the winner.

One of the unfortunate consequences has been that early adopters and developers have had to waste time implementing both protocols, or have had to make a guess about the correct choice. This has left the implementers vulnerable to changes in the marketplace. It now appears that for a host of reasons, some of which are detailed below, RSVP-TE is the preferred option within the IETF, which has decided to halt further work on CR-LDP. Although new work on CR-LDP is strongly discouraged by the IETF, it does not mean that CR-LDP will be buried immediately. There is some interest from other standards bodies in keeping CR-LDP alive and making extensions to cover new features. Additionally, major equipment vendors that have invested heavily in CR-LDP may continue to support it. The IETF, however, has decided that CR-LDP (RFC 3212) will never be progressed beyond its current Proposed Standard status—that is, it will never become a full standard.

9.8.1 Why Are There Two Protocols?

MPLS developed very rapidly in a highly competitive commercial environment. As the traffic engineering requirements crystallized, equipment vendors were already experimenting with two approaches based on existing protocols and deployments. The IETF, not wanting to show commercial bias and recognizing that there was no evidence that either of the protocols was fatally flawed, allowed the development and standardization of both with the intention of seeing which proved to be more popular among implementers and deployers.

9.8.2 Applicability and Adoption

Both CR-LDP and RSVP-TE have turned out to be suitable for MPLS traffic engineering. In terms of building services in the Internet to support quality of service, VPNs, or Voice over IP, each offers a similar capability set when suitably extended by the various additional drafts that are being written within the IETF. Both protocols can be managed in much the same way and the IETF's Management Information Bases (MIBs) are suitable for both protocols.

Although there are experimental networks using CR-LDP and others using RSVP-TE, one of the major driving forces influencing implementers and Service Providers has been the simple fact that Cisco and Juniper have both chosen to provide MPLS traffic engineering based on RSVP-TE. In order to interoperate and to sell into the same market, other vendors must also implement RSVP-TE.

One counterweight which has yet to fully come into play is the preference apparently shown within the International Telecommunications Union (ITU) for CR-LDP as a hard-state protocol.

9.8.3 Comparison of Functionality

Table 9.10 shows a summary of the main functions of CR-LDP and RSVP-TE and shows how they compare. No single function is necessarily a show-stopper

Table 9.10 Comparative Summary of Features of CR-LDP and RSVP-TE

Feature	CR-LDP	RSVP-TE
Transport	TCP	Raw IP
LSP Merging and Multipoint-to-point LSPs	Yes	Yes
Traffic Description and Resource Reservation	Yes	Yes
MTU Size Exchange	Not without new extensions to LDP	Yes
Traffic Control	Forward path	Nominally reverse path, but forward path in many implementations
Resource Sharing	No	Yes
Multicast	No	No (but new IETF drafts address it)
Security	Yes (through TCP security and IPsec)	Yes (through MD5 applied to RSVP)
Explicit Routing	Yes	Yes
Route Recording	Yes (through Path Vector)	Yes
Rerouting	Yes	Yes
Route Pinning	Yes	Yes, but requires Record Route
Policy Control	Implicit	Explicit
Exchange of Layer 3 Protocol Identifiers	No	Yes
LSP State Maintenance	Hard state	Soft state
LSP Refresh	Not required	Periodic, hop-by-hop in both directions
High Availability and Restart	Available through additions	Inherent in refresh

for the adoption of one protocol or the other, since it is always possible to invent protocol extensions to add new features. For example, if route pinning was determined to be a significant requirement in RSVP-TE without the use of Record Routes and the resignaling of the Path message using an Explicit Route, a new flag could be added (perhaps in the Session Attributes) to control pinning exactly as it is controlled in CR-LDP. Conversely, if the Path Vector in CR-LDP was determined to be inadequate for route recording it could be extended or added as a new TLV.

More significant in the comparison of function have been the two "philosophical" differences between the protocols: the underlying transport and the debate over soft versus hard protocol state. The two issues are to a large extent linked.

CR-LDP, in using TCP, is able to take advantage of the reliable delivery of its transport and so does not need to implement any handshaking to ensure that messages arrive. It is able to know that state, once established, persists until it is torn down or until the transport notifies it of a failure. This makes CR-LDP protocol state hard. RSVP-TE uses raw IP, which means that individual protocol messages might be lost or delivered out of order. Based on RSVP, RSVP-TE handles this situation not through protocol handshakes but through protocol state refresh messages which are required to prevent LSPs for timing out.

Many people favor hard state because they find it predictable and clean; soft state, for them, is messy and unpredictable, with the potential for routes to change and leave resources dangling. Further, they consider the overhead of the state refresh messages that are needed in RSVP-TE to keep the LSPs up and active to be excessive and a potential inhibitor to scalability. In practice, however, the refresh reduction schemes developed for RSVP are equally applicable to RSVP-TE and cut the overhead of LSP maintenance significantly.

The use of TCP also allows CR-LDP to inherit whatever security is being used by TCP. Although TCP is vulnerable to denial of service attacks, CR-LDP can benefit from whatever security and authentication techniques are applied to the TCP connections it uses. RSVP-TE, on the other hand, must implement its own security and authentication, and the RSVP-TE implementations must be updated to take up any new security developments.

9.9 Prioritizing Traffic in MPLS

IP traffic flows may be prioritized within the Internet through the use of Differentiated Services (see Chapter 6). This allows higher-priority packets to overtake those of lower priorities, making preferential use of queuing mechanisms, resource availability, and fast links.

The use of resource affinities within CR-LDP and RSVP-TE allows LSPs to be set up using specific link types, and explicit routing allows LSPs to be directed down chosen paths. This provides some of the function for Differentiated

Services over MPLS, but it does not cover the full range. Specifically, it does not define how an LSR should prioritize the traffic on one LSP compared to that on another, and it does not indicate how individual labeled packets on an LSP should be handled.

RFC 3270 defines procedures and protocol extensions for the full support of Differentiated Services over MPLS by describing how LSPs may be set up with specific priorities, and how packets within an individual LSP may be assigned priorities. Readers may find it helpful to familiarize themselves with Section 6.3 on Differentiated Services before continuing.

9.9.1 Inferring Priority from Labels

If each LSP that is set up is associated with a DiffServ Ordered Aggregate (OA), then all of the traffic on the LSP can be assigned the same Per Hop Behavior Scheduling Class (PSC) and drop precedence at an LSR. This allows traffic from different LSPs to be differentiated at transit LSRs. If the ingress LSR places traffic onto LSPs according to its DiffServ Behavior Aggregates (BAs), then the features of DiffServ can be achieved within an MPLS network.

LSPs that are established to carry traffic associated with specific OAs by associating the DiffServ class with a label are called L-LSPs.

For this process to operate, it is necessary that the relationship between the L-LSP and the PSC and drop precedence be understood at each transit LSR. This information can be statically configured across the network or can be signaled through the MPLS label distribution protocol. Note, however, that as with Diff-Serv there is no obligation on an LSR to prioritize the LSPs in the same way or even to differentiate between the traffic flows at all.

Figure 9.79 shows the new objects added to RSVP-TE and to LDP (and, hence, to CR-LDP) to signal the PSC mapping for an L-LSP. These objects are

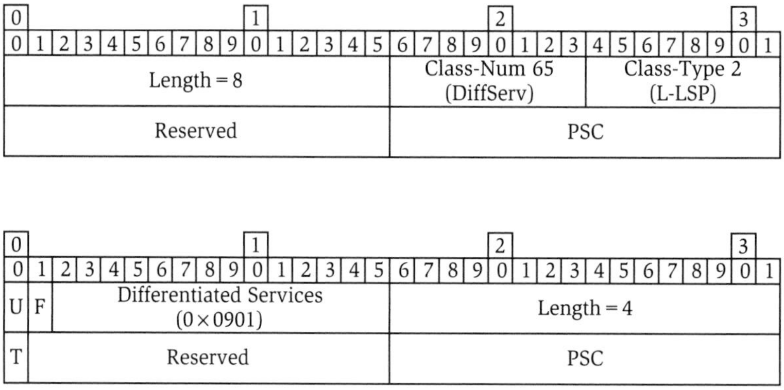

Figure 9.79 RSVP-TE DiffServ Object and LDP DiffServ TLV for L-LSPs.

added to the Path and Label request messages, respectively, as optional objects. In RSVP-TE the new DiffServ Object should be placed between the Session Attributes object and the Policy Object. In LDP and CR-LDP the new DiffServ TLV should be placed with the optional TLVs. Note that L-LSPs can be supported in LDP by placing the DiffServ TLV in the Label Mapping message. The PSC is encoded as a 16-bit number.

In the LDP DiffServ TLV the setting of the U- and F-bits are up to the source LSR and could both be set to zero if the ingress wishes full DiffServ support across all LSRs in the network, or both set to 1 if the ingress is content to have the DiffServ function applied within the network wherever it can be.

9.9.2 Inferring Priority from Experimental Bits

Recall that an MPLS shim header includes 3 bits called the experimental bits (EXP bits). If not used for any other purpose, these bits allow an MPLS packet to be assigned to one of eight categories. If each bit setting is assigned to a DiffServ BA, basic differentiation of traffic may be achieved on the LSP within the network. More precisely, each EXP bit setting can be interpreted as specifying a specific PSC and drop precedence. This provides considerably more granularity than simply inferring priority from labels, and can help to reduce the number of LSPs required to provide extensive differentiation of traffic but does require that the label switching engine is able to examine the EXP bits. LSPs that use the EXP bits to differentiate traffic are called E-LSPs.

Two pieces of information must be signaled by the MPLS traffic engineering protocol for this process to work. First, all LSRs on the LSP must be made aware that they can interpret the EXP bits as indicating a PSC, and second, the LSRs must have a common understanding of the meanings of the EXP bits and the "ranking" of the PSCs that they encode. Note, however, that as with DiffServ there is no obligation on an LSR to prioritize the packets in the same way or even to handle the EXP bits at all.

The mapping from the EXP field to the PSC and drop precedence can be different for each LSP and can be preconfigured at each LSR or signaled during LSP setup. Preconfigured mappings can be defined as defaults for the LSR or can be derived from other information such as the source and destination points of the LSP. Signaling the EXP bit to PSC mapping requires the addition of extra information to the signaling messages.

Figure 9.80 shows the new objects added to RSVP-TE and to LDP (and, hence, to CR-LDP) to signal the EXP-bit to PSC mappings for E-LSPs. This process reuses the new objects introduced for L-LSPs and differentiates them using different C-Types in RSVP-TE and a type bit in LDP. Note that E-LSPs can be supported in LDP by placing the DiffServ TLV in the Label Mapping message.

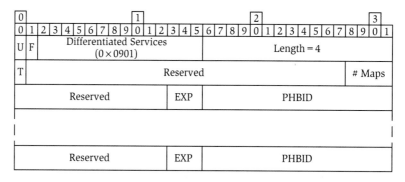

Figure 9.80 RSVP-TE DiffServ Object and LDP DiffServ TLV for E-LSPs.

A counter in the new objects indicates how many EXP bit to PSC mappings are defined—this is not strictly needed since it can be deduced from the length of the object. Each EXP to PSC mapping contains the setting of the EXP bits and a PHBID encoded as a 16-bit number.

In the LDP DiffServ TLV the T-bit is used to indicate that the TLV defines an E-LSP and is set to zero. The settings of the U- and F-bits are as described in the preceding section.

It is acceptable for fewer than eight mappings to be signaled, in which case it is a local configuration matter how each LSR will handle traffic with other EXP bit settings.

9.9.3 New Error Codes

With the introduction of new function it is necessary to define new error codes. For MPLS DiffServ support, the new error codes are shown in Tables 9.11 and 9.12. The LDP status codes are carried on Notification messages and the RSVP-TE codes are carried on PathErr messages only.

Table 9.11 New LDP Status Codes for Differentiated Services

Status Code	E-Bit Setting	Meaning
0x01000001	0	Unexpected DiffServ TLV
0x01000002	0	Unsupported PHB
0x01000003	0	Invalid EXP < -- > PHB mapping
0x01000004	0	Unsupported PSC
0x01000005	0	Per-LSP context allocation failure

Table 9.12 New RSVP-TE Error Codes and Values for Differentiated Services

Error Code	Error Value Setting	Meaning
27		Differentiated Services error
	1	Unexpected DiffServ TLV
	2	Unsupported PHB
	3	Invalid EXP < -- > PHB mapping
	4	Unsupported PSC
	5	Per-LSP context allocation failure

9.9.4 Choosing Between L-LSPs and E-LSPs

The choice between L-LSPs and E-LSPs must be governed by the capabilities of transit nodes in the network. It may be possible to route LSPs only through LSRs that support these DiffServ extensions, but if those LSRs are few then the consequent traffic congestion may be worse than allowing diverse paths without using any Differentiated Services.

If sufficient DiffServ-capable LSRs exist, the capabilities of the LSRs still come into play since some nodes may not be able to examine the EXP bits of each packet and act accordingly. Such LSRs will not handle E-LSPs in any beneficial way, and if there are a significant number of them in the network, L-LSPs will provide the only way to differentiate traffic.

The total number of LSPs may also influence the choice. If an L-LSP is to be installed for each PSC there may turn out to be an unmanageably large number. In this case it makes sense to use E-LSPs to cut the number to an eighth.

If the aim of the deployment is to differentiate services between a source and destination pair, then E-LSPs provide a good solution and differentiation can be limited to within a single LSP. If the aim is to differentiate all traffic across an LSR, then either solution may be suitable, depending on implementation, with L-LSPs making it possible to apply a coarser filter on traffic without the need to examine packets.

Using MPLS it is possible to establish traffic protection schemes that protect individual LSPs or groups of LSPs. One model for this would protect only the traffic having certain PSC and drop characteristics. In this model it would be impossible to protect only some of the traffic on an LSP, and the use of L-LSPs may be required to differentiate the protected and unprotected traffic.

Some layer two protocols include certain service parameters akin to Differentiated Services. For example, ATM can indicate the drop precedence using the CLP flag in the cell header, Frame Relay similarly uses the DE flag, and 802.1 allows User Priority to be encoded. The availability of these features and their limits may influence the choice of DiffServ LSP. Because the shim header is not examined in ATM and Frame Relay and only the single drop precedence bit can be used, it may provide better control to use L-LSPs.

Under some circumstances it may be desirable to establish a set of parallel LSPs to handle traffic with different PSCs but to share resources within the network. This makes a lot of sense when the purpose of traffic differentiation is considered, and it would allow the traffic on the higher-priority LSPs to use the shared resources at the expense of the traffic on the lower-priority LSPs. All this could be achieved without affecting the resource usage of LSPs outside the group. This technique is equally applicable to L-LSPs and E-LSPs and can be achieved either through static configuration or by utilizing the resource sharing capabilities of the signaling protocols—RSVP-TE is, perhaps, best suited to this since it can place all of the LSPs into the same session and automatically share resources.

9.10   BGP-4 and MPLS

As has already been discussed, one of the operational modes for Downstream Unsolicited label distribution is driven by the appearance of new routes in the local routing table. As these routes are advertised by the routing protocols, labels for the routes can be advertised by the label distribution protocols.

A possible optimization is to combine the two efforts and have the routing protocol distribute labels. Just such an idea has been applied by the IETF in RFC 3107 for the Border Gateway Protocol (BGP) routing protocol.

Readers are advised to familiarize themselves with BGP by reading Section 5.8 of this book before continuing.

9.10.1 Distributing Labels for BGP Routes

As BGP distributes a route in a BGP Update message, the label mapping information for that route can be piggybacked in the same message. This has several advantages.

If two adjacent LSRs are also BGP peers, then distributing labels using BGP avoids the need to run any other label distribution protocol between the LSRs. This simplifies the management and operation of the LSRs.

More usual, however, BGP peers exist across the network from each other. The BGP-capable LSRs exist at the edge of the network, providing connectivity to other networks, and are classed *exterior LSRs*. Other LSRs in the network are called *interior LSRs* and only carry traffic within the network—they do not participate in BGP.

In Figure 9.81 Host X needs to send traffic to Host Y. The path will traverse three networks. Consider how the routing information has been propagated— within network 3 reachability information for Host Y is fully propagated by the IGP, router G speaks BGP to router D to communicate reachability into network 3, and the IGP in network 2 distributes the information on how to reach router G. Finally, in network 1 the IGP distributes routes to reach router C.

Within networks 1, 2, and 3, LDP may be used to distribute labels corresponding to the IGP routes, giving us the three LSP segments {A, B, C, D},

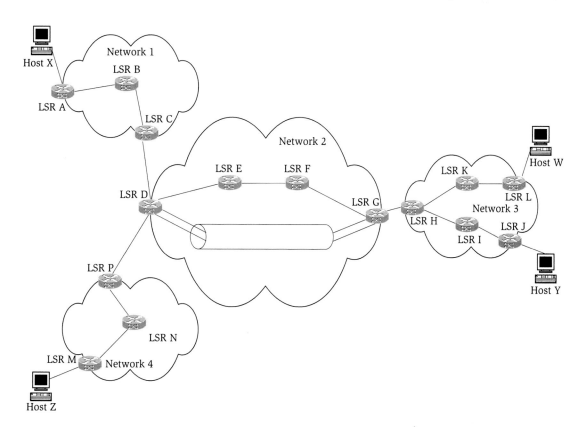

Figure 9.81 Using BGP to connect LSPs through a Tunnel.

{D, E, F, G}, and {G, H, I, J}. To pass traffic from one host to the other it is desirable to set up a single end-to-end LSP. This could be achieved by splicing the three segments together, but attractive as this may seem, it breaks down very quickly when new hosts are added that need to share the common route across the core network (network 2). What we actually need is to set up an MPLS tunnel across network 2 to carry the end-to-end LSPs.

The labels distributed by LDP within network 2 provide the basis for the tunnel and we now need to distribute end-point labels constituting the routes in the external networks. It would be possible to have remote LDP adjacencies between the BGP peers D and G, but if BGP Route Reflection is being used it makes sense to extend it to distribute labels directly associated with the routes it distributes. When this is done, the LSP segments in networks 1 and 3 are spliced using a "single" hop from LSR D to LSR G that is routed down the LSP tunnel from D to G using label stacking. Distribution of labels can be achieved by piggybacking a label in the BGP Update message using the Multiprotocol Extension attribute. The format is shown in Section 9.10.2.

9.10.2 New and Changed Message Objects

A BGP speaker indicates that it is capable of processing piggybacked label advertisement by using the Capabilities Optional Parameter on the Open message. It uses the Multiprotocol Extensions capabilities code (value 1) and advertises the Address Family Identifier and Subsequent Address Family Identifier pairs available, as shown in Figure 9.82. A Subsequent Address Family Identifier value of 4 is used to indicate that a label will be distributed.

If the use of label advertisement is successfully negotiated, and once an LSP exists between a pair of BGP peers (as between LSRs D and G in Figure 9.81), the peers may start to advertise labels using BGP. This is done using the Multiprotocol Reachable Network Layer Reachability Information Extension Attribute on an Update message, as shown in Figure 9.83. Again, the SAFI value of 4 is used to indicate that a label is being sent, and the label itself is encoded in the Network Layer Reachability Information (NLRI) field at the end of the attribute. Note that the length of the NRLI is given in bits not bytes, but that the prefix field is padded with reserved bits up to a full byte boundary.

0		1		2		3	
0 1 2 3 4 5 6 7	8 9 0 1 2 3 4 5	6 7 8 9 0 1 2 3	4 5 6 7 8 9 0 1				
Parameter code = 2 (Capabilites)	Parameter Len = 6	Capability code = 1 (Multiprotocol)	Capability Len = 4				
Address Family Identifier (AFI)		Reserved	SAFI = 4 (Label)				

Figure 9.82 BGP Capabilities optional parameter for multiprotocol support with label exchange.

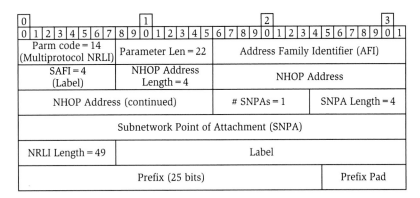

0										1										2										3	
0	1	2	3	4	5	6	7	8	9	0	1	2	3	4	5	6	7	8	9	0	1	2	3	4	5	6	7	8	9	0	1
Parm code = 14 (Multiprotocol NRLI)								Parameter Len = 22								Address Family Identifier (AFI)															
SAFI = 4 (Label)								NHOP Address Length = 4								NHOP Address															
NHOP Address (continued)																# SNPAs = 1								SNPA Length = 4							
Subnetwork Point of Attachment (SNPA)																															
NRLI Length = 49								Label																							
Prefix (25 bits)																								Prefix Pad							

Figure 9.83 A BGP Multiprotocol NRLI Extension Attribute for label exchange.

9.10.3 Constructing MPLS VPNs

RFC 2547 describes how to establish BGP/MPLS VPNs. It does not introduce any new protocol extensions, but describes how Service Providers may use MPLS within their backbone network to forward traffic while using BGP to distribute routes. The process essentially uses the information distributed by BGP to trigger the establishment of tunnels like that shown in Figure 9.81.

If this process is combined with BGP distribution of labels, extensive MPLS connectivity can be achieved across backbone networks.

VPNs are described in more detail in Section 15.2.

9.11 Further Reading

MPLS Technology and Application, by Bruce Davie and Yakhov Rekhter (2000). Morgan Kaufmann. This gives a thorough history of IP switching protocols and techniques as well as a detailed introduction to MPLS.

Traffic Engineering with MPLS, by Eric Obsorne and Ajay Simha (2002). Cisco Press. This book is a hands-on guide to the use of Cisco routers to provide traffic engineered services in a MPLS network.

The MPLS Working Group has a web page that includes links to RFCs and Internet drafts for MPLS: www.ietf.org/html.charters/mpls-charter.html. Some key RFCs are:

RFC 3031—Multiprotocol Label Switching Architecture
RFC 3036—LDP Specification
RFC 3107—Carrying Label Information in BGP-4

RFC 3209—RSVP-TE: Extensions to RSVP for LSP Tunnels

RFC 3212—Constraint-Based LSP Setup Using LDP

RFC 3270—Multiprotocol Label Switching (MPLS) Support of Differentiated Services

RFC 3468—The Multiprotocol Label Switching (MPLS) Working Group Decision on MPLS Signaling Protocols

Chapter 10

Generalized MPLS (GMPLS)

The cores of most modern networks do not switch packets even if they are carrying packet-based data. The networks are built from optical fibers, and the bandwidth is divided up by lambda (frequency or wavelength) or timeslot through *time division multiplexing* (TDM). Switches in these core networks switch timeslots, wavelength, wavebands, or entire fibers from an input port to an output port.

The traditional approaches to provisioning switches in core networks have utilized manual planning and configuration. This has often resulted in setup times for new services measured in days or weeks. Turn-down of services is also slow and because there is no central control it is a process fraught with the risk of affecting other data traffic, leading to many resources being left in service rather than risking accidentally turning off the wrong one.

It became obvious that improvements to the management of core networks could be made using control protocols. These could be linked with traffic engineering engines to place traffic more optimally within the networks.

Generalized MPLS (GMPLS) is a set of extensions to MPLS traffic engineering signaling protocols (CR-LDP and RSVP-TE) and to traffic engineering routing protocols (OSPF and IS-IS) to provide a common, standardized suite for controlling core networks. GMPLS is built on MPLS because the switching notions are very similar and because there is benefit in leveraging the proven technology of MPLS.

One new protocol, the Link Management Protocol (LMP), is defined as part of GMPLS. LMP allows adjacent switches to discover, configure, and monitor the data links that join them. The properties discovered and advertised between nodes in LMP are fed to the routing protocols, which distribute them so that the correct links can be chosen to support the requirements of the LSPs signaled by the signaling protocols.

This chapter explores the control plane additions made to MPLS to support other media apart from packet switching. Readers are advised to familiarize themselves with MPLS (see Chapter 9) before embarking on this chapter.

10.1 A Hierarchy of Media

Set out in the following sections are a variety of ways in which data entering a node can be switched to leave the node on the next hop toward its destination. The methods of switching can be seen to be hierarchical in terms of the granularity with which they switch, and LSPs can be set up to carry data at a specific switching granularity. These LSPs can be established as nested tunnels, provided that the switching capability of the outer tunnel is of no finer granularity than the payload LSP, and provided that (as is the nature of tunneled traffic) the payload traffic does not need to be switched before it reaches the end of the outer tunnel.

10.1.1 Layer Two Switching

Media that recognize cell/frame boundaries and may be capable of switch sub-packet quantities are called *layer-2 switching capable* (L2SC), in reference to the layered protocol architecture described in Chapter 1. Examples include ATM hardware that forwards cells based on the VPI/VCI that they carry, and Ethernet bridges that forward frames based on their MAC addresses.

10.1.2 Packet Switching

MPLS is an example of packet switching. Each received packet is examined and switched to be sent out of a different port. Packet switching has the advantage of flexibility and allowing small data flows to share a common network link, but it has the disadvantage that each received packet must be examined to determine how it should be switched—this can significantly limit the throughput of packet switches. Nodes that switch packets are said to be *packet switch capable* (PSC).

10.1.3 Time Division Multiplexing

The bandwidth on a network link can be divided up into timeslots. In this model, the signal is seen as a sequence of data frames with F frames each of size S being sent every second (giving a total bandwidth of F*S). Data flows are allocated to one or more of the F frames, giving them dedicated bandwidth and allowing their timeslots to be switched as discrete quantities. Since multiple packets can be placed in individual frames using simple concatenation, this is an optimization over packet switching that is enhanced by the fact that the switching can be driven by a clock without the need to examine the data.

This process is known as *time division multiplexing* (TDM). SONET and SDH are examples of how data can be divided in this way.

10.1.4 Lambda Switching

Within a fiber, the available bandwidth can be divided up by frequency or wavelength (also known as lambdas) according to the capabilities of the hardware. Some hardware transmits only a single frequency on a fiber (this is common in TDM systems) and other hardware multiplexes move wavelengths onto a single fiber. Coarse Wave Division Multiplexing (CWDM) places relatively few wavelengths on a fiber, but Dense Wave Division Multiplexing (DWDM) can put 20, 40, 80, or many more wavelengths on a single fiber. Each wavelength is capable of carrying a fixed maximum bandwidth (typically 2.5 GB or 10 GB), so the number of wavelengths increases the amount of data that can be sent down a single fiber.

A node that is *lambda switch capable* (LSC) breaks out the individual wavelengths from the incoming fiber and switches them independently to go out on different fibers. Some switches are capable of modifying the frequency by regenerating the signal, but others can only switch the signal as received.

10.1.5 Waveband Switching

Waveband switching collects a group of physically adjacent frequencies from one fiber and switches them together as a single unit to another fiber. This can offer optimizations where switching resources are limited.

10.1.6 Fiber and Port Switching

All of the wavelengths on a single fiber may be collected together and considered as a single unit. The contents of the fiber may be switched by a *fiber switch capable* (FSC) node from an incoming port to an outgoing port without any attempt to switch at a finer granularity. Port or fiber switching is the coarsest granularity of switching available.

10.1.7 Choosing Your Switching Type

Choosing the switching type for an LSP is largely based on the capabilities of the hardware. An LSP that traverses MPLS packet switches must utilize that type of switching. Some networks will be constructed from nodes with different switching capabilities, and some nodes will support multiple switching technologies on different interfaces or even on the same interface. For example, some optical switches are capable of switching individual lambdas or whole fibers.

Where an LSP starts in a packet switched network, traverses an optical network, and ends up in a second packet switched network, the switching type of the LSP must be packet-based at the edges but may be restricted to lambda-based in the core. Although it is possible to modify the switching type of the LSP as it transits the core, another possibility is to tunnel the PSC LSP through an LSC LSP. Since the bandwidth granularity of the LSC LSP is likely to be high compared with the PSC flow, this approach offers the possibility of tunneling multiple PSC LSPs through the same LSC LSP and thereby making more efficient use of the available resources.

10.1.8 What Is a Label?

Having established that LSPs can be set up to switch data at different granularities, it is necessary to identify exactly what a label is in each switching mode. Simply put, a label is the identifier for the quantity that is switched, so just as in MPLS a label identifies all packets that are switched in the same way, so in GMPLS a label identifies all data that are switched in the same way.

For example, in an optical switch a label may identify a particular lambda. The switching operation is defined as {incoming port, incoming lambda} maps to {outgoing port, outgoing lambda} and it is the responsibility of signaling in GMPLS to exchange the label information that identifies the lambdas.

10.2 Generic Signaling Extensions for GMPLS

GMPLS signaling is built on MPLS-TE signaling. This is not just a convenience that reduces the amount of new protocol development required, but it reflects the fact that GMPLS as a concept grew out of MPLS-TE and uses many of the same terms and concepts.

MPLS has two defined signaling protocols, both of which have been extended for use in GMPLS. However, the authors of the drafts, learning the lessons of the past, did as much as possible to make the extensions generic and protocol-independent. This was achieved by determining the function required and the consequent information that needed to be passed between nodes. This information was then defined in common data formats which can be carried in new objects in RSVP-TE or TLVs in CR-LDP. This section describes these common formats and explains the functions they are used to provide.

Note that there is no equivalent of LDP in GMPLS. GMPLS is a traffic engineering technology.

It should be emphasized that GMPLS is a superset of MPLS. That is, all of the function defined for MPLS is available in GMPLS. Packet switching is just one flavor of GMPLS.

10.2.1 Generic Labels

MPLS labels are encoded as 23 bits within a 32-bit integer. This allows GMPLS labels up to 32 bits to be carried in the same fields within the signaling protocols, although new type indicators are needed within the signaling protocols so that the protocols know that all 32 bits are relevant. 32 bits is sufficient to carry

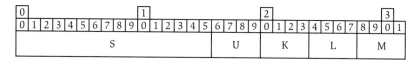

Figure 10.1 GMPLS label format for SONET and SDH TDM labels.

Table 10.1 The Interpretation of the Five Fields in a GMPLS TDM Label

Field	Usage	Notes
S	Index of an STS-3/AUG-1 inside an STS-N/STM-N multiplex	Only significant for SONET STS-N (N > 1) and SDH STM-N (N > 0), and must be set to zero and ignored for STS-1 and STM-0
U	Index of an STS-1_SPE/VC-3 within an STS-3/AUG-1	Only significant for SONET STS-N (N > 1) and SDH STM-N (N > 0), and must be set to zero and ignored for STS-1 and STM-0
K	Index of a TUG-3 within a VC-4	Only significant for an SDH VC-4 structured in TUG-3s, and must be set to zero and ignored in all other cases
L	Index of a VT_Group/TUG-2 within an STS-1_SPE/TUG-3 or VC-3	Must be set to zero and ignored in all other cases
M	Index of a VT1.5_SPE/VC-11, VT2_SPE/VC-12, or VT3_SPE within a VT_Group/TUG-2	Must be set to zero and ignored in all other cases

a large proportion of the required label types: port or fiber identifiers are usually integers, and lambdas are usually indicated by their wavelength in nanometers, although this is a local matter and it would be equally valid to indicate the chosen lambda by counting through the available grid. Generic SONET and SDH labels for use in TDM can also be encoded within 32 bits, as shown in Figure 10.1.

The TDM Label fields are described in detail in an Internet Draft that will soon be made into an RFC. The subject of TDM could easily fill a whole book itself, and the interpretations of the fields given in Table 10.1 are only intended to provide an overview.

As with all GMPLS generalized labels, the interpretation of a TDM label is context sensitive and is not encoded within the label or within the signaling objects that carry the label. It is left up to the implementation to know the capabilities of the link and to interpret the label within that context and with reference to the traffic parameters that describe the resources being requested.

There are several cases within GMPLS in which 32 bits is not sufficient to hold a label, and in any case the intention of GMPLS is to be sufficiently generalized to handle new technologies as they come along. For this reason, the generalized label is not limited to 32 bits but is defined by the length of the protocol object that carries it. More specifically, the size of the label is context specific, being

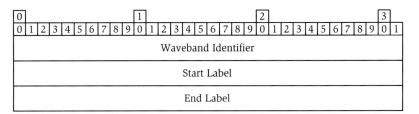

Figure 10.2 Waveband labels include an identifier, a start label, and an end label.

defined by the capabilities of the link, the request made for the label, and the traffic parameters. For example, in TDM arbitrary noncontiguous concatenation of timeslots may be represented by a series of TDM labels.

Figure 10.2 shows another label type that requires more than 32 bits. Some hardware may be capable of switching a set of contiguous wavelengths known as a *waveband* as a single switching operation. The waveband label is identified in the signaling protocol by a distinct label type.

10.2.2 Requesting Labels

MPLS signaling messages that request LSP setup include an object that indicates the payload protocol that will be carried by the LSP. For GMPLS, the label request shown in Figure 10.3 must indicate that GMPLS is requested and must also provide a little extra information about the LSP that is being established.

The Encoding Type shown in Table 10.2 describes how the data will be presented to the transport medium and so what type of LSP is requested. For example, an optical system such as DWDM would request an LSP that handles data encoded as "lambda." The GPID shown in Table 10.3 has a similar use to the level three protocol identifier (L3PID) in MPLS—that is, it identifies the payload traffic that will use the LSP. In addition to the values defined in the table, normal L3PID values (standard Ethertypes) may also be used. The Switching Type field shown in Table 10.4 has been the cause of more confusion than any other field within GMPLS. It indicates the granularity at which it is acceptable to switch the LSP at transit nodes and is necessary to handle links and switches that can operate at different levels within the media hierarchy. For example, some optical switches may be able to switch whole fibers or individual lambdas, in which case the ingress may want to control the switching behavior to

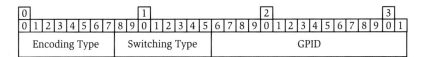

Figure 10.3 The Generalized Label Request.

Table 10.2 GMPLS Encoding Types

Encoding Type	Meaning
1	Packet
2	Ethernet
3	ANSI/ETSI PDH
4	Reserved
5	SDH ITU-T G.707 / SONET ANSI T1.105
6	Reserved
7	Digital wrapper
8	Lambda (photonic)
9	Fiber
10	Reserved
11	FiberChannel

Table 10.3 GMPLS Switching Types

Switching Type	Meaning
1	Packet-Switch Capable-1 (PSC-1)
2	Packet-Switch Capable-2 (PSC-2)
3	Packet-Switch Capable-3 (PSC-3)
4	Packet-Switch Capable-4 (PSC-4)
51	Layer-2 Switch Capable (L2SC)
100	Time-Division-Multiplex Capable (TDM)
150	Lambda-Switch Capable (LSC)
200	Fiber-Switch Capable (FSC)

not use fiber switching so that subsequent LSPs using the same incoming fiber can be switched to different outgoing fibers.

10.2.3 Negotiating Labels

Label allocation in GMPLS, as with MPLS, is decided by the downstream node on any link; it advertises the label back to the upstream node using the signaling protocol. In GMPLS, however, labels map to network resources, and contention can arise if the downstream node does not select the right label. This is perhaps

Table 10.4 GMPLS Generalized Protocol Identifiers that Supplement Standard Ethertypes

GPID	Meaning	Transport Technology
0	Unknown	All
1	Reserved	
2	Reserved	
3	Reserved	
4	Reserved	
5	Asynchronous mapping of E4	SDH
6	Asynchronous mapping of DS3/T3	SDH
7	Asynchronous mapping of E3	SDH
8	Bit synchronous mapping of E3	SDH
9	Byte synchronous mapping of E3	SDH
10	Asynchronous mapping of DS2/T2	SDH
11	Bit synchronous mapping of DS2/T2	SDH
12	Reserved	
13	Asynchronous mapping of E1	SDH
14	Byte synchronous mapping of E1	SDH
15	Byte synchronous mapping of 31 * DS0	SDH
16	Asynchronous mapping of DS1/T1	SDH
17	Bit synchronous mapping of DS1/T1	SDH
18	Byte synchronous mapping of DS1/T1	SDH
19	VC-11 in VC-12	SDH
20	Reserved	
21	Reserved	
22	DS1 SF asynchronous	SONET
23	DS1 ESF asynchronous	SONET
24	DS3 M23 asynchronous	SONET
25	DS3 C-bit parity asynchronous	SONET
26	VT/LOVC	SDH
27	STS SPE/HOVC	SDH
28	POS – No scrambling, 16-bit CRC	SDH
29	POS – No scrambling, 32-bit CRC	SDH

30	POS – Scrambling, 16-bit CRC	SDH
31	POS – Scrambling, 32-bit CRC	SDH
32	ATM mapping	SDH
33	Ethernet	SDH, Lambda, Fiber
34	SONET/SDH	Lambda, Fiber
35	Reserved (SONET deprecated)	Lambda, Fiber
36	Digital wrapper	Lambda, Fiber
37	Lambda	Fiber
38	ANSI/ETSI PDH	SDH
39	Reserved	SDH
40	Link Access Protocol SDH	SDH (LAPS – X.85 and X.86)
41	FDDI	SDH, Lambda, Fiber
42	DQDB (ETSI ETS 300 216)	SDH
43	Fiber Channel-3 (Services)	Fiber Channel
44	HDLC	SDH
45	Ethernet V2/DIX (only)	SDH, Lambda, Fiber
46	Ethernet 802.3 (only)	SDH, Lambda, Fiber

best illustrated using Figure 10.4, in which three LSPs are desired across an optical network. The edge nodes have lasers of different wavelengths which are identified through generalized labels, but the transit nodes are pure optical switches—that is, they can switch wavelengths received on one fiber to go out of another fiber, but they cannot convert one wavelength to another.

In the example, two LSPs have already been set up. One {A, C, D, E} uses one wavelength, λ_1 (gray), and the other {B, C, D, F} uses wavelength λ_2 (black). Now a request for a third LSP {A, C, D, F} is issued. The signaling protocol (RSVP-TE or CR-LDP) sends the LSP setup request (Path or Label Request) along the path of the LSP to F. Node F selects an available label (that is, wavelength) and since λ_1 is available, it may allocate this and signal it back to node D. Node D is happy to use λ_1 on the interface toward node F, and now needs to select a suitable wavelength for use on the interface from node C. But Node D is a pure optical switch and cannot modify wavelengths so it must use the same lambda on both incoming and outgoing interfaces. It must choose λ_1, but that wavelength is already in use between nodes C and D, and the LSP setup must be failed.

Clearly what is required is some way for upstream nodes to indicate to downstream nodes which labels are available to constrain the choice made by

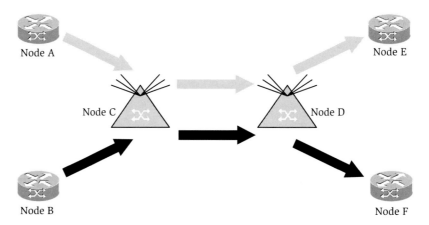

Figure 10.4 Label allocation conflict in an optical network.

the downstream node. The GMPLS label set provides this function by allowing the upstream nodes to list all available labels.

In Figure 10.4, the node B adds a label set to the setup request for the third LSP. It lists all the labels it can support that are not already in use: perhaps $\{\lambda_1, \lambda_3, \lambda_4, \lambda_5, \lambda_6\}$ noting that λ_2 is not listed because it is being used to support an existing LSP. When the request reaches node C, the label set is updated according to the switching capabilities of the transit node. In this case, since it is a pure optical switch, it must exclude λ_1 from the list and cannot add any new values; it sends out the label set $\{\lambda_3, \lambda_4, \lambda_5, \lambda_6\}$. Node D does not need to exclude any further labels, but also cannot add any. The label set arrives at node F and allows the choice of a label that will be acceptable all the way back along the path.

The application of label sets is by no means limited to pure optical switches. It can provide useful control of label selection for optimized switching in a variety of switches, including those that do support label conversion.

GMPLS defines the content of the label set as shown in Figure 10.5. The action field describes the nature of the set—type zero (inclusion) shows a list of labels that are available, type 1 (exclusion) shows a list of labels that are not available, type 2 (inclusion range) gives the start and end points of a range of labels that are available, and type 3 (exclusion range) gives a range of labels not available. The label type field allows the signaling protocols to indicate the label type carried in the set: all labels in one set must be of the same type. The elements of the label set itself may be complex and not just single labels. This allows the members to be wavebands or concatenated timeslots as identified by the label type field.

The upstream nodes may want to exert more control over the selection of labels at downstream nodes. Sending a label set with just one member is a possible solution, but it may limit the choice too much. The GMPLS suggested label

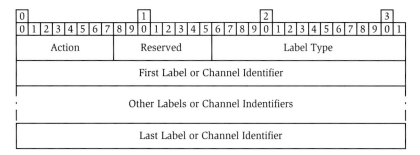

Figure 10.5 The GMPLS label set.

concept allows an upstream node to make a strong suggestion of the label that should be chosen, but allows the downstream node to choose a different label if it wants to. The suggested label is carried on the LSP setup request and simply looks like a generalized label.

The concept of label suggestion is particularly useful to reduce LSP setup in switches in which hardware components may take some time to program. For example, some optical switches use micromirrors that may take tens of milliseconds to direct and stabilize. Without label suggestion, the time to set up an LSP across n nodes is

$$T_n = 2(n-1)(mpt) + n(spt)$$

where *mpt* is the message propagation time and *spt* is the switch programming time.

Label suggestion, however, allows the upstream nodes to perform switch programming on the forward path (during setup request propagation) and to send the setup request onward even before they start to program their hardware. In this case, the time for LSP establishment may drop as low as

$$T_n = 2(n-1)(mpt) + (spt)$$

Of course, there is some chance that some or all of the labels supplied in the LSP setup responses will differ from the labels preprogrammed into the hardware, but this situation is no worse than if the upstream nodes had waited for the responses without taking any action.

GMPLS also allows for very detailed control of the labels used on some or all of the links that an LSP traverses. A strict, fully specified hop in an explicit route may be followed by a new subobject that mandates the label that must be used on the link to the next node. Note that specifying a label in an explicit route after a loose hop or for a hop that is not fully specified would be ambiguous and so is not allowed. This form of *explicit label control* has many applications in traffic engineered networks, especially those that contain a mix of nodes that can and cannot convert labels. It is also useful in optical networks where the impairments caused by the choice of different wavelength can be factored into the way in which LSPs are established. A final use of labels in explicit routes allows the selection or indication of a final port, wavelength, or timeslot on which to send the payload traffic when it reaches the end of the LSP.

10.2.4 Bidirectional Services

MPLS is limited to unidirectional LSPs. This is usually not an issue in packet switched applications because separate LSPs can be set up for the reverse direction traffic as required, and these reverse LSPs can use different paths as necessary. GMPLS, however, is often applied to networks that are fundamentally bidirectional (such as those carrying voice traffic) and where it is appropriate for traffic flowing in both directions to share the same links. To achieve this, bidirectional LSPs are needed.

It might have been possible to derive a method of establishing two parallel LSPs, one in each direction, sharing the same paths and tied together. Indeed, some early implementations took this approach, using the recorded route on the forward LSP to feed an explicit route on the reverse LSP. However, this method is clumsy and hard to manage, so GMPLS includes a mechanism to request setup of a single, bidirectional LSP.

For a bidirectional LSP to work, the labels used by traffic traveling in the reverse direction (egress to ingress) must be distributed by the upstream nodes to the downstream nodes. Note that terminology at this point gets very confusing! Upstream, downstream, ingress, and egress are generally interpreted with respect to the initial LSP setup request. That is, the node that requests the LSP is the ingress and is upstream of all other nodes, and the target of the LSP setup is the egress and is downstream of all the other nodes. That data flow from downstream to upstream (egress to ingress) is just a fact of bidirectionality. This traffic may be usefully described as reverse direction traffic.

Since LSP setup uses just one exchange of messages (Path and Resv, or Label Request and Label Mapping) the label advertisement for reverse direction traffic must be made on the LSP setup request. This is done using an Upstream Label which looks just like a generalized label and tells the downstream node which label it must use to send reverse direction traffic on this LSP.

There is a considerable risk that the downstream node will not be able to use the supplied upstream label because of hardware or other restrictions. If this is the case, it must reject the LSP setup. This leaves the upstream node to guess another value for the upstream label and try again. In the case of pure optical switches the failure may have to be passed back further through the network before it can be resolved. The potential need for multiple setup requests probing different upstream labels is addressed by allowing the downstream node that rejects a bidirectional LSP setup request to include an Acceptable Label Set that tells the upstream node which labels would have been acceptable to the downstream node. Acceptable Label Sets look like and are managed in the same way as label sets.

It is a requirement of GMPLS that the reverse path be considered complete by the time the LSP setup request has completed processing at the egress node. At this point it is acceptable for traffic to start to flow in the reverse direction along the LSP. On the face of it, this means that switch programming must be done at each node before the request is forwarded downstream, thus reversing the setup latency gains made by using a suggested label (see the previous section). However, it may be possible to make some assumptions about the uniformity of programming behavior at each node so that setup requests can be forwarded at once with the programming happening in the background, and the egress node pausing a short while before declaring the reverse data path open. Another option favored by some implementations that use RSVP-TE is to program in the background, and for the egress node to request confirmation of LSP establishment from the ingress (using ResvConf) before sending data on the reverse path.

Both of these alternatives, nonstandard approaches to handling bidirectional LSP setup, require that all nodes in the network behave in the same way—something that may be unlikely when mixing equipment from different vendors.

10.2.5 Protection Services

The ability to provision end-to-end connections that are capable of surviving network outages so that data can be delivered continuously is very important in telecom applications. There are two ways of providing protection for an LSP in the network shown in Figure 10.6. The first approach actually establishes two parallel LSPs, for example, from LSR A to LSR L through {A, E, F, G, L} and {A, H, J, K, L}. These are designated *primary* and *backup* LSPs, the primary carrying traffic until it is disrupted, at which time the traffic is switched to the backup.

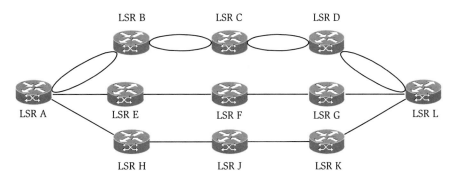

Figure 10.6 Protection services in GMPLS.

Figure 10.7 GMPLS Protection Request.

Table 10.5 GMPLS Protection Link Flags

Flag	Name	Meaning
0x01	Extra Traffic	The LSP may use links that currently protect other LSPs. If the link is required to carry active traffic for the protected LSP, this LSP may be preempted.
0x02	Unprotected	The LSP should not use any link protection.
0x04	Shared	A shared link protection scheme such as $1{:}n$ protection should be used.
0x08	Dedicated 1:1	Dedicated one-for-one link protection should be used.
0x10	Dedicated 1+1	Dedicated one-plus-one link protection should be used.
0x20	Enhanced	An enhanced protection scheme giving better protection than dedicated one-plus-one link protection should be used.

Alternatively, the protection of the data path can be provided by using links that are themselves protected so that if there is a break it will not disrupt the traffic. The path {A, B, C, D, L} in Figure 10.6 would support such an LSP. Both forms of protection can be utilized at the same time.

GMPLS is designed to allow protected LSPs to be requested. The GMPLS Protection Object shown in Figure 10.7 can be included in the LSP setup request to indicate through the S-flag whether this is a primary (set to zero) or secondary (set to 1) LSP. Additionally, link flags can be set to require that the LSP use only links that provide at least the level of protection specified. The link flags are shown in Table 10.5 and may not be combined (that is, they are not really flags!).

10.2.6 Managing Connections and Alarms

LSPs in GMPLS often require the activation of physical resources such as the turning on of a laser. It is often useful to be able to establish an LSP in a test mode, determining the path and reserving the resources without actually activating them. At the same time, management of the hardware alarms (that is, notifications of hardware errors) may be desirable so that the act of establishing or tearing down an LSP does not, of itself, cause alarms to be raised.

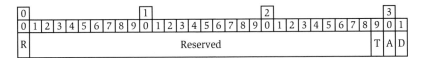

Figure 10.8 The GMPLS Administrative Status bits.

Table 10.6 The GMPLS Administrative Status Bits

Bit	Meaning
R	This bit is used to force an end-to-end response to the change in Administrative Status. When the bit is set, the receiving edge node should reflect the object back (with this bit cleared) in the appropriate signaling message.
T	The Testing bit is used to put the LSP into testing mode. The actions taken are implementation and media dependent, but this could allow the LSP to be set up without reservation of resources, proving the path without tying up resources.
A	The Administrative bit is used to put the LSP into an administrative down state. This might be used to turn off alarm reporting during LSP setup. Note that setting this bit indicates down not up.
D	The Deletion bit is used to indicate that the LSP is about to be torn down or request that it be torn down. This can be used to achieve alarm-free LSP teardown.

The GMPLS Administrative Status object allows an LSP end point (ingress or egress) to change the administrative status of the LSP. The precise actions of the nodes on the LSP are not defined, but instead, the bits are defined to cause local actions appropriate to setting the status of the LSP. Figure 10.8 shows the contents of the GMPLS Administrative Status object that is common to RSVP-TE and CR-LDP. Table 10.6 explains the meanings of the bits within the object.

The example message flow for RSVP-TE in Figure 10.27 shows the use of the Administrative Status object to achieve alarm-free LSP establishment and teardown.

10.2.7 Out of Band Signaling

Many transport media do not include the ability to identify individual packets. Indeed, the purpose of high-speed media and switches is to transport data with a much greater granularity than individual packets. Thus, a switch that is responsible for switching entire wavelengths from one fiber to another will not examine the contents of the signal, both for speed and because it often lacks the ability to do so—a pure optical switch, for example, can split wavelengths from a fiber and direct them to other ports, but does not include the electronic components to convert the light signal to electronics and extract the individual packets.

This may pose a problem for signaling components in GMPLS since those components need to be able to exchange control messages using IP packets. In MPLS, those packets flow along the same links as the packet data and can easily be distinguished from the data through their ports and addresses, the IP Router Alert flag, and the Next Protocol indication in the IP header. This option is not available in GMPLS for some transport media and it is necessary for the control channel to be discrete from the data channel—the control signaling is *out of band*.

There is a range of possibilities for out of band signaling. A well-known lambda or timeslot may be reserved for use by the control channel: this is in fiber out of band signaling. Alternatively, the control channel may utilize a separate link, perhaps following a distinct path: this is out of band out of fiber signaling. Figure 10.9 shows how the control channel may be run through a routed IP network to provide control of multiple parallel transport links between a pair of LSRs.

There are two aligned issues to be handled for out of band signaling. It is necessary to deliver the signaling messages to the right nodes even though they follow separate paths, and it is important to identify the link that is to carry the LSP since the control message no longer arrives on that link. The first problem is handled by the signaling protocols and the way that they utilize IP, but the second issue needs the addition of GMPLS Interface Identifiers. These are presented as TLV (type-length-variable) structures so that they can be placed in different objects and so that multiple interfaces can exist within one object. The type field indicates what type of address can be found in the variable field, and the length gives the length of the whole TLV in bytes. The defined type values are shown in Table 10.7.

The IPv4 and IPv6 address types are encoded as usual. For the other three interface identifier types the interface is identified by an IPv4 address followed by an index, as shown in Figure 10.10.

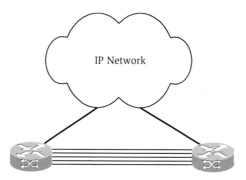

Figure 10.9 An out of band control channel connection may be provided through a single IP connection to an IP network for multiple parallel data channels.

Table 10.7 GMPLS Interface Identifier Types

Type	Length	Usage
1	8	IPv4 Address
2	20	IPv6 Address
3	12	Interface Index
4	12	Downstream Component Interface
5	12	Upstream Component Interface

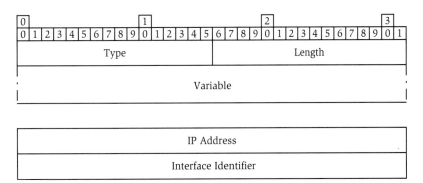

Figure 10.10 Interface identification in GMPLS is expressed through one or more TLVs. Component interfaces use IPv4 addresses and an interface identifier.

10.2.8 Choosing to Use GMPLS Signaling

There are three questions to consider before adopting GMPLS as a provisioning service in a network. Is a signaling mechanism appropriate in the network? Would MPLS provide all of the required functionality? Is there some other suitable signaling mechanism?

Optical transport networks have historically been provisioned manually. That is, operators have visited each switch using remote configuration tools such as Telnet or SNMP (see Chapter 13) to program the switching operations at each switch. Such manual configuration is not only time consuming, it is error-prone because an operator may have to enter hundreds of commands before an end-to-end data connection is fully established. The combination of configuration time and the planning time necessary to place the data service correctly has meant that the roll-out of new services has frequently taken days or even months, even when the hardware resources exist and are lying unused within the network. Slow provisioning like this can lead to unhappy or lost customers. Attempts to reduce the planning time for service delivery can often result in connections being routed badly and network resources being stranded, unreachable, and unusable.

In a similar way, when a service is no longer required, manual configuration is necessary to de-provision all associated resources across the network. This process is equally error-prone and can be scary to an operator who is also supporting high-profile, high-paying customers. It is better to be safe than sorry, so in some cases resources are left in place, provisioned but unused, and unusable by any other service.

An automated provisioning service like that provided by GMPLS can activate new services in a matter of seconds and can be tied to path computation engines to derive optimal paths through the network and to avoid stranding resources as unreachable. At the same time, a service that has been provisioned through signaling can be tracked by signaling so that all of the resources can be easily released when the service is no longer required. In this way the use of a signaling protocol in an optical transport network can significantly reduce operation expenditure and capital expenditure since better use can be made of fewer resources.

Having established that a signaling protocol is desirable, the choice must still be made between GMPLS and other standard and proprietary protocols. The obvious advantage of a standardized protocol suite that is designed for interoperability must be weighed against the immaturity of the standards. At the time of writing, the deployed base of GMPLS is relatively small, although it should be of some comfort that GMPLS builds on proven MPLS technology and that interoperability tests between vendors have been successful. From the perspective of this book, the choice between GMPLS and other standardized signaling/routing protocol suites such as PNNI is simple—GMPLS is an IP-based set of control protocols that utilize proven and installed IP infrastructure and is easily integrated into existing IP networks.

The choice between MPLS and GMPLS in a traffic engineered network applies only where the network is capable of layer-2 or packet switching. The decision here is largely evolutionary since GMPLS supports all of the capabilities of MPLS. Although it is possible for a single switch to support MPLS and GMPLS at the same time on the same interface, note that the process is slightly more than trivial since MPLS and GMPLS use marginally differing objects. Where networks are only switching frames/cells or packets it is likely that the short-term decision will be in favor of MPLS, but as GMPLS becomes proven, and as the need to support interaction between different switching types grows, GMPLS will become universal in all label switching networks.

10.3 Choosing RSVP-TE or CR-LDP in GMPLS

The choice between RSVP-TE and CR-LDP in GMPLS is the same as that for traffic engineered MPLS described in Section 9.8. However, it should be noted that the standardization process for GMPLS was some eighteen months behind that for MPLS-TE, with the result that by the time the GMPLS RFCs had been published the IETF had already decided that there should be no new work on CR-LDP. In consequence, the chance of the adoption of CR-LDP for GMPLS looks to be less than negligible.

10.4 Generalized RSVP-TE

RSVP-TE (see Chapter 9) can easily be extended for use as a signaling protocol for GMPLS. A few new objects are needed to carry the additional information described in Section 10.2, and a single new message is added to allow more direct notification of errors than was previously supported by the protocol. However, the basic message exchanges remain unchanged.

The sections that follow identify changes to RSVP-TE above and beyond the inclusion of generic GMPLS objects within the signaling messages. Section 10.4.5 lists the new objects used to carry all of the new information, and the sections that follow show how the protocol messages are constructed for GMPLS message exchange.

10.4.1 Enhanced Route Control

RSVP-TE as used in MPLS includes the ability to record labels within the Record Route object (RRO) on Path and Resv messages. Since GMPLS allows for bidirectional LSPs, there is a label in each direction and these must both be recorded in the RRO to provide full informational feedback about the LSP. One of the reserved flags bits is used (as shown in Figure 10.11) to indicate the direction of the label. If the U-bit is zero (as it would be in MPLS) the label is for the forward path, but if it is set to one, the label is an upstream label for use in the reverse direction.

GMPLS also allows the Explicit Route Object (ERO) to contain information controlling which labels are used on a specific hop between a pair of nodes by including an Explicit Route Label Subobject, as shown in Figure 10.12. As with the RRO, the U-bit indicates the direction in which the label must be applied.

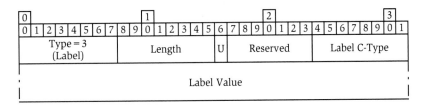

Figure 10.11 The modified Record Route Subobject for recording bidirectional labels in GMPLS.

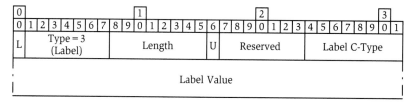

Figure 10.12 The new GMPLS Explicit Route Subobject for explicit label control.

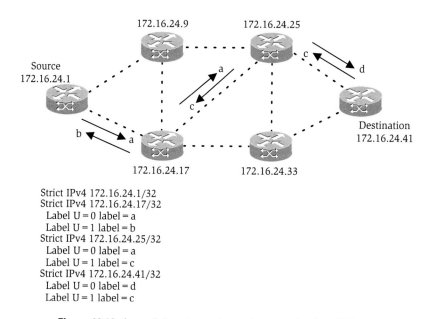

Strict IPv4 172.16.24.1/32
Strict IPv4 172.16.24.17/32
  Label U = 0 label = a
  Label U = 1 label = b
Strict IPv4 172.16.24.25/32
  Label U = 0 label = a
  Label U = 1 label = c
Strict IPv4 172.16.24.41/32
  Label U = 0 label = d
  Label U = 1 label = c

Figure 10.13 An explicit route may be used to control path and labels.

The L-bit indicates whether the subobject is loose or strict—and for this type of subobject must be set to zero and ignored.

There are several other restrictions placed on the use of a label subobject within an ERO to make sure that there is no ambiguity in the application of the label requirement. The label subobjects are defined to apply to the link between the current node and the node identified by the subobject that immediately precedes the label subobjects. This node must be identified unambiguously, so the subobject that precedes the label subobjects must be fully explicit (for example, a 32-bit IPv4 prefix), not an Autonomous System number, and must be a strict hop. Figure 10.13 shows how an ERO might be constructed to achieve label control through a simple network for an LSP from the source (172.16.24.1) to the destination (172.16.24.41). The path is forced to include the two transit LSRs 172.16.24.17 and 172.16.24.25, and labels are mandated on each hop.

EROs and RROs can also contain GMPLS interface identifiers to allow control and reporting of interfaces when there are parallel links between a pair of nodes.

10.4.2 Reducing Protocol Overheads

RSVP was designed to be flexible to routing changes and to make resource reservations on the new paths, leaving the old paths to timeout and release their resources for use by other traffic flows. The protocol uses a process of refreshing state between nodes to keep the state active: for this reason RSVP state is known as a *soft state* protocol. Although soft state is good for managing IP microflows, it is less appropriate for traffic engineering, where the path is more stable. It is even less suitable in some GMPLS networks where rerouting is a very controlled process.

The overhead of message exchange to maintain soft state is a considerable concern in many networks and although it can be addressed using the standard RSVP refresh reduction techniques (see Chapter 6) there remain concerns about reliable message delivery. These are addressed in GMPLS by making every message carry a message ID, just like a Path message does in RSVP refresh reduction. In this way, each message can expect an acknowledgment, and the sender can determine whether the message should be resent. Although the Message ID object is optional on GMPLS messages, in practice it is used on all messages apart from Hellos.

An optimization can be made in GMPLS to facilitate LSP clean-up after error events or after egress initiated teardown. In RSVP-TE, a network failure causes a PathErr to be sent upstream and leaves the ingress responsible for sending a PathTear to release resources. Similarly, if the egress node wishes to end the LSP it may send ResvTear and wait to receive a PathTear. In GMPLS, a new flag (the Path State Removed Flag—value 0x4) is added to the Error Spec object in the PathErr message to indicate that state has already been removed by the downstream nodes. This removes the need for further message exchanges as shown in Figure 10.14.

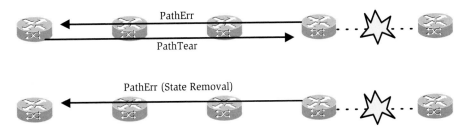

Figure 10.14 The State Removal flag on a PathErr message reduces the number of messages exchanged during tidy-up after LSP failure.

10.4.3 Notification Requests and Messages

An increasingly important aspect of network design is the ability to recover from failures of links or nodes. Ideally, this should be automatic and should result in minimal disruption of data transfer. There are three phases in providing this service: error detection, error notification, and error recovery. Error detection is largely a matter for hardware, although the RSVP Hello message exchange can be used to detect certain failures. Error recovery is specific to the system and the level of service being provided—traffic may be automatically switched to backup dedicated LSPs, or new LSPs may be signaled on demand.

Error notification, however, falls within the scope of the signaling protocol. RSVP-TE has the PathErr and ResvErr messages to propagate information about network failures, but these messages are forwarded hop-by-hop, requiring protocol processing at each node. This could be slow, and since one of the objectives of failure reporting is to switch the traffic to the new path as quickly as possible, a new message, the Notify message, is introduced into RSVP-TE for GMPLS. This new message is addressed and sent directly (perhaps requiring IP forwarding, but not needing any intervention by higher-level protocols) to the node that will effect the recovery of the LSP. This has the added advantage of being able to traverse a path through the network that is selected by the routing protocol and does not follow the LSP.

When an error occurs, the detecting nodes need to send a message upstream and downstream to notify repair points that they must take some form of recovery action. In Figure 10.15 the link between LSRs D and E fails and this is noticed by the two nodes. LSR D is responsible for sending a notification upstream and LSR E must send one downstream. But how do they know that Notify messages are desired, and how do they know where to send them?

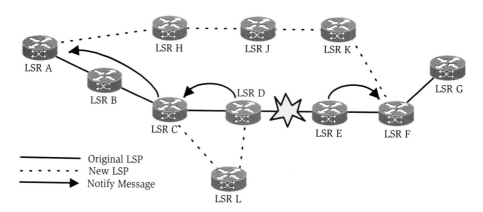

Figure 10.15 The use of Notify messages in an RSVP-TE GMPLS network.

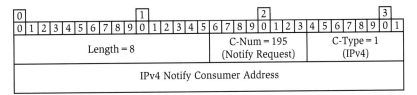

Figure 10.16 The RSVP-TE GMPLS IPv4 Notify Request object.

The answer is that a new message object, the Notify Request object shown in Figure 10.16, may be placed in Path and Resv messages to request that the Notify message be generated. If present on a Path message, the object indicates that a Notify message should be sent upstream and gives the address to which the message should be sent. If present on a Resv message, the Notify Request object indicates the node to which a Notify message should be sent in the downstream direction. It is even possible that for management reasons the consumer of the Notify message could be another node completely disjointed from the LSP.

As a Path or Resv message passes through the network, nodes may replace the address in the Notify Request object, substituting their own addresses so that they see the Notify messages. In Figure 10.15 an LSP is set up from LSR A to LSR G. LSR A adds a Notify Request object to the Path message so that it will know about any problems with the LSP. When the Path message reaches LSR C, it substitutes its own address because it knows that it has limited capabilities to repair the LSP. Similarly, the Resv contains a Notify Request object from LSR G, and LSR F substitutes its address. When an error occurs on the link between LSRs D and E, both LSRs notice the problem. LSR D sends a Notify message to LSR C, and LSR E sends one to LSR F. Since LSR C is unable to repair the LSP it sends a Notify message onward to LSR A, where the traffic can be diverted to a new LSP.

The Notify message can be sent to alert nodes to other events beyond link failures. For example, when a resource recovers after a failure, a Notify message can be sent allowing traffic to be reverted to the preferred path.

The format of the Notify message is shown in Section 10.4.6. It allows for multiple LSPs associated with the same error to be reported on the same Notify message. This has the considerable advantage of reducing the storm of messages that might be generated as the result of a single error.

10.4.4 Graceful Restart

An important feature of out of band signaling (see Section 10.2.7) is that a disruption to the control plane does not necessarily imply any effect on the data plane. RSVP and RSVP-TE may assume that the failure to receive a Path or Resv refresh indicates that the local state should be released, but in GMPLS it may be

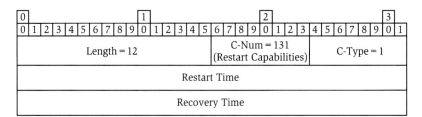

Figure 10.17 The Restart Capabilities Object carried in Hello messages in GMPLS.

desirable to maintain the LSP so that data traffic is not affected. Similarly, in RSVP-TE the failure to receive Hello messages can be an indication that the link or adjacent node has failed.

GMPLS modifies this behavior by allowing LSPs to persist even when the control channel is down. An additional object on the Hello messages, the Restart Capabilities Object shown in Figure 10.17, indicates that the adjacent nodes are capable of surviving control plane faults. When Hello messages have not been received, an LSR must stop expecting to receive refresh messages and not time-out any LSPs. If Hellos have not been recovered within the time indicated by the Restart Time field (specified in milliseconds) then the LSR should declare the LSPs failed. A Restart Time of minus one (0xffffffff) is used to indicate an indefinite wait, allowing the distinction to be drawn between restarting the control plane and operating the data plane without any control plane.

Once Hello message exchange has been recovered, the LSRs need to resynchronize state. If the Recovery Time field on the new Hello message is set to zero, then no state was retained and the LSRs must treat the LSPs as having failed and must reestablish them as necessary. Otherwise, the field indicates how long it will take to resynchronize state—after this period, any LSPs that have not been resynchronized should be treated as failed.

Resynchronization is largely a matter of exchanging Path and Resv messages; however, there is the possibility that although the data plane is fully programmed and operational, only the upstream node is actually aware of the label that is in use. When it sends a Path message with a Label Set and Suggested Label, it indicates that the label is already in use by also adding a Recovery Label object to the message. This object is identical to the Suggested Label object but carries a different C-Num.

10.4.5 New and Changed Message Objects

A few new error codes have been added for GMPLS. These are listed in Table 10.8.

Table 10.9 lists the Class Numbers for the new message objects introduced into RSVP-TE for GMPLS. Where new Class Types have been added to existing Class Numbers, these are also shown.

Table 10.8 New RSVP-TE Error Codes Introduced for GMPLS

Error Value	Error Code	Meaning
24	11	Routing problem/Label set
24	12	Routing problem/Switching type
24	14	Routing problem/Unsupported encoding
24	15	Routing problem/Unsupported link protection
25	4	Notify error/Control channel active state
25	5	Notify error/Control channel degraded state

Table 10.9 New RSVP-TE Objects Introduced for GMPLS

C-Num	C-Type	Notes
19	4	Generalized Label Request Object. Used in a Path message in place of a Label Request object when GMPLS is to be used instead of MPLS. It is differentiated from a Label Request Object by the C-Type only, and is according to its C-Num just a variant of a Label Request object. The object carries the Encoding Type, Switching Type, and G-PID of the LSP as defined in Section 10.2.2.
16	2	Generalized Label Object. Used in a Resv message in response to a Path that carried a Generalized Label Request. It is differentiated from a Label object by the C-Type only, and is according to its C-Num just a variant of a Label object. It carries a Generalized Label as described in Section 10.2.1.
16	3	Waveband Label Object. When the Generalized Label Request asks for a waveband label an object of this type is returned in the Resv carrying a waveband label, as described in Section 10.2.1. It is also just a variant of a Label Object.
129	2/3	Suggested Label Object. Used on a Path message to make a strong suggestion to the downstream node of which label should be allocated for forward direction traffic. The label is encoded as described in Section 10.2.1.
36	2/3	Label Set Object. The set of labels that would be acceptable to the upstream node if allocated by the downstream node for forward traffic. The structure of a label set is described in Section 10.2.3.
35	2/3	Upstream Label Object. Defines by its presence that a bidirectional LSP is being established and indicates to the downstream node the label that must be used for reverse direction traffic. Bidirectional LSPs are discussed in Section 10.2.4. This object carries a label as described in Section 10.2.1.
130	2/3	Acceptable Label Set Object. Used by a downstream node when it rejects a Path message that was asking to set up a bidirectional LSP. Lists those labels that would be acceptable to the downstream node if they were selected in an Upstream Label object by the upstream node. Bidirectional LSPs are discussed in Section 10.2.4. This object carries a label set as described in Section 10.2.3.

Table 10.9 *Continued*

C-Num	C-Type	Notes
195	1/2	Notify Request Object. Carried on a Path or Resv message as described in Section 10.4.4 to identify (using an IPv4 address if the C-Type is 1 or an IPv6 address if it is 2) the recipient of any Notify message that may be sent.
37	1	GMPLS Protection Object. Defines the level of protection that is required from the underlying links to support this LSP and indicates whether this LSP is a primary or backup LSP. The contents of the object are described in Section 10.2.5.
196	1	Administrative Status Object. Used to control the status of the LSP as described in Section 10.2.6.
3	3/4	Interface Identified RSVP Hop Object. Enhanced RSVP Hop object to indicate which link is used for the LSP.
6	3/4	Interface Identified Error Spec Object. Enhanced Error Spec object reporting the link that is at fault.
131	1	Restart Capabilities Object. Present on a Hello message to indicate that state should be resynchronized after restart.
34	2/3	Recovery Label Object. Present on a Path message to restore an LSP using a label that is already in use.

10.4.6 Message Formats

The message formats are structurally unchanged from RSVP-TE, but new message objects are added, and so it is useful to show them again in full in Figures 10.18 through 10.21. The format of the Flow Descriptor remains unchanged from RSVP-TE (see Section 9.7.9). The new Notify message is also shown in Figure 10.22.

10.4.7 Message Exchanges

The message exchanges are also largely unchanged from RSVP-TE. Figure 10.27 demonstrates alarm-free LSP establishment, error notification, and alarm-free teardown. At step 1 LSR A starts to set up an LSP by sending a Path message. It sets the Administrative Status flags to show that the LSP is administratively down (that is, alarms are disabled) and adds a Notify Request object requesting that it be notified of any problems.

The Path message is propagated to LSR D, which responds with a Resv (step 2) as normal. When the Resv reaches LSR A the LSP has been established and can start to carry traffic. LSR A enables alarms by sending a further Path

```
< Path Message > ::=        < Common Header >
                            [ < INTEGRITY > ]
                            [[ < MESSAGE_ID_ACK > | < MESSAGE_ID_NACK > ] ... ]
                            [ < MESSAGE_ID > ]
                             < SESSION >
                             < RSVP_HOP >
                             < TIME_VALUES >
                            [ < EXPLICIT_ROUTE > ]
                             < LABEL_REQUEST >
                            [ < PROTECTION > ]
                            [ < LABEL_SET > ... ]
                             < SESSION_ATTRIBUTE > ]
                            [ < NOTIFY_REQUEST > ]
                            [ < ADMIN_STATUS > ]
                            [ < POLICY_DATA > ]
                             < SENDER_TEMPLATE >
                             < SENDER_TSPEC >
                            [ < ADSPEC > ]
                            [ < RECORD_ROUTE > ]
                            [ < SUGGESTED_LABEL > ]
                            [ < RECOVERY_LABEL > ]
                            [ < UPSTREAM_LABEL > ]
```

Figure 10.18 Formal definition of the GMPLS Path message.

```
< Resv Message > ::=        < Common Header >
                            [ < INTEGRITY > ]
                            [[ < MESSAGE_ID_ACK > | < MESSAGE_ID_NACK > ] ... ]
                            [ < MESSAGE_ID > ]
                             < SESSION >
                             < RSVP_HOP >
                             < TIME_VALUES >
                            [ < RESV_CONFIRM > ]
                            [ < SCOPE > ]
                            [ < NOTIFY_REQUEST > ]
                            [ < ADMIN_STATUS > ]
                            [ < POLICY_DATA > ]
                             < STYLE >
                             < flow descriptor list >
```

Figure 10.19 Formal definition of the GMPLS Resv message.

```
< PathErr Message > ::=      < Common Header >
                             [ < INTEGRITY > ]
                             [[ < MESSAGE_ID_ACK > | < MESSAGE_ID_NACK > ] . . . ]
                             [ < MESSAGE_ID > ]
                              < SESSION >
                              < ERROR_SPEC >
                             [ < ACCEPTABLE_LABEL_SET > ]
                             [ < POLICY_DATA > ]
                              < SENDER_TEMPLATE >
                              < SENDER_TSPEC >
                             [ < ADSPEC > ]
                             [ < RECORD_ROUTE > ]
                             [ < SUGGESTED_LABEL > ]
                             [ < RECOVERY_LABEL > ]
                             [ < UPSTREAM_LABEL > ]
```

Figure 10.20 Formal definition of the GMPLS PathErr message.

```
< ResvErr Message > ::=      < Common Header >
                             [ < INTEGRITY > ]
                             [[ < MESSAGE_ID_ACK > | < MESSAGE_ID_NACK > ] . . . ]
                             [ < MESSAGE_ID > ]
                              < SESSION >
                              < RSVP_HOP >
                              < ERROR_SPEC >
                             [ < SCOPE > ]
                             [ < ACCEPTABLE_LABEL_SET > ]
                             [ < POLICY_DATA > ]
                              < STYLE >
                              < error flow descriptor >
```

Figure 10.21 Formal definition of the GMPLS ResvErr message.

```
< Notify message > ::=       < Common Header >
                             [ < INTEGRITY > ]
                             [[ < MESSAGE_ID_ACK > | < MESSAGE_ID_NACK > ] . . . ]
                             [ < MESSAGE_ID > ]
                              < ERROR_SPEC >
                              < notify session list >
```

Figure 10.22 Formal definition of the new GMPLS Notify message.

```
< notify session list > ::=     < upstream notify session > | < downstream notify session >
                                [ < notify session list > ]
```

Figure 10.23 Formal definition of the Notify Session List on the GMPLS Notify message.

```
< upstream notify session > ::=     < SESSION >
                                    [ < ADMIN_STATUS > ]
                                    [ < POLICY_DATA > ... ]
                                    < SENDER_TEMPLATE >
                                    < SENDER_TSPEC >
                                    [ < ADSPEC > ]
                                    [ < RECORD_ROUTE > ]
                                    [ < SUGGESTED_LABEL > ]
                                    [ < RECOVERY_LABEL > ]
                                    [ < UPSTREAM_LABEL > ]
```

Figure 10.24 Formal definition of the Upstream Notify Session: a single element in a Notify Session List on the GMPLS Notify Message.

```
< downstream notify session > ::=     < SESSION >
                                      [ < POLICY_DATA > ... ]
                                      < flow descriptor list >
```

Figure 10.25 Formal definition of the Downstream Notify Session: a single element in a Notify Session List on the GMPLS Notify message.

```
< Hello Message > ::=     < Common Header >
                          [ < INTEGRITY > ]
                          < HELLO >
                          [ < RESTART_CAP > ]
```

Figure 10.26 Formal definition of the GMPLS Hello message.

message (step 3) carrying an Administrative Status object with the Reflect flag set and the Administrative Status flag cleared. As each LSR receives and processes the Path message it enables alarms on its hardware and propagates the Path message until it reaches the egress, LSR D. Since the Reflect flag is set, LSR D must respond with a Resv carrying the Administrative Status object (step 4) so that there is a full handshake and LSR A knows that the LSP is fully operational.

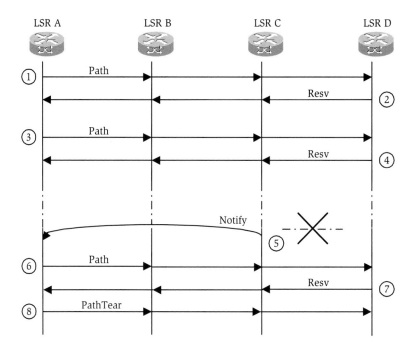

Figure 10.27 Alarm-free LSP establishment and teardown with a link failure and Notify message.

After some time there is a failure on the data link between LSRs C and D. LSR C notices this failure and sends a Notify message (step 5) as requested by LSR A. LSR A decides to teardown the LSP, avoiding alarms, so it sends a Path message (step 6) carrying the Administrative Status object with the Reflect and Administrative Status flags set. As this Path message propagates, each LSR disables alarms on its hardware until the Path reaches LSR D. Since the Reflect flag is set, LSR D must respond with a Resv carrying the Administrative Status object (step 7) so that there is a full handshake and LSR A knows that alarms have been disabled on the LSP and it is safe to send a PathTear (step 8).

10.5 Generalized CR-LDP

As stated in Section 10.3, even though CR-LDP has been specified as a signaling protocol for GMPLS it is unlikely that it will ever be significantly deployed. For that reason a discussion of the extensions to the protocol would be largely academic. However, for completeness, the sections that follow list the new TLVs, and show how they are placed in the messages.

Table 10.11 New CR-LDP TLVs Introduced for GMPLS

Type	TLV
0x0824	Generalized Label Request
0x0825	Generalized Label
0x0826	Upstream Label
0x0827	Label Set
0x0828	Waveband Label
0x0829	Label ER-Hop
0x082A	Acceptable Label Set
0x082B	Administrative Status Object
0x082C	Interface ID
0x082D	IPv4 Interface ID
0x082E	IPv6 Interface ID
0x082F	IPv4 IF_ID Status
0x0830	IPv6 IF_ID Status

10.5.1 New TLVs

Table 10.11 lists the new TLV codes defined in CR-LDP to support GMPLS. The CR-LDP specification for GMPLS defines no new error codes and makes use of the error codes already defined for LDP and CR-LDP.

10.5.2 Message Formats

Table 10.12 shows the presence of the new GMPLS objects and the preexisting objects in CR-LDP messages for GMPLS.

10.6 Hierarchies and Bundles

The concepts of hierarchies of LSPs and bundles of links are closely aligned concepts in GMPLS that are both used to improve scalability. They are described in separate IETF documents that are also distinct from the main MPLS and GMPLS specifications, so that they may form add-ons to the core signaling function.

The scalability of GMPLS may be improved by creating a hierarchy of LSPs so that many LSPs are transported across the network encased in a single LSP tunnel. This can be achieved through the following steps:

Table 10.12 TLV Presence on CR-LDP Messages for GMPLS

Message	TLV	Presence
Label Request	Message ID	Mandatory
	FEC TLV	Mandatory
	LSPID TLV	Mandatory for CR-LDP
	Generalized Label Request TLV	Mandatory for GMPLS in CR-LDP
	ER-TLV	Optional for CR-LDP
	Traffic Parameters TLV	Optional for CR-LDP
	Route Pinning TLV	Optional for CR-LDP
	Resource Class TLV	Optional for CR-LDP
	Preemption TLV	Optional for CR-LDP
	Upstream Label TLV	Optional for GMPLS in CR-LDP
	Label Set TLV	Optional for GMPLS in CR-LDP
	Administrative Status TLV	Optional for GMPLS in CR-LDP
	Hop Count TLV	Optional
	Path Vector TLV	Optional
Label Mapping	Message ID	Mandatory
	FEC TLV	Mandatory
	Generalized Label TLV	Mandatory for GMPLS in CR-LDP
	Label Request Message ID TLV	Mandatory (downstream on demand)
	LSPID TLV	Optional for CR-LDP (required if on Label Request)
	Traffic Parameters TLV	Optional for CR-LDP (required if on Label Request)
	Administrative Status TLV	Optional for GMPLS in CR-LDP
	Hop Count TLV	Optional
	Path Vector TLV	Optional

- A Label Switching Router (LSR) creates traffic engineered LSP between itself and some other (usually nonadjacent) LSR.
- Once the LSP is established, it is advertised as a traffic engineering link (TE link) in the routing protocol at the same level as the links that actually support it. This creates a "virtual" Forwarding Adjacency (FA) between the LSRs at the ends of the LSP.

- Other LSRs can now use this FA as they compute paths for new LSPs and those LSPs can be directed to use the new TE-link (that is, can be sent through the tunnel).
- As LSPs traverse the virtual TE-link, label stacking is used to carry them through the tunnel.

No new protocol objects are required to support FAs and LSP hierarchies in this way. The IETF document simply contains an explanation of this procedure and guidance on how to assign and advertise interface identifiers for the LSP tunnel.

A scalability issue may also arise in GMPLS where there are very many parallel links between a pair of nodes. It is impractical to advertise each link separately through the routing protocol since this would swamp it and is essentially unnecessary if all of the links have similar properties. Instead, the links can be gathered together into *bundles* that are represented as a single TE-link. Having done this, however, it is necessary to be able to disambiguate the *component links* of the bundle so that LSPs can be placed on specific links.

Where the level of switching corresponds to the granularity of the link (most notably in fiber switching when the bundled links are fibers) the label is sufficient to distinguish the links within the bundle and no further work is required. However, where the label of itself is not enough (for example, lambda switching on fibers that are bundled) a new piece of information must be signaled.

The choice of component link on any hop is always made by the upstream LSR. It indicates the component link to use by including the Interface Identification information defined in the core GMPLS documents. The interface address identifies the TE link and the interface identifier identifies the link within the bundle. In this way, component links can also be mandated in explicit routes and reported in recorded routes.

Certain constraints are applied to link bundling to make the process manageable. All component links in a bundle must begin and end on the same pair of LSRs, have the same traffic engineering metric, and have the same set of resource classes at each end of the links.

Note that a Forwarding Adjacency may be a component link of a bundle so that, in the most extreme case, a bundle can be constructed from a mix of point-to-point links and FAs.

10.7 OSPF and IS-IS in GMPLS

The routing extensions to OSPF and IS-IS in support of GMPLS are built on the traffic engineering extensions to those protocols described in Section 8.5. This is wholly appropriate because GMPLS is simply an extension to the traffic engineering model in which a new meaning for bandwidth is applied to a variety of link types.

Only a few additional pieces of information need to be exchanged between routers to enable a GMPLS network. These are described in the following sections. It will be seen that many of them provide the details needed by a routing protocol or path computation engine to satisfy the service requests signaled during LSP setup using GMPLS. Looking ahead to Section 10.9 on LMP, it will be seen that many of these link characteristics may be discovered through the message exchanges of LMP.

10.7.1 A New Meaning for Bandwidth

In the traffic engineering extensions to OSPF and IS-IS the available bandwidth is advertised to help understand where resources are available and to place traffic or LSPs in the best possible way. In GMPLS the granularity of resource allocation may be limited. For example, a fiber may have a total of 160 GB per second of bandwidth available, but that bandwidth might only be available in 2.5 GB lumps corresponding to individual lambdas—this governs the maximum LSP bandwidth that can be allocated on the link. At the same time, for packet and TDM technologies it may be advantageous to control the lower size limit of bandwidth allocations on a link to help prevent the link from becoming swamped.

Add to this the need to reserve bandwidth for use at different priorities and to allow advertisement of resource availability according to the preemption schemes within MPLS and GMPLS and there is a batch of new link-related bandwidth information that needs to be added to the OSPF and IS-IS advertisements.

Bandwidths are expressed as 4-byte IEEE floating point numbers of bytes per second.

10.7.2 Switching and Protection Capabilities

Two further link properties that are important factors in choosing how to route LSPs in GMPLS are switching and protection capabilities. The switching capabilities shown in Table 10.13 indicate how traffic received on a link can be switched by the receiving node. The switching capabilities of a link are reported in OSPF and IS-IS along with the bandwidths available. If a link supports more than one switching capability, each capability must be reported along with the bandwidths supported in that mode. Note that the values used are noncontiguous decimals.

Some links provide protection of data traffic by actually comprising more than one physical connection. GMPLS allows an LSP to request that it use only this type of link to provide an extra level of protection for its data. For the LSP can be routed only over such links, the level of support offered by a link must also be advertised by the routing protocol. The protection types shown in Table 10.14 are defined as in GMPLS signaling. Unlike switching capabilities, these values

Table 10.13 Link Switching Capability Values

Value	Link Switching Capability
1	Packet-Switch Capable-1 (PSC-1)
2	Packet-Switch Capable-2 (PSC-2)
3	Packet-Switch Capable-3 (PSC-3)
4	Packet-Switch Capable-4 (PSC-4)
51	Layer-2 Switch Capable (L2SC)
100	Time-Division-Multiplex Capable (TDM)
150	Lambda-Switch Capable (LSC)
200	Fiber-Switch Capable (FSC)

Table 10.14 Link Protection Capability Values

Value	Link Protection Capability
0x01	Extra Traffic
0x02	Unprotected
0x04	Shared
0x08	Dedicated 1:1
0x10	Dedicated 1 + 1
0x20	Enhanced

may be combined bit-wise to allow multiple protection capabilities to be reported in one go.

10.7.3 Shared Risk Link Groups

A group of links that share a resource whose failure may affect all of the links in the same way can be grouped together as a *Shared Risk Link Group* (SRLG). A single link may belong to multiple SRLGs; for example, eight fibers that share the same conduit could be grouped into one SRLG, but separate SRLGs would identify the fact that after unbundling, four of the fibers are connected to one shelf in a switch while the other four are connected to another shelf. A backhoe judiciously applied to the conduit is likely to affect all eight fibers, but a toma-hawk applied to one of the shelves will affect only four of the fibers. Knowing the SRLGs to which links belong can be useful when establishing protected LSPs since the primary and backup paths can be selected to use links that do not share any (configured) failure risks.

An SRLG is identified by a 32-bit number that is unique within an IGP routing domain. The method of ensuring this uniqueness is outside the scope of any protocols and the whole business is a matter for configuration. However, once the SRLGs have been configured, they can be advertised as link properties by OSPF or IS-IS so that the path computation engines placing LSPs in the network can take advantage of the information.

10.7.4 OSPF Message Objects

A TE link between two nodes may be unnumbered, in which case the LSR at each of the links assigns an identifier to the link. This identifier is a nonzero 32-bit number that is unique within the scope of the LSR that assigns it. To support unnumbered links in routing, the local link identifiers must be advertised. In OSPF a node can communicate its Link Local Identifier to its neighbor using a link local opaque LSA, as shown in Figure 10.28.

New sub-TLVs of the Link TLV shown in Figure 10.29 are introduced to distribute the information described in the previous sections. The Link Local/Remote Identifier sub-TLV is used to reference the unnumbered interface identifier if the link is not numbered—if the remote identifier is not known at the time of advertisement, a value of zero is used.

The Link Switching Capabilities sub-TLV includes the bandwidths and switching types supported by the link. If the switching type is Packet, Layer-2, or TDM, additional parameters are included at the end of the sub-TLV.

The Shared Risk Link Group sub-TLV shown in Figure 10.30 can occur at most once in the Link TLV and is used to identify the link with one or more SRLGs. An SRLG identifier is a 32-bit value, and the contents of this sub-TLV is

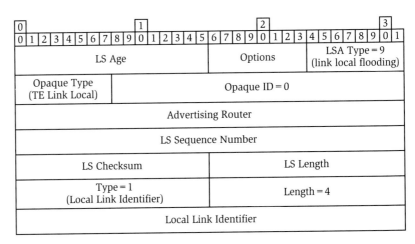

Figure 10.28 The OSPF opaque TE Link Local LSA.

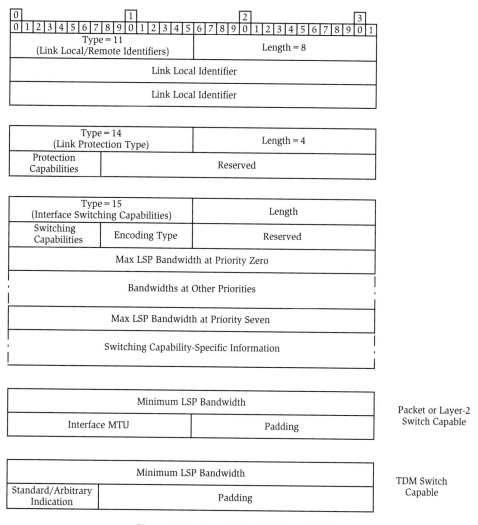

Figure 10.29 New OSPF sub-TLVs for GMPLS.

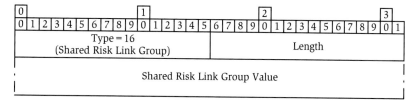

Figure 10.30 The OSPF Shared Risk Link Group (SRLG) sub-TLV.

an unordered list of SRLG identifiers. The length of the sub-TLV determines the size of the list.

10.7.5 IS-IS Message Objects

The Link Local/Remote Identifiers sub-TLV shown in Figure 10.31 may be carried in the Extended IS Reachability TLV to identify the local and remote ends of an unnumbered link. If the remote identifier is unknown, it is set to zero. The Link Protection and Link Switching sub-TLVs, also shown in Figure 10.31, may each appear at most once in the Extended IS Reachability TLV.

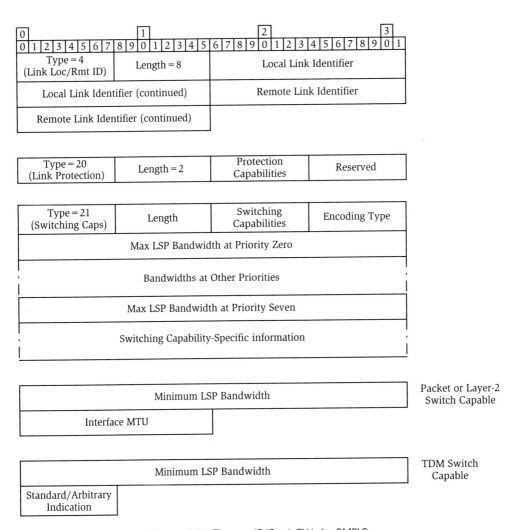

Figure 10.31 The new IS-IS sub-TLVs for GMPLS.

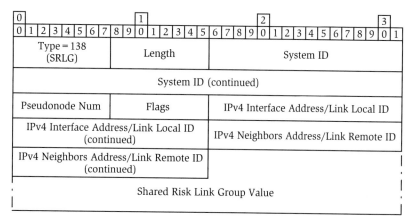

Figure 10.32 The IS-IS Shared Risk Link Group (SRLG) TLV.

The Shared Risk Link Group TLV shown in Figure 10.32 is used to identify the link with one or more SRLGs. An SRLG identifier is a 32-bit value, and the contents of this sub-TLV is an unordered list of SRLG identifiers. The length of the sub-TLV determines the size of the list.

10.7.6 Choosing Between OSPF and IS-IS in GMPLS

The choice between routing protocols in GMPLS may be somewhat more free than the choice when extending IP routing networks to support traffic engineering or MPLS since there is often no deployed routing infrastructure in the optical transport networks to which GMPLS is applied. However, if GMPLS is to be used for packet switching, then the choice of routing protocol may be constrained by existing deployed technologies.

From a functional standpoint there is no particular reason to choose one protocol over the other. The choice at the time of writing is influenced by a few relatively minor considerations.

- Existing technology owned by the switch manufacturer must be taken into consideration, it being considerably easier to extend one routing implementation than to construct a new one.
- Service Provider preferences, which may range from deployment experience to religious zeal, may be an issue.
- Interactions with other routing components at the edge of the GMPLS network will affect the choice. It will increasingly be the case that traffic engineering information is leaked between networks to allow the control of core optical networks from the packet networks that surround them. This control may utilize GMPLS in a peer-to-peer fashion or operate a well-defined signaling

interface such as the Optical Interworking Forum's User-to-Network Interface (the OIF-UNI). Whichever solution is used, it may be found to be easier to leak the required TE and routing information if the core network uses the same routing protocol as the surrounding networks.

10.8 Optical VPNs

Optical Virtual Private Networks are still at a conceptual stage. The aim is to provide edge-to-edge connectivity across an optical network for users or user networks. The connectivity would be managed within the core network in the same way that IP VPNs are currently managed, and a secure site-to-site connectivity would be provided as if by a private optical network.

Some models of the Optical VPN represent it as a single switch from the point of view of the user networks. This is represented in Figure 10.33. The switch has a series of ports, each of which can handle a set of labels. To achieve connectivity, the user networks request that the switch be programmed to map traffic from {input port, input label} to {output port, output label} as shown in Table 10.15. Under the covers, these requests are translated to LSP setup requests across the optical core. At the time of writing it is unclear whether the concept of an Optical VPN will require any additional routing or signaling objects.

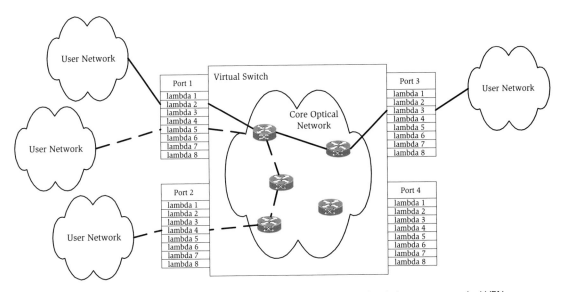

Figure 10.33 The core optical network may be represented as a virtual switch to support optical VPNs.

Table 10.15 The Label Forwarding Information Base (LFIB) for the Virtual Switch and Optical LSPs Represented in Figure 10.33

Incoming Port	Incoming Lambda	Outgoing Port	Outgoing Lambda
1	2	3	3
1	5	2	4

10.9 Link Management Protocol (LMP)

The optical networks in which GMPLS may operate present a number of new management issues.

- How can two switches learn the capabilities and identifiers of links that connect them without requiring coordinated configuration?
- How can the routing protocol be protected from having to advertise multiple parallel links in a bundle of fibers?
- Is there a way to detect and isolate faults in optical networks where some switches do not utilize electronic components on the data path (pure photonic switches)?

These questions are addressed by the Link Management Protocol (LMP), which is run between pairs of adjacent nodes. LMP also includes features to authenticate neighbors to protect against malign interference in a network.

LMP was originally specified to run over raw IP, but concerns about the proliferation of protocols and the shortage of IP protocol numbers has led it to be moved to run over UDP. This is not a big deal since LMP is a relatively light-weight protocol.

LMP messages are built from a common header followed by a series of objects. In many ways this is similar to the format of RSVP messages, and formal definitions of the messages are presented in the same BNF notation. Figure 10.34 shows how the common header and all of the objects are built. The header begins with a version number for LMP (version 1 is currently in use) and includes a Message Type field to indicate what sort of LMP message is being passed. The full list of message types is given in Table 10.16. The message length is in bytes and includes the whole message, including the header itself. The Flags field has 2 bits defined: 0x01 is used to request that the control channel be brought down gracefully, 0x02 indicates that there was some failure and that previous LMP state has been lost.

All LMP objects have the same format as is illustrated in Figure 10.34. The first bit is set to zero to indicate that the object that follows contains nonnegotiable information, and to one to show that the parameters may be negotiated. Perversely, the next field, the Class type field, is a qualifier for the subsequent Class field.

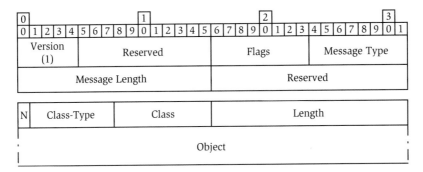

Figure 10.34 LMP common message header and object formats.

Table 10.16 LMP Message Types

Message Type	Message	Message Type	Message
1	Config	11	TestStatusSuccess
2	ConfigAck	12	TestStatusFailure
3	ConfigNack	13	TestStatusAck
4	Hello	14	LinkSummary
5	BeginVerify	15	LinkSummaryAck
6	BeginVerifyAck	16	LinkSummaryNack
7	BeginVerifyNack	17	ChannelStatus
8	EndVerify	18	ChannelStatusAck
9	EndVerifyAck	19	ChannelStatusRequest
10	Test	20	ChannelStatusResponse

The Class identifies the object family and the Class-Type shows the use to which the object is put; together they fully identify the purpose of the object. The Length field gives the length of the entire object, including the common fields.

Message IDs are used in LMP for correlation of requests and responses. Each request carries a unique ID and the associated response returns the ID so that the originator can tie the two together. Message IDs could be incrementing integers or might be implemented as pointers to memory on the originating node. Since each message is acknowledged and uniquely identified, a rapid retransmission algorithm can be used to protect against lost messages—note that UDP does not give this level of protection.

The LMP specification includes state machines. These state machines serve to give a representation of the expected behavior of an LMP node and, if implemented as they stand, would give a functional yet suboptimal implementation.

10.9.1 Links, Control Channels, and Data Channels

A channel is an independent connection between a pair of nodes. Control channels carry signaling, routing, and other control messages; data channels carry data. In an in-band packet network such as Ethernet, there is usually a single channel between a pair of nodes that carries control messages and data, but in out-of-band signaling networks, the control channel will be a reserved wavelength in a fiber, or a reserved timeslot, or perhaps an Ethernet link that runs parallel to the fiber. If there are multiple parallel fibers between two nodes, each is identified as a data channel but it is not necessary to have a control channel for each.

LMP requires that the addresses of control channels are configured at each node, although control channel discovery could be operated by using the broadcast address 244.0.0.1. To maintain an LMP adjacency, it is necessary to have at least one active control channel between the two nodes. More than one control channel is acceptable and will provide a degree of robustness.

An LMP control channel is brought into use when one end sends a Config message. The Config message identifies the local end of the control channel and carries negotiable parameters to apply to the use of LMP between the two nodes. The receiver of a Config message replies with a ConfigAck message to accept the parameters and supply its own identifiers. It also includes the node, control channel, and message identifiers from the received message so that there is no ambiguity. If the receiver of the Config message wishes to negotiate the configuration, it sends a ConfigNack message including its preferred configuration parameters. The formal definitions of the Config messages are given in Figure 10.35, and Figure 10.36 shows how the messages are built byte by byte.

In LMP the Node ID is defined for a node running OSPF as the address contained in the OSPF Router Address TLV, and for a node running IS-IS and advertising the TE Router ID TLV it is the same as the advertised Router ID.

```
< Config Message > ::=        < Common Header >
                              < LOCAL_CCID > < MESSAGE_ID >
                              < LOCAL_NODE_ID > < CONFIG >
< ConfigAck Message > ::=     < Common Header >
                              < LOCAL_CCID > < LOCAL_NODE_ID >
                              < REMOTE_CCID > < MESSAGE_ID_ACK >
                              < REMOTE_NODE_ID >
< ConfigNack Message > ::=    < Common Header >
                              < LOCAL_CCID > < LOCAL_NODE_ID >
                              < REMOTE_CCID > < MESSAGE_ID_ACK >
                              < REMOTE_NODE_ID >
                              < CONFIG >
```

Figure 10.35 Formal definition of the LMP Config, ConfigAck, and ConfigNack messages.

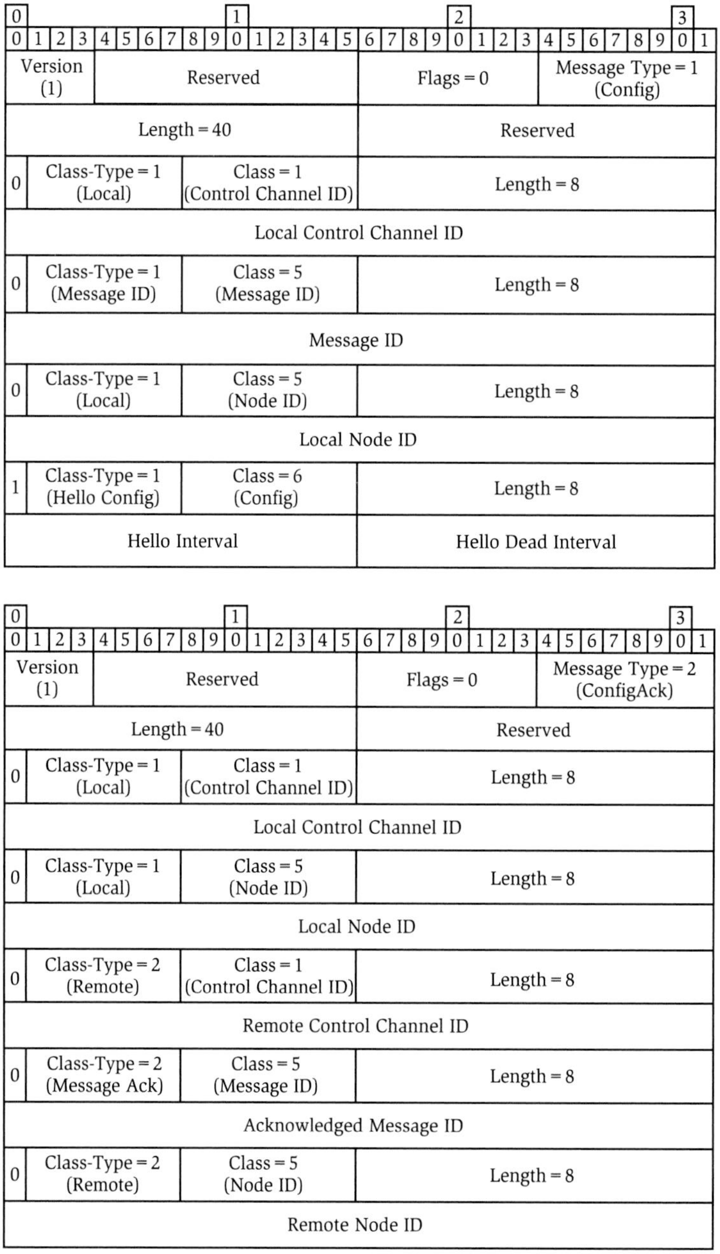
0 1 2 3
0 1 2 3 4 5 6 7 8 9 0 1 2 3 4 5 6 7 8 9 0 1 2 3 4 5 6 7 8 9 0 1
Version (1)
Reserved
Flags = 0
Message Type = 1 (Config)
Length = 40
Reserved
0
Class-Type = 1 (Local)
Class = 1 (Control Channel ID)
Length = 8
Local Control Channel ID
0
Class-Type = 1 (Message ID)
Class = 5 (Message ID)
Length = 8
Message ID
0
Class-Type = 1 (Local)
Class = 5 (Node ID)
Length = 8
Local Node ID
1
Class-Type = 1 (Hello Config)
Class = 6 (Config)
Length = 8
Hello Interval
Hello Dead Interval
0 1 2 3
0 1 2 3 4 5 6 7 8 9 0 1 2 3 4 5 6 7 8 9 0 1 2 3 4 5 6 7 8 9 0 1
Version (1)
Reserved
Flags = 0
Message Type = 2 (ConfigAck)
Length = 40
Reserved
0
Class-Type = 1 (Local)
Class = 1 (Control Channel ID)
Length = 8
Local Control Channel ID
0
Class-Type = 1 (Local)
Class = 5 (Node ID)
Length = 8
Local Node ID
0
Class-Type = 2 (Remote)
Class = 1 (Control Channel ID)
Length = 8
Remote Control Channel ID
0
Class-Type = 2 (Message Ack)
Class = 5 (Message ID)
Length = 8
Acknowledged Message ID
0
Class-Type = 2 (Remote)
Class = 5 (Node ID)
Length = 8
Remote Node ID

Figure 10.36 The LMP Config and ConfigAck messages and their constituent objects.

In other cases, the Node ID should be globally unique and must be sufficiently unique to allow any one node to distinguish its peers. The Control Channel ID (CCID) is required to be unique on any one node.

A class type is defined for the Config object to carry LMP Hello timers. The values are presented in milliseconds and show how often the LMP Hello message (see the following paragraphs) should be sent and after what period without the receipt of a Hello message the control channel should be declared as dead. It is possible that as the need arises for further configuration of LMP control channels new Config class types will be defined.

It is possible that both ends of a control channel will send a Config message simultaneously. This contention is resolved by the nodes performing a numerical comparison of the node IDs used (as unsigned integers)—the node with the higher ID "wins" and does not respond to the received Config message.

A class type is defined for the Config object to carry LMP Hello timers. The values are presented in milliseconds and show how often the LMP Hello message (see the following paragraph) should be sent and after what period without the receipt of a Hello message the control channel should be declared as dead. If the use of Hellos is not supported, both fields are set to zero. It is possible that as the need arises for further configuration of LMP control channels new Config class types will be defined.

The formal definition of the Hello message is shown in Figure 10.37. As well as the local control channel identifier, the message contains a Hello object. This object holds 32-bit transmit and receive Hello Sequence Numbers. The transmit number must start at 1 for a new control channel, and the receive number reflects back the most recently received transmit number with zero indicating that no Hello has yet been received. The numbers wrap to 1 (not zero).

Figure 10.38 shows the establishment and maintenance of a pair of control channels between two nodes. Configuration negotiation was necessary during the setup of the first control channel. One is designated primary and the other backup—the primary carries the LMP message exchanges for managing the data channels. Hellos are used to keep the control channels active, and when the primary fails, the management traffic is switched to the other.

Between a pair of adjacent switches there may be a large number of physical links (such as optical fibers). As described in Sections 10.6 and 10.7, it makes a lot of sense to bundle these links so that the routing protocol is not over-burdened, and to manage the resulting TE Link as a single entity.

```
< Hello Message > ::=     < Common Header >
                          < LOCAL_CCID > < HELLO >
```

Figure 10.37 Formal definition of the LMP Hello message.

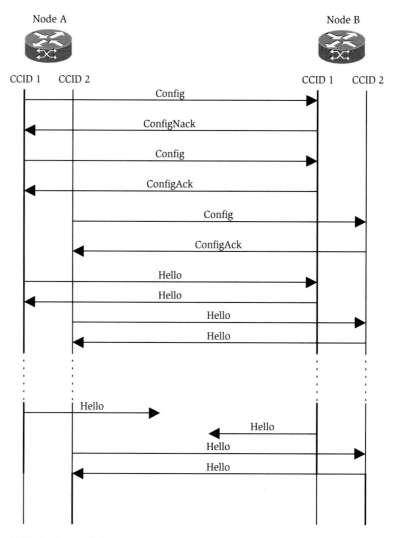

Figure 10.38 Dual control channel establishment in LMP showing configuration negotiation and control channel switchover after failure.

However, even if individual links or fibers are not identified through the routing protocol they still need to be indicated by the signaling protocol so that both peers understand which physical link is to be used to carry a specific data flow. GMPLS uses the link ID for this purpose, but there is still a need for the nodes to agree on the identifiers assigned to each link. This agreement can be achieved through configuration, but LMP allows for a protocol-based exchange of link identifiers.

In fact, LMP contains procedures for exchanging link identifiers, verifying the connectivity of links, and exchanging link properties so they can be grouped into a single TE link. These features are discussed in the following sections.

10.9.2 Discovering and Verifying Links

Link verification is the process in LMP that leads to the discovery of the connectivity of data links between a pair of nodes. Initially, one node knows its local identifiers for the data links that it believes connect to the adjacent node, but it does not know the state of these links nor the identifiers used by the other node to refer to them. It needs this information if it is to successfully signal connections such as LSPs using the links. In GMPLS, LSRs use the interface ID mappings determined by LMP link verification to signal exactly which link is to carry an LSP.

The link verification process is bounded by the exchange of BeginVerify/BeginVerifyAck and EndVerify/EndVerifyAck messages. The node that wishes to verify the links sends BeginVerify and the partner node responds with a positive acknowledgment or a BeginVerifyNack if it is unable or unwilling to comply. When the verification process is complete, the initiator sends an EndVerify message, and this is acknowledged by the responder. As with Config messages, these messages carry message IDs to match responses to their requests. Additionally, a 32-bit Verify ID (class 10, class type 1) is provided on the BeginVerifyAck and used on the EndVerify exchange to disambiguate multiple simultaneous link verifications. The formal definitions of the LMP messages are shown in Figure 10.39.

```
< BeginVerify Message > ::=          < Common Header >
                                     < LOCAL_LINK_ID >  < MESSAGE_ID >
                                     [ < REMOTE_LINK_ID > ]
                                     < BEGIN_VERIFY >
< BeginVerifyAck Message > ::=       < Common Header >
                                     [ < LOCAL_LINK_ID > ]
                                     < MESSAGE_ID_ACK >
                                     < BEGIN_VERIFY_ACK >  < VERIFY_ID >
< BeginVerifyNack Message > ::=      < Common Header >
                                     [ < LOCAL_LINK_ID > ]
                                     < MESSAGE_ID_ACK >  < ERROR_CODE >
< EndVerify Message > ::=            < Common Header >
                                     < MESSAGE_ID >  < VERIFY_ID >
< EndVerifyAck Message > ::=         < Common Header >
                                     < MESSAGE_ID_ACK >  < VERIFY_ID >
```

Figure 10.39 Formal definitions of the LMP Link Verification control messages.

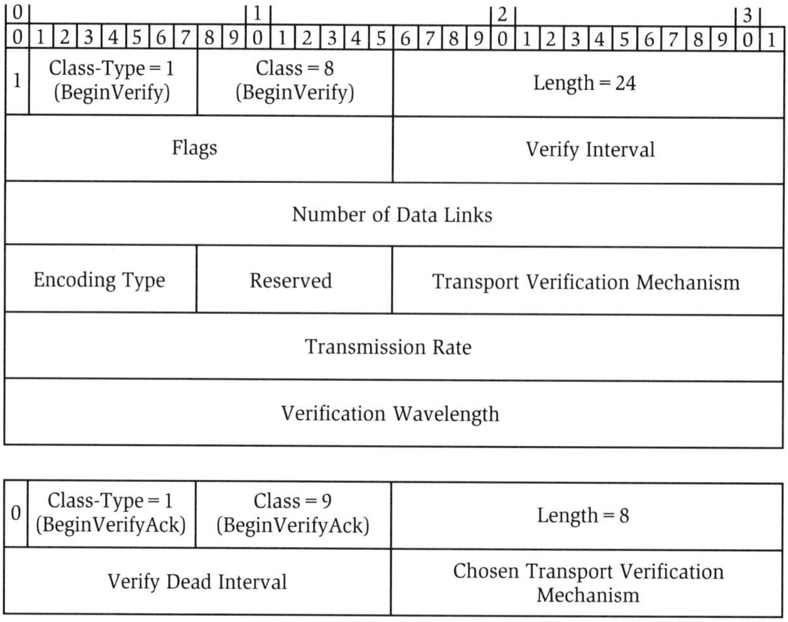

Figure 10.40 BeginVerify and BeginVerifyAck objects for LMP.

The link verification process may be applied to all TE links between a pair of nodes or may be limited to a single TE link specified by using a nonzero local link ID. If the remote ID of the TE link is known, it may also be supplied. If the verification is for a single TE link, the response contains the other node's identifier of the TE link.

The BeginVerify and BeginVerifyAck objects are shown in Figure 10.40. The BeginVerify object is used to describe the verification procedure that will be applied. As shown in the figure, the object contains a field that identifies the transport verification mechanism to be used. This is important because transport verification requires some interference with the data signal to identify which data channel is in use. Ideally, LMP would send a packet down the data channel being verified and the receiver would spot the packet, enabling it to both verify that the data channel is active and to match the source link ID to its own link ID. The LMP Test message shown in Table 10.17 is defined for this purpose, but it can only be used when the source has the ability to insert Test messages into the data channel and the destination has the ability to detect them. This is often not the case in optical and TDM switches, so other methods of indicating the data channels are used—in TDM, the overhead bytes are used, and in optical networks there are proposals to signal simply by turning lasers on and off. For these nonpacket cases, the Test message is sent over the control channel and the selected transport verification mechanism is applied to the data channels. Figure 10.41 lists the defined transport verification mechanisms.

Table 10.17 LMP Transport Verification Mechanisms

Bit Setting	Transport Verification Mechanism
0x0001	J0–16: 16 byte J0 Test Message
0x0002	J0–64: 64 byte J0 Test Message
0x0004	DCCS: Test Message over the Section/RS DCC
0x0008	DCCL: Test Message over the Line/MS DCC
0x0010	J0-trace: J0 Section Trace Correlation
0x0020	J1–16: 16 byte J1 Test Message
0x0040	J1–64: 64 byte J1 Test Message
0x0080	J2–16: 16 byte J2 Test Message
0x0100	J1-trace: J1 Path Trace Correlation
0x0200	J2-trace: J2 Section Trace Correlation
0x4000	Loss of Light and out of band Test messages
0x8000	Payload: Test Message transmitted in the payload

```
< Test Message > ::=    < Common Header >
                        < LOCAL_INTERFACE_ID > < VERIFY_ID >
```

Figure 10.41 Formal definition of the LMP Test messages.

The initiator of the verification process may set several bits to indicate the mechanisms it supports on the link and the responder must select just one mechanism.

The sequence of events during link verification can be seen in the chart in Figure 10.42. After the exchange of BeginVerify and BeginVerifyAck (step 1) the initiator loops through the links to be tested (step 2). For each link it sends a Test message (step 3) and, if the message is not sent in the payload, it sets the transport characteristics on the link to be tested. The responder receives the Test message and, if appropriate, checks for the transport characteristics. Once it has determined which link is being tested it responds with a TestStatus-Success message if everything is OK (step 4) or a TestStatusFailure if there is a problem (step 5). The initiator acknowledges the TestStatus message (step 6) and moves on to test the next link (step 7). When all links have been tested, the initiator ends the process with an EndVerify message, which is acknowledged (step 8).

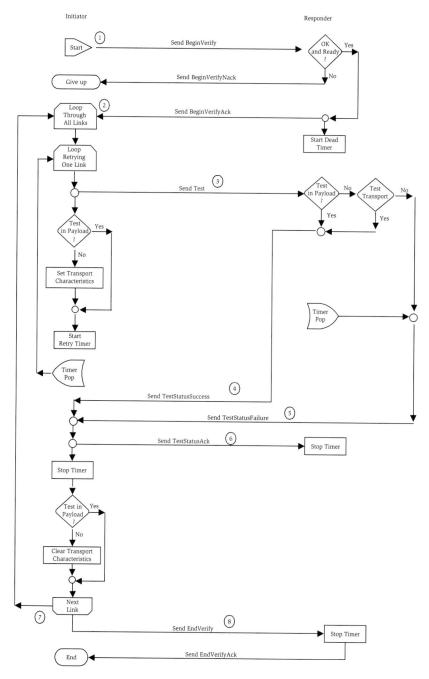

Figure 10.42 Flow of control during LMP link verification.

```
< TestStatusSuccess Message > ::=    < Common Header >
                                     < LOCAL_LINK_ID > < MESSAGE_ID >
                                     < LOCAL_INTERFACE_ID >
                                     < REMOTE_INTERFACE_ID > < VERIFY_ID >
< TestStatusFailure Message > ::=    < Common Header >
                                     < MESSAGE_ID > < VERIFY_ID >
< TestStatusAck Message > ::=        < Common Header >
                                     < MESSAGE_ID_ACK > < VERIFY_ID >
```

Figure 10.43 Formal definition of the LMP Test messages.

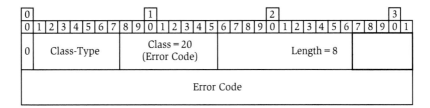

Figure 10.44 The LMP Error Code Object.

Table 10.18 LMP Error Codes Depend on the Object Class Type and May Be Combined to Report Multiple Errors Simultaneously

Class	Class Type	Error Code	Meaning
20	1	0x01	Link verification procedure not supported.
20	1	0x02	Unwilling to verify links.
20	1	0x04	Unsupported link verification transport mechanism.
20	1	0x08	Link_ID configuration error.
20	1	0x10	Unknown object C-Type in BeginVerify message.
20	2	0x01	Unacceptable nonnegotiable Link Summary parameters.
20	2	0x02	Renegotiate Link Summary parameters.
20	2	0x04	Invalid TE_Link Object in Link Summary.
20	2	0x08	Invalid Data_Link Object in Link Summary.
20	2	0x10	Unknown TE_Link Object C-Type in Link Summary.
20	2	0x20	Unknown Data_Link Object C-Type in Link Summary.

The formal definitions of the TestStatusSuccess, TestStatusFailure, and TestStatusAck messages are given in Figure 10.43.

The LMP Error Code object shown in Figure 10.44 is included in Begin-VerifyNack messages and in LinkSummaryNack messages (see the following section). A simple 32-bit error code is supplied to indicate the reason for the failure. The class-type is used to qualify the error, and error code values are chosen from those listed in Table 10.18. The values are bit-sensitive so that multiple issues may be reported in a single error code.

10.9.3 Exchanging Link Capabilities

Once nodes have established data channel connectivity using the link verification procedures, it may be useful for them to exchange information about the capabilities of the data channels. This is particularly important where the data channels between a pair of nodes have different qualities. The Link Property Summarization exchange can also be used to verify the integrity of link configuration if link identifiers are configured rather than discovered using Link Verification.

Link Summarization consists of the exchange of LinkSummary and LinkSummaryAck/Nack messages. Each LinkSummary message may report on multiple data channels that belong to a single TE link. The Ack message simply agrees to the distributed parameters, but the Nack message includes an error code to indicate the failure reason and may list the data channels that are being failed if the failure does not apply to all of the data channels in the original LinkSummary message. Figure 10.45 shows the formal definition of the LinkSummary messages.

The TE_Link object identifies the TE link to which the component data channels belong. The object, shown in Figure 10.46, contains the local and remote link identifiers as used by the routing protocol. Versions are defined for IPv4, IPv6, and unnumbered links. A Flags field indicates whether the LMP optional procedures Link Verification (0x01) and Fault Management (0x02) are supported for data channels on this TE link.

```
< LinkSummary Message > ::=          < Common Header >
                                     < MESSAGE_ID > < TE_LINK >
                                     < data link list >
< LinkSummaryAck Message > ::=       < Common Header >
                                     < MESSAGE_ID_ACK >
< LinkSummaryNack Message > ::=      < Common Header >
                                     < MESSAGE_ID_ACK > < ERROR_CODE >
                                     [ < data link list > ]
< data link list > ::=               < DATA_LINK > [ < data link list > ]
```

Figure 10.45 Formal definition of the LMP LinkSummary messages.

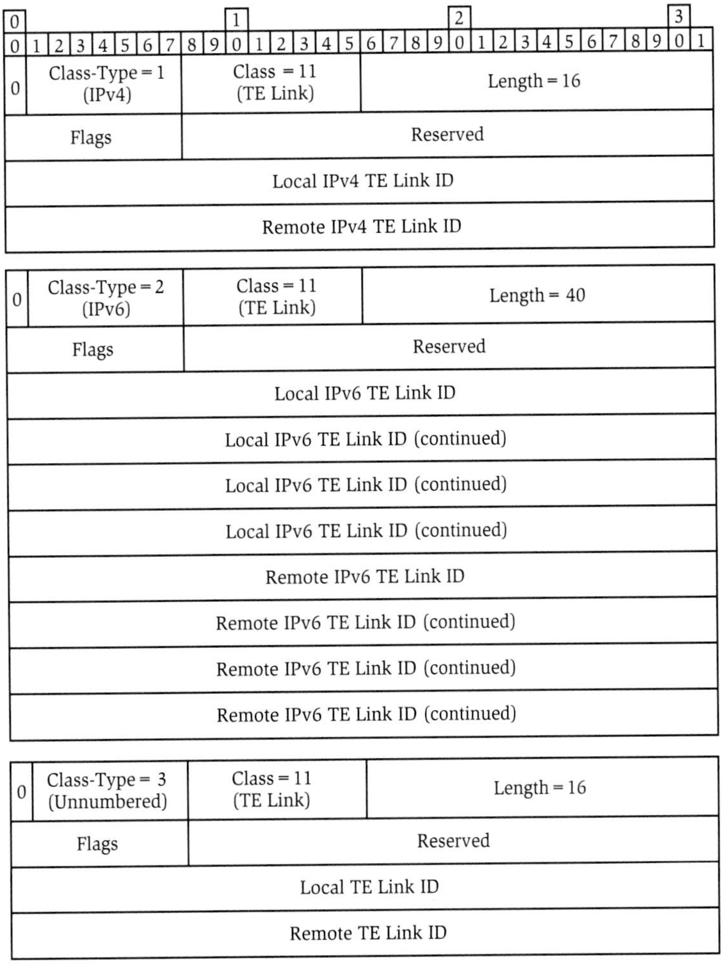

Figure 10.46 The three LMP TE_Link objects.

The Data_Link object, shown in Figure 10.47, is used to describe an individual data channel. The object consists of a common header (there are three variants for IPv4, IPv6, and unnumbered link identification), and a series of subobjects. The common header is formed as for the TE_Link object, so only the IPv4 variant is shown in the figure. The flags in the common header indicate whether the link is a port as opposed to a component link (0x01), whether the data link is currently allocated for user traffic (0x02), and whether the data link is currently in a failed state and not suitable for user traffic (0x04). The subobjects are presented as TLVs with a single byte for each of the Type and Length fields. The Length field gives the length of the entire subobject, including the Type and Length fields.

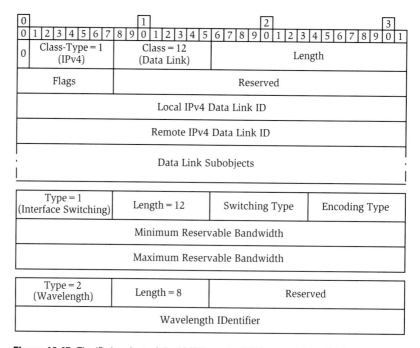

Figure 10.47 The IPv4 variant of the LMP Data_Link Object together with its subobjects.

10.9.4 Isolating Faults

Some optical switches are "transparent," meaning that they switch and propagate light signals without examining them. They may switch data by fiber, wavelength, or time slot without inspecting the signal itself. In consequence, if the signal fails because of some fault upstream they simply may not notice.

The worst case of this behavior would result in the failure not being detected until the signal reached the egress node where it was due to be converted back to an electrical signal to be forwarded into a packet switched network. In order to repair connections by means such as rerouting traffic to back-up paths it is necessary to localize the fault, otherwise the repair may be inefficient or might continue to utilize the failed link.

LMP provides a mechanism to isolate and report on faults. The process is initiated by a downstream node that detects a problem on a data link. This node sends a ChannelStatus message upstream using the control channel and immediately receives an acknowledgement. The upstream node receiving a ChannelStatus that reports a failure knows that it is safe to destructively examine the data signal, and checks to see whether it is receiving a satisfactory signal from its upstream neighbor. If it is receiving a good signal, the fault has been isolated and the upstream node returns a ChannelStatus message to say that the link is

< ChannelStatusRequest Message > ::=	< Common Header > < LOCAL_LINK_ID > < MESSAGE_ID > [< CHANNEL_STATUS_REQUEST >]
< ChannelStatusResponse Message > ::=	< Common Header > < MESSAGE_ID_ACK > < CHANNEL_STATUS >
< ChannelStatus Message > ::=	< Common Header > < LOCAL_LINK_ID > < MESSAGE_ID > < CHANNEL_STATUS >
< ChannelStatusAck Message > ::=	< Common Header > < MESSAGE_ID_ACK >

Figure 10.48 Formal definition of the LMP ChannelStatus messages.

fine. If the upstream node is not receiving a good signal, it sends a Channel-Status upstream and downstream to its neighbors to report the problem. Note that it is possible for the upstream node to have already spotted the fault when it receives the ChannelStatus from its downstream neighbor.

Nodes may request channel status information at any time using the ChannelStatusRequest and ChannelStatusResponse exchange. This may be particularly useful at boot-up, when it is desirable to find out the status of all of the links. The formal definitions of the ChannelStatus Messages are shown in Figure 10.48. Figure 10.49 shows the ChannelStatusRequest and ChannelStatus objects carried on these messages. Figure 10.50 shows a simple scenario in which the data channel failure is detected downstream from the actual failure and is isolated using LMP.

The ChannelStatusRequest may list individual data channels to be reported or may omit the ChannelStatusRequest object to learn about all data channels associated with the TE link identified by the Local Link ID. The A-bit in the Channel Status object defines whether the data channel is carrying active traffic (1) or not (zero). The D-bit indicates the direction of the link that is being reported—the directions are relative to data traffic, with 1 indicating transmit and zero meaning receive. Three channel status values are currently defined: 1 means "Signal OK," 2 means "Signal Degraded," and 3 means "Signal Failed."

The Channel Status message can also be used to indicate that the data channel has been repaired and is available for traffic.

10.9.5 Authentication

Confidentiality is not considered a requirement of LMP, but it is necessary to authenticate message senders to protect against spoofing, which might disrupt

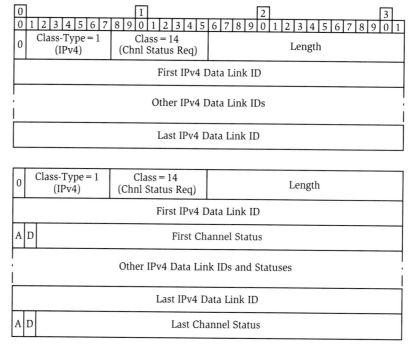

Figure 10.49 The IPv4 variants of the LMP ChannelStatusRequest and ChannelStatus Objects.

data services. This is especially important where the control channel passes through an arbitrary IP cloud on its way between two nodes that are adjacent in the data plane. The LMP draft suggests that LMP security is in the domain of the IP and UDP transport mechanisms and recommends the use of IPsec.

10.9.6 Choosing to Use LMP

LMP is not an essential building block within a GMPLS network, but if offers flexibility and reduces configuration overheads as network complexity increases. Initial deployments of GMPLS networks are likely to be small and carefully controlled. They will rely heavily on manual configuration so that all aspects can be monitored.

As the networks grow and more links are brought into service, the overhead of manual configuration of links will become excessive. Additional intricacy will arise as GMPLS networks are built out of switches from different vendors that have dissimilar configuration interfaces and different link and switching capabilities. LMP provides a standardized and interoperable way to integrate such networks.

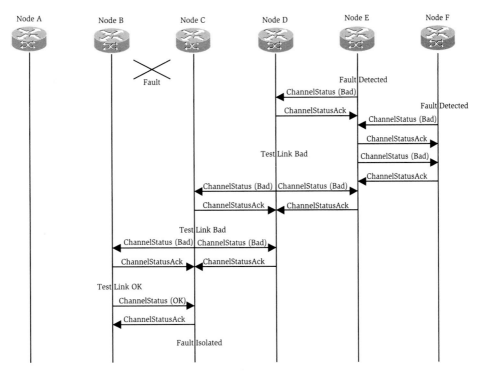

Figure 10.50 LMP message exchange for fault isolation and reporting.

10.10 Further Reading

At the time of writing, there are no reference books giving suitable background material on Generalized MPLS. Some White Papers may be found on the Internet at various sources. A good starting point is the MPLS Resource Center at http://www.mplsrc.org.

The CCAMP Working Group has a web page that includes links to RFCs and Internet drafts for GMPLS: www.ietf.org/html.charters/ccamp-charter.html. Some key RFCs and drafts are:

RFC 3471—Generalized MPLS—Signaling Functional Description
RFC 3472—Generalized MPLS Signaling—CR-LDP Extensions
RFC 3473—Generalized MPLS Signaling—RSVP-TE Extensions
draft-ietf-ccamp-gmpls-architecture—Generalized Multi-Protocol Label Switching Architecture
draft-ietf-ccamp-gmpls-routing—Routing Extensions in Support of Generalized MPLS

draft-ietf-ccamp-ospf-gmpls-extensions—OSPF Extensions in Support of Generalized MPLS

draft-ietf-isis-gmpls-extensions—IS-IS Extensions in Support of Generalized MPLS

draft-ietf-mpls-hierarchy—LSP Hierarchy with Generalized MPLS TE

draft-ietf-mpls-bundle—Link Bundling in MPLS Traffic Engineering

draft-ietf-ccamp-lmp—Link Management Protocol

draft-ietf-ccamp-lmp-test-sonet-sdh—SONET/SDH Encoding for Link Management Protocol Test Messages

Chapter 11

Switches and Components

Up to this point the term *switch* has been used to refer to a node that runs routing and signaling code to control the behavior of hardware that is responsible for switching data from one port to another based on some form of label. These Label Switching Routers (LSRs) are actually composites with a presence in the routing, control, and data planes.

This chapter looks at switches that reside solely in the data plane and are controlled by external components using IP-based protocols. These protocols should be distinguished from the pure management protocols described in Chapter 13 because they are (or can be) closely tied to the signaling protocols, making it possible to separate the control and data planes.

Three protocols for controlling switches are presented. The General Switch Management Protocol (GSMP) is focused on MPLS style switches and can handle ATM, Frame Relay, and MPLS labels. The work under way in the ForCES Working Group of the IETF is focused on separating the control and forwarding planes in IP routers/switches; it is at an early stage, but bears examination. Finally, consideration is given to the attempt to extend the Link Management Protocol (LMP—see Chapter 10) to allow optical switches to be separated into distinct demultiplexing and switching components.

11.1 General Switch Management Protocol (GSMP)

Version three of the General Switch Management Protocol (GSMP) is specifically designed for the management of label switches. It recognizes that switching components may lack the ability to run complex routing and signaling protocols, and so provides an all-purpose set of functions designed to allow management of the switch by external components which have these capabilities.

GSMP was originally specified before the invention of MPLS and focused on ATM and Frame Relay switches, but it became apparent that the concepts were equally applicable to MPLS, and version three of the protocol was developed to handle ATM, Frame Relay, and MPLS label switching. The concept of switching Forwarding Equivalence Classes (FECs) was also added to enable IP switches and Label Edge Routers (LERs) to dispatch IP packets on to LSPs. The protocol itself is designed to be run over any transport medium, and specifications exist for GSMP over ATM, Ethernet, and TCP. Running GSMP over IP using TCP gives the most generic solution for remote connectivity and fits within the context of this book.

GSMP version 3 is defined in RFC 3292 and does not currently specify support for GMPLS, but work is progressing in the IETF to address this function.

11.1.1 Distributed Switches

The GSMP model separates the switch from the *controller* so that the components in the data plane are kept as simple as possible. As shown in Figure 11.1 the controller, which may be a signaling router or a management station, communicates with the switch using GSMP. The separation between the controller and the switch is arbitrary. In some implementations the switch and the control may be physically colocated but use GSMP to achieve a clean architectural separation, and in other cases the switches and controllers may be significantly separated and use routed IP links over which to run GSMP.

This separation offers an architectural simplicity where the separation is not relevant to the function of the switches and opens up new possibilities for multivendor switching environments. The downside of GSMP is that it increases the amount of control flow necessary to establish an LSP, and introduces new links that are vulnerable to breaks and security attacks.

Figure 11.2 shows a larger-scale picture of GSMP in use in a network. The IP cloud may contain signaling routers that exchange MPLS control messages, and may also route GSMP messages from management stations. The signaling routers are not required to be physically adjacent to the switches.

One switch may be controlled by multiple controllers, and a single controller may control multiple switches. A switch may even be divided into multiple logical switches, each of which is presented to GSMP as a *partition* of the switch. This may aid in management, especially if the switch is used to manage different label spaces for different purposes.

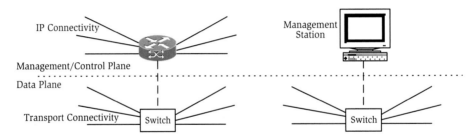

Figure 11.1 GSMP allows a clean separation of the data plane from the management and control

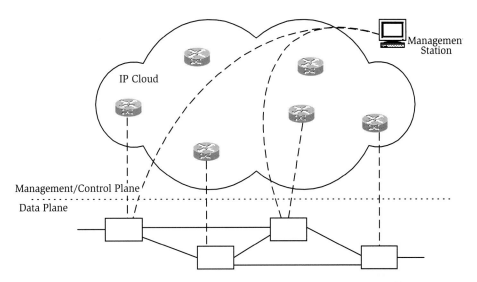

Figure 11.2 Each switch communicates with one or more controllers using GSMP.

11.1.2 Overview of GSMP

GSMP operates in an IP network using TCP. Switches act as the servers and listen on the reserved port 6068. A controller opens a TCP connection to a switch and exchanges Adjacency messages to negotiate the GSMP version and operational parameters to use.

The protocol is based on request–response exchanges. Each request from the controller contains an identifier and a flag to say whether a response is required. Success responses contain only the necessary response information, but failure responses are formatted exactly as the request was and include a result code indicating the reason for failure.

Switches may also issue unsolicited status messages to the controllers to report on asynchronous events in the data plane. The switch may request a response to such messages but does not usually do so.

GSMP message types are distinguished by numeric codes, and the messages are divided into functional groups as shown in Table 11.1. A GSMP implementation is not required to support all of the defined messages.

11.1.3 Common Formats

All GSMP messages except for the Adjacency message have a common header, as shown in Figure 11.3. The header is prefixed by a 4-byte encapsulation header containing the GSMP Ethertype and a length indicator when the message is sent over TCP. The Length field in this encapsulation header shows the length in

Table 11.1 GSMP Messages Arranged by Functional Grouping

Functional Group	Message Type	Message	Required Support
Adjacency Management	10	Adjacency Message	Mandatory
Configuration	64	Switch Configuration	Mandatory
	65	Port Configuration	Mandatory
	66	All Ports Configuration	Mandatory
	67	Service Configuration	Optional
Port Management	32	Port Management	Mandatory
	33	Label Range	Optional
Connection Management	16	Add Branch	Mandatory
	17	Delete Branches	Mandatory
	18	Delete Tree	Optional
	20	Delete All Input	Optional
	21	Delete All Output	Optional
	23	Move Input Branch	Optional
	22	Move Output Branch	Optional
	26/27	Move Input/Output Branch Specific to ATM VPCs	Optional
Reservation Management	70	Reservation Request	Mandatory
	71	Delete Reservation	Mandatory
	72	Delete All Reservations	Optional
State and Statistics Reporting	48	Connection Activity	Optional
	49	Port Statistics	Mandatory
	50	Connection Statistics	Optional
	52	Report Connection State	Optional
Event Notification	80	Port Up	Optional
	81	Port Down	Optional
	82	Invalid Label	Optional
	83	New Port	Optional
	84	Dead Port	Optional

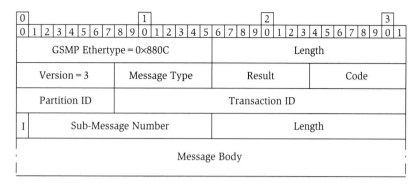

Figure 11.3 The GSMP common message format with its 4-byte TCP encapsulation header.

bytes of the GSMP message that follows and does not include the Ethertype and Length fields.

The fields of the common header indicate the version of GSMP (version three), the message type (see Table 11.1), a result field used to request a response when included on a request message or to indicate the type of response on a response message, a result code for failure responses (refer to RFC 3292 for a very long list of failure codes), and a partition ID to identify the virtual switch that is being controlled. Message exchanges are bunched as transactions so that a single request may have multiple coordinated responses—all responses to a single request must carry the transaction ID from the request, and each request must use a new transaction ID.

The Submessage Number field is used to coordinate messages that must be segmented because they exceed the Maximum Transmission Unit (MTU) size of the IP network. In non-IP networks it is the responsibility of the GSMP implementations to segment and reassemble GSMP messages, and each segment is sent with a full GSMP header and uses the same transaction ID. The first segment has the I-bit set and uses the submessage number to state the total number of segment messages used. Other segment messages use the submessage number to indicate their position in the sequence of segments. Since TCP/IP is capable of segmentation and reassembly in its own right, this feature need not and would generally not be used when running GSMP over IP.

The last common field shows the length in bytes of the entire GSMP message, including the common header and the message body, but not including the TCP encapsulation header. That is, the value in the two length fields shown in Figure 11.3 should be the same.

Labels are an essential commodity in GSMP; they are what the protocol is all about. Since labels are used on many of the GSMP messages, common formats are defined as shown in Figure 11.4. Each label is prefixed by a 4-byte structure comprising a Flags field, an indication of the type of label that follows, and the length of the label that follows in bytes. The flag definitions are shown in

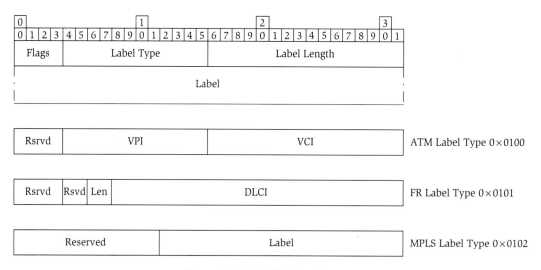

Figure 11.4 The GSMP label formats.

Table 11.2 The GSMP Label Flags

Value	Shorthand	Meaning
0x8		Reserved.
0x4	S	Label stacking is in use.
0x2	V	The label is a VPI label and the VCI field is unused.
0x1	C	The label range may be used for multipoint connections.

Table 11.2. If label stacking is indicated, this label is not the bottom label in a label stack and other labels follow—thus, a single label would not have this flag set.

Forwarding Equivalence Classes (FECs) are also considered as labels in GSMP because they are programmable, switchable quantities. Since FECs can be constructed from a series of FEC elements, the FEC label shown in Figure 11.5 is slightly more complex than the labels shown in the preceding figures. At the moment, GSMP supports only FEC elements that are address prefixes—the element type 0x02 is used to identify this element type.

11.1.4 Establishing Adjacency

Before GSMP messages can be exchanged between controller and switch to control the switches behavior, the controller must establish connectivity with the switch. The switch listens on port 6068 and the controller establishes a TCP connection with that port. It uses this connection to exchange Adjacency messages with the

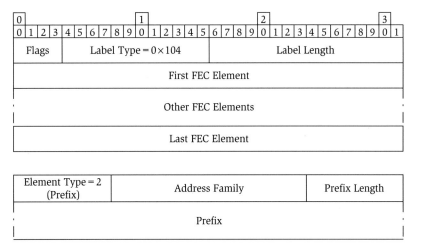

Figure 11.5 The GSMP FEC formats.

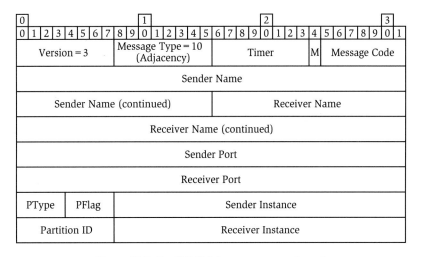

Figure 11.6 The GSMP Adjacency message format.

switch, using the message format shown in Figure 11.6. There are four Adjacency messages, all of which use the same format. They are differentiated by the setting of the Message Code field: Synchronize (SYN) 0x01, Synchronize Acknowledgement (SYNACK) 0x02, Acknowledgement (ACK) 0x03, and Reset Acknowledgement (RSTACK) 0x04.

The procedure for establishing a GSMP adjacency is as follows. RFC 3292 defines a state machine to help explain the sequence of events. A three-way handshake is used.

The controller sends a SYN message containing its sender name (the MAC address is suggested) and specifying the local TCP port ID. It also supplies a unique sender instance to distinguish this instance of an adjacency from previous instances. The PType field is used to request switch partitions: zero means no partitions and 1 indicates a request for a fixed partition. The P-Flag qualifies the partition request, with the value 1 indicating that the partition is new, and the value 2 showing that the partition is being recovered. (Note that the GSMP state machines also support initiation of adjacencies by the switches using the M-bit to indicate whether the sender of the SYN message is the master [1] or slave [0].

The switch receiving the SYN checks that the parameters are OK and responds with a SYNACK. It copies the Sender fields from the SYN to the Receiver fields of the SYNACK and fills its own information into the Sender fields. If a partition was requested, the switch responds by setting the PType field to 2 to indicate that a fixed partition has been assigned.

Upon receiving a SYNACK, the controller completes the handshake by sending an ACK.

The timer value on the messages is specified in hundreds of milliseconds (that is, tenths of seconds) and tells the receiver the rate at which the sender will retransmit unresponded messages. The adjacency, once established, is kept alive by periodic exchanges of ACKs. The same timer is used to generate an ACK, and when an ACK is received, it should be responded to with another ACK, provided that an ACK has not already been sent within the time interval.

11.1.5 Switch Configuration

The Switch Configuration message body shown in Figure 11.7 is sent by the controller to set and retrieve the global switch configuration parameters of the switch using a standard message header. If the switch does not support the parameters passed, it may include in its response a set of acceptable configuration parameters. The exchange of request–response continues until the switch is

0		1		2		3
0 1 2 3 4 5 6 7	8 9 0 1 2 3 4 5	6 7 8 9 0 1 2 3	4 5 6 7 8 9 0 1			
MType	MType	MType	MType
Firmware Version Number		Window Size	
Switch Type		Switch Name	
Switch Name (continued)			
Max Reservations			

Figure 11.7 The GSMP Switch Configuration message body.

successfully configured and no other messages may be exchanged before this process is complete.

The MType is used to indicate the reservation model requested/supported in the switch. Currently, only the value 0x00 is defined as the GMPLS default model. In the request, the first MType is the requested value. In a success response, the MType is returned as requested, but in a failure response the first MType is set to zero and the other three may be set to zero or to other supported values to suggest to the controller values that it might try next.

The other fields are returned by the switch on the response and tell the controller about the capabilities of the switch. The Window Size is the number of unacknowledged GSMP messages that the switch can handle without the risk of dropping some. The Max Reservations field indicates the number of reservations that can be programmed into the switch. The other fields (Firmware Version Number, Switch Type, and Switch Name) are specific to the manufacturer of the switch—the MAC address may be used as the Switch Name.

The Port Configuration and All Ports Configuration message bodies are used to request the configuration of one or all of the switch ports, again using standard message headers. The Port Configuration message consists of a single Port Record (Figure 11.8) used to request and return the configuration of a specific port, and the All Ports Configuration request is just a header and the response consists of a series of Port records prefixed by 2 reserved bytes and a 2-byte count of Port Records.

The 32-bit port number is used to identify the port on the switch, and the port session number gives context in time so that GSMP connection or switch resets can be detected. The Event Sequence Number is set to zero when the port is initialized and is incremented by one each time the port detects an asynchronous event that the switch would normally report via an Event message. The Event Flags report the asynchronous events that have occurred on the port since the Event flags were last cleared. The defined bits are shown in Table 11.3.

Just one Port Attribute Flag is defined: 0x8000 indicates that any clashes found when branches are added will result in the new branch replacing the old, rather than in a failure. The Port Type tells the controller the switching type of the port and may be set to ATM (1), Frame Relay (2), or MPLS (3). A single Service Type Flag is defined: 0x80 indicates that service specifications are found at the end of the port record. The Data Fields Length is a piece of redundant information that gives the length in bytes of the rest of the port record.

The Label Range Block is preceded by a 32-bit header and consists of a series of pairs of labels of the appropriate format for the port type (see Figure 11.4). FEC labels may not be used to construct label ranges. The first label in a pair is treated as the inclusive low end of a label range, and the second label is the inclusive high end of the range. The number of pairs of labels is given in the Label Range Count, and the Label Range Length indicates the size in bytes of the Label Range Block. The flags P, M, L, R, and Q are shown in Table 11.4. The

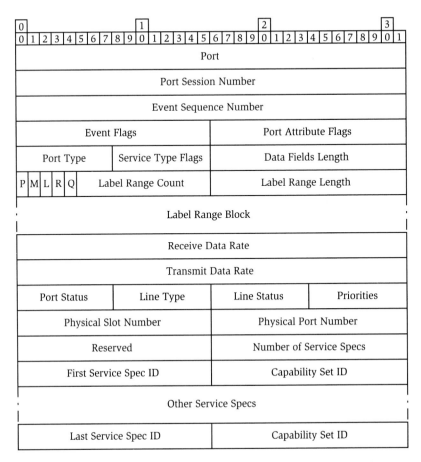

Figure 11.8 The Port Record used in GSMP Port Configuration and All Ports Configuration messages.

Table 11.3 The Events Bits Used to Report the Occurrence of Asynchronous Events in GSMP

Event Bit	Event
0x8000	Port Up
0x4000	Port Down
0x2000	Invalid Label
0x1000	New Port
0x0800	Dead Port
0x0400	Adjacency Event

Table 11.4 The Label Range Flags in GSMP

Flag	Meaning
P	VP switching is supported if the port type is ATM.
M	Each output branch of a point-to-multipoint tree may be assigned a different label.
L	Logical multicast is supported.
R	The switch is capable of reallocating its label range and accepts the Label Range message.
Q	This switch port is capable of handling the Quality of Service messages.

Table 11.5 The Port and Line Status Field Values for GSMP

Status Field	Report/Request	Value	Meaning
Port	Report/Request	1	Available
	Report/Request	2	Unavailable
	Report/Request	3	Internal loopback mode
	Report/Request	4	External loopback mode
	Report/Request	5	Bothway loopback mode
	Request	6	Reset input port and all connections originating there
	Request	7	Reset Event flags
	Request	8	Set transmission data rate
Line	Report	1	Up
	Report	2	Down
	Report	3	Test

flags in the first label are used as defined in Table 11.4 to describe the properties of the labels in the entire label range.

Receive and Transmit Data rates are quoted in cells per second for ATM links and bytes per second for other links. These fields seriously constrain the use of GSMP with switches that support high data rates.

The defined values for the Port and Line Status fields are given in Table 11.5. The line type is taken from the iftype definitions managed by the Internet Assigned Numbers Authority (IANA). The GSMP specification suggests that only the values shown in Table 11.6 are applicable. The Priorities field says how many priorities

Table 11.6 Line Types for Use in GSMP

Port Type	Line Type	Line Type Value
Unknown	other	1
MPLS	ethernetCsmacd	6
	ppp	23
ATM	atm	37
FR	frameRelayService	44

are supported by the port. Each Service Specification gives a service identifier and capabilities identifier to correlate the switch's capabilities on the port.

11.1.6 Port Management

The Port Management message (body shown in Figure 11.9) is used to set the status of the port into any of the modes shown in Table 11.5 or to request any of the indicated functions. If the function requests it, the port transmit data rate is set to the value supplied. One flag (0x8000) is defined to request that the port be put into connection replace mode—if the switch does not support this mode on this port it will respond with an error. The Duration field gives the period in seconds for which the port should be held in loopback mode if it is set into that mode by the request and if it is not cleared from that mode by a subsequent command.

The Event Flags report the recent asynchronous events, and Flow Control Flags are used to turn on or off flow control of asynchronous events using the same bit-settings as are used in the Events Flag (see Table 11.3).

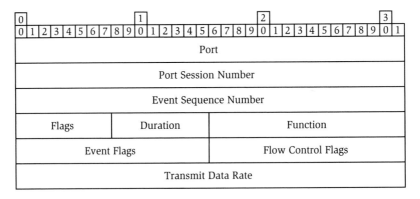

Figure 11.9 The GSMP Port Management message body.

If the switch supports dynamic modification of the label range on a port, the Label Range message may be used by the controller. This message contains the Port and Port session Number followed by a Label Range Block, as shown in Figure 11.5. Again, FEC labels may not be used to construct label ranges.

11.1.7 Connection Management

Finally, the GSMP adjacency is ready for use—the switch and ports are configured, and reservations have been defined. The controller can now start to provision the switch to switch traffic. Each cross-connection through the switch is referred to as a *tree*. Each leg of the cross-connect (that is, each port/label pair) is known as a *branch* of the tree. A tree may be point-to-point or point-to-multipoint, but not multipoint-to-point. This is not to say that GSMP does not support multipoint-to-point cross-connections but rather that the trees that thread the conceptual database of cross-connections are rooted firmly in a single input branch.

Connection management consists of adding, deleting, and moving branches. Note that although branches are theoretically just input or output legs, they are always specified using both input and output port/label pairs so that the context of cross-connection can be made. When a branch is added using the Add Branch message (body shown in Figure 11.10), the input and output ports and labels are specified. The port session number is applied to the input port. If a reservation has already been defined, it is referenced through the reservation ID, but if it has not been defined and if resource reservation is still desired, the

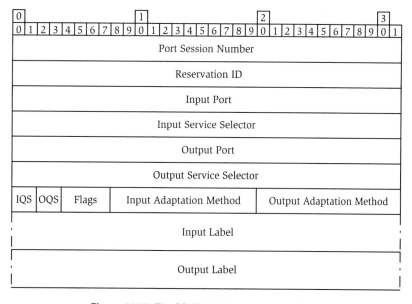

Figure 11.10 The GSMP Add Branch message body.

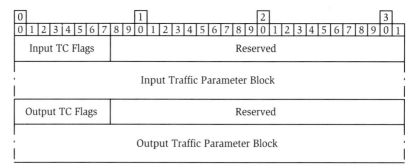

Figure 11.11 The GSMP Traffic Parameters used on Add Branch and Reservation messages.

IQS and OQS fields may be set to 0x2 and the traffic parameters block shown in Figure 11.11 is appended to the message. The adaptation method is used to define the adaptation framing that may be in use when moving traffic from one port type to another port type—three values are defined: PPP (0x100), FRF.5 (0x200), and FRF.8 (0x201).

The Delete Branches message reverses the effect of the Add Branch message. The message lists one or more sequences of Input Port, Output Port, Input Label, and Output Label as represented on an original Add branch message.

Various messages exist to achieve wholesale deletion of connections. The Delete Tree message is supplied with the Input Port and Input Label and deletes all branches from the tree. The Delete Input/Output Port messages delete all branches that utilize the specified port in the given direction.

Input and output branches can also be moved from one tree to another by supplying the old and new ports and labels in the Move Input/Output Branch messages. This process may be supported atomically by some switches, meaning that data can be redirected without the risk of packet loss that would occur if the old branch were first deleted and then the new branch added.

11.1.8 Prereservation of Resources

Resources may be requested as branches are added as described in the previous section. Alternatively, they may be prereserved so that they cannot be used for some other connection.

The Reservation Request message looks exactly like the Add Branch message, with the exception that the reservation ID is used to identify the new reservation. The traffic parameters shown in Figure 11.11 would normally be present to define the reservation required, but the message can be used simply to reserve cross-connection resources.

The Traffic Control flags are bit sensitive and are defined in Table 11.7. They indicate traffic shaping behavior to be applied by the switch.

Table 11.7 GSMP Traffic Control Request Flags

Value	Shorthand	Meaning
0x80	U	Usage parameter control requested
0x40	D	Packet discard requested
0x20	I	Ingress shaping to the peak rate and delay variation tolerance requested
0x10	E	Egress shaping to the peak rate and delay variation tolerance requested
0x08	S	Egress shaping to the sustainable rate and maximum burst size requested
0x04	V	ATM virtual channel merge requested
0x02	P	Indicates that the traffic block pertains to a whole Ingress Port

The contents of the Traffic Parameter Blocks depend on the service model in use and reuse the definitions from the ATM, IntServ Controlled Load, CR-LDP, and Frame Relay specifications. DiffServ is not supported in this version of GSMP

Reservations can be deleted one at a time using the Delete Reservation message, which uses the Reservation ID to identify the reservation to be removed. Alternatively, all reservations on the switch can be deleted at once using the Delete All Reservations message.

11.1.9 Events, State, and Statistics

Asynchronous events can be reported by switches to their controllers through unsolicited messages. The switch may request acknowledgement of these messages by setting the Result field in the message header, but it would not normally do so. All event messages have the same message body, as shown in Figure 11.12. Four messages exist to report changes in port status to Up or Down, and to show when a port is added or deleted. One further event message is used to report to the controller that one or more cells or frames were received on the

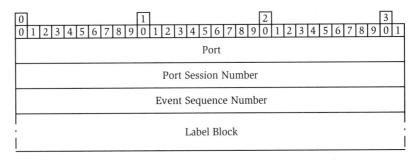

Figure 11.12 The common body of the GSMP Event messages.

specified port with an unexpected or invalid label. The messages are distinguished only by their message types. The label block is relevant only for the invalid label event.

Switches may be capable of collecting traffic statistics based on connections or ports. These statistics can be read by the controller, which may issue Port Statistics or Connection Statistics messages to the switch. The statistics requests supply the port ID and a label block, although the latter is ignored if the request is for port statistics. Note that the port session number is not used in these messages. Responses replicate the information from the request and append a well-ordered series of 64-bit counters, as listed in Table 11.8. Counters that are not relevant for a particular connection or port are set to zero.

A simplified form of statistics reporting is provided by the Connection Activity Request/Response messages (body shown in Figure 11.13). Each request asks for the current value of a traffic counter for one or more connections. If the switch does not support per-connection traffic counting it will return a failure, but if it is able to count traffic it returns the most recent count of traffic on the connection. RFC 3292 does not specify the units that should be counted by this field, but if the input cell/frame counts are maintained it might be reasonable to use these. The controller compares the returned value with the previous value to determine if the connection is active. If the switch does not keep per-connection traffic counts but can determine that the connection is active, it may report this information by setting the flag value 0x02 in the response.

The Report Connection State message can be used to request that the switch report the current state of a single connection or all of the connections

Table 11.8 GSMP Counters Reported on Statistics Messages

Counter	What It Counts
Input Cell	Cells received on the port or connection.
Input Frame	Frames received on the port or connection.
Input Cell Discard	Cells discarded owing to input queue overflow on the port or connection.
Input Frame Discard	Frames discarded owing to input queue overflow on the port or connection.
Header Checksum Error	Incoming cells or frames discarded because of checksum errors on this port or connection.
Input Invalid Label	Incoming cells or frames discarded on a port because of an invalid or unexpected label.
Output Cell	Cells transmitted on the port or connection.
Output Frame	Frames transmitted on the port or connection.
Output Cell Discard	Cells discarded owing to output queue overflow on the port or connection.
Output Frame Discard	Frames discarded owing to output queue overflow on the port or connection.

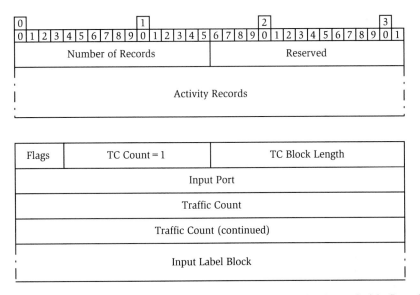

Figure 11.13 The body of the GSMP Connection Activity messages showing an Activity Record.

on a port. The state of a connection is reported as the input port and label followed by a series of one or more output ports and labels. This effectively allows the controller to display the tree of branches rooted at a particular input branch.

11.1.10 Choosing to Use GSMP

GSMP has grown as more management and configuration possibilities have arisen. The result is a simple request–response protocol with a somewhat heavy array of messages and parameters as it tries to be generic in an area often filled with vendor hardware–specific features.

When used in conjunction only with management stations, GSMP is a direct competitor with SNMP (see Section 13.4). GSMP offers a generic, media-nonspecific management protocol, but lacks many of the details that are specific to the switching carried out for different transport types. Similarly, GSMP is not well placed to report on and manage switches that are primarily controlled by signaling protocols since none of the details of the signaling are reported to the controller.

Various issues exist in regard to keeping GSMP up to date with the emergence of new technologies. The current version of GSMP has limitations on the bandwidths that can be represented, does not support GMPLS, and cannot make DiffServ resource reservations. These features will be added by the IETF over the course of time, but until then GSMP cannot be used in switches that need those features.

Nevertheless, a vendor hoping to supply switch components or dumb switches who wishes to concentrate on hardware development rather than routing and signaling software should think hard about GSMP and the opportunities it offers for a generic, standardized, IP-based interface.

11.2 Separating IP Control and Forwarding

Many, maybe even most, implementations of network nodes recognize that there should be some form of separation between the control plane components that are responsible for running routing, signaling, and management applications and the forwarding engine that handles packets within the data plane. Packet forwarding is obviously on the critical path and will be handled by specialist hardware or by high-priority software components. The control plane components are responsible for managing the forwarding engine by issuing it instructions.

Where the forwarding is in software, the separation between control plane and forwarding engine can be blurred, but a well-architected implementation will recognize that multiple control sources may want to manage the same forwarding engine without contention and without affecting the performance of data forwarding. This leads to the instigation of some form of API between the components and, as often as not, this is a message-passing interface that allows the forwarding components to process management instructions in their own context and at their own pace.

If the forwarding components are on specialist hardware, the interface between control plane and forwarding engine is forced. Messages must be passed in some manner, perhaps across a backplane, to the forwarding hardware so that it can be managed.

Having acknowledged this form of separation between control plane and forwarding engine it is a simple step to consider a greater geographical separation. This allows the management or control plane component to be remote and to instruct the forwarding engine over a link that may itself run IP. In fact, there is no reason why this link cannot be multihop, carrying the instructions through a routed network using IP.

11.2.1 The ForCES Working Group and Netlink

The Forwarding and Control Element Separation (ForCES) Working Group in the IETF is chartered to investigate the separation of forwarding and control components of IP routers. As addition to framing this research in terms of an architecture and formal requirements, the group aims to produce a control protocol running over an IP transport protocol such as TCP or SCTP for the purpose of managing the forwarding components remotely. This protocol may be an existing protocol (with or without modification) or may be a wholly new protocol.

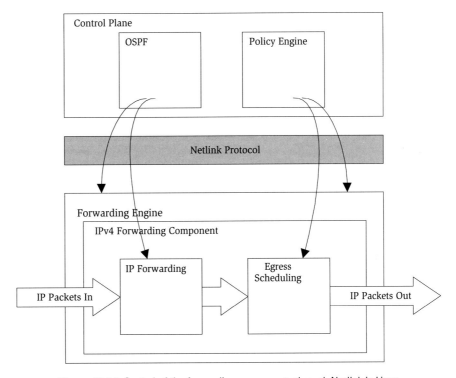

Figure 11.14 Control of the forwarding components through Netlink in Linux.

ForCES is examining the Linux Netlink protocol as being potentially suitable for use as a management protocol for separated forwarding components. Although Netlink serves as an intrakernel messaging system, as an interprocess communication scheme, and as a configuration tool for other non-IP network services (such as decnet), these very abilities make it potentially suitable to act as a configuration tool for IP forwarding services, and Netlink is used in this way within Linux, as shown in Figure 11.14.

Although Netlink as shown in this figure is clearly used within a single component running Linux, there is no reason why the Control Plane and Forwarding Engine should reside in the same location. Netlink could be run over a transport link such as one provided by TCP. In fact, since Netlink is already specified as a message-passing protocol to fit within the internal architecture of Linux, and since it is already used to manage and control the forwarding components of an IP data forwarder, it is well placed to be adopted by the IETF as the preferred protocol for ForCES.

Netlink messages are built from a common header, a single service template, and service-specific TLVs, as shown in Figure 11.15. Message types are specific to the services managed and constitute the basic operations such as add, delete, and inspect. The services are the managed entities (interfaces, addresses, routes, etc.)

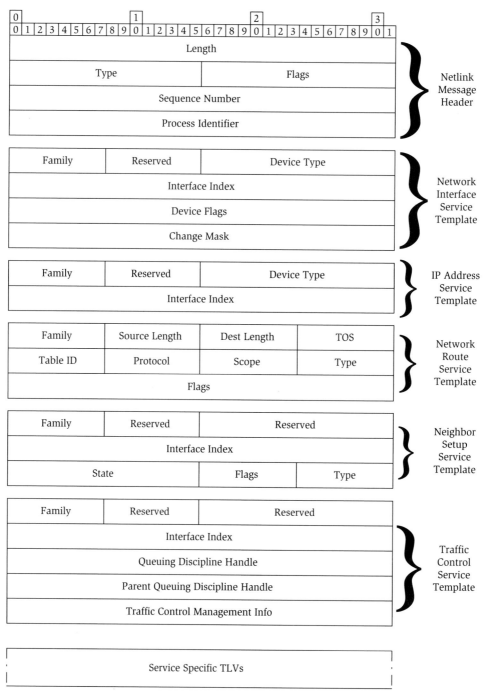

Figure 11.15 Netlink messages are built from a common header, a service template, and service-specific TLVs.

and the service template contains the information necessary to identify the managed entity and to qualify the message type. Where additional information is necessary, such as in configuration or in reporting of statistics, additional TLVs that are specific to the service type are appended to the message.

11.3 LMP-WDM

LMP-WDM is an extension to the Link Management Protocol (LMP) for use within Wave Division Multiplexing (WDM) switches. That is, it is a version of LMP that is run between the components of a switch rather than across a network.

11.3.1 Distributed WDM Architectures

Many hardware companies specialize in the manufacture of Add-Drop Multiplexors (ADMs) or Optical Switches (OXCs) and do not necessarily integrate both functions into their products. Even when they do, they see architectural or commercial benefits to separating the components. The separation normally applied collects the ADM together with any line amplifiers as a single component called the Optical Line System (OLS).

In such a distributed model there are optical links between the ADM and the OXC that need to be configured, verified, and monitored. Doing this will enable the OXC to correctly understand the resources that are available to it and will help it isolate faults. Many of the features necessary for this function are already provided by LMP, so it is natural to extend the protocol for use between the OXC and OLS. This extended protocol is called LMP-WDM and is shown in Figure 11.16.

11.3.2 Control Channel Management

The use of LMP-WDM assumes that some form of control channel exists between the OXC and the OLS. This may be a dedicated lambda or an Ethernet link. To distinguish between control channels set up between OXCs and those between an OXC and an OLS, a new type of the Config object is introduced for inclusion on the Config message, where it is used in addition to the existing Config object if the control channel is used for LMP-WDM. The LMP-WDM_CONFIG object is shown in Figure 11.17. The W-flag is set to indicate that the sending node supports LMP-WDM on this control channel. The O-flag indicates that the sender of the message is an OLS.

11.3.3 Link Management

No changes to the messages are required for link verification, but it should be noted that the links tested during LMP-WDM link verification are components

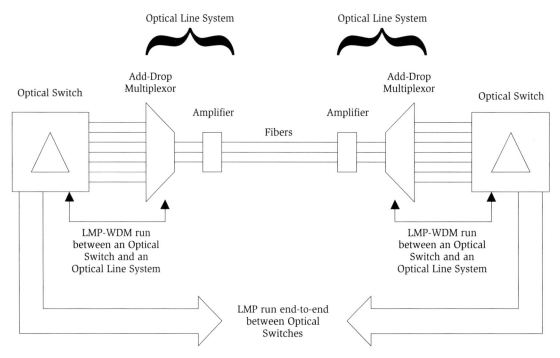

Figure 11.16 LMP-WDM runs between an optical switch and an optical line system.

0									1										2										3	
0	1	2	3	4	5	6	7	8	9	0	1	2	3	4	5	6	7	8	9	0	1	2	3	4	5	6	7	8	9	0	1

0	Class Type (lmp-wdm_config)	Class = 6 (Config)	Length = 8
W O	Reserved		

Figure 11.17 The LMP-WDM Config Object used on the Config message in LMP-WDM.

(segments) of the links that would be tested in LMP link verification between a pair of OXCs. Therefore, it is important not to run the two link verification procedures at the same time.

Several useful additions may be made to the link summarization process to report the characteristics of the optical links between the OXC and the OLS. The Link Summary message contains a series of Data Link objects, each describing a single link, and each containing a sequence of subobjects formed as TLVs. Figure 11.18 shows the new Data Link subobjects defined for LMP-WDM. Note that the TLV type identifiers have not yet been formally assigned.

Most of the fields in these new TLVs are self-explanatory. The BER estimate shown is the sign-reversed exponent of the estimated bit error rate of the link;

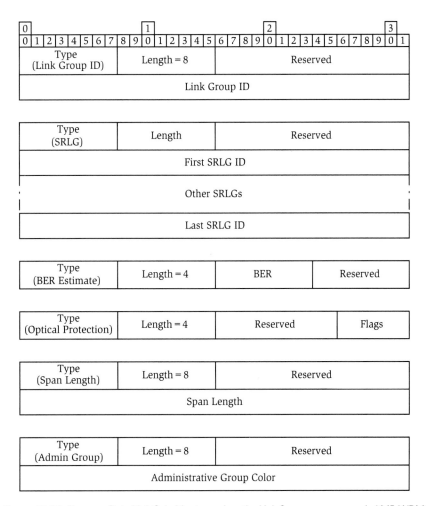

Figure 11.18 The new Data Link Subobjects used on the Link Summary message in LMP-WDM.

that is, if the link is expected to drop 1 bit in every 100,000,000,000 bits it has a BER of 10^{-11} and the field in the TLV contains the value 11. The protection bits are identical in values and meaning to those defined for GMPLS (see Chapter 10). The span length is the fiber length between the OXC and OLS in meters.

11.3.4 Fault Management

Fault management is also inherited from LMP. A new variant of the Channel Status object is introduced to report the status of the links within a link group as identified on the Link Summary message. The Link Group Channel Status

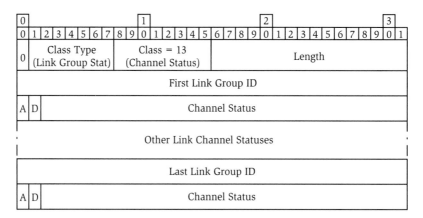

Figure 11.19 The new Link Group Channel Status Object used on the Channel Status messages in LMP-WDM.

object shown in Figure 11.19 is included on the Channel Status and Channel Status response messages.

On a Channel Status message the Link Group ID of 0xFFFFFFFF is reserved to indicate a request to report on all of the channels in all of the link groups in the TE link. The Channel Status field and the A- and D-flags are inherited unchanged from LMP.

11.4 Further Reading

GSMP is developed within the IETF by the GSMP Working Group. The GSMP Working Group has a web page that includes links to RFCs and Internet drafts for GSMP: www.ietf.org/html.charters/gsmp-charter.html. Some key RFCs and drafts are:

RFC 3292—General Switch Management Protocol V3
RFC 3293—GSMP Packet Encapsulations
RFC 3294—GSMP Applicability

The ForCES Working Group has a web page that includes links to Internet drafts for forwarding and control separation: www.ietf.org/html.charters/forces-charter.html. Some key drafts are:

draft-ietf-forces-requirements—Requirements for Separation of IP Control and Forwarding
draft-ietf-forces-netlink—Netlink as an IP Services Protocol

LMP-WDM falls within the remit of the CCAMP Working Group, and links to related Internet drafts can be found at www.ietf.org/html.charters/ccamp-charter. html. The key draft is:

draft-ietf-ccamp-lmp-wdm—Link Management Protocol (LMP) for DWDM Optical Line Systems

Chapter 12
Application Protocols

There are many Internet application protocols providing ways for applications to communicate in an IP environment to achieve a common task. It would be impossible to cover them adequately here—even some books dedicated exclusively to the topic struggle to provide sufficient material on all of the common protocols.

This chapter is intended to give the background to standardized Internet application protocols and to illustrate how they function and how they make use of IP and IP transport services by examining a few of the very common and most important protocols.

The Domain Name System protocol (DNS) is an important facilitator. It is used to associate host and domain names with specific IP addresses allowing, for example, a Universal Resource Locator (URL) such as http://www.elsevier.com to be converted to an IP address (165.193.122.135) to allow IP messages to be routed to the correct destination.

Telnet is a simple character-based protocol that provides user access to remote systems. It is a popular method for users to log in and access the command line interfaces of computers and network devices without having to have a terminal that is directly attached. Telnet is also used as an "application transport" mechanism for some other applications, and parts of the protocol (such as the authentication options) are incorporated into other application protocols.

The File Transfer Protocol (FTP) is used extensively in the Internet to copy files from one place to another. It is transaction oriented and focuses on the reliable transfer of bulk data using TCP as its transport protocol.

The Trivial File Transfer Protocol (TFTP) achieves the same function as FTP but operates over UDP. The unreliability of data transfer over UDP places a different set of requirements on TFTP, making it a subtly different protocol and giving it significantly different application characteristics.

The Hypertext Transfer Protocol (HTTP) could be described as *the* protocol that has made the Internet a popular success. It is used to publish and read hypertext documents across the World Wide Web—that is, to read web pages.

12.1 What Is an Application?

Applications are programs that are run for or on behalf of users to address specific service requests made by the users. Some applications such as word processors can operate in a self-contained environment, taking input from the user through access devices such as keyboards, mice, and microphones, and sending output to screens, printers, or disks. Other applications are designed to interact with remote computers, sending or retrieving information as files, emails, or web pages. In practice, the line is blurred; applications that store data on disks may access remote file systems, and applications that are intended to provide access to remote computers can be applied to the local host.

Applications that provide some form of access to remote sites are usually formed in two parts: a *client* that receives instructions from the user and that sends requests to the remote *server*.

12.1.1 Clients and Servers

Figure 12.1 shows how client and server applications may connect across the Internet in a many-to-many relationship. A client on one host may access servers

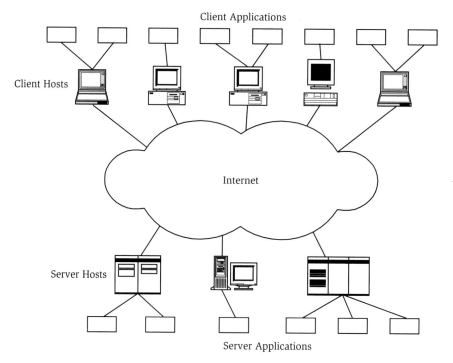

Figure 12.1 Client and server applications connect across the Internet in many-to-many relationships.

on multiple remote hosts, and a server application may serve multiple applications running on the same or different hosts. A host may run multiple instances of the same application—usually this applies only to the client application, but it could also be the preferred solution on the server. A client application may provide access for one or more users on the client host.

For a client–server model to work, it is necessary for the server application to exist and be running at the remote site. Some systems achieve this by leaving the server running as a *daemon*, that is as a passive background process that waits for requests from the client. Others may choose to load the server only on demand, when a request is received from the client.

It is not enough, however, to have a client and a server; there must also exist a communication path between them. This path consists not only of a physical link, but also requires a data transport mechanism. This is what the whole of this book (and, indeed, the whole of the Internet) has been leading up to—IP provides an excellent way of transferring data between computers whether it be routed or switched data, and the IP transport protocols lift the burden of data delivery from the application.

So now we have a client and a server ready to exchange requests and responses across the Internet. But will they understand each other? Even applications, it is clear, need a set of rules to govern the languages they speak to one another. These application protocols are heavily tailored to the requirements of the applications themselves—there is little in common between them except the fact that most of them are text-based rather than binary encoded. That is, the applications exchange strings of printable characters to formulate requests and responses rather than using the bits and bytes that are common in the lower-layer protocols.

12.1.2 Ports

Ports provide a handy way of identifying the communication flows between a client and its server. Since multiple clients and servers may be running on a single host, the IP address is not enough to distinguish the conversations, and so traffic is labeled with the source and destination port.

Typically, a server application will listen on a well-known port so all clients know how to get in touch with it. The client selects its own source port and sends a message through the transport protocol to the host on which the server is running, targeting the server's port. The server replies back to the client's port. In some cases the server may choose to vary its port ID on the response so that subsequent communications are moved away from the well-known port on which it is listening for new connections from other clients. Once the client and server ports are established, the client and server can carry out their conversation without any risk of confusing traffic from other clients on other hosts, or from other instances of the client application on the same host.

The scope of *well-known* as applied to the port on which the server listens is an interesting point. For all application protocols defined by the IETF, there is a well-known port for each transport protocol over which the application protocol may be run. These port IDs are tracked by IANA and, in general, the same port number is used by one application protocol over all transport protocols. Although these standard port numbers serve as defaults in the Internet, some system operators choose to vary them on their hosts. Of course, this works only if the client is configured to know the correct port ID, otherwise it will fail to connect to the server. Variance of server port ID may be done for security reasons (although it does not provide a great deal of security, some operators see a great benefit in using a higher number port ID that does not require root privileges), to distribute per-port traffic load, or to distinguish server resources accessible through different ports.

TCP and UDP ports are described in Section 7.1.2.

12.2 Choosing a Transport

Applications exchange data and must choose a means of communicating the data between client and server. In the Internet this comes down to choosing an IP transport protocol or simply sending raw IP data. IP transport protocols are described in Chapter 7.

On the whole, designers of application protocols and implementers of applications want to be protected from issues of out-of-order delivery, data corruption, and message loss. They see no need to reinvent the wheel and are happy to take advantage of the transport services that can be provided by existing protocols. For this reason, it is rare for an application protocol to operate using IP packets directly.

The choice of transport protocol depends on the services that the application needs. In general, applications try to use the lighter-weight UDP whenever they can get away with it, both because there is a shorter setup time for communications between client and server, and because there is less overhead per byte sent. However, when an application needs to transfer data reliably and in order, it will usually choose to use TCP. There is one important exception to this rule: Some applications need to transfer large amounts of data in a reliable way but cannot afford the large code space needed for a TCP implementation—these applications use UDP and must abort and restart their work if any error is detected (see Section 12.5.8 for a description of TFTP, an example of such a protocol).

Applications that are specified to use SCTP are rare simply because SCTP is such a new protocol. Work is being done to investigate which application protocols would benefit from the move to SCTP, but until there is a wider deployment of this transport protocol, it is unlikely that it will gain much use except in specialized fields.

12.2.1 Choosing to Use Sockets

Sockets are described in Section 7.3.8. They are a nearly standard programming interface to IP and IP transport protocols that allow applications to be written in a portable way and run on different systems, getting the same level of access to the IP transport. Sockets implementations themselves provide a level of queuing of messages and buffering of data that is of great help to an application implementer. Note that sockets implementations exist to provide access to UDP and TCP. Direct access to IP (without the use of a transport protocol) is often provided through *raw sockets*, although there is not universal support for this in operating systems. Work on SCTP sockets is progressing, and where SCTP support is available, it is usually through a sockets-like interface.

Although sockets are a roughly standardized solution, it should be noted that they are not part of the specification of IP or the IP transport protocols but are only a means of access to them. Many application implementations choose to use sockets because of their convenience or because they provide the only access to the IP or IP transport support in the systems in which they will run.

12.3 Domain Name System (DNS)

So far, all discussion of communication between hosts and routers in the Internet has focused on the use of IP addresses. IP addresses are, however, inconvenient for users who (unless they are particularly gifted, or don't get out enough) find remembering 12-digit numbers a drag. Wouldn't it be nicer to define an alias for each node in the network and allow the user to use that? The Domain Name System (RFC 1034 and RFC 1035) defines naming conventions for hosts and ways to resolve names into IP addresses.

12.3.1 Host Names

Assigning names to network nodes gives rise to two problems: distribution of configuration information and guaranteeing uniqueness. In small, privately administered networks, host names are defined for each machine connected to the network, and a network administrator manages a list of mappings between names and IP addresses. Each host may even have multiple names or aliases. When users want to access a certain machine they add an entry to a system file on their computer (for a UNIX user this is */etc/hosts*) defining the name to address mapping—this is analogous to putting an entry in your address book. More commonly, the network administrator periodically distributes a master copy of the host names file so that all users can access new computers.

As the size of a network grows, and particularly when connectivity is made to the Internet, the task of managing host names becomes too much for even a team of administrators. The first issue to resolve is how to keep host names unique—bear in mind the many hundreds of computers that their users have named "enterprise," "voyager," "barney," and "wilma." This problem is tackled by making host names hierarchical across the Internet and distributing responsibility for managing each level of the name. Confusion is reduced by making the names entirely case insensitive.

Names of the form www.elsevier.com are familiar to users of the Internet, especially those who use web browsers. These are names of specific hosts attached to the Internet. The name is a hierarchy of components read with increasing granularity from right to left—demarcation between levels in the naming hierarchy is provided by the period ".". In this case, the name tells us that the host belongs to a corporation (*com*), that the corporation's registered Internet name is *elsevier*, and that the host in question is that assigned as the World Wide Web server.

There are only a few general suffixes (the highest level in the naming hierarchy) defined within the Internet and these are administered separately by different organizations which are responsible for registering and assigning the next level of name. Table 12.1 lists the common name suffixes.

The "*int*" suffix was originally set aside for all hosts based at international sites, but it was soon realized that this approach was both parochial and impractical as there are more than a few computers outside the United States. The "int" suffix is now used by a few truly international bodies (such as http://www.un.int), and individual country codes are assigned as suffixes to allow the devolution of management to national bodies so that, for example, www.northwalescavingclub. org.uk is the machine that provides World Wide Web server access to the web pages belonging to the North Wales Caving Club, which is based in the United Kingdom. Note, however, two quirks when a national suffix is used: corporate names use "co" instead of "com," and educational (or academic) names use "ac" in place of "edu."

The waters, however, are muddy! Host names within the United States do not generally bother with a national suffix ("us"), and instead use the suffixes

Table 12.1 Some of the Standard Internet Host Name Suffixes

Name Suffix	Usage
com	Commercial
edu	Educational
gov	Governmental
mil	Military
net	Network provider
org	Organization (such as a club or a nongovernmental organization)

shown in Table 12.1. This has led many companies based outside of the United States to register in the "com" name space because it gives the impression that they are truly international businesses. At the same time, individuals wanting to put personal information onto the World Wide Web often manage to register for names in the "com" hierarchy, giving the false impression that they are operating a business. What is more, *redirection* of domain names means that web sites need not actually be hosted in the country to which the name refers. The island state of Niue in Polynesia (population roughly 2000) has been assigned the nationality suffix "nu," and the country enjoys a nice business selling domain names. Recent pushes toward deregulation have introduced the "biz" and "info" suffixes, and some people would like to do away with the structure of domain names entirely, making names such as *http://myteam.is.the.best* a possibility.

Each formal suffix is administered by a body to which an organization, company, or individual must apply to register the next level in the name hierarchy (*elsevier* or *northwalescavingclub*). This moves the name administration responsibility out to the organization, which must ensure name uniqueness. For example, Elsevier may have individual servers responsible for supporting World Wide Web access and for email, and they could name these www.elsevier.com and email.elsevier.com.

An organization can continue to extend the hierarchy to as many levels as it wants, so that individual PCs within different departments might be named karyn.editorial.elsevier.com and tracy.hospitality.elsevier.com.

It has become conventional for certain services to be provided by hosts with well-known prefixes, so Elsevier might have two hosts called www.elsevier.com and ftp.elsevier.com providing access for web browsing and for FTP (see Section 12.5). In practice, however, it is quite likely that these services are provided by the same machine and that this machine is called voyager (or barney, wilma, or enterprise). This is not a problem because one host can have three aliases, in this case voyager.elsevier.com, www.elsevier.com, and ftp.elsevier.com can all map to the same IP address.

What is more, the North Wales Caving Club (a group of impoverished spelunkers) has not purchased a server and a permanent connection to the Internet. Instead, they have rented domain name hosting from a larger organization. In this case, the host name maps to the IP address of some other organization's computer, which probably also hosts web pages for many other groups. There may be thousands of fully-qualified host names that map to the same IP address.

This leaves one remaining issue: how to get the information that maps a host name to an IP address onto the host system that wants to reach a specific remote host, since regardless of how the user knows a remote host, data must be sent using IP addresses. It is certainly possible for users to place entries in their host names file, but this doesn't answer the problem of how they discover the IP address to which to configure. It might also be possible to redistribute a table of all host name to IP address mappings from some central authority to all users, but this table would be impractically large. Instead, a protocol is provided to allow a client to send a request into the Internet to discover the IP address to use to reach a specific host name. This is the DNS protocol.

12.3.2 The DNS Protocol

The DNS protocol is designed to help a client to resolve a host name into an IP address. If the host does not have an entry for the host name in its host name file, it can send a request to a DNS server. The request simply asks, "Given this host name (or IP address), what is the IP address (or host name)?" The DNS server sends back a response which repeats the question to avoid confusion, and then gives an answer. If a DNS server does not know the answer, it may respond with a negative response, "unknown," or may choose to ignore the request.

DNS requests and responses generally use UDP datagrams. This is appropriate because they are simple request–reply exchanges, and if the client does not get a response, it can always ask again. The client sends a request to the IP address of its DNS server, targeting the well-known port 53. The server listens on that port and returns the response to the client's source port. TCP can also be used, and may be preferred when large amounts of data need to be transferred—the maximum data size supported for DNS over UDP is 512 bytes, and some queries (notably transfers of the full set of information owned by a server—zone transfers) will definitely require more data. On the other hand, there is considerable overhead associated with establishing a TCP connection, and for normal request–response exchanges UDP is a better mechanism.

A client may know about more than one DNS server and should choose a preferred server, using the others only when it gets no answer from its selected server. If the client does not know the address of any DNS server, it may broadcast or multicast its request, still targeting port 53. If the client gets multiple replies it should choose one (usually the first) as its preferred DNS server, but may store the other server addresses in case the first server stops responding at some time in the future.

12.3.3 Distribution of DNS Databases

The full database of all host name to IP address mappings would be enormous. It is impractical to store it in a single place, both because of its size and because the components of the database are managed disparately. This gives rise to a distributed DNS database managed by multiple servers across the Internet.

When the client in Figure 12.2 wishes to access the Elsevier web pages, it needs to map the host name www.elsevier.com to an IP address. It first looks in its local host name file, but if it can't find an entry it sends a request to its local DNS server. The local DNS server has a more extensive host name file applying to all of the computers in its network, but since the Elsevier node is not local it

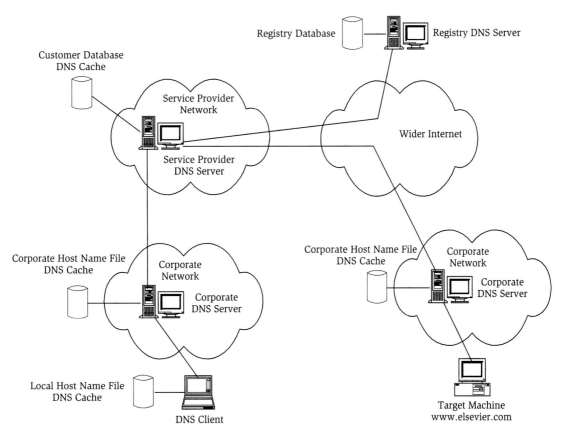

Figure 12.2 DNS requests are passed from server to server until a response can be returned.

doesn't know about it. This DNS sever, however, has access to the outside world through some Service Provider, and so it makes a proxy DNS request for the client—that is, it makes an identical request to the Service Provider's DNS server. The DNS server in the Service Provider maintains a large table of customers and may be able to resolve the Elsevier host name, but if it can't it needs to find out information from a higher authority—it asks the DNS server responsible for the registry based on the host name suffix. This, too, is a proxy request.

The registry DNS server does not contain the answer to the host name to IP address question. If it did, it would contain the unmanageably large mapping table. It does, however, know who is responsible for the next level of hierarchy in the name—it knows the IP address of the DNS server in the Elsevier corporate network. Rather than send a proxy request (which would mean that the response came back to it), the DNS server responds with a "don't ask me, ask him" message, telling the Service Provider DNS server to send its request direct to the

Elsevier corporate DNS server which knows the IP address of the web server and is able to respond. The response carrying the IP address of the target machine is passed back, server to server, until it is given back to the client, which can now send its IP messages.

In practice there may be many more levels of hierarchy and the request may be forwarded many times (as shown in Figure 12.2) before an answer is sent.

The information giving mappings from host name to IP address is usually pretty stable over time. It is not necessary for every node to fire off a request each time it needs to look up a host name. In fact, if it did, the network might easily become swamped with DNS requests and responses. Clients often maintain a cache of recent DNS responses so that they can use them to perform mappings. Entries in this cache usually timeout after a while so that the client will not use stale information. Each DNS response carries a time-to-live value that helps the client manage its cache, and when a client reboots, it usually throws away the whole cache.

Similarly, DNS servers maintain a cache of DNS replies that they have forwarded. This enables them to answer requests for the same host name much more speedily. DNS caches on DNS servers are also subject to time-to-live values and, to stop them from becoming too big, may discard entries using some function of the frequency of request for the host name and the time the entry has left to live.

12.3.4 DNS Message Formats

DNS messages consist of requests and responses. The request obviously contains the question, and the response includes the answer. To help disambiguate responses to different requests, the response also contains the question. Multiple questions may be included in the same request, and so responses may include multiple answers—in fact, multiple answers could be provided for the same question. All messages also start with a common header, and may end with additional information provided by the server, as shown in Figure 12.3.

The common header is shown in Figure 12.4. It contains a Request ID used to correlate replies, an Opcode (operation code) to show what the request/reply is asking, and an Rcode to indicate the result. The DNS Opcodes and Rcodes are shown in Tables 12.2 and 12.3. The Inverse Query (opcode 1) is used to map from an IP address back to a name—this function is optional and need not be

```
< DNS Message > ::=    < common header >
                       < question > [ < question > ...]
                       [ < answer > ...]
                       [ < authority > ...]
                       [ < additional info > ...]
```

Figure 12.3 The formal definition of a DNS message.

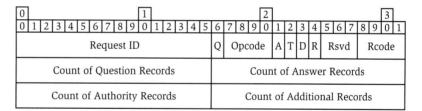

Figure 12.4 The DNS common Message header.

Table 12.2 DNS Opcodes

Opcode	Request Type
0	A standard query
1	An inverse query
2	A server status request

Table 12.3 DNS Rcodes

Rcode	Meaning
0	No error condition (success or message request).
1	Format error—The DNS server could not decode the request.
2	Server failure—The DNS server encountered an internal error processing the request.
3	Name Error—The name in the request does not exist.
4	Not Implemented—The DNS server does not support the type of request.
5	Refused—The DNS server refused the request for policy reasons such as security.

supported by DNS servers. Also included in the header are the five bit flags explained in Table 12.4.

The second part of the header consists of four counts. Each indicates the number of records of a particular type that follow the header and may be zero. The records always appear in the same order as the counts and correspond to the components of the message shown in Table 12.2.

Question Records are encoded as shown in Figure 12.5, but Answer, Authority, and Additional Records share a common resource record format, shown in Figure 12.6. Names in Question Records and Resource Records are encoded using a special format that replaces the periods with counts of the number of characters

Table 12.4 DNS Message Header Bits

Bit	Meaning
Q	Query/Response bit: zero means this is a query; 1 means it is a response.
A	Authoritative Answer bit: set to 1 if this response is from a DNS server that is an authority for the name being queried. In this case, there is no possibility of the response being from an out-of-date cache.
T	Truncation bit: set to 1 if a response has been truncated to fit within the requirements of the transport mechanism.
D	Recursion Desired bit: set to 1 on a query if the client wishes the DNS servers to pursue an answer recursively.
R	Recursion Available bit: set to 1 on a response to a query that did not have the Recursion Desired bit set, if the server responding would have been able to support recursion had it been requested.

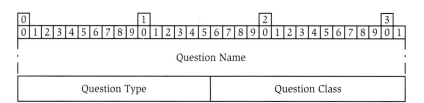

Figure 12.5 The DNS Question Record.

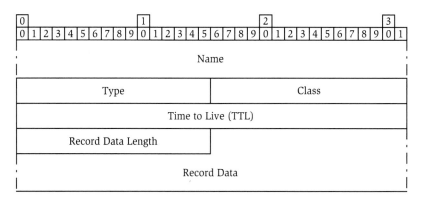

Figure 12.6 The DNS Resource Record used for Answer, Authority, and Additional Records in Response messages.

in the next segment of the name. Thus, the name www.elsevier.com would be encoded as:

```
3 w w w 7 e l s e v i e r 3 c o m 0
```

Note the final zero to indicate that no more name segments follow. Since names encoded in this way may be an arbitrary length, and since the name fields are not padded, subsequent fields and records may begin on any byte boundary.

The Question Record includes two fields to present the type and class of the question. The commonly used values for the Type field are shown in Table 12.5. The Class field is intended to indicate the use to which the data is put, for example, the type of network from which the name comes. Only two class values are used in the Internet: the value 1 indicates "The Internet" and the value 255 means "Any Class."

Note that the questions listed in Table 12.5 all refer to the information that is being solicited by the query if the request opcode is zero (a normal query). In all cases, the information supplied is a host or domain name. On the other hand, if the request Opcode is 1 (inverse query), the answer is supplied in the request using the answer field, and the question is returned in the response with question type indicating "host address."

The three other record types (Answer, Authority, and Additional Information) use a standard format, as shown in Figure 12.6. Common records return the name that was queried and provide additional information in record data. The Type and Class fields are subsets of the values used in the query record and are shown in Table 12.5. No value greater than 128 is used in a common record.

The Time to Live (TTL) field indicates in seconds for how long the information supplied in the response will remain valid. This allows the receiver to know for how long it may retain the information in its own cache. Note that the TTL field cannot take account of the transmission delay between server and client since the two nodes do not have synchronized clocks.

The record data returned is specific to the type of record and to the question that was asked. For example, an answer record for a simple host name look-up (Opcode 0, question class 1) would contain the IP address that is mapped from the supplied host name. IP addresses are encoded in hexadecimal; the IP address 172.0.8.12 would be presented as 0xac00080c.

Authority records indicate the authoritative DNS name server for a name resolution. Authority records may be present on responses even when those responses provide answers to the original questions. This allows a client to determine which server is responsible for the name to address mapping. The client may then requery the correct server for a definitive response. An authority record may also be present on a response that does not provide the answer, allowing a registry server (as shown in Figure 12.2) to tell a client to redirect its request to another DNS server.

Additional information that the server thinks may be of use to the client is placed in additional records. This information may be other addresses, other host names, test strings, or may be application defined.

Table 12.5 Question Type Codes

Question Type	Meaning
1	A host address
2	An authoritative name server
5	The canonical name for an alias
6	Marks the start of a zone of authority
10	A null RR—unformatted data for experimental usage
11	A well-known service description
12	A domain name pointer
13	Host information
14	Mailbox or mail list information
15	Mail exchange
16	Text strings
252	A request for a transfer of an entire zone—that is, all of the information for which the DNS server contains the authoritative copy
253	A request for mailbox-related records
255	A request for all records

12.3.5 Extensions to DNS

As befits a topic so central to the way the Internet works, there are well over 50 RFCs relating to DNS. Some of them discuss implementation problems and observed deployment characteristics, but others provide extensions to cover a variety of features, from IPv6 to security. Other DNS RFCs are concerned with defining new DNS resource records to encode a whole range of information, from geographic location to security keys. As the amount of information that a DNS server can hold is increased, DNS gets closer to being a generalized distributed database with a simple access protocol.

12.4 Telnet

In the early days of computing, a user at a remote site could perform interactive operations on a mainframe computer by typing commands at a terminal. Terminals were essentially dumb devices that had point-to-point connectivity with the main computer. The terminals were either manufactured by the supplier of the computer or were made by a second company following the strict specifications for connectivity to the computer. The only problems with this form of connectivity were the number of point-to-point links needed for multiple users, each with his own terminal.

As the demand for computing power increased, additional computers became available at different sites and the users wanted to access them. If the computers were made by different manufactures (and sometimes even when they came from the same company) each one needed a terminal with different characteristics. This often left users needing multiple terminals on their desks and resulted in rats' nests of cabling—a fine situation if you manufacture terminals or cables, but not a lot of fun if you are trying to fit lots of equipment into your tiny cubicle.

These issues led to the development of the Telecommunications Network Protocol (Telnet) to provide a standardized way for terminals to communicate with host computers, regardless of their type. The workstations needed to be a bit smarter to run the Telnet client software, but at this time desktop PCs were being introduced, so that was possible. Telnet servers needed to be implemented on the host computers—this function was quickly integrated into many standard operating systems, and where it was not available with legacy equipment, terminal servers could be installed to convert from Telnet back to the data format expected by the hosts. Running Telnet over an Internet transport protocol also tidied up the cabling because a single connection to the Internet was enough to allow a user to connect to any number of hosts.

The before and after network diagrams shown in Figure 12.7 illustrate the reduction in cabling and terminals upon moving to use an IP network with Telnet used to provide terminal connectivity.

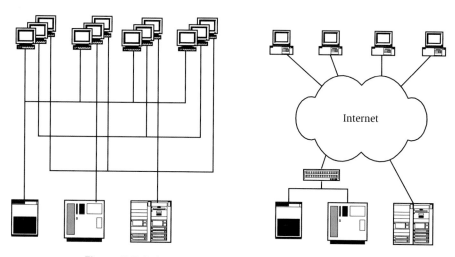

Figure 12.7 Before and after—remote workstation connectivity.

12.4.1 Choosing Between Character and Graphical Access

Over time, Telnet has become almost universal. A user wanting to log on to a remote host can use Telnet. Telnet is usually provided as the means to establish remote command line interface access to remote devices from the dumbest power controllers to the most modern optical switches.

Although Telnet offers only a character-based command interface, it is still immensely popular. This type of interface is, after all, the type of interface that users have come to expect when they connect to a remote device. Command line interfaces are pretty much ubiquitous.

As a result, Telnet clients are supplied as part of most operating systems, and there is a plenitude of Telnet tools and applications for most platforms. Telnet servers are built into all server operating systems, guaranteeing that, as long as there is IP connectivity, it will be possible to access the server.

Graphical interfaces have, of course, gained control of desktop computing, with most single-user operating systems offering "Windows-like" front-ends. Although much progress has been made to make remote access available through graphical interfaces through the work of the Open Group consortium and the advent of products such as Microsoft's NetMeeting, these applications require that complex server programs are run on the remote computer to allow a user to gain access. These programs often do not exist because the remote computer is old, runs an operating system that doesn't support graphical access, or is a specialized piece of equipment (such as a switch or a router) that does not have processing capacity for such server applications. For these situations, Telnet remains an excellent solution for remote access.

12.4.2 Network Virtual Terminal

One of the major issues to be resolved to enable Telnet to work is the conversion of keystrokes on a terminal to characters at the server. This may seem trivial until you understand that different terminals and keyboards have different ways of representing characters and control commands, and that different servers have different expectations. To give two simple examples: Many large IBM computers use a character encoding called Extended Binary Coded Decimal Interchange Code (EBCDIC) in which the character *A* is represented by the single hexadecimal byte 0xC1, but most other computers use the American Standard Code for Information Interchange (ASCII) in which the same character is represented by 0x41; many desktop computers represent end-of-line markers with two characters (carriage return and line feed), but servers, especially UNIX servers, use only the line feed character.

Clearly, for two computers to communicate using Telnet, there may need to be a translation. Several options exist to make this work. Each workstation could determine the characteristics of each server to which it intends to attach and could perform the necessary translations, but this requires the workstation to have a high level of sophistication when, ideally, we want to keep workstations as simple as possible. Alternatively, the servers could be responsible for performing the translations so that clients can be kept simple. This alternative puts the complexity for translation into the server, where it may also be inappropriate, for example, when providing simple Telnet access to a device. In any case, whether the translation is implemented on the client or the server, a large number of translation functions may be needed to map all of the possible encodings, and these functions must continually be updated as new devices are introduced.

The solution is embodied in Network Virtual Terminal (NVT), documented by RFC 854, the base RFC that defines the Telnet protocol. This document describes an imaginary terminal within the network and defines the character encodings it uses. All workstations using Telnet are required to perform their own translations so that the data they send looks as if it had been generated by one of these virtual terminals. Each Telnet server is required to accept data formatted as though it had come from a virtual terminal. In this way each participating node, client, or server is responsible for implementing precisely one translation function, mapping data between its own format and the NVT format. Lucky implementations discover that their own encoding is close to or identical to NVT and that their translation function is trivial.

An NVT is defined to be a device capable of sending and receiving data. It has a keyboard through which a user can enter data to be sent, and a printer capable of displaying received data. The device operates in half-duplex mode, meaning that it buffers characters received from the keyboard until it has assembled a full line of text before it submits that line to the host server. This makes editing of the entered characters and cancellation of the whole line a local matter.

The character code set is based on the 7-bit ASCII code (known at the time of the RFC as USASCII) with several key modifications, as set out in Table 12.6. The characters are transmitted in 8-bit bytes.

12.4.3 How Does Telnet Work?

Telnet uses TCP as its transport protocol. The Telnet server listens on the well-known port 23 and responds to the client on the client's chosen port. The server may also offer other ports, and this can be useful to distinguish between connections to different devices when the connectivity is provided through a concentrator or terminal server, as shown in Figure 12.7.

Telnet transactions are remarkably simple, and it will be a relief to readers who have struggled bravely through RFCs of a hundred pages and more to discover that RFC 854 is only 15 pages long, including the definition of NVT.

Telnet character flows are presented to TCP for transmission. In the normal case, the client does this only when the end of a line is reached—that is, when the user presses the "Enter" or "Return" key. There is nothing, however, that prevents the client from sending data to the server one character at a time,

Table 12.6 NVT Control Characters and Their Meanings

NVT Code	Short Name	Meaning
0	NULL	Do nothing.
7	BEL	Bell. Produces an audible or visible signal (which does not move the print head).
8	BS	Back Space. Moves the print head one character position toward the left margin.
9	HT	Horizontal Tab. Moves the printer to the next horizontal tab stop.
10	LF	Line Feed. Moves the printer to the next print line, keeping the column.
11	VT	Vertical Tab. Moves the printer to the next vertical tab stop.
12	FF	Moves the printer to the top of the next page, keeping the same column.
13	CR	Carriage Return. Moves the printer to the left margin of the current line.
255	IAC	Interrupt as Command. Treat the next byte as a control command defined by the Telnet protocol.

although such behavior is very inefficient. The server sends data to the client in blocks of one or more lines, depending on whether it is spooling a job to the printer or just writing a message to the user's screen.

Telnet control commands and options are embedded in the character flow and are indicated by the IAC character (0xff). The IAC character is used to indicate that the next character represents a control command. This ensures that characters with the same numeric value as control commands that are not preceded by IAC are not interpreted as commands. In some cases (such as option negotiation), the control command is followed by one or more other characters. This is either a well-defined sequence (such as for the DO command when precisely one option character follows) or is bounded by an end-of-sequence marker command, itself preceded by the IAC character (such as with the SB and SE commands).

Initially, only a few control commands were defined (as shown in Table 12.7), and these were single-byte codes, sometimes with optional parameters. These remain central to the operation of Telnet, but over time new commands have been added to support additional options and extensions. Telnet has spawned over one-hundred RFCs defining extensions and ways of handling specific terminal types. Some relate to hardware behavior, such as those that describe functional mappings for the IBM 3270 and 5250 families of terminals and controllers. Others offer extensions for encryption and other security features. There is even one (RFC 1097) describing the transmission and display of subliminal messages.

Table 12.7 Telnet Control Commands

Code	Short Name	Meaning
240	SE	End of subnegotiation parameters.
241	NOP	No operation. Do nothing—useful to delete control sequences without removing characters from the data flow.
242	DM	Data Mark. This control character is sent as the only byte of data in an urgent TCP packet to clear the data path to the other party by flushing all data stored for processing at the receiver. This is used as part of the Telnet synchronization process.
243	BRK	Break. Indicates that the Break key or the Attention key was hit. The effect may be system dependent, and the command is provided to offer a character encoding for a keystroke that is not within the normal NVT character set.
244	IP	Interrupt Process. Suspend, interrupt, abort, or terminate the remote Telnet process. This is used when a user believes his process is in an unending loop, or when an unwanted process has been inadvertently activated. IP may be used by other protocols that use Telnet as an application-level transport when they wish to terminate their use of Telnet.
245	AO	Abort Output. Process through all queued data without sending it to the output device. If some data has been prepared but not yet sent to the output device, the prepared data should be silently dropped. To clear data that is buffered within TCP, it may also be necessary to use the synchronization process.
246	AYT	Are You There? Send back to the NVT some visible (that is, printable) evidence that the remote end of the Telnet conversation is still active and that the AYT command was received.
247	EC	Erase Character. The recipient should delete the last preceding undeleted character or print position from the data stream, if possible. If the data has already been sent to the output device this may result in over-printing (compare with the BS character 0x08), so it is preferable to maintain whole lines within the sender, allowing editing in place and the transmission of whole lines.
248	EL	Erase Line. The recipient should delete characters from the data stream back to, but not including, the last "CR LF" sequence sent over the Telnet connection. This function is unlikely to be supported by output devices, but is useful for managing lines of text within input buffers.
249	GA	Go Ahead. When the process at one end of a Telnet connection cannot proceed without input from the other end, the process transmits the GA command to solicit further data. This mechanism allows Telnet to be managed as half-duplex.
250	SB	Indicates that what follows is subnegotiation of the indicated option.
251	WILL	Indicates the desire to begin performing, or confirmation that you are now performing, the indicated option.

Table 12.7 *Continued*

Code	Short Name	Meaning
252	WON'T	Indicates the refusal to perform, or continue performing, the indicated option.
253	DO	Indicates the request that the other party perform, or confirmation that you are expecting the other party to perform, the indicated option.
254	DON'T	Indicates the demand that the other party stop performing, or confirmation that you are no longer expecting the other party to perform, the indicated option.

The DM command (242) is used as part of the Telnet synchronization procedure. This is used by one end of the Telnet connection to flush or clear the data path from it to the other end of the connection. The command is sent on its own in an Urgent TCP packet. Such packets are received in order, but are prioritized for processing. The receiving Telnet process discards any queued output as if it were processing an IP command and also flushes (by reading and discarding) all TCP data for the Telnet connection up to the offset indicated by the TCP packet carrying the DM command (hence, its name).

The Telnet synchronization provides more drastic measures than the AO and IP commands and may result in lost data and lost control commands; however, synchronization processing is required to notice and act on IP, AO, and AYT commands embedded in the data it discards. Conventionally, an IP command is sent as normal data immediately before the urgent DM command so that proper cleanup will occur even if the receiver does not prioritize urgent TCP data.

Many of the Telnet commands (SB, SE, DO, DON'T, WILL, WON'T) are concerned with negotiation of Telnet parameters. This is discussed in a partner document, RFC 855. Basic option negotiation consists of one party sending a request that it should be allowed to use the option, or that the other party should use the option. The WILL command is an offer to use an option and the DO command is a request that the option be used. The WILL and DO commands are mutual acknowledgments, but WON'T is a refusal of the DO command, and DON'T is the refusal of the WILL command.

DO, DON'T, WILL, and WON'T are single-character command codes, as shown in Table 12.7, but are always followed by an additional code to indicate the option being negotiated. The list of options is maintained by the Internet Assigned Numbers Authority (IANA). The effect of this is that a three-character sequence is transmitted, as shown by the example in Figure 12.8, in which the option code for the Echo option is 1.

Some options require negotiation of more parameters than just the basic enablement of the options. In these cases, both parties agree to discuss the use of the option by using the will/do exchange and the option indicator. They then embark on subnegotiation of the additional parameters. The initiator sends an

```
Server sends:      IAC DO ECHO

                   FF FD 01
```

Figure 12.8 An example of an Option Request.

```
Server sends:    IAC DO TERMINAL-TYPE

                 FF FD 18

Client sends:    IAC WILL TERMINAL-TYPE

                 FF FB 18

Server sends:    IAC SB TERMINAL-TYPE SEND IAC SE

                 FF FA 18 53 45 4E 44 FF F0

Client sends:    IAC SB TERMINAL-TYPE IS IBM-3278-2 IAC SE

                 FF FA 18 49 53 20 49 42 4D 2D 33 32 37 38 2D 32 FF F0
```

Figure 12.9 A simple subnegotiation exchange showing retrieval of the client terminal type.

SB command to indicate the start of subnegotiation and immediately follows it with the option code to indicate which option is being negotiated. It then supplies the additional parameters in a format that is specific to the option. At the end of the sequence of additional parameters, it sends SE. Note that if any of the parameters has the value 255, the character must be presented twice so that it is not interpreted as the IAC character. Figure 12.9 gives a simple example of the use of the SB and SE commands. Note that the option code for Terminal-Type is 24 (0x18) and that the parameters are passed as text.

12.4.4 Telnet Authentication

One Telnet option is an important feature used by several other character-based application protocols such as FTP. In many application services it is important to verify the user's identity on the server before granting the user's application access to restricted resources or information. From the user's perspective this process takes the form of prompts for his user name and password, but this information must be handed off through the Telnet protocol to the server (if authentication was done at the client, a malicious or careless client could let anyone access the server).

Telnet authentication can use one of a huge range of authentication schemes, from simple Kerberos ticket exchange to various forms of encryption. All use the Authentication option (option code 37). As shown in Figure 12.10, which is taken from RFC 2941, the server and client first agree to use the authentication option—if the client refused, the server would simply drop the

Server sends:	IAC DO AUTHENTICATION
Client sends:	IAC WILL AUTHENTICATION
Server sends:	IAC SB AUTHENTICATION SEND
	KERBEROS_V4 CLIENT|MUTUAL
	KERBEROS_V4 CLIENT|ONE_WAY IAC SE
Client sends:	IAC SB AUTHENTICATION NAME "joe"
	IAC SE
Client sends:	IAC SB AUTHENTICATION IS KERBEROS_V4 CLIENT|MUTUAL AUTH
	4 7 1 67 82 65 89 46 67 7 9 77 0 48 24 49
	244 109 240 50 208 43 35 25 116 104 44 167 21 201 224 229
	145 20 2 244 213 220 33 134 148 4 251 249 233 229 152 77
	2 109 130 231 33 146 190 248 1 9 31 95 94 15 120 224
	0 225 76 205 70 136 245 190 199 147 155 13
	IAC SE
Server sends:	IAC SB AUTHENTICATION REPLY
	KERBEROS_V4 CLIENT|MUTUAL ACCEPT
	IAC SE

Figure 12.10 An example of Kerberos version four authentication in Telnet.

connection. Then the server uses subnegotiation to tell the client what forms of authentication are acceptable—if the client can't operate any of the required authentication methods it must drop the connection.

If the client can operate one of the requested authentication methods, it sends the username and follows it with authentication information (in the figure, this is a Kerberos version 4 ticket). If the server accepts the authentication it sends an acceptance notification. If the authentication fails, the server may send a failure notification or simply disconnect the connection.

12.4.5 Telnet Applications

Telnet applications are very common. Usually the user requests a connection to a specific host name or IP address. If a host name is specified, the application will need to look up the correct IP address using the local mapping tables and possibly resorting to the DNS protocol (see Section 12.3). The user may also supply the server port ID if some port other than the default port (23) is to be used.

Most Telnet applications offer a command line interface for managing the Telnet connection and requesting options, although some perform this function only through pull-down menus and check-boxes. Since Telnet is a command line application, a special escape sequence is required to tell the application that the option-management text being typed is not intended for transmission as normal data but should be intercepted and handled by the client application. This command sequence varies from implementation to implementation, but is often the Control key held down while the Right Square Bracket key is pressed (shown as "^]" or "CTRL+]"). Some common Telnet commands are shown in Table 12.8.

Table 12.8 Common Telnet Application Commands

Command	Meaning
Close	Close current connection but keep the Telnet application active
Display	Display operating parameters
Help	Print help information
Open	Connect to a remote server
Quit	Quit the Telnet application, closing the current connection
Set	Set an option (type "set ?" for a list)
Status	Display status information
Unset	Clear an option (type "unset ?" for a list)
?	Print help information

12.5   File Transfer Protocol (FTP)

The File Transfer Protocol (FTP) provides an excellent example of a transaction-based application protocol that operates over TCP. The transfer of bulk data in the format of files quickly grew to be a key use of the Internet in its early days, and the development of a protocol to effectively and reliably allow a user on one computer to access files on a remote computer exercised a lot of effort, with almost 50 of the first 1000 RFCs concerning themselves with the issue.

After much debate, a stable and reworked version of the FTP specification was published as RFC 959 in 1985. This version extends, but does not substantially modify, the previous version RFC 765 published 5 years earlier.

These days it is relatively unusual for a new implementation of FTP to be coded. Most operating systems include FTP as part of their IP stack, and there is no need to code a new one. This has many advantages for stability and interoperability.

12.5.1 A Simple Application Protocol

FTP addresses some basic requirements. It can transfer one or more files between two computers, regardless of their operating system, character representation, file format, or the type of link connecting the computers. It is, however, a transfer rather than an access protocol—this means that the contents of files can be examined or changed only on the local computer.

What could be simpler than a protocol to copy a file from one place to another? Simplistically, only a single command is required: "copy < source file path and name > < destination file path and name >". But FTP contains 33 standard commands, most of which require some end-to-end signaling. FTP implementations typically include further commands designed either to provide local functions or to map as shorthand onto standard commands. To manage the conversation that these commands and their responses generate, and to maintain context for that conversation, FTP has been designed as a connection-oriented protocol. This complicates the protocol further.

FTP is a client–server protocol. An FTP client is an application that a user may utilize to get files from (or put them to) a remote host. The remote host must run an FTP server to catch and respond to the user's requests. Although an FTP client may choose to implement a small subset of the protocol and the user commands, the server must be prepared to respond to any of the defined operations.

From a user's perspective, the operations are nevertheless relatively simple. With some variations, the commands available to a user are relatively standard, allowing a user to move from one system to another with ease and making it possible to write scripts that use FTP to automatically transfer files irrespective of the system on which they are run. Table 12.9 shows some of the common

Table 12.9 Typical FTP Client Commands Available to a User

Command	Operation
open	Connect to the FTP server on a remote host
user	Log in as a specific user on a remote host
close/disconnect	Disconnect from the remote FTP server
quit/bye	Disconnect from the remote FTP server and exit the client application
pwd	Display the current directory on the remote host
cd	Change the current directory on the remote host
lcd	Change the current directory on the local host
ls/dir	List the files in the current directory on the remote host
mkdir	Make a new directory on the remote host
rmdir	Remove a directory on the remote host
get/recv	Retrieve a file from the remote host
put/send	Copy a file to the remote host
delete	Delete a file on the remote host
rename	Rename a file on the remote host
append	Append the contents of a local file to a file on the remote host
mget	Retrieve multiple files for the remote host
mput	Copy multiple files to the remote host
mdelete	Delete multiple files on the remote host
ascii	Set the file transfer mode to ASCII (text) and convert text formatting characters between the local and remote host formats
binary	Set the file transfer mode to binary and do not attempt to examine or modify the contents of the files
prompt	Prompt the user between each of a set of operations
literal/quote	Send a specific command direct to the protocol

user commands offered by an FTP client application. The size of the list demonstrates the extent of the protocol that is needed to support all of the features that are necessary to offer a user a high-function file transfer utility.

The FTP client does not actually need to be a command-line application using the operations listed in Table 12.9. It may be implemented with a graphical user interface, and most web browsers also include FTP client capabilities. Regardless of the form of the FTP client, however, all implementations must include the same standard protocol features defined by RFC 959.

12.5.2 Connectivity Model

The FTP connectivity model shown in Figure 12.11 has two connections between client and server. The Control Connection is used to exchange commands and responses with the client sending one or more commands as the result of a user request, and the server responding with at least one response for each command. The Data Connection is used to transfer file data.

Both the control and data connections use TCP to transport their messages. The control connection is established between the client port (C) and the server port (S) where C and S have default values of 21. The control connection ports may be varied only by agreement between the client and server implementations external to the FTP protocol itself. The data connection is established, by default, between the client port (C) and the server port (S-1). Using a distinct port on the server helps prevent control commands from being blocked behind large amounts of data on what might be a very busy server, but there is no special need to use a distinct client port. The data connection ports may be varied by the client issuing the PORT command to vary the client side port and the PASV command to set the server-side port (see Section 12.5.5).

The control channel is initiated by the client initiating a TCP connection to port (S) on the server. The data connection, however, is initiated by the server in response to a data transfer command (such as RETR or STOR, Section 12.5.5). The data connection supports two-way traffic—that is, the same data connection may be used for sending and receiving files at the same time. When a file transmission has completed, the data connection may be closed or it may be left open for further file transfer.

Note that it is possible to run the client command generator and client data transfer process on different hosts. That is, the control and data connections do

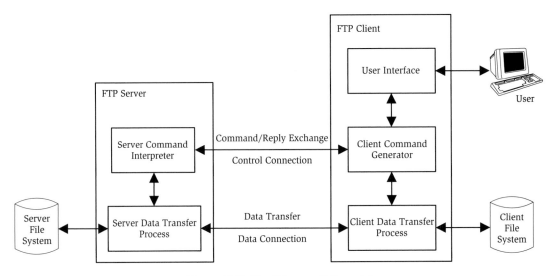

Figure 12.11 The FTP connectivity model.

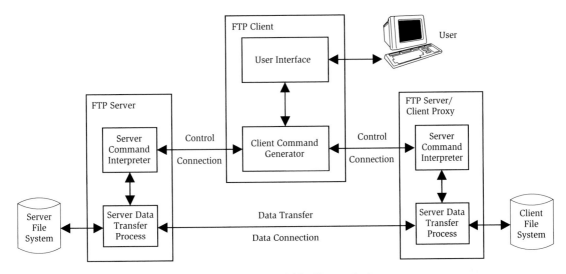

Figure 12.12 The FTP connectivity model for file transfer between two servers.

not need to be parallel, and FTP can be used to transfer data to or from a third node. For this to work, there must be an FTP client data transfer process running on the third node and listening on the correct port. Further, FTP may be used to exchange data between two nodes, neither of which is the client, by configuring two control connections as shown in Figure 12.12 and by issuing the appropriate commands to the two servers.

12.5.3 FTP Message Format

FTP control messages use a small part of the Telnet protocol when they are sent on the control channel. This has the advantage that no new protocol encodings are required, and FTP can be reduced to a text-based command–response protocol. Control requests are presented as four (or sometimes three) case-insensitive character strings to identify the operation and are followed by the text strings that constitute the parameters to the request. Parameters are separated by spaces. The command interpreter at the FTP server is constructed pretty much as an interpreter would be built to handle commands entered by a user at a command line interface. So, in BNF format, a command looks like the following example, where < SP > is the Telnet space character and < CRLF > is the Telnet carriage return line feed character:

< command string > [< SP > < parameter > ...] < CRLF >

Some parameters are encoded as a sequence of bytes represented as decimal numbers separated by commas:

< d > < , > [< d > < , > ...]

For example, the hexadecimal number 0xc0ffee would be transmitted as the string 192,255,238.

Although Telnet is used as the transmission protocol for FTP control messages, only a small subset of the Telnet function needs to be supported by the FTP server. In particular, the FTP server does not need to support editing by the client of the control commands—in practice, it is unlikely that the FTP client (which is a program and not a user) would need or want to do this.

Synchronization and confirmation of file transfer actions are achieved using FTP replies. Each command generates at least one reply although, as with the login/password sequence, some command–reply exchanges may be entirely embedded within others. Replies may indicate success, an intermediate state, or failure.

An FTP reply consists of a three-digit number that indicates to the client the exact result of the command and position in the processing. It is encoded as three alphanumeric characters. The number may be followed by a space and a text string intended for display and interpretation by the client's user. The whole reply is terminated by a Telnet end-of-line code.

12.5.4 Managing an FTP Session

Once a TCP connection has been set up for the control connection, the client must indicate to the server who the user is, what account the user is accessing, and in which directory the user is working. The control connection management commands are shown in Table 12.10.

Table 12.10 The FTP Access Control Commands

Command	Parameters	Use
USER	user name	Identify the user ID to be used on the server. This transaction may require additional user information to be entered through a subsequent command—for example, a password.
PASS	password	Exchange the password for the user ID on the server.
ACCT	account name	Set the user account information if it differs from the default for the user ID in use.
REIN		Reinitialize. Terminate a user session, allowing the current file transfer to complete, but remain connected.
QUIT		Terminate the user session as for the REIN command, allowing file transfer to complete, but then disconnect the control connection.
CWD	path name	Change the user's working directory on the server without the user having to change the user or account details.
CDUP		Change directory to parent directory (that is, up one level in the hierarchy). This is a special case of the CWD command in which no parameter needs to be passed.
SMNT	path name	Structure mount to another directory or file system without the user having to change the user or account details.

12.5.5 Data Connection Control

As described in Section 12.5.2, data connections are set up by the server on demand. That is, if a client does not issue any command that requires the transfer of data to or from the server, no data connection is established. When the client requests the exchange of data between the client and server using one of the commands described in Section 12.5.1, the server initiates a TCP connection either using the default ports or using the ports and IP addresses indicated by the client.

The client may use any of the commands shown in Table 12.11 to control the exchange of data. It may set the local and remote port IDs and it may configure the data types exchanged.

Data is transmitted to or from the client in a byte format selected by the client. This allows clients to be simpler and places all data conversion intelligence in the server. Files may contain text or binary data. A text file may be stored on a given machine in one of two popular encodings, ASCII or EBCDIC, and conversion between the encodings may be necessary. The TYPE command allows the client to specify the encoding that it will use for data it sends, or the format in which it expects to receive data. The server is responsible for performing any conversion to and from its own preferred encoding. Similarly, there are several standards for the way in which control information is stored in a text file—for example, some systems mark line ends with two control characters < CR > < LF > (carriage return and line feed) but others simply use < LF > . The TYPE command also allows a client to state the control encoding that it expects to be used for all data transfers, leaving the server to convert to and from its own preferred encoding.

Binary files are subject to no translation by the server, but a fourth option allows a local format (for example, double-byte characters) to be used by the client. Although the bytes on the wire are single bytes, the TYPE command may be used to indicate how the bytes should be combined to produce the extended bytes used by the client.

There are three FTP data transmission modes which may be selected by the user using the MODE command. The stream mode is the default mode and results in bytes being sent as a continuous stream. When the file transmission is complete, the data connection is closed by the sender, which tells the receiver that the file operation is done. Although TCP is in use and so transmission is relatively secure, the stream mode has a weakness because, should the data connection fail for any reason, the receiver will believe that file transmission has completed successfully and will close the file containing only partial data.

The block and compressed modes of data transmission do not close the data channel when file transmission is complete, and use explicit indications to mark the end of files. This overcomes the weakness in the stream mode and has the added advantage that the data connection remains open for further file transfers.

In the block mode, the data is transmitted as one or more blocks of data each preceded by a header. The block mode header is shown in Figure 12.13. The byte count indicates the number of bytes that are present in the block that follows the header, and the descriptor flags provide information about the data

Table 12.11 The FTP Data Connection Management Commands

Command	Use
PORT	Data Port: Overrides the default IP address and port ID to be used on the data connection. The parameters are broken up into 8-bit fields and transmitted as a series of decimal numbers separated by commas. Thus, a PORT command would be transmitted as $PORT < SP > a1,a2,a3,a4,p1,p2$ where $< SP >$ is the space character, a1–a4 are the decimal representations of the bytes of the IP address, and p1–p2 are the decimal representations of the port ID.
PASV	Passive: This command puts the server into passive listen mode on a data connection. The server's reply includes the IP address and port ID on which it is listening.
TYPE	Sets the data representation type of the transferred data based on the data representation and storage capabilities of the client. It is assumed that the server will have greater data translation characteristics than the client. The parameters indicate the data type and are separated by a space. The first parameter is a single character denoting the encoding type as follows: A—ASCII (the default setting) E—EBCDIC I— Image (that is, binary) L—Local format. For ASCII, EBCDIC, and binary files, a second, optional parameter indicates the presence of control characters that may need translation between client and server formats as follows: N—No printer control characters are included (the default setting) T—Telnet control characters are used C—Carriage return control characters are used. Local format files also indicate the byte size as a count of bits expressed as a decimal number.
STRU	File structure: A single character indicates the file structure as follows. F—File: no record structure (the default setting) R—Record structure applies P—Page structure applies.
MODE	Transfer Mode: A single character indicates the transfer mode for data on the data connection as follows: S—Stream (the default value) B—Block C—Compressed.

block, as shown in Table 12.12. The flags are bit sensitive, so multiple flags may be set in one header.

Two flags require further description. Flag 0x20 indicates that there is possibly a problem in the data block, but allows it to be transmitted so that the remainder of the file will also be sent (rather than aborting the transmission). Flag 0x10 indicates that the data in this block is not file data but is a checkpoint.

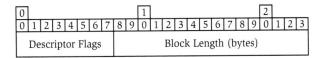

Figure 12.13 The FTP block mode data transmission block header.

Table 12.12 FTP Block Mode Data Transmission Descriptor Flags

Descriptor Flag	Meaning
0x80	End of data block is EOR
0x40	End of data block is EOF
0x20	Suspected errors in data block
0x10	Data block is a restart marker

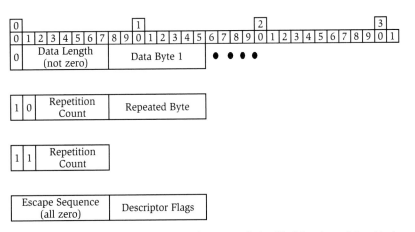

Figure 12.14 The FTP compressed mode data transmission block header and data blocks.

Checkpoints are used to restart interrupted transmissions (see the REST command in Table 12.13) and may, for example, be a block count or byte count.

The compressed mode of file transmission combines a simple form of data compression with the block mode already described. A single byte header is used in the compressed mode, as shown in Figure 12.14. There are four forms, indicated by the setting of the first 1 or 2 bites in the header. The first form allows for a block of up to 127 uncompressed bytes. The second form allows for the repetition (up to 63 times) of a single specified byte. The third form encodes the repetition (up to 63 times) of a filler character specific to the file type—a space is used for text files and zero is used for binary files. The last form presents an escape character followed by the descriptor flags defined for the block mode of data transmission and shown in Table 12.13.

Table 12.13 The FTP File Transfer Commands

Command	Parameters	Use
RETR	Path and file name	Retrieve the specified file from the server and store it in the current directory of the client.
STOR	Path and file name	Store a copy of the specified client file on the server in the current directory of the server, overwriting the file on the server if it already exists.
STOU	Path and file name	Store Unique: Behaves as the Store command except that a unique file name is generated on the server. The file name is reported on the FTP reply.
APPE	Path and file name	Append the contents on the specified client file to the named file in the current directory on the server, creating the file if it does not already exist.
ALLO	File size ["R," record size]	Allocate system storage space on the server in preparation for file transfer. This command is not typically required except in old file systems. The file size is given in bytes. An optional parameter is preceded by the letter R and gives the record size in bytes.
REST	Checkpoint	Restart: Move the read/write pointer on the server and client to a specific offset checkpoint within the transferred files in preparation to resuming the file transfer.
RNFR	Path and file name	Rename From: Specifies the source path and file name on the server for a rename operation. This command must be followed by a RNTO (Rename To) command that specifies the destination of the rename operation.
RNTO	Path and file name	Rename To: Specifies the destination path and file name on the server for a rename operation. This command must be preceded by a RNFR (Rename From) command that specifies the source of the rename operation.
ABOR		Abort the previous FTP command, if it has not completed, and any associated data transfer. Files that were created as a result of the previous command should be deleted. The data connection may be closed as a result of this command.
DELE	Path and file name	Delete the specified file from the server.
RMD	Path name	Remove Directory: Remove the specified directory from the server.
MKD	Path name	Make Directory: Create the specified directory on the server.
PWD		Print the working directory on the server.
LIST	Path name	List the files in the specified directory on the server or in the current directory on the server if the path name supplied is null. Note that the returned list of files is sent as a data stream over the data connection.

NLST	Path name	Name List: Operates as the LIST command except that the returned information contains only a list of the file names in the specified directory separated by carriage return and line feed characters. No other information (such as file sizes, permissions, creation dates) is provided, allowing the list to be more easily handled by automated processes such as the FTP user *mget* operation.
SITE	System-specific	Site Parameters: Set system-specific site parameters on the server. These parameters and their encoding are specific to server systems and outside the scope of FTP.
SYST		System: Retrieve a keyword indicating the operating system running on the server.
STAT		Status: If issued while a file transfer operation is in progress, this command causes the server to respond with the current status of the file transfer. If issued outside the scope of a file transfer, the server responds with general information about the state of the FTP process.
STAT	Path and file name	Status: If issued outside the scope of a file transfer the server returns the same information as for a LIST command for the specified file, but returns the information over the control channel. This operation may be useful to check the success of commands that cause file creation or deletion.
STAT	Path name	Status: If issued outside the scope of a file transfer, the server returns implementation-specific information such as a list of file names in the specified directory, or details about the path specified. The information is returned over the control channel. This operation may be useful to check the success of an MKD or RMD command.
HELP	Command name	Return help information about the specified command or general help information if no command is specified.
NOOP		No Operation: The server returns a reply but performs no other action. This allows the client to verify the connectivity of the control channel.

12.5.6 Moving Files in FTP

With the control channel in place and the parameters set for the data channel, the client can start to transfer files. Files are managed by a series of commands, shown in Table 12.13. These are largely self-explanatory and correspond to the commands that would be issued to perform the same operations on a local file system. Note, however, that only server path and file names are used. It is up to the FTP client to provide functions to map to local (that is, client) path and file names.

The only operation that requires two path and file names is the rename command. The rename operation is split into two distinct commands giving the old and new path and file names. This helps to restrict the length of the individual FTP commands because the path names may be fairly long.

Many of the commands listed in Table 12.13 complete with a reply on the control channel and need no further exchange, but some of them require data transfer (which is, after all, the whole point of FTP). When data transfer is needed, a data connection is set up as described in the previous section. When the data transfer is complete, the data connection is torn down to indicate the end of the file if the data transmission mode is stream. Otherwise, the data connection is left up for use by further file transfers or until it is closed by the client.

12.5.7 FTP Replies

As previously described, each FTP command generates at least one reply message. Replies are formed as Telnet messages, comprising a three-digit number presented in ASCII followed optionally by a space and parameter text. The whole message is terminated with a carriage return line feed, so the message looks like

$$< \text{reply code} > [< \text{space} > < \text{parameter text} >] < \text{CRLF} >$$

The first digit of the reply code is used to indicate the status of the command for which the reply was generated, as shown in Table 12.14, the second digit indicates the purpose of the reply message, as shown in Table 12.15, and the final digit qualifies the reply.

The defined reply codes are indicated in Table 12.16. Where specific interpretation may be placed on the parameter text by the FTP client, the figure shows the format that must be followed. Otherwise, the parameter text is free-form and intended for display to the user at the user interface.

Some replies may require more than one line and may include multiple reply codes. For example, help text or a system message may include multiple lines of text to be displayed to the user. Such replies are sent as a nested series of messages where the first message uses a hyphen "-" instead of a space to separate the reply code from the first line of text. Subsequent lines are carried in separate messages and do not begin with a reply code, but the last line in the last

Table 12.14 The FTP Reply Code First Digit Indicates the Status of the Command

Reply Code First Digit	Meaning
1	Command has not currently completed.
2	Command has completed (ready for next command).
3	Command is awaiting another command before processing can continue.
4	Command cannot currently be processed (but may be acceptable if issued again).
5	Command cannot be processed.

Table 12.15 The FTP Reply Code Second Digit Indicates the Type of Reply

Reply Code Second Digit	Meaning
1	The reply relates to the syntax of the command (success or failure).
2	The reply is informational.
3	The reply relates to the status or control of a connection.
4	This value is not used.
5	The reply conveys information about the file or directory.

Table 12.16 The FTP Reply Codes

Code	Meaning and Parameter Text
110	Restart marker reply. The parameter text must be present and must be of the form $MARK < SP > yyyy < SP > = < SP > mmmm$ where $< SP >$ is the space character, $yyyy$ is the client process data stream marker, and $mmmm$ is the server's equivalent marker.
120	Service not ready. The parameter text of the form nnn shows that the service will be ready in nnn minutes.
125	Data connection already open; transfer starting.
150	File status okay; about to open data connection.
200	Command okay.
202	Command not implemented, superfluous at this site.
211	System status, or system help reply.
212	Directory status.
213	File status.
214	Help message.
215	NAME system type. The parameter encodes a decimal number that indicates the system type from a list managed by IANA.
220	Service ready for new user.
221	Service closing control connection; the user will be logged out if currently logged in.
225	Data connection open; no transfer in progress.
226	Closing data connection; requested file action was successful.
227	Entering Passive Mode; the parameter text reads $a1,a2,a3,a4,p1,p2$ where a1–a4 are the digits representing the bytes of an IP address, and p1–p2 are the digits of a port ID.
230	User logged in; proceed.

Table 12.16 *Continued*

Code	Meaning and Parameter Text
250	Requested file action okay, completed.
257	Path name created; the parameter text returns the path name created.
331	User name okay; need password.
332	Need account for login.
350	Requested file action pending further information.
421	Service not available; closing control connection.
425	Can't open data connection.
426	Connection closed; transfer aborted.
450	Requested file action not taken; file unavailable.
451	Requested action aborted; local error in processing.
452	Requested action not taken; insufficient storage space in system.
500	Syntax error, command unrecognized or cannot be fully parsed.
501	Syntax error in parameters or arguments.
502	Command not implemented.
503	Bad sequence of commands.
504	Command not implemented for that parameter.
530	Not logged in.
532	Need account for storing files.
550	Requested action not taken; file unavailable or not found, or access permissions insufficient.
551	Requested action aborted; page type unknown.
552	Requested file action aborted; exceeded storage allocation.
553	Requested action not taken; file name not allowed.

message must begin with the same reply code and use the space to indicate that the sequence of replies is ending. If one of the lines itself begins with a number, padding with some other character must be inserted at the start of the line to avoid confusion—that is, to prevent the client from interpreting the line as a new reply. Thus, for example, the series of messages shown in Figure 12.15 might be used.

Replies, especially system information messages, may be *spontaneous*. That is, they may be generated by the server without reference to a specific client command to inform the user of important or interesting (or entirely banal) system

Message 1:	"211 – This is the first line of a multiline message. < CRLF > "
Message 2:	"This is the second line and does not use a reply code. < CRLF > "
Message 3:	" < SP > 112 is the telephone emergency code in Europe. < CRLF > "
Message 4:	"211 < SP > The final line begins with the same reply code. < CRLF > "

Figure 12.15 An FTP reply may span multiple lines with special use of the reply code.

events. Such replies may simply be sent to the client, but are more usually held by the server until another reply is sent in response to a command.

12.5.8 Could It Be Simpler? Trivial FTP

The previous sections make it clear that FTP is a fairly complex protocol. It has evolved to handle a range of different data formats, encoding, and application uses. As a result there are a lot of commands and options to be supported. RFC 959 makes it clear that an FTP server can choose to support a minimal subset of the commands (USER, QUIT, PORT, STRU, RETR, STOR, and NOOP) and options (ASCII nonprint data type, stream mode, and file or record structure). However, most implementations include the full function set to ensure that they are as useful as possible.

That FTP runs over TCP makes it quite heavyweight for simple or small transactions. Some uses need to transfer just a few bytes, or are run by trimmed-down software stacks that do not have access to TCP. For example, an application may simply need to send a short log file to a remote event server, or a diskless device (like a router of a switch) may need to use software burned on to a chip to load a more extensive program from a remote server. In these cases, FTP is not suitable and an alternative protocol, the Trivial File Transfer Protocol (TFTP), is used.

The client TFTP application offers its users a subset of the FTP commands. Typically, only the *connect, get, put, ascii,* and *binary* operational commands are supported, and here the similarity ends. TFTP uses UDP as its transport protocol, making file transfer far less reliable but significantly reducing the overhead both in the number of control and management bytes sent on the wire and in the code that needs to be implemented by the client. This makes TFTP popular for the applications described in the preceding paragraph.

TFTP version two is described in RFC 1350, dated 1992. It draws on some of the processes embedded in TCP because it has to address some of the same issues when transferring data over fundamentally unreliable lower layers. In particular, TFTP uses retransmission and acknowledgement schemes based on those used in TCP.

The messages and responses in TFTP are transmitted as the contents of UDP datagrams. Each message is indicated by a 2-byte message code (or Opcode), as indicated in Table 12.17. Parameters are encoded as ASCII strings and are

Table 12.17 The TFTP Message Types (Op Codes) and Parameters

Op Code	Meaning
1	Requests a file to be read from the server and stored on the client.
2	Requests a file to be opened for write on the server and copied from the client.
3	The message contains data being transferred.
4	The message acknowledges a data message.
5	Reports an error.

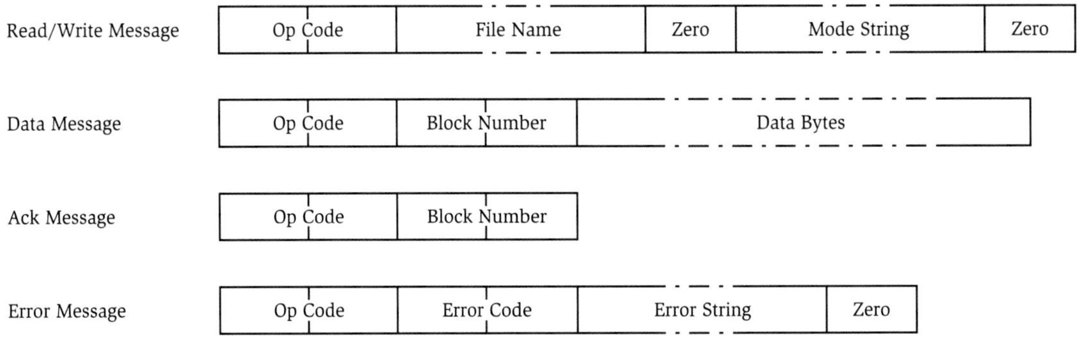

Read/Write Message	Op Code	File Name	Zero	Mode String	Zero

Data Message	Op Code	Block Number	Data Bytes

Ack Message	Op Code	Block Number

Error Message	Op Code	Error Code	Error String	Zero

Figure 12.16 The TFTP message showing the bytes that make up the messages.

null terminated, with the exception of transferred data which is presented in its native form and is not specially terminated.

The format of the TFTP messages is shown in Figure 12.16. Read and write requests carry two parameter strings. The first indicates the path and file name to be used as the source or destination on the server, and the second parameter gives the file transfer mode. The file transfer mode must be one of the three following case-insensitive ASCII strings: "netascii," "octet," or "mail." Netascii is used to indicate that the contents of the file must be transmitted in ASCII and that the server is responsible for translating to and from its own text representation. Octet indicates that the file should be read or written on the server as transmitted. The mail mode is used by simple mail applications that can leverage the data transfer procedures of TFTP to pass mail messages between users. In this case, the file name is replaced by a mail recipient (for example, a user name) and the format of the data is treated as if the mode were netascii.

Data messages carry up to 512 bytes of data. All data messages apart from the last one in a file transfer must be full (that is, must contain 512 bytes). The receipt of a data message carrying fewer than 512 bytes is taken as indicating the end of the file (so that if a file is an exact multiple of 512 bytes, an additional, empty data message must be sent to terminate the file transfer). Each data message contains a block number, and when the message has been received an acknowledgment message is sent allowing the sender to send the next block. Block numbers run from 1 to 65,535 and increase by 1 each time, allowing the sender and receiver to detect and discard packets that are being duplicated in the network and delivered out of order. If the sender does not receive an acknowledgement in a reasonable time period it can retransmit the data message—block numbers help protect the receiver from processing duplicate blocks if the acknowledgement message was lost.

An acknowledgement message with block number zero is used to confirm the receipt of a write request to let the client know that it can start sending data.

Errors can be reported using the error message, which contains an error code to indicate the nature of the problem and an error string to display to the client or to place in a system log. The error codes are shown in Table 12.18, but the error messages are implementation specific and may be zero length. Note that there is very little error handling in TFTP and all errors except that of an unknown source port are deemed fatal and cause the abortion of the file transfer.

TFTP servers listen on port 69 to receive read or write requests. These messages carry the source port ID that the client will use to handle subsequent messages. When the server sends its first response, it must send to the client's port ID, but may use a different port itself so that it may continue to listen on port 69 for more requests from the same or other clients. The client must send all subsequent messages for the file transfer to the server's port. This exchange is illustrated in Figure 12.17.

The FTP data block size of 512 bytes is now seen as something of a limitation, especially for transferring large files on reliable links. Extensions have been defined in RFCs 2347, 2348, and 2349 to allow the client to pass additional configuration parameters in a read or write message. The parameters are identified

Table 12.18 TFTP Error Codes

Error Code	Meaning
0	Not defined. Error message may provide more details.
1	File not found.
2	Access violation. Insufficient privileges to access file.
3	Disk full or allocation exceeded.
4	Illegal TFTP operation.
5	Unknown transfer ID.
6	File already exists.
7	No such user.

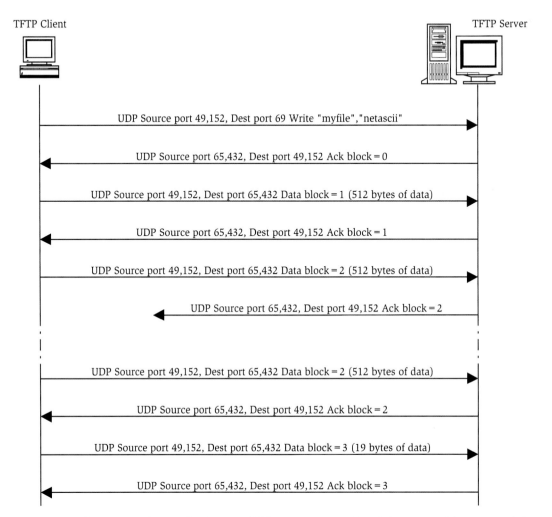

Figure 12.17 TFTP message exchanges showing use of UDP ports, message acknowledgments, and data retransmission.

by keywords (such as "blocksize") and are followed by numeric values. These extensions also allow the client to specify the timeout period after which an unacknowledged data message will be resent, and the total size of the file being transferred.

12.5.9 Choosing a File Transfer Protocol

Other file transfer protocols were also designed and published. The Simple File Transfer Protocol (SFTP) aimed to fill the gap between TFTP's simplicity and FTP's complexity, the Background File Transfer Protocol (BFTP) addresses the issue of making file transfer lower priority than other traffic on busy networks, and the Sender-Initiated/Unsolicited File Transfer Protocol (SIFT/UFT) allows a client to distribute files in advance of a request from a user. However, despite these and other proposals, FTP and TFTP have grown to be the standard protocols for file transfer in the Internet.

Many of the pros and cons of FTP and TFTP have been described in the preceding sections. The issues for consideration are security, robustness, reliability (all strengths of FTP), simplicity of implementation, and minimization of transmitted overhead (benefits of TFTP). It should be noted that the very simplicity of TFTP has often proved to be a double-edged sword. Because only a small amount of code is needed for a TFTP implementation, it is often rewritten from scratch, leading to deployed TFTP implementations that are poorly tested and infamous for their bugs.

TFTP does not include the facility for the server to solicit a user name or password from the client. Although this is a benefit both in reducing the size of the TFTP implementation and in addressing the problem of how a diskless device would know its user ID and password at boot time, it does make a TFTP server a significant security risk. For this reason, TFTP servers are run only where absolutely necessary and are given very limited access to the server file system. Further, TFTP does not include directory browsing facilities, which limits its usefulness to a human user.

Another approach to the issue of sharing data across the Internet is to allow remote access to files rather than to push and pull copies of the files. The Network File System (NFS) was originally published in the IETF as RFC 1094. This document described a protocol for remote file access developed by Sun Microsystems designed to be portable across different machines, operating systems, network architectures, and transport protocols. NFS became very popular on UNIX-based file servers and, since it was independent of transport protocols, it could be used easily in the Internet where, because it had sufficient built-in features, it was run over UDP. Version four of NFS was published as RFC 3010—this version includes security improvements and support for features such as file locking and device mounting.

12.6 Hypertext Transfer Protocol (HTTP)

The Hypertext Transfer Protocol (HTTP) is one of the most extensively used Internet application protocols. It is used to communicate between web browsers and web servers, to read information from web pages, or to send responses such as completed forms or checked boxes. Most users of the Internet are familiar with the applications that use HTTP, but since these applications are well hidden behind the graphical interfaces of web browsers, it is rare for anyone to be familiar with (or even aware of) the protocol working away in the background.

The World Wide Web is facilitated by a set of standards that define how objects are formatted so that they can be universally interpreted, how their locations may be expressed so that they can be easily found, and how they are moved around within the Internet. The sections that follow introduce the Hypertext Markup Language (HTML) and Universal Resource Locators (URLs), which address the first two of these standards, before moving on to a more detailed discussion of the Hypertext Transfer Protocol (HTTP) that is used to exchange information within the web.

12.6.1 What Is Hypertext?

A markup language is a method of presenting documents in a common character set (ASCII) with formatting instructions embedded in the text using *tags* that can be easily distinguished from the text and tell the application displaying or printing the document how to behave. Coders familiar with strings in the C language will recognize that the escape character "/" and the parameter format character "%" are forms of tags.

All word processors use some form of tagging to represent formatting within the documents they produce. The tagging, indicating such things as indentation, font, and text color, usually makes use of proprietary encodings so that the document, when saved to disk, is in some binary form that is hard or impossible for other applications to interpret.

Hypertext is immensely popular within documents that have multiple cross-references or key definitions and are read by a user electronically. The user may point and click at key words or locations on diagrams using a mouse or similar device, and the application will load a new document or jump to another part of the text. Conventionally, keywords or phrases that form such *hypertext links* are indicated in the text using special coloration and are, perhaps, underlined. In the source document, hypertext links are supported through special tags that define the word or phrase to be linked from, and that provide the location (file name or tag) to which to link.

The Hypertext Markup Language (HTML) is a standard set of tags with common and well-understood meanings that is used extensively within the Internet. The advantage of a standard set of tags is that any application can read the file and take the same meaning from the formatting instructions. HTML goes one step further and restricts the character set available for tags to only those characters that are printable so that HTML documents may even be read by entirely dumb text editors.

The precise layout of an HTML document when it is displayed or printed is the responsibility of the application that is reading the document. It may choose to limit the support for certain tags, and map others to the same output style. The standard meanings of the tags make it easy for the application to produce consistent and legible output.

Designers of web sites were once very familiar with the details of HTML, but over time applications have been written that allow HTML documents to be written using standard graphical or word processor interfaces. This speeds the production of web pages yet still produces an HTML document that can be read by any application.

HTML version 2 is defined in RFC 1866 as the result of a collaborative effort between the IETF and the World Wide Web Consortium (W3C). Since HTML is not a protocol it is not covered further in this book.

12.6.2 Universal Resource Locators (URLs)

Hypertext links offer a facility for point-and-click references between documents or parts of the same document. When the user clicks on the link, the browser is redirected to another piece of text in the same document or in another file. Simple hypertext links may point to a tag or label within a single document. If the link jumps to another file, the link target must be expressed as a path name, file name, and tag. If the link takes the reader to a file that is stored on another computer, the target representation must also include an identifier of the host on which the file is stored.

Since the whole purpose is to provide standardized access to files across the Internet and to allow one file to contain links to another that may be stored at another location, it is important to use a common notation for the target of links. As with HTML, this allows application-independent navigation of hypertext links.

Universal Resource Locators (URLs) are defined in RFC 1738 and build on the definition of host names set out in Section 12.3.1 of this book. Each URL indicates the service used to access the resource (for example, HTTP, email, or FTP), the host location (expressed as an IP address or a host name), the port through which to access the server at the target host (that is, a TCP or UDP port number), and the path and file name of the resource. Figure 12.18 shows the abstract definitions of URLs according to the service type *scheme*. Note that several of the components are optional and may take defaults—for example, on a web browser the scheme itself is optional and defaults to HTTP, and the port number is usually omitted and defaults to the standard port number for the protocol used to access the server for a given scheme. URLs are a subset of the Universal Resource Identifiers (URIs) that can be used to identify any object,

```
file://[ < host_name_or_address > ]/ < path_and_file_name >
http:// < host_name_or_address >  [: < port > ]/ < path_and_file_name >  [ < additional_tags > ]
mailto: < user_name >  @  < host_name_or_address >
gopher:// < host_name_or_address >  [: < port > ]/ < path_and_file_name >
telnet:// < user >  [: < password > ] @  < host_name_or_address >  [: < port > ]
```

Figure 12.18 Common Universal Resource Locator abstract representations.

file, or person in a unique and globally recognizable way. A URL is special because it includes the method of access to the identified resource.

When users enter a URL at the command prompt of their application, or click on a hypertext link that references a URL, the application uses the service type to determine what application protocol and method to use to access the link and then uses the host name or IP address to direct the application protocol to the right place. If a host name has been supplied, the application must use the DNS (see Section 12.3) to resolve the name to an IP address.

HTTP URLs may also include additional tags such as "?" to indicate labels or values that form part of the URL as the result of a user filling out a form. The "?" symbol is often seen in the URL of a search result such as *http://www.mysearch.com/search?q=jam&ie=UTF-8&oe=UTF-8&hl=en&meta=.* The "#" is used to indicate a place marker tag within the specified file.

12.6.3 What Does HTTP Do?

Having accepted the value of distributed document storage and of hypertext links that span files stored at different locations, there is a need for a standard-ized access protocol that allows applications to retrieve and send documents and files across the Internet. An early application protocol designed to access remotely stored documents was called Gopher (a vague and aged pun on the pronunciation of "go for"), and it is described in RFC 1436. Gopher was developed as an application to allow users to search and retrieve documents held at remote sites. It originally had a menu-based user interface that let the user select hosts, paths, or files to search or retrieve. The files would then be stored on the local host and the user could access them using the appropriate applications. As well as providing a client–server application protocol for finding and searching files, Gopher served as a front-end to other application protocols such as FTP for file retrieval.

As graphical user interfaces grew in popularity Gopher was clearly inadequate. It's "clunky" menu interface was no match for a snazzy graphic, but more important was the fact that it did not integrate document browsing with docu-ment retrieval. So, using the opportunities offered by HTML, web browsers were developed to offer users high-function applications that could access and browse remotely stored files. But as the function of web browsers grew, it became necessary to invent a new protocol by which they could communicate with the servers that stored the files. This protocol is the Hypertext Transfer Protocol (HTTP).

HTTP is described by RFC 2616 as "a generic, stateless, protocol which can be used for many tasks beyond its use for hypertext." This is a pretty wide definition, but fairly summarizes HTTP's capabilities. The previous version of the protocol (RFC 2068) included the description "object-oriented" because the specification of the protocol dwelt (perhaps excessively) on the implementation concepts that defined objects to be processed and methods to manipulate them.

The protocol itself uses requests and responses. A client wishing to perform some operation on a remote server sends requests using TCP to the default port 80 on the server and waits for a reply. Each request or reply message uses an HTTP message header that may be followed by a message body encoded using common content encoding techniques called Multipurpose Internet Message Extensions (MIME), which are described further in Section 12.6.4. HTTP applications may optionally use a KeepAlive exchange to keep the TCP connection open when the applications are otherwise silent for a long period.

HTTP clients are often referred to as *user agents*, and the servers on which the data that they access is stored are called *origin servers*. The data itself is known as an *entity*, and a client may retrieve it from or store it on an origin server. The client need not be directly attached to the origin server, but may use the services of a *proxy server*. A proxy is an intermediary program that acts as both a server (with respect to the client) and a client (with respect to the origin server) and makes requests on behalf of the client. A proxy may forward the request unmodified or may add value for the benefit of the client. Proxies are commonly used to provide access into and out of private networks both for security and to allow DNS resolutions to be carried out only on the server.

Gateway servers also intercede between clients and an origin server, but they act as though they were actually the origin server by returning the requested data so that the client may not be aware that it is talking to the gateway rather than the origin server. The gateway adds value by retrieving the data from the origin server, perhaps using some other protocol rather than HTTP and by performing content translation so that the data is in the form requested by the client.

Proxies and gateways are allowed to *cache* entities that they have previously retrieved in response to earlier client requests. If this is the case, a request from a client may be serviced more quickly without the need to exchange requests and responses with the origin server. Cache entries have a limited lifetime specified by the origin server when it first sends out the data, and a client may also ask that a request is serviced using real data from the origin and not using cached entries.

An HTTP request–response exchange is said to consist of a chain of requests and a chain of responses. The term *chain* refers to the fact that the request may be passed from user agent to proxy server, between proxy servers, and to a gateway before it finally reaches the object server. The response is passed back through a chain. The chain may be cut short at any point if a proxy server or gateway has a cache of the requested resource.

The operations a client may request from a server are known as *request methods*. The term *method* is a carryover from the object-oriented origins of the protocol and simply refers to the set of functions that must be executed by the server to support the request. The HTTP request methods are listed in Table 12.19.

Table 12.19 The HTTP Request Methods

Request Method	Use
OPTIONS	This method is a request to the server for information about the communication options along the path from the client to the server. This allows a client to find out its options with regard to a resource and a server, without initiating an operation on the resource.
GET	The GET method is the principle use of HTTP during web browsing. It is used to retrieve the entity identified by a URL carried in the request. A GET request may be qualified by additional parameters that retrieve data only if the object has (or has not) been modified since a specified date or time, or if tags stored with the object match (or don't match) those supplied on the request. A GET may also be restricted to a partial GET that requests that only part of the entity be transferred. The entities returned on responses to GET requests may be cached by gateways and proxies subject to permissions and lifetimes given on the response.
HEAD	The HEAD method is identical to GET except that the server does not return any entity data on the response. This can be used to find out data sizes and encodings to establish whether there is any point in beginning a real transfer. It may also be used to determine whether a cached version of an entity is still up-to-date.
POST	The POST method supports functions such as the posting by a client of a message to a bulletin board. This also covers the return of a completed form to a server process. In all cases the data uploaded to the server is subordinate to a resource that has previously been retrieved from the server using a GET.
PUT	A client uses the PUT method to independently store data on a server. This is distinct from the POST operation because there is no dependency on a previous GET. The entities stored on a server in this way may be cached by proxies and gateways as the request passes through so that the entity is available in answer to GET requests from other clients. Note that if the request is failed by the server, the cached copies should be removed.
DELETE	The DELETE method is used by a client to remove a resource from a server. As a success response is processed by gateways and proxies, they should also remove their copies of the deleted entity from their caches.
TRACE	The TRACE method is used to invoke a remote, application-layer loop-back of the request message. The final recipient of the request SHOULD reflect the message received back to the client as the entity-body of an OK response.
CONNECT	This CONNECT method is reserved for use by a proxy that can tunnel requests for or over other protocols.

> **gopher**\'gō-fər\ *n* [origin unknown] **1**: a burrowing edible land tortoise (*Gōpherus polyphemus*) of the southern U.S. **2 a**: any of several burrowing rodents (family *Geomyidae*) of western North America and the southern U.S. that are the size of a large rat and have large cheek pouches opening beside the mouth **b**: any of numerous small ground squirrels (genus *Citellus*) of the prairie region of North America closely related to the chipmunks.

12.6.4 Multipurpose Internet Message Extensions (MIME)

Many application-level protocols, such as those used for email and web access, are character-based. That is, although they exchange bytes, those bytes are assumed to be restricted to a limited set of characters that are printable or control printing. Such characters use only the low-order 7 bits in each 8-bit byte. This is fine when the applications are exchanging simple, printable text. It is even OK when the data includes formatting instructions that are encoded using a text-based tagging system such as HTML. But it does not allow the protocols to exchange binary files such as images, audio clips, or executables. These files use all 8 bits of each byte, and any attempt to treat them as printable text would result in corruption as the top bit of each byte was discarded. These constraints even apply to text files that use extended character sets as required for accented letters in foreign languages.

The solution is to use an encoding technique called the Multipurpose Internet Message Extensions (MIME). MIME allows a body of data to be described using standard headers and then presented through a mapping into the printable character set. Three basic encodings are supported by MIME—the first two do not modify the bytes that are transparent, but indicate that the data is either *7-bit-plain-text* (that is, contains only printable characters) or is *quoted-printable* (being built mainly from printable characters with the inclusion of an occasional print control character expressed as an escape character "=" followed by a byte of 8-bit binary data).

The third encoding is called *base64* and it is used to convey binary files. Each 3 bytes of 8-bit binary data are mapped into 4 bytes of 7-bit printable characters. This process is not as simple as it might at first seem, and requires five RFCs (2045–2049) to describe it fully. Nevertheless, the basic principle can be seen in Figure 12.19. The source binary bytes are grouped into 3-byte sequences and are mapped bit-for-bit into the low-order 6 bits of a group of 4 index bytes. These indexes are used to generate a sequence of four characters from within the acceptable payload character set. (Note that this

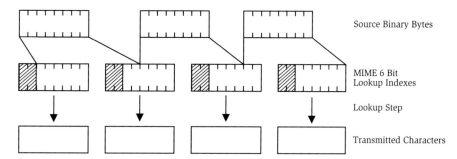

Figure 12.19 The base64 method of encoding binary data as printable characters for transmission by text-based application protocols.

index-based translation is necessary because the values such as zero and 1 are not acceptable characters.) The process may be reversed using the same look-up table.

The remainder of the MIME drafts concentrate on the additional text-based fields that are necessary in application protocol messages to describe the media types and encodings used in the message bodies.

12.6.5 HTTP Message Formats

HTTP is an application protocol and its messages are text-based. That is, the control part of each message is made up of a series of fields, each of which is a text string tag. The payload (for example, the file being transferred) is encoded using MIME as described in the previous section.

Each HTTP message uses the standard encoding of an application text message as defined in RFC 822. That is, the message is built up from a common request or status header, an arbitrary number of message headers, and a message body, as shown in Figure 12.20. Note that the slightly idiosyncratic usage of the CRLF character occurs because there is a CRLF embedded in the definitions of Request-Line and Status-Line, as shown in Figure 12.21. The Request-Line and Status-Line segregate requests from responses.

generic-message::=	(Request-Line | Status-Line)
	*(message-header CRLF)
	CRLF
	[message-body]

Figure 12.20 The standard Internet text message format as used by HTTP

Request-Line::=	Request-Method SP Request-URI SPHTTP-Version CRLF
Status-Line::=	HTTP-Version SP Status-Code SP Reason-Phrase CRLF
HTTP-Version:=	"HTTP" "/" 1*DIGIT "." 1*DIGIT

Figure 12.21 HTTP requests and responses use the Request Line and Status Line respectively as the first part of their messages.

The Request-Method is the operation that the client wishes to perform on the server and is encoded as a single-word tag, as shown in Table 12.19. The Request-URI specifies a Universal Resource Locator on which the request operation is performed.

The Status Code is a three-digit response code that indicates the result of the request. The first digit indicates a class of result, as shown in Table 12.20. The second and third digits give the detailed response codes listed in Table 12.21. HTTP status codes have become so familiar that they are beginning to creep into the English language. For example, the 404 status code is used to indicate that the requested resource (file, web page, etc.) was not available—it is now finding use to refer to someone who is away from his desk, or slow to absorb new information.

The Reason-Phrase carries user-visible text explaining the error or status. The text may span multiple lines by including line feed characters, but must not include carriage returns since that would be confused with the end of the Status-Line.

Using these constructs, simple request and status lines such as those shown in Figure 12.22 can be constructed. These lines, combined with the message body encoding described in the previous section, give the basic building blocks for HTTP messages. However, as shown in Figure 12.20, HTTP messages also contain message headers, and these are specific to the message request being sent or responded to.

The full definition of a request message is shown in Figure 12.23. It is constructed from a request-line as shown in Figure 12.21, followed by one or more message headers chosen from general-headers, request-headers, and entity-headers. General-headers are message headers that may be present on requests and responses to describe the service requested or provided. Request headers may only be present on request messages and allow the client to pass additional information about the request, and about the client itself, to the server. Entity-

Table 12.20 HTTP Responses Carry a Three-Digit Status Code, the First Digit of Which Indicates the Class of Result

Status Code First Digit	Meaning
1	Informational. Request received, continuing to process
2	Success. The request was successfully received, understood, and accepted
3	Redirection. Further action must be taken by the client to complete the request
4	Client Error. The request contains bad syntax and cannot be fulfilled by the server
5	Server Error. The server failed to fulfill an apparently valid request

Table 12.21 HTTP Response Status Codes

Status Code	Meaning	Status Code	Meaning
100	Continue	404	Not Found
101	Switching Protocols	405	Method Not Allowed
200	OK	406	Not Acceptable
201	Created	407	Proxy Authentication Required
202	Accepted	408	Request Timeout
203	Nonauthoritative Information	409	Conflict
204	No Content	410	Gone
205	Reset Content	411	Length Required
206	Partial Content	412	Precondition Failed
300	Multiple Choices	413	Request Entity Too Large
301	Moved Permanently	414	Request-URI Too Large
302	Found	415	Unsupported Media Type
303	See Other	416	Requested Range Not Satisfiable
304	Not Modified	417	Expectation Failed
305	Use Proxy	500	Internal Server Error
307	Temporary Redirect	501	Not Implemented
400	Bad Request	502	Bad Gateway
401	Unauthorized	503	Service Unavailable
402	Payment Required	504	Gateway Timeout
403	Forbidden	505	HTTP Version Not Supported

```
GET www.elsevier.com/index.html HTTP/1.1
HTTP/1.1 408 Server timed out attempting to service request
```

Figure 12.22 Example HTTP Request and Status lines.

headers are used to describe the content of the message-body and may be present on requests and responses whenever a message-body is present.

Similarly, the response message may contain a sequence of message-headers chosen from general-headers, response-headers, and entity-headers, as shown

```
Request::=    Request-Line
              *( (general-header |
                  request-header |
                  entity-header )
              CRLF)
              CRLF
              [message-body]
```

Figure 12.23 The full definition of an HTTP Request message.

```
Response::=   Status-Line
              *( ( general-header |
                  response-header |
                  entity-header )
              CRLF )
              CRLF
              [message-body]
```

Figure 12.24 The full definition of an HTTP Response message.

in Figure 12.24. The response-headers may only be present on responses and allow the server to pass additional information about the response, and about the server itself, to the client.

Each message header begins with a common format. This is a single word tag followed by a colon separator. The list of message-headers is extensive. Each has a formal definition and usage rules, making RFC 2616 a document of 176 pages. There is, therefore, insufficient space to describe them in detail in this book; however, Tables 12.22 through 12.25 list them and give a short description of each.

12.6.6 Example Messages and Transactions

By way of a brief example of HTTP in use, consider the HTTP client in Figure 12.25. A user at the client wants to access the web page http://www.elsevier.com/index.html, that is, to read the file index.html from the root directory of the server www.elsevier.com. The client connects to a proxy server (proxy.yournetwork.net) which is responsible for servicing requests either by retrieving cached entities or by forwarding the requests to the origin server.

Table 12.22 The HTTP General-Header Tags and Uses

Tag	Use
Cache-Control	Specifies directives to be obeyed by all caching mechanisms along the request–response chain.
Connection	Allows the sender to specify options that are desired for that particular connection.
Date	The date and time at which the message was originated.
Pragma	Used to include implementation-specific directives that might apply to a recipient along the request–response chain.
Trailer	Indicates that the given set of header fields is present in the trailer of a message encoded with chunked transfer-coding.
Transfer-Encoding	Indicates what (if any) type of transformation has been applied to the message body to safely transfer it between the sender and the recipient.
Upgrade	Allows the client to specify which additional communication protocols it supports and would be prepared to use if the server finds it appropriate to switch protocols; used by a server in a response if it is a switching protocol.
Via	Used by gateways and proxies to indicate the intermediate protocols and recipients between the user agent and the server on requests, and between the origin server and the client on responses.
Warning	Used to carry additional information about the status or transformation of a message which might not be reflected in the message.

The request sent by the client is shown in Figure 12.26 with spaces and carriage returns exactly as it would be sent. The request is a GET of the file index.html from the root directory. The HTTP version is 1.1. The target host is www.elsevier.com—no port ID is specified, allowing the use of the default port. The message was sent on April 1st just before noon GMT.

The client has specified that it is willing to receive a cached copy of the file provided that cache is no older than 300 seconds (5 minutes). It has also specified that it is prepared to accept the file only if the message body is encoded as HTML text and is not compressed or otherwise formatted by the sending server ("identity").

By way of reference to the servers, the client has inserted the email address of the user that is currently logged on at the client, and the product name, version number, and build release information of the client application.

When the request reaches the proxy server, it discovers that it has a copy of the required file in its cache and that the copy has been there for only 4 minutes so is acceptable to the client. It doesn't need to forward the request to the origin server, but can build and send the response shown in Figure 12.27 prepended to the data from the file.

Table 12.23 The HTTP Request-Header Tags and Uses

Tag	Use
Accept	Specify media types that are acceptable for the response.
Accept-Charset	Indicate which character sets are acceptable for the response.
Accept-Encoding	Similar to Accept, but restricts the content-encodings.
Accept-Language	Similar to Accept, but restricts the set of natural languages.
Authorization	Consists of credentials containing the authentication information of the user agent for access to the resource being requested.
Expect	Used to require specific behavior by the server.
From	An email address for the human user who controls the requesting user agent.
Host	The Internet host and port number of the resource being requested.
If-Match	Used to make a method conditional on matches with the supplied entity tags.
If-Modified-Since	Used to make a method conditional on the entity having been modified since the date and time specified.
If-None-Match	Makes a method conditional on no matches with the supplied entity tags.
If-Range	Allows the client to request a specific part of an entity.
If-Unmodified-Since	Makes a method conditional on the entity not having been modified since the date and time specified.
Max-Forwards	Limits the number of proxies or gateways that can forward the request to the next inbound server.
Proxy-Authorization	Allows the client to identify itself (or its user) to a proxy that requires authentication.
Range	Indicates that the message body contains a part of the entity.
Referer [sic]	Allows the client to specify, for the server's benefit, the address (URI) of the resource from which the Request-URI was obtained. Note that the tag is misspelled.
TE	Indicates what extension transfer-encodings the client is willing to accept in the response and whether or not it is willing to accept trailer fields in a chunked transfer-encoding.
User-Agent	Contains information about the user agent originating the request.

The response begins with the HTTP version number and the status code 200 ("OK"). The server includes a warning message for the benefit of the client application or the user to let the user know that the file comes from a cache—it uses the general warning code 199 that indicates a message to be logged or displayed. After a date stamp, the server also includes the age of the cached

Table 12.24 The HTTP Response-Header Tags and Uses

Tag	Use
Accept-Ranges	Allows the server to indicate its acceptance of range requests for a resource.
Age	Conveys the sender's estimate of the amount of time since the response (or its revalidation) was generated at the origin server; useful when the response is generated from a cache.
ETag	The current value of the entity tag for the requested entity; the entity tag may be used for comparison with other entities from the same resource.
Location	Redirects the recipient to a location other than the Request-URI for completion of the request or identification of a new resource.
Proxy-Authenticate	A challenge that indicates the authentication scheme and parameters applicable to the proxy for this Request-URI.
Retry-After	Indicates how long the failed service is expected to be unavailable.
Server	Information about the software used by the origin server to handle the request.
Vary	Indicates whether a cache is permitted to use the response, while it is fresh, to reply to a subsequent request without revalidation.
WWW-Authenticate	A challenge that indicates the authentication scheme(s) and parameters applicable to the Request-URI.

file that it is returning—since 240 is less than 300, the client will be happy with this file.

The server now describes the content of the message body. The content is HTML text, which meets the client's requirements. The content encoding is not shown because the default encoding (no compression or modification) is used. The length of the message body is a little over 4 kilobytes.

Two further fields describe the file as it is stored on the origin server. It was last modified on March 26th and any cached copies of the file on proxy servers or on the client, should expire at the start of May.

12.6.7 Securing HTTP Transactions

It is increasingly important for HTTP transactions to be secured so that they cannot be intercepted or forged. Without this facility online commercial transactions would be vulnerable to fraud and the use of credit cards over the Internet would be very unwise. Chapter 14 is dedicated to security considerations within the Internet, and includes a specific section describing two approaches to making HTTP secure.

Table 12.25 The HTTP Entity-Header Tags and Uses

Tag	Use
Allow	The set of methods supported by the resource identified by the Request-URI.
Content-Encoding	Used as a modifier to the media-type. Its value indicates what additional content encodings have been applied to the message-body, and, thus, what decoding mechanisms must be applied.
Content-Language	Describes the natural language(s) of the intended audience for the entity. Note that this might not be the full set of languages used within the message-body.
Content-Length	Indicates the size of the entity (that is, the message-body) in a decimal number of bytes. In the case of the HEAD method, this is the size of the entity that would have been sent had the request been a GET.
Content-Location	May be used to supply the location for the entity enclosed in the message when that entity is also and primarily accessible from another location.
Content-MD5	An MD5 digest of the entity-body for the purpose of providing an end-to-end message integrity check. Not advised as a security mechanism.
Content-Range	Sent with a partial entity to specify where it lies within the full entity.
Content-Type	Indicates the media type of the message-body. In the case of the HEAD method, this is the media type that would have been sent had the request been a GET.
Expires	Gives the date and time after which the entity data carried in a response should be considered stale.
Last-Modified	Indicates the date and time at which the origin server believes the entity was last modified.

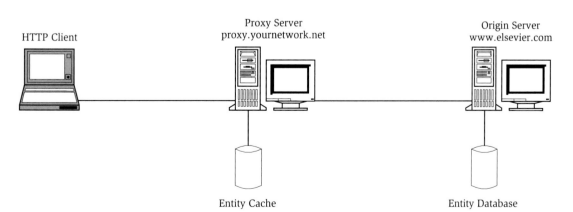

Figure 12.25 An HTTP client with proxy server and origin server.

```
GET/index.html HTTP/1.1
Host: www.elsevier.com
Date: Tue, 01 April 2004 11:59:01 GMT
Cache-Control: max-age 300
Accept: text/html
Accept-Encoding: identity
From: ethelred.2@palace.gov.uk
User-Agent: FriendlyAppl/v.7.2 build/147b
```

Figure 12.26 An example HTTP Request message.

```
HTTP/1.1 200
Warning: 199 proxy.yournetwork.net:80 This file comes from a proxy cache
Date: Tue, 01 April 2004 11:59:37 GMT
Age: 240
Content-Type: text/html
Content-Length: 17152
Last-Modified: Wed, 26 Mar 2004 16.31.12 GMT
Expires: Thu, 01 May 2004 12:00:00 GMT
```

Figure 12.27 An example HTTP Response message.

12.7 Choosing an Application Protocol

There are too many Internet application protocols even to consider presenting them in a simple list. Some of the more common protocols that have not been covered in this chapter are shown in Tables 12.26 through 12.29, which also list the IETF RFCs that define them. Some other application protocols make advanced Internet services available and are discussed in Chapter 14.

Table 12.26 Common Internet Application Protocols for Device Management

BOOTP	RFC 951	Bootstrap Protocol. An IP/UDP bootstrap protocol that allows a diskless client machine to discover its own IP address, the address of a server host, and the name of a file to be loaded into memory and executed.
DHCP	RFC 2131	Dynamic Host Configuration Protocol. A framework for passing configuration information to hosts on a TCP/IP network. A development of BOOTP.
NTP	RFC 958	Network Time Protocol. A protocol for synchronizing a set of network clocks using a set of distributed clients and servers.

Table 12.27 Common Internet Application Protocols for Remote Access

RLOGIN	RFC 1282	A feature a little like Tenet that allows login to a computer from a remote site.
RPC	RFC 1831	Remote Procedure Call. Like RLOGIN, RPC is a means to access services on a remote computer. RPC makes these services available as functional units for use by an application running without user intervention.
NFS	RFC 3010	Network File System. Provides remote access to files over the Internet.
Gopher	RFC 1436	A character-based protocol for publishing and accessing text files. A precursor to HTTP.

Table 12.28 Common Internet Application Protocols for Mail and News

SMTP	RFC 821	Simple Mail Transfer Protocol. Allows messaging agents to exchange email messages.
POP3	RFC 1939	The Post Office Protocol version 3. A protocol for client mail applications to use to retrieve mail stored for them by a mail server.
IMAP	RFC 2060	Internet Mail Access Protocol. Allows users to store their messages on a remote server. Unlike POP3, the messages may continue to be stored on the remote server, from where they may be read and manipulated.
NNTP	RFC 977	Network News Transfer Protocol. A protocol for the distribution, inquiry, retrieval, and posting of news articles using a reliable stream-based transmission of news.

Table 12.29 Common Internet Application Protocol for Directory Services

LDAP	RFC 2252	Lightweight Directory Access Protocol v3. A directory access protocol that provides both read and update access.

12.8 Further Reading

There are as many books on Internet application protocols as there are protocols themselves.

TCP/IP Clearly Explained, by Peter Loshin (1999). Academic Press. This provides sound overviews of many application protocols, including those covered here.

Internet Application Protocols: The Definitive Guide, by Eric Hall (2004). O'Reilly. A brand new text that promises to give a good explanation of many of the application protocols in the Internet.

HTTP: The Definitive Guide, by Brian Totty, David Gourley, Marjorie Sayer, Anshu Aggarwal, and Sailu Reddy (2002). O'Reilly. This is a thorough and readable introduction to HTTP.

The key RFCs for the Domain Name System are as follows:

RFC 1034—Domain Names—Concepts and Facilities
RFC 1035—Domain Names—Implementation and Specification

There are over 100 RFCs referring to Telnet. Most define additional options for use in specific environments. Some key RFCs are:

RFC 854—Telnet Protocol Specification
RFC 855—Telnet Option Specifications
RFC 1097—Telnet Subliminal-Message Option
RFC 2941—Telnet Authentication Option

File transfer protocols are covered in a host of RFCs. Some of the key ones are:

RFC 906—Bootstrap Loading Using TFTP
RFC 913—Simple File Transfer Protocol
RFC 959—File Transfer Protocol
RFC 1068—Background File Transfer Program (BFTP)
RFC 1350—TFTP Revision 2
RFC 1440—SIFT/UFT: Sender-Initiated/Unsolicited File Transfer
RFC 2347—TFTP Option Extension
RFC 2348—TFTP Blocksize Option
RFC 2349—TFTP Timeout Interval and Transfer Size Options
RFC 2428—FTP Extensions for IPv6
RFC 3010—NFS version 4 Protocol

HTML and URLs are worked on by the IETF in cooperation with the World Wide Web Consortium, which can be found at http://www.w3c.org. Some important RFCs on HTML, URLs and HTTP are:

RFC 1738—Uniform Resource Locators
RFC 1866—Hypertext Markup Language—2.0

RFC 2045 through RFC 2049—Multipurpose Internet Mail Extensions
RFC 2396—Uniform Resource Identifiers (URI): Generic Syntax
RFC 2616—Hypertext Transfer Protocol—HTTP/1.1

The Open Group works to standardize applications. Their web site is http://www.opengroup.org.

Chapter 13

Network Management

This chapter gives an overview of centralized and standardized techniques for remote management of the devices that make up a network. The term *network management* is used to cover all aspects of configuration, control, and reporting that are useful to a network operator who is trying to understand how a network is functioning, commissioning new equipment, directing traffic along specific paths, or performing maintenance on parts of the network.

We begin with a brief description of the benefits of network management and then discuss some common techniques for the collection of operational statistics and the motivation for doing so. The chapter moves on to compare the benefits of proprietary configuration methods with standardized approaches. There follow individual sections introducing some of the standardized management models, including Management Information Bases (MIBs), the Simple Network Management Protocol (SNMP), the Extensible Markup Language (XML), and the Common Object Request Broker Architecture (CORBA). After a discussion of the differences between the management models, the chapter concludes with a section describing the Common Open Policy Service (COPS) protocol and the use of Policy within modern networks.

The chapter is not intended to present each management mechanism in detail but rather to give a working overview. Where specific protocol-related components exist they are highlighted and described.

13.1 Choosing to Manage Your Network

At some level all network devices require some management. Even the most simple devices have physical management needs as they are commissioned and connected to a power supply. But most devices need some form of configuration to tell them what role they are to play in the network and precisely how to behave. Even when auto-configuration protocols like DHCP (see Chapter 2) are used to dynamically assign IP addresses and to download basic configuration information, a network operator will want to use management operations to inspect the devices to discover what addresses they are using.

In practice, many network devices are complex animals, requiring a large number of configuration parameters. Many, if not most, of these parameter can usually use default values, but fine tuning may be necessary to ensure optimal functioning of the network, and that requires some form of management access to the device.

At the same time, it is crucial to the understanding of the operation of a network to be able to inspect each node and observe how it is behaving. What resources are active and how much traffic are they carrying? Who has provisioned those connections that are causing a bottleneck for the CEO's emails? Why can't I send any packets to that host? The background information needed to answer these types of question ranges from basic state information about the devices, through detailed data concerning the inner functioning of the devices and thorough statistics recording the number of errors, packets, and bytes.

In order to get the most meaning out of management information retrieved from a device, it is usually decomposed in a logical and modular fashion. So, for example, one might be able to access data about a whole router, the line cards on the router, the interfaces on each line card, the protocol components running on the router, and so on. Conversely, configuration is most flexible when it can be applied to the same logical components of the system.

A final management requirement is the ability to provision new services. This may require commissioning resources at each node along a path through the network, or if a signaling protocol is in use, simply issuing management requests to the starting point of the new connection.

So, at many levels it is impossible to operate a network without some form of management. The remainder of this chapter examines how to use standardized approaches to produce a coherent management strategy for the whole of the network, making it possible to debug the network more effectively and to reduce the management resources required to operate a network constructed from computers from different vendors.

Network management is an area in which most Internet Service Providers (ISPs) seem to struggle. The nature of their networks is constantly changing, and the market is continually driving them to provide new and different services. These changes put a strain on existing network management tools and require the Service Providers to race to adapt their techniques to their customers' requirements. In previous years, managed Internet services were the highest requirement, but these days, enterprises are looking for their Service Provider to support intranet or extranet services. This means that the Service Provider needs to provide an entire "network" to an individual enterprise customer and not just a set of simple and unrelated connections to the Internet. The new network services are provided to the customer as Virtual Private Networks (VPNs) across a common shared network infrastructure owned by the Service Provider. This sharing of network resources provides a new challenge to the network management capabilities of the Service Provider who must now be able to partition resources and share them between customers.

13.2   Choosing a Configuration Method

There are many ways to configure devices, from automatic configuration protocols such as BOOTP and DHCP, through command line interface and configuration files to graphical user interfaces. These techniques may use a mixture of proprietary manufacturer information and techniques and standardized protocols and data formats. As will be shown in the following sections, there are benefits and disadvantages to using the vendor-specific approaches, but the standardized methods give a great benefit in providing a centralized and coherent view of the network.

13.2.1   Command Line Interfaces

The easiest management tool for a manufacturer of network equipment to write is a command line interface (CLI), sometimes known as a craft interface (CI). A CLI is a set of text-based commands issued by the operator at a terminal. The commands have specific (sometimes complex and esoteric) syntaxes specified by the manufacturer and are very specific to the hardware being managed. This means that an operator running a network of diverse nodes from different manufacturers must learn the command language for each node—no small task. Fortunately, devices from one manufacturer tend to use the same commands where there is an overlap of function, and the same syntaxes for all commands. Because devices that perform the same functions need roughly the same configuration, and because vendors recognize the difficulties of managing networks built from hardware from many different vendors, there is a tendency for CLIs to look quite similar, with convergence on the command syntaxes used by the incumbent manufacturers. This has obvious benefits, but can also be frustratingly confusing when the syntaxes are so similar as to make the differences hard to remember.

In its simplest form, the CLI requires that the operator be present at a terminal directly attached to the device being managed. This is not viable in large networks in which the routers and switches are distributed over a large geographic area and are often installed in inaccessible places. Remote console access can be achieved running a product such as a terminal server which the user connects to using Telnet and which is physically connected to the device as though it were a local terminal.

Alternatively, if the device supports TCP and runs a Telnet server, the operator can log in using Telnet and run the CLI. In either case, the user can manage the device remotely and must visit the location in which the equipment is installed only in the event of a catastrophic failure.

It is a considerable inconvenience to an operator to have to reconfigure a device each time it is restarted (that is, power cycled), so most devices store their configuration data in some form. It is not really important whether this information is on a local hard disk, in flash memory, or in a file held on a remote server and accessed through some means such as the Trivial File Transfer Protocol (TFTP). The effect is the same: the device is able to recover its configuration by reading a file and commence operation without any further management intervention. Such configuration files may be stored in any format, and could be simple binary files which are easily read into memory and have meaning only to the software that is using them, but a more sensible approach is to record the configuration commands necessary to recreate the required state and to replay the file as though it were being typed by the operator. Command-based configuration files have the advantages that they can be inspected and understood by an operator, they can be edited so that new configuration is automatically picked up on reboot, and they are more easily proofed against software version upgrades.

It should be noted that the one great benefit of a CLI is that it is easily able to give a very fine level of control over a device and allows a user to examine every last detail of the device's operation. Debug commands are rarely available in any other form.

13.2.2 Graphical User Interfaces

Graphical User Interfaces (GUIs) are a more user-friendly configuration tool. The operator does not need to remember a command language, but is led through a series of screens with spaces to fill in the necessary configuration information. Default values are provided automatically and context-sensitive help is often available. Advanced GUIs support point-and-click provisioning in which an operator can achieve a high level of management using a mouse to select devices and components and to drag and drop configuration objects.

The biggest benefit to a GUI is the way in which data retrieved from devices can be displayed. Although it is possible to just show tables of data as in the CLI output, these tables can be easily enhanced to allow the user to click on any piece of information to drill down further and see more details. Better still, the GUI can provide graphical representations of information, tracking data against time or mapping resources in physical space. A GUI can, for example, build a picture of a device by learning from it what components it has that are installed and operational, and can present this to the operator as though he were looking at the real device. Similarly, by connecting to multiple devices in the network, the GUI can present a single, graphical view of the entire network.

This latter feature means that the GUI must be capable of operating remotely and must not be limited to direct access on the managed device. Remote GUI access can be achieved in a variety of ways, including through the X/Open remote console protocols, but this requires that the complex graphical manipulation and presentation is performed on the managed device. It is more common to place the bulk of the function at the central management site on a dedicated computer and to have the GUI-based management program contact the managed devices using some form of communications protocol.

The GUI can be implemented "over the top of" the CLI so that all commands issued at the GUI are mapped to CLI commands which are sent to the managed device using Telnet. Data that is displayed by the GUI can be collected in the same way before being massaged to make the pretty screens. Alternatively, GUIs may use their own communications protocols and data formats to talk to devices with the benefit of a more condensed information exchange since only the raw data is sent without the lengthy text control commands and output strings.

There is still a place for configuration files in systems that are managed using a GUI. There is, however, a less obvious way to store the data. If the GUI is implemented over the top of the CLI either locally or for remote transmission, then it is obvious to store the configuration using the CLI commands, but if the GUI is implemented using direct access to configuration data structures it is often tempting for an implementer to build a binary configuration store. This loses the benefits of the text-based configuration file described in the previous section and makes it difficult to handle a system with a GUI and CLI, so the most common approach is to convert the GUI configuration into the equivalent CLI commands before storing the information.

It is worth noting that despite the user-friendly aspects of a GUI, an experienced network operator or field engineer will often prefer to use the CLI. The CLI gives access to a finer level of control and a greater amount of information than the GUI, even if that information is not always formatted in the most readable way. Further, many engineers claim that they can operate with the CLI much faster than they can handle a GUI.

13.2.3 Standardized Data Representations and Access

Network managers dream of having a single application that they can use to manage their entire network. This application must be capable of controlling all of the devices in the network, and of collecting and integrating the information and statistics stored on each device. The advantages for the operator are a coherent view and a less complex management task because he doesn't have to learn to speak the different command languages for the different equipment vendors and the different dialects for the different devices and models from the same vendor.

One approach to building the global network management tool is to incorporate modules designed to talk to each of the individual components and map these to a common display and control component. This is hard work for the writer of a management application since he has to keep up with the latest command syntaxes and products produced by each vendor. This is, however, a viable solution, especially if a modular approach is taken.

One easier way to produce a global management tool is to make the individual vendors responsible for the modules that manage all of their devices and to make those modules distinct (usually running on separate computers) with a *northbound interface* to the global application. This can be seen in Figure 13.1, in which the operator works at a Network Management System (NMS) or through an Operations Support System (OSS) such as Telcordia's TIRKS or NMA. Use of an OSS allows the operator to utilize sophisticated provisioning and accounting services, and the OSS uses a scripting language such as TL1 to pass CLI-like commands on to the NMS. The NMS is the global management application that communicates to many Element Management Systems (EMSs), each of which is responsible for managing a collection of devices of the same type. It is the EMS that the equipment vendor supplies as a distinct module for incorporation into the whole management network.

As shown in Figure 13.1, the operator may have access to the EMSs where he uses proprietary CLIs and GUIs to control the devices. But if the operator is working at the NMS or OSS there must be a channel of communications between the NMS and each EMS. This is popularly referred to as a *northbound interface* to the EMS. There are two requirements for this communication: that the messages be understood universally (there must be a common communications protocol), and that the data be comprehensible (there must be a common data format). The popular standard for NMS to EMS communications is the Common Object Request Broker Architecture (CORBA) described later in this

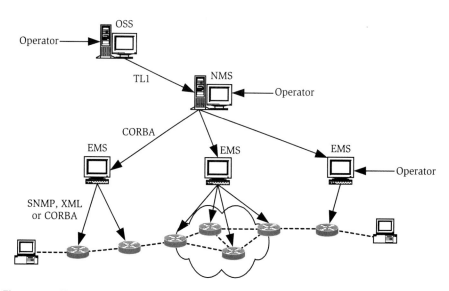

Figure 13.1 The management network can be built up from a series of management systems so that the operator can use a single, central management server.

chapter. CORBA provides a standardized way for the NMS to access data objects managed by each EMS, and a way for the equipment vendors or EMS authors to publish a database format for the NMS to access—these formats can become standardized, making the job even simpler.

The EMS is now free to manage the devices themselves. Each equipment vendor may take a different approach to the management of its devices, as described in the previous section, but it is increasingly popular to use one of a small set of standardized protocols and data formats. There is a clear advantage for vendors because they are able to leverage lots of existing code when they produce a new device and they do not have to make substantial upgrades to their EMS to support the new product. Three popular standards-based configuration techniques have emerged: CORBA, the Simple Network Management Protocol (SNMP), and the Extensible Markup Language (XML). If CORBA is used by the EMS to manage its devices, the mapping between NMS and device is particularly simple for the EMS, but otherwise a conversion component must be written.

However, once the devices support a standardized configuration protocol, there is less need for an EMS. It does continue to add management features specific to the vendor's equipment, but it gets in the way of centralized management from the NMS and affects management performance if translations are required on every command. For this reason, the EMS is increasingly dropped from the picture and the NMS communicates with the devices directly using one of the standardized protocols.

13.2.4 Making the Choice

Making the choice between configuration methods may be constrained by what protocols and techniques are supported by the equipment in your network. At the worst, you will need to use the CLI on each piece of equipment, operating via Telnet and possibly with the use of a terminal server.

If standardized management protocol support is available there are many advantages to using it, but it should not be forgotten that there will often be more detail and flexibility available through proprietary configuration interfaces than are available through the standards. Nevertheless, except for the configuration of advanced features or for debugging, the benefits of a consolidated management system dictate the use of a standardized technique.

13.3 The Management Information Base (MIB)

One problem in the management of networks is deciding how the statistics and configuration data should be represented. Each device (switch, router, host, etc.) will have different configuration requirements and internal data structures according to its implementation. Similarly, each network management tool will have different commands and management screens displaying and requiring subtly different pieces of information. Nevertheless, any two devices that perform the same function in the network (for example, two OSPF routers) require substantially the same configuration to enable them to operate their IP-based protocols. This means that all that is required is a common, standardized way to represent the data while it is moved between management station and device. The management tools are free to collect and display the information in whatever way they choose, and the devices can store the information and use it (or discard it) as they see fit.

For each protocol that it develops, the IETF produces a standard set of operational configuration and statistics information necessary for successful configuration and management of a device that runs the protocol. This information is published in separate RFCs for each protocol and constitutes a module from the global network Management Information Base (MIB).

The MIB is an ordered, structured view of all of the information in all networks, all at the same time. This is a pretty ambitious claim which is, in fact, true only within the global uniqueness of identifiers such as IP addresses and router identifiers. The secret to meeting this aim lies in the way that data values (or *objects*) are given unique *object identifiers* (OIDs) in a hierarchical and somewhat long-winded way.

To illustrate this, consider the part of the *OID tree* shown in Figure 13.2. This shows the root of the tree and the branches down as far as some individual

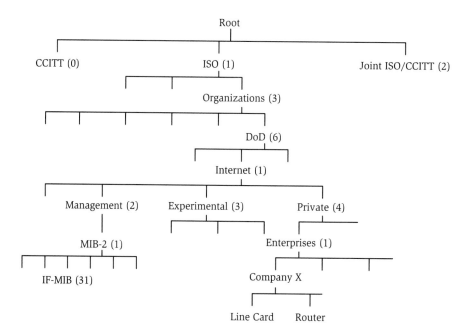

Figure 13.2 The OID tree from its root shown at the top of the example.

MIB modules. As can be seen, the MIB is broken into branches according to the standards-making body. Within the ISO branch, the American Department of Defense is responsible for the Internet. So all Internet OIDs begin with the value 1.3.6.1 using dot notation to represent the OID. Standardized IETF MIB modules are assigned from the MIB-2 branch of the Management branch, but those that are still under development usually come from the Experimental branch. Another branch is designated for private use and allows enterprises (companies, network operators, research establishments, etc.) to develop their own MIB modules. So, for example, OIDs in proprietary Cisco MIB modules begin 1.3.6.1.4.1.9 where the digit "9" has been assigned to denote Cisco.

Below these points in the OID tree come the individual MIB modules. A MIB module contains all of the configuration and reporting information for a single type of logical component. This may be a line card or router, as shown for Company X in Figure 13.2, or may be a component of a protocol such as an interface as managed by the IF-MIB module. In other words, MIB modules are defined to manage all instances of a single type of manageable entity.

MIB modules comprise individual *scalar objects* and *MIB tables*. On a managed object (for example, a router) the scalar objects can be thought of as global variables, and a MIB table can be thought of as an array of control blocks. Just as an implementation might need several types of control blocks, so a MIB module may include more than one table.

The scalar objects are each assigned a single object identifier within the MIB module. Thus, in the Interfaces MIB (IF-MIB) module documented in RFC 2863, there is an object called ifTableLastChange that records the time at which the Interface Table was last changed. This object is assigned the OID 5 from within the MIB module, giving it the full OID 1.3.6.1.2.1.31.1.5 where the penultimate "1" indicates that this is an object in the MIB.

Each table is also assigned an OID within the MIB module. So, for example, the Interfaces Receive Addresses Table (ifRcvAddressTable) in the IF-MIB module that is used to list all of the addresses that can be used on an interface has the value 4. Each table is made up of a series of *MIB rows* or *entries*. An entry is the equivalent of a single instantiation of a control block and is made up of a sequence of objects, each with its own object identifier. The ifRcvAddressTable contains three objects: the address itself, the current status of the address (available for use or not), and the volatility of the address on the interface assigned the OIDs 1, 2, and 3, respectively, so that the address object (ifRcvAddressAddress) has the full OID 11.3.6.1.2.1.31.1.1.4.11 where the penultimate 1 indicates that this is an entry in the table. Thus, all of the addresses in this table form a conceptual column in the table with the same OID.

Rows in MIB tables are distinguished by indexes. Indexes are object values within the table or within some other MIB table on which this one depends. In our example of the Interfaces Receive Addresses Table, there are two indexes. The *primary index* is the interface identifier itself, a value stored in a separate table, and the secondary index is the interface receive address in the ifRcvAddressAddress

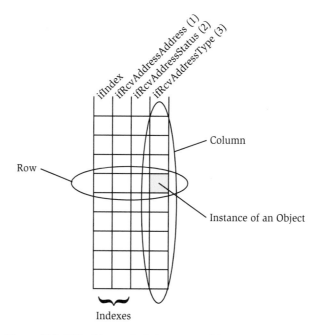

Figure 13.3 MIB tables are built from rows with conceptual columns.

object. Using these two indexes it is possible to select an individual row in the table and find out about a specific address on a specific interface. Alternatively, using just the primary index, and a "get next" operation, it is possible to read each of the addresses in use on a given interface. The table format is shown in Figure 13.3.

13.3.1 Representing Managed Objects

The Structure of Management Information (SMI) is specified in RFC 2578. It describes a subset of the Abstract Syntax Notation One (ASN.1) that may be used to define MIB modules and to encode MIB objects when they are passed from one node to another in management requests. ASN.1 was devised by the Open Standards Organization (OSI) and provides a text-based, macro language that may be used to define data structures in a form that is both intelligible to humans and machine readable. At the same time, ASN.1 also provides a set of rules for encoding data when it is passed on the wire between network nodes called the Basic Encoding Rules (BER). These rules provide for a very efficient (that is, requiring the smallest number of bytes) way to pass data along with its data types, but are somewhat complicated by flexibility of

ASN.1 to handle complex and nested data structures—a feature not required for MIB modules.

The SMI lays out a minimal subset of data types and constructs from ASN.1 and extends these concepts to support the specific requirements of MIB modules. These data types are shown in Table 13.1. They form the basis of more complex data types or *textual conventions* that can be defined within MIB modules. Textual conventions usually define interpretations to place on an object of a specific type. For example, the MPLS Textual Conventions MIB module defines MplsBitRate as an integer number of thousands of bits per second with a special meaning assigned to zero, as shown in Figure 13.4. Any other MIB module may *import* this textual convention and is thereby saved the effort of redefining it and also benefits from a consistent definition of bit rates. The SMI also defines some important macros used to embed useful information (such as the status of the object, a description, and display hints), and to define common concepts such as MIB objects and modules.

Table 13.1 The Eleven Basic Data Types Defined in the SMI

Data Type	Meaning
INTEGER	Signed 32-bit integer.
OCTET STRING	A series of bytes, each greater than or equal to 0 and less than or equal to 255.
OBJECT IDENTIFIER	An OID that can be displayed in dot notation.
Integer32	The same as INTEGER except that it is guaranteed to never need more than 32 bits for a two's complement representation.
Unsigned32	Unsigned 32-bit integer.
Counter32	A 32-bit integer used to count events (such as the number of packets received). When the value of an object of this type reaches 4,294,967,295, it wraps to 0.
Gauge32	A counter that can go up or down to register the number of instances of some object. Unlike Counter32 it cannot increment beyond 4,294,967,295, and does not wrap to zero. Similarly, it does not increment below zero.
Counter64	A 64-bit version of Counter32. This is particularly useful when counting things that are very fast (for example, bytes on a high-capacity link), and the SMI mandates that Counter64 be used for any counter that may wrap more frequently than once an hour.
TimeTicks	An unsigned 32-bit integer counting hundredths of seconds and wrapping to 0.
Opaque	An OCTET STRING wrapper of any arbitrary ASN.1 construct.
IpAddress	A sequence of 4 bytes containing an IPv4 address. Note that this data type is deprecated and new MIB modules use Unsigned32 for the same purpose.

```
MplsBitRate::=TEXTUAL-CONVENTION
DISPLAY-HINT "d"
STATUS current
DESCRIPTION
    "If the value of this object is greater than zero,
    then this represents the bandwidth of this MPLS
    interface (or Label Switched Path) in units of
    '1000 bits per second.'
    The value, when greater than zero, represents the
    bandwidth of this MPLS interface (rounded to the
    nearest 1000) in units of 1000 bits per second.
    If the bandwidth of the MPLS interface is between
    ((n * 1000) – 500) and ((n * 1000)+499), the value
    of this object is n, such that n > 0.
    If the value of this object is 0 (zero), this
    means that the traffic over this MPLS interface is
    considered to be best effort."
SYNTAX— Unsigned32 (0|1..4294967295)
```

Figure 13.4 A textual convention allows multiple MIB modules to import the same construct and meaning without having to redefine it.

13.4 The Simple Network Management Protocol (SNMP)

Once the management station and the managed devices have a common view of the management data (that is, MIB objects) all that remains is to provide a mechanism for the management station to create, write, read, and delete those objects. This is achieved using the Simple Network Management Protocol (SNMP) which, like anything that calls itself "simple," should be taken with a pinch of salt.

SNMP is an application-level protocol that can use any transport mechanism. In practice, it is most often used with UDP using port 161 since that is mandatory for conformance with the SNMP standards. Other transport protocols are sometimes used in a misguided attempt to handle some of the security issues covered in Section 13.4.2. TCP is occasionally chosen when a management application does not handle lost messages.

13.4.1 Requests, Responses, and Notifications

SNMP is a client–server protocol. Management agents connect to the managed devices and issue requests. Managed devices return responses.

The basic requests are very simple. They are GET and SET to read and write to an individual MIB object identified by its OID and, if the object is in a table, by the appropriate index values. Index objects are read and write protected—there is no need to specifically read an index because it is always supplied in a GET request and returned in a GET response to give context to the read request, and clearly it would be a bad idea to allow the index of a row to be changed dynamically. Some MIB modules also make some of their objects read only so that the device may report information (such as statistics) without it being modifiable by an external component. Other than these restrictions, however, GET and SET are quite straightforward in their operation.

However, it would be hugely inefficient to manage the configuration of a remote device one object at a time, so SNMP allows multiple objects within a single MIB row to be read or written in a single request. That is, a single GET or SET command can operate on multiple objects within a single row. Further, the GET-BULK command allows a management station to read multiple rows from a table, improving the retrieval time when an entire table is being read. Similarly, the GET-NEXT request allows a management agent to "walk" the OID tree to find the next object in a MIB row, or more usually to navigate a MIB table (which may be sparsely populated) reading one row at a time.

Row creation and deletion are special functions that are handled using the SET command and not through their own special messages. MIB rows contain a special writable object called the *row status* that is used to control the creation and deletion of the row. When a management station creates a row for the first time, it writes the value "create" to the row status object—if the row already exists, the operation will be failed by the managed device. If the row creation was successful, the management status goes on to write the other objects, and when the row is ready for use, it sets the row status to active. At this point, the configuration information is available and the device or component can be activated.

At any time the management station can move the row back into the "not ready" state by writing that value into the row status object. This effectively takes the row back into the state it was in as it was being created. To delete the row, the row status is set to the value "deleted" and the managed device must stop the corresponding process or device and delete the corresponding information.

A final SNMP message called a TRAP (sometimes known as a notification) may be issued by the managed device to report a specific event (for example, the crossing of a threshold).

13.4.2 SNMP Versions and Security

MIB data is encoded for transmission using the Basic Encoding Rules (BER) from the ASN.1 specification in the International Standard ISO 8825. This is a compact way of representing data and data types on the wire. For consistency, BER is also used for encoding SNMP messages, with the added advantage that the messages can be specified using the ASN.1 text notation.

SNMP messages are built from an SNMP header and an SNMP protocol data unit (PDU). The header is quite short and contains a protocol version number. The PDU contains the request and any data.

There are three versions of SNMP. The original version of SNMP was produced at the end of the 1980s. SNMPv1 turned out to be too simple in many respects, not having sufficiently powerful requests and using the limited SMIv1 to build its PDUs. After several abortive attempts, the IETF produced SNMPv2 and documented it in RFC 1901 as an experimental protocol. At the same time, work began on SMIv2, which was finally documented as RFC 2578, and SNMPv2 messages may carry only PDUs built using SMIv2.

SNMPv1 and SNMPv2 have considerable security concerns. Even on networks in which the data exchange is secured (for example, by using the facilities of IPsec) there is no control within these versions of SNMP as to who on the secure network is allowed to perform SNMP operations and access the objects in this MIB module. That is, any user on the network who can exchange UDP packets with the managed device will be able to examine and modify the MIB objects. This is clearly undesirable, so SNMPv3 includes application-level cryptographic authentication to enable individual users to be authenticated. SNMPv3 differs from SNMPv2 in the message header only—the PDUs are the same and both use SMIv2.

The IETF recommends strongly that deployment of SNMPv1 and SNMPv2 should be avoided, and that SNMPv3 be used instead. Further, they recommend that cryptographic authentication be implemented and enabled so that it is a matter for the network operator to manage the legitimacy of access to the management information on each device.

13.4.3 Choosing an SNMP Version

As explained in the preceding section, the IETF has some strong views about which version of SNMP should be deployed. In practice, however, although SNMPv1 is pretty well deprecated except in a relatively small number of older devices, SNMPv2 saw significant deployment and new devices are still being shipped that support only SNMPv2.

Therefore, although SNMPv3 is the ideal, management stations need to be able to support both SNMPv2 and SNMPv3 for the foreseeable future. All new devices should, however, be produced with support for SNMPv3, and it is reasonable to assume that management software will support SNMPv3 so that it is no longer necessary for a device to include SNMPv2 support.

13.5 Extensible Markup Language (XML)

The Extensible Markup Language (XML) is a subset of the Standard Generalized Markup Language (SGML) specified in the International Standard ISO 8879. XML defines data objects known as *XML documents* and the rules by which applications access these objects. XML documents look very much like Hypertext Markup Language (HTML) documents (for example, World Wide Web pages), but XML document specifications include strict definitions of the data type in each field of an object. This makes XML documents applicable to database formats, whereas HTML documents are more suited for text management. Thus, while presentation instructions (such as "center this text and print it in Arial twelve point") are part of SGML, they are not relevant to XML but are highly important in HTML.

In effect, XML provides encoding rules for commands that are used to transfer and update data objects. The syntax of these commands can be precisely specified and can be automatically parsed by a simple text-based application. Just as in HTML, formatting and control are managed using text *tags* that delimit the data, but unlike in HTML, the semantics of a tag is not global, but is specific to a given XML document. The data itself is presented as strings of bytes with each string enclosed by a pair of tags known as a single *XML element*. ISO 8879 defines how tags are used to enclose XML elements and what the meaning of the tags is (in other words, how the tags cause the receiving application to operate on the data in the XML element).

The collection of tags in an XML document is referred to as the *markup data*. The markup data not only gives instructions on the interpretation of individual data elements, but defines how the elements are associated, and also describes the purpose of the entire document and its applicability.

XML is developed by the World Wide Web Consortium (W3C) based on SGML. SGML was standardized in the mid-1980s and work on XML started in 1996, reaching its first standard (or Recommendation) in 1998. As such, XML is neither a communications protocol, nor tied to use within the Internet, but its applicability and increasing popularity as a configuration and management tool for Internet devices makes it worthy of further examination.

13.5.1 Extensibility and Domains of Applicability

Key to the nature of XML is its extensibility. XML elements can be defined as they are needed to fulfill the needs of specific document uses. Network management is one such area of use or *domain*, and subdomains might be defined for the management of a type of network element (for example, a router) or even for a specific make and model of a network element.

It is important to note that the definition of new XML elements is not the same as the definition of new tags or syntaxes within XML. Tags and syntaxes are standardized, meaning that all XML documents can be successfully parsed by any correctly implemented XML engine regardless of the domain to which the document applies. The semantics of an XML element may, however, only be understood within its domain of applicability.

The documents used within a specific domain will use a well-known set of XML elements, tags, and markup data. Knowledge of this information is useful to implementers since it governs the amount of code they have to write to construct and parse XML and to interpret XML elements. XML documents for a domain are described in a *document type definition* (DTD) and, conversely, a document identifies the domain to which it belongs by indicating the DTD. Note that DTDs may be nested as subsets of other DTDs so that a document that conforms to a child DTD will also conform to the parent.

13.5.2 XML Remote Procedure Calls

XML is a data encoding technique that can be used to represent data and data requests that are transmitted between components on a single node or across a network. It does not define what data should be transferred (that is the responsibility of the application developer, and any data including ASN.1 encoded SNMP data can be encapsulated in XML), nor does it define how the XML documents should be exchanged.

XML documents may be transferred using any data or file transfer process. Various processes have been applied, from UDP or TCP, through FTP and HTTP (see Chapter 12 for a description of the File Transfer Protocol and the Hypertext Transfer Protocol). The early uses of XML utilized a remote procedure call (RPC) mechanism based on HTTP—this made good sense because XML is closely related to HTML, which HTTP is designed to carry, and because HTTP contains basic get and put operations.

XML-RPC is still in use and has been successful, but it is considered by some to have too much overhead. A more object-oriented approach was desired, and so the Simple Object Access Protocol (SOAP) was devised.

13.5.3 Simple Object Access Protocol (SOAP)

The Simple Object Access Protocol (SOAP) is a lightweight protocol for exchange of XML documents over an underlying transport protocol. It supports transactions on distributed objects in a web-based environment by defining how remote procedure calls and responses may be represented within messages that may be sent between participating network elements.

SOAP messages are encoded in XML, which makes them reasonably easy for a human to read. The whole message is contained in an *envelope* and comprises an optional header and a mandatory body. The header contains control information about the message (things like priority and destination) and is not always required because in most cases the default behavior can be applied and the assumed destination is the receiver of the message. SOAP does allow messages to be relayed, however. That is, a SOAP message from node A to node C may be sent on a transport connection from node A to node B and relayed by the SOAP component on node B, which sends the message onward on a connection to node C. This feature requires that the header includes the target node for the message. The SOAP body contains the XML operations and data being transferred, as shown in Figure 13.5.

```
< env:Envelope xmlns:env = "http://www.w3.org/2003/05/soap-envelope" >
  < env:Header >
    < t:transaction xmlns:n = "http://elsevier.com/exmaple-msg"
            env:mustUnderstand = "true" >
    < n:priority > Low < /n:priority >
    < n:expires > 2005–10–15T23:59:59–05:00 < /n:expires >
    display
  < /t:transaction >
< /env:Header >
< env:Body >
    < dsp:text > This message is displayed. < /dsp:text >
  < /env:Body >
  < /env:Envelope >
```

Figure 13.5 An example SOAP message carrying a message to be displayed.

```
< env:Envelope xmlns:env = "http://www.w3.org/2003/05/soap-envelope"
        xmlns:m = "http://www.example.org/timeouts"
        xmlns:xml = "http://www.w3.org/XML/1998/namespace" >
  < env:Body >
  < env:Fault >
  < env:Code >
    < env:Value > env:Sender < /env:Value >
    < env:Subcode >
      < env:Value > m:MessageTimeout < /env:Value >
    < /env:Subcode >
  < /env:Code >
  < env:Reason >
    < env:Text xml:lang = "en" > Sender Timeout < /env:Text >
  < /env:Reason >
  < env:Detail >
    < m:MaxTime > P5M < /m:MaxTime >
  < /env:Detail >
  < /env:Fault >
  < /env:Body >
  < /env:Envelope >
```

Figure 13.6 An example SOAP fault message.

The SOAP envelope may alternatively contain a SOAP fault construct. This is used to report errors and has several mandatory components, including an error code for the fault, a text string describing the fault, and the identifier of the reporting node. Figure 13.6 shows a sample fault message copied from the SOAP specification.

13.5.4 XML Applicability to Network Management

XML is a useful management tool, and some network equipment vendors support only XML and their proprietary CLI. XML lends itself to the easy development of web-based management applications that can read and write network configuration information from and to remote devices.

It is relatively simple to use a DTD to generate the screens that an application will display, and this is an important point since each vendor's device managed through XML is likely to have a different DTD even if the function of the devices is similar.

XML is, however, a comparatively verbose way of encoding data. The tags are usually descriptive, meaning that several text words may be used to encapsulate a single piece of data. This is a large overhead compared with a binary encoding of a known structure, but it is also a great strength because the format and meaning are encoded in XML in a way that can be simply parsed by the recipient. The overhead of XML encoding is overcome to some extent by compression algorithms built into the protocols used to transfer XML documents.

13.6 Common Object Request Broker Architecture (CORBA)

The Common Object Request Broker Architecture (CORBA) is a distributed management architecture that takes an object-oriented approach to management. CORBA includes the specification of the managed objects, the communications and requests that are exchanged between management applications and the managed objects, and the requests, access control, security, and relationships between the objects.

CORBA is developed by the Object Management Group (OMG), which was founded in 1989 and is currently developing version 3.0 of the CORBA specification.

13.6.1 Interface Definition Language (IDL)

Each managed object (for example, a device, a line card, or a connection) is represented in CORBA by a CORBA object. The object is defined by an *object interface*, which (much as in an object-oriented programming language) indicates the accessible fields within an object, the operations that can be performed on the object, and the relationship between the object and other objects. Relationships with other objects are defined through inheritance.

The Interface Definition Language (IDL) is an object-oriented language specified by the OMG to describe object interfaces. IDL uses a subset of the C^{++} programming language, but extends it with a small set of additional constructs to support the type of object management that is needed in the context of network management. The most notable extension is the *any* data type, which can be used to represent an unknown or unspecified data type.

13.6.2 The Architecture

CORBA is a client–server architecture. The client is a management agent that performs operations on objects which are controlled by the server. The client and server are connected by the Object Request Broker (ORB) which is responsible for correlating the location of the client and server and managing the communications between them. This architecture protects the client from knowledge of the location of the server for each object and allows local and remote objects to be managed in a uniform way.

The Object Management Architecture (OMA) is illustrated in Figure 13.7. Central to the architecture is the ORB that is responsible for relaying the client's requests to the correct component at the correct location. Client requests are typically passed to the ORB through an Application Interface developed for the specific management application. Application Interfaces are usually developed for specific purposes or management applications, although because these purposes are sometimes common they may be standardized by the OMG. The ORB delivers the requests to the appropriate components, which may be local or remote. Common Facilities are utilities or operations oriented toward applications, and they may be common across multiple applications such as system and task management, operations on distributed document handling, and information management such as the embedding of an object from one application within a document from another application. Common Object Services (COS) are the

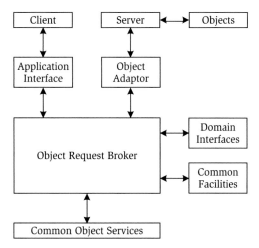

Figure 13.7 The Object Management Architecture reference model as defined by the Object Management Group.

underlying common functions used by the ORB to answer the requests issued by the client. COS includes the necessary components to ensure end-to-end delivery of object transactions, and also common services that range from object location and naming, through the management of object relationships, persistence and lifecycles to timing, security, and event notifications.

The Domain Interfaces are a collection of components that serve purposes similar to those of the Common Facilities and Common Object Services, but have scope limited to a particular application (that is, to a specific domain). These components are specified as part of the object definition, but if any of them is discovered to be common across multiple domains, it may be standardized and moved into the set of common components.

Finally, the ORB delivers object operations to the server for application to the objects themselves through the Object Adaptor. Like the Application Interface, the Object Adaptor is domain specific (that is, it is developed for managing a specific set of objects) and implementation specific, converting between the standard ORB requests and the local server implementation. In particular, the Object Adaptor may convert between the public and standard form of an object and the local storage format.

Figure 13.8 shows the interaction between the ORB and the client and server in more detail. It also shows the information repositories that are held at the client and server. The Interface Repository is held on the client and contains information about how the objects are handled, such as the interfaces and data attributes. The Implementation Repository is held on the server and contains the information that allows the ORB to locate and manage the objects; it also contains the active values of the fields within the object.

There are three components that provide the Application Interface from client to ORB. The ORB interface is a standard abstract interface to the ORB defined by the CORBA specification to allow application implementations to be decoupled from the ORB with an abstract representation of the objects. The IDL stub provides a mapping of object formats between the local application and the ORB. This mapping is important when the local application has not been coded using an IDL programming language—ORB development kits typically support mappings to standard languages (for example, C, C^{++}, and Java) and provide IDL compilers to allow new objects to be defined in IDL and converted to the local programming language. The third Application Interface component is the Dynamic Invocation Interface (DII) that provides direct access to the request–response mechanism of the ORB, including an IDL stub but with full awareness of the format of the objects.

Similarly, at the server, there are three components that provide access to the Implementation Repository. The ORB interface supplies the same level of standard abstract interaction on the server that it does on the client. The other two components interact with the ORB through the Object Adaptor described in the preceding paragraphs. The IDL Skeleton fulfills the same role on the server that the IDL stub does on the client:it provides a mapping between the standard

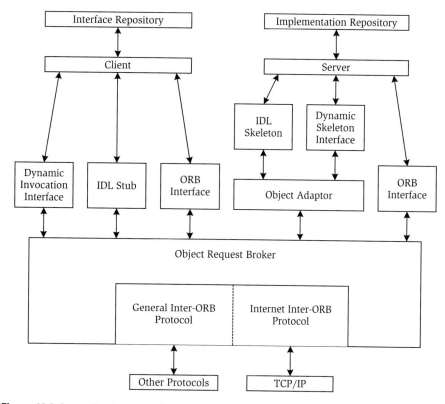

Figure 13.8 Interaction between client, server, and an ORB is handled by a set of components that provide abstraction and mapping functions. Communication between ORBs is provided by a general protocol with a specific adaptation to bridge the gap to TCP/IP.

object formats and the local formats stored in the Implementation Repository. The Dynamic Skeleton Interface (DSI) provides direct access to the request–response mechanism of the ORB, including an IDL Skeleton, but with full awareness of the format of the objects.

Figure 13.8 also shows how the ORB communicates with other client or server ORBs. The ORBs talk to each other using the General Inter-ORB Protocol (GIOP) that defines a set of application-level messages and data representations for transactions between ORBs. GIOP may be carried over a variety of transport protocols, but we are interested only in transport over the Internet. For this purpose, CORBA requires that an additional adaptation layer be used to bring the level of function of TCP/IP up to the requirements of GIOP and to make visible the IP addresses of the nodes on which objects reside. The combination of GIOP and this adaptation layer is known as the Internet Inter-ORB Protocol (IIOP). GIOP and IIOP are described further in the next section.

13.6.3 CORBA Communications

CORBA's General Inter-ORB Protocol is defined along with CORBA by the Object Management Group (OMG). GIOP is a generic object exchange protocol designed to be mapped onto any connection-oriented transport protocol. The OMG lists the objectives of GIOP as simplicity, scalability, low cost, generality, and architectural neutrality. GIOP attempts to achieve these goals by defining a set of assumptions about the underlying transport mechanism, messages to carry the data and data manipulation requests across the transport mechanism, and a list of syntaxes for the representation of IDL data types within the messages.

The GIOP Common Data Representation (CDR) defines how objects and data are encoded within messages. There are several key points to note:

- All data types are aligned on their natural boundaries to make it easier for applications to read and write data to messages. This has the obvious consequence that messages may be larger than strictly required, but makes application implementation more simple. Note that as data objects are placed in a message, they may need to be prepadded to bring the message up to the correct byte offset.
- Integers are supplied in messages in the sender's native format. This differs from the normal process in which all integers are transferred in "wire format" with the most significant byte first. Again, this allows for a simpler implementation—a sender never has to manipulate data before placing it in a message. A flag in each GIOP message indicates the sender's integer format and the receiver need only manipulate the data from a message if its own integer format is different.
- Other encodings (such as ASN.1 for SNMP requests) may be encapsulated as octet strings (that is, transparent streams of bytes) within the CDR.
- The CDR includes a construct called an *indirection* that allows one part of a message to point to data in another part of the message. This enables a degree of compression so that repeated data need only be present in the message once.

GIOP is a client–server protocol. The client is responsible for initiating a connection (using the underlying transport mechanism) with the server, and initiating the communications. In early versions of GIOP the server was not allowed to send request messages—it could only respond to requests from the client so that if two nodes wished to operate on each other's data objects it was necessary to maintain two connections between them. Although this added some simplicity to implementations in which only a unidirectional service was needed, the limitation has been relaxed in later versions of GIOP to allow bidirectional request exchanges on a single connection with the distinction of client and server diminished to connection management.

All GIOP messages begin with a common header, as shown in Figure 13.9. The first 4 bytes contain the magic cookie "GIOP" encoded in ASCII. The next two fields give the version number—the current version is 1.3, but any

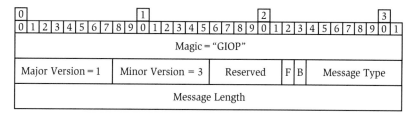

Figure 13.9 The common format of a GIOP message.

implementation supporting version 1.x must also support version 1.y for each y < x. The F-bit indicates whether this is the last or only fragment of a message (zero) or whether further fragments will follow (one). The B-bit shows how the integers in this message (including the subsequent Message Length field) are encoded—zero means the integers are Big-Endian and one means Little-Endian. The Message Type field indicates what the message is for, using values from Table 13.2. The Message Length gives the length of the remaining message, excluding the common header in bytes.

Each GIOP message starts with the common message header and continues with some message-specific fields, including a 4-byte request identifier to help correlate responses and fragments. The data is presented as a series of data values. On a Request message the data values are the input parameters to the object operation, and on a Reply they are the output parameters. Data values in a GIOP message can be represented by the BNF encoding shown in Figure 13.10. Each value begins with an integer value tag to identify the data type. The value tag may optionally (according to the value of the value tag) be followed by strings giving a codebase Universal Resource Locator (URL) and type information to help locate the data in a repository. Then comes the data itself (called the *state*). Alternatively, the value tag may be replaced by an indirection to the data, or a special tag to show that no data is present.

The state may be a sequence of one or more bytes (called octets) or may be a nested sequence of values, allowing data structures to be represented as shown in Figure 13.11. Note that there is support for splitting large (that is, of many bytes) data values across messages by chunking them. The end tag is used to indicate the end of a series of data chunks or the end of a nesting of values.

The tags are all long integers (that is, of 4 bytes) and use values from Table 13.3. Note that the chunk size tag is really just a count of the size of the chunk.

Connections are initiated in GIOP by a client. It uses the transport mechanism to open a connection to the server. In early versions of GIOP only the client was able to send Request, LocateRequest, and CancelRequest messages, and only the server could send CloseConnection. In more recent versions the distinction between client and server is limited to connection establishment. The connection

Table 13.2 GIOP Messages

Message Type	Message
0	Request. Sent by the client (or the server if bidirectional GIOP is in use) to invoke a CORBA object that is to read, write, or otherwise operate on an object. Request messages carry unique request identifiers that are used to correlate replies and fragments.
1	Reply. Sent in response to a Request to return data that is read or to return the result of the operation in the request. A flag in the Request indicates whether a Response should be sent.
2	CancelRequest. Sent by the sender of a Request to attempt to cancel it before the receiver acts on it and sends a Reply.
3	LocateRequest. Sent to determine whether the receiver is capable of performing the requested operation on the specified object. The LocateReply can affirm or deny the request and can also redirect the request to another location. Note that these results are identical to the response to a Request message carried by a Reply, but that the LocateRequest does not carry the full data, which is useful if redirection is likely.
4	LocateReply. Sent in response to a LocateRequest.
5	CloseConnection. Sent by either end of a connection to indicate that the sender intends to close the connection and that any outstanding Requests sent to it will not receive a Reply and will not be acted on.
6	MessageError. Reports a general, high-level parsing error such as an unsupported version number or an unknown message type. More detailed message-specific errors are handled in Reply messages.
7	Fragment. The Fragment message is used to continue and complete a sequence of message fragments started by a Request or Reply that has the F-bit in the common header set to 1 to indicate that the data has been fragmented between multiple messages.

< value > ::=	< value_tag > [< codebase_URL >] [< type_info >] < state > | < indirection_tag > < indirection > | < null_tag >

Figure 13.10 The basic encoding of values in GIOP messages.

gives context to the request identifiers used in the messages and (obviously) transports the messages.

TCP/IP provides reliable connection-oriented transport and so should be suitable for use by GIOP, but TCP/IP is limited by the failure or closure of connections. In particular, TCP does not provide a graceful shutdown whereby data "in the pipe" is flushed before the connection is torn down. This is a requirement of GIOP because the server may send CloseConnection and then shut the connection down—if this operation is attempted in TCP, the CloseConnection

< state > ::=	< octets > |
	< value_chunk > [< end_tag >] |
	< value > [< end_tag >]
< value_chunk > ::=	< chunk_size_tag > < octets >
< octets > ::=	octet [< octets >]

Figure 13.11 The encoding of data values within a GIOP message may be a series of bytes, chunks of data, or nested data types.

Table 13.3 The GIOP Tag Values

Tag	Fixed Value	Minimum Value	Maximum Value
indirection_tag	0xffffffff		
end_tag		0x80000001	0
null_tag	0		
chunk_size_tag		1	0x7ffffeff
value_tag		0x7ffff00	0x7ffffff

message may be lost, leaving the client unsure whether a new invocation is required because the previous connection failed or whether the old connection was closed under the control of an application. To bridge this gap, an additional adaptation layer is added to GIOP to make the Internet Inter-ORB Protocol (IIOP). Since IIOP is a minimum requirement of a conformant CORBA implementation, and since TCP/IP is almost ubiquitous, the term IIOP is used interchangeably with GIOP. IIOP is also defined by the OMG in the base CORBA specification along with GIOP.

The first requirement of IIOP is to extend the object profiles to contain the host on which the object is located and the port through which it can be accessed. The host is presented as a string that may contain a partially or fully specified host name (that is, a name such as "enterprise," or a fully qualified domain name for the host such as "enterprise.accounts.mycompany.com"), or the IP address of the host presented in dotted notation (for example, "192.231.79.52"). The port number identifies the TCP port on which the server (that is, the identified host) will be listening.

IIOP modifies the procedure for closing a connection by stipulating that the receiver of a CloseConnection message must close the connection. This takes the responsibility for connection closure away from the sender of the message and allows the process to complete successfully.

13.7 Choosing a Configuration Protocol

Choosing between CORBA, XML, and SNMP is not simple even if you have decided to use a standardized technique rather than one of the proprietary configuration mechanisms built into your equipment. SNMP is well established, with MIB modules designed within the IETF, often by the people who wrote the protocols that are being managed. The MIB modules offer a great deal of detail and fine control, but to some extent this is a downfall since the level of detail increases the apparent complexity of a MIB module for the reader or the implementer. The argument is often made that MIB modules are too complex and are consequently hard to understand. In the end, the amount of information that needs to be managed is static regardless of the protocol used to manage it; there is a constant amount of information needed to control and operate a device no matter how that information is transferred to the device. This means that discussions about the quantity of managed data are bogus and all that remains to be considered are the encodings and protocols.

XML provides an encoding technique that is at once easy to extend, readable by a human, and easy for a program to parse. Its downside is that its very readability makes it verbose, although compression techniques in the transport protocol may help to ameliorate this. XML is unquestionably easy and quick to develop and for this reason it is beginning to gain considerable popularity.

CORBA has an established foothold, especially with the larger Service Providers where the structured management network shown in Figure 13.1 is popular. Since CORBA is so often a requirement as a northbound interface from EMSs, it may make sense to offer CORBA support on the managed devices. Note that CORBA is also popular with object-oriented programmers because of its inherent object-oriented nature and the ready availability of ORB components in C^{++} and Java.

SNMP remains the most-deployed network management protocol. Despite fears about security, SNMPv2 is widely used and MIB modules give a well-known and detailed breakdown of the configuration data. Although ASN.1 is initially hard to get into, with familiarity the text representation is easy to read and can be automatically parsed to generate management applications and source code for clients and servers.

Note that is possible to mix and match. One option that is sometimes used is to maintain the configuration data in MIB format, but to transfer it as bulk data using CORBA or XML. This can avoid some of the security concerns of the earlier SNMP versions while continuing to use the detailed MIB modules.

13.8 Choosing to Collect Statistics

Successful network operation is not just about configuring devices, but also requires constant monitoring of the status of the links and nodes that make up the network to detect faults, congestion, and network "hot spots." For Service Providers to achieve contracted levels of service, they must be continuously aware of the load within their network and must discover node and link failures as quickly as possible.

SNMP provides notifications through trap messages to alert the management station when key events occur, although it is of the nature of networking failures that they may themselves prevent the delivery of any notification messages. SNMP also gives access to counters that provide basic statistical information about the traffic flows through a specific interface or device, and a management station may read these counters repeatedly to get a view of the change in network usage.

It should be borne in mind that the process of collecting network statistics in real time may have a detrimental effect on the operation of the network. This is not quite Heisenberg's Uncertainty Principle, but repeated requests to read data at many nodes can cause a lot of additional traffic and may congest the network around the central location at which the data is accumulated. For this reason, network statistics should be collected in a very structured way for day-to-day operation, focusing on entry and exit points to networks rather than on every link and node within the entire network. This has the benefit of policing internetwork agreements as well as checking to see which external links are close to their limits. Figure 13.12 shows how only certain links in a network might be monitored.

At the same time, multiple collection points can be used within the network to share the load of statistics collection. These intermediate collection points

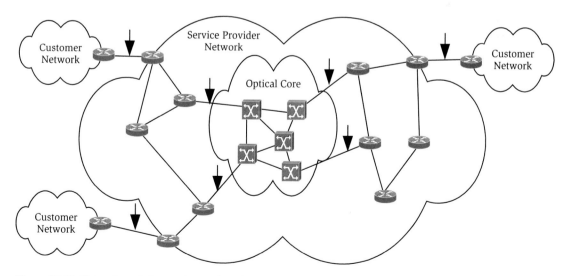

Figure 13.12 Network statistics can be monitored at specific points in a network (shown by the arrows) to gain a good view of overall operations without overloading the network.

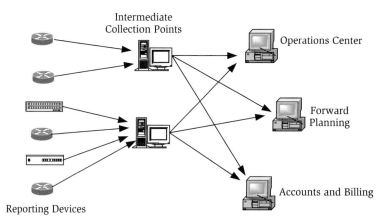

Figure 13.13 A hierarchy of collection points for network statistics reduces the associated traffic and offloads some of the processing requirements.

serve to coalesce the data sets into a single useful group of statistics before forwarding the information to the central collection point. In particular, since some statistics are used for billing, some for fault detection, some for long-term planning, and some for service maintenance, the intermediate collection points can filter the statistics and send information to the appropriate consumer while still providing just a single point of contact for each device. This hierarchy is shown in Figure 13.13.

Although SNMP may provide access to the necessary statistical information, it is not the best choice for network monitoring because it is request–response based. The client (or collection point) must issue read requests to the server (the device being monitored) in order to read the information. Further, the MIB modules are structured for wide configuration reporting rather than pure statistics gathering. These two factors mean that SNMP introduces a considerable overhead if it is used for this purpose.

As an alternative, the NetFlow architecture was devised by Cisco and is now being considered for standardization by the IETF. NetFlow is based on a series of record formats specifically designed to contain statistical information and to allow devices to report bulk data to their collection points. An important consideration is that the maintenance and dispatch of the NetFlow records should have the smallest possible impact on the ability of the device to forward data.

The NetFlow records can be collected by the device and sent periodically (based on a timer or a threshold) to the collection point, usually using a file transfer protocol such as FTP. An intermediate collection point can operate on the data and then send it onward. Since NetFlow is not an IP protocol, it is not discussed further in this book.

13.9 Common Open Policy Service Protocol (COPS)

Policy control is a variation of network management. It recognizes that when configuration requests arrive through signaling protocols rather than through management protocols, each network node is responsible for applying some policy to decide how to treat the requests. This policy may be local (specific to the node making the decision) or applicable across a wider domain, and the decision can be made at each node or devolved to centralized policy servers.

Note that when devices are managed through a management protocol there is still a policy that governs what resources can be provisioned in support of which services, but that policy is usually applied by the network operator in consultation with a management application.

The IETF defined a framework for policy control in RFC 2753 and the Common Open Policy Service (COPS) protocol to convey policy requests between clients and servers in RFC 2748.

13.9.1 Choosing to Apply Policy

When resources in a network are reserved to support service management for Integrated Services or RSVP (see Chapter 6) they are removed from general availability and are held for exclusive use by a specific data stream. This happens solely on the say-so of the requesting node—usually the node that will be sending or receiving the data. This requesting node knows the characteristics of the data being transferred and what network resources will be required to support it, so the reservation request asks for what is needed.

A node in the network receives many such requests but has only limited resources available. It must decide which requests should be satisfied and which rejected. These decisions obviously take into account the available bandwidth, and may consider authentication data (is the request from a valid neighbor?) and request priority (as in RSVP-TE for MPLS—see Chapter 9). However, in a large network additional policy-based decisions need to be made to determine whether precious resources should be tied up for use by data flows between particular applications at the source and destination nodes.

It is not necessary to make these policy decisions at each node in the network. It is sufficient to consider the requests as they pass into and out of policy administrative domains. Once a request has entered such a domain, the nodes within the network may consider that the local domain policy has been satisfied and can reserve the resources as requested. This is shown in Figure 13.14. Policy checking on departure from an administrative domain may not be necessary, but network operators may want to distinguish between reservation requests that are satisfied entirely within their network and the financial cost of resources reserved outside their network.

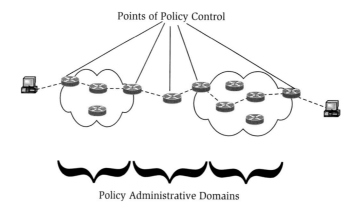

Figure 13.14 Policy is enforced at the boundaries of administrative domains.

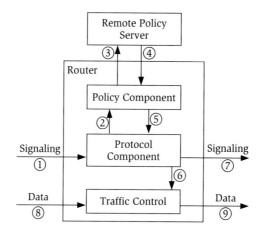

Figure 13.15 Policy is the responsibility of a distinct component within a network node and may require the assistance of a remote policy server.

The points of policy control shown in Figure 13.14 may be configured with sufficient information to make policy decisions on their own. This would certainly be the case for simple policies, but for more complex decisions based on detailed information about the topology and players in the network—and possibly a frequently changing networkwide policy—the points of policy control must consult an external policy server.

Figure 13.15 shows how a router that makes policy decisions might be constructed. When a reservation request is received by the signaling component of the router (step 1) it consults the local policy component (step 2). If the policy control component on the router cannot make a decision it consults a remote policy server (step 3). The policy decision (step 4) is relayed by the local policy component to the signaling component (step 5), which is able to make the required resource reservations (step 6) before signaling to the next node in the network (step 7). Finally, the data can flow, making use of the reserved resources (steps 8 and 9).

Figure 13.16 shows the full architecture for policy-based decision making. The IETF has named a point of policy control a Policy Enforcement Point (PEP). The PEP receives a policy request and consults its Local Policy Decision Point (LPDP), which may involve examination of a cache of locally stored policy information. If the LPDP is unable to make a decision, the PEP consults a remote Policy Decision Point (PDP) on another node in the network. Since the PDP is remote from the PEP, the two nodes must use a protocol to communicate—the IETF has specified the Common Open Policy Service (COPS) protocol for this purpose. The PEP fills the role of a client, making policy inquiries or requests to the PDP server.

The PDP has much more information available to it and can apply the full policy rules to produce an answer for the PEP, which it returns using the COPS protocol. However, as the size of networks grows it may be infeasible for a single PDP server to retain all of the information necessary to make proper policy decisions about all possible traffic flows. The architecture handles this by allowing both the LDPD and PDP to read additional policy data from a full (and probably distributed) policy database using whatever protocol is suitable (perhaps the Lightweight Directory Access Protocol, or maybe SNMP).

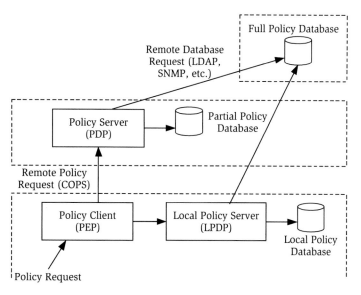

Figure 13.16 The policy architecture allows for local decisions, and the consultation of a remote policy database.

13.9.2 The COPS Protocol

The COPS protocol defined in RFC 2748 is a client–server protocol. A single PEP may maintain COPS sessions with zero, one, or more remote PDPs, and multiple PEPs may exist on a single node with sessions to the same or different PDPs. COPS runs over TCP using the well-known port number 3288 (0xCD8). Servers listen on this port for connections from all clients. Multiple PEPs on the same node, communicating with the same PDP, may share a TCP connection. Each COPS message uses a field in the COPS messages called the Client Type to identify the type of PEP and a Handle object within the message to identify the PEP itself so that exchanges with the server are fully disambiguated.

Once the TCP connection has been established, a client opens COPS communications with the server by sending a Client-Open message. If the server is willing to work with the client, it responds with a Client-Accept message. Alternatively, the server may reject the client using a Client-Close message giving reason codes and, optionally, returning a redirection IP address and port number to refer the client to a different PDP.

Once a TCP connection is open and active for COPS communication, some action must be taken to monitor the state of the connection and the remote COPS partner. This is the same issue that arises in all protocols that use TCP as a transport and wish to have timely detection of connection failures (see BGP-4 and LDP in Chapter 5 and Chapter 9). Timeliness is important because the policy request may be made in the course of signaling or data management and a lengthy delay would affect other nodes in the network.

COPS uses a KeepAlive message to monitor the status of the TCP connection. The PEP sends a KeepAlive message using a random variance on a timer sent to it by the PDP in the Client-Accept message. If the server does not receive a KeepAlive, it declares the connection dead, but if it does receive a KeepAlive, it immediately echoes it back to the client, allowing the client to monitor the connection as well. If multiple client types are active on the same connection, there is still only the need for one KeepAlive exchange using the smallest of the timer values received on the Client-Accept messages.

The client is now able to make policy requests to the server and receive the decisions. This exchange is achieved using three messages: the Request and Decision messages are obvious, and the Report-Status message is used to confirm that the client has taken the policy action as instructed by the server. The Report-Status part of the exchange is important because future policy decisions made by the server may be based on previous decisions. For example, the client may make several requests for the reservation of bandwidth, and the server may be policing an upper bound; clearly it is important for the server to know whether the bandwidth was actually reserved so that it can correctly police the upper limit.

With this in mind, the server also needs a mechanism to update itself on the status of policy-based decisions acted on by the client. If the server is reset, or if the TCP connection fails and is restarted, the server must get a fresh picture of the policy state information acted on by the client. It does this by sending a Synchronize-State-Request, which causes the client to respond with a series of Report-State messages, followed by a Synchronize-Complete message so that the server does not go on waiting for further state.

Finally, the client may send a Delete-Request-State to the server to let it know that the resources associated with a previous policy request have now been released.

Figure 13.17 shows COPS messages exchanged between a PEP and PDP. Initially, the client opens communications with the server (step 1), and then KeepAlive messages are exchanged (step 2). At step 3 the PEP makes a policy request, receives a decision, and notifies the PDP that it has acted on the decision. At step 4 the PDP decides that it wants to resynchronize its state, so it sends a Synchronize-State-Request and the PEP responds with a series of

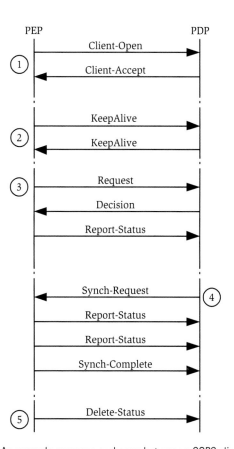

Figure 13.17 An example message exchange between a COPS client and server.

Report-State messages followed by a notification that it has finished. Finally, the client has finished with activities for which it made the policy request and so notifies the server (step 5).

13.9.3 COPS Message Formats

All COPS messages begin with a common header, as shown in Figure 13.18. The current version of COPS is version one, and this is given in the first field of the message. The S-bit is set to show that the current message was solicited by a previous COPS message. The Opcode field shows the operation that this message is performing—that is, it identifies the message type using values from Table 13.4. As described in the preceding section, the Client Type identifies the type of PEP, which is particularly useful when multiple PEPs are sharing a TCP connection. It is also important so that the PDP knows how to interpret the request and information supplied. Client type values are shown in Table 13.5. The final field in the common message header gives the size of the entire message (including the header) in bytes.

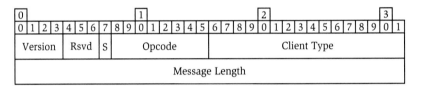

Figure 13.18 The common message header for all COPS messages.

Table 13.4 The COPS Message Operation Codes

Opcode	Abbreviation	Message
1	REQ	Request
2	DEC	Decision
3	RPT	Report State
4	DRQ	Delete Request State
5	SSQ	Synchronize State Request
6	OPN	Client-Open
7	CAT	Client-Accept
8	CC	Client-Close
9	KA	KeepAlive
10	SSC	Synchronize Complete

Table 13.5 The COPS Client Types

Client Type	Meaning
0x0001 – 0x3FFF	Reserved for use in IETF standards.
1	RSVP policy client as described in RFC 2749.
2	DiffServ policy client as described in RFC 3317.
0x4000 – 0x7FFF	Reserved for private implementations. Not tracked by the Internet Assigned Numbers Authority (IANA) and not defined in any standards.
0x8000 – 0xFFFF	Reserved for registration by other organizations. Tracked by IANA.
0x8001 – 0x8004	IP Highway.
0x8005	Fujitsu.
0x8006 – 0x8007	HP OpenView.
0x8008	PacketCable.

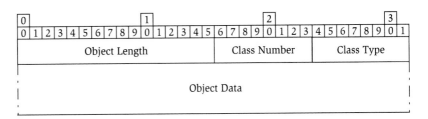

Figure 13.19 COPS messages are composed of objects which use a common format.

COPS messages are composed of objects in the same way as in RSVP (see Chapter 6). After the message header there is a series of objects, each one encoded using the format shown in Figure 13.19. The Object Length shows the length in bytes of the entire object (including the first three fields) and must be a multiple of four. The Class Number (C-Num) is used to identify the type of the object and the Class Type (C-Type) provides a subqualification. The COPS C-Nums are listed in Table 13.6.

The COPS messages built from the objects listed in Table 13.6 can be represented in BNF (just as for RSVP). Figure 13.20 shows the request message, which is the most complicated. The client handle and context objects are mandatory, but all of the other objects are optional. Note that multiple client-specific information objects and multiple LDPD decision objects may be present using the sequences defined below the message. As with all COPS messages,

Table 13.6 The COPS Class Numbers

C-Num	Meaning
1	Handle. A free-form identifier that is unique within the context of a client type on a particular TCP connection between PEP and PDP. Used to identify policy state to correlate requests, decisions, state reports, and deletions. The contents of the handle are at the discretion of the client implementation and might be (for example) a control block pointer.
2	Context. Indicates why a request has been issued by a client. Bit flags indicate whether there was an incoming protocol message or admission control request, a resource allocation request, a request to send a message, or a configuration request. A 16-bit integer is available to carry the message type of the causal event.
3	In Interface. The incoming interface to which a policy request applies. The object carries an interface index and an IPv4 or IPv6 address.
4	Out Interface. The outgoing interface to which a policy request applies. The object carries an interface index and an IPv4 or IPv6 address.
5	Reason code. The reason a policy state was deleted in a delete request message. RFC 2748 specifies a long list of possible reasons and subreasons, including signaled state removal, management intervention, preemption, timeout, and route change. These values are managed by IANA.
6	Decision. The result returned from the PDP. There are five C-Types defined for this object. C-Type 1 defines a mandatory object in the decision message which indicates whether the request was successful or not. This object may repeat in the decision message to present the other C-Types, which supply policy, admission control, and signaling protocol information specific to the client type.
7	LPDP Decision. A PEP with access to a local policy decision point may still wish to send a request message to a remote PDP for correlation or for further checking. This allows quick decisions to be made locally and to be validated in the background. In this case, the PEP sends the details of the local decision in a set of objects identical to the Decision objects but with a different C-Num.
8	Error. This object is used to convey COPS protocol errors (that is, not failures of policy). It is carried on a decision message to reject a malformed or unknown request message, or on a client-close for other errors.
9	Client-Specific Info. Used to provide additional information about a client on a client-open request. The information may indicate a named configuration for the client or may be specific to the client type.
10	KeepAlive Timer. The value of the KeepAlive timer to be used by the client is returned by the server in this object on the client-accept message. This is a 4-byte object, but the first 2 bytes are reserved. The second 2 bytes give the time value in seconds, with zero implying infinity (that is, no timer is run).
11	PEP Identification. A null-terminated ASCII string that uniquely identifies the PEP to the PDP. The IPv4 address in dot notation is often used. Note that this object must be padded to a multiple of 4 bytes using trailing nulls and that the length of the object includes these nulls.

12	Report Type. Used in the report-state message to indicate whether the decision was successfully implemented or not. A third value indicates that the message is being sent in response to a synchronize-state request.
13	PDP Redirect Address. A PDP that rejects a client-open request may include this object on the client-close message to suggest a different IP address and/or port number that the client should use to successfully open a connection. IPv4 and IPv6 versions of the object are defined.
14	Last PDP Address. Used by the PEP on a client-open message to indicate the address and port number of the PDP that it last successfully connected to for a client of this client type. IPv4 and IPv6 versions of the object are defined.
15	Accounting Timer. A timer specified in seconds by the PDP on a client-accept message. The PEP should generate unsolicited report-state message sequences (that is, without waiting to receive a synchronize-state request) on this time interval. If the timer is set to zero, no such messages are sent by the PEP.
16	Message Integrity. Used on all messages if message authentication is configured by the PEP and PDP for their communications. The object contains a key identifier, a sequence number which is incremented for each message to protect against replay attacks, and a message digest produced by a hashing algorithm operating on the message contents and the key identified by the key ID. For more information on message authentication see Chapter 14.

```
< Request Message > ::=     < Common Header >
                            < Client Handle >
                            < Context >
                            [ < IN-Int > ]
                            [ < OUT-Int > ]
                            [ < ClientSIs > ]
                            [ < LPDPDecisions > ]
                            [ < Integrity > ]
< ClientSIs > ::=           < ClientSI >
                            [ < ClientSIs > ]
< LPDPDecisions > ::=       < LPDPDecision >
                            [ < LPDPDecisions > ]
< LPDPDecision > ::=        [ < Context > ]
                            < LPDPDecision: Flags >
                            [ < LPDPDecision: Stateless Data > ]
                            [ < LPDPDecision: Replacement Data > ]
                            [ < LPDPDecision: ClientSI Data > ]
                            [ < LPDPDecision: Named Data > ]
```

Figure 13.20 The COPS request message may include multiple client-specific information objects and a series of local PDP decisions.

```
< Decision Message > ::=        < Common Header >
                                < Client Handle >
                                < Decisions >  |  < Error >
                                [ < Integrity > ]
< Decisions > ::=               < Decision >
                                [ < Decisions > ]
< Decision > ::=                < Context >
                                < Decision: Flags >
                                [ < Decision: Stateless Data > ]
                                [ < Decision: Replacement Data > ]
                                [ < Decision: ClientSI Data > ]
                                [ < Decision: Named Data > ]
```

Figure 13.21 The COPS decision message either returns a series of policy decisions or an error.

the order of objects shown is required for every message built and sent, but a receiver should be prepared to receive the objects in any order, provided that context and meaning is not lost.

The decision message shown in Figure 13.21 also has the potential for multiple objects because many pieces of decision information may be present for each of several decision options. Alternatively, if there was a formatting problem with the request message, there might be no decision objects, but an error object instead.

The remaining eight COPS messages are considerably simpler and are shown together in Figure 13.22. Note that if authentication is not in use, the KeepAlive message is almost trivial.

13.9.4 The Policy Information Base

The above is all very well, but the policy information that is exchanged using COPS and stored in policy databases needs some structure and format. Initial policy uses were specified using text (see RFC 2749 that describes the use of COPS in support of RSVP), but this is neither sufficiently precise to be safe, nor easily extensible as more client types are produced. In particular, there may be common concepts such as interfaces that are shared between policy data for different clients—it would be helpful if this information could be configured and managed coherently.

The IETF recognized that the information to be managed was not dissimilar to that for device configuration and management and that the Management Information Base (MIB) described in Section 13.3 already had an infrastructure suitable for specifying and encoding such data. So the Policy Information Base (PIB) was born.

```
< Client-Open > ::=                    < Common Header >
                                       < PEPID >
                                       [ < ClientSI > ]
                                       [ < LastPDPAddr > ]
                                       [ < Integrity > ]
< Client-Accept > ::=                  < Common Header >
                                       < KA Timer >
                                       [ < ACCT Timer > ]
                                       [ < Integrity > ]
< Client-Close > ::=                   < Common Header >
                                       < Error >
                                       [ < PDPRedirAddr > ]
                                       [ < Integrity > ]
< Keep-Alive > ::=                     < Common Header >
                                       [ < Integrity > ]
< Synchronize State > ::=              < Common Header >
                                       [ < Client Handle > ]
                                       [ < Integrity > ]
< Report State > ::=                   < Common Header >
                                       < Client Handle >
                                       < Report-Type >
                                       [ < ClientSI > ]
                                       [ < Integrity > ]
< Synchronize Complete > ::=           < Common Header >
                                       [ < Client Handle > ]
                                       [ < Integrity > ]
< Delete Request > ::=                 < Common Header >
                                       < Client Handle >
                                       < Reason >
                                       [ < Integrity > ]
```

Figure 13.22 The bulk of the COPS messages are relatively simple, comprising just a few objects each.

The PIB is in many ways very similar to the MIB. It has tables and rows to contain the information about instances of specific devices and managed entities. These may range from the capabilities and restrictions of devices and interfaces, through the resources and bandwidth, to the specific data flows and policy request. PIBs are specified using the ASN.1 Basic Encoding Rules just as MIBs are and they use the same basic data types defined in the Structure of Management Information (SMIv2 in RFC 2578). RFC 3318 defines a framework Policy Information Base in the context of Policy Decision Points and defines some basic textual conventions for use by other PIB modules.

13.10 Further Reading

MPLS Network Management: MIBs, Tools, and Techniques, by Thomas Nadeau (2003). Morgan Kaufmann. Although focused primarily on the management of MPLS networks through SNMP and MIBs, this book provides a good introduction and comparison of SNMP, CORBA, and XML, and includes a chapter on NetFlow.

Simple Network Management Protocol and the Management Information Base

Essential SNMP, by Douglas R. Mauro and Kevin J. Schmidt (2001). O'Reilly. This explains how SNMP works and examines some of the commercially available SNMP packages.

Understanding SNMP MIBs, by David Perkins and Evan McGinnis (1996). Prentice-Hall. This book covers all of the guts of how MIB modules are put together and how they work.

SNMP and the MIB are described in the following RFCs.

RFC 2578—Structure of Management Information Version 2 (SMIv2)
RFC 2579—Textual Conventions for SMIv2
RFC 3411—An Architecture for Describing SNMP Management Frameworks
RFC 3412—Message Processing and Dispatching for the Simple Network Management Protocol
RFC 3413—Simple Network Management Protocol (SNMP) Applications
RFC 3414—User-based Security Model (USM) for SNMPv3
RFC 3416—Version 2 of the Protocol Operations for the Simple Network Management Protocol
RFC 3417—Transport Mappings for the Simple Network Management Protocol (SNMP)
RFC 3512—Configuring Networks and Devices with Simple Network Management Protocol (SNMP)

Abstract Syntax Notation One (ASN.1) is defined in International Standard ISO 8824. The Basic Encoding Rules for ASN.1 can be found in International Standard ISO 8825.

Extensible Markup Language and the Simple Object Access Protocol

XML in a Nutshell, by Elliotte Rusty Harold and W. Scott Means (2002). O'Reilly. This tells you all you need to know to get started in XML.

For more information about XML visit the World Wide Web Consortium's web page at *http://www.w3c.org*.

Several IETF RFCs are concerned specifically with XML.

RFC 3076 — Canonical XML Version 1.0
RFC 3470 — Guidelines for the Use of Extensible Markup Language (XML)
within IETF Protocols

Common Object Request Broker Architecture

Advanced CORBA Programming with C++, by Michi Henning and Stephen
Vinoski (1999). Addison-Wesley. This book gives a programmer's slant on
CORBA, tying it closely to the C++ programming language, but explaining all
of the essentials.

CORBA/IIOP Clearly Explained by Michael Hittersdorf (2000). AP Professional.
This book gives a thorough overview of CORBA and introduces the Internet
Inter-ORB Protocol (IIOP).

Information about CORBA can be found on the Object Management Group's
web site at http://www.omg.org. A full list of the CORBA specifications can be
found at http://www.omg.org/technology/documents/corba_spec_catalog.htm.

Statistics

More information about NetFlow can be found at the Cisco web site: http://
www.cisco.com.

Policy

Policy-related standards can be found in the following RFCs.

RFC 2578 — Structure of Management Information Version 2 (SMIv2)
RFC 2748 — The COPS (Common Open Policy Service) Protocol
RFC 2749 — COPS Usage for RSVP
RFC 2753 — Framework for Policy-based Admission Control
RFC 3048 — COPS Usage for Policy Provisioning
RFC 3159 — Structure of Policy Provisioning Information
RFC 3317 — Differentiated Services Quality of Service Policy Information Base
RFC 3318 — Framework Policy Information Base

Chapter 14

Concepts in IP Security

No topic related to the Internet, with the possible exceptions of the free availability of pornography and the plague of unwanted spam email, has received more attention in the mainstream media than "security." For the average user the concerns are predominantly viruses that may infect their personal computers, causing inconvenience or damage to their data. Increasingly we also hear about white-collar e-criminals who steal personal financial details or defraud large institutions after illegally gaining entry to their computer systems.

We are also now all familiar with catastrophic failures of parts of the Internet. Although these are sometimes caused by bugs in core components (such as routers) or by the perennial backhoe cutting a cable or fiber, they are increasingly the responsibility of individuals whose sole joy is to pit their wits against those who maintain the Internet. Sometimes known as *hackers,* these people attempt to penetrate network security, or cause disruption through *denial of service attacks* for a range of motives.

Corporate espionage is of relatively little concern to most people, but within every forward-looking company there is a person or a department responsible for keeping the company's secrets safe. At the same time, the populist war against terrorism invokes contradictory requirements—that the government should be able to keep its information private while at the same time examining the affairs of suspects without them being able to hide their communications.

Whatever the rights and wrongs of the politics and sociology, Internet security is a growth industry. This chapter provides an overview of some of the issues and shows the workings of the key security protocols. It introduces the security algorithms without going into the details of the sophisticated mathematics behind encryption algorithms or key generation techniques. For this type of information the reader is referred to the reference material listed at the end of the chapter.

The first sections of the chapter examine the need for security, where within the network it can be applied, and the techniques that may be used to protect data that is stored in or transmitted across the network. There then follows a detailed examination of two key security protocols: IPsec, which provides security at the IP packet level, and Transport Layer Security (TLS), which operates at the transport layer and provides the Secure Sockets Layer

(SSL). After a brief discussion of some of the ways to secure Hypertext Transfer Protocol (HTTP) transactions, which are fundamental to the operation of web-based commerce, the chapter describes how hashing and encryption algorithms are used in conjunction with keys to detect modification of data or to hide it completely—the Message Digest Five (MD5) hashing algorithm is presented as the simplest example. The chapter concludes with an examination of how security keys may be securely exchanged across the network so that they may be used to decrypt or verify transmitted data.

14.1 The Need for Security

It is fair to say that when the Internet was first conceived, security was not given much consideration. In fact, the whole point of the Internet was to enable information to be shared and distributed freely. It is only as a greater number of computers have been connected together, and the sort of information held on computer and distributed across the Internet has grown in quantity and sensitivity, that network security has become an issue.

There are two fundamental issues. First, there is a need to keep information private for access only by authorized parties. Whether it is classified government material, sensitive commercial information, your credit card number, or just a note suggesting that you meet your friend in the bar in half an hour, there is strong motivation to protect any information sent across the Internet from prying eyes. This desire extends beyond protection of data transmitted over the Internet, and should also be considered to cover the safeguarding of files stored on computers attached to the Internet, and access to computing resources and programs. Some of the solutions to this issue can be seen by users on private networks as they are required to log on to their workstations, password protect key documents, and digitally sign their emails.

The second security issue concerns protection of the infrastructure of the Internet. This covers prevention of attacks on the configuration of devices in the network, theft of network resources, and the malicious jamming of nodes or links with spurious data that makes it impossible for legitimate messages to get through.

Somewhere between these two cases comes prevention of unauthorized access to secure locations on computers. This access may be in order to read privileged information, or it may be to replace it with something else, or even simply to delete it. A popular gag among hackers is to replace the content of a web site with slogans or pictures that are neither relevant nor helpful to the cause that the site was promoting.

The Internet has been shown repeatedly to be quite fragile. The accidental misconfiguration of a key router may result in large amounts of data looping or being sent off into a void. Malicious changes to routing information may have a similar effect. At the time of writing, the English-language web site of the Arab news service al-Jazeera is unreachable because someone has stolen" its DNS entry on several key servers, resulting in all attempts to reach http://www.aljazeera.net being redirected to another site that displays an American patriotic message. Such intervention in the smooth operation of the Internet, although no doubt a great deal of fun to the perpetrator, is at best an inconvenience for the normal user of the Internet. For the commercial organizations that depend on exchanging information across the Internet or on customers visiting their web sites, these disruptions are a more serious matter.

Various techniques are used to compromise Internet security. The most obvious technique involves simply impersonating another user to access that user's computer. Remote access protocols such as Telnet and FTP make this particularly easy. Of course, data that is sent on the Internet can be examined quite easily using a sniffer, provided access to a computer on the network can be gained or a sniffer can be hooked up to the network at some point.

Even when passwords and authentication or encryption are used, it may be possible for someone to capture a sequence of commands and messages and replay them at a later time to gain access. Such *replay attacks* can at least confuse the receiving application and waste system resources, but may return information such as encryption keys, or may provide access to applications on a remote server.

Denial of service attacks result in degradation of service to legitimate network users. There is no immediately obvious benefit to the perpetrator, although the example in the next section describes how denial of service may be used to trick network operators into giving away their secrets. Denial of service is increasingly a tool of "Internet anarchists" who target organizations with whom they have a disagreement and block access to or from those organizations' private networks.

14.1.1 Choosing to Use Security

On the face of it, it would seem that anyone would be crazy to consider using the Internet without steeping themselves and their computers in the deepest security. Yet most individual users connect their personal computer to the Internet daily without significant consideration of the risks to their data, and only those whose computers are attached to the Internet for prolonged periods of time using high-speed links consider that they are at risk. Even a large proportion of corporations apply only the simplest *gatekeeping* security to prevent unwarranted access into their private networks, and take little or no precautions for the safety of the data that they send across the Internet.

To some extent this is a statistical question: What are the chances of a hacker stumbling across my computer? The answer is that it is currently fairly unlikely, unless you draw attention to yourself, for example, by being a hated multinational corporation with a reputation for polluting the environment, or by writing textbooks on Internet security. The statistical trend, however, may not be in our favor and, just as we have all become aware of the dangers of computer viruses and have equipped ourselves with software to detect and remove viruses, so we will need to protect our computers from hackers who write or use programs that search the Internet for unsecured computers.

There are other trade-offs to consider, too. Not the least of these is price, and although a lot can now be done for the home computer at a very low price, the best corporate Internet security comes at a greater cost. There are also performance costs associated with data encryption and authentication as the algorithms used perform multiple computations on each byte of data that is transmitted. The effect on the rate of data transmission can be reduced by using dedicated security hardware that is optimized for the computations that are needed, but that pushes the price up again. Work is also progressing to develop faster algorithms that are equally secure.

The last consideration is the complexity of a fully secure system. In many cases there are configuration issues to be addressed as security keys must be entered into the system at the sender and receiver—some of these issues can now be solved using key distribution protocols (see Section 14.8). And the complexity of a security system may lead to maintenance problems, with confusion and misjudgment by network operators, as illustrated by the following cautionary (and possibly apocryphal) tale from the early days of networking.

A bank used to transport all its computer data on tape every night from a major branch to its head office. The bank installed a computer link between the sites to make the transfer more efficient and timely. Not being entirely ignorant, they applied a simple encryption algorithm to the data.

As time went by, the bankers became uncomfortable that their encryption algorithm might be too easy to crack, so they bought an upgrade to the software that had a far more sophisticated encryption routine. In due course, they upgraded the software and left the program to run overnight. To their consternation, the next morning they discovered that the data received at the head office was garbled and couldn't be decoded. A quick experiment showed that if they turned off the encryption, the data was transmitted fine, but with encryption enabled the computer at the head office was unable to make sense of the data.

With pressure mounting and the bank due to open, the manager made the obvious decision; the new encryption software was broken and must be disabled for the transmission. So, the data was sent to head office unencrypted and business went on as usual. The software developers were called but could find nothing wrong with their programs, and so, eventually, hardware engineers came to inspect the leased line between the offices. They, of course, found the point at which the criminals had intercepted the data and mangled everything that was encrypted, allowing through anything that was in the clear. Examination of the bank's records showed that once the nightly transaction had started without encryption, the resourceful thieves had inserted their own records into the data and had siphoned off their share of the money.

14.2 Choosing Where to Apply Security

Security within an IP network can be applied at any or all of a set of different levels. Physical security governs the connectivity and access to private networks; protocol-level security controls and safeguards the essential protocols that make the Internet work; application security can be used to protect sensitive data and to limit access to applications; transport and network layer security is used to protect data flows across public or exposed networks and connections.

Choosing between these options is as much a matter of strategic network planning as it is a requirement for protecting individual pieces of data. Security consultants expend a great deal of effort helping their customers pick exactly the right combination of options to achieve a secure and yet manageable system since it is often the case that increased security is paid for through ever more complex configuration requirements. The consequences of a poorly designed security system extend beyond the problems described in the previous section—an overzealous or badly administered scheme can bar or frustrate legitimate users. The sections that follow briefly outline the levels at which security can be applied.

14.2.1 Physical Security

Perhaps the most obvious and strongest form of security is a physical break in the connectivity. It is very hard for an intruder to gain access to your network or data if there no connections to the outside world. This approach still forms the foundation of many corporate security models, but as networks grow in size they often include links that are hard to protect (for example, those that run between buildings) and this introduces a vulnerability which a determined outsider may exploit. At the same time, external access to and from the wider Internet and for dial-up connectivity is now almost ubiquitous. Although certain physical connectivity constraints can be applied to both dial-up links and more permanent external links, the gates stand open welcoming the hacker into private networks and offering malicious or just nosy individuals the scope to examine private data exchanges.

Even when there are physical connections from a private network to the outside world, there are some connectivity constraints that can be applied to help bar the doors. On dial-up links caller ID detection or call-back facilities can limit unauthorized access, and permanent links to the Internet are, of course, both few and wellknown. Nevertheless, such physical security can provide only limited protection for the private network and gives no safeguard for data once it has left the privacy of the corporate network. Software safeguards are needed.

Some simple software configuration control measures can be made at a physical level to enhance security. These techniques are referred to as *Access*

Control (see Section 14.3.1) and are used to limit the access available to a node or network by source IP address and by user ID and password.

14.2.2 Protecting Routing and Signaling Protocols

Chapter 5 focused on routing protocols that are used to distribute information about links and reachability so that IP packets can be successfully delivered. Although the information distributed by these protocols is not very sensitive (some network providers may want to keep their network topology secret), the protocols themselves are vulnerable to malicious attacks that can cause a breakdown in the services provided to end users—a denial of service attack. For example, if someone injected OSPF messages into a network that appeared to advertise a low-cost link from one side of the network to the other, this might find its way into the paths computed by all or most of the nodes in the network, causing traffic to be misrouted and possibly lost entirely.

Similarly, signaling and other IP-based protocols are used to manage network resources and to direct traffic along specific paths. These protocols are also vulnerable to attack, particularly from message replay or spoofing.

Routing and signaling protocols typically offer some security protection through authentication schemes (discussed in Section 14.3.2). These processes allow nodes to verify that a message really was sent by the partner from which it appears to come and, combined with sequence numbering schemes within the protocols themselves, also protect against replay attacks.

In practice, however, authentication is rarely used by deployed routing and signaling implementations. This has something to do with the configuration and management overheads (each node must know a security key for use when authenticating a message from each other node with which it might communicate), and also derives from the fact that network providers are able to apply other security schemes (physical, access control, and network level) to achieve the same ends.

14.2.3 Application-Level Security

For a majority of users the most important aspect of IP security is the protection of their user data as it is transferred across the network. It has been argued that the greatest facilitator of the recent exponential growth of the Internet has been the development of reliable and truly secure techniques for encrypting data. Without these mechanisms it is unlikely that Internet commerce would have become so popular because the sensitive nature of financial details (such as credit card numbers) limits the likelihood of people participating in online transactions across a public network.

Similarly, commercial information is widely regarded as being sufficiently sensitive that it should be protected from prying eyes. The fact that the overwhelming percentage of corporate data is so banal as to be tedious, and that this information outweighs valuable data to such an extent as to hide it quite efficiently, is rightly not considered as an effective security measure. The enthusiastic and determined criminal will be willing to wade through thousands of unimportant emails that set out lunch arrangements or discuss the latest ballgame, in the hope of discovering something of value. Companies, therefore, do not send information "in the clear" across the Internet. Data in file transfers and email exchanges are routinely encrypted as they are transferred between company sites over public networks.

Application security normally takes one of two forms. First, the user can encrypt or password protect the data to be transferred. Many applications such as word processors or file compression tools allow the user to require the use of a password before the file can be opened. This password is usually encrypted and stored within the file so that the receiving application requires the user to enter the same password before the data can be viewed. All nontrivial applications assume that the use of a password also implies that the data should be encrypted—this is wise since the application in question is not the only tool that could be used to examine the file.

The second application security mechanism is embedded in the applications that are used to transfer files or data as distinct from those that the user uses to operate on the data. For example, email programs often allow the user to encrypt individual emails so that the recipient must specify a password before being allowed to read what was sent. An equally important concept is secure exchange of data on web-based transactions—using security extensions to the Hypertext Transfer Protocol (HTTP) described in Chapter 12, it is possible for a user to send and receive sensitive data such as credit card numbers using encryption techniques.

A final concept that is popular, especially in email exchanges, is the digital signature. This technique allows the receiver to verify that the message being read was really sent by the apparent author, and that the message has not been modified by a third party.

Application security has strengths and weaknesses. It allows the user full control of the level of security applied to different transactions, but at the same time it allows the user to make a mistake or simply forget to take appropriate measures. Security modules must be implemented for each application since the rules and methods for applying security within each application protocol differ. Although these modules should be able to share common libraries for encryption and decryption, the applications are developed by different software companies and cannot necessarily rely on the presence of a third-party security library that the consumer would have to purchase and install. So each application may need to include its own security implementation. The alternative to this is offered by applying security across the board to all traffic at a lower layer, as described in the next two sections, but this may mean that more security is used than is actually required, slowing data transfer.

14.2.4 Protection at the Transport Layer

Transport protocols (described in Chapter 7) are responsible for delivering data on behalf of applications over an IP network. Different transport-layer protocols provide different levels of service, ranging from simple datagram dispatch to guaranteed in-order delivery of data.

The more sophisticated transport protocols include some elements of security that may be used by applications that do not, themselves, include modules that offer secure data transfer. This has the advantage of collecting together all security code in a single place (the transport stack module) and relieving applications from having to include such features. On the other hand, the security enhancements are not available in all transport protocols (for example, the popular User Datagram Protocol—see Section 7.2), which limits the popularity of transport-layer security.

Perhaps the biggest issue with transport-layer security is that it does not hide or protect important fields in the transport protocol headers. These fields indicate the source and destination of the data and give clues to the purpose of the message exchanges. Additionally, these unprotected fields are fundamental to the successful delivery of the data: if they are modified, the service may be interrupted.

14.2.5 Network-Level Security

The best alternative to application-level security is provided at the network layer where the whole content of IP packets, and even the IP headers themselves, are secured. This solution has many advantages. It is available for all IP traffic between any pair of end points, so it is useful to protect application data and also can be used to secure routing and signaling exchanges.

IP security (IPsec) is the mainstay of network level security and is described in Section 14.4. It is used to authenticate the sender of messages, to verify that message data has not been tampered with, and to hide information from prying eyes. IPsec is used for a wide range of applications, from protecting signaling and routing flows to providing Virtual Private Networks (VPNs) across the public Internet, as described in Chapter 15.

14.3 Components of Security Models

Security is achieved by building on the three distinct components described in the sections that follow. These are Access Control, in which limits are placed on the ability of a remote system or user to access the local system; authentication, in which the sender's identity and the data they send is authenticated to be genuine and free from modification; and encryption, in which the data is protected by a cipher. These components may be applied at all levels within the network.

14.3.1 Access Control

Access controls provide some of the simpler, but also most widespread, forms of security. Building on the concept of physical security, in which there is no connectivity to the outside world, access controls attempt to limit the users who can connect to a network, host, or application. The most familiar access control comes in the form of user names and passwords; before users can access a given application they must supply their name and password. In many operating systems and applications it is possible to configure user groups that have different privileges—users are assigned to a specific group and this limits what activities they can perform, with only the most privileged user group being able to access the most sensitive data and perform security-related tasks (such as assigning users to groups).

User name and password protection provides a simple lock and key mode of access control, and with it comes the problem of the user who leaves the door open. What happens if a user connects to an application and then walks away from the computer? Couldn't someone else happen by and use the other user's access permissions? To help combat this, many applications automatically log users out after a period of inactivity, and some even prompt users to reenter their password every so often regardless of activity.

But just as someone may lend a friend their ATM card and tell them their PIN so that they can be saved a trip to the bank, so user names and passwords may not be treated to particularly high levels of secrecy. In addition, passwords have to be remembered by users who may have accounts on many computers and so they tend to be common words or names. Programs used by hackers to attempt to gain access to computer systems by repeatedly trying user names and passwords take these human failings into account and are coded to try the default password settings first (things like "password") and then run through a series of well-known common passwords, before resorting to words selected from a dictionary. It is an interesting anthropological note that the password "NCC1701D" (the serial number of the starship *Enterprise*) is one of the most common passwords.

A further level of security can be achieved by using a dedicated computer or program known as a *firewall* to provide a security gateway between your private network and the outside world. The firewall is inserted between the private domain and the public network as shown in Figure 14.1. Normally, access to and from the Internet would be provided by connectivity to a gateway router, but in this case all exchanges between the private network and the Internet also go through the firewall router.

Firewalls are responsible for applying access control. They filter the IP packets that they forward based on many properties, including source and destination IP address, payload protocol, transport port number, and any other quality that the security manager deems appropriate. The simplest configurations are called *IP Access Lists* and are lists of remote IP addresses that are allowed to

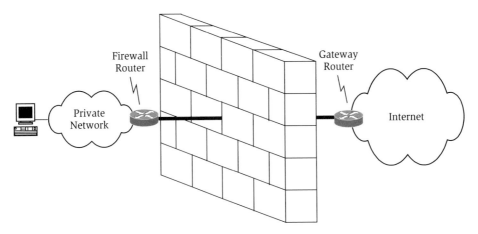

Figure 14.1 A firewall gateway provides additional security by filtering packets that are sent between a private network and the Internet.

source messages that will be passed into the private network through the firewall. Other common filters limit access only to designated hosts (destination IP addresses) and even then restrict incoming packets to those that carry a particular protocol (such as TCP) and target specific port numbers (such as port 80 for web access). Packets that are not allowed through are simply discarded—no special error message is returned because this would surely help a hacker discover a way to penetrate the security.

Filters applied at firewalls can be inclusive or exclusive (or both)—that is, they may be a list of packets that are allowed through, or a list of packets that will be denied access. There are advantages and disadvantages to each approach and a trade-off must be made between the cost of misconfigurations that allow inadvertent access and those that block legitimate use. The latter can normally be fixed quite simply and (provided that the security manager does not panic or overreact when responding to an annoyed user) it is usually considered better to build up a profile of users and packet types that are allowed access than to try to list each of the sources that are not allowed.

A further firewall model inserts an additional computer between the firewall router and the gateway router. This computer serves as an application gateway, and all connections from one side of the firewall to the other are terminated and regenerated at this node, as shown in Figure 14.2. The application gateway can be made additionally secure by applying access control on each side so that the only connections allowed are between the private network and the application gateway, and between the application gateway and the Internet. The application gateway maps connection requests onto connections to real hosts within the private network, hiding those nodes from the outside world—a feature similar to that supplied by HTTP proxies. Similarly, such gateways may

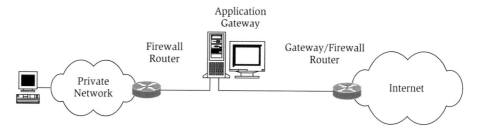

Figure 14.2 Application security may be enhanced by the use of an application gateway positioned between two firewall routers.

map application protocols or even network protocols, providing access to the Internet for proprietary or nonstandard networks.

Firewall security may actually be condensed to run on a single box so that an application gateway may be combined with a firewall router, or a home computer may run simple access control on its dial-up connection to the Internet.

Firewalls are a popular security solution because they are a simple concept and they provide a single point of security management. This allows the responsibility for security to be placed in the hands of a single person who has only to manage and configure a single computer. Such an approach is also cheap to implement, requiring the addition of only one network element and providing security through a simple software solution. On the other hand, this form of packet filtering may cause an undesirable bottleneck in the path of legitimate data traffic since all packets must pass through the one point of connection and each must be subject to a series of checks against the configured rules.

In the end, however, access control is of only limited efficacy. Malicious users may impersonate others either by stealing their user names and passwords, or by changing their IP addresses to get through the firewall. The very nature of the firewall includes the crack through which an intrusion may occur.

This means that full security must be achieved through more complex techniques described in the sections that follow.

---

fire wall *n*: a wall constructed to prevent the spread of fire

---

14.3.2 Authentication

Authentication serves two purposes: it validates that the user or the sender of a message is who they claim to be, and it ensures that the message received is genuine and has not been tampered with. At an application level, authentication is usually provided through a user ID and password exchange building on the application access control mechanisms already described. Application-level authentication is most often applied to transactions or sessions (that is, at a relatively high level), although individual components of transactions may be authenticated through the use of digital signatures.

At a per-message level in routing, signaling, and transport protocols, or in IP itself, authentication usually takes the form of a validation process applied to parts or the whole of the message being transported. The sender runs an algorithm over the whole of the message (usually in conjunction with a secret string called a *key*) and includes the output from the algorithm with the message that is sent. The receiver runs the same algorithm over the message using the same key and checks that its result is the same as the one it received. Any attempt by a third party to modify the message will cause the receiver's answer to differ from the one in the message. Since the key is not transmitted, and since it is known only to the sender and the receiver, the attacker cannot patch up the message to defeat the authentication process.

The use of sequence numbers within the protocol messages protected by an authentication scheme helps defeat replay attacks because a replayed message with an incremented sequence number will fail the authentication test, and a replayed message without a change to the sequence number will be rejected by the protocol.

14.3.3 Encryption

Authentication is all very well, but it does not protect the privacy of data that is sent through a public network or over public connections. This data is exposed and may easily be read by anyone using reasonably simple technology. The obvious risks to passwords, financial details, and confidential information require the use of other techniques to hide or encrypt the data that is sent.

Encryption techniques on the Internet are not really that dissimilar to those used in all of the best spy movies. Some formula is applied to the source data to convert it into a stream of apparently meaningless characters. This information can then be safely transmitted across the Internet to the recipient, who applies another formula to decrypt the message and discover the data.

Successful encryption algorithms rely on the fact that someone who intercepts a message cannot readily decrypt it. The first approach to this technique is to keep the encryption and decryption formulae secret—if the algorithms are good, no one will be able to interpret the messages that are exchanged. The problem with this technique is that the algorithm must be well known for the security process to have wide application, which defeats its efficacy as a primary security measure.

The solution is to enhance the encryption algorithms with keys. These keys provide additional input to the encryption and decryption processes, making them unique even when the algorithms are well known. The keys are private to the sender and receiver of the messages.

Encryption may be applied at any level within the network. In many cases, applications or users encrypt all or part of the data they want to send—this is, for example, how credit card details are exchanged during commercial transactions on the World Wide Web. In other circumstances, the transport or network protocols are asked to provide encryption on behalf of the applications—the most widespread encryption and authentication technique at the network layer is provided by IPsec, discussed in the next section.

Authentication and encryption may be applied independently or in combination.

14.4 IPsec

IP security (IPsec) defines a standard way in which IP datagrams may be authenticated or encrypted when they are exchanged between two nodes. The security architecture for IPsec is described in RFC 2401, and RFC 3457 explains some common scenarios in which IPsec may be used. The protocol extensions for IPsec are defined in RFC 2402 (authentication) and RFC 2406 (encryption) and are explained in the sections that follow.

Secure packet exchanges using IPsec occur between a pair of cooperating nodes that establish a *Security Association* (SA). The SA essentially defines the type of security (authentication and/or encryption), the algorithms, and the keys to be applied to all IP packets exchanged between the nodes. As a point of precision, SAs are actually unidirectional, but it would be normal to instantiate them in both directions using the same characteristics with the possible exception of the keys, which might be different for each direction.

IPsec may be deployed end-to-end between host computers or across the network by proxy security servers on behalf of the hosts. That is, the SA may extend from data source to data sink, or may cover only part of the path between the two end points.

14.4.1 Choosing Between End-to-End and Proxy Security

Figure 14.3 shows the difference between end-to-end security and the proxy model. In the end-to-end case, the Security Association extends from the source to the destination and packets are fully encrypted or authenticated along the whole length of their path. This is the maximally secure solution.

For proxy security, a node part-way along the data path (a proxy) is responsible for applying IPsec to the IP packets and transferring them to another proxy which validates or decrypts the packets before passing them on to the final destination.

Proxy security has the obvious drawback that the packets are exposed for part of their path. However, it has many positive points that make it useful and popular. First, it reduces the implementation complexity at the end points—in the proxy model, one proxy may serve multiple end points, allowing the security code to be concentrated just on the proxies. This process extends to allow a

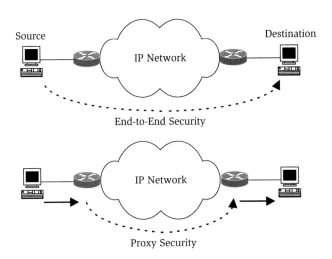

Figure 14.3 IPsec may be applied in an end-to-end model or across only part of the network using proxy security.

single SA to carry traffic belonging to multiple data streams. This is possible if several hosts served by one proxy want to communicate with other hosts served by a second proxy. In this mode of operation, the IP packets from the data streams are grouped together and treated to the same security measures and forwarded to the same remote proxy as if down a *tunnel*.

A final advantage of the proxy model is that, in IPsec, it hides the source and destination IP information as packets traverse the core network. As will be seen in later sections, when packets enter the IPsec tunnel they are completely encapsulated in a new IP packet that flows between proxies—this increases the security by not exposing the end points of the data flows.

End-to-end security is used when individual remote nodes connect into networks (for example, when dialing in through a public network). Proxy security is used when using a public network to connect together networks belonging to the same company to form a virtual private network (VPN).

14.4.2 Authentication

As described in Section 14.3.2, authentication is achieved by processing the message with a key. This is illustrated in Figure 14.4. In IPsec the IP header, data payload, and a key are processed through an authentication algorithm to produce authentication data. This authentication data is placed in an *Authentication Header* inserted between the IP header and the payload. The Authentication Header is shown in Figure 14.5.

The hashing algorithm is performed on the whole IP packet to be transmitted— that is, the IP header and the data. The value generated by the hashing process

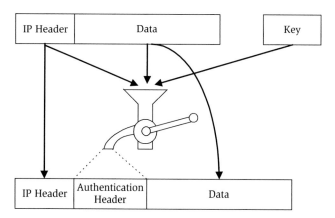

Figure 14.4 IPsec authentication is used to verify that the sender of a message is legitimate and that the message has not been tampered with.

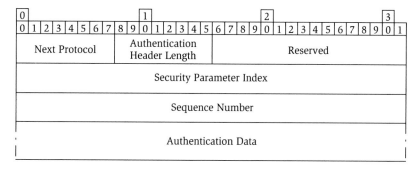

Figure 14.5 The IPsec authentication header is inserted into IP packets to carry authentication information.

is placed in the Authentication Data field of the Authentication Header and transmitted to the destination. At the destination, the algorithm is performed again on the IP header and the data (but not the Authentication Header) using the same key. The result is compared with the transmitted authentication data to verify that no modification of the packet has occurred. This process and the format of the IPsec Authentication Header is described in RFC 2402.

Any authentication algorithm may be used, and plenty are defined. IPsec places a requirement on implementations that at least the Message Digest Five (MD5) algorithm is supported (see Section 14.7.1). It is (obviously) a requirement that both the sender and the receiver know which authentication algorithm is in use, and the values of the keys. IPsec does not discuss how this information is exchanged or configured, but Section 14.8 describes some possibilities.

One issue should be immediately apparent: some of the values in the IP header may legitimately be modified as the packet traverses the network and this will invalidate the authentication process. To avoid this problem the hashing algorithm is applied to the IP packet with certain key fields (TTL, ToS, checksum, and flags) set to zero. Further, the next protocol field is modified by the insertion of the Authentication Header; it is set to 51 (0x33) to indicate that an Authentication Header is present. The hashing algorithm is applied to the IP packet at the source before the insertion of the Authentication Header, and at the destination it is performed after the removal of the Authentication Header. The Authentication Header, shown in Figure 14.5, carries the payload protocol for restoration into the IP header, and indicates its own length for ease of removal.

One last observation should be made about the insertion of an Authentication Header. The presence of the header may cause the IP packet size to exceed the MTU size for the link into the network. If fragmentation is not allowed, the size of source data packets must be modified before authentication can be used because, otherwise, the packet may be fragmented. Note that fragmentation at the source node is no different from fragmentation within the network—it is performed on the whole IPsec packet, including the Authentication Header (there is no question of one Authentication Header per fragment) and so the fragments must be reassembled at the destination before they can be authenticated.

The Authentication Header (shown in Figure 14.5) includes a Security Parameter Index (SPI) that is used to identify the Security Association that manages this packet. Given a source and destination address pairing, the SPI uniquely identifies the security context, telling the receiver which algorithms and keys to apply. The SPI should be generated randomly to reduce predictability and to limit the chances of a restarting node accidentally reusing an old Security Association. The SPI values 0 through 255 are reserved. A Sequence Number is designed to help prevent denial of service attacks in which malicious parties capture and replay packets or sequences of packets. The sequence number may help the destination node determine that received packets are duplicates or are out of order and discard them without further processing. Finally, the Authentication Header contains the output of the hashing algorithm in a field that will vary in length depending on the algorithm in use.

Authentication can be applied in the end-to-end model or using proxies: in each case the format of the message is the same.

14.4.3 Authentication and Encryption

When data is encrypted an encryption algorithm is fed with a stream of data and an encryption key. The output is a new stream of data that may be longer than the original data. When IPsec encryption is used in end-to-end mode, the data part of the source IP packet is encrypted and transported with the original IP header. The encrypted data is named the *Encapsulated Security Payload* (ESP) and is placed between an ESP header and trailer, as shown in Figure 14.6.

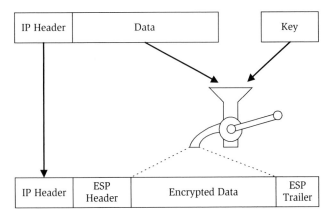

Figure 14.6 IPsec encryption may be applied to the IP payload data in the end-to-end security model.

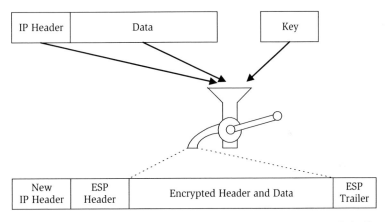

Figure 14.7 When IPsec encryption is used in the proxy security model the whole IP packet is encrypted and encapsulated in a new packet.

In proxy IPsec encryption the whole source IP packet (header and data) is encrypted as shown in Figure 14.7. A new packet is built with a new IP header that handles the passage down the tunnel from one proxy to the other. The data of this new packet is the encrypted source packet encapsulated between an ESP header and trailer.

Many encryption algorithms exist, and they operate on keys of varying complexity. A massive industry has grown up around the conflicting desires of privacy and transparency, conspiracy and law enforcement. Suddenly, mathematicians who devise these procedures discover that they can be popular if they work in this field. IPsec mandates that implementations must

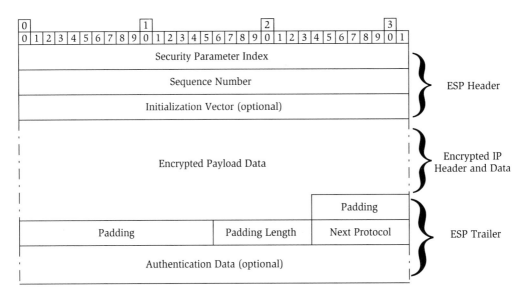

Figure 14.8 In IPsec encryption an IP packet is converted into an Encapsulating Security Payload packet.

at least support the Data Encryption Standard (DES). This algorithm is discussed in Section 14.7.

The IPsec encryption process is described in RFC 2406. The ESP packet format shown in Figure 14.8 starts off simply enough. After the normal IP header, which carries a next protocol value of 50 (0x32) to indicate that an ESP header is present, the ESP header begins with an SPI and Sequence Number that are used in the same way as they are in the authentication process described in the previous section. From here on, however, the packet seems to be a bit of a mess! It is easiest to understand how it is constructed by working from the end toward the beginning.

If authentication is in use in addition to encryption, this will be known to both the source and the destination and a piece of authentication data (the output from the hashing algorithm) with a well-known length will be appended to the packet. In front of this, comes a single byte that identifies the protocol of the encrypted payload. In the IP case described here this field does not appear to be necessary—surely we know that the payload is an IP packet?—but there is no reason this method of encryption and encapsulation shouldn't be used to carry non-IP traffic across an IP network. In our case, if proxy security is in use, the next protocol field is set to 0x04 to indicate IPv4, otherwise the next protocol field is copied from the next header field of the original IP header and indicates the payload type.

Continuing to work backwards through the packet, we reach a count of padding bytes. The padding is present at the end of the encrypted payload data and serves several purposes.

- It may be necessary to ensure that the Next Protocol field ends on a 4-byte boundary, which is an encoding requirement.
- Some encryption algorithms may function over data that is presented only in multiples of a certain number of bytes (such as 4, 8, or 16). Padding is therefore necessary to bring the number of bytes in the IP header and data up to the right number of bytes.
- It may be advantageous to vary the length of packets being sent across a network to better hide the operations being carried out. A trivial example could be the transfer of a password; although the encryption algorithm will hide the password, the packet length could expose the length of the password. Adding padding helps to mask this information.

Working further backwards we reach the encrypted data itself. This is the IP header and data that is being sent across the network. The last field we reach is the optional Initialization Vector. This field is specific to the encryption algorithm and includes any information needed by the decryption algorithm before it can operate—some algorithms include this field directly with the data and others extract specific meanings that guide their operations.

If IPsec is not used to protect the data at the network layer, then the next alternative is to use some form of protection at the transport layer, as described in the next section.

14.5 Transport-Layer Security

Transport-layer security is provided by the Transport Layer Security Protocol (TLS) defined in RFC 2246. This protocol is in fact two small protocols designed to run over TCP, being inserted between applications and the transport protocol usually through the use of the *Secure Sockets Layer* (SSL).

The TLS Handshake Protocol is used to correlate what encryption and authentication operations are used on the TCP connection—these may also include data compression. The TLS Record Protocol provides a mechanism for the exchange of handshake messages and is responsible for authentication and encryption of data exchanged over TCP connections. It uses standard algorithms to hash or encode the data that is passed to it over the secure sockets API. The sockets API allows applications to stream data in arbitrary blocks, but most encryption algorithms operate on records of a defined length, so the first thing the TLS Record Protocol must do is buffer data to build up complete records ready for processing. Conversely, large blocks of data must be segmented into records of 2^{14} bytes or less so that they may be properly handled. Figure 14.9 shows how the protocols are arranged and where the Sockets and Secure Sockets APIs fit in.

Annoyingly, the message formats in RFC 2246 are specified in a notation a little like "C" or XDR so that they appear as data structures. For most purposes this may be sufficient because the structures can simply be picked up, made to

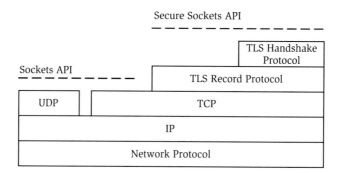

Figure 14.9 The Secure Sockets Layer provides an additional level of function above TCP.

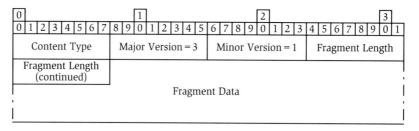

Figure 14.10 The Transport Layer Security record format.

Table 14.1 Defined Values for the TLS Record Content Type

Value	Meaning
20	Change of cipher specification
21	TLS alert
22	Handshake message
23	Data

compile, and used to build and decode messages, but it should be recalled that although structure packing rules may vary by compiler the message formats on the wire must remain constant. The format of the basic TLS record is shown in Figure 14.10. Records are sent as the payload of IP packets with the next header field set to 56 (0x38) to indicate TLS. The Content Type field indicates whether the record is carrying data or is being used to manage the process; the defined values are shown in Table 14.1. The protocol version number is 3.1 and is encoded in two fields (the value 3.1 is historic: TLS is based on a previous protocol called SSL, the protocol that provided the Secure Sockets Layer, which had reached version 3.0 when TLS version 1.0 was invented).

Each TLS Record message may contain a control message or data. If the data (or control message) is too large to fit into one message it must be fragmented and sent in a series of messages. Each fragment may not be larger than 2^{14} bytes after it has been subject to decompression. The use of data compression or data encryption for the payloads of the data messages is selected through configuration or through the use of the TLS Handshake Protocol described in the following section.

14.5.1 The Handshake Protocol

The TLS Handshake Protocol is optional in transport-layer security. It is used to dynamically negotiate and exchange security parameters (algorithms, keys, etc.) for use within the context of a TCP connection. If the Handshake exchanges are not used, security parameters must be exchanged through some other means (for example, manual configuration).

Handshake messages are carried in TLS Record Protocol exchanges. The record type 23 (handshake) is used, and one or more record fragments may be used to carry the message (note that the maximum handshake message length is 2^{24} and that a fragment can carry only 2^{14} bytes). Each message has a common format, giving the message type and length, and is then followed by message-specific fields. This is shown in Figure 14.11 with the Record Protocol header.

The Handshake Protocol is an end-to-end protocol—the messages are exchanged between the TCP TLS client and server across the network. The basic exchange of messages is initiated by the client sending a Client Hello, as shown in Figure 14.12. The Client Hello indicates the client's desire to establish a security session on this TCP connection, defines a session ID, and lists the security and compression algorithms the client supports and is willing to use.

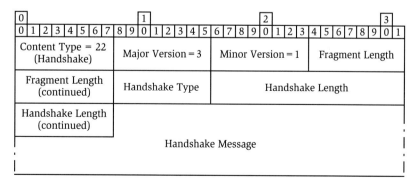

Figure 14.11 Transport Layer Security Handshake Protocol messages are carried in TLS records and have a common header.

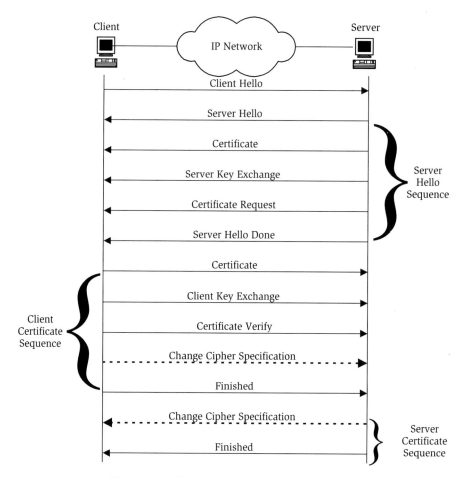

Figure 14.12 The TLS handshake message exchange.

The server responds with a series of messages that define the server's security parameters. The Server Hello message acknowledges the Client Hello and narrows the lists of security and compression algorithms down to just one of each. The Certificate and Server Key Exchange messages are optional and are used to convey security information (the identity of the server and the server's security keys, respectively) if required. Similarly, the server may optionally send a Certificate Request if it wishes the client to identify itself in a secure way. The server indicates that it has completed this sequence of messages by sending a server Hello Done message.

The client now embarks upon a sequence of messages to pass its certification information to the server. Some of the messages are optional, depending upon whether the server sent an optional request. The Certificate message identifies the client in response to a Certificate Request. The Client Key Exchange message is identical in format to the Server Key Exchange message and reports the client's security parameters. The client confirms that the certificate sent by the server (if one was sent) is acceptable by sending a Certificate Verify message. Now the protocol needs to switch from unencrypted message exchange (which it has used so far) to encoded messages. It wants to do this by sending a trigger message so that the receiver also knows that encryption is in use, so it sends a Change Cipher Spec message. But the Change Cipher Spec message is not part of the Handshake Protocol; it is a TLS Record Protocol message. This allows it to be used even when the Handshake Protocol is not in use, for example, when encryption information is configured or exchanged in some other way. Once the use of the cipher has been enabled, the client completes its sequence of messages with a Finished message.

The ball is now back with the server. All that remains for the server to do is enable its own use of encryption for messages sent on the connection. It does this by sending a Change Cipher Spec message followed by a Finished message.

The order of messages shown in Figure 14.12 is important. The only permissible deviation is when an optional message is not included.

The sequence of messages shown in Figure 14.12 may also be reinitiated during the life of a secure TCP connection to renegotiate the security parameters. This may be desirable if the transactions carried on the connection suddenly reach a point at which additional security is needed, or if the connection has been open for a configured time such that the client or server believes it is time to change the key. In this case the client may send a new Client Hello to restart the exchange, or the server may send a Hello Request to trigger the client to send a Client Hello.

Figure 14.13 shows the TLS Handshake Protocol messages converted from their pseudo "C" to byte format. Many of the fields are enumerations of options or types or encryption options and the lists of values can be looked up in RFC 2246. Certificates and the distinguished names of certifying authorities are taken from the ISO's X.509 directory standards. Keys, key information, and signatures are dependent on the encryption algorithms and options selected.

The Finished message bears a little further examination. The message exchange up to and including the Change Cipher Spec message has been in the open (assuming that a lower-layer security system such as IPsec is not in use), which means that it was vulnerable to interception and manipulation. What is needed is a way to verify that the received messages were identical to those sent. The Finish message does this by performing an authentication hashing algorithm on the combined byte stream produced by concatenating together some of the messages and security information already exchanged. The 12-byte authentication data in the Finish message is the output of the Pseudo Random Function (PRF) defined in RFC 2246. The input to the PRF is as follows.

- The Master Secret (a 48-byte secret key shared between the end points).
- A Finished Label (the text string "client finished" or "server finished").

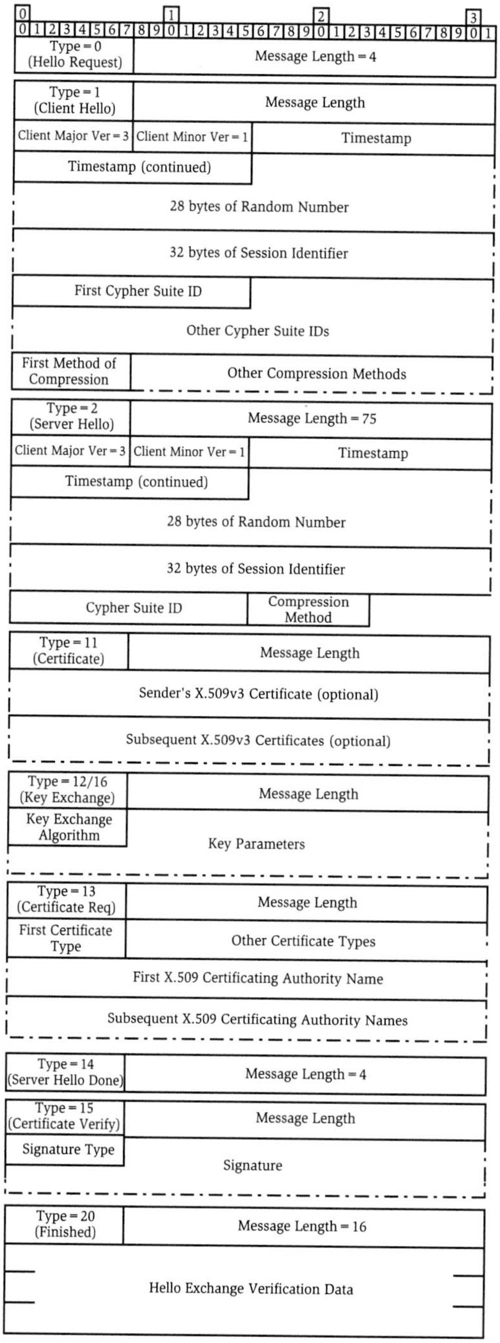

Figure 14.13 Transport Layer Security Handshake Protocol messages are specified in RFC 2246 using a notation similar to "C," but may be converted into byte format.

- The output of two distinct hashing algorithms, each applied to the concatenation of all of the Handshake Protocol messages sent by this node on this session up to this point in time (not including this message, not including the Record Protocol headers, and not including the Hello Request message if it was sent).

The two hashing algorithms used are Message Digest Five (MD5) and Secure Hash Algorithm One (SHA-1).

14.5.2 Alert Messages

TLS alert messages have the fragment length set to 2 and carry 2 bytes of error information. The first byte indicates the severity of the error (1 means warning, 2 means fatal), and the second byte indicates the specific error using a value from Table 14.2. When an error is detected on a TLS connection, the node identifying the problem sends an alert message—this may be in response to a message that forms part of the handshake procedure, or may report an error with data exchanged on the connection. When a fatal alert message is sent or received, both parties immediately close the connection without sending any further messages and are required to forget any session-identifiers, keys, and secrets associated with the connection.

14.6 Securing the Hypertext Transfer Protocol

Securing the Hypertext Transfer Protocol (HTTP), described in Chapter 12, was an important advance in Internet security that made possible much of today's web-based commerce in a secure environment. Without a solution to security issues in the World Wide Web it is unlikely that the Internet would have grown beyond a giant information base, and online shopping as we know it would never have taken off.

Two strategies have evolved. The first is called the Secure Hypertext Transfer Protocol (S-HTTP) and offers a set of extensions to HTTP. The second approach, called HTTPS, involves running standard HTTP communications over TCP using the Secure Sockets Layer (SSL).

S-HTTP is described in RFC 2660, and is a set of extensions to HTTP described in Chapter 12. A single new HTTP method is defined; the *Secure* method allows clients to initiate an exchange of encryption and key information so that subsequent data messages may be encrypted or digitally signed. RFC 2617 offers client–server identity authentication functions through additional fields for standard HTTP methods.

S-HTTP is less used than HTTPS because S-HTTP leaves the HTTP message headers exposed. In HTTPS, the entire HTTP communication is packaged within SSL (see Section 14.5) and is completely encrypted. For HTTPS operations, URLs

Table 14.2 TLS Alert Messages Carry a Descriptive Error Code

Error Code	Severity	Meaning
0	Warning	close_notify: Notifies the recipient that the sender will not send any more messages (data or control) on this connection. The receiver should respond with a close_notify to terminate the session. This is a warning message so that the remote node may respond.
10	Fatal	unexpected_message: Indicates a protocol violation.
20	Fatal	bad_record_mac: Authentication of a received record has failed.
21	Fatal	decryption_failed: Decryption failed because of the format of the encrypted data.
22	Fatal	record_overflow: The record length received was too large.
30	Fatal	decompression_failure: Decompression produced an invalid record (for example, the record length was too large after decompression).
40	Fatal	handshake_failure: Could not agree on an acceptable set of connection parameters during the handshake process.
42	Warning	bad_certificate: A certificate was corrupt.
43	Warning	unsupported_certificate: An unsupported certificate type was used.
44	Warning	certificate_revoked: A certificate was revoked by the signer.
45	Warning	certificate_expired: A certificate has expired.
46	Warning	certificate_unknown: A certificate was unusable for some other reason.
47	Fatal	illegal_parameter: Some parameter exchanged during the handshake process was out of range or unknown.
48	Fatal	unknown_ca: A Certificate Authority certificate could not be matched.
49	Fatal	access_denied: The certificate is valid but does not afford the requested access according to local policy.
50	Fatal	decode_error: A message could not be decoded because of an encoding error or a parameter out of range.
51	Warning	decrypt_error: A handshake cryptographic operation failed, including being unable to correctly verify a signature, decrypt a key exchange, or validate a finished message.
60	Fatal	export_restriction: An attempt to export a key failed.
70	Fatal	protocol_version: Recognized but unsupported protocol version received.
71	Fatal	insufficient_security: Specific handshake failure when the server requires more security than the client has offered.
80	Fatal	internal_error: An internal programming error or resource shortage has occurred.
90	Warning	user_canceled: Abort the current handshake process. Should be followed by a close_notify.
100	Warning	no_renegotiation: Reject cipher renegotiation for an active session.

are prefixed with *https://* and port number 443 is used in place of the standard HTTP port 80.

When users start to access a secure web site using HTTPS they usually see a dialog box prompting them to accept the certificate sent from the web server. This implies a close implementation tie-up between the HTTP engine and the protocol stack implementing the SSL.

Securing HTTP communications allows users to build semiprivate web sites, which lets companies provide web-based access to their corporate email systems. This has been developed so that many companies offer their customers selective access to sensitive sites that hold customer-specific details shared between the supplier and consumer (such as, databases of reported faults, software patches for download, etc.).

14.7 Hashing and Encryption: Algorithms and Keys

Hashing and encryption algorithms are used for the most basic authentication procedures and for the highest security encryption of data. Each algorithm takes as input the raw data to be transmitted and a key. A key is a binary value that is used to lock and unlock the data. Keys vary in length from 32 bits to 256 bits or larger—for any specific algorithm it is generally the case that the larger the key, the more difficult it is to crack the encryption code.

As described in the preceding sections, authentication algorithms use the data and key to generate an authentication code. The receiver can run the same algorithm with the same key on the received data and compare the resulting authentication code to the one transmitted with the data. Encryption algorithms use the key to convert the data into a series of apparently meaningless bytes that the receiver must unscramble before they can be used. The data may be unscrambled using a paired algorithm and a partner key corresponding to those used for encryption, or the same algorithm and the same key may be used, depending on the encryption technique employed.

The most basic hashing algorithm is the cyclic redundancy check (CRC) described in Chapter 2. CRC is used in IP to validate that data has not been accidentally modified, for example, by errors during the transmission process. It is valuable for that purpose and will discover a very high proportion of accidental errors, but it is absolutely no use as an authentication algorithm since there are well-known procedures for modifying the CRC value for any change made to the data. More complex hashing algorithms are used for authentication in conjunction with a security key.

Encryption algorithms tend to be more complex and have longer keys. The standard minimum encryption algorithm is the Data Encryption Standard (DES) described in Section 14.7.2, but many more sophisticated approaches have been developed. There are two keying techniques used in cryptography; the *secret key* model has already been described and functions by the sender and receiver both knowing (and keeping secret) the key so that they can successfully exchange data. This is a fine procedure, but as already explained it requires some form of key exchange between end points. This is not only insecure, because someone might intercept this key exchange, but it is dependent on the trustworthiness of both the sender and the receiver since, for example, once the receiver knows the sender's key he can impersonate the sender or intercept other encrypted data.

Curiously, the solution to this problem is to make the key public knowledge. In *public key* cryptography one algorithm but two keys are used: one to encrypt the data and the other to decrypt it. One of these keys is freely advertised but the other is kept secret. So, for example, a node wishing to receive secret data would advertise the encryption key to use, but would keep secret the decryption key. The remote node would use the advertised (public) encryption key to encode the data and would send it to the recipient where it could be decoded using the secret key. Conversely, a node wishing to prove its identity will advertise a public decryption key, but keep secret its encryption key—in this way anyone can decode its *digital signature* and know that only the owner of the secret encryption key can have sent the message. This technique can be extended to message digest techniques to provide public key authentication.

In practice, algorithms that use two keys (*dual key algorithms*) are more complex and slower to operate since they require each byte of data to be handled many times. This makes them far from ideal for use in bulk data transfer, but fortunately a solution exists. A secret key algorithm is used to encode the data (that is, it is encrypted using an algorithm that can be encoded and decoded using a single key) and the secret key itself is encrypted using a public key algorithm. The encrypted secret key need only be exchanged once for each transaction and can be used to decode all of the data.

14.7.1 Message Digest Five (MD5)

The simplest authentication hashing algorithm in popular use is the Message Digest version 5 (MD5) algorithm described in RFC 1321; RFC 1828 describes how to apply the algorithm to authentication. Support for this algorithm is mandated in several protocols (such as RSVP) and must be supported as a minimum requirement of IPsec. MD5 produces a 16-byte authentication code (the *message digest*) from data of any length with or without a key of any length. Without a key, MD5 can be used like the CRC to detect accidental changes in data. It can be applied to individual messages, data structures, or entire files. But since a hacker could readily recompute the message digest and so mask a malicious change to the data, a key is used (appended or prepended to the data) to make it impossible for a third party to determine the correct MD5 authentication code of a modify packet.

Figure 14.14 shows some sample code to implement the MD5 authentication algorithm by way of evidence that even the simplest authentication algorithms

```
/* Function to perform MD5 digest hashing on a buffer with a key */
/* Returns the message digest in a 16 byte string that is supplied */
void MD5(char *input_buffer, char* input_key, char *output_digest)
{
  u_int32 digest[4];
  u_int32 bit_count[2];
  u_char work_buffer[64];
  u_char pad_buffer[64]={
        0x80, 0, 0, 0, 0, 0, 0, 0, 0, 0, 0, 0, 0, 0, 0, 0,
          0, 0, 0, 0, 0, 0, 0, 0, 0, 0, 0, 0, 0, 0, 0, 0,
          0, 0, 0, 0, 0, 0, 0, 0, 0, 0, 0, 0, 0, 0, 0, 0,
          0, 0, 0, 0, 0, 0, 0, 0, 0, 0, 0, 0, 0, 0, 0, 0};
  u_char bit_string[8];
  u_int32 _buffer_len=strlen(input_buffer);
  u_int32 key_len=strlen(input_key);
  u_int32 pad_len;
  u_int32 ii, jj;

  /* Pre-initialize the digest to well-known values */
  /* Placing the low order bytes first, the 16 bytes */
  /* should be filled with 0x01 23 45 67 89 ab cd ef */
  /*             0xfe dc ba 98 76 54 32 10 */
  digest[0]=0x67452301;
  digest[1]=0xefcdab89;
  digest[2]=0x98badcfe;
  digest[3]=0x10325476;
  /* initialize the bit counts */
  bit_count[0]=0;
  bit_count[1]=0;

  /* Start the digest with the key */
  if (key_string !=NULL) {
    _MD5_work(&digest, &bit_count, key_string, key_len, &work_buffer);
    /* Pad to the next 64 byte boundary */
    pad_len=key_len % 64;
    if (pad_len !=0)
      _MD5_work(&digest, &bit_count, &pad_buffer, pad_len, &work_buffer);

  /* Perform first pass MD5 calculation on the string */
  _MD5_work(&digest, &bit_count, input_buffer, buffer_len, &work_buffer);

  /* Update the digest with the key (again) */
  if (key_string !=NULL)
    _MD5_work(&digest, &bit_count, key_string, key_len, &work_buffer);

  /* Pad the combined string to a length of 56 modulo 64 */
  /* The value 56 leaves sufficient space for the 8 byte string */
  /* representation of the message length */
  /* Update the digest with the padding */
  pad_len=(bit_count[0]/8) % 64;
  if (pad_len>56)
    pad_len=pad_len - 56;
```

Figure 14.14 Continued

```
    else
      pad_len=56+64 - pad_len;
    if (pad_len !=0)
      _MD5_work(&digest, &bit_count, &pad_buffer, pad_len, &work_buffer);

    /* Convert the bit count into a string and add it to the digest */
    /* This fits into the last 8 bytes of the work buffer */
    for (ii=0; ii < 2; ii++)
      for (jj=0; jj < 4; jj++)
        bit_string[jj+(ii * 4)]=(u_char)((bit_count[ii] >> (jj * 8)) &0xff);
    MD5_work(&digest, &bit_count, &bit_string, 8,&work_buffer);

    /* Move digest data into the output string */
    for (ii=0; ii<4; ii++)
      for (jj=0; jj<4; jj++)
        output_digest[jj+(ii * 4)]=(u_char)((digest[ii] > (jj * 8)) &0xff);

    return;
}

/* Function to process a buffer in 64 byte pieces */
void _MD5_work (u_int32 *digest, u_int32 *bit_count, u_char- *input_buffer,
                u_int32- len, u_char- *work_buffer)
{
  u_int32 bytes_needed;
  u_int32 offset=0;
  /* Is the work buffer partially full? */
  /* If so, how many bytes are needed to fill it up? */
  bytes_needed=64 - ((bit_count[0]/8) % 64);

  /* Update count of number of bits added by this string */
  bit_len=len * 8;
  bit_count[0] +=bit_len;
  if (bit_count[0] < bit_len)
    bit_count[1] ++;
  /* Don't forget to handle the case where len * 8 overflows */
  bit_count[1] += ((u_int32)len >> 29);

  /* Try to fill up the work buffer and do the hash */
  while (len > bytes_needed) {
    memcpy(work_buffer[64 - bytes_needed], input_buffer[offset], bytes_needed);
    _MD5_hash(digest, work_buffer);
    len-=bytes_needed;
    offset+=bytes_needed;
    bytes_needed=64;
}

  /* Copy any spare bytes into the work buffer */
  if (len > 0) {
    assert(len < 64);
    memcpy(work_buffer[0], input_buffer[offset], len);
}
```

```
  return;
}

/*  Function to do the actual MD5 hashing  */
void _MD5_hash(u_int32 *digest, u_char *work_buffer)
{
  u_int32 work_digest[16];
  u_int32 ii, jj;
  u_int32 a = digest[0], b = digest[1], c = digest[2], d = digest[3];

  /*  Convert 64 bytes of buffer into integers  */

  for (ii=0; ii < 16; ii++)
    for (jj=0; jj < 4; jj++)
      work_digest[ii]+=( (u_int32)(work_buffer[(ii * 4)+jj]) << (jj * 8) );
  /*  Now do the ghastly MD5 magic  */
  /*  The following code is taken from RFC1321 and is copyright RSA Data Security,  */
  /*  Inc. to which the following copyright notice applies.  */
  /*  Copyright (C) 1991-2, RSA Data Security, Inc. Created 1991. All rights reserved  */
  /*  License to copy and use this software is granted provided that it is identified  */
  /*  as the "RSA Data Security, Inc. MD5 Message-Digest Algorithm" in all material  */
  /*  mentioning or referencing this software or this function.  */
  /*  License is also granted to make and use derivative works provided that such  */
  /*  works are identified as "derived from the RSA Data Security, Inc. MD5 Message  */
  /*  Digest Algorithm" in all material mentioning or referencing the derived work.  */
  /*  RSA Data Security, Inc. makes no representations concerning either the  */
  /*  merchantability of this software or the suitability of this software for any  */
  /*  particular purpose. It is provided "as is" without express or implied warranty  */
  /*  of any kind.  */
  /*  These notices must be retained in any copies of any part of this documentation  */
  /*  and/or software.  */
#define F(x, y, z) (((x) &(y)) | ((~x) &(z)))
#define G(x, y, z) (((x) &(z)) | ((y) &(~z)))
#define H(x, y, z) ((x) ^ (y) ^ (z))
#define I(x, y, z) ((y) ^ ((x) | (~z)))
#define ROTATE_LEFT(x, n) (((x) << (n)) | ((x) >> (32-(n))))
#define FF(a, b, c, d, x, s, ac)                          \
        (a)+=F ((b), (c), (d))+(x)+(u_int32)(ac); \
        (a)=ROTATE_LEFT ((a), (s));                \
        (a)+=(b);
#define GG(a, b, c, d, x, s, ac)                          \
        (a)+=G ((b), (c), (d))+(x)+(u_int32)(ac); \
        (a)=ROTATE_LEFT ((a), (s));                \
        (a)+=(b);
#define HH(a, b, c, d, x, s, ac)                          \
        (a)+=H ((b), (c), (d))+(x)+(u_int32)(ac); \
        (a)=ROTATE_LEFT ((a), (s));                \
        (a)+=(b);
#define II(a, b, c, d, x, s, ac)                          \
        (a)+=I ((b), (c), (d))+(x)+(u_int32)(ac); \
        (a)=ROTATE_LEFT ((a), (s));                \
        (a)+=(b);
```

Figure 14.14 Continued

```
/*  Round 1  */
FF (a, b, c, d, x[ 0],  7, 0xd76aa478);
FF (d, a, b, c, x[ 1], 12, 0xe8c7b756);
FF (c, d, a, b, x[ 2], 17, 0x242070db);
FF (b, c, d, a, x[ 3], 22, 0xc1bdceee);
FF (a, b, c, d, x[ 4],  7, 0xf57c0faf);
FF (d, a, b, c, x[ 5], 12, 0x4787c62a);
FF (c, d, a, b, x[ 6], 17, 0xa8304613);
FF (b, c, d, a, x[ 7], 22, 0xfd469501);
FF (a, b, c, d, x[ 8],  7, 0x698098d8);
FF (d, a, b, c, x[ 9], 12, 0x8b44f7af);
FF (c, d, a, b, x[10], 17, 0xffff5bb1);
FF (b, c, d, a, x[11], 22, 0x895cd7be);
FF (a, b, c, d, x[12],  7, 0x6b901122);
FF (d, a, b, c, x[13], 12, 0xfd987193);
FF (c, d, a, b, x[14], 17, 0xa679438e);
FF (b, c, d, a, x[15], 22, 0x49b40821);

/*  Round 2  */
GG (a, b, c, d, x[ 1],  5, 0xf61e2562);
GG (d, a, b, c, x[ 6],  9, 0xc040b340);
GG (c, d, a, b, x[11], 14, 0x265e5a51);
GG (b, c, d, a, x[ 0], 20, 0xe9b6c7aa);
GG (a, b, c, d, x[ 5],  5, 0xd62f105d);
GG (d, a, b, c, x[10],  9, 0x2441453);
GG (c, d, a, b, x[15], 14, 0xd8a1e681);
GG (b, c, d, a, x[ 4], 20, 0xe7d3fbc8);
GG (a, b, c, d, x[ 9],  5, 0x21e1cde6);
GG (d, a, b, c, x[14],  9, 0xc33707d6);
GG (c, d, a, b, x[ 3], 14, 0xf4d50d87);
GG (b, c, d, a, x[ 8], 20, 0x455a14ed);
GG (a, b, c, d, x[13],  5, 0xa9e3e905);
GG (d, a, b, c, x[ 2],  9, 0xfcefa3f8);
GG (c, d, a, b, x[ 7], 14, 0x676f02d9);
GG (b, c, d, a, x[12], 20, 0x8d2a4c8a);

/*  Round 3  */
HH (a, b, c, d, x[ 5],  4, 0xfffa3942);
HH (d, a, b, c, x[ 8], 11, 0x8771f681);
HH (c, d, a, b, x[11], 16, 0x6d9d6122);
HH (b, c, d, a, x[14], 23, 0xfde5380c);
HH (a, b, c, d, x[ 1],  4, 0xa4beea44);
HH (d, a, b, c, x[ 4], 11, 0x4bdecfa9);
HH (c, d, a, b, x[ 7], 16, 0xf6bb4b60);
HH (b, c, d, a, x[10], 23, 0xbebfbc70);
HH (a, b, c, d, x[13],  4, 0x289b7ec6);
HH (d, a, b, c, x[ 0], 11, 0xeaa127fa);
HH (c, d, a, b, x[ 3], 16, 0xd4ef3085);
HH (b, c, d, a, x[ 6], 23, 0x4881d05);
HH (a, b, c, d, x[ 9],  4, 0xd9d4d039);
HH (d, a, b, c, x[12], 11, 0xe6db99e5);
HH (b, c, d, a, x[ 2], 23, 0xc4ac5665);
HH (c, d, a, b, x[15], 16, 0x1fa27cf8);
```

```
/*  Round 4  */
II (a, b, c, d, x[ 0],  6, 0xf4292244);
II (d, a, b, c, x[ 7], 10, 0x432aff97);
II (c, d, a, b, x[14], 15, 0xab9423a7);
II (b, c, d, a, x[ 5], 21, 0xfc93a039);
II (a, b, c, d, x[12],  6, 0x655b59c3);
II (d, a, b, c, x[ 3], 10, 0x8f0ccc92);
II (c, d, a, b, x[10], 15, 0xffeff47d);
II (b, c, d, a, x[ 1], 21, 0x85845dd1);
II (a, b, c, d, x[ 8],  6, 0x6fa87e4f);
II (d, a, b, c, x[15], 10, 0xfe2ce6e0);
II (c, d, a, b, x[ 6], 15, 0xa3014314);
II (b, c, d, a, x[13], 21, 0x4e0811a1);
II (a, b, c, d, x[ 4],  6, 0xf7537e82);
II (d, a, b, c, x[11], 10, 0xbd3af235);
II (c, d, a, b, x[ 2], 15, 0x2ad7d2bb);
II (b, c, d, a, x[ 9], 21, 0xeb86d391);

/*  Finally update the digest and return  */
digest[0]+=a;
digest[1]+=b;
digest[2]+=c;
digest[3]+=d;
return;
}
```

Figure 14.14 Code to implement MD5 authentication.

are nontrivial. The guts of the algorithm are the RSA Data Security, Inc. MD5 Message-Digest Algorithm and are copied from RFC 1321. In the code, a top-level function, *MD5()*, is called with a data buffer and a key; it returns a 16-byte authentication code. This function processes the following strings in turn: the key, padding up to a 64-byte boundary, the data buffer, the key, and more padding. Each string is passed to *_MD5_work()*, which chops the data into 64-byte segments and passes them to *_MD5_hash()* to be processed through the algorithm.

MD5 has been discovered to have some security flaws, and work is ongoing to develop fixes and to devise more secure alternatives.

14.7.2 Data Encryption Standard (DES)

The Data Encryption Standard (DES) is the basic encryption algorithm mandated by IPsec. It was standardized by the U.S. National Bureau of Standards as Federal Information Processing Standards Publication 46–2 (superceding FIPS 46-1). DES is a federally approved mathematical algorithm for encrypting and decrypting binary-coded information.

DES uses a minimum 64-bit key of which 56 bits are available to define the key itself, and 8 bits (one per byte) are used to provide error detection on the key itself. The eighth bit in each byte is set to give parity in the byte—that is, it is set so that there are an even number of bits set to 1 within the byte.

Four modes of DES operation are defined, each providing an increased level of complexity and, thus, a better level of security. The Electronic Codebook (ECB) mode is the direct application of the DES algorithm to encrypt and decrypt data, deriving its name from the way secret messages used to be encoded and decoded by hand using a book of codes. The Cipher Block Chaining (CBC) mode is an enhanced mode of ECB that chains together blocks of cipher text to increase the size and therefore complexity of the encoded data. The Cipher Feedback (CFB) mode uses previously generated cipher text together with the message to be encoded as input to the DES algorithm, effectively chaining together the source message with a pseudorandom stream of bytes. The Output Feedback (OFB) mode is identical to CFB except that the previous output of the DES is used as input in OFB.

The DES algorithm is sufficiently complex to warrant its exclusion from this book. For a detailed description of the process refer to the National Institute of Standards and Technology web page listed at the end of this chapter.

14.8 Exchanging Keys

The generation and distribution of keys is fundamental to the operation of security systems. Historically, keys have been "randomly" generated at a central location and distributed to the encryption and decryption sites using the most reliable methods available. Often, this has involved writing the key down on a piece of paper that is then carried to the computers concerned, where it is manually entered into the system. Presumably, the message self-destructed a few seconds later.

Computers have made it possible to achieve a new degree of randomness in key generation and also to distribute keys more freely, but a significant problem is that keys cannot be encrypted when they are transmitted—if they were the user would not be able to interpret them. This means that the most sensitive piece of data, the key to all of the rest of the data, is sent in the open and is easy to intercept.

As described in Section 14.7, dual key cryptography algorithms allow the receiver to tell the sender a public key to use to encode secret data while retaining a separate secret key to decode the data. Since the public key is used only for encryption it does not matter that other users might view it. The secret key that is used to decrypt the messages is never exposed. This method can be used to encrypt other keys that need to be exchanged across public networks—a useful feature since dual key encryption algorithms are considerably more burdensome to operate if applied to all messages.

Key exchange is, therefore, an important aspect of Internet security and is the subject of several protocols. These protocols are also used to allow encryption/ decryption partners to negotiate which algorithms and features they will use on the Security Association they maintain.

The Internet Key Exchange (IKE) described in RFC 2409 is the merger of two previous protocols: the OAKLEY key exchange protocol (RFC 2412) and the Internet Security Association and Key Management Protocol (ISAKMP; RFC 2408). The reader might wonder why the merged protocol has a numerically lower RFC number than one of the constituent parts, but this is just an editorial issue as a batch of RFCs were all published at the same time. In all senses, IKE and ISAKMP/OAKLEY are identical.

14.8.1 Internet Key Exchange

ISAKMP provides the necessary negotiation facilities to agree on the level of security required and the algorithms to use. It also allows end points to exchange keys in the most secure fashion possible. It is also important to note that the protocol includes strong authentication of the end points so that a node may know for certain that it is really talking to the correct remote node—otherwise it would be possible for an impostor to participate in a conversation using all of the security techniques and being sent the prized data in a form that it would be able to decrypt.

The first job of ISAKMP is to establish the SA between the end points. This function is taken from ISAKMP and requires a message exchange over TCP or UDP using port number 500 to initiate the SA, negotiate options, exchange public keys, and exchange identity certification information. The elements here are not dissimilar to those described for the Transport Layer Security handshake protocol in Section 14.5.1, although the message flows are different.

Each ISAKMP message begins with a common message header that identifies the message and the SA to which it applies. The body of the message is made up of a series of payloads. The type of the first payload is indicated in the common header, and each payload announces the type of the subsequent payload if one exists. The format of the payloads depends on their type. Figure 14.15 shows the ISAKMP common header with two payloads. The initiator and responder cookies identify the SA at the end points. The protocol version defined by RFC 2408 is 1.1. The Message ID is a randomly generated number created by the sender of a request message and echoed in a response, allowing correlation with minimal risk of collision. The Message Length is given in bytes and covers the whole message, including the header. The Exchange Type indicates the ISAKMP mode of operation and so dictates which payloads are required—possible values for this field are shown in Table 14.3. Three flags are used as follows:

A – Authentication Only: The payloads of this message should be subjected to authentication but not encryption.

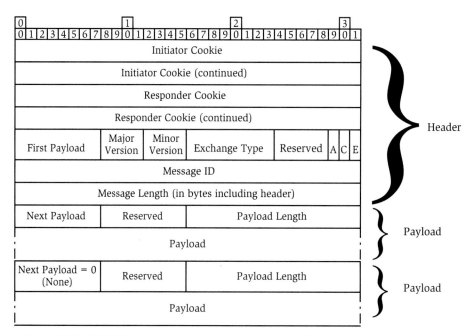

Figure 14.15 ISAKMP messages comprise a common header followed by one or more payloads.

C – Commit: Used to request (force) a complete message exchange before the contents of a message are put into use.

E – Encrypted: Indicates that the payloads are encrypted using the agreed encryption algorithm.

The First Payload field of the ISAKMP header indicates the type of the first payload element in the message body. Each payload element also contains a Next Payload field to indicate the type of the next payload. These types are listed in Table 14.4. Each payload also includes a Length field that indicates the length of the payload in bytes, including the Next Payload and Length fields.

The Exchange Types listed in Table 14.4 dictate how the ISAKMP end points exchange information—that is, which payload elements they send in which messages. The main differences are in how the elements are combined and therefore how much protection is available to the information that is sent. In general there is a trade-off between sending a few messages packed with unprotected information, and sending more messages in which the information in the later messages is protected by security negotiated by the earlier messages.

Figure 14.16 illustrates the messages exchanged when an SA is established using the Base Exchange. In step 1 the initiator sends a request carrying the Security Association, Proposal, and Transform payloads to show that it wants to

Table 14.3 ISAKMP Exchange Types Carried in the Common Message Header

Exchange Type	Meaning
0	None.
1	The Base Exchange is designed to allow the Key Exchange and Authentication-related information to be transmitted together. Combining the Key Exchange and Authentication-related information into one message reduces the number of round-trips at the expense of not providing identity protection.
2	The Identity Protection Exchange separates the Key Exchange from the Identity and Authentication-related information providing protection of the identity information at the expense of two additional messages since identities are exchanged under the protection of a previously established common shared secret.
3	The Authentication Only Exchange provides for the transmission of only authentication-related information. This exposes the authentication feature without the extra expense of computing keys. When using this exchange during negotiation, none of the transmitted information will be encrypted.
4	The Aggressive Exchange allows the security association, key exchange and authentication payloads to be transmitted together in a single message. This reduces the number of round-trips at the expense of not providing identity protection.
5	The Informational Exchange provides a one-way transmission of information that can be used for security association management.

establish a Security Association and to advertise the types of security it wants to apply and the algorithms that it supports. It also includes a Nonce payload to randomize the message. The responder checks that the Nonce is new and, if it is willing to establish a Security Association, responds with the precise subset of security options and algorithms that will be applied (step 2). The initiator then generates keys and sends them together with proof of its identity (step 3) and the responder completes the exchange with its keys and proof that it is who it says it is. The SA is now fully established and data transfer can begin. Note that since the identities and keys are sent on the same message, the identities cannot actually be protected by the security mechanisms.

The Identity Protection Exchange provides protection for the identity exchange. This is achieved by introducing an additional message exchange and sharing out the payloads as shown in Figure 14.17. The Nonce is moved from the initial exchange (steps 1 and 2) to the new exchange (steps 3 and 4) that also swaps keys. Once the keys are known they can be applied to all subsequent messages and so the identity exchanges (steps 5 and 6) can be protected by the authentication algorithms and sent along with a Hash payload.

Alternatively, the Aggressive Exchange cuts the number of messages sent to a bare minimum, as shown in Figure 14.18. In this case, the initiator reduces its

Table 14.4 ISAKMP Payload Types Identify the Components of Messages

Payload Type	*Meaning*
0	No more payloads.
1	Security Association Parameters. Sets the context for the establishment of a security association by specifying the use to which this association will be put. Contains a Domain of Interpretation (DOI) field that is set to the value 1 to indicate IPsec.
2	The Proposal payload defines the identity of the security association and includes the operational protocol (IPsec, TLS, OSPF, etc.) and the cookies (sometimes known as the Security Parameter Index or SPI) used in that protocol to represent the association.
3	The Transform payload suggests or agrees on the security processes and algorithms available or chosen for use on the security association.
4	The Key Exchange payload is used to exchange keys.
5	The end points identify themselves using the Identification payload, which is context specific depending on the Domain of Interpretation and the identity type chosen.
6	A Certificate payload provides strong authentication of the identity of an end point using one of a variety of standardized means.
7	The Certificate Request payload can be included in any message and requests that the remote node immediately respond with a message that includes a Certificate payload. (Compare with the Certificate Request in the TLS handshake protocol.)
8	The Hash payload is included in messages if the use of message authentication has been agreed to. The payload contains the output of the hashing algorithm applied to all or part of the message as negotiated using the Transform payload.
9	The transform payload may also negotiate the use of digital signatures. If so, the Signature payload is included in all messages to authenticate their origins.
10	A pseudorandom identifier is included in the Nonce payload to help prevent against replay attacks. The value of this identifier is changed for each instance of the security association, but is constant for the life of one association. Since the Nonce is only present in encrypted messages it is not externally visible and can be verified to be consistent on all messages in one association and a super-security-conscious end node can keep track of previous values to protect against an intruder replaying previous messages.
11	The Notification payload contains information data specific to the DOI context.
12	The Delete payload officially "contains a protocol-specific security association identifier that the sender has removed from its security association database and is, therefore, no longer valid." That is to say, it is used to terminate a security association.
13	ISAKMP messages may optionally include Vendor ID payloads to identify the communicating implementations.

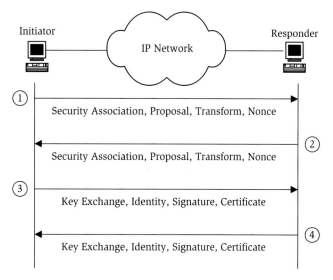

Figure 14.16 The ISAKMP messages and payloads exchanged during the establishment of a security association using the Base Exchange.

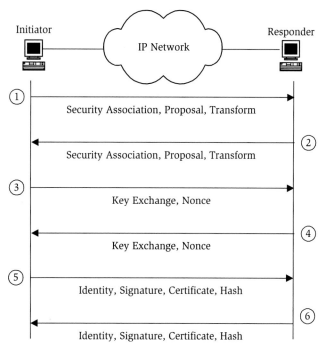

Figure 14.17 The ISAKMP Identity Protection Exchange provides additional security during the establishment of a security association.

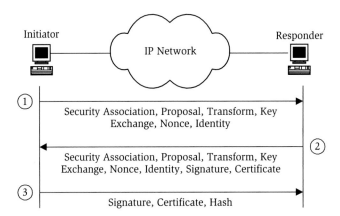

Figure 14.18 The number of messages exchanged to set up a security association can be kept down to just three using the Aggressive Exchange.

Proposal and Transform options so that the responder has no choice other than acceptance or refusal. The initiator can therefore generate its keys up front and it sends these on the initial message along with its identity (step 1). The responder replies with all information in one go (step 2), leaving the initiator to certify its identity and maybe use the authentication algorithm to protect this final stage (step 3).

> **nonce**\'nän(t)s\ *n* [**ME** *nanes*, alter. (fr. incorrect division of *then anes* in such phrases as *to then anes* for the one purpose) of *anes* one purpose, irreg. fr. *an* one, fr. **OE** *an*]: the one, particular, or present occasion, purpose, or use < for the ~ >

14.9 Further Reading

Personal Encryption Clearly Explained, by Pete Loshin (1998). IP Professional. This book provides a comprehensive introduction to the use of security in the Internet and other networks.

Virtual Private Networks—Making the Right Connection, by Dennis Fowler (1999). Morgan Kaufmann. Fowler describes the use of IPsec to provide secure connections between private networks. It also provides a good introduction to user authentication and to key management and exchange.

Applied Cryptography: Protocols, Algorithms, and Source Code in C, by Bruce Schneier (1995). John Wiley & Sons. This is a good starting point for those who want to dig deeper into the way that encryption is made to work.

The following lists show specific RFCs and other standards broken down by topic.

Security Considerations

RFC 1281—Guidelines for the Secure Operation of the Internet
RFC 2411—IP Security—Document Roadmap
RFC 2828—Internet Security Glossary

IPsec

RFC 2401—Security Architecture for the Internet Protocol
RFC 2402—IP Authentication Header
RFC 2406—IP Encapsulating Security Payload (ESP)
RFC 3457—Requirements for IPsec Remote Access Scenarios

Other Security Protocols

RFC 2246—The TLS Protocol Version 1.0
RFC 2617—HTTP Authentication: Basic and Digest Access Authentication
RFC 2660—The Secure HyperText Transfer Protocol
RFC 2818—HTTP Over TLS

Algorithms

Data Encryption Standard:[FIPS-46-2], from the U.S. National Bureau of Standards, http://www.itl.nist.gov/div897/pubs/fip46-2.htm

RFC 1321—The MD5 Message-Digest Algorithm
RFC 1828—IP Authentication Using Keyed MD5
RFC 2405—The ESP DES-CBC Cipher Algorithm with Explicit IV

Key Exchange

SKEME: A Versatile Secure Key Exchange Mechanism for Internet, by Hugo Krawcyzk. ISOC Secure Networks and Distributed Systems Symposium, San Diego, 1996.

RFC 2408—Internet Security Association and Key Management Protocol (ISAKMP)
RFC 2409—The Internet Key Exchange (IKE)
RFC 2412—The OAKLEY Key Determination Protocol

Chapter 15
Advanced Applications

This chapter examines some of the advanced uses for the Internet Protocol that are being developed and are gaining in importance in the world of networking. Some techniques have been around for a while and are well established, and others are more experimental. Each has a clear application within the Internet that makes it a technology that is particularly relevant to users.

Many uses of IP require a special technique whereby IP traffic is passed from one point in the network to another without examination by transit nodes. This process is called tunneling and it facilitates such functions as traffic engineering and mobile IP. This chapter examines several ways of packaging or encapsulating IP traffic so that it can be tunneled across an IP network.

Virtual Private Networks (VPNs) are a major growth area for Service Providers. VPNs allow customers' private networks to be joined together across the Internet, producing cost savings for the customers and the Service Providers as permanent leased lines are replaced with IP connectivity. VPNs introduce a series of challenges for management and security, and these problems have led to a considerable number of solutions. This chapter introduces some of these approaches and provides a comparison.

Mobile IP also presents some interesting challenges to Internet protocols. Internet protocols are often built on connection-oriented transport protocols and use hierarchical address spaces, but the very nature of mobile networking makes these transport and addressing features inappropriate. Such issues are closely related to, but distinct from, the problems addressed by IP telephony for cabled or wireless networks. All these topics are examined along with a discussion of how to carry voice over IP.

The invention of new applications is limited only by imagination, and many new ideas have recently been developed into protocols and products. In consequence, this chapter can only be an introduction to some of the topics. Suggestions for further reading are provided at the end of the chapter.

15.1 IP Encapsulation

Tunneling is a significant technology both in traffic engineering and in Virtual Private Networks (VPNs). A tunnel may be viewed by the end points as a *virtual wire*, making it appear that they are connected by a single hop from a management perspective. That is, the end points of the tunnel need only be aware of each other's addresses and can rely on some other technology to carry data between them.

There are many tunneling techniques that exist at the data-link layer, below the level of IP. These include the Layer 2 Tunneling Protocol (L2TP), X.25, Frame Relay, and ATM. These tunneling techniques are beyond the scope of this book, and the sections that follow concentrate on tunneling mechanisms that use IP to build the tunnels.

15.1.1 Tunneling Through IP Networks

Tunneling provides a convenient way to gather together IP packets that are to be treated in the same way (forwarded along the same route, given the same treatment under a traffic management regime, etc.). This makes the use of tunnels particularly pertinent in traffic engineering, as described in Chapter 8.

At the same time, tunneling can be used to separate addressing schemes within the IP world. This allows enterprise networks to use private address spaces when they communicate across the Internet without worrying about how the Internet itself or other enterprise networks also connected to the Internet will react to their addresses. In effect, the communicating enterprise networks are connected by a virtual wire across the Internet and their traffic cannot leak out to other domains. This form of tunneling provides the basis for VPNs described in Section 15.2.

Figure 15.1 provides a simple illustration of tunneling in use. The tunnel is routed along a path from router to router across the core network, but from the

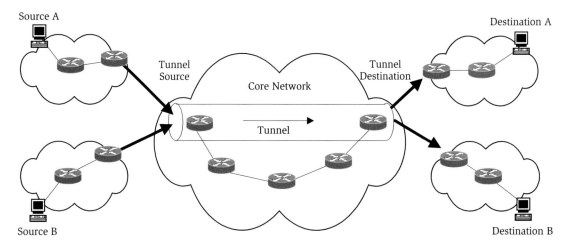

Figure 15.1 Tunneling in use.

perspective of the traffic passing from Source A to Destination A, and from Source B to Destination B the tunnel is a single hop from beginning to end. All the traffic entering the tunnel is treated in the same way through the core network.

15.1.2 Generic Routing Encapsulation

Generic Routing Encapsulation (GRE) was designed as a generic mechanism for carrying one protocol within another and was originally specified in RFC 1701 but later modified and simplified by RFC 2784. The basic mechanism shown in Figure 15.2 places a packet from the payload protocol into a packet of another protocol (the delivery protocol) preceded by a GRE header. This allows payload protocol packets to be carried across a network that supports only the delivery protocol.

The GRE header is shown in Figure 15.3. The Version field indicates the version of GRE. This is currently set to zero even though RFC 2784 represents the second version of GRE. This allows backwards compatibility with implementations of RFC 1701 since the only changes are the deprecation of options. These options would be carried in the first 4 bits of the Reserved-0 field of the header and, since an RFC 2784 implementation does not use these bits, if they are received as nonzero then they have been set by an RFC 1701 implementation and the packet must be discarded.

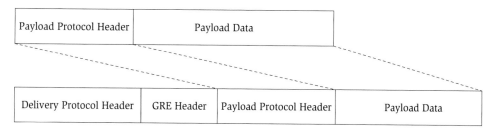

Figure 15.2 Generic Routing Encapsulation is used to encapsulate arbitrary protocols.

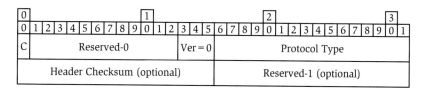

Figure 15.3 The Generic Routing Encapsulation header.

The Protocol Type field indicates the payload protocol. Values are chosen from the list of Ethertypes managed by the Internet Assigned Numbers Authority (IANA). The GRE header checksum is optional since there is such a very small amount of data in the GRE header. If it is present, the C-bit is set at the start of the header and an additional 16-bit reserved field is used to pad the header to a 32-bit boundary.

Since this book is devoted to the Internet, we must consider two scenarios. The payload protocol may be IP or the delivery protocol may be IP. In fact, there is no reason why both protocols should not be IP and this technique can be used to tunnel IP traffic through an IP network as an alternative to IP in IP encapsulation described in Section 15.1.3.

If the delivery protocol is IP, the next protocol field in the header carries the value 47 to indicate that a GRE header is present. If the payload protocol is IPv4, the Protocol Type field in the GRE header has the value 0x0800 (2048).

15.1.3 IP in IP Encapsulation

Perhaps the simplest form of tunnels is provided by IP in IP encapsulation. In this case, an IP packet entering the tunnel is simply given an additional IP header and sent on its way. The new header carries the source and destination addresses of the end points of the tunnel, and its payload is the entire original IP packet (header and payload). This process is defined in RFC 2003 and is the preferred way of delivering IP packets from a home station to a mobile station in Mobile IP (see Section 15.3). Figure 15.4 illustrates IP in IP encapsulation where packets between Hosts A and B, and between Hosts C and D are encapsulated

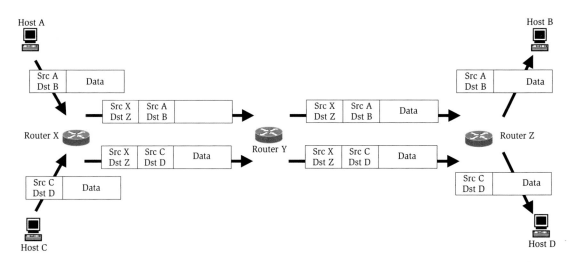

Figure 15.4 IP in IP tunneling showing how an additional IP header is imposed on the encapsulated packet giving the source and destination of the tunnel.

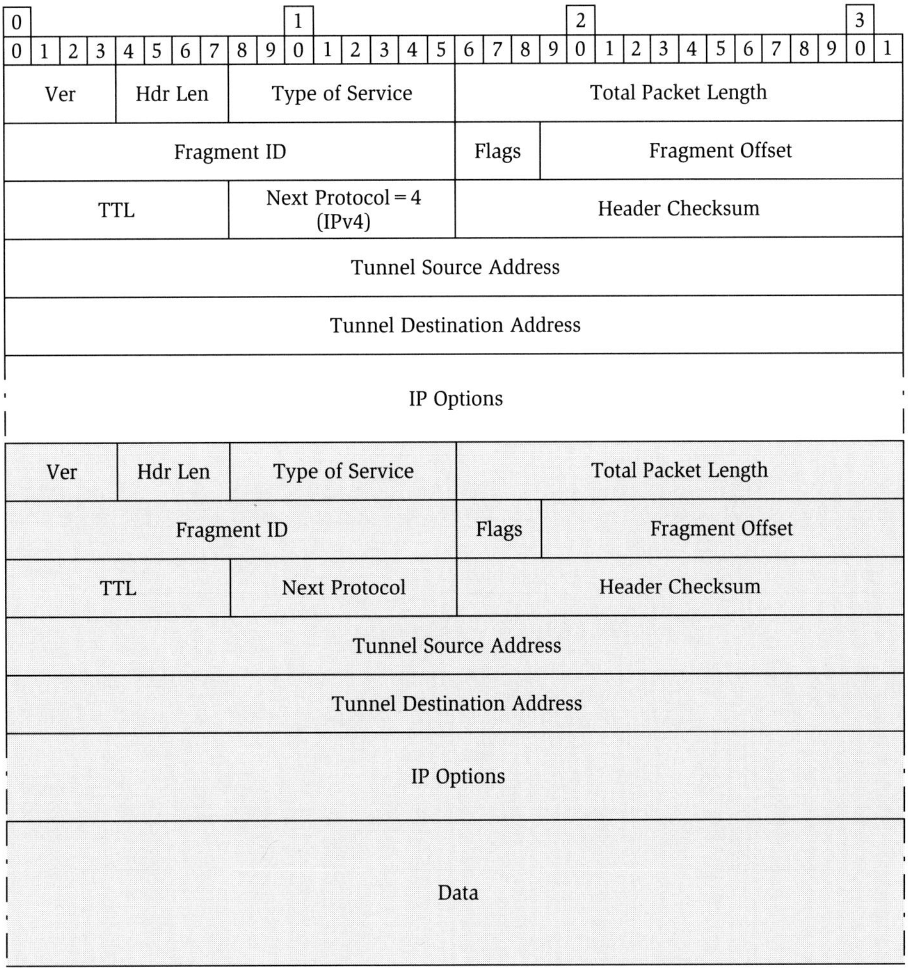

0										1										2										3	
0	1	2	3	4	5	6	7	8	9	0	1	2	3	4	5	6	7	8	9	0	1	2	3	4	5	6	7	8	9	0	1

Ver	Hdr Len	Type of Service	Total Packet Length
Fragment ID		Flags	Fragment Offset
TTL	Next Protocol = 4 (IPv4)	Header Checksum	
Tunnel Source Address			
Tunnel Destination Address			
IP Options			
Ver	Hdr Len	Type of Service	Total Packet Length
Fragment ID		Flags	Fragment Offset
TTL	Next Protocol	Header Checksum	
Tunnel Source Address			
Tunnel Destination Address			
IP Options			
Data			

Figure 15.5 IP in IP encapsulation places an additional IP header in front of the IP packet to be transmitted. The new header indicates that the payload is IP by using a next protocol value of 4.

to be passed down a tunnel from router X to Router Z. Figure 15.5 shows how the IP in IP packet is constructed.

Figure 15.5 shows an IPv4 packet encapsulated in IPv4. There is no reason why other combinations of IPv4 and IPv6 should not be used. In the example the new header is shown in white and the encapsulated packet (header and data) is shown in gray. The fields of the new header are partially inherited from the encapsulated packet but are mainly specific to the encapsulation. The Version, Fragment ID, Flags, and Fragment Offset are all handled as for normal IP within the context of the tunnel. The Header Length and Header Checksum in the new header apply to the new header, and the Total Packet Length indicates the size of the new packet (that is, the length of both headers and the data). The Type of Service byte is usually copied from the encapsulated packet but may be enhanced for specific treatment in the tunnel. The Time to Live (TTL) field is not copied from the encapsulated packet but is set to a value intended to control the life of the packet within the tunnel. When a packet is forwarded into a tunnel its TTL is decremented by one, treating the tunnel as a single hop. Sometimes an attempt is made to decrement the TTL of the encapsulated packet to reflect the tunnel length—this can only be done if it is known to what value the TTL of the encapsulating packet is set when it enters the tunnel and is not recommended by RFC 2003.

Most important, the protocol field of the encapsulating packet header is set to four to indicate that the payload is an IPv4 packet—that is, that IP in IP encapsulation is in use. As mentioned before, the source and destination addresses in the encapsulating packet header identify the end points of the tunnel, not the source and destination of the encapsulated packet. The IP options of the encapsulating packet are not usually copied from the encapsulated packet.

15.1.4 Minimal IP Encapsulation

One of the concerns about IP in IP encapsulation as described in Section 15.1.3 is the overhead introduced by adding a full IP header. Where the data payload per packet is low, this may result in an unacceptably high ratio of control information to transported data. On the other hand, where the data packets are large, the introduction of a whole new IP header may cause undesirable packet fragmentation.

One approach to reduce the overhead of IP in IP encapsulation is suggested in RFC 2004. In this case the original IP header is modified and a new Minimal Forwarding Header is inserted between the IP header and the IP data as shown in Figure 15.6.

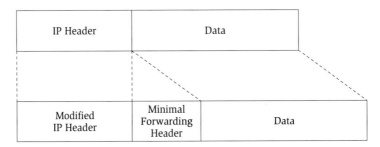

Figure 15.6 Minimal IP encapsulation modifies the IP header and inserts a Minimal Forwarding header.

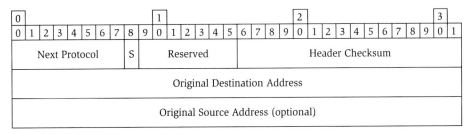

Figure 15.7 The Minimal Forwarding Header used in minimal IP encapsulation.

The modified IP header is a copy of the original IP header and only five fields are changed. The source and destination addresses are changed to reflect the start and end of the tunnel (just as in IP in IP encapsulation). The total packet length is incremented by the size of the Minimal Forwarding Header, and the checksum is recomputed on the new header. The Next Protocol field is set to 55 to indicate that minimal IP encapsulation is in use and that the data immediately after the IP header is a Minimal Forwarding Header.

Note that the TTL from the original header is copied into the modified header and is decremented for each hop along the tunnel. This differs from the behavior of IP in IP encapsulation.

The Minimal Forwarding header inserted between the modified header and the data is shown in Figure 15.7. It is used to preserve the fields from the original IP header that are overwritten when the header is modified. These three fields are the next protocol (indicating what protocol is contained in the payload data), and the original source and destination addresses. A checksum is also applied to the Minimal Forwarding Header to preserve its integrity.

A further optimization can be achieved where the start of the tunnel is also the source of the original IP packet since it is not necessary to pass the source address a second time. In this case the original source address is omitted from the Minimal Forwarding Header and the S-bit is set to indicate that the shorter form of the header is in use.

When the packet emerges from the end of the tunnel the Minimal Forwarding Header is removed and its fields are copied back into the main IP header. The header checksum is recalculated and the packet is forwarded toward its final destination.

15.1.5 Using MPLS Tunnels

Carrying IP traffic in MPLS Tunnels is described in Chapter 9. In summary, MPLS introduces a small MPLS header (the shim header) to encapsulate each IP packet, and the MPLS packets are switched based on the label values in that header. MPLS may be used to encapsulate any protocol, but can only be forwarded over MPLS-capable networks, which include ATM and Frame Relay networks.

Table 15.1 A Comparison of IP Tunneling Mechanisms

	GRE	IP in IP	Minimal IP Encapsulation	IPsec	MPLS
Security	None	None	None	Strong	Weak
Support for Traffic Engineering	No	No	No	No	Yes
Multiple Data Streams	Yes	Yes	Yes	No	Yes
Signaling Requirements	Data link	Data link	Data link	Key exchange	Full
Transit Node State	No	No	No	No	Yes
End Node State	No	No	No	Yes	Yes

15.1.6 Choosing a Tunneling Mechanism

The choice of tunneling mechanism will be driven by many factors, not least of which is the availability of implementations on source and destination nodes. Some application suites require the use of a particular tunneling technique, and others are more flexible but still mandate that a specific basic tunneling method must be available in all implementations. Table 15.1 gives a brief comparative summary of some of the properties of different tunneling mechanisms.

Note that all tunneling mechanisms require some form of end-to-end signaling to agree on the form of tunneling to be used. In some cases this can be a simple link-level agreement, but in others more extensive signaling is required to establish tunneling information.

15.2 Virtual Private Networks (VPNs)

Virtual Private Networks (VPNs) are a major growth area with the Internet. Using standardized protocols, companies are able to connect their private networks using the economical and highly available resources of the Internet while, at the same time, protecting their data from prying eyes.

The growth in popularity of VPNs has been accompanied by an explosion in techniques for providing this function. Most of these techniques utilize standardized approaches, but each uses different protocols and each has its own benefits and disadvantages. There is not space in this book to do more than provide a brief overview of some of the IP-related solutions. Interested readers are referred to the bibliography at the end of this chapter.

15.2.1 What Is a VPN?

The basic building block of a VPN is a private network. Consider an office network or the computers in a college campus. Organizations that own these networks often connect them together using dedicated resources such as leased lines, fibers, microwave links, or simple dial-up telephone lines. When they do this they are extending their private networks to span multiple sites.

These dedicated links between sites can be very long and consequently expensive. But connections to the Internet are typically short and relatively cheap. Why not replace dedicated long-distance resources with shared public resources such as the Internet?

A good example of this would be a home worker or traveling salesman who uses a modem to access his company network. The modem can be configured to call up the head office and provide connectivity to the office network, but this could involve expensive long-distance phone calls. On the other hand, Internet Service Providers offer points of presence in most cities, allowing dial-up access for the price of a local call—free in the United States. The same principle applies to connecting static sites and, in fact, the financial savings may be greater since dedicated lines may be billed regardless of whether they are carrying data. This connectivity is demonstrated in Figure 15.8, in which two companies (imaginatively named Company A and Company B) each have two sites with private networks—the companies connect them across the Internet.

Such networks create only the illusion of being private. That is, the data that is sent between the private networks passes through the public network and is therefore vulnerable to interception, forgery, or accidental misdelivery. These networks are consequently known as Virtual Private Networks, and

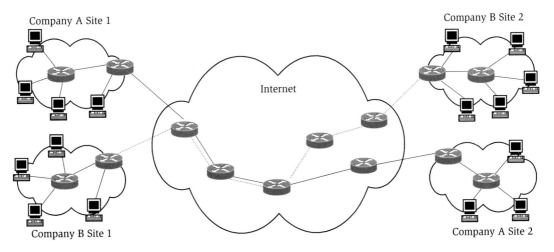

Figure 15.8 Virtual Private Networks consist of private networks connected together through a public network.

considerable effort is expended to ensure the integrity of the data sent between the private sites.

15.2.2 Tunneling and Private Address Spaces

One of the options provided by a VPN is that the addresses within the private networks may be kept private. This allows the companies in Figure 15.8 to use identical address spaces, and lets each have hosts that have the same addresses.

If the private networks were entirely distinct (that is, if their components were connected together using private dedicated resources) the use of identical address spaces would not be an issue and there would never be a problem distinguishing between two hosts with the same address. However, since IP packets from Company A Site 1 are sent across the Internet to Company A Site 2 there is obvious scope for confusion and misdelivery. How do the routers in the Internet know which is the real intended recipient of the packets?

One answer to this problem lies with tunneling using any form of IP encapsulation: GRE, IP in IP, or a data-link layer mechanism such as the Layer 2 Tunneling Protocol (L2TP). This makes it possible to build a tunnel across the Internet. So, in Figure 15.8, Sites 1 and 2 of Company B are connected by a tunnel represented by the dotted line. This tunnel could be seen as a virtual wire and some VPN management technologies allow the customers (that is the companies that own the private sites) to manage their connections across the Internet as emulated wires.

In fact, tunneling like this starts to address some of the security issues with VPNs since a properly configured router at the edge of the Internet will guarantee that the packets are kept within their correct tunnels and delivered to the proper remote edge router for decapsulation and delivery to the right private network. However, tunneling on its own does not provide a strong security model since packets within the Internet are still susceptible to interception, and the edge routers can still be misconfigured. Further consideration of the security of VPNs is given in Section 15.2.4.

15.2.3 Solutions Using Routing Protocols

A serious concern with layer-2 tunneling solutions for VPNs is that they don't scale well. Each tunnel models a wire or physical connection, so if there are n sites participating in the VPN there is the need to configure and manage $n(n-1)/2$ connections. An alternative is to provide a single hub node that acts as a clearinghouse for all data for the VPN—this cuts down the number of links to just n but leaves the hub node as a single point of failure that could break connectivity for the whole VPN. These topologies are illustrated in Figure 15.9. This is, of course, no more complex than managing the physical links that were needed in the truly private network, but since we are using the Internet, which

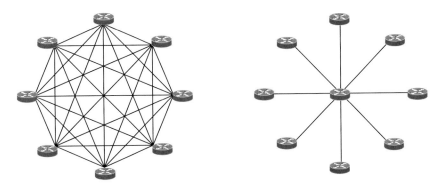

Figure 15.9 Full mesh connectivity with tunnels does not scale well, but the hub-and-spokes topology has a single point of failure.

is equipped with a host of automatic signaling and routing protocols, surely we can do better.

We most certainly can do better. Using IP tunneling techniques, it is only the end points of the tunnels that are nailed down; the actual paths of the tunnels are left up to the routing protocols within the Internet. Although this may reduce the configuration within the core network, it doesn't reduce the effort at each of the edge nodes. It is still necessary to configure mappings of private destination IP addresses into tunnels—that is, the IP address of the far end of the tunnel must be configured for the address of each node within the VPN. Although this process may be simplified by using suitable subnetworks, the configuration effort is still significant.

This issue can be handled quite elegantly by using the routing protocols that run over the Internet to exchange VPN connectivity information between edge nodes. In short, an edge node can advertise that to reach a certain set of IP addresses within a given VPN other routers should send packets to it.

There are two approaches to the use of routing protocols to support VPNs. Each recognizes that the edge nodes (the nodes that provide access from the private networks to the Internet) need to retain separate routing tables for each VPN that they support. This allows a packet from one VPN to be encapsulated and correctly routed across the Internet to the corresponding edge node that will forward it onward within the private network. The routing tables are often called *virtual routing tables* and are distinguished by unique identifiers assigned to each VPN.

The first solution uses a separate instance of a routing protocol to support each virtual routing table. Tunnels are set up between each of the edge points that provide access to the VPNs as before, but the configuration and management of these tunnels is greatly improved by running an Interior Gateway Protocol (IGP) such as OSPF through the tunnels. Each tunnel end point is presented as a virtual interface through which the IGP advertises its routing

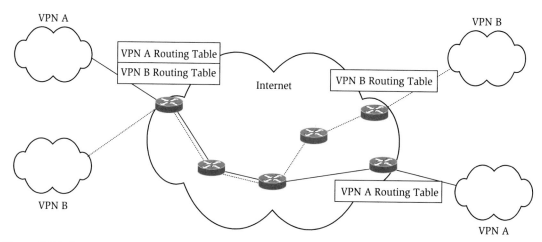

Figure 15.10 Separate routing tables are maintained for each VPN using information exchanged by IGPs along tunnels between VPN access nodes.

information. The tunnel appears as a single-hop link between the tunnel end points.

In this way, the full reachability information for the nodes within a VPN is distributed to every node that participates in the VPN, but is not visible within the core of the network and is not sent to nodes that do not participate in the VPN since the IGP only sends its messages on the virtual interfaces (tunnels) configured as part of the VPN.

Since a single edge node may provide access for multiple VPNs, it must keep the routing information for each VPN separate. Additionally, it must keep the VPN information distinct from the normal routing information for the core network. This can be achieved simply by using a distinct routing table for each use—the tables are usually indexed by a VPN identifier. A separate instance of the IGP is used to construct each routing table with each instance running on distinct interface, be it a physical interface or a virtual (tunnel) interface. This is illustrated in Figure 15.10.

Distribution of reachability/routing information across a core network is one of the problems that the Border Gateway Protocol (BGP, see Section 5.8) was designed to address. The second VPN routing protocol solution utilizes a single instance of BGP to distribute information for all VPNs. This approach is illustrated in Figure 15.11. It extends BGP to allow the inclusion of a VPN identifier in the information distributed. This immediately allows multiple virtual routing tables to be exchanged between all edge nodes, and with the minimum of fuss, VPN connectivity is established.

Note that in both cases, the routing protocol is being used to distribute the addresses of edge nodes that provide access to nodes within the VPN. IP tunneling is still used to deliver VPN packets across the Internet.

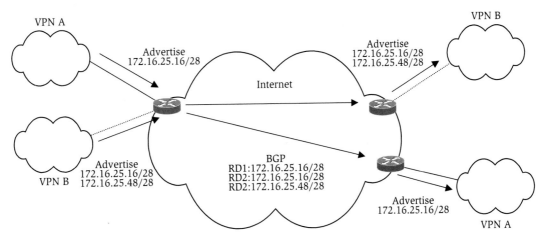

Figure 15.11 BGP may use Route Distinguishers to facilitate advertisement of addresses belonging to different VPNs.

15.2.4 Security Solutions

IPsec is discussed in Chapter 14. It is essentially a tunneling protocol devised to securely transport IP across a public network. IPsec has considerable potential in VPN implementation because it offers a full suite of security features from encryption and authentication to protection against replay. A neat feature of IPsec tunnels is that they are connectionless and do not require that the tunnel end points store any protocol state information (although they do need to manage security information such as keys, which may be distributed automatically or configured manually).

On the other hand, IPsec has the performance hit of encrypting all data—but since VPN data security is often a requirement, some form of encryption would likely be performed anyway. Another disadvantage to the use of IPsec is that it is hard to demultiplex data streams from a single IPsec tunnel, so a single tunnel may need to be set up between each pair of VPN nodes that exchange data.

Solutions to this second problem involve the use of some other tunneling mechanism in addition to IPsec. IPsec can be applied to the whole tunnel (that is, tunneling the tunnel itself through IPsec) or multiple IPsec tunnels can be multiplexed together into a single tunnel of some other technology.

15.2.5 MPLS VPNs

MPLS can be used to set up tunnels through an MPLS capable network as described in Chapter 9.

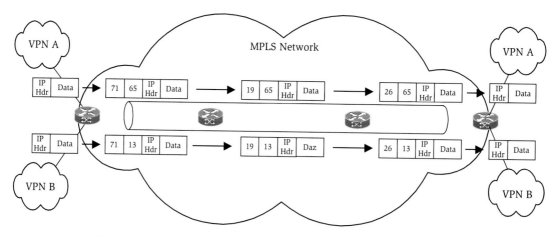

Figure 15.12 MPLS may be used to connect multiple VPNs through a single tunnel.

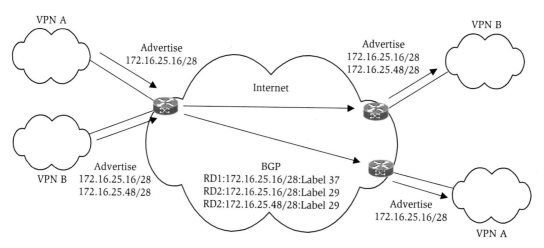

Figure 15.13 An example showing the information distributed for a BGP MPLS VPN.

These tunnels can be used to establish layer-2 VPNs in ATM, Frame Relay, or other MPLS-capable networks. Each tunnel provides a virtual wire between source and destination to connect different parts of the VPN. Alternatively, MPLS packets can be encapsulated in some other tunneling mechanism to allow them to be transported across the IP core network. This second choice may be particularly useful when MPLS is used within the VPN, or when many edge points each provide access to multiple VPNs, and it is desirable to reduce the number of tunnels across the network, as shown in Figure 15.12.

A hybrid VPN solution that utilizes both BGP and MPLS is described in RFC 2547 and is being further developed within the IETF. This solution is scalable and flexible. BGP is used to advertise which edge nodes provide access to which VPNs, the reachability information for addresses in each VPN at each edge node, and an MPLS label used to identify which VPN is targeted. Packets sent across the core are given an MPLS label that allows the receiver to immediately distinguish to which VPN it should deliver the data. As the packets traverse the core they may be encapsulated in IP, GRE, IPsec, or MPLS tunnels. An example of the information distributed for a BGP MPLS VPN is shown in Figure 15.13.

15.2.6 Optical VPNs

Optical VPNs are a new concept concerned with the automatic provisioning of data services through an optical core. The networks that are being connected together in this case are likely to be fragments of a Service Provider's whole network. The core network providing the optical connectivity is sometimes referred to as a *Service Provider's Service Provider*.

Section 10.8 gives an example of how GMPLS may be used to establish an Optical VPN and how the core network can be viewed as a single virtual switch switching data between access interfaces.

15.2.7 Choosing a VPN Technology

At the time of writing, VPNs are one of the biggest growth areas within the Internet. The solutions described in the preceding sections are only some of the popular approaches, and there are probably more methods available than there are vendors selling VPN-enabled equipment. As might be expected, the debate over which solutions provide the best connectivity, security, ease of maintenance, and speed of provisioning is highly colored by the implementations that the vendors have to offer, and is not necessarily influenced by reality.

Nevertheless, one of the most important factors in choosing a VPN technology must be its availability in proven and tested equipment. Table 15.2 lists some of the more important considerations when building a VPN and highlights which solutions are strongest for each feature.

Perhaps the most hotly debated topic is scalability. How much extra configuration is required? How much additional routing or signaling information must be exchanged? This issue affects the question of whose responsibility it is to maintain the VPN, since the Service Provider's customers would like to buy VPN services without the need to configure their own equipment, yet they do not trust their Service Providers to protect their data from misdelivery or from hackers. Many tunneling solutions can be implemented by the Customer Edge (CE) equipment or by the Provider Edge (PE) equipment, further widening the choice.

Table 15.2 A comparison of some VPN technologies

	Layer Two Tunneling	IP Tunneling	IPsec	MPLS	Virtual Router	BGP	BGP/MPLS
Customer Equipment Needs to Be Aware of VPN	Yes	Yes if CE manages tunnels, no if PE owns tunnels	Yes	No	No	No	No
Customer Equipment Needs to Be Configured for VPN	Yes	Yes if CE manages tunnels, no if PE owns tunnels	Yes	No	No	No	No
Network Equipment Needs to Be Aware of VPN	No	No if CE manages tunnels, yes if PE owns tunnels	No	Yes	Yes	Yes	Yes
Scalability at Provider Edge	Good	Moderate if CE manages tunnels, poor if PE owns tunnels	Moderate	Moderate	Poor	Moderate	Moderate
Data Security	Some based on integrity of hardware	Good	None	Some based on integrity of hardware	None	None	Some based on integrity of hardware
Traffic Engineering in the Network	No	Limited with DiffServ	No	Yes	Limited with DiffServ	Limited with DiffServ	Yes

15.3 Mobile IP

Today's computers are smaller and more mobile than they once were. Processing power that used to take up a whole air-conditioned room can now be easily carried around and used anywhere. At the same time, connectivity to the Internet has become easier and more diverse. A user may now disconnect his computer in the office and reconnect from another site within the same office or elsewhere. Connectivity may be achieved through established networking technologies such as Ethernet, through dial-up lines, or using wireless networking. In the latter case, the point of attachment may change even while the user is connected since the user may travel between base stations of a wireless LAN or a mobile phone system.

The infrastructure to support IP telephony and IP over dial-up links is discussed in subsequent sections of this chapter. This section examines the problems and solutions for handling IP when a host's physical location changes.

15.3.1 The Requirements of Mobile IP

Mobile IP allows a node to change its point of attachment to the Internet without needing to change its IP address. This is not simply a configuration simplification, but can facilitate continuous application-level connectivity as the node moves from point to point.

A possible solution to this problem would be to distribute routes through the network to declare the node's new location and to update the routing tables so that packets can be correctly dispatched. This might, at first, seem attractive, but it is a solution that scales very poorly since it would be necessary to retain host-specific routes for each mobile host. As the number of mobile hosts in the Internet increases (and the growth of web access from mobile devices such as cell phones and palm-tops is very rapid) it would become impractical to maintain such tables in the core of the Internet.

The solution developed by the IETF involves protocol extensions whereby packets targeted at a mobile host are sent to its home network (as if the host were not mobile) and passed to a static (nonmobile) node called the node's *home agent*. The mobile host registers its real location with the home agent, which is responsible for forwarding the packets to the host.

If the mobile host is at home (attached to its home network), forwarding is just plain old IP forwarding, but if the host is roving, packets must be tunneled across the Internet to a *care-of address* where the host has registered its attachment to a *foreign agent*. At the care-of address (the end of the tunnel) the packets are forwarded to the mobile host. This is illustrated in Figure 15.14.

Note that this tunneling process is only required in one direction. Packets sent by the mobile host may be routed through the network using the standard IP procedures.

It is worth observing that although mobile IP can be used to address any IP mobility issue, its use within wireless LANs and mobile phone networks might be better served by link-layer (that is, sub-IP) procedures such as link-layer handoff. These processes are typically built into the link-layer mechanisms and involve less overhead than mobile IP. Such processes do, however, require that the mobile host remains logically connected within the IP subnet to which its address belongs—it becomes the responsibility of the link layer to maintain connections or virtual connections into that subnet.

An alternative to tunneling in mobile IP might be to use source routing within IP. IPv4 has been enhanced with optional extensions to support source routing (see Chapter 2). However, since the source routing extensions to IPv4

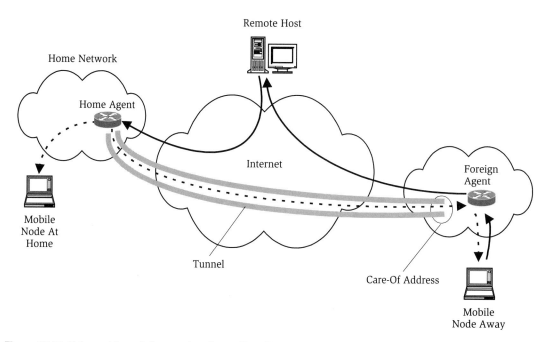

Figure 15.14 If the mobile node is away from home, IP traffic is sent to a Home Agent and tunneled across the Internet to a Foreign Agent for delivery to the mobile node.

are a relatively new development and are in any case optional, many (or even most) deployed IPv4 nodes do not support them. This means that they are not a lot of use for developing mobile IP services over existing IPv4 networks. They may be of more use in new networks that are being constructed for the first time since the Service Providers can insist on these extensions from their equipment vendors.

IPv6 (see Chapter 4) offers some alternatives to tunneling for mobile IP by using the routing extension header. In this way the mobile node can establish communications with its home agent and then use information learned to directly route packets to the destination, bypassing the home agent. Since this feature is built into IPv6 and so supported by all IPv6 implementations, it makes IPv6 a popular option for mobile IP deployments.

15.3.2 Extending the Protocols

Specific protocol exchanges are necessary to allow the mobile node to register with either its Home Agent or some remote Foreign Agent. Similarly, once a mobile node has registered with a Foreign Agent, a further registration process with the Home Agent is needed to get it to redirect traffic and to supply the

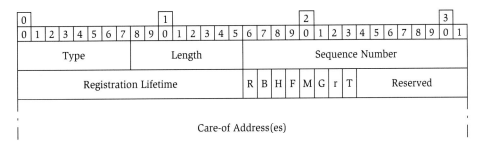

Figure 15.15 The mobile IP Agent Advertisement ICMP TLV.

Table 15.3 The Agent Capability Flags Within the Mobile IP Agent Advertisement ICMP TLV

Flag	Meaning
R	The mobile nodes must complete registration procedures to make use of this foreign agent.
B	The agent is busy and will not accept registrations from additional mobile nodes.
H	This agent offers service as a home agent on the link on which this Agent Advertisement message was sent.
F	This agent offers service as a foreign agent on the link on which this Agent Advertisement message was sent.
M	This agent supports receiving tunneled datagrams (from the home agent) that use minimal encapsulation as defined in RFC 2004 (see Section 15.1.4).
G	This agent supports receiving tunneled datagrams (from the home agent) that use GRE encapsulation as defined in RFC 2784 (see Section 15.1.2).
r	Reserved (must be zero).
T	This agent supports reverse tunneling as defined in RFC 3024.

care-of address. Additionally, Foreign Agents may advertise their capabilities so that mobile nodes that connect to them know that registration for mobile IP is an option. The messages to support these functions are described in RFC 3344.

Mobile nodes discover available home and foreign agents through extensions to the ICMP router discovery process (see Chapter 2). The agents advertise their mobile IP capabilities through new TLVs, shown in Figure 15.15, that follow the Router Advertisement fields in an ICMP Router Advertisement Message. The TLVs give the capabilities of the agent and list a set of useable care-of addresses and the length of validity of the registration. The meanings of the capabilities bit flags are shown in Table 15.3.

Note that regardless of the capability set advertised, a foreign agent must always support IP in IP encapsulation as defined in RFC 2003 (see Section 15.1.3). This is the favored tunneling mechanism.

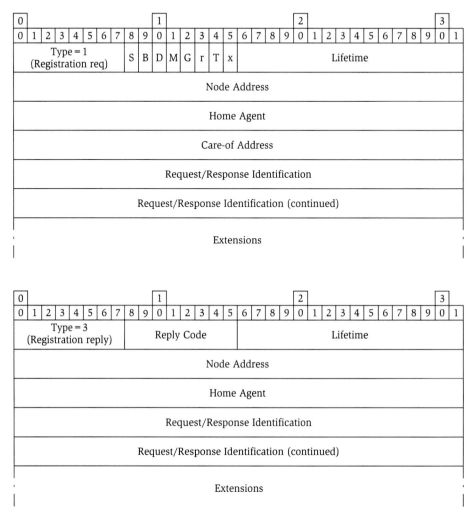

Figure 15.16 The Mobile Node Registration Request and Reply messages.

A mobile node tells its home agent about its care-of address using a registration procedure built as a new miniprotocol that uses UDP as its transport. The UDP port number 434 is reserved for agents to listen on for incoming registration requests from mobile nodes. The registration is a simple request–reply exchange using the messages shown in Figure 15.16.

The capability bits in the Registration message are inherited with some modification from the ICMP Advertisement message flags shown in Table 15.3—their precise meanings are given in Table 15.4. The Request/Response Identification is a 64-bit random number used by the requester to prevent replay attacks by malicious agents. The Reply Code in the Reply message indicates the success or failure of the request—a host of rejection reasons are allowed, as shown in Table 15.5.

Table 15.4 The Capability Flags Within the Mobile IP Registration Request Message

Flag	Meaning
S	This bit indicates that the mobile node is requesting that this binding supplement rather than replace the previous binding.
B	The mobile node requests that broadcast datagrams be tunneled to it along with any datagrams that are specifically addressed to it.
D	The mobile node will itself decapsulate datagrams that are tunneled to the care-of address. That is, the mobile node is colocated with the care-of address.
M	The mobile node requests the use of minimal encapsulation tunneling as defined in RFC 2004 (see Section 15.1.4).
G	The mobile node requests the use of GRE encapsulation tunneling as defined in RFC 2784 (see Section 15.1.2).
r	Reserved (must be zero).
T	The mobile node requests the use of reverse tunneling as defined in RFC 3024 (see below).
x	Reserved (must be zero).

Table 15.5 Mobile IP Registration Reply Message Reply Codes

Reply Code	Meaning
0	Registration accepted
1	Registration accepted, but simultaneous mobility bindings unsupported

Rejections from the Foreign Agent

64	Reason unspecified
65	Administratively prohibited
66	Insufficient resources
67	Mobile node failed authentication

Table 15.5 *Continued*

Reply Code	Meaning
68	Home agent failed authentication
69	Requested Lifetime too long
70	Poorly formed Request
71	Poorly formed Reply
72	Requested encapsulation unavailable
73	Reserved and unavailable
74	Requested reverse tunnel unavailable
75	Reverse tunnel is mandatory and T-bit not set
76	Mobile node too distant
77	Invalid care-of address
78	Registration timeout
79	Delivery style not supported
80	Home network unreachable (ICMP error received)
81	Home agent host unreachable (ICMP error received)
82	Home agent port unreachable (ICMP error received)
88	Home agent unreachable (other ICMP error received)
Rejections from the Home Agent	
128	Reason unspecified
129	Administratively prohibited
130	Insufficient resources
131	Mobile node failed authentication
132	Foreign agent failed authentication
133	Registration Identification mismatch
134	Poorly formed Request
135	Too many simultaneous mobility bindings
136	Unknown home agent address
137	Requested reverse tunnel unavailable
138	Reverse tunnel is mandatory and T-bit not set
139	Requested encapsulation unavailable

Extensions to the Request and Reply messages exist to convey authentication details. The extensions are defined as TLVs for use in communication between the different components of the mobile IP network. Thus, there are extensions for Mobile-Home Authentication, Mobile-Foreign Authentication, and Foreign-Home Authentication.

15.3.3 Reverse Tunneling

In some environments, routers examine not only the destination IP address, but also the source IP address, when making a decision about how to forward a packet. This processing allows the router to make some attempts to filter out spoofed packets. However, in mobile IP, the source IP address of a packet sent by the mobile node may be unexpected within the context of the foreign network and may be discarded by a router. This undesirable problem is overcome by tunneling packets from the mobile node back to the Home Agent, and having the Home Agent forward them from there. This process, known as reverse tunneling, effectively reverses the path of packets that are sent to the mobile node.

Ideally, reverse tunnels would be established by the mobile nodes; however, this only works if the mobile node is colocated with the care-of address. If a Foreign Agent is used to provide the care-of address, the reverse tunnel is managed by the Foreign Agent. There are two options:

1. In the Direct Delivery style of reverse tunneling the mobile node sends packets directly to the Foreign Agent as its default router and lets the Foreign Agent intercept them, and tunnel them to the Home Agent.
2. In the Encapsulating Delivery style of reverse tunneling the mobile node sends packets to the Foreign Agent using a tunnel. The Foreign Agent decapsulates the packets and retunnels them to the Home Agent.

Signaling extensions for reverse tunneling are defined in RFC 3024 and basically involve the use of the T-bit shown in Tables 15.3 and 15.4, and the reply codes 74–76, 79, and 137–139 shown in Table 15.5.

15.3.4 Security Concerns

The standards for mobile IP mandate the use of strong authentication cryptography for the registration process between a mobile node and its home agent. This is the most vulnerable part of the mobile IP process and might, if intercepted or spoofed, cause the interception or diversion of all traffic sent from the home agent to the mobile node on behalf of the remote point of contact. Strong authentication may also be used between the mobile node and the Foreign Agent and between the Foreign Agent and the Home Agent. Agent discovery messages are not subject to authentication because there is currently no IP-based authentication key distribution protocol.

The data exchanged between hosts participating in mobile IP may also be encrypted. Any of the standard approaches may be used (see Chapter 5), giving rise to three models. In the first, the source of the data encrypts it and sends it through the home agent to the mobile node, which decrypts it. In the second model, the home agent chooses whether to encrypt the data it forwards according to whether the mobile node is away from or at home—in this way data forwarded to a roving mobile node is encrypted across the unknown part of the network and is decrypted by the mobile node. In the final model, IPsec is used as the tunneling protocol between the home and foreign agent and the mobile node does not need to have encryption/decryption capabilities.

15.4 Header Compression

A significant amount of data traffic may be overhead, introduced by the protocols that carry the traffic. For example, as described in Section 7.5, the use of RTP, UDP, and IP can require 40 bytes of control data to be sent with each data packet. If the data is a short audio sample (maybe only 16-bytes) the overhead is 70 percent. This can make the difference between being able to provide an adequate service over a slow link and providing unacceptable quality with distortion and loss.

To address this, a lot of thought has gone into ways to reduce the protocol overhead without losing the important information that it carries. It goes without saying that if the protocol information were entirely redundant, it would be discarded. One of the popular solutions is the compression of the protocol headers. This is described further in this section.

15.4.1 Choosing to Compress Headers

The benefits of header compression are clear: The proportion of data traffic to protocol overhead can be increased with the result that higher data throughput can be achieved. Header compression is, however, a point-to-point technology. It relies on the fact that between a pair of network nodes, there are only minor changes in protocol information from one packet to the next, and that those changes are largely predictable. It is still necessary for each node to decompress protocol header information to discover how to process each packet. This requires that every node must be able to handle compression and decompression, and introduces a significant processing overhead at each hop across the network.

If links have limited bandwidth and sufficient processing power is available, header compression may bring significant improvements in quality of service.

Header compression is usually negotiated as a quality of the layer-2 network connection between a pair of nodes. This is appropriate both because this is the layer that knows the bandwidth capabilities of the link, and because everything above this layer may be compressed—it is important that the peers know whether or not to use compression. For example, CSLIP and PPP (described in Section 15.8), use connection-time parameter negotiation to determine whether header compression will be used on the links they manage.

15.4.2 IP Header Compression

In an individual IP data flow between a single source and destination, most of the fields in the IP header remain unchanged from one packet to the next. In fact, most of the fields in the IP, UDP, and RTP headers for a single flow do not change between packets. Figure 15.17 shows shaded in gray those fields that do not change in consecutive packets. It is easy to imagine, therefore, some form of per-flow compression algorithm that does not retransmit these fields for every packet.

Additionally, two fields, the IP Packet Length and the UDP Length, can be considered as redundant in most networking technologies because the network layer (Ethernet, PPP, etc.) also carries an indication of the entire packet length. These two fields can therefore be safely dropped from transmitted packets.

Further, one more IP field and two of the RTP fields can be described as predictable. The IP Fragment ID and the RTP sequence number predictably

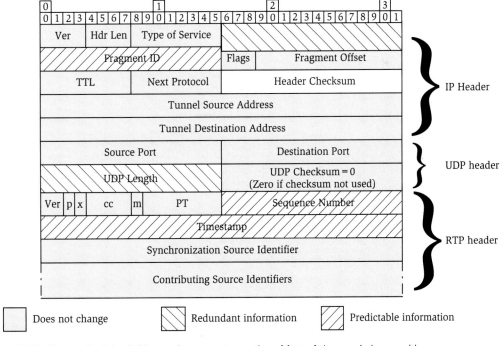

Figure 15.17 Nearly all of the fields remain constant over time. Most of the remainder are either entirely redundant or predicable.

increase by one for each packet sent, and the RTP timestamp increases according to the packet rate exchanged in the RTP session parameters. These three fields could also be excluded.

Examining the full set of fields shown in Figure 15.17, we see that only one field remains: the IP Header Checksum. But if no other field in the IP header is needed, we can also remove this field. So it appears that no header, neither IP, nor UDP, nor RTP, is needed—this, it turns out, is a bit of an over-simplification.

The receiver of a compressed packet (the *decompressor*) must be able to reconstitute the headers so that the packet can be processed by the IP and higher-layer software. To do this it must receive its first packet in an uncompressed form (that is, with all headers present), and must store the fields in a state block within the context of the packet flow. When each new compressed packet for the context arrives, the decompressor can rebuild the headers using the stored data.

To establish the context for a compressed packet (so that the decompressor can restore the IP, UDP, and RTP header fields) an end-to-end, connection-oriented identifier must be exchanged. The Context Session Identifier (CID) may be 16 bits long (allowing up to 65,536 contexts) or can be trimmed to 8 bits if no more than 256 contexts are required. When the initial full packet is sent to establish the invariant values of the headers, the redundant length fields in the headers are used to carry the CID for the context, as shown in Figure 15.18. The first bit of the IP Packet Length field is used to indicate whether an 8- or 16-bit CID is in use. When compressed packets are sent, they begin with a flag to indicate whether an 8- or 16-bit CID is used and then the CID itself.

As described in the preceding paragraphs, the IP Fragment ID and the RTP Sequence Number are predictable, but they are not entirely redundant since they serve to discover out-of-order or lost packets. This processing can, however, reasonably be reduced to just 4 bits, providing the same function, albeit with

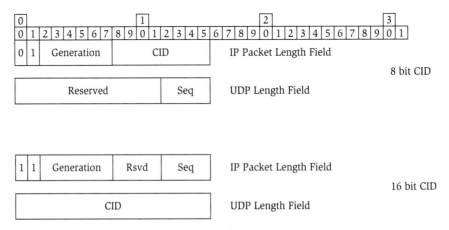

Figure 15.18 A Context Session Identifier (CID) is encoded in the redundant IP Packet Length and UDP Length fields as an 8- or 16-bit quantity.

a smaller window. When full headers are sent the sequence number is also carried in the superfluous length fields, as shown in Figure 15.18. The sequence number is used on compressed packets together with the CID to fully identify the packet. Note that the location of the sequence number changes according to whether an 8- or 16-bit CID is used. A Generation field is also present to support nondifferential coding of UDP packets with IPv6, but for IPv4, the generation number is set to zero.

The option now exists for the sender of a packet (the *compressor*) to send the packet as normal uncompressed IP, with full headers but replacing the header fields with CIDs (that is, preparing the decompressor to receive compressed packets), or as compressed IP. Further, the sender may elect to compress all of the headers or just the IP and UDP headers. (This second option is, of course, popular when RTP is not in use.)

This is all very well, but the receiving node needs some way to determine whether the network layer payload is normal IP, full headers with the length fields replaced with CIDs, compression of just IP and UDP, or a fully compressed packet. Fortunately, most link-level protocols such as Ethernet and PPP have some way of indicating the payload protocol. This mechanism is already used to indicate that the payload is IP, and can be extended to indicate that a packet is IP with CIDs (FULL_HEADER), compressed IP and UDP (COMPRESSED_UDP), or fully compressed including RTP (COMPRESSED_RTP). The numeric values for these symbolic constants belong to the definitions of the link-level protocols and are typically managed by IANA.

Two further payload packet types are required. The first, COMPRESSED_NON_TCP, uses full header compression but includes an extra 2 bytes to carry the Fragment Identification field from the IPv4 header. This may be useful on links that have high packet loss ratios since it will help to identify lost packets. A final packet type, CONTEXT_STATE, is used to allow a decompressor to request that the compressor sends a packet with full headers to refresh the decompressor's state for the context. It might do this periodically to check that it is in synch, after a large number of changes, or after it has detected an error.

Figure 15.19 shows the format of a standard COMPRESSED_UDP packet. The context is carried in the first 1 or 2 bytes (depending on whether 8- or 16-bit CIDs are in use)—the figure shows an 8-bit CID. The I-bit is used to indicate whether an IP Fragment Identifier Delta is present. After the header come two optional fields: the UDP checksum (if in use in the context) and the IP Fragment Identifier Delta (if indicated by the I-bit). After this comes the UDP payload which may comprise a full RTP header and payload. As indicated by its name, the Fragment Identifier Delta field does not provide the new fragment identifier, but gives the delta (that is, the change) from the last value sent.

The COMPRESSED_RTP packet shown in Figure 15.20 works in a similar way to the COMPRESSED_UDP packet. The CID is followed by four flags, that include the I-bit with the same meaning as for the compressed UDP packet. Of the other flags, the M-bit is the RTP Marker Bit, but the other two flags (the S-bit and the

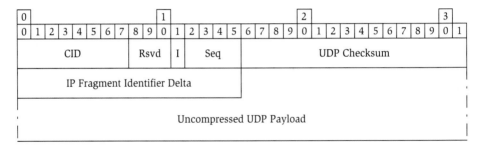

Figure 15.19 A COMPRESSED_UDP packet showing an 8-bit CID, IP Fragment ID, and UDP Checksum.

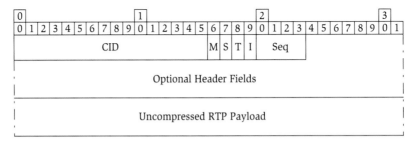

Figure 15.20 A COMPRESSED_RTP packet showing a 16-bit CID.

T-bit) are used to indicate that deltas are supplied for the RTP Sequence Number and the RTP Timestamp, respectively.

If indicated by the S- and T-bit, the deltas are treated like the IP Fragment Identifier Delta. That is, they provide an indication of the amount of change in the respective field, not an absolute value of the field.

Special meaning is given if the M-, S-, T-, and I-bits are all set to 1. In this case, an extra byte is present after the (optional) UDP checksum. This extra byte gives the real values of the 4 bits and the CC field (count of RTP Contributing Source Identifiers). This process allows a way for RTP Mixers to indicate changes in the contributors to the RTP flow. The new list of Contributing Source Identifiers is placed in the optional header fields as shown in Figure 15.21.

The CONTEXT_STATE packet shown in Figure 15.22 is used to request that the compressor sends uncompressed packets to resynchronize the state. The CD Type field is set to 1 to indicate that 8-bit CIDs are used, and to 2 to use 16-bit CIDs. There follows a count of the total number of CIDs for which errors are being reported. Each CID is presented followed by an I-bit that indicates whether a FULL_HEADER packet is required (I-bit is set to 1) or whether the error is only advisory and the compressor can choose to ignore it (I-bit is clear).

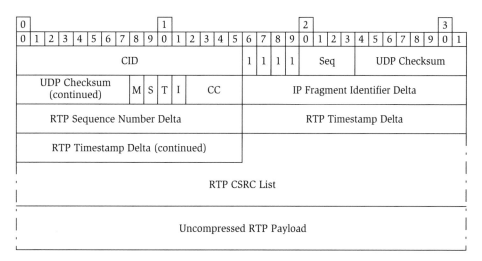

Figure 15.21 A COMPRESSED_RTP packet showing the presence of all of the optional header fields.

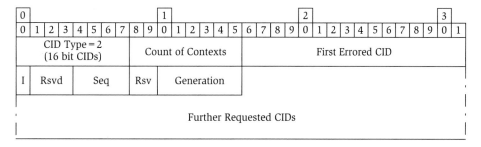

Figure 15.22 A CONTEXT_STATE packet using 16-bit CIDs.

Also, for each CID in error, the CONTEXT_STATE packet includes a sequence number and a generation ID. These fields are taken from the last good packet received for the context.

15.4.3 MPLS and Header Compression

The use of MPLS tunnels provides an interesting way to protect network nodes from the need to participate in header compression and decompression. Although MPLS introduces a further overhead (a 4-byte shim header) to each packet, it is an end-to-end technology which allows the packet with the compressed header to be sent along the whole tunnel without any need to decompress the header. In effect, the tunnel becomes a single hop between two compression-capable nodes.

To use MPLS tunnels in this way it is necessary for the tunnel end points to negotiate the use of header compression just as with any sub-IP transport mechanism. Some early proposals within the MPLS Working Group of the IETF suggest the inclusion of new Compression Request and Compression Response objects in the RSVP-TE protocol during LSP establishment. An alternative is clearly manual configuration.

Of course, the addition of a shim header is itself a concern because this goes contrary to the objective of reducing the number of bytes of protocol overhead that flow on the link. Where MPLS is used over some other layer-2 networking technology such as PPP, the MPLS header itself may be compressed using the same factors as before—given a context for the LSP, the label and other bits of the shim header do not change from one packet to another. Furthermore, when a label stack is present, the labels lower down the stack do not change either.

This compression technique may also be applied where the MPLS packets are transported over a network technology where the label is embedded in the connection information of the lower-layer protocol. For example, in ATM and Frame Relay, the MPLS label is carried by the vpi/vci or DLCI respectively. In these cases, the shim header is even more easily compressed.

Technical work for the compression of MPLS headers was begun in the MPLS Working Group of the IETF but was taken over by the MPLS Forum which took responsibility for all areas of voice over MPLS.

15.5 Voice Over IP

Carrying voice over IP is of increasing interest. Some office-based phone systems are being built around dedicated IP networks that have no IP connections to the outside world. Other phone systems allow telephones to be connected to the office LAN, making cabling simpler. At the same time, the prospect of "free" long-distance telephone calls made over the Internet is hugely attractive.

The main issue with carrying voice over an IP network is maintaining sufficient quality. Delayed or lost packets can render speech incomprehensible, and unlike broadcast audio which can be buffered and played when fully received, telephone conversations must retain real-time qualities to be of any use.

RSVP (see Chapter 6) can be used within the network to ensure that suitable network resources are reserved and made available to maintain the quality of the voice traffic. At the same time, RTP (see Chapter 7) can be used to manage the real-time delivery of voice data. In many networks, the proportional cost of the packet headers associated with the transport protocols may be unacceptable and it is necessary to use one of the compression techniques described in Section 15.4.

Some consideration must be given to the address space needed when delivering voice services over IP networks. If every telephone were made IP-capable

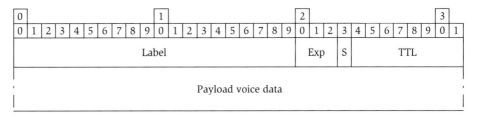

Figure 15.23 Voice data may be carried through MPLS networks without the use of IP or transport protocol headers.

there are concerns that the IPv4 address space would be insufficient. IPv6 is, therefore, often implemented for use by voice over IP devices.

One last component that may be used in voice over IP applications is a signaling protocol. This is needed to place calls and provide the value-added services commonly found in telephone systems. IP telephony is the subject of Section 15.6.

15.5.1 Voice Over MPLS

Voice may, of course, also be carried through MPLS-capable networks. IP data streams carrying voice data can be packaged up as MPLS packets with a shim header and forwarded through an MPLS network. Note, however, that MPLS traffic engineering signaling (see Chapter 9) involves the determination of a data path and the reservation of resources along that path. This may make the use of IP and transport protocols unnecessary, leading to the direct encapsulation of voice traffic as the payload of MPLS packets, as illustrated in Figure 15.23.

For voice over MPLS to be successfully supported, both ends of the MPLS Label Switched Path (LSP) must agree that the payload will be voice traffic. This allows the receiver to interpret it correctly and deliver it to the correct application. Additionally, the transit nodes in a voice over MPLS network must not attempt to forward the traffic if the LSP becomes broken—there are no protocol headers present by which to do this.

15.6 IP Telephony

IP telephony is the business of placing telephone calls using IP-based signaling protocols. Telephony is not limited to establishment of telephone calls, but also demands the provision of extensive additional services related to billing, customer information, and customer assistance. The data channels for IP telephony may also utilize IP as described in the previous section, but that is by no means a requirement.

Much of the work for IP telephony has been done by the International Telecommunications Union (ITU). There are Working Groups within the IETF for the associated work areas and these groups focus on ensuring that there is a common approach to standardization and that the IP telephony standards are appropriate for use within the Internet.

15.6.1 The Protocols in Brief

The protocols for IP telephony are many and complex. To attempt anything but the briefest overview would require at least a whole book. The list of protocols in Table 15.6 and Figures 15.24 and 15.25 are intended to give a flavor of the complexity of the IP telephony scene.

Table 15.6 Some of the Key Protocols in IP Telephony

Protocol	Summary
CORBA	Common Object Request Broker Architecture. A common way to represent and manage network elements and resources (see Chapter 13).
H.225.0	A member of the H.323 protocol suite used for signaling and call control in ITU networks.
H.245	A member of the H.323 protocol suite used for capabilities exchange and for managing the data flow in ITU networks.
H.248	The ITU name for the protocol known in the IETF as MEGACO.
H.323	A suite of protocols including H.225.0 and H.245 that comprise the ITU signaling suite for IP telephony. The H.323 standard also specifies the transport protocols to be used for signaling and the protocols to use to carry the data.
ISUP	ISDN user part. The higher-layer protocol within the SS7 protocol suite (q.v.) that is responsible for call management.
MEGACO	The Media Gateway Control Protocol: RFC 3015. The joint effort between the IETF and the ITU (where it is known as H.248) for the replacement and extension of MGCP (q.v.).
MGCP	The Media Gateway Control Protocol. A protocol used to control media gateways that convert data between formats, such as between telephone systems and IP networks.
RAS	Registration, Admission, and Status. A subset of the functions of H.225.0 signaling that are run over UDP.
RSVP	Resource ReSerVation Protocol for reserving network resources on the data path in IP networks (see Chapter 6) or in MPLS networks (see Chapter 9).
RTCP	Real-Time Transport Control Protocol. Allows measurement and control of the behavioral characteristics of traffic that uses RTP (see Chapter 7).
RTP	Real-Time Transport Protocol for delivery of real-time data such as audio (see Chapter 7).
SIP	Session Initiation Protocol: RFC 3216. An IP-based control protocol used to establish and manage end-to-end sessions in IP networks.
SS7	The family of signaling protocols used in the Public Switched Telephone Network.

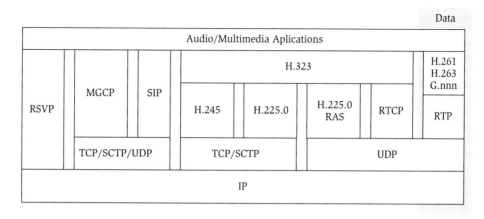

								Data
		Audio/Multimedia Aplications						
				H.323				H.261 H.263 G.nnn
RSVP	MGCP	SIP	H.245	H.225.0	H.225.0 RAS	RTCP		RTP
	TCP/SCTP/UDP		TCP/SCTP			UDP		
				IP				

Figure 15.24 How the IP telephony protocols fit together.

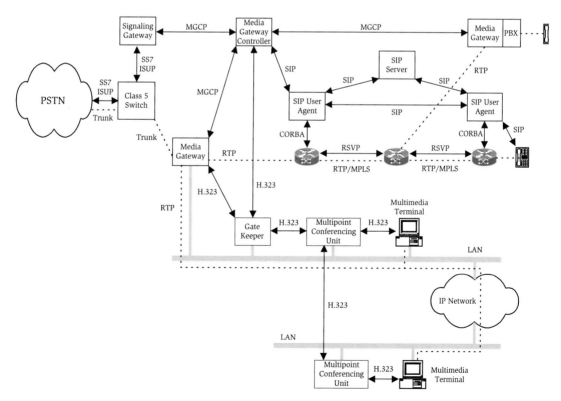

Figure 15.25 Some of the components of an IP telephony system showing the signaling and control protocols.

Figure 15.24 shows how the protocols listed in Table 15.6 are built on each other. The gray area on the right of the figure shows the protocols used to carry data. The remainder are all signaling protocols.

The very busy diagram in Figure 15.25 shows some of the components of an IP telephony system with the protocols that run between the components. The data path is shown with a dotted line. For simplicity, H.323, H.225.0, and H.245 are all shown as H.323. Note that in a deployed system it would be common for some of the components to be coresident in a single box.

15.7 IP and ATM

Asynchronous Transfer Mode (ATM) networks continue to enjoy popularity and have been extensively deployed. Some of these networks use dynamic switched virtual circuits (SVCs)—ATM connections established using Private Network to Network Interface (PNNI) the ATM signaling protocol. Other networks rely on statically configured permanent virtual circuits (PVCs).

Where ATM links provide point-to-point connectivity between IP-capable nodes, little further work is required: the link is no different from any point-to-point link. However, in most cases the ATM network provides connectivity between a large set of IP nodes. In this case, the network may be modeled as a single multidrop connection (like an Ethernet) or as a collection of point-to-point links.

Whichever approach is taken, there is a requirement to map IP addresses to ATM virtual circuits so that packets can be transferred to the next hop on their IP paths. This section briefly discusses some of the solutions that have been developed. Full details can be found in the documents produced by the ATM Forum.

15.7.1 IP Over ATM (IPOA)

Two issues must be addressed to carry IP traffic over ATM. The first is address resolution where the next hop IP address is mapped to a virtual circuit, and the second is encapsulation of the IP data in ATM cells.

IP over ATM (IPOA) is a set of rules for running ARP over a well-known ATM circuit, and for provisioning ATM circuits to handle IP traffic between peers. The use of ARP allows a source of IP traffic to determine the ATM destination to which to send the packet when broken into cells. Dynamic circuit provisioning ensures that connections are only set up where necessary.

Data encapsulation may map the IP data direct into the AAL5 SDU as shown in Figure 15.26. This approach is fine provided that only IP data is placed on the virtual circuit, but it is often desirable to be able to carry more than one protocol as a payload on a single virtual circuit. The problem here is not the encapsulation of data, but demultiplexing the data when it arrives at the destination since the receiver needs a way to determine to which application to deliver the data. The

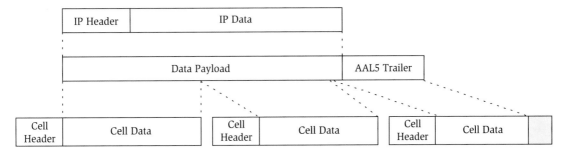

Figure 15.26 Direct AAL5 encapsulation and mapping to ATM cells.

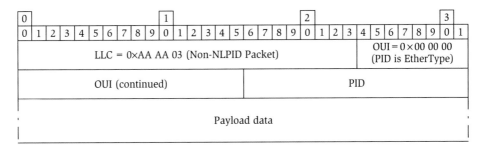

Figure 15.27 AAL5 LLC/SNAP encapsulation.

solution to this is to use IEEE 802.2 Logical Link Control and 802.1 Subnetwork Attachment Point (LLC/SNAP) headers to identify the payload, as shown in Figure 15.27. The LLC value 0xAAAA03 indicates that a SNAP header follows. The Organizational Unit Identifier (OUI) value zero says that the following 2-byte protocol Identifier (PID) field should be interpreted as an EtherType value (for example, 0x0800 IPv4, 0x0806 ARP). The completed SDU is packaged into cells just as before. It is a quality of the ATM circuit whether direct AAL5 encapsulation is used or whether LLC/SNAP headers are also used.

15.7.2 Multiprotocol Over ATM (MPOA)

A set of standards were developed for Multiprotocol Over ATM (MPOA) operation. Although these standards are largely unimplemented, they merit brief examination because of the problem they were trying to solve.

MPOA addresses communication between ATM switches that are themselves capable of bridging or routing function. This must be distinguished from the case addressed by IPOA where routing function is provided by external routers. Figure 15.28 illustrates three networks. In the first network IPOA is used to establish connectivity between routers A and B, and B and C on distinct IP subnetworks across the ATM cloud. In the second network, the routing function

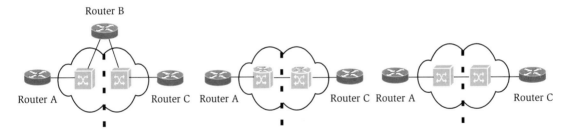

Figure 15.28 IPoA requires external routers, but MPOA enables routing or bridging within the network.

is moved onto the ATM switch so that data may be more directly switched from one virtual circuit to another. In the third diagram the ATM switches are capable of bridging and may "short-cut" data across the network.

The great hope of MPOA exponents was not the ability to route packets, but the facility to set up bridges between IP subnetworks, thereby replacing the bridging routers that span the subnetworks. In order to achieve this a new ATM protocol, the Next Hop Resolution Protocol (NHRP), was invented. NHRP turned out to be relatively complex to implement and to manage. Multiple servers were needed to resolve target addresses and great care was needed to limit the domain that NHRP was run in to avoid routers conspiring with NHRP to build forwarding loops where traffic was passed from one bridge to another over ATM circuits without any decrease of the TTL of the payload.

Figure 15.30 shows how data is encapsulated for bridging in an MPOA network. By way of an example, Ethernet 802.3/Ethernet is shown as the payload. The LLC indicates that no NLPID is used and so the next field is the Organizational Unit Identifier. The value 0x0080C2 indicates 802.1. The protocol identifier shows the link level encapsulation—in this case 802.3. Two variants of each PID are provided: The range 0x0001 to 0x0006 shows inclusion of the full 802.3/ Ethernet, 802.4, 802.5, FDDI, or 802.6 frame. The range 0x0007 to 0x000B indicates the same frame types but excludes the original checksum from the frame, thus, saving a couple of bytes that don't need to be transmitted since ATM has its own ways of ensuring data integrity. Note that the checksum must be recomputed and restored when the frame emerges from the ATM network.

Using MPOA encapsulation, the PDUs sent through the ATM network may be routed or bridged. Routed PDUs are encapsulated using the LLC type value 0xFEFE03. The LLC header is followed by a 1-byte ISO Network Layer Protocol Identifier (NLPID) that identifies the protocol type of the payload. This format is shown in Figure 15.29. The NLPID values are administered by ISO and the ITU-T. Note that IP traffic could theoretically be carried directly using MPOA encapsulation using an NLPID value of 0xCC, but that this is considered illegal, and IP traffic must be carried using the IPoA encapsulation shown in Figure 15.30. Perhaps the most interesting NLPID value is 0x83, which indicates IS-IS traffic.

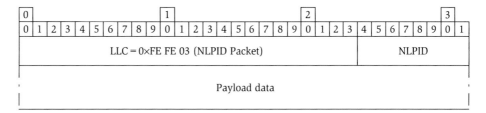

Figure 15.29 MPOA encapsulation for routed traffic.

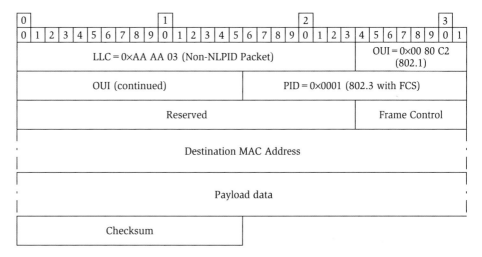

Figure 15.30 MPOA encapsulation for bridged traffic showing an 802.3 example.

In the end, although the facility to bridge between IP subnetworks without an intervening router was desirable, MPOA never really took off because of the inherent danger of NHRP forwarding loops, the complexity of implementation, the lack of support for multicast, and the provision of equivalent function using LAN Emulation (LANE).

15.7.3 LAN Emulation

LAN Emulation (LANE) saw some work within the IETF, but was fully developed by the ATM Forum. It provides a way to enhance an ATM network such that it appears to behave like a bridged LAN by the addition of LANE servers.

The LANE servers provide address resolution services to allow clients to map between MAC and ATM addresses facilitating unicast traffic through ATM virtual circuits preprovisioned as PVCs or set up on demand as SVCs. Additionally, clients may send multicast and broadcast traffic to a Broadcast Server that is responsible for replicating the traffic to the right destinations (possibly through other Broadcast Servers). The Broadcast Server also enables a client to send unicast traffic without a specific virtual circuit to the destination ATM address by passing it to the server for dispatch. Although this would be inefficient for significant quantities of data, it is very useful for short exchanges since it avoids the overhead of setting up and tearing down a virtual circuit.

LANE uses the encapsulation formats shown for MPOA to carry 802.3/Ethernet and 802.5 traffic. Note that FCS bytes are not included and that the 3 "reserved" bytes are used as a LANE message header.

15.7.4 MPLS Over ATM

As was described in Chapter 9, MPLS is well suited to run across an ATM network since MPLS labels can be mapped to ATM virtual path and circuit identifiers to leverage the switching nature of ATM hardware. Note that the control plane for MPLS remains based on IP and that this means that adjacent MPLS-enabled ATM switches must have a point-to-point method of exchanging IP packets. This is usually provided over a default virtual circuit using the encapsulation discussed in Section 15.7.1.

15.8 IP Over Dial-Up Links

Dial-up links are used by many home-based PCs to access the Internet. They are a special case of serial links that used to be (and sometimes still are) used to connect equipment to a dedicated physical port on a computer (for example, a workstation to a mainframe). However, dial-up links to the Internet are less rigid than connections to a specific port and require that IP is run by the PCs so that data can be forwarded beyond the Internet Service Provider's computer that has answered the phone.

Two network level protocols have been developed to carry IP traffic over serial phone lines. The first, Serial Line Internet Protocol (SLIP) is very simple and was devised only as a short-term solution although, as is often the case, once it was in use it was hard to displace. The second protocol, Point-to-Point Protocol (PPP), is more sophisticated and includes elements of link control. PPP is now the preferred link protocol for carrying IP over dial-up serial lines.

15.8.1 Serial Line Internet Protocol (SLIP)

The Serial Line Internet Protocol (SLIP) is simply a data encapsulation protocol. It addresses two simple issues for the receiver: How do I know when an IP packet is starting? How do I know when the IP packet has completed? The first question is important because the receiver is otherwise simply receiving a series of idle bytes on the line. The second question could be answered by the receiver

0×c0	IP Header	IP Data	0×c0

Figure 15.31 SLIP uses the END byte to encapsulate IP packets on the wire.

looking inside the IP packet and finding the length indicator, but this would require placing IP intelligence in the line device which really should be as dumb as possible.

Figure 15.31 shows that SLIP encapsulates IP packets with a single special byte called the SLIP END byte with value 0xc0. When a receiver sees this byte, it has finished receiving one IP packet and is ready to receive a new packet, so the same byte can be used to begin and end an encapsulation. The sender should send 0xc0 as the idle byte on the wire.

But what if the data in the IP packet contains a byte with value 0xc0? This would cause the receiver to prematurely terminate the received packet. SLIP uses an ESCAPE byte with value 0xdb to indicate that the 0xc0 was present in the initial data stream and replaces the 0xc0 byte with 0xdc. When the receiver sees 0xdb, it discards that byte and converts the next byte (0xdc) back to 0xc0.

But now, what if the IP packet contained a byte with value 0xdb? The receiver would treat this as the ESCAPE byte and would exclude it from the received packet. This is handled by the sender inserting a new ESCAPE byte and converting the 0xdb to 0xdd. This process is shown in Figure 15.32.

And that's it! There is nothing more to SLIP. RFC 1055, which defines the protocol as a small piece of C code, spends as much time considering the issues with the use of SLIP as it does defining it.

One of the concerns with SLIP was its use over slow links. This is not particularly an issue with SLIP *per se*, but with the transmission of IP, UDP, and TCP over phone connections which used to peak at a stunning 2400 bits per second. In particular, the issue of the burden of IP headers (as discussed in

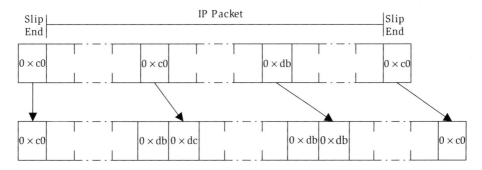

Figure 15.32 SLIP uses the ESCAPE byte (0xdb) to indicate the presence of bytes with special values in the IP packet.

Section 15.4) is relevant. Compressed SLIP (CSLIP) was introduced several years later to handle this problem.

CSLIP uses IP header compression that takes advantage of the fact that the link is point-to-point and that the bulk of the contents of the IP and TCP headers (around 20 bytes each) does not change significantly from one packet to the next. The logic described in RFC 1144 (known eponymously as Van Jacobson compression) forms the basis of header compression described in Section 15.4 and will not be covered further here. Where SLIP is still used today, it usually incorporates the IP header compression techniques.

15.8.2 Point-to-Point Protocol

SLIP was never intended to be a permanent solution and was acknowledged in RFC 1055 to have several issues beyond the need to handle IP header compression solved in CSLIP. It has no error detection or correction mechanisms, and it is only designed to carry IP traffic, making it very restrictive when compared to other networking protocols. Finally, SLIP assumes that both ends of a link either already know or have no need to know the addresses of the other end of the link.

To resolve these deficiencies, the Point-to-Point Protocol (PPP) was developed over a period of years and stabilized as RFC 1661. PPP features data encapsulation just like SLIP, but it uses the High-Level Data Link Control (HDLC) protocol as a basis for encapsulating datagrams over point-to-point links. This features an END byte with value 0x7e to mark the start and end of packets, and escape sequences are used to protect real data bytes with that value.

HDLC framing calls for a 1-byte address field and a 1-byte control field. PPP uses an address of 0xff (the all-purpose broadcast address) and a control value of 0x03 (which states that the user data will be transmitted in an unsequenced frame). The next 2 bytes indicate the payload protocol allowing PPP to carry multiple network layer protocols (like AppleTalk and Netware, and of course, IP). The assigned protocol value for IP is 0x21.

Now comes the data (the IP packet), which is usually constrained to a maximum of 1500 bytes and is followed by a checksum applied to the whole of the PPP frame between the END flags, and finally an END flag to mark the end of the packet. This is all shown in Figure 15.33.

A further feature of PPP is that it includes a management protocol to control the serial connection by initiating and terminating the use of the link, and by negotiating line parameters including the operation of PPP. The Link Control Protocol (LCP) is contained in RFC 1661 and allows optimizations such as dropping of the address and control bytes.

A further set of related protocols (the Network Control Protocols—NCPs) have different variants for each payload protocol carried by PPP. NCP allows the ends of the link to negotiate options such as IP header compression and to perform dynamic assignment of IP addresses to hosts that connect over dial-up links so that they may play a part in the network to which they connect.

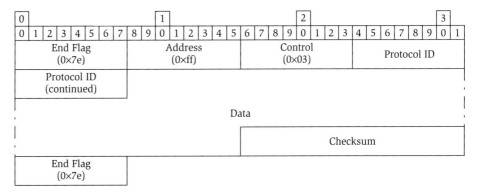

Figure 15.33 Data in PPP is encapsulated with additional control bytes.

15.8.3 Choosing a Dial-Up Protocol

The choice between SLIP, CSLIP, and PPP is relatively simple. Although SLIP and CSLIP are still supported in many environments, PPP is much preferred because of its error detection capabilities. Most Internet Service Providers use PPP for dial-up access, although a quick experiment reveals that few offer support for header compression.

15.8.4 Proxy ARP

Figure 15.34 shows a simple network with Ethernet connectivity. Several modems provide dial-in access, and the modems are served by two separate routers which provide connectivity into the network. When the client dials in it may be connected to any one of the modems.

The routers typically do not bridge between the network and the dial-up link, but only route packets that are targeted at the IP address of the client. This

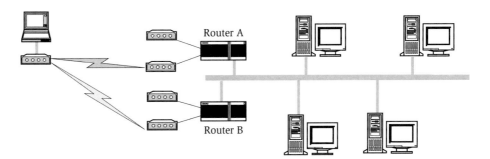

Figure 15.34 When dial-up connections are used, proxy ARP is usually enabled.

is all very well, but the hosts on the local network need to discover an Ethernet address to use when they want to send a packet to the dial-up client. Under normal circumstances, the hosts would use ARP to discover this, but their ARP requests will go unanswered since they are not bridged through to the dial-up client.

The solution is to have the network node that services the modem respond to the ARP requests on behalf of the dialed-in client. It returns a proxy ARP response, effectively giving its Ethernet address as the one to be used to reach the client's IP address. It is then responsible for routing the IP packets onto the correct link.

An interesting situation may occur if the client disconnects and dials in again within a short period of time. If the new connection goes to a modem supported by the same router there is no problem—the ARP tables at other nodes on the network will still hold the correct Ethernet address to use to reach the client. But if, in the example in Figure 15.34, the second connection is made to a modem served by router B, the ARP tables on the hosts in the network will be out of date, and until the entries in those tables timeout, it will be impossible to deliver packets correctly.

There are two solutions to this issue. The first is for the router to use UnARP to remove entries from ARP tables in the network when the client disconnects. The second option is for the router that receives the second connection to issue a Gratuitous ARP notification to replace any old information held in the network. Either approach works well. For more information on ARP, see Chapter 2.

15.9 Further Reading

IP Encapsulation

The following RFCs describe some of the tunneling mechanisms available for IP networks:

RFC 1702—Generic Routing Encapsulation over IPv4 networks
RFC 2003—IP Encapsulation within IP
RFC 2004—Minimal Encapsulation within IP
RFC 2784—Generic Routing Encapsulation (GRE)

Virtual Private Networks

Virtual Private Networks—Making the Right Connection, by Dennis Fowler (1999). Morgan Kaufmann. This book thoroughly explains the concepts behind VPNs from the perspectives of security and technology.

VPN Technologies—A Comparison, by Jon Harrison (2003). This is a White Paper from Data Connection Ltd. that offers an excellent introduction to the very many VPN solutions.

Two RFCs give additional information:

RFC 2547—BGP/MPLS VPNs
RFC 2917—A Core MPLS IP VPN Architecture

Mobile IP

Mobile IP is discussed by the Mobile IP Working Group of the IETF. Their web site is http://www.ietf.org/html.charters/mobileip-charter.html. Some key RFCs are:

RFC 2005—Applicability Statement for IP Mobility Support
RFC 2794—Mobile IP Network Access Identifier Extension for IPv4
RFC 3024—Reverse Tunneling for Mobile IP
RFC 3344—IP Mobility Support for IPv4

Header Compression

RFC 2507—IP Header Compression
RFC 2508—Compressing IP/UDP/RTP Headers for Low-Speed Serial Links
RFC 2509—IP Header Compression over PPP
RFC 3409—Lower Layer Guidelines for Robust RTP/UDP/IP Header Compression

The MPLS Forum produces interoperability agreements covering, among other things, MPLS header compression. Their web site is http://www.mpls forum.org.

Voice Over IP

The MPLS Forum produces interoperability agreements covering, among other things, Voice over MPLS. Their web site is http://www.mplsforum.org.

Telephony

IP Telephony, by Bill Douskalis (2000). Prentice-Hall. This provides a good description of IP telephony and also explains the reasoning behind IP compression.

The Telecommunications Standards Sector of the International Telecommunications Union (ITU) is called the ITU-T (formerly the CCITT). It develops standards for IP telephony jointly with the IETF. Their web site is http://www.itu.int/itu-t.

The IETF's IP Telephony Working Group maintains a web page at http://www.ietf.org/html.charters/iptel-charter.html, while the Session Initiation Protocol Working Group has a page at http://www.ietf.org/html.charters/sip-charter.html.

Media gateway control is worked on by the Megaco Working Group located at http://www.ietf.org/html.charters/megaco-charter.html.

Some important RFCs are:

RFC 2824—Call Processing Language Framework and Requirements
RFC 2871—A Framework for Telephony Routing over IP
RFC 3219—Telephony Routing over IP (TRIP)
RFC 3216—SIP: Session Initiation Protocol
RFC 3312—Integration of Resource Management and Session Initiation Protocol (SIP)

RFC 3428—Session Initiation Protocol (SIP) Extension for Instant Messaging
RFC 2805—Media Gateway Control Protocol Architecture and Requirements
RFC 3015—Megaco Protocol Version 1.0
RFC 3054—Megaco IP Phone Media Gateway Application Profile

IP and ATM

The ATM Forum developed and continues to pursue standards and interoperability agreements for all aspects of ATM. Their web site is http://www.atmforum.com. Some important RFCs relevant to carrying IP over an ATM network are:

RFC 1932—IP over ATM: A Framework Document
RFC 2022—Support for Multicast over UNI 3.0/3.1 based ATM Networks
RFC 2225—Classical IP and ARP over ATM
RFC 2226—IP Broadcast over ATM Networks
RFC 2331—ATM Signalling Support for IP over ATM — UNI Signalling 4.0 Update
RFC 2601—ILMI-Based Server Discovery for ATMARP
RFC 2684—Multiprotocol Encapsulation over ATM Adaptation Layer 5

IP over Dial-Up

Several RFCs describe the lower-layer protocols for carrying IP over dial-up links.

RFC 1055—Nonstandard for Transmission of IP Datagrams over Serial Lines
RFC 1144—Compressing TCP/IP Headers for Low-Speed Serial Links
RFC 1661—The Point-to-Point Protocol
RFC 1662—PPP in HDLC-like Framing

Concluding Remarks

A company or individual can make a fortune from successful prediction of the future, but it is not easy. When we ask, "How will the Internet develop next?" we must look at an evolutionary process driven by user demand, Service Providers' willingness to invest, manufacturers' readiness to make new developments, and the standards bodies' enthusiasm for embracing new work.

Perhaps the biggest area of potential growth for the Internet is IPv6. Much has been made of the motivation for IPv6 and whether it is really necessary, but the momentum is beginning to build. In 2001 the Japanese Government spent around $70 million on IPv6 verification testing and experimentation, and set a deadline of 2005 for all businesses dealing with the government and for all government agencies to use IPv6. Many forward-looking governments, including the British and American Governments, have IPv6 tasks forces charged with the responsibility of determining what action needs to be taken to ensure a smooth transition to IPv6. In June 2003 the American Department of Defense (DoD) announced that all new equipment purchased after October 2003 to participate in the Global Information Grid (see the next section) must be IPv6 enabled and that all DoD traffic will transition to IPv6 by the year 2008. And gradually more experimental networks are being rolled out with many now carrying live traffic. But although this represents a major configuration nightmare and requires the roll-out of much new hardware and software, it isn't a dramatic new technological development.

It is possible to gain some insight into the up-and-coming new areas by monitoring the activity of the IETF. A crude tool is the number of people attending Working Group meetings when the IETF gathers every four months. By that standard it is possible to determine which areas of work are receiving a lot of attention and where most work is currently going on. For example, at the IETF meeting in Washington, D.C. in November 1999, there were nearly 800 people present for the MPLS Working Group meeting. This was a huge turn-out, with all of the seats filled and people sitting on the floor in the aisles. MPLS was a new and hot topic at the time.

At the moment, the IETF Working Groups that deal with Virtual Private Networks (VPNs) are seeing a lot of activity. VPNs are a major growth area for Service Providers since they involve a service that is easily billable and readily understood by the customers. Such was the amount of work, that the IETF recently made the decision to split the single Provider Provisioned Virtual Private Network (PPVPN) Working Group into two groups. This created the Layer Two VPN (L2VPN) and the Layer Three VPN (L3VPN) Working Groups dedicated to deriving VPN solutions architected at the data-link layer and the network layer, respectively. IETF VPN protocol extensions are well advanced through standardization and are already seeing significant deployment.

This may give us the key to one of the areas in which the Internet will develop. Service Providers are looking to provide new services that are easily recognized as benefits by the consumer and for which the Service Provider can charge. As Niel Ransom, CTO of Alcatel, said recently: "...the future is about creating billable services." Into this category, along with VPNs come mobile IP, mobile VPNs (MVPNs), and the carriage of voice over IP. Again, the standards in these areas are well developed and deployed to lesser or greater extent. MVPN is an interesting development to provide an emulation of a secure, private mobile or wireless network using the common, shared, and generally insecure resources of the public mobile or wireless networks. It is without doubt that the ability to access emails and to surf the Web from small, hand-held, wireless devices will be a growth sector in the next few years, and the standardization of IP-based protocols to place telephone calls and to carry voice traffic over the Internet will lead to a surge in that area too.

IP telephony is an example of another burgeoning area, that of IP-based control protocols. In the last few years there have been a lot of new application and signaling protocols that use IP and IP-based transport as their foundation. Some of these, like GMPLS and LMP, although now standardized, are still in the early stages of deployment and may or may not take off according to the pressures from the market place. The scope for new application and control protocols is really only limited by imagination and market support for, although the IETF likes to see a clear statement of a problem before it works on a new protocol, there is nothing quite like the commercial drive of competing equipment manufacturers with a host of customers clamoring to give them money.

IP telephony also leads to the general theme of media distribution with video streaming, and voice and video conferencing being high on the list of requirements. This brings us to the tricky subject of multicast networking, an area with reasonably well-developed standards but very poor take-up by Service Providers, with only slow growth in the Multicast Backbone, the MBONE. It would seem that either the networking technologies are not yet suitable or the market is not making enough of a noise. Recent developments in signaling point-to-multipoint connections for MPLS and GMPLS networks may indicate that this is the way forward with a more rigid, connection-oriented approach to multicast traffic.

Another critical area for the future of the Internet is reflected in the fact that "security" has become a popular buzz-word. Computers need to be protected from viruses and hackers, and networks themselves need to be protected against abuse and denial of service attacks. Data sent across the network need to be protected from prying eyes, and governments are at the same time champions of their need to be able to protect their own data and their requirement to be able to examine everyone else's messages and files. The security sector of the

Internet is bound to continue to grow as a result both of the interesting challenges and the very real commercial demand for solutions.

Optical networking was a bright hope in the years leading up to the writing of this book, but the downturn in the telecoms marketplace slowed developments in this area considerably. However, the protocols described in Chapter 10 are now stable, and many have been deployed and are used to manage traffic in optical networks. As the industry recovers and the demands for bandwidth continue to grow, optical devices will be in greater demand and photonic switches (that is, devices that switch light signals from one fiber to another without converting the signal to an electronic form) will doubtlessly be deployed in the core of optical networks. These developments will call upon the features of GMPLS protocols to make it possible to operate these switches dynamically, and will offer the network users such services as on-demand bandwidth and optical VPNs.

It is worth noting as a final comment that enterprise networks do not necessarily have the same requirements as the Internet. Routing and security are typically simpler, but the demand may be higher for integrated voice and data traffic. These distinctions, of course, get fudged as the enterprise network is connected to or across the Internet.

The Global Information Grid

The Global Information Grid (GIG), or simply the Grid, has been described as Internet II, or the Son of Internet. It is a massive network being built by the U.S. Department of Defense (DoD) designed to connect "war fighters" anywhere in the world. It uses its own infrastructure, which is distinct from that of the Internet, but will have many similarities.

The requirements were recently stated by Brigadier General Bud Bell of the U.S. Air Force: We want "a Web-based, browser-enabled, self-healing network that uses commercial off-the-shelf (COTS) applications to support existing and projected business practices while integrating data elements across all legacy systems protected by a multi-level secure environment that we can trust in war." That means that the Grid must provide all U.S. military personnel with the network connectivity they require at any time and in any place so that they can get information in a timely, reliable, and secure way. For that reason, the DoD is keen to emphasize that bandwidth must never be a limiting factor; but other factors such as end-to-end communication capabilities, seamless interoperability between components, bandwidth on demand, robustness and resilience, and integration of data, voice, and video services within one network are likely to be significant forces in the shape of the network that is built.

It is noteworthy that one of the driving forces behind today's Internet was the ARPANET (the Advanced Research Projects Agency Network), with its feet firmly rooted in the requirements of the DoD. It is not unreasonable to expect, therefore, that the average Internet user will see some benefits fall out from this project. However, although the Grid will use lots of the latest technology and will push the frontiers of bandwidth and computing power, there is no intention to make this network available for general use. This means that Internet users might not see firsthand benefits from the Grid, but may have to wait for new developments to filter down.

Three factors will benefit tomorrow's Internet users more rapidly. First, the DoD is a large purchasing organization and many salesmen would kill to get approval for sales to build the Grid. This means that when the DoD asks for a new function manufacturers will jump to build it into their product lines, and that means that most if not all of that function will become generally available. Second, the DoD is naturally cautious about deploying brand-new unproven technology in the field where the lives of its soldiers and politicians may be at risk. They demand that new developments are fully tested in real networks carrying real data—that is, in the Internet. The final factor is commercial reality. When push comes to shove, a considerable financial saving can be made by the U.S. Government if it utilizes commercial network infrastructures, and this is likely to result in substantial upgrades to the infrastructure of the Internet's backbone which may benefit all users.

The Grid is not to be confused with Grid. Grid is the practice of interconnecting geographically disjoint computers for the purpose of sharing processing power, not just data and information. Unlike cluster computing, the processor power of remote computers is under real-time control and does not require a centralized scheduler, but can react according to the other demands on the systems. At the moment, consumers of this Grid are mainly research establishments that have large or super-computers and periodically have very big problems to solve using a lot of processing power. Grid computing places interesting requirements on the network that connects the participating computers.

Further Reading

You can follow the activities of the IETF's PPVPN working groups at http://www.ietf.org/html.charters/l2vpn-charter.html and http://www.ietf.org/html.charters/l3vpn-charter.html.

Mobile VPNs are described in *Mobile VPN: Delivering Advanced Services in Next Generation Wireless Systems*, by Alex Shneyderman and Alessio Casati (2002). Wiley.

Internet2 is a not-for-profit consortium of universities and companies working to develop and deploy advanced network applications and technology with a view to improving the performance and function of the Internet. You can find out more at their Web site, http://www.internet2.edu.

The American government ran a successful Next Generation Internet project which was wound up in the year 2002. See http://www.ngi.gov for more details.

Work now continues on the Large Scale Networking (LSN) project described at http://www.itrd.gov/pubs/blue01/lsn.html, to bring more consumers and data onto the Internet and to increase its bandwidth and function.

The Global Grid Forum is a consortium of researchers working to improve distributed computing through "Grid" technologies. They can be found at http://www.gridforum.org.

Index

7-bit-plain-text encoding, 621
802.2 standard, 18–19

A

Abort chunks, 347–348
ABRs (area border routers), 136–137, 170–172, 174, 176–177, 417
Abstract nodes, 433
Abstract Syntax Notation One. *See* ASN.1 (Abstract Syntax Notation One)
Acceptable Label Sets, 502–503
Access control, 681–682, 685–687
ACK (Acknowledgement) message, 555, 556
Acknowledgement message, 303
Active peers, 406–407
Adaptive real-time protocols, 265
Add Branch message, 561
Add-Drop Multiplexors. *See* ADMs (Add-Drop Multiplexors)
Address Family Identifier pair, 488
Address messages, 409–411
Address Resolution Protocol. *See* ARP (Address Resolution Protocol)
Address spaces, 37–38, 40–41
Address Withdraw message, 411
Adjacency and GSMP (General Switch Management Protocol), 554–556
Adjacency messages, 551, 554–556
Adler 32-bit checksum, 340
Administrative groups, 450
Administrative Status object, 505, 519–520

Admission control component, 258–259
ADMs (Add-Drop Multiplexors), 569
Adspec object, 262, 271, 281, 294, 464, 468
AFI (Address Family Indicator), 205
AFI (Authority and Format Identifier), 180
Aggregate Route-Based IP Switching. *See* ARIS (Aggregate Route-Based IP Switching)
Aggregation, 117–118
al-Jazeera Web site, 678–679
All Ports Configuration message body, 557
All Routers addresses, 90
All Routers group, 90
All Systems addresses, 90
All Systems group, 90
All Systems Group Membership Query, 91
Anycast addresses, 99–101
Appliances and IP addresses, 93
Application gateway, 686–687
Application interfaces, 653–654
Application layer, 5
Application Plane, 7–8
Application protocols, xxi, xxiii, 5, 307, 575
    FTP (File Transfer Protocol), 598–611
    HTTP (Hypertext Transfer Protocol), 615–630
    protecting data, 35
    selecting, 630–631
    Telnet, 588–597
    TFTP (Trivial FTP), 611–614
    well-known port, 578

Application-level protocols, character-based, 621
Application-level security, 682–683
Applications
    automatic log outs, 685
    client, 576–577
    data distribution, 83–84
    hard real-time requirements, 261
    listen mode, 320
    managing data delivery for real-time, 354
    preventing fragmentation, 34
    quality of service requirements, 252
    receipt of out-of-order fragments, 33
    reducing controlled load token bucket, 265
    SCTP, 578
    selecting type of service to implement, 265–266
    server, 576–577
    session management, 5
    stream of data, 9
    TCP (Transmission Control Protocol), 578
    transactions, 7–8
    UDP, 578
    use of separate datagrams, 31
    using multicast, 83–84
    well-known port numbers, 311
Area Addresses TLV, 187
Area border routers. *See* ABRs (area border routers)
Areas, 136–137
    ABRs, 176
    aggregation at borders, 171
    algorithm performance, 175–176
    backbone of AS, 170

Areas (*continued*)
choosing to use, 175–177
decrease in SPF, 175
hiding parts of networks, 175
increasing management
complexity of network, 177
increasing robustness of
routing protocol, 175
IS-IS, 181, 184
nesting, 170
number of routers in, 176
OSPF (Open Shortest Path
First), 156, 170–172
routing decisions, 175
scalability issues, 176
ARIS (Aggregate Route-Based
IP Switching), 397
ARP (Address Resolution
Protocol), 23, 49–53, 74
ARPANET (Advanced Research
Projects Agency Network),
765
ASBRs (autonomous system
border routers), 177, 199
leaking external routing
information, 219
transferring information
transparently across IS-IS
routing domain, 193–194
ASCII (American Standard Code
for Information
Interchange), 590
AS-Confederacy-Sequence
segment identifier, 222
AS-Confederacy-Set segment
identifier, 222
ASICs, 46
ASM (Any Source Multicast), 236
ASN.1 (Abstract Syntax Notation
One), 644, 647, 673–674
ASs (autonomous systems), 118
client-server relationship
between BGP speakers,
220–221
community identifiers, 214
confederations, 221–222
forwarding packets out of,
217–218

multihoming, 211–213
numbers, 119
routing protocols, 119
routing traffic between, 199–200
Association Initiation chunk,
342–343
Associations
aborting, 347
active, 346
half-open, 345
managing, 342, 344
multiplexing more than one
data stream, 348
negotiating terms, 342
non-fatal errors, 347
orderly closure, 346–347
periodically probing, 346
returning unsupported
parameters, 345
SCTP (Stream Control
Transmission Protocol),
339, 341–348
sequenced and numbered
flow of bytes, 348–352
TCB (Transmission Control
Block), 347
timer, 345
timestamp, 346
Asynchronous Transfer Mode.
See ATM (Asynchronous
Transfer Mode)
ATM (Asynchronous Transfer
Mode), 14–17, 376, 386
inferred labels, 390
IP, 752–756
IP datagrams, 30
layer 2 VPNs, 732
VCI (Virtual Circuit Identifier),
390
VPI (Virtual Path Identifier),
390
ATM Forum Web site, 762
ATM networks, 169
AAL5 (ATM Adaption
Layer 5) PDU (Protocol
Data Unit), 390
PNNI (Peer Network to Network
Interconnect), 398

PVCs (permanent virtual
circuits), 752
SVCs (switched virtual
circuits), 752
ATM switches and GSMP
(General Switch
Management Protocol),
549
Audio streaming, 83–84
Authentication
application level, 687–688
IPsec (IP security), 690–695
IPv6, 109
ISAKMP (Internet Security
Associating and Key
Management Protocol),
711
LMP (Link Management
Protocol), 545–546
messages not tampered with,
687–688
Mobile IP, 741
OSPF routers, 156–157
per-message level, 688
RIP, 150–151
RIPv1 routers, 154
RIPv2 routers, 154
routers, 189
routing protocols, 682
signaling protocols, 682
TCP connections, 695
Telnet, 595–597
validating user or sender,
687–688
Authentication algorithms, 703
Authentication extension header,
109
Authentication header, 690–691
Authentication Information TLV,
189
Authoritative DNS name server,
587
autonomous system border
routers. *See* ASBRs
(autonomous system
border routers)
Autonomous systems. ASs
(autonomous systems)

B

Backbone networks, 119
Background File Transfer
    Protocol. *See* BFTP
    (Background File
    Transfer Protocol)
Backup designated router, 168–169
Backup LSPs, 503
Bacus-Naur Form. *See* BNF
    (Backus-Naur Form)
Bandwidth
    conflict between demand and
        availability, 265
    IS-IS, 524
    limitations on, 264–265
    OSPF (Open Shortest Path
        First), 524
    timeslots, 492
    wavelengths, 493
Basic Encoding Rules. *See* BER
    (Basic Encoding Rules)
BeginVerify object, 538
BeginVerifyAck object, 538
BeginVerify/BeginVerifyAck
    message, 537
BeginVerifyNack message, 542
Bell, Bud, 765
BER (Basic Encoding Rules),
    645–647
BFTP (Background File Transfer
    Protocol), 614–615
BGMP (Border Gateway Multicast
    Protocol), 235–236, 241
BGP (Border Gateway Protocol),
    xxii, 116, 245
    AS (autonomous systems),
        199–200
    advanced functions, 214–217
    communities, 214
    dampening route flap, 216–217
    distributing external routing
        information, 219
    distributing labels for routes,
        486–488
    example Update message,
        217
    exterior LSRs, 487
    exterior routing, 199–200

Interior Gateway Protocol,
    217–220
interior LSRs, 487
IPv4 routes, 214
IPv6 addressing, 214
multi-protocol support, 215–216
Next Hop address, 215
peers, 487
point-to-point protocol, 200
processing piggybacked label
    advertisement, 488
route distinguisher, 216
running across AS borders, 219
running with AS, 219
SAFIs (Subsequent Address
    Family Identifiers), 205
selecting, 222–223
SNPA length, 216
TCP (Transmission Control
    Protocol), 200
Update message, 486
VPNs (Virtual Private
    Networks), 216, 730, 733
withdrawing routes, 208–209
BGP messages, 200
    BGP Identifier, 203
    BGP Notification message,
        205–208
    Capability Codes, 203–204
    exchanging, 202–203
    header, 201
    KeepAlive message, 203
    length, 201
    Multi-Exit Discriminator
        attribute, 212–213
    Multiprotocol Capability,
        204–205
    Notification message, 203
    Open message, 202–203
    Route Refresh message, 208
    SAFI (Subsequent Address
        Family Identifier), 205
    types, 201
    Update message, 208–214
    well-known attributes, 210
BGP networks, 216
BGP peers, 200, 205, 208
BGP routers, 200, 203

BGP speakers, 201, 219
    client-server relationship
        between, 220–221
    AS number, 203
    requesting complete and
        immediate update of all
        routes, 208
    routes for variety of protocols
        and uses, 205
    time before declaring session
        dead, 203
BGP-4 (Border Gateway Protocol 4),
    199–223
    MPLS, 486–489
    TCP (Transmission Control
        Protocol), 337
Bidirectional LSPs, 502–503
Big-Endian integers, 657
Binary files, 621
Bits, xxiv
BNF (Backus-Naur Form),
    xxv–xxvi, 281, 468
BOOTP (Bootstrap Protocol),
    23, 53–54, 316
BOOTP server, 53
Bootstrap Protocol. *See* BOOTP
    (Bootstrap Protocol)
Border Gateway Multicast
    Protocol. *See* BGMP
    (Border Gateway Multicast
    Protocol) and BGMP-4
Branches, 561
Bridges, 42–44
Bridging, 4
Bridging table, 43
Broadcast addresses, 39
Broadcasting, 79, 168–169
Broadcasts, 39
    datagrams, 79
    looping traffic, 43
    prune protocols and, 225–226
Bundle message, 297–298
Bundles, 523
BYE packet, 360
Bypass tunnels, 438
Byte streams, broken into
    integers, 35
Bytes, xxiv

C

Candidate list, 144
Care-of-address, 735, 737
Categorizing packets, 249
CBT (Core Based Tree) protocol, 236, 240–241
CCAMP working group, 305
CCAMP Working Group Web site, 547, 573
CDI (Context Session Identifier), 744–745
CE (Customer Edge) equipment, 733
Cell phones and IP addresses, 93
Cell Switching Router. *See* CSR (Cell Switching Router)
Cell tax, 15
Cells, 14–15
Certificate message, 698
Certificate Request message, 698
Certificate Verify message, 699
Chain, 619
Change Cipher Spec message, 699
Channels, 533–537
ChannelStatus message, 544–545
Character flows and Telnet, 591–592
Checkpoints, 604–605
Checksum algorithm, 36
Checksum TLV, 189
Checksums
    error and datagrams, 66
    ICMP messages, 65
    IGMP messages, 88
    IP, 35–37
    IPv6, 111–112
    LSPs (Link State PDUs) PDU, 192
    optimizing calculations, 36
    OSPF messages, 156
    PIM messages, 227
    reducing processing time, 35
    standard IP, 35
    TCP (Transmission Control Protocol), 322, 324
    transmitted with data, 35
    TTL field, 36

UDP (User Datagram Protocol), 314–316
UDP Lite, 317
Ch-LSP FEC element, 412
Chunks, 339, 340–341, 348
CI (craft interface), 637
CIDR (Classless Inter-Domain Routing), 113, 116–118
Cisco routers, 181
Cisco Web site, 383, 675
Class A addresses, 40
Class B addresses, 40, 117
Class C addresses, 39–40
Class D addresses, 84–85
Class-full routing, 118
Classless Inter-Domain Routing. *See* CIDR (Classless Inter-Domain Routing)
Classless routing, 117
Client applications, 576–577
Client Key Exchange message, 698–699
Client-Accept message, 666
Client-Close message, 666
Client-Open message, 666
Clients
    cache of recent DNS responses, 584
    DHCP capable, 54
    file for more DHCP options, 55
Client-server model, 577
Client-server protocols
    COPS (Common Open Policy Service Protocol), 666
    FTP (File Transfer Protocol), 598
    GIOP (General Inter-ORB Protocol), 656
    CLIs (command line interfaces), 400, 637–638
    CLNP (Connectionless Network Protocol), 4, 179
    CloseConnection message, 659
    Coarse Wave Division Multiplexing. *See* CWDM (Coarse Wave Division Multiplexing)
Coloring packets, 253–255

command line interfaces. *See* CLIs (command line interfaces)
Common Facilities, 653
Common Object Request Broker Architecture. *See* CORBA (Common Object Request Broker Architecture)
Common Object Services. *See* COS (Common Object Services)
Common Open Policy Service. *See* COPS (Common Open Policy Service) protocol
Communities, 214
Community attribute, 214
Complete Sequence Number PDU. *See* CSNP (Complete Sequence Number PDU)
Component links, 523
Components, 7–8
Compound objects, 283
Compressed packets, 744
COMPRESSED_NON_TCP packet type, 745
COMPRESSED_RTP packet type, 745–746
COMPRESSED_UDP packet type, 745
Compression Request object, 748
Compression Response object, 748
Computers, 1–3
Computing paths, 142–147
Confederacy route advertisement, 222
Confederations, 221–222
Config message, 533, 535, 569
Config object, 535, 569
ConfigAck message, 533
ConfigNack message, 533
Configuration methods
    CLIs (command line interfaces), 637–638
    GUIs (graphical user interfaces), 638–639
    standardized data representations and access, 639–641

Configuration protocols, selecting, 660
Configuration Sequence Number TLV, 407
Congestion
  detection, 368
  dropping packets, 256
Congestion window, 333
Connection Activity Request message, 564
Connection Statistics message, 564
Connectionless, 26
Connectionless Network Protocol. *See* CLNP (Connectionless Network Protocol)
Connection-oriented protocols, 318
Connection-oriented transport, 312
Connections, state of, 564–565
Connectivity, propagating information, 115
Conservative Label Retention, 418
Constrained Shortest Path First. *See* CSPF (Constrained Shortest Path First)
Constraint-based LSP Setup Using LDP. *See* CR-LDP (Constraint-based LSP Setup Using LDP)
Constraint-based routing, 373, 436
Constraint-based signaling protocol, 438
  CR-LDP (Constraint-Based LSP Setup Using LDP), 439–456
  Extensions to RSVP-TE (RSVP for LSP Tunnels), 456–478
Context Session Identifier. *See* CDI (Context Session Identifier)
CONTEXT_STATE packet type, 745, 746–747
Control channels
  managing, 569
  out-of-band signaling networks, 533
Control Connection, 600

Control plane, 7
Control plane protocols, IP-based, 397–398
Control protocols, 3, 7
Control signaling, out of band, 506
Controlled Load service, 265
Controllers, 550
  establishing connectivity with switch, 554–555
  reporting asynchronous events to, 563
Conversations, xix
COPS Decision message, xxvi
COPS messages, 666, 668–673
COPS (Common Open Policy Service) protocol, xxiii, 663, 666–667, 670–671
CORBA (Common Object Request Broker Architecture), xxiii, 640–641, 652, 660
  Application Interface, 654
  Application interfaces, 653
  architecture, 653–655
  client-server architecture, 653
  CloseConnection message, 659
  Common Facilities, 653
  communications, 656–659
  CORBA object, 652
  COS (Common Object Services), 653–654
  DII (Dynamic Invocation Interface), 654
  Domain Interfaces, 654
  DSI (Dynamic Skeleton Interface), 655
  GIOP (General Inter-ORB Protocol), 655, 656
  how objects and data are encoded in messages, 656
  IDL (Interface Definition Language), 652–653, 654
  IDL Skeleton, 654–655
  IIOP (Internet Inter-ORB Protocol), 655, 659
  Implementation Repository, 654–655
  indirection, 656

  Interface Repository, 654
  Object Adaptor, 654
  object interfaces, 652
  OMA (Object Management Architecture), 653–654
  ORB (Object Request Broker), 653–655
CORBA object, 652
Core, 224
Core Based Tree protocol. *See* CBT (Core Based Tree) protocol
Core networks, controlling, 491
Corporate-espionage, 677
COS (Common Object Services), 653–654
Cost, 143
COTS (commercial off-the-shelf) applications, 765
CRC (cyclic redundancy check), 12, 314, 703
CR-LDP (Constraint-based LSP Setup Using LDP), xxii, 435, 439
  applicability and adoption, 479–480
  CBS (committed burst size), 443, 445
  CDR (committed data rate), 443, 445
  choosing FEC, 440–441
  coloring LSP, 450
  DiffServ TLV, 483
  Downstream On Demand mode, 439
  EBS (excess burst size), 443, 445
  Explicit Route Hop TLVs, 441, 443
  Explicit Route TLV, 441
  explicit routes, 439, 441–443
  FEC element, 440–441
  generalized, 520–521
  GMPLS, 508–509, 520–521
  identifying LSP, 441
  IP address Explicit Route Hops, 443
  Label Abort message, 453

CR-LDP (*continued*)
 Label Mapping message, 448, 453
 Label Release message, 449, 453
 Label Request message, 447–449, 453
 Label Withdraw message, 453–454
 Local CR-LSP Id, 441
 loop detection mechanisms of LDP, 440
 LSP priorities, 451
 LSPID Explicit Route Hop TLV, 443
 message flows, 427, 453
 Notification message, 447–448, 451–453
 PBS (peak burst size), 443, 445
 PDR (peak data rate), 443, 445
 PDUs, 454
 peak rate token bucket, 444
 pinning LSP, 448–450
 Preemption TLV, 451
 priorities assigned to LSPs, 439
 protocol state, 481
 re-routing LSP, 448–450
 resource affinities, 481
 Resource Class TLV, 450
 re-using mechanisms from LDP, 439–440
 versus RSVP-TE, 479–481
 signaling PSC mapping for L-LSP, 482
 similarity to LDP, 440
 status codes, 451–452
 Status TLV, 451
 summary of main functions, 480–481
 TCP (Transmission Control Protocol), 481
 TLVs, 440–451
 traffic parameters, 439, 443–448
 Traffic Parameters TLV, 443–447
CR-LDP messages, 452–455
CSNP (Complete Sequence Number PDU), 195–196

CSPF (Constrained Shortest Path First), 145–147
CSR (Cell Switching Router), 396
CWDM (Coarse Wave Division Multiplexing), 493
cyclic redundancy check.
 See CRC (cyclic redundancy check)

D
Daemons, 577
Data
 delivery and SCTP (Stream Control Transmission Protocol), 350
 end-to-end delivery, 4
 IP fragmentation, 30–34
 packaging, 9–10
 protecting path, 504
 Telnet servers, 591
 urgent, 329–330
Data buffers and TCP (Transmission Control Protocol), 333
Data channels, 533–537
Data chunk, 349–351
Data Connection, 600
Data distribution, 83–84
Data Encryption Standard.
 See DES (Data Encryption Standard)
Data events, 240
Data flows
 controlled load service, 260
 datagram delay, 262, 264
 defining session, 287
 merging in RSVP, 277–280
 modification requests, 298
 new, 298
 quality of service, 260
 removing from merge, 279
 requirements, 257
 routing, 371–372
 state refresh messages, 298
 worst case non-rate-based transit time variation, 263–264

Data Link objects, 570
Data packets, 16–17, 367
Data Plane, 7–8
Data streaming, 83–84
Data traffic, 7
Data transfer
 SCTP (Stream Control Transmission Protocol), 348–352
 TCP (Transmission Control Protocol), 322–324
Data transfer protocols, 2–3
Datagrams, 25
 amount of data carried by, 26–27
 arriving out of order, 33
 best path to forward, 115–116
 broadcast, 79
 checksum errors, 37, 66
 connectionless, 26, 313
 control information, 26
 Datagram Identifier field, 31–32
 determining end of, 33
 DF (Don't Fragment) bit, 34
 discarding non-secure, 76
 expired TTL, 67
 failure to deliver, 70
 formats, 26–30
 forwarding or discarding, 85, 87
 fragment re-assembly, 33–34
 fragmenting, 27, 30–34, 75
 Header Checksum field, 29
 headers, 26
 identifier, 27
 identifying sender of message, 29
 intended destination, 29
 IP, 30, 32, 42
 IPv6, 102–103, 107
 length of, 26–27
 Loose Route option, 62–63
 MF (More Fragments), 33
 MTU (Maximum Transmission Unit), 75–76
 number of hops before timing out, 27–28
 versus packets, 26
 payload data, 26

preventing fragmentation, 34
prioritizing, 26
protocol identifier, 28–29
protocol version, 26
real destination of, 62
Record Route option, 61–63
redirecting information,
    67–68, 70
reporting errors, 64–77
sending as broadcast
    datagram, 80–81
sending multiple copies, 79–80
sequences that never
    complete, 33
size of, 30
source node control over path,
    61–62
Source Route option, 62–63
Strict Route option, 62–63
time limit for delivery of,
    260–262
timer problems, 67
timestamps, 63
tracking path through
    network, 61
transport protocols, 312–313
TTL failure, 66
TTL (Time to Live) field, 27–28
Type of Service byte, 26
unfragmented, 33
unicast traffic, 79
unreachable destination, 70
Data-link exchanges, 4
Data-link layer addresses, 37
Data-link layer broadcasts and
    routers, 81
Data-link layer protocols, 3,
    24–25, 376
Data-link layers, 4
    datagrams as broadcast
        datagram, 80–81
    frames, 10
    hosts, 24
    including multicast concept, 81
    IP datagrams, 42
    IPv6, 107–108
    MTU, 10
    stream of data, 10

Data_Link object, 543
Data-link protocols, 2
    802.2 standard, 18
    ATM (Asynchronous Transfer
        Mode), 14–16
    dial-up networking, 18
    Ethernet, 10–12
    PoS (Packet over SONET),
        16–17
    Token Ring, 12–14
Decision message, 666, 672
Decompressor, 744
Default route, 45
Delete Branches message, 562
Delete Input message, 562
Delete Reservation
    message, 563
Delete Tree message, 562
Delete-Request-State
    message, 667
Denial of service attacks, 677,
    679, 682
Dense Wave Division
    Multiplexing. See DWDM
    (Dense Wave Division
    Multiplexing)
Dense-mode multicast protocols,
    223, 225–227
DES (Data Encryption Standard),
    694, 703, 709–710
Designated routers, 167–169
Destination area and ABRs,
    176–177
Destination options extension
    headers, 105
Destination Service Access Point.
    See DSAP (Destination
    Service Access Point)
Destination Unreachable ICMP
    message, 66, 70, 75–76
Devices
    CLIs (command line
        interfaces), 637–638
    identifying, 3
    management, 635–636
    physical level, 3
    storing configuration data,
        637–638

DHCP (Dynamic Host
    Configuration Protocol),
    23, 53–56, 59, 74
DHCP messages, 56–57
Dial-up networking, 18, 59
Dial-up protocols, 759
Differentiated Services. See
    DiffServ (Differentiated
    Services)
Differentiated Services Code
    Point. See DSCP
    (Differentiated Services
    Code Point)
DiffServ (Differentiated Services),
    xxii, 49, 249, 372, 481
    BAs (Behavior Aggregates), 482
    coloring packets, 253–255
    different qualities of service,
        256
    DSCP (Differentiated Services
        Code Point), 253
    facilitating real-time
        applications, 265
    functional model, 255–256
    identifying DSCP, 253–254
    versus IntServ, 266
    LSP, 486
    OA (Ordered Aggregate), 482
    prisoner's dilemma, 257
    scalability issues, 257
    selecting, 257
DiffServ networks, 253–254
DiffServ Object, 483
Diffusing computations, 242
Digital signatures, 683, 704
DII (Dynamic Invocation
    Interface), 654
Dijkstra, E. W., 144
Dijkstra algorithm, 193
Dijkstra Shortest Path First
    algorithm, 144–145
Direct routing, 42
Diskless workstations and RARP
    (Reverse ARP), 52
Distance Vector Multicast
    Routing Protocol. See
    DVMRP (Distance Vector
    Multicast Routing Protocol)

Distance vector protocols, 125, 129–131, 139, 246
  advertised connectivity metric, 143
  choosing how to compute paths, 147
  path computation model, 142–143
  RIP (Routing Information Protocol), 147–155
Distance vector routing
  distribution of routing information, 143
  Hello protocol, 132–133
  policies, 138
  routers sending information over links, 132
Distance vectors, 125–131
Distributed switches and GSMP (General Switch Management Protocol), 550
Distributing
  labels and RSVP-TE, 458
  routing information, 124–142
  traffic, 369
Distribution tree, pruning, 225–226
DNS (Domain Name System), xxiii, 575
  distribution of DNS databases, 582–584
  DNS message formats, 584–588
  DNS protocol, 582
  extensions to, 588
  host names, 579–582
  question type codes, 588
DNS databases, distribution of, 582–584
DNS messages, 584–588
DNS name server, 587
DNS servers, 582–584
document type definition. See DTD (document type definition)
Documents and hypertext, 616–617

Domain Name System. See DNS (Domain Name System)
Domain names, redirection of, 581
Domain Specific Part. See DSP (Domain Specific Part)
Dotted decimal notation, 37
Downstream on Demand label distribution, 411–418
Downstream Unsolicited label distribution, 398–399, 411–418
dRFC 2212 – (Specification of Guaranteed Quality of Service), 305
DSAP (Destination Service Access Point), 18
DSCP (Differentiated Services Code Point), 253–255
DSI (Dynamic Skeleton Interface), 655
DSP (Domain Specific Part), 180–181
DTD (document type definition), 650, 652
Dual IS-IS, 179
Dual key algorithms, 704, 710
DVMRP (Distance Vector Multicast Routing Protocol), 224, 227, 232–233, 235
DWDM (Dense Wave Division Multiplexing), 493
Dynamic address assignment, 53–59
Dynamic Host Configuration Protocol. See DHCP (Dynamic Host Configuration Protocol)
Dynamic Invocation Interface. See DII (Dynamic Invocation Interface)
Dynamic ports, 311
Dynamic Skeleton Interface. See DSI (Dynamic Skeleton Interface)
Dynamic traffic engineering, 373–374

E
EBCDIC (Extended Binary Coded Decimal Interchange Code), 590
Echo Reply ICMP message, 71
Echo Request ICMP message, 71–72, 75–76
ECMP (Equal Cost Multi-Path), 146, 369, 372
ECN (explicit congestion notification), 375–376
Edge nodes, 729, 730
Edge router, 233
EF (Expedited Forwarding) PHB, 255
EGPs (Exterior Gateway Protocols), 119, 139, 199–223, 245
EIGRP (Enhanced Inter-Gateway Routing Protocol), 147, 242
Element Management Systems. See EMSs (Element Management Systems)
E-LSPs, 483–486
EMSs (Element Management Systems), 640
Encapsulated Security Payload. See ESP (Encapsulated Security Payload)
Encryption, 683, 688–689
  end-to-end mode, 692
  IPsec (IP security), 692–695
  IPv6, 109–110
  keys, 688
  Mobile IP, 742
  proxy, 693
  TCP connections, 695
  VPNs, 731
Encryption algorithms, 703–704
  DES (Data Encryption Standard), 709–710
  multiples of certain number of bytes, 695
Endpoints, 309
End-to-end delivery of data, 4
End-to-end protocol, 697
End-to-end security, 689–690
EndVerify message, 539

EndVerify/EndVerifyAck message, 537
Enhanced Inter-Gateway Routing Protocol. *See* EIGRP (Enhanced Inter-Gateway Routing Protocol)
Entities, 403–409, 619
Entries, 643
Envelopes, 650–651
Ephemeral ports, 311
Epoch, 299
Equal Cost Multi-Path. *See* ECMP (Equal Cost Multi-Path)
EROs (Explicit Route Objects), 509–511
Error detection, 34–37, 308, 512
Error notification, 512
Error Notification message, 407
Error recovery, 512
Error Spec Object, 272, 284, 285, 290–292
Errors
    ICMP reporting and detection, 65
    TFTP (Trivial FTP), 613
Error_Spec object, 511
ES-IS, 242–243
ESP (Encapsulated Security Payload), 109–110, 692, 694
ESs (end systems), 179
/etc/hosts file, 579
Ethernet, xxiv, 1
    802.3 standard, 10
    channels, 533
    collisions, 11
    CRC (cyclic redundancy check), 12
    data speeds, 10–11
    direct routing, 42
    frames, 11–12
    hubs, 11
    MAC addresses, 11
    maximum PDU, 31
    messages, 11
    multi-access technology, 11
    nodes discarding frames, 13
    payload length, 11–12

payload type indicator, 12
PDU (Protocol Data Unit) maximum size, 30
point-to-point technology, 11
popularity, 12
repeaters, 42
sending multiple copies of datagram, 79–80
Start Delimiter byte, 11
switches, 11
unacceptable number of collisions, 42
Events and GSMP (General Switch Management Protocol), 563–565
Exchanging keys, 710–716
EXP bits (experimental bits), 483–484
explicit congestion notification. *See* ECN (explicit congestion notification)
Explicit Route Hop TLVs, 441, 443
Explicit Route Label Subobject, 509–510
Explicit Route Object, 459, 462
Explicit Route Objects. *See* EROs (Explicit Route Objects)
Explicit Route Subobjects, 459
Explicit Route TLV, 441
Explicit routes, 400, 439
    abstract nodes, 433
    CR-LDP (Constraint-Based LSP Setup Using LDP), 441–443
    fully specified addresses, 433
    interface address, 433
    loopback addresses, 433
    loose hops, 434–435, 448
    MPLS, 433–436
    RSVP-TE, 459–460
    strict hops, 434–435, 448
Extended Binary Coded Decimal Interchange Code. *See* EBCDIC (Extended Binary Coded Decimal Interchange Code)
Extended IS Reachability TLV, 379–380

Extensible Markup Language. *See* XML (Extensible Markup Language)
Extension headers, 105, 108
Extensions to RSVP-TE (RSVP for LSP Tunnels), 456–478
Exterior Gateway Protocols. *See* EGPs (Exterior Gateway Protocols)
Exterior LSRs, 487
External attributes LSA, 178
External LSA, 177
External Reachability Information TLV, 193

F
FANP (Flow Attribute Notification Protocol), 396
FAs (Forwarding Adjacencies), 393
FDDI, 1, 30, 42
FEC (Forwarding Equivalence Class), 391–392, 412–413
    GSMP (General Switch Management Protocol), 554
    switching, 549–550
FEC element, 440–441
FF Flow Descriptor, 283
FF (Fixed-Filter) style, 283, 464–465
FIB (forwarding information base), 122
Fiber switching, 493
File Transfer Protocol. *See* FTP (File Transfer Protocol)
File transfer protocols, 615
Files
    moving in FTP, 607–608
    synchronization and confirmation of transfer actions, 602
    transferring, 598–611
FilterSpec Objects, 271, 279–280, 293, 459, 469
Finished message, 699
Firewalls, 685–687

Five-layer IP model, 7
Fixed Filter style, 469
Flapping, 216
Fletcher's checksum, 164, 181, 182–183, 192
Flow Attribute Notification Protocol. *See* FANP (Flow Attribute Notification Protocol)
Flow control
    ICMP, 70
    increasing amount of, 550
    TCP (Transmission Control Protocol), 324–329
Flow Descriptor, 516
Flow Descriptor List, 469
Flows and RSVP, 270–271
FlowSpec objects, 271, 279–280, 283, 294, 464
ForCES (Forwarding and Element Control Separation) Working Group, xxiii, 549, 566–569
ForCES Working Group Web site, 572
Foreign agents, 735–738
Forwarding, 115–116, 142
Forwarding Adjacencies. *See* FAs (Forwarding Adjacencies)
Forwarding Adjacency and bundles, 523
Forwarding and Element Control Separation Working Group. *See* ForCES (Forwarding and Element Control Separation) Working Group
Forwarding Equivalence Class. *See* FEC (Forwarding Equivalence Class)
forwarding information base. *See* FIB (forwarding information base)
Fragment Identifier Delta, 745
Fragmentation
    datagrams, 27
    IP data, 30–34
    IPv6 datagrams, 107–108

Frame Relay, 376, 386, 732
    inferred labels, 390
    networks, 169
    switches and GSMP (General Switch Management Protocol), 549
Frames, 10
    Ethernet, 11–12
    hosts, 24
    Token Rings, 13–14
FSC (fiber switch capable), 493
FTP (File Transfer Protocol), xxiii, 575, 598
    access control commands, 602
    BFTP (Background File Transfer Protocol), 614–615
    binary files, 603
    block mode, 603–604
    checkpoints, 604–605
    commands, 598–599
    compressed mode, 603, 605
    connectivity model, 600–601
    Control Connection, 600
    data block size, 613–614
    Data Connection, 600
    data connection control, 603–607
    file transfer commands, 606–607
    flags, 604
    MODE command, 603
    moving files, 607–608
    PASV command, 600
    PORT command, 600
    rename command, 607
    replies, 602, 608–611
    session management, 602
    SFTP (Simple File Transfer Protocol), 614
    SIFT/UFT (Sender-Initiated/Unsolicited File Transfer Protocol), 615
    spontaneous replies, 610–611
    stream mode, 603
    TCP (Transmission Control Protocol), 337
    text files, 603
    transferring files, 598
    TYPE command, 603

FTP clients, 598–599, 601, 607
FTP messages, 601–602
FTP servers, 598, 601–602, 611
full mesh of sessions, 219–220
FULL_HEADER packet type, 745, 746

G

Gap acknowledgement blocks, 351
Gateway to Gateway Protocol. *See* GGP (Gateway to Gateway Protocol)
Gateways, 44, 119, 139, 619
General Inter-ORB Protocol. *See* GIOP (General Inter-ORB Protocol), 655–659
General Switch Management Protocol. *See* GSMP (General Switch Management Protocol)
Generalized CR-LDP, 520–521
Generalized Multiprotocol Label Switching. *See* GMPLS (Generalized Multiprotocol Label Switching)
Generalized RSVP-TE, 509–520
Generic Routing Encapsulation. *See* GRE (Generic Routing Encapsulation)
GGP (Gateway to Gateway Protocol), 245
GIG (Global Information Grid), 765–766
GIOP (General Inter-ORB Protocol), 655–659
Global Grid Forum Web site, 767
Global Information Grid. *See* GIG (Global Information Grid)
Global management tool, 639–640
Global unicast addresses, 95–97
GMPLS (Generalized Multiprotocol Label Switching), xx, xxi, xxii, 265, 386, 491
    Acceptable Label Sets, 502–503
    Administrative Status object, 505

allowing LSPs to persist, 514
automated provisioning service, 508
bidirectional services, 502–503
bundles, 521–523
choosing between OSPF, 529–530
context-specific label size, 495–496
CR-LDP, 508–509, 520–521
defining content of label set, 500
detailed control of labels, 501
Encoding Type, 496
ERO (Explicit Route Object), 509–510
error codes, 514–516
Error_Spec object, 511
explicit label control, 501–502
Explicit Route Label Subobject, 509–510
Generalized Protocol Identifiers supplementing standard Ethertypes, 498–499
generic labels, 494–496
generic signaling extensions, 494–508
GMPLS signaling, 507–508
GPID, 496
granularity of resource allocation, 524
hierarchies, 521–523
improving scalability, 521–523
interface address, 523
Interface Identifiers, 506
interpretation of TDM label, 495
IS-IS, 523–530
labels, 494, 497
link id, 536
LMP (Link Management Protocol), 491, 537
managing connections and alarms, 504–505
many parallel links between nodes, 523
message formats, 521

messages carrying message id, 511
negotiating labels, 497–502
OSPF (Open Shortest Path First), 523–530
out of band signaling, 505–506
protected LSPs, 504
protection capabilities, 524–525
protection services, 503–504
requesting labels, 496–497
routing protocols, 529–530
RRO (Record Route object), 509
RSVP (Resource Reservation Protocol), 266
RSVP-TE, 508–520
signaling, 494, 506
switching capabilities, 524
Switching Type, 496
upstream node and labels, 501–502
GMPLS messages, 511
Gopher, 618, 620
Grades of service, 249
Graft function, 226
graphical user interfaces. See GUIs (graphical user interfaces)
Gratuitous ARP, 50
GRE (Generic Routing Encapsulation), 28, 721–722
Group membership LSA, 231
Group Membership Query message, 88
Group Membership Report, 89–91
Groups and IGMP (Internet Group Management Protocol), 87–88
GSMP (General Switch Management Protocol), xxii–xxiii, 45, 549–550
ACK message, 556
Add Branch message, 561
adding features, 565
Adjacency messages, 554–556
All Ports Configuration message body, 557
asynchronous events, 558, 560
ATM switches, 549

Connection Activity Request message, 564
connection management, 561–562
Connection Statistics message, 564
cross-connections, 561
Delete Branches message, 562
Delete Input message, 562
Delete Reservation message, 563
Delete Tree message, 562
distributed switches, 550
establishing adjacency, 554–556
events, 563–565
failure code, 553
FECs (Forwarding Equivalence Classes), 554
Frame Relay switches, 549
increasing amount of control flow, 550
Label Range message, 559, 561
labels, 553–554
line types, 560
Output Port message, 562
overview, 551
Port Configuration message body, 557
Port Management message, 560–561
Port Statistics message, 564
pre-reservation of resources, 562–563
Report Connection State message, 564–565
request-response exchanges, 551
request-response protocol, 565
Reservation Request message, 562
Response message, 564
selecting, 565–566
state, 563–565
state machines, 556
statistics, 563–565
Switch Configuration message body, 556–560

GSMP (*continued*)
SYN message, 556
SYNACK message, 556
Traffic Control flags, 562–563
Traffic Parameter Blocks, 563
trees, 561
version, 553
GSMP messages, 551–554
GSMP Working Group Web site, 572
Guaranteed service, 260–262, 265
Guard bytes, 34
GUIs (graphical user interfaces), 638–639

H
Hackers, 677, 685
Handle object, 666
Handshake messages, 697
Hardware
managing alarms, 504
problems transient and repetitive, 216–217
waveband, 496
Hashing algorithms
CRC (cyclic redundancy check), 703
MD5 (Message Digest version 5), 704–709
HDLC (High-Level Data Link Control), 758
Header compression
benefits of, 742
CDI (Context Session Identifier), 744–745
IP, 743–747
MPLS, 747–748
Header extensions, 4
Headers, 4
datagrams, 26
protecting against random corruptions, 36–37
Heartbeat Acknowledgement chunk, 346
Heartbeat chunk, 346
Hello Ack Object, 467
Hello Adjacency, 404–405

Hello Done message, 698
Hello messages, 157–159, 467–468, 470, 535
Configuration Sequence Number TLV, 407
ignoring, 404
LDP (Label Distribution Protocol), 403–405
not received, 514
targeted, 404
UDP packets, 404
Hello Object, 467, 535
Hello PDUs, 185–190
Hello protocol, 132–133, 245–246
Hello Request object, 467
Hierarchies and MPLS, 393–396
Higher-layer protocols, 28
High-Level Data Link Control. *See* HDLC (High-Level Data Link Control)
high-order DSP. *See* HO-DSP (high-order DSP)
HO-DSP (high-order DSP), 181
Hold Timer, 403
Holding priority, 437
Home agent, 735, 736
Horizon, 130
Host Address FEC element, 412
Host names, 579–582
Hosts, 44
aliases, 581
communicating with other hosts, 39
data-link layer, 24
default route, 45
discovering route to, 70–74
frames, 24
grades of service, 249–250
IPv6, 97
multihomed, 211–212
multiple instances of application, 577
raw IP, 297
route table, 45
routing function within, 45
set of, 100
silent, 152

static configuration of router addresses, 74
testing reachability, 70–74
Hot Standby Router Protocol. *See* HSRP (Hot Standby Router Protocol)
HSRP (Hot Standby Router Protocol), 243–245
HTML (Hypertext Markup Language), 616–617
HTML documents, 616–617, 649
HTTP (Hypertext Transfer Protocol), xxiii, 6, 575, 615
applications and KeepAlive exchange, 619
capabilities, 618
example message and transactions, 626–629
general warning code 199, 628
MIME (Multipurpose Internet Message Extensions), 621–622
operation of, 618–620
request or reply message, 619
request-response exchange, 619
securing transactions, 630
security, 683, 701, 703
status code, 628
TCP (Transmission Control Protocol), 337
text-based messages, 622
URLs, 618
version number, 628
HTTP clients, 619–620
HTTP messages, 619, 622–626
HTTP servers, 619
HTTPS, 701, 703
Hub router, sending datagrams, 224
Hubs, 11
Hypertext, 616–617
Hypertext Markup Language. *See* HTML (Hypertext Markup Language)
Hypertext Transfer Protocol. *See* HTTP (Hypertext Transfer Protocol)

I

IAC character (0xff), 592
IANA (Internet Assigned
    Numbers Authority), xx,
    xxvii, 28–29, 95
  AF (Assured Forwarding)
    PHBs, 255
  assigning Class D addresses, 85
  iftype definitions, 559
  managing allocation of DSCP
    values, 255
  port ids, 578
  port numbers, 311
  Telnet options, 594
IANA Web site, 29
I-BGP (Interior BGP), 217–220
  full mesh of sessions, 219–220
  peers, 219
ICANN, 38
ICMP (Internet Control Message
    Protocol), 23–24, 243
  Communication
    Administratively
    Prohibited code, 76
  discovering routers, 74–75
  discovering routers in
    network, 64
  error messages, 62, 64–67, 76
  error reporting and diagnosis,
    65–70
  flow control, 70
  path MTU discovery, 75–76
  ping, 64, 70–74
  protocol identifier, 28
  return notifications when
    packets are discarded, 37
  route tracing facilities, 76
  Router Advertisement
    Message, 737
  security implications, 76–77
  Source Quench message, 333
  traceroute, 64, 70–74
ICMP routers, discovery process,
    737–738
IDI (Initial Domain Identifier),
    180
IDL (Interface Definition
    Language), 652–654

IDL Skeleton, 654–655
IDP (Initial Domain Part), 180
IDRP (Inter-Domain Routing
    Protocol), 243, 245
IEEE 802 series of standards, 21
IEEE Web site, 21
IESG (Internet Engineering
    Steering Group), xxvi
IETF (Internet Engineering Task
    Force), xx, xxvi–xxvii
  MBONED (MBONE
    Deployment Working
    Group), 235
  multicasts, 84
IETF Web site, xxvii, 365
IFMP (Ipsilon Flow Management
    Protocol), 396
IGMP (Internet Group Message
    Protocol), xxii, 79, 87–91
  extensions to, 238
  messages, 87–91
  packets, 232
  protocol identifier, 28
IGMPv3, 238
IGP (Interior Gateway Protocol),
    119, 139, 376, 729–730
  BGP, 217–220
  OSPF (Open Shortest Path
    First), 155–179
IGRP (Inter-Gateway Routing
    Protocol), 242
IIOP (Internet Inter-ORB
    Protocol), 655, 659
IKE (Internet Key Exchange), 711
Implementation Repository,
    654–655
InARP (Inverse ARP), 52
In-band packet networks, 533
Independent control, 417
Indirect routing, 42
Indirection, 656
Infinity, 152–154
Information distribution
    protocols, 2–3
Initial Acknowledgement chunk,
    342, 345
Initial Domain Identifier. See IDI
    (Initial Domain Identifier)

Integers, xxiv, 657
Integrated IS-IS, 179
Integrated Services. See IntServ
    (Integrated Services)
Integrity Challenge
    message, 295
Integrity Object, 294–295
Integrity Response
    message, 295
Interdomain protocols, 224, 239
Inter-Domain Routing Protocol.
    See IDRP (Inter-Domain
    Routing Protocol)
Inter-Domain Routing
    Protocol Information
    TLV, 193–194
Interface Addresses TLV, 187
Interface Definition Language.
    See IDL (Interface
    Definition Language)
Interface Repository, 654
Interfaces
  IPv6, 97
  IS-IS, 180
  set of, 100
  TCP connections, 319
Inter-Gateway Routing Protocol.
    See IGRP (Inter-Gateway
    Routing Protocol)
Interior BGP. See I-BGP (Interior
    BGP)
Interior Gateway Protocol.
    See IGP (Interior Gateway
    Protocol)
Interior LSRs, 487
Intermediate destination, 107
Intermediate Systems Neighbors
    TLV, 188, 192–193
Intermediate-System to
    Intermediate-System. See
    IS-IS (Intermediate-System
    to Intermediate-System)
Internal Reachability Information
    TLV, 192–193
International Standards
    Organization. See ISO
    (International Standards
    Organization)

Internet, xix
  AS (autonomous systems),
    118–119
  EGPs (Exterior Gateway
    Protocols), 139
  evolution of, xx
  forwarding, 115
  grades of service, 249
  hop-by-hop forwarding, 142
  limitations on bandwidth,
    264–265
  MBONE (Multicast
    Backbone), 234–236
  multicast routing, 234
  routing, 115
Internet Assigned Numbers
    Authority. *See* IANA
    (Internet Assigned
    Numbers Authority)
Internet Control Message
    Protocol. *See* ICMP
    (Internet Control Message
    Protocol)
Internet Drafts, xxvi
Internet Engineering Steering
    Group. *See* IESG (Internet
    Engineering Steering Group)
Internet Engineering Task Force.
    See IETF (Internet
    Engineering Task Force)
Internet Group Message Protocol.
    See IGMP (Internet Group
    Message Protocol)
Internet Inter-ORB Protocol.
    See IIOP (Internet
    Inter-ORB Protocol)
Internet Key Exchange. *See* IKE
    (Internet Key Exchange)
Internet Protocol. *See* IP (Internet
    Protocol)
Internet protocols, xix–xxi
Internet RAP (Route Access
    Protocol), 243
Internet Security Associating and
    Key Management Protocol.
    See ISAKMP (Internet
    Security Associating and
    Key Management Protocol)

Internet2 Web site, 766
IntServ (Integrated Services),
    xxii, 249, 257, 267, 372
  C error term, 262, 264
  characterizing traffic, 264
  choosing service type, 265–266
  Controlled Load service, 260,
    265
  D error term, 263–264
  describing traffic flows, 258–259
  versus DiffServ, 266
  end nodes collecting resource
    information, 262–264
  guaranteed service, 260–262,
    265
  real-time data traffic, 264
  reporting capabilities, 262–264
  selecting, 264–265
  specific uses for services, 266
  token bucket, 258–259,
    261–262
Inverse ARP. *See* InARP (Inverse
    ARP)
IP (Internet Protocol), 4, 23
  advanced functions, 59–63
  advanced uses, 719
  ARP (Address Resolution
    Protocol), 49–53
  ATM (Asynchronous Transfer
    Mode), 752–756
  BOOTP messages, 53
  bridges, 42–59
  checksum, 35–37
  connecting across network
    types, 24–25
  connection oriented, 318
  CRC checksum, 324
  data fragmentation, 30–34
  datagrams, 25–30
  delivering datagrams, 42–59
  Differentiated Services, 481–482
  discarding packets, 37
  dynamic address assignment,
    53–59
  encoding problems, 67, 68
  error detection, 34–37
  External Reachability
    Information TLV, 193

Fragment Identifier Delta, 745
header compression, 743–747
Interface Addresses TLV, 187
Internal Reachability
    Information TLV, 192–193,
    193
label switching, 386
lazy reassembly of fragments,
    33–34
local delivery, 46–47
loopbacks, 46–47
Loose Route option, 62–63
options, 59–63
over dial-up links, 756–760
packet switching, 386
protocol identifiers, 316
Record Route option, 61–63
recording, 61–63
reporting datagram errors,
    64–77
revisions, 25
route control, 61–63
routing, 44–46, 371–372
RSVP-TE, 481
separating control and
    forwarding, 566–569
size of datagram, 30
sockets, 579
Source Route option, 62–63
source routing, 371
standard checksum, 35
Strict Route option, 62–63
switching, 44–46
Timestamp option, 63
traffic flows, 481
type of service, 47–79
unreliability, 83
as unreliable delivery
    protocol, 37
usage, 42–59
IP Access Lists, 685–687
IP addresses, 24, 29, 579
  address spaces, 37–38
  allocating, 40
  appliances, 93
  assigned to identify
    interfaces, 93
  assigning, 38

broadcast addresses, 39
cell phones, 93
classes, 38–39, 116–117
detecting nodes with same, 53
discovering, 23
dotted decimal notation, 37
dynamic assignment, 53–59
endpoints, 309
formats, 37–38
grouping into subnetworks,
    139–140
host names, 581
IPv4, 37–41
managing, 23
mapping to MAC addresses,
    42
multiple for nodes, 38
NAT (Network Address
    Translation), 41
netmask, 39–40
ports, 309–310
prefix, 40
private networks, 41
qualifying, 309
resolving host name to, 582
structure, 38
as unique identifier, 38
IP datagrams
data-link layer, 42
IGMP messages, 87
SCTP packets, 339
IP encapsulation, xxiii, 719–722,
    724–725
IP header
CE (Congestion Encountered)
    bit, 375
delimiting sequence of
    options, 61
ECT (ECN-Capable Transport)
    bit, 375
encoding of DSCP field,
    254
Fragment Offset field, 33
IGMP messages, 88
size limit, 59
ToS (Type of Service) byte,
    49, 375
ToS field, 253

IP in IP encapsulation, 722–724,
    737–738
IP messages
bundling RSVP messages
    together, 297–298
TCP messages, 322
IP multicast, 81, 116
IP networks, xxiv
CSPF (Constrained Shortest
    Path First), 145
managing IP networks with,
    252
managing services, 251–252
OSPF (Open Shortest Path
    First), 198
policing traffic flows, 252
RIP (Routing Information
    Protocol), 147–155
security, 681
segmenting and reassembling
    GSMP messages, 553
traffic prioritization, 252
tunneling through, 720–721
IP over ATM. See IPoA (IP over
    ATM)
IP packets
distributing to LSPs, 550
packet loss, 52
Security Association, 692
IP routers, xxiv
IP security. See IPsec
    (IP security)
IP switches, 45–46, 549–550
IP switching, 396
IP telephony, 749–752, 764
IP telephony protocols, 20
IP Telephony Working Group
    Web site, 761
IP traffic and MPLS tunnels, 725
IP transport protocols, 578–579
IP-based control plane, 397–398
Ipconfig program, 59
IPoA (IP over ATM), 752–753
IPsec (IP security), xxiii,
    294–295, 684
authentication, 690–695
authentication algorithm,
    691–692

authentication header,
    690–692
DES (Data Encryption
    Standard), 694
encryption, 692–695
encryption algorithms,
    693–694
end-to-end security, 689–690
ESP (Encapsulated Security
    Payload), 692, 694
hashing algorithm, 690–691
MD5 (Message Digest Five)
    algorithm, 691–692
Proxy security, 689–690
SA (Security Association), 689
secure packet exchanges, 689
Sequence Number, 692, 694
SPI (Security Parameter
    Index), 692, 694
Ipsilon Flow Management
    Protocol. See IFMP (Ipsilon
    Flow Management
    Protocol)
IPv4 (IP version four), 23, 25
address space limits, 93
BGP (Border Gateway
    Protocol), 214
choosing between IPv6 and,
    110–113
downstream interface of
    address, 287, 289
interface address, 100
interoperation with IPv6, 111
IP addresses, 37–41
IPv4 packet encapsulated,
    723
LSP Tunnel Session, 458
packets, 26
popularity, 110
source route control, 103–104
tunneling traffic, 111
IPv4 addresses
IPv6, 110–111
size of, 94–95
IPv4 networks and Mobile IP,
    735–736
IPv4 packet encapsulated IPv4,
    723

IPv6 (IP version six), 763
  additional header information,
    103
  anycast addresses, 99–100
  authentication, 109
  checksums, 111–112
  choosing between IPv6 and,
    110–113
  constraints, 94
  data-link layer, 107–108
  defined option types, 105
  destination options extension
    headers, 105
  documenting, 94
  downstream interface of
    address, 287, 289
  effect on other protocols, 112
  encryption, 109–110
  end-to-end MTU values, 108
  ESP (encapsulating security
    payload) extension header,
    109–110
  extension headers, 103–109
  fragmentation header,
    108–109
  gradual deployment of, 110
  hop-by-hop extension header,
    104–105
  hosts, 97
  interfaces, 97
  intermediate destination, 107
  interoperation with IPv4, 111
  IPv4 addresses, 110–111
  LSP Tunnel Session, 458
  multicast addressing, 98
  Next Header field, 103
  NSAP (Network Service
    Access Point) addresses, 99
  number of addresses to be
    processed, 105, 107
  options, 103–110
  protocol support for, 94
  requirements for options, 105
  routing extension header, 105
  Routing Type field, 105
  security, 109
  Segments Left field, 105, 107
  source route control, 103–104

  tunneling traffic, 111
  UDP datagrams, 316
  unicast addresses, 99
IPv6 addresses
  addresses with special
    meaning, 100–101
  BGP (Border Gateway
    Protocol), 214
  formats, 95–102
  FP (Format Prefix), 95, 97
  global unicast addresses,
    95–97
  group ids, 100
  increasing size of address
    space, 95
  interface address, 99
  Interface Id, 97
  Link Local Unicast IPv6
    Addresses, 97
  NLA Id (Next Level
    Aggregation Id), 97, 99
  picking, 101–102
  Public Topology, 97
  represented with hexadecimal
    encoding, 95
  reserved, 100
  Site Level Aggregation Id, 99
  Site Local Unicast IPv6
    Addresses, 97–98
  Site Topology, 97
  size of, 94–95
  SLA Id (Site Level
    Aggregation Id), 97
  structure of, 95
  subnetwork address, 99
  TLA Id (Top Level
    Aggregation Id), 97
  Top Level Aggregation Id, 99
IPv6 datagrams, 102–103, 107–108
IPv6 unicast addresses, 99
IPv6 Working Group, 94
IPv6 Working Group Web site,
  114
IRTF (Internet Research Task
  Force) Service
  Management Research
  Group, 306
IS Neighbors Hello TLV, 192–193

ISAKMP (Internet Security
  Associating and Key
  Management Protocol),
  711–716
ISAKMP messages, 711–712
ISDN, 2
IS-IS (Intermediate-System to
  Intermediate-System), xxii,
  99, 116, 141, 223–224
  addressing, 180–181
  adjacency maintenance,
    185–190
  advanced features, 197
  area boundaries on links, 181
  Area Id, 181
  areas, 181, 184
  backbone area, 181, 184
  bandwidth, 524
  data encapsulation, 180–181
  deployment pattern, 198
  Dijkstra Shortest Path First
    algorithm, 144–145
  distributing link state
    information, 190–194
  distribution protocol, 197
  Extended IS Reachability
    TLV, 528
  Fletcher's checksum, 164,
    181, 182–183, 192
  GMPLS, 523–530
  hard limit on path lengths/
    costs, 193
  header length, 184
  Hello PDU, 185–190
  HO-DSP (high-order DSP), 181
  implementation simplicity, 197
  interfaces, 180
  ISO (International Standards
    Organization), 198
  L1 Multi-Access Hello PDU,
    186–187
  L2 Multi-Access Hello PDU,
    186–187
  levels of hierarchy, 181
  linear sequence number
    space, 191
  Link Local/Remote Identifiers
    sub-TLV, 528

Link Protection sub-TLV, 528
Link Switching sub-TLV, 528
looping of routing information
    between levels, 380
LSPs (Link State Protocol Data
    Units), 379
message objects, 528–529
neighbor discovery, 185–190
NET (Network Entity Title),
    181
non-IP addressing domains,
    193
NSAP Selector, 181
versus OSPF, 196–198
packets, 197
PDUs (protocol data units),
    180, 184–185
Point-to-Point Hello PDU, 186
protocol identifier, 28
protocols routed by, 197
reliable exchange of LSPs
    between routers, 194
remaining lifetime of LSPs, 191
S bit, 381
scalability, 197–198
security, 197
Shared Risk Link Group
    TLV, 529
SNPA (Subnetwork Point of
    Attachment), 180
SRLGs, 526, 529
support for areas, 197
synchronizing databases,
    195–196
TCP/IP and CLNP as separate
    addressing spaces, 179
TE Router ID TLV, 533
TLVs, 190–194
TLVs relevant to IP systems,
    185, 187
traffic engineering extensions,
    523
U-bit, 380–381
IS-IS messages, 180–181
IS-IS networks, 177
IS-IS TE Internet Draft, 380
IS-IS Working Group, 198
IS-IS-TE, 379–381

ISO (International Standards
    Organization), 4, 99,
    179–180, 198
ISO 8824, 674
ISO 8825, 647, 674
ISO 8879, 648, 649
ISO 10589, 185, 189–190
ISO address, 180–181
ISO N4053, 243
ISPs (Internet Service Providers),
    18
    allocating IP addresses, 40
    network management, 636
    points of presence, 727
    segmenting Internet into
        separate domains, 199
ISs (intermediate systems), 179
ITU (International
    Telecommunications
    Union), 749
ITU (International
    Telecommunications
    Union) standard H.323,
    354
ITU-T Web site, 761

J
Jacobson, Van, 333
Jitter
    guaranteed service, 261
    RTP (Real-time Transport
        Protocol), 355

K
KeepAlive exchange, 619
KeepAlive message, 407–408
Keep-Alive message, 666–667
Keys, 688, 703
    exchanging, 710–716
    randomly generating, 710

L
L1 Multi-Access Hello PDU,
    186–188
L1/L2 routers, 181, 184

L2 Multi-Access Hello PDU,
    186–188
L2SC (layer-2 switching capable),
    492
L2VPN (Layer Two VPN)
    Working Group, 763–764
L3VPN (Layer Three VPN)
    Working Group, 763–764
Label Abort message, 453
Label Abort Request message, 423
Label Distribution Protocol. *See*
    LDP (Label Distribution
    Protocol)
Label distribution protocols, 397
Label Edge Routers. *See* LERs
    (Label Edge Routers)
Label Forwarding Information
    Bases. *See* LFIBs (Label
    Forwarding Information
    Bases)
Label Mapping message, 411–415,
    420–422, 426–427, 448, 453
    DiffServ TLV, 483
    Hop Count TLV, 414
    Label Request Message Id
        TLV, 418
    Path Vector TLV, 414
Label Object, 464, 469
Label Range message, 561
Label Release message, 420–423,
    426–427, 449, 453
Label Request message, 415,
    420–422, 426, 447–449,
    453
Label Request Object, 458
Label Request Object on a Path
    message, 458
Label stack, 393–394
Label subobject, 463
Label swapping, 389–390
Label Switched Paths. *See* LSPs
    (Label Switched Paths)
Label switches, managing,
    546–566
Label switching, 386–388
Label Switching Routers. *See*
    LSRs (Label Switching
    Routers)

Label Withdraw message,
    419–420, 427, 453–454
Labels
    address prefix, 412
    distributing, 411–417, 458
    formats, 413
    fully-qualified host address,
        412–413
    GMPLS, 494
    GSMP (General Switch
        Management Protocol),
        553–554
    inferring priority from, 482
    mode of distribution, 417–418
    MPLS, 494
    no longer valid, 419
    retention mode, 418
    stopping use of, 419–423
    switching modes, 494
Lambdas, 493
lamda switch capable. *See* LSC
    (lambda switch capable)
LAN Emulation. *See* LANE (LAN
    Emulation)
LAN (Local Area Network)
    technologies, 1
LANE (LAN Emulation), 755–756
Layer 2 VPNs, 732
Layer Three VPN. *See* L3VPN
    (Layer Three VPN)
    Working Group
Layer Two VPN. *See* L2VPN
    (Layer Two VPN) Working
    Group
layer-2 switching capable. *See*
    L2SC (layer-2 switching
    capable)
Layer-two switching, 492
LCP (Link Control Protocol), 758
LDP (Label Distribution
    Protocol), xxii, xxiv, 171
    adding constraints, 439–440
    address advertisement and
        usage, 409–411
    Address List TLV, 411
    Address messages, 409–411
    Address Withdraw message,
        411

advertisement of labels, 401
break in session, 429
Conservative Label Retention,
    418–419
control conversation between
    adjacent LSRs, 401
CR-LDP (Constraint-Based
    LSP Setup Using LDP)
    extension, 430
DiffServ TLV, 483–484
discovery of LDP-capable
    adjacent LSRs, 401
distributing labels, 411–417
Downstream On Demand
    label distribution, 411–418,
    426–427
Downstream On Demand LSP,
    426
Downstream Unsolicited
    distribution, 411–418
downstream unsolicited
    independent mode, 171–172
entities, 403–409
error cases, 423–424
Error Notification message,
    407, 416
event notification, 423–424
extensibility, 401
extensions, 430
fault tolerance, 429–430
Fault Tolerant LDP extension,
    430
Graceful Restart extension, 430
Hello Adjacency, 404–405
Hold Timer, 403
Hop Count TLV, 416–417
independent control, 417
KeepAlive message, 407–408
Label Abort Request message,
    423
label distribution mode,
    417–418
Label Mapping message,
    411–415, 420–422, 426–427
Label Release message,
    420–423, 426–427
Label Request message,
    420–422, 426

label requests, 415
label retention mode, 418
Label Withdraw message,
    419–420, 427
Liberal Label Retention,
    418–419
loop detection, 415–416
message flow examples,
    426–428
network failure, 426–427
Notification message,
    423–424, 426–427
ordered control, 417
Path Vector Limit, 407
Path Vector TLV, 417
PDUs (Protocol Data Units),
    401
peers, 403–409
Receiver LDP Identifier, 407
SCTP, 429–430
Session Initialization message,
    406–408
sessions, 403–409
status codes, 424–425, 484
stopping use of labels,
    419–423
surviving network outages,
    429–430
TCP (Transmission Control
    Protocol), 337, 429
transport protocols, 429
UDP, 429
version of, 401
withdrawal of labels, 401
LDP messages, 401–403
LDP peers, 403
LDP routers, 406
LDP sessions, 405–406
Least cost path, 143
Leave Group Report message, 89
LERs (Label Edge Routers), 550
Level of service, 261
LFIBs (Label Forwarding
    Information Bases),
    389–390
    actions needed for
        tunneling, 395
    dynamic label distribution, 397

Liberal Label Retention, 418
LIH (Logical Interface Handle), 289
Link Control Protocol. *See* LCP (Link Control Protocol)
Link Local Unicast IPv6 Addresses, 97
Link Management Protocol. *See* LMP (Link Management Protocol)
Link Property Summarization exchange, 542
Link state, 145–146, 232
Link State Advertisements. *See* LSAs (Link State Advertisements)
Link state databases, 132–134
    OSPF router synchronization, 159–161
    periodically refreshing, 135
    routers synchronizing, 195–196
Link state information, 143
    amount exchanged, 136
    LSPs (Link State PDUs), 190–194
    OSPF (Open Shortest Path First), 190
Link State Protocol Data Units. *See* LSPs (Link State Protocol Data Units)
Link state protocols, 223–224, 247
    advertised connectivity metric, 143
    extending, 141
    IS-IS, 223–224
    OSPF (Open Shortest Path First), 223–224
    routers with same view of resources, 143
    scaling issues, 136
Link state routers, 185
Link state routing, 131
    age limit on information advertised by LSA, 135
    coherent policy for route selection, 132
    distinguishing between LSAs referring to same link, 135

grouping routers into areas, 136–137
    levels of hierarchy, 137
    path computation algorithms, 132
    peers, 132–133
    policies, 138
    routers computing shortest path, 144
Link state routing protocols
    carrying basic resource availability information, 147
    choosing how to compute paths, 147
    counting schemes to generate LSA sequence numbers, 135
    IS-IS (Intermediate-System to Intermediate-System), 179–196
    lollipop-shaped sequence number space, 135–136
    selecting, 196–198
Link Summary message, 570–571
Link-level protocols, 745
Links
    bundles, 523
    LMP (Link Management Protocol), 533–537
    managing, 569–571
    protection capabilities, 524–525
    SRLG (Shared Risk Link Group), 525–526
    switching capabilities, 524
LinkSummaryNack message, 542
Little-Endian integers, 657
LLC (Logical Link Control) protocols, 18–19
L-LSPs, 482–483
    versus E-LSPs, 485–486
LMP (Link Management Protocol), xxii, 317, 491, 531, 549
    adjacency, 533
    authentication, 545–546
    BeginVerifyNack message, 542
    CCID (Control Channel Id), 535
    channels, 533–537

ChannelStatus message, 544–545
ChannelStatus object, 545
ChannelStatusRequest object, 545
Config message, 533, 535
ConfigAck message, 533
ConfigNack message, 533
data channels, 533–537
Data_Link object, 543
EndVerify message, 539
Error Code object, 542
error codes, 541
exchanging link capabilities, 542–543
Hello message, 535
Hello timers, 535
isolating faults, 544–545
link discovery, 537–542
Link Property Summarization exchange, 542
link verification, 537–542
links, 533–537
LinkSummaryNack message, 542
Message Ids, 532
Node Id, 533, 535
protocol-based exchange of link identifiers, 536
Raw IP, 531
selecting, 546
state machines, 532
TE_Link object, 542
Test message, 538, 539
TestStatus message, 539
TestStatusAck message, 542
TestStatusFailure message, 542
TestStatusSuccess message, 539, 542
transport verification mechanism, 538–539
UDP, 531
LMP messages, 531, 537
LMP objects, 531–532
LMP-WDM, xxiii, 569–572
LMP-WDM_CONFIG object, 569
Load balancing, 146

Local Area Network technologies. *See* LAN (Local Area Network) technologies

Local CR-LSP Id, 441

Local delivery and IP, 46–47

Local Policy Decision Point. *See* LPDP (Local Policy Decision Point)

Localhost, 46

Logical AND, 39

Logical connections, xix, 8

Logical Interface Handle. *See* LIH (Logical Interface Handle)

Logical Link Protocols. *See* LLC (Logical Link Control) protocols

Lollipop sequence number space, 191

Loopback address, 123

Loopbacks and IP, 46–47

Loose hops, 434–435, 448

Loose route, 62–63

Loose Route option, 62–63

LPDP (Local Policy Decision Point), 665

LSA header, 178–179

LSAs (Link State Advertisements), 133–135, 161–166
    advertisement-specific data, 161
    aging, 135
    carrying information across OSPF AS, 177–178
    header, 161–162
    Length field, 164
    Link State Checksum, 164
    Link State Database entry, 162
    Link State Id field, 169
    not aging out of link state database, 163
    opaque, 178–179
    referring to same link, 135
    timers and actions in OSPF, 163
    types of information, 163–164
    updating, 162
    verifying contents, 164

LSC (lambda switch capable), 493

LSN (Large Scale Networking) Web site, 767

LSP (link state packet), 133–135

LSPID Explicit Route Hop TLV, 443

LSPs (Label Switched Paths), 389–390, 432
    acknowledging, 194
    activating physical resources, 504
    assigning to administrative group, 450
    associating packets with, 391
    automatically setting up, 400
    backup, 503
    bidirectional, 502–503
    bypass tunnels, 438
    changing administrative status, 505
    choosing switching type, 493–494
    classes of service, 391
    coloring, 450, 466
    committed data rate, 445
    DiffServ OA (Ordered Aggregate), 482
    explicit routes, 433
    hierarchy of, 521–523
    holding priority, 437
    identifying, 458–459
    limits, 194
    managing network, 431
    manual configuration, 400, 438
    mapping data to, 391–392
    merging, 459
    nesting, 393–396
    network resources automatically managed, 431
    pinning, 448–450
    preemption, 437
    pre-signaled backup, 438
    primary, 503
    priorities, 439, 451
    protection for, 503–504
    PSC (Per Hop Behavior Scheduling Class), 482
    re-routing, 448–450
    setting up, 400

    setup priority, 437
    as TE link (traffic engineering link), 522
    traffic characteristics of, 443–448
    tunneling, 393–396

LSPs (Link State Protocol Data Units), 190–194, 379

LSRs (Label Switching Routers), 389–390, 522, 549
    distributing labels between, 401–430
    Label Space Identifier, 401–402
    link failure, 411
    mapping between IP routes, 409–410
    resynchronizing state, 514
    Router Id, 402
    routing look-up based on egress address, 433
    scalability, 393
    unused resources, 446

M

MAC (Media Access Control) addresses, 3, 49, 101–102
    Ethernet, 11
    IP datagrams, 42

Make-before-break, 473

Make-before-break routing, 464

Management Information Bases. *See* MIBs (Management Information Bases)

Management interactions, 7

Management Plane, 7–8

Management protocols, 3

Markup data, 649

Markup language, 616

MAU (Multiple Access Unit), 13

Maximum Transmission Unit. *See* MTU (Maximum Transmission Unit)

MBGP (Multiprotocol BGP), 241

MBONE (Multicast Backbone), 764
    growth, 234–235
    MSDP (Multicast Source Discovery Protocol), 241

MBONE Deployment Working
    Group. *See* MBONED
    (MBONE Deployment
    Working Group)
MBONED (MBONE Deployment
    Working Group), 235
MD5 (Message Digest Five)
    algorithm, 157, 691–692,
    701, 704–709
MD5() function, 709
Media, L2SC (layer-2 switching
    capable), 492
Media Access Control addresses.
    See MAC (Media Access
    Control) addresses
Merge point, 275
Mesh networks, 44
Message Ack Object, 298
Message digest, 704
Message Digest Five algorithm.
    See MD5 (Message Digest
    Five) algorithm
Message flows
    CR-LDP (Constraint-Based
    LSP Setup Using LDP), 453
    examples, 426–428
    reserving resources, 267–270
    RSVP-TE, 472–476
Message Id Multicast List Object,
    303
Message Id object, 511
Message Identifier Object, 298–300
Message Nack object, 301
Message objects, 286–296
Message replay, 682
Messages, 10
    addressing information, 3
    control information, 3
    diagrammatic representation,
    xxiv
    error detection, 34–37
    Ethernet, 11
    exchanging, 5
    guard bytes, 34
    headers, 4
    identifying source and
    destination of, 3
    payload data, 3–4

simple sum, 34–35
TLV (type-length-variable)
    component objects, 401
trailer, 4
Metcalfe, Robert, 1
MIB modules, 660
    statistics, 662
    textual conventions, 645
MIB rows, 643
MIB tables, 643
MIBs (Management Information
    Bases), xxiii, 641–645
    BER (Basic Encoding Rules),
    647
    data, 374
    row status, 647
MIME (Multipurpose Internet
    Message Extensions), 619,
    621–622
Minimal IP encapsulation, 724–725
Mixer, 356, 360
Mobile hosts, 735
Mobile IP, xxiii, 734, 764
    authentication, 741
    care-of-address, 735, 737
    encryption, 742
    extending protocols, 736–741
    Foreign Agents, 735–737
    Home Agent, 736
    IP in IP encapsulation, 722–724
    IPv4 networks, 735–736
    link-layer procedures, 735
    mobile hosts, 735
    mobile nodes, 737–738
    requirements, 735–736
    reverse tunneling, 741
    security, 741–742
    tunneling, 735
Mobile IP Working Group Web
    site, 761
Mobile nodes, 738–739, 741
MOSPF (Multicast OSPF), 224, 241
    enterprise networks, 235
    multi-area networks, 232
    source-based trees, 231–232
MPLS (Multiprotocol Label
    Switching), xx, xxi, xxii, 14,
    45, 223, 241, 372, 382–383

BGP-4, 486–489
bypass tunnels, 438
choosing between L-LSPs and
    E-LSPs, 485–486
computation of diverse paths,
    432
constraint-based routing, 436
constraint-based signaling
    protocol, 438–439
control protocols, 385
converging paths, 392
Differentiated Services, 482
DiffServ support, 484
dynamically reserving and
    updating resources, 431
E-LSPs, 483–484
Experimental bits, 391
explicit routes, 433–436
facilitating improved traffic
    engineering, 400
FEC (Forwarding Equivalence
    Class), 391–392
FTN (FEC to Next Hop Label
    Forwarding Entry)
    mapping table, 392
fundamentals, 388–397
grooming traffic, 437
header compression, 747–748
hierarchies, 393–396
inferred labels in switching
    networks, 390
inferring priority, 482–484
label swapping, 389–390
labels, 385, 388, 494
LDP (Label Distribution
    Protocol), 401–430
LDP Downstream On Demand
    label distribution, 433
LFIB (Label Forwarding
    Information Base), 389–390
L-LSPs, 482–483
load-sharing and traffic
    grooming decisions, 431
look-up tables for nodes, 385
LSP (Label Switched Path),
    xxiv, 389–390, 431–432
LSP preemption, 437
managing network, 437–438

MPLS (*continued*)
mapping data to LSP, 391–392
multiple tunnels sharing
resources, 470
new error codes, 484–485
packet switching, 492
packets identification, 393–394
PHP (Penultimate Hop
Popping), 395
PNNI (Peer Network to
Network Interconnect), 398
prioritizing data, 391
prioritizing traffic, 481–486
processing rules for explicit
route, 434–436
protection schemes for LSPs,
486
recovery procedures, 431, 438
reducing amount of routing
information, 387
reserving resources, 436–437
routing and signaling
protocols for, 385
RRO (Record Route object), 509
RSVP (Resource Reservation
Protocol), 266
selecting, 396–397
shim header, 388
SLAs (service level
agreements), 436
SPF (shortest path first)
algorithm, 432
strong link to IP, 398
traffic engineering, 257,
431–439, 457
traffic routed between LSPs,
431
tunnels, 393–396, 725, 731–733
unidirectional LSPs, 502
virtual circuit switched
overlay to Internet routing
model, 433
VPNs, 731–733
MPLS (Multiprotocol
Label-Switching), 6
MPLS Forum Web site, 761
MPLS network, 389–390
MPLS Over ATM, 756

MPLS Resource Center Web site,
547
MPLS Textual Conventions MIB
module, 645
MPLS VPNs, constructing, 489
MPLS Working Group, 305, 385,
401
MPLS Working Group Web site,
430, 489
MPOA (Multi-Protocol Over
ATM), 753–755
Mrouted program, 232
MSDP (Multicast Source
Discovery Protocol),
235–236, 241
MTP2, 353
MTU (Maximum Transmission
Unit), 10, 34, 75–76, 313
Multi-access broadcast link, 186
Multi-access networks, xxiv
broadcasting, 168–169
Hello PDU, 188
OSPF (Open Shortest Path
First), 167–169
Multicast
additional management
overhead, 83
challenges to routers, 223
choosing, 79–84
data sent to special address, 81
forwarding paradigms in
routers, 83
groups, 84
IETF, 84
MAC addresses, 101
NTP (Network Time
Protocol), 100
security, 83
special routing protocols, 83
unreliability of IP, 83
Multicast addresses, 83–87
Class D addresses, 84–85
correctly assigning, 84–85
IPv6, 98
ranges, 85
RIPv2, 152
scope field, 100
Multicast applications, 83–84

Multicast architecture, 236–238
Multicast Backbone. *See* MBONE
(Multicast Backbone)
Multicast Backbone Deployment
working group Web site, 248
Multicast datagrams, 84–85, 87
Multicast distributions tree, 225
Multicast groups, 87–88, 90
Multicast IP datagram, 81
Multicast IP delivery, 79
Multicast IP multimedia
conferencing, 84
Multi-cast links, 122
Multicast networks, 292
Multicast OSPF. *See* MOSPF
(Multicast OSPF)
Multicast protocols, 91, 225–227,
247–248
BGMP (Border Gateway
Multicast Protocol), 241
CBT (Core Based Trees)
protocol, 240–241
dense-mode, 223
driven by data or by control
events, 240
interdomain routing protocols,
224
link state protocols, 223–224
MBGP (Multiprotocol BGP),
241
MOSPF, 241
MSDP (Multicast Source
Discovery Protocol), 241
pull principle, 223
push principle, 223
selecting, 239–240
shared tree, 224–225
source-based, 224
sparse-mode, 223
Multicast resource sharing,
280–281
Multicast routing, 116
dense-mode multicast
protocols, 225–227
DVMRP (Distance Vector
Multicast Routing
Protocol), 232–233
Internet, 234

MBONE (Multicast Backbone), 234–236
MOSPF (Multicast OSPF), 231–232
multicast architecture, 236–238
PIM-SM (Protocol Independent Multicast Sparse-Mode), 227–230
RIP, 154
sparse-mode protocols, 227
Multicast Source Discovery Protocol. *See* MSDP (Multicast Source Discovery Protocol)
Multicast traffic, 85
Multicast trees, 85, 224–225
Multihoming, 211–213, 338
Multimedia conferencing, 84
Multiple Access Unit. *See* MAU (Multiple Access Unit)
Multiprotocol BGP. *See* MBGP (Multiprotocol BGP)
Multiprotocol Extensions capabilities code, 488
Multiprotocol Label Switching. *See* MPLS (Multiprotocol Label Switching)
Multiprotocol Label Switching networks, 171
Multi-Protocol Over ATM. *See* MPOA (Multi-Protocol Over ATM)
Multipurpose Internet Message Extensions. *See* MIME (Multipurpose Internet Message Extensions)
MVPNs (mobile VPNs), 764

N
Nagel algorithm, 329
NAT (Network Address Translation), 41, 97, 113
NBMA (non-broadcast multi-access) networks, 169
Nesting areas, 170
NET (Network Entity Title), 181, 184

NetFlow, 375, 383, 662
Netlink, 566–569
Netmask, 39–40
NetMeeting, 267, 354
Network Access Point. *See* NSAP (Network Service Access Point)
Network Address Translation. *See* NAT (Network Address Translation)
Network architecture, 7–8
Network computers, 7
Network Control Protocols. *See* NPCs (Network Control Protocols)
Network Entity Title. *See* NET (Network Entity Title)
Network File System. *See* NFS (Network File System)
Network Layer Protocol Identifiers. *See* NLPIDs (Network Layer Protocol Identifiers)
Network layer protocols, xxi, 4
Network Layer Reachability Information. *See* NLRI (Network Layer Reachability Information)
Network layers, 4–5, 307
gateways, 44
MTU, 10
packets, 10
stream of data, 9
Network management, 635
configuration method, 637–641
COPS (Common Open Policy Service Protocol), 663–673
CORBA (Common Object Request Broker Architecture), 652–660
devices, 635–636
global management tool, 639–640
meaning from information, 636
MIB (Management Information Base), 641–645
modules, 639
provisioning new services, 636

SNMP (Simple Network Management Protocol), 646–648
statistics, 660–662
XML (Extensible Markup Language), 648–652
Network management protocols, 374
Network Management System. *See* NMS (Network Management System)
Network masks, 117
Network protocols
detecting error, 309
layered model, xxi
point-to-point exchanges, 307
Network providers and SLAs (Service Level Agreements), 381
Network Time Protocol. *See* NTP (Network Time Protocol)
Network Virtual Terminal. *See* NVT (Network Virtual Terminal)
Networked computers, 7–8
Network-level security, 684
Networks
addressing schemes, 24
areas, 136–137
assigning subnets to each link, 123
ATM, 169
avoiding building looped segments, 43
congestion, 256
connecting across types, 24–25
data frame size, 24
data-link layer protocols, 24
discovering what paths and links are available, 368
distributing traffic, 369
error detection, 308
Frame Relay, 169
guaranteeing service level, 261
least cost path, 143
listing routers, 188
monitoring and policing traffic flows, 256

Networks (*continued*)
  packet switching, 387
  point-to-point
    communications, 309
  predetermining paths, 146–147
  preferred routes converging,
    433
  prioritizing data, 391
  prioritizing packets, 253–257
  quality of service, 251, 256
  reclassifying traffic, 256
  recovering from failures of
    links or nodes, 512
  requesting node, 663
  routing tables, 115
  RSVP adapting to changes in,
    274–277
  shortest path, 143
  slash 24 address, 40
  subnetting, 117
  TDM (time division
    multiplexing), 491
  understanding utilization,
    374–376
  value of, 1
  X.25, 169
Next Generation Internet
    Web site, 766
Next Hop. *See* NHOP (Next Hop)
Next hop address, 115
Next Hop Resolution Protocol.
    See NHRP (Next Hop
    Resolution Protocol)
Next hop router, 42
NFS (Network File System), 615
NHOP (Next Hop), 289
NHRP (Next Hop Resolution
    Protocol), 754
NLPIDs (Network Layer Protocol
    Identifiers), 188, 754
NLRI (Network Layer Reachability
    Information), 208
NMS (Network Management
    System), 640
Nodes
  advertising details of links, 132
  announcing presence on
    network, 49–50

ARP caches, 50–51
ARP Reply, 52
capable of IP routing, 386
changing point of attachment
    to Internet, 735–736
configured with BOOTP
    server's address, 53
FSC (fiber switch capable), 493
home agent, 735
interface address, 46
local address, 38
loopback addresses, 46–47
LSC (lambda switch capable),
    493
mapping tables, 50
multiple IP addresses, 38
periodically retransmitting
    IP to MAC address
    mapping, 51
ports, 309
PSC (packet switch capable),
    492
querying network to
    determine address
    mapping, 51–52
terminating protocols, 5–6
unable to supply timestamp,
    63
non-broadcast multi-access
    networks. *See* NBMA
    (non-broadcast
    multi-access) networks
Nonce, definition of, 716
Non-IP networks and GSMP
    messages, 553
Nontransient errors, 65–66
Northbound interface, 640
Notification message, 423–427,
    447–448, 451–454, 484
Notify message, 512–513, 516
Notify Request object, 513
NPCs (Network Control
    Protocols), 758
NSAP (Network Service Access
    Point), 181
NSSA (not so stubby areas),
    172–173
Ntop, 375

NTP (Network Time Protocol),
    100, 317
Numbered links, 122–124
NVT (Network Virtual Terminal),
    590–592

O

OAKLEY key exchange protocol,
    711
Object Adaptor, 654
object identifiers. *See* OIDs
    (object identifiers)
Object interfaces, 652
Object Management Architecture.
    See OMA (Object
    Management Architecture)
Object Management Group. *See*
    OMG (Object Management
    Group)
Object Management Group
    Web site, 675
Object Request Broker. *See* ORB
    (Object Request Broker)
Objects, 642
  COPS messages, 669, 672
  RSVP, 286–296
  RSVP messages, 457
  transport verification
    mechanism, 538–539
Octet, xxiv
Offline traffic engineering, 373–374
OID tree, 642–643
OIDs (object identifiers), 642
OIF-UNI (Optical Internetworking
    Forum's User-to-Network
    Interface), 530
OLS (Optical Line System), 569
OMA (Object Management
    Architecture), 653–654
OMG (Object Management
    Group), 652
On-demand label distribution,
    399
One's complement, 316
One's complement addition,
    35–36

One's complement checksum, 35–37
Opaque LSAs (Link State Advertisements), 178–179, 377
Open Group Web site, 633
Open Group Web site, The, 306
Open message, 202–203, 488
Open Shortest Path First. *See* OSPF (Open Shortest Path First)
Open Standards Organization. *See* OSI (Open Standards Organization)
Open Systems Interconnection. *See* OSI (Open Systems Interconnection) protocols
Operation error chunk, 347–348
Operations Support System. *See* OSS (Operations Support System)
Optical Line System. *See* OLS (Optical Line System)
Optical networking, 765
Optical switches, 544
Optical Switches. *See* OXCs (Optical Switches)
Optical transport networks, 507–508
Optical VPNs (Virtual Private Networks), 530–531, 733
ORB (Object Request Broker), 653–655
Ordered control, 417
Origin servers, 619
OSI (Open Standards Organization), 179, 644
OSI (Open Systems Interconnection) protocols, 4
OSI seven-layer model, 1
OSPF (Open Shortest Path First), xxii, 116, 141, 143–145, 155–179, 223–224
  adjacencies, 167
  adjacency of peers, 157
  advanced features, 197
  advertising link state, 161–166

aging out old state from database, 163
areas, 156, 170–172
Authentication Data field, 157
Authentication Length field, 157
available open links, 145
backup designated router, 168–169
bandwidth, 524
choosing to use areas, 175–177
cryptographic authentication, 157
deployment pattern, 198
designated routers, 167–169
Dijkstra Shortest Path First algorithm, 144–145
distribution protocol, 197
external attributes LSA, 178
Fletcher's checksum, 164, 181, 182–183
GMPLS, 523–530
Hello message, 157–159, 167
implementation simplicity, 197
interacting with other autonomous systems, 177–178
IP networks, 198
IPv4-centric outlook, 155
versus IS-IS, 196–198
Key Id field, 157
Link Local Identifier, 526
Link Local/Remote Identifier sub-TLV, 526
Link State Acknowledgement message, 166
Link State Age field, 163
link state and distance vector modes, 172
link state information, 157, 190
Link State Request message, 160
Link State Type field, 163
Link State Update message, 166
Link Switching Capabilities sub-TLV, 526

Link TLV, 526
Link Type field, 165
LSA (Link State Advertisement), 161–166
LSAs (link state advertisements), 163
message formats, 155–157
message objects, 526–528
multi-access networks, 167–169
Network Mask field, 157
NSSA (not so stubby areas), 172–173
opaque LSAs, 178–179, 377
OSPF messages, 155–157
packets, 197
point-to-point links, 165
protocol identifier, 28
protocols routed by, 197
Router Address TLV, 533
Router LSA, 165
Router Type field, 165
scalability, 197–198
security, 197
Shared Risk Link Group sub-TLV, 526, 528
SRLGs advertised as link properties, 526
stub areas, 172
summary LSA, 172
support for areas, 197
TOS (Type of Service) basis, 165–166
traffic engineering extensions, 523
type of link advertised, 165–166
type-1 metrics, 173
versions, 155
virtual links, 174–175, 193
OSPF Database Description message, 159–161
OSPF messages, 155–157
OSPF routers
  authentication, 156–157
  connection failure, 159
  Database Description Sequence Number, 160
  demand circuit option, 159

OSPF routers (*continued*)
  designated router, 159
  Hello Interval, 157
  largest MTU, 160
  link state, 161, 232
  Link State Update message,
    161, 168
  neighbor discovery, 157–159
  opinion of network mask, 157
  option flags, 158
  Router Priority byte, 158–159
  synchronizing database state,
    159–161
OSPF Working Group, 198
OSPF-TE, 377–379
OSPF-TE Router Address TLV, 380
OSS (Operations Support
  System), 640
Out of band signaling, 505–506,
  513
Outgoing interface, 115
Out-of-band signaling networks,
  533
Output Port message, 562
OXCs (Optical Switches), 569

P
Packaging data, 9–10
Packet forwarding, 566
Packet over SONET. *See* PoS
  (Packet over SONET)
packet switch capable. *See* PSC
  (packet switch capable)
Packet switched networks, 367
Packet Switched Telephone
  Network. *See* PSTN (Packet
  Switched Telephone
  Network) connections
Packet switching, 386–387, 492
Packets, 10
  address-based forwarding, 47
  associating with LSP, 391
  basic categorization, 270
  categorizing, 249
  classifying, 256
  versus datagrams, 26
  destination addresses, 37

discarded by IP, 37
dropping, 256
forwarding based on service
  type, 47, 49
imposing labels on, 394
IS-IS, 197
label stack, 393–394
labeling in MPLS, 388
OSPF (Open Shortest Path
  First), 197
prioritizing, 49, 250, 253–257
sensitive part, 317
switching, 45
traffic conditioning, 256
Padding TLV, 190
Parameter Problem ICMP
  message, 66–68, 76
Partial Sequence Number PDU.
  See PSNP (Partial Sequence
  Number PDU)
Passive peers, 406
Passwords, 685
PASV command, 600
Path messages, 267–269, 281,
  460–461, 464, 466, 468,
  472, 474, 516, 519
  Administrative Status object,
    520
  Adspec object, 271
  collecting information, 271
  Message Ids, 303
  Notify Request object, 513
  preventing propagation, 271
  refreshing, 274
  RSVP node, 298
  Sender Descriptors, 469
  Sender TSpec, 271
Path MTU discovery, 75–76
Path sequences, 140–141
Path sets, 140–141
Path Vector Limit, 407
Path vector protocols, 247
  amount of information to be
    propagated, 138
  BGP-4 (Border Gateway
    Protocol 4), 199–223
  choosing how to compute
    paths, 147

large number of destinations,
  139
path computation model, 143
policy-based routing
  decisions, 137
quantity of routing
  information, 139
route summarization, 138
valid routes, 138
Path vector routing, 137, 144
Path vectors, 137–141
PathErr messages, 272–274,
  284–285, 290, 471, 476,
  484, 511–512
Paths
  choosing how to compute,
    147
  composed parameters, 262
  least cost, 143
  load-balance traffic across,
    146
  LSP (Label Switched Path),
    389–390
  modifying costs, 369–370
  predetermining, 146–147
  shortest, 143
PathTear message, 269, 283, 472,
  474–476, 511
Patricia Tree, 120
Payload data, 3–4, 26
PDPs (Policy Decision Points),
  665–668
PDUs (protocol data units),
  10, 180
  accidental corruption, 189
  context of, 401
  CR-LDP (Constraint-Based
    LSP Setup Using LDP), 454
  header, xxiv, 401–402
  Header Length field, 184
  headers, 401
  IRPD (Intradomain Routing
    Protocol Discriminator)
    field, 184
  Maximum Area Addresses
    field, 185
  maximum size of, 194
  PDU Type field, 185

System Identifier Length field, 184
TLV (type-length-variable) format, 184
types, 185
variable-length fields, 184
PE (Provider Edge) equipment, 733
Peer Network to Network Interconnect. *See* PNNI (Peer Network to Network Interconnect)
Peering agreements, 119
Peers
  active, 406
  BGP (Border Gateway Protocol), 487
  LDP (Label Distribution Protocol), 403–409
  link state databases, 132–134
  passive, 406
  routers, 133
Penultimate Hop Popping. *See* PHP (Penultimate Hop Popping)
PEPs, 666–668
Per Hop Behavior Scheduling Class. *See* PSC (Per Hop Behavior Scheduling Class)
Per-Hop Behavior. *See* PHB (Per-Hop Behavior)
Perlman, Radia, 191
permanent virtual circuits. *See* PVCs (permanent virtual circuits)
PHB (Per-Hop Behavior), 254
PHOP (Previous Hop), 289
PHP (Penultimate Hop Popping), 395
Physical communications, 5
Physical connections, xix
Physical connectivity, 1–2
Physical layer, 4, 10
Physical links, 25
Physical security, 681–682
Physical transport network, 8
PIB (Policy Information Base), 672–673

PIM (Protocol Independent Multicast), 235
PIM messages, 227–229
PIM-SM (Protocol Independent Multicast-Sparse Mode), 91, 224, 227–230
Ping, 64, 70–74, 76
PNNI (Peer Network to Network Interconnect), 398
PNNI (Private Network to Network Interface), 752
PNNI (Private Network to Node Interface), 14
Point-to-multipoint trees, 561
Point-to-Point Hello PDU, 186
Point-to-point links
  OSPF (Open Shortest Path First), 165
  routers, 186
  as subnetwork, 122
Point-to-Point Protocol. *See* PPP (Point-to-Point Protocol)
Point-to-point trees, 561
Poison reverse split horizon, 130
Policies, 137–141, 253
Policy control, 258, 663–665
Policy Decision Points. *See* PDPs (Policy Decision Points)
Policy Information Base. *See* PIB (Policy Information Base)
Policy Object, 295–296
Policy-based decision-making, 665
Policy-based routing, 137–138
POP3 (Post Office Protocol), 337
PORT command, 600
Port Configuration message body, 557
Port Management message, 560–561
Port numbers, 311
Port Statistics message, 564
Port switching, 493
Ports
  client applications, 577
  dynamic, 311
  ephemeral, 311
  GSMP management, 560–561
  IP addresses, 309–310

  private, 311
  registered, 311
  server applications, 577
  transport protocols, 309–311
  UDP (User Datagram Protocol), 316
  well-known, 311, 577–578
PoS (Packet over SONET), 16–17
Post Office Protocol. *See* POP3 (Post Office Protocol)
PPP (Point-to-Point Protocol), 16–18, 200, 758–760
PPVNP Working Groups Web sites, 766
Preemption Priority Policy element, 465
Prefix FEC element, 412
Prefix length, 117
Pre-reservation of resources, 562–563
Presentation layer, 5, 9
Previous Hop. *See* PHOP (Previous Hop)
Primary index, 643
Primary LSPs, 503
Prioritizing data, 391
Prioritizing traffic, 368, 481–486
Priority-based algorithm, 256
Prisoner's dilemma, 257
Private address spaces, 728
Private Network to Network Interface. *See* PNNI (Private Network to Network Interface)
Private networks and IP addresses, 41
Private ports, 311
Privileges, 685
Process domains, 242
Propagating connectivity information, 115
protocol data units. *See* PDUs (protocol data units)
Protocol exchanges, xxiv, 151–153
Protocol identifiers, 316
Protocol Independent Multicast. *See* PIM (Protocol Independent Multicast)

Protocol Independent Multicast-Sparse Mode. *See* PIM-SM (Protocol Independent Multicast-Sparse Mode)
Protocol layer, 35
Protocols, xix, xx–xxi
  AFI (Address Family Indicator), 205
  control, 3
  data transfer protocols, 2–3
  data-link, 10–19
  data-link layer, 3
  effect of IPv6 on, 112
  encoding and transferring data, 2
  extending for Mobile IP, 736–741
  extensions to, 112
  header compression, 742–748
  identifying message source and destination, 3
  information distribution, 2–3
  IP telephony, 749–752
  layered model, xxi
  management, 3
  operational configuration and statistics information, 642
  OSI seven-layer model, 6
  relationship between, 19–20
  RIPv2 version indicator, 148
  SCTP (Stream Control Transmission Protocol), 353
  support for IPv6, 94
  TCP (Transmission Control Protocol), 337
  UDP (User Datagram Protocol), 316–317
Protocols Supported TLV, 188
Proxies, caching entities, 619
Proxy ARP, 53, 759–760
Proxy DNS request, 583
Proxy security, 689–690
Proxy servers, 619, 626, 628
Pruning distribution tree, 225–226
PSC (Per Hop Behavior Scheduling Class), 482
PSC (packet switch capable), 492

Pseudo message header, 315
PSNP (Partial Sequence Number PDU), 194
PSTN (Packet Switched Telephone Network) connections, 338
Public key, 710
Public key cryptography, 704
Pull principle, 223
Push principle, 223
PVCs (permanent virtual circuits), 14, 752

Q
Quality of service, 251
Queues, 251, 256
Quoted-printable encoding, 621

R
Random Early Detection mechanism. *See* RED (Random Early Detection) mechanism
Random-walk routing, 142–143
Ransom, Niel, 764
RAPI (RSVP API), 267, 306
RARP (Reverse ARP), 52–53
Raw IP, 429
  hosts, 297
  LMP (Link Management Protocol), 531
  Next Protocol field, 316
  versus UDP, 316
Raw sockets, 579
Real links, 193
Real-time data traffic, 264
Real-time services, 257–266
Real-time Transport Control Protocol. *See* RTCP (Real-time Transport Control Protocol)
Real-Time Transport Protocol, 84
Real-time Transport Protocol. *See* RTP (Real-time Transport Protocol)
Receiver LDP Identifier, 407

Record Route Object, 460–464, 468–469
Record Route objects. *See* RROs (Record Route objects), 509
Record Route option, 61–62
Record Route Subobjects, 462
Recording IP, 61–63
RED (Random Early Detection) mechanism, 375
Redirect ICMP message, 66–68, 70, 75
Refresh reduction, 297–303
Registered ports, 311
Registration message, 738–739, 741
Registry DNS server, 583
Rendezvous point, 224
Repeaters, 42
Replay attacks, 679
Reply message, 73, 739, 741
Report Connection State message, 564–565
Report-State message, 667
Report-Status message, 666
Request message, 657, 666
Request methods, 619–620
Requesting node, 663
Request-Line object, 622–623
Request-response protocol, 565
Reservation Request message, 562
Reserving resources, 249, 266–304
  choosing to, 267
  message flows, 267–270
  MPLS, 436–437
  RSVP-capable network, 268
  styles, 279–280
Resource Reservation Protocol. *See* RSVP (Resource Reservation Protocol)
Resources
  collecting information about, 268
  pre-reservation of, 562–563
  requests, 464–465
  reservations, 464–465
  reserved, 268

reserving, 249, 266–304, 436–437
standard classification, 257–266
Resources classes, 450
Response messages, 151–152, 564
Restart Capabilities Object, 514
Resv Confirm Object, 293–294
Resv messages, 267–269, 274–275, 281, 283, 458, 460–461, 464–465, 472, 474, 516
Administrative Status object, 519
Flow Descriptor List, 469
FlowSpec object, 271
formal definition, 469
Message Ids, 303
Notify Request object, 513
refreshing, 275
RSVP node, 298
Sender Descriptor, 468
ResvConf messages, 269, 285, 290, 457
ResvErr message, 272–274, 284–285, 290, 471, 512
ResvTear message, 270, 283, 475, 511
Reverse ARP. *See* RARP (Reverse ARP)
reverse path lookup. *See* RPL (reverse path lookup)
Reverse tunneling, 741
RFCs (Request For Comments), xxvi–xxvii
RIB (routing information base), 121–122
RIP (Routing Information Protocol), xxii, 116
authentication, 150–151
distance vector protocols, 154
distributing routing information, 152
infinity, 152, 154
link failures, 154
message formats, 148–150
multicast routing, 154
network size limitation, 154
overloading route entry, 150–151

protocol exchanges, 151–153
Request message, 152
response messages, 151–152
RIP messages, 148–150
RIPv2, 148
route withdrawal, 153
security, 154
simple to implement, 154
small networks, 154
timers managing exchanges, 152
widely deployed, 154
RIP messages, 148–151
RIP networks, 152
RIP routers, 152–153
RIPv1 routers, 153–154
RIPv2
backwards compatibility with RIPv1, 153–154
multicast address, 152
protocol version indicator, 148
security, 150–151
RIPv2 routers, 153–154
Routable router identifier, 123
Route advertisements
confederacy, 222
inclusion of entire path in, 137
size of, 137
Route aggregation, 140
Route caches, 120–121
Route coloring, 214
Route control, 61–63
Route distinguisher, 216
Route flap, 216–217
Route import filtering, 121
Route reflection, 220–221
Route Refresh message, 208
Route summarization, 138
Route table, 45
Route tagging, 150
Router Advertisement Message, 737
Router ids, 47
Router information, 133–135, 141
Router LSA, 165
Router tables, 126–127
Routers, 42, 44–45
admission control component, 258–259

agreement on constraints, 145
allocating configurable resources, 255
applying different polices, 138
area addresses supported, 185
area identifier, 156
ASBRs (autonomous system border routers), 119
authentication, 189
breaking up routing space, 170
building and using routing tables, 119–122
candidate list, 144
capabilities, 188
computing shortest path, 144
database of available links, 132
data-link layer address, 49
data-link layer broadcasts, 81
default route, 120
distance vectors, 125–131
easily identifying routing loops, 137
explicit route, 120
feedback on, 74–75
FIB (forwarding information base), 122
flooding process, 133
forwarding datagrams on available paths, 146
forwarding datagrams with IP broadcast addresses, 81
forwarding or discarding datagrams, 85, 87
grades of service, 249–250
grouping into areas, 136–137
having same view of resources, 143
Hello protocol, 132–133
hop-by-hop forwarding, 142
ICMP discovery, 74–75
informing sender of better route, 67–68, 70
input, 121
knowledge of network topology, 44
limiting visibility to routing tables, 130

link failure, 133
link state information, 143
listing, 188
load balancing, 146
loopback address, 123
LSA (link state advertisement), 133–135
LSA aging, 135
LSP (link state packet), 133–135
LSPs (Link State PDUs), 191
mapping table, 49
monitoring liveliness of links between, 132
multi-access broadcast link, 186
multicast challenges, 223
multicast datagrams, 84
multicast routing protocols, 91
multidrop link, 49
next hop router, 42
number in area, 176
numbered links, 122–124
OSPF virtual adjacency, 175
packet priority, 49
passing full path between, 144
peers, 132–133
point-to-point links, 49, 186
poison reverse split horizon, 130
policy decisions, 664–665
policy-based filters for routes, 122
priority, 187
random-walk routing, 142–143
reading statistics from, 374
real links, 193
registering with adjacent routers, 90
reliable exchange of LSPs between, 194
responding to membership query, 91
responsibilities, 16
retransmitting LSPs, 191
RIB (routing information base), 121–122
route aggregation, 140
route import filtering, 121

router IDs, 47, 122–124
routes, 120
routing decision engine, 122
routing IP flows, 371–372
routing tables, 45, 115
routing trees, 144
RPL (reverse path lookup), 85, 87
security and RIPv2, 150–151
sending and receiving BGP messages, 201
sharing information, 377
sharing routing information between multicast routing protocols, 234
soliciting routing information, 129
soliciting routing table updates from peers, 152
speed of discovering changes, 130
synchronizing link state databases, 195–196
timer for routes in routing table, 128–129
transit, 219
triggered updates, 128
unique identifier, 156
unnumbered links, 122–124
use of same routing path, 143–144
virtual links, 175, 193
Routers Solicitation ICMP message, 75
Routes
    definition of, 180
    RSVP-TE management, 459–464
    withdrawing, 208–209
Routing, 115
    AS (autonomous systems), 118–119
    aggregation, 117–118
    BGP-4 (Border Gateway Protocol 4), 199–223
    CIDR (Classless Inter-Domain Routing), 116–118
    classless, 117

constraint-based, 373
direct, 42
flexibility, 386
indirect, 42
IP, 44–46
IP flows, 371–372
IP multicast, 116
IS-IS (Intermediate-System to Intermediate-System), 179–196
link failure, 126–127
make-before-break, 464
multicast routing, 223–233
multicast tree, 85
network address, 117
next hop address, 115
OSPF (Open Shortest Path First), 155–179
outgoing interface, 115
policies, 122
random-walk, 142–143
RIP (Routing Information Protocol), 147–155
routing tables, 386
service-based routing, 372–373
subnetwork addresses, 117
supporting unnumbered links, 526
switches, 386
versus switching, 387–388
Routing algorithms, 115–116
Routing by rumor, 125
Routing decision engine, 122
Routing extensions for traffic engineering, 376
    IS-IS-TE, 379–381
    OSPF-TE, 377–379
Routing information
    ABRs leaking, 170–171
    choosing routing model, 141–142
    decrease in quality of routing decisions, 176
    distance vectors, 125–131
    distributing, 124–142
    DVMRP (Distance Vector Multicast Routing Protocol), 232–233

increased benefit of reduced,
176
link state routing, 131–137
modifying, 137
path sequences, 140–141
path sets, 140–141
path vectors, 137–141
policies, 137–141
re-advertising, 128–129
RIP distributing, 152
topology information
describing network, 132
routing information base. *See* RIB
(routing information base)
Routing Information Protocol.
See RIP (Routing
Information Protocol)
Routing metric, 130–131
Routing models
choosing, 141–142
choosing how to compute
paths, 147
CSPF (Constrained Shortest
Path First), 145–146
ECMP (Equal Cost Multi-Path),
146
OSPF (Open Shortest Path
First), 143–145
single constraint to route, 145
TE (traffic engineering),
146–147
Routing paths, computing,
142–147
Routing Plane, 7–8
Routing protocols, 6–7, 20, 44,
115–116, 141, 241
all available routes, 122
ASs (autonomous systems),
119
authentication, 682
BGP (Border Gateway
Protocol), 245
denial of service attack, 682
EGP (Exterior Gateway
Protocol), 245
EIGRP (Enhanced
Inter-Gateway Routing
Protocol), 242

ES-IS, 242–243
extending, 141
GGP (Gateway to Gateway
Protocol), 245
GMPLS, 529–530
Hello Protocol, 245–246
historic, 245–246
HSRP (Hot Standby Router
Protocol), 243–245
IDPR (Inter-Domain Policy
Routing), 245
IDRP (Inter-Domain Routing
Protocol), 243
IGRP (Inter-Gateway Routing
Protocol), 242
Internet RAP (Route Access
Protocol), 243
piggy-backing information on,
141
protecting, 682
Prune message, 225
route tagging, 150
router ids, 47
routing trees, 224
shared trees, 239
tunnels, 729
VPNs (Virtual Private
Networks), 728–730
VRRP (Virtual Router
Redundancy Protocol),
243–245
Routing tables, 42, 47, 115, 386
building, 119–122
configuring, 124–125
construction of, 120
Dijkstra algorithm, 144–145
efficiently searching, 120
flushing, 130
implementation of, 119–120
limiting visibility to, 130
look-up times, 120–121
optimum route, 126
as ordered list, 120
Patricia Tree, 120
rapid look-up, 143
repopulating, 128
subnetwork addresses, 117
TOS-based routing, 166

updating, 115, 120, 208
usage, 119–122
Routing trees, 145, 224–225
Routing-based label distribution,
398–399
Row status, 647
RPL (reverse path lookup), 85, 87
RROs (Record Route objects),
509, 511
RSTACK (Reset Acknowledgement)
message, 555
RSVP (Resource Reservation
Protocol), xxii, 249, 266,
456–457
Acknowledgement message,
303
adapting to changes in
network, 274–277
Adspec object, 262, 294
aggregation of traffic flows,
304
Bundle message, 297–298
choosing transport protocol,
296–297
collecting information about
resources, 268
confirming reservations,
293–294
control state, 268
describing traffic, 457
describing traffic flow, 294
discovering, 271–272
error codes, 290–292
Error Spec Object, 272, 284,
290–292
explicit padding of objects,
287
extensions, 297, 457
failure to receive Path or Resv
refresh, 513
FilterSpec Objects, 271,
279–280, 293
FilterSpecs, 459
flows, 270–271
FlowSpec Object, 279–280, 294
Hop Object, 283–284, 287–289
identifying message senders,
293

RSVP (*continued*)
  implementations, 268
  Integrity Object, 294–295
  interval between refresh
    messages sent to refresh
    state, 289–290
  jittering refresh intervals, 289
  LIH (Logical Interface
    Handle), 289
  link failure, 466–467
  list of addresses of senders, 292
  malformed messages, 292
  managing admission control
    policy, 295–296
  merge point, 275
  merging flows, 277–280
  Message Ack Object, 298
  message flows for resource
    reservation, 267–270
  Message Id Multicast List
    Object, 303
  Message Nack object, 301
  message objects, 286–296
  message refresh processing
    and rerouting, 275
  multicast flows, 280
  multicast resource sharing,
    280–281
  multiple tunnels sharing
    resources, 470
  NetMeeting, 267
  NHOP (Next Hop), 289
  nodes timing out, 275
  objects and formats, 286–296
  operating over raw IP, 296
  Path messages, 267–269,
    271, 274
  PathErr messages, 272–274,
    284–285
  PathTear messages, 269, 283
  PHOP (Previous Hop), 289
  Policy Object, 295–296
  Preemption Priority Policy
    element, 465
  processed overhead, 457
  protecting against message
    spoofing, 294–295
  protocol identifier, 28, 471

  refresh reduction, 297–304,
    511
  refreshing state between
    nodes, 511
  reporting errors, 272–274
  requesting, 271–272
  reserved resources, 268
  reserving, 271–272
  restricting hops on path, 286
  Resv Confirm Object, 293–294
  Resv messages, 267–269, 271,
    274–275
  ResvConf messages, 269
  ResvErr message, 272–274,
    284–285
  ResvTear message, 270, 283
  re-use by RSVP-TE, 457
  RSVP Hop Object, 284
  RSVP Hot Object, 287–289
  RSVP Scope Object, 292
  RSVP-capable and
    RSVP-incapable nodes, 264
  Scope Object, 292
  Sender Template Object, 271,
    459
  Sender TSpec object, 294
  service parameters encoding,
    260
  Session Object, 270, 286–287,
    458–459
  sessions, 270–271
  as soft state protocol, 277, 511
  Source Message List Object,
    303
  specifying reservation
    requirements, 457
  split points, 280–281
  Srefresh (Summary Refresh
    message), 303
  Srefresh (Summary Refresh)
    message, 301, 303
  Style Object, 279, 283, 293
  styles for resource reservation,
    279–280
  Time Values Object, 289
  traffic control component, 271
  UDP, 297
  Voice over IP, 267, 748

  RSVP API. *See* RAPI (RSVP API)
  RSVP messages, 268
    BNF (Backus-Naur Form), 281
    bundling, 304
    Checksum field, 285
    confirming reservation, 285
    encapsulated in IP packets, 296
    epoch, 299
    FF Flow Descriptor, 283
    FF (Fixed-Filter) style, 283
    Flow Descriptor List, 251, 283
    formats, 281–286
    header, 285
    Length field, 285
    mandatory and optional
      objects, 281
    message identifier, 298–300
    Message Identifier Object,
      298–299
    message type field, 285
    objects, 457
    ordering of objects within, 281
    packaging multiple together,
      297–298
    Path Message, 281
    Resv message, 281, 283
    ResvConf message, 285
    RSVP-capable routers, 296
    SE (Shared-Explicit) style, 283
    Send TTL field, 286
    Sender Descriptor, 281
    uniquely identifying, 298
    WF (Wildcard-Filter) style, 283
  RSVP node, 298
  RSVP routers, 298
  RSVP Working Group, 305
  RSVP-capable network, 268
  RSVP-capable routers, 296
  RSVP-TE, xxii, 435
    admission control, 471
    Adspec object, 464
    alarm-free LSP establishment,
      516
    alarm-free teardown, 516
    applicability and adoption,
      479–480
    attributes, 465–466
    BNF (Backus-Naur Form), 468

coloring LSP, 466

Compression Request object, 748

Compression Response object, 748

controlled re-routing of LSP, 457

versus CR-LDP, 479–481

detecting errors, 466–468

DiffServ Object, 483

distributing labels, 458

Downstream on Demand label distribution, 458

enhanced route control, 509–511

error codes and values, 471

error notification, 516

Explicit Route Object, 459, 462

explicit routes, 459–460

failure to receive Path or Resv refresh, 513

FF Flow Descriptor, 469

FF (Fixed Filter) reservation style, 464–465

FilterSpec Object, 469

Fixed Filter style, 469

Flow Descriptor, 516

FlowSpec objects, 464

generalized, 509–520

GMPLS, 508–520

graceful restart, 513–514

Hello Ack Object, 467

Hello message, 467–468, 470

Hello Object, 467

Hello Request object, 467

identifying LSPs, 458–459

IP, 481

Label Object, 463–464, 469

Label Request Object on a Path message, 458

link failure, 466–467

listing Flow Descriptors, 469

LSP setup, 472

LSP teardown, 472

maintaining connectivity, 466–468

make-before-break, 473

message exchanges, 516–520

message flows, 472–476

message formats, 516

network failure, 476, 511

notification requests and messages, 512–513

Notify message, 512, 516

Path message, 460–461, 464, 466, 468, 472, 474

PathErr message, 471, 476, 512

PathTear message, 472, 474–476

policy considerations, 471

preemption, 465–466

Preemption Priority Policy element, 465

priorities, 465–466

protocol identifier, 471

protocol state, 481

Record Route Object, 460–464, 469

reducing protocol overheads, 511

re-routing LSPs, 473

resource affinities, 481

resource requests and reservation, 464–465

Resv message, 458, 460–461, 464–465, 472, 474

ResvConf message, 457

ResvErr message, 471, 512

ResvTear message, 475

re-use of RSVP, 457

route recording, 460–462

routing tunnels, 466

SE (Shared Explicit) reservation style, 464–465

security, 471

Sender Object, 474

Sender Template Object, 459

Session Attribute Object, 463–466

Session Attributes object, 474

Session Object, 458–459

setting up and re-routing LSPs, 473–475

Shared Explicit style, 469

signaling PSC mapping for L-LSP, 482

state refresh, 467

status codes, 484

summary of main functions, 480–481

summary of messages and objects, 468–470

transport protocol, 470–471

WF (Wildcard Filter) reservation style, 464–465

RSVP-TE messages, 476–478

RTCP (Real-time Transport Control Protocol)

  Application packet, 362

  BYE packet, 360

  Message Type field, 356

  packet types, 358–362

  purposes, 358

  registered server port numbers, 354

  RR (Receiver Report), 360–362

  RTP (Real-time Transport Protocol), 354

  SDES (Sender Descriptor) packet, 358–360

  Source Description Chunks, 359

  Source Description items, 359–360

  SR (Sender Report), 360–362

  transferring application control information, 362

RTCP messages, 356

RTP (Real-time Transport Protocol), xxii, 234–235

  amount of control information transmitted in data packet, 363

  choosing transport, 363

  detecting packet loss, 356

  header compression techniques, 364

  identifying source in session, 356

  jitter, 355

  joining session, 358–359

  managing data, 354–358

RTP (*continued*)
mixer, 356, 360
multiple data sources
combined to form single
stream, 356
overhead, 364
Receiver Reports, 364
registered payload types,
357–358
registered server port
numbers, 354
RTCP (Real-time Transport
Control Protocol), 354
SCTP, 363
selecting, 363–364
Sender Reports, 364
TCP (Transmission Control
Protocol), 363
timestamp of payload data,
355
UDP, 354, 363
version number, 355
Voice over IP, 748
RTP header, 355–356
timestamp of payload data,
355

S
SA (Security Association), 689,
711–712
SAFIs (Subsequent Address
Family Identifiers), 205
Sample networks, xxiv
Scalability
label switching, 386
LSRs, 393
Scalar objects, 643
SCTP (Stream Control
Transmission Protocol),
xxii, 5, 20, 307
Abort chunk, 347
Adler 32-bit checksum, 340
applications, 578
association establishment and
management, 341–348
Association Initiation chunk,
342

associations, 339
chunk types, 341
Cumulative TSN
Acknowledgement, 351–352
Data chunk, 349–350
data delivery, 350
data transfer, 348–352
features, 338
gap acknowledgement blocks,
351
Heartbeat Acknowledgement
chunk, 346
Heartbeat chunk, 346
Host Name Address
parameter, 344
implementing, 352–353
Initial Acknowledgement
chunk, 342, 345
IPv4 Address parameter, 344
IPv6 Address parameter, 344
lack of availability, 353
LDP, 429–430
MAC (Message Authentication
Code), 345
messages within connection,
338
multihoming, 338
multiple streams between pair
of end points, 338
network-level fault tolerance,
338
Operation error chunk, 347
port numbers, 339
protocol identifier, 28
protocols, 353
RTP (Real-time Transport
Protocol), 363
security, 338
Selective Acknowledgement
chunk, 351–352
Sender Heartbeat Information,
346
Shutdown Acknowledgement
chunk, 347
sockets, 579
sockets API, 353
State Cookie Echo chunk,
344–345

State Cookie parameter, 344
versus TCP, 353
Unrecognized Parameter, 345
user data messages, 350
SCTP header, 339–340
SCTP messages, 338–341
SCTP packets
bundling multiple messages,
338
chunks, 339–341
Data chunk, 351
Heartbeat Acknowledgement
chunk, 346
IP datagrams, 339
length, 340
SCTP header, 339
Shutdown Acknowledgement
chunk, 346
Shutdown Complete chunk,
346–347
Shutdown Request chunk,
346
source and destination
addresses, 346
three-way handshake, 346
SDES (Sender Descriptor) packet,
358–360
SDH (Synchronous Digital
Hierarchy), 16–17, 495
SDLC, 2
SE (Shared Explicit) style,
464–465
SE (Shared-Explicit) style, 283
Searching routing tables
efficiently, 120
Secret key, 710
Secret key model, 703–704
Secure Hash Algorithm One.
See SHA-1 (Secure Hash
Algorithm One)
Secure Hypertext Transfer
Protocol. *See* S-HTTP
(Secure Hypertext Transfer
Protocol)
Secure method, 701
Secure sockets API, 695
Secure Sockets Layer. *See* SSL
(Secure Sockets Layer)

Security, 677, 764–765
  access control, 681–682,
    685–687
  application-level, 682–683
  authentication, 687–688
  clear text password, 189
  complexity of system, 680
  cost, 680
  denial of service attacks, 679
  digital signatures, 683
  encryption, 683, 688–689
  encryption algorithms, 703–707
  end-to-end, 689–690
  exchanging keys, 710–716
  firewalls, 685–686
  hashing algorithms, 703–707
  HTTP (HyperText Transfer
    Protocol), 701, 703
  ICMP implications, 76–77
  impersonating another user,
    679
  IP network, 681
  IPsec (IP security), 689–695
  IPv6, 109
  IS-IS, 197
  keeping information private,
    678
  limiting unauthorized access,
    681
  Mobile IP, 741–742
  model components, 684–689
  multicast, 83
  NAT (Network Address
    Translation), 41
  need for, 678–680
  network-level, 684
  OSPF (Open Shortest Path
    First), 197
  password protection, 683
  performance costs, 680
  physical, 681–682
  physical break in connectivity,
    681
  protecting routing and
    signaling protocols, 682
  protection at transport layer,
    684
  protection from hackers, 680

  protection of infrastructure of
    Internet, 678
  protection of user data, 682
  proxy, 689–690
  replay attacks, 679
  RIP, 154
  RIPv2, 150–151
  RSVP-TE, 471
  SCTP (Stream Control
    Transmission Protocol),
    338
  sniffers, 679
  SNMP (Simple Network
    Management Protocol),
    647–648
  TFTP (Trivial FTP), 615
  transport-layer, 695–701
  unauthorized access to secure
    locations, 678
  VPNs (Virtual Private
    Networks), 728, 731
  where to apply, 681–684
Security Association. *See* SA
  (Security Association)
Security gateways, 76
Security Parameter Index. *See* SPI
  (Security Parameter Index)
Segment, 322
Selective Acknowledgement
  chunk, 351–352
Sender Descriptor, 281, 468
Sender Descriptor Chunks, 360
Sender Descriptor packet. *See*
  SDES (Sender Descriptor)
  packet
Sender Object, 474
Sender Reports, 364
Sender Template Object, 271,
  281, 459, 468
Sender TSpec Object, 281, 294, 468
Sender-Initiated/Unsolicited File
  Transfer Protocol. *See*
  SIFT/UFT (Sender-Initiated/
  Unsolicited File Transfer
  Protocol)
Serial Line Internet Protocol. *See*
  SLIP (Serial Line Internet
  Protocol)

Server applications, 576–577
Server Hello message, 698
Server Key Exchange message,
  698
Service Level Agreements.
  See SLAs (Service Level
  Agreements)
Service Management Research
  Group, 306
Service Providers
  DNS server, 583–584
  quality of service, 252
Service Provider's Service
  Provider, 733
Service-based routing, 372–373
Services
  applications selecting type,
    265–266
  best-effort delivery, 251
  methods of managing, 251–253
Session Attributes Object,
  463–466, 474
Session Initialization messages,
  406–408, 411, 416
Session layer, 5, 9
Session Object, 270, 286–287
Sessions, 200
  defining for data flow, 287
  exchanging information about
    addresses, 408
  FTP management, 602
  initialization, 406
  label space, 407
  LDP (Label Distribution
    Protocol), 403–409
  qualifying details, 465
  rejecting, 407
  RSVP, 270–271
  sending parameters, 407
  state machine for
    initialization, 408
Setup priority, 437
Seven-bit ASCII code, 591
sFlow, 375, 383
SFTP (Simple File Transfer
  Protocol), 614
SGML (Standard Generalized
  Markup Language), 648, 649

SHA-1 (Secure Hash Algorithm
One), 701
Shared Explicit style, 469
Shared Risk Link Groups.
See SRLGs (Shared Risk
Link Groups)
Shared tree multicast routing
protocols, 224–225
Shared trees, 239–240
Sharing resources
computation of, 279
merged flows or parallel
flows, 283
multicast, 280–281
Shim, definition of, 388
Shim header, 388
Shortest path, 143
Shortest Path First algorithms.
See SPF (Shortest Path
First) algorithms
S-HTTP (Secure Hypertext
Transfer Protocol), 701,
703
Shutdown Acknowledgement
chunk, 346–347
Shutdown Complete chunk,
346–347
Signaling protocols, 7
authentication, 682
automatically setting up
LSPs, 400
choosing IP-based control
plane, 397–398
constraint-based, 438–439
downstream unsolicited label
distribution, 398–399
explicit route, 400
message replay, 682
on-demand label distribution,
399
operation of, 397
optical transport network, 508
protecting, 682
routing-based label
distribution, 398–399
RSVP (Resource Reservation
Protocol), 266
spoofing, 682

traffic engineering, 399–400
usage, 400
Signaling Transport Working
Group, 365
Silent hosts, 152
Simple File Transfer Protocol.
See SFTP (Simple File
Transfer Protocol)
Simple Mail Transfer Protocol.
See SMTP (Simple Mail
Transfer Protocol)
Simple Network Management
Protocol. *See* SNMP
(Simple Network
Management Protocol)
Simple Object Access Protocol.
See SOAP (Simple Object
Access Protocol)
Single Source Multicast
architecture. *See* SSM
(Single Source Multicast)
architecture
SIP, 353
Site Local Unicast IPv6
Addresses, 97–98
SLAs (Service Level
Agreements), 381, 436
SLIP (Serial Line Internet
Protocol), 756–758
Slow start, 333
SMI (Structure of Management
Information), 644–645
SMTP (Simple Mail Transfer
Protocol), 337
SNAP (Sub-Network Access
Protocol) header, 19
Sniffers, 679
SNMP (Simple Network
Management Protocol),
xxiii, 374, 641, 646, 660
application-level
cryptographic
authentication, 648
GET and SET requests, 647
GET-BULK command, 647
GET-NEXT request, 647
MIBs (Management
Information Bases), 438

notification messages, 661
notifications, 646–647
request-response based, 662
requests, 646–647
responses, 646–647
security, 647–648
SET command, 647
statistics, 661
TRAP message, 647
versions, 647–648
SNMP messages, 648
SNPA (Subnetwork Point of
Attachment), 180
SOAP (Simple Object Access
Protocol), 650–651
SOAP messages, 650–651
Sockets, 318, 579
Sockets API, 319, 334, 353, 695
Sockets interface, 334
Soft state protocol, 277, 511
SONET (Synchronous Optical
Network), 16–17, 492, 495
SONET links, 16
Source Description Chunks, 359
Source Description items, 359–360
Source Message List Object, 303
Source node, 61–62
Source Quench message, 70, 333
Source Route option, 62–63
Source routing, 371, 382
choice of route, 372
problems with, 63
Source Service Access Point.
See SSAP (Source Service
Access Point)
Source-based multicast routing
protocols, 224
Source-based trees, 231–232
Sparse-mode protocols, 226–227,
239, 240–241
SPF (Shortest Path First)
algorithms, 145–146, 432
SPF (shortest path first) routing,
367–368
SPI (Security Parameter Index),
692
Split horizons, 130
Split points, 280–281

Spoofing and signaling protocols, 682

Srefresh (Summary Refresh) message, 301, 303

SRLGs (Shared Risk Link Groups), 382, 525–526

SSAP (Source Service Access Point), 18

SSL (Secure Sockets Layer), xxiii, 695, 701

SSM (Single Source Multicast) architecture, 236–238

Standard Generalized Markup Language. *See* SGML (Standard Generalized Markup Language)

Standard header, 4

State, 563–565, 657

State Cookie Echo chunk, 344–345

State machine, definition of, 555

Statistics, 660–662

Status-Line object, 622–623

Stream Control Transmission Protocol. *See* SCTP (Stream Control Transmission Protocol)

Strict hops, 434–435, 448, 450

Strict route, 62–63

Strict Route option, 62–63

Structure of Management Information. *See* SMI (Structure of Management Information)

Stub areas, 172

Style Object, 279, 283, 293

Subnets
anycast addresses, 100–101
IPv6 unicast addresses, 99
prefixes, 99

Subnetting, 40–41, 117

Subnetwork addresses, 117, 122

Subnetwork Point of Attachment. *See* SNPA (Subnetwork Point of Attachment)

Subnetworks
CIDR, 117
grouping IP addresses into, 139–140

Subsequent Address Family Identifier pair, 488

Subsequent Address Family Identifiers. *See* SAFIs (Subsequent Address Family Identifiers)

Summary LSA, 171, 177

Summary Refresh message, 303

SVCs (switched virtual circuits), 14, 752

Switch Configuration message body, 556–560

switched virtual circuits. *See* SVCs (switched virtual circuits)

Switches, 45–46
asynchronous events, 563
capabilities of, 557
collecting traffic statistics, 564
Ethernet, 11
global switch configuration parameters, 556–560
number of reservations programmed into, 557
partition of, 550
reducing LSP setup, 501
reservation model requested/ supported, 557
routing, 386
separating from controller, 550
as servers, 551
supporting high data rates, 559
unsolicited status messages, 551

Switching
choosing type, 493–494
FECs (Forwarding Equivalence Classes), 549–550
fiber, 493
hierarchy of media, 492–494
IP, 44–46
lambda, 493
layer-two, 492
port, 493
versus routing, 387–388
waveband, 493

Switching networks and inferred labels, 390

SYN (Synchronize) message, 555–556

SYNACK (Synchronize Acknowledgement) message, 555–556

Synchronize Acknowledgement message. *See* SYNACK (Synchronize Acknowledgement) message

Synchronize message. *See* SYN (Synchronize) message

Synchronize-Complete message, 667

Synchronize-State-Request message, 667

Synchronous Digital Hierarchy. *See* SDH (Synchronous Digital Hierarchy)

Synchronous Optical Network. *See* SONET (Synchronous Optical Network)

T

Tag Distribution Protocol. *See* TDP (Tag Distribution Protocol)

Tag switching, 396–397

Tags, 616

Targeted frames, looping, 43

TCB (Transmission Control Block), 347

TCP (Transmission Control Protocol), xxii, 5, 20, 307, 318
Acknowledgement Numbers field, 326–328
acknowledgements, 324–329
applications, 578
BGP (Border Gateway Protocol), 200
BGP-4 (Border Gateway Protocol), 337
checksums, 324
congestion window, 333
connection-oriented protocols, 318

TCP (*continued*)
  CR-LDP, 481
  data buffers, 333
  data transfer, 322–324
  enhancing, 337
  flow control, 324–329
  FTP (File Transfer Protocol),
    337
  HTTP (Hypertext Transfer
    Protocol), 337
  implementing, 331–334
  importance of, 318
  keep alive mechanism, 332
  LDP (Label Distribution
    Protocol), 337, 429
  maximum segment size, 336
  Nagel algorithm, 329
  network congestion, 333–334
  POP3 (Post Office Protocol),
    337
  protocol identifier, 28
  protocols, 337
  reliable transport protocol,
    318
  reliable transport services, 336
  RTP (Real-time Transport
    Protocol), 363
  versus SCTP, 353
  segment acknowledgement,
    326
  slow start, 333
  SMTP (Simple Mail Transfer
    Protocol), 337
  sockets, 318, 579
  sockets interface, 334
  stop-start transfer of data,
    328
  TCP connection establishment
    message, 320
  Telnet, 337, 591
  timers, 332
  versus UDP, 336–337
  urgent data, 329–330
  window scaling, 336
  Window Size field, 326–328
TCP connections, 200, 319–321
  authentication, 695
  closing, 330–331
  control information
    exchanged by endpoints,
    334–336
  encryption, 695
  failure timeouts, 407
  idle, 332
  interfaces, 319
  measuring round-trip time, 336
  MTU size, 336
  performance optimization, 336
  sequence numbers, 332–333
  sockets API, 319
TCP header, 324, 329–330
TCP messages, 318
  Acknowledge flag, 320
  checksums, 322
  data message, 322
  Finish flag, 330–331
  Flags bits, 321
  header, 319
  IP messages, 322
  number of segment, 324
  pseudo header, 324
  Push flag, 323
  reassembling, 322
  retransmitting segments,
    325–326
  segment, 322
  sequence number of next
    byte, 324
  Synchronize flag, 320
TCP options, 334–336
TCP packets, fragmentation of,
  322–323
TCP stack, 320, 322
TCP/IP
  GIOP (General Inter-ORB
    Protocol), 658–659
  IS-IS, 179
TDM (time division
  multiplexing), 16, 492, 495
TDP (Tag Distribution Protocol),
  396–397
TE (traffic engineering), 146–147,
  367–368
  complexity, 382
  constraints on computing
    paths, 382
  discovering network
    utilization, 374–376
  dynamic, 373–374
  ECMP (equal cost multipath),
    369
  ECN (explicit congestion
    notification), 375–376
  future developments, 382–383
  guaranteeing availability of
    single, stable address, 380
  limitations, 382
  maximizing performance of
    network connections, 381
  modifying path costs, 369–370
  MPLS (Multiprotocol Label
    Switching), 382–383,
    431–439
  offline, 373–374
  path computation, 381
  routers, 371–372
  routing decisions, 373
  routing extensions for, 376–381
  routing IP flows, 371–372
  service-based routing, 372–373
  signaling protocols, 399–400
  source routing, 382
  SRLGs (Shared Risk Link
    Groups), 382
  tunneling, 382
  tunnels, 371–372, 720
  usage, 381–383
Telecommunications Network
  Protocol. *See* Telnet
TE_Link object, 542
Telnet, xxiii, 575, 589
  applications, 597
  authentication, 595–597
  Authentication option (option
    code 37), 596
  AYT command, 594
  character and graphical
    access, 590
  character flows, 591–592
  Command Line Interfaces, 438
  commands, 597
  control commands and
    options, 592–594
  DM command (242), 594

DO command, 594
flushing or clearing data path, 594
IAC character (0xff), 592
negotiation of parameters, 594–595
NVT (Network Virtual Terminal), 590–591
operation of, 591–595
popularity of, 590
reduction in cabling and terminals, 589
SB and SE commands, 595
special escape sequence, 597
synchronization procedure, 594
TCP (Transmission Control Protocol), 337, 591
transactions, 591
translations for, 590–591
as transmission protocol for FTP control messages, 602
Urgent TCP packet, 594
WILL command, 594
workstations, 591
Telnet messages, 608
Telnet servers, 589–591
Terminals, 588–589
Test message, 538–539
TestStatus message, 539
TestStatusAck message, 542
TestStatusFailure message, 542
TestStatusSuccess message, 539, 542
Textual conventions, 645
TFTP (Trivial File Transfer Protocol), xxiii, 53, 316, 575, 611–615
TFTP clients, 611
TFTP messages, 612
TFTP servers, 613
Throughput-based algorithm, 256
time division multiplexing. See TDM (time division multiplexing)
Time Exceeded ICMP message, 66–67, 72
Time Expired ICMP error message, 72

Time Values Object, 289
Timers and TCP (Transmission Control Protocol), 332
Timeslots, 492
Timestamp Request ICMP message, 73
Timestamps
associations, 346
datagrams, 63
TLS Handshake Protocol, 695–701
Certificate message, 698
Certificate Request, 698
Certificate Verify message, 699
Change Cipher Spec message, 699
Client Hello message, 697
Client Key Exchange message, 698–699
Finished message, 699
Hello Done message, 698
PRF (Pseudo Random Function), 699, 701
Server Hello message, 698
Server Key Exchange message, 698
TLS (Transport Layer Security) protocol, xxiii, 695, 701, 702
TLS Record Protocol, 695–701
TLVs (type-length-variables), 54, 59
CR-LDP (Constraint-Based LSP Setup Using LDP), 440–451
extension headers, 105
Hello PDUs, 187–190
IS-IS, 190–194
LSPs (Link State PDUs), 190–194
relevant to IP systems, 185, 187
TCP options, 334
Token bucket, 258–259, 261–262
Token Rings, 1, 12–14
amount of jitter, 42
PDU (Protocol Data Unit) maximum size, 30
Tokens, 13
TOS-based routing, 166
Traceroute, 64

gathering addresses of nodes that datagram passes through, 73
ICMP, 70–74
IP Record Route option, 73
measuring time for datagram to travel network, 73
plotting route through network, 72–74
route recording properties, 71
UDP datagrams, 72
Traffic
distributing, 369
policing, 258
predicting levels of service, 257
prioritizing, 250, 368
Traffic conditioning, 256
Traffic control component, 271
traffic engineering. See TE (traffic engineering)
Traffic flows
aggregation, 304
controlled load service, 260
describing, 258–259
IP, 481
level of service, 259
maximum packet size, 259
minimum policed unit, 259
peak rate, 259
regulated predictability, 437
standard classification, 257–266
staying within parameters, 260
time limit for delivery of datagrams, 260–262
token bucket, 258–259
Traffic parameters, 439, 443–448
Trailer, 4
Transactions, 7–8
Transferring files, 598
Transient errors, 65–66
Transit routers, 219
Transmission Control Block. See TCB (Transmission Control Block)
Transmission Control Protocol. See TCP (Transmission Control Protocol)

Transmission Sequence Number. *See* TSN (Transmission Sequence Number)

Transport Area Working Group, 365

Transport Area Working group, 318

Transport layer, 5, 9–10, 307

Transport Layer Security protocol. *See* TLS (Transport Layer Security) protocol

Transport Plane, 8

Transport protocols, xxi, 5, 6, 20, 684
  addresses, 309–311
  choosing, 307–308
  choosing for RSVP, 296–297
  complexity of implementation, 309
  congestion detection, 368
  connection-oriented transport, 312
  datagrams, 312–313
  ECN, 375–376
  end points, 309
  end-to-end, 307
  LDP, 429
  ports, 309–311
  protecting data, 35
  reasons for using, 308–309
  reducing capacity for data transport, 309
  reliable delivery, 311–312
  RSVP-TE, 470–471
  RTP (Real-time Transport Protocol), 354–364
  SCTP (Stream Control Transmission Protocol), 307, 337–353
  secure data transfer, 684
  security, 684
  selecting, 578–579
  TCP (Transmission Control Protocol), 307, 318–337
  UDP (User Datagram Protocol), 307, 313–318

Transport-layer security, 684, 695–701

TRAP message, 647

Trees, 561–562

Triggered updates, 128

Trivial File Transfer Protocol. *See* TFTP (Trivial File Transfer Protocol)

TSL Record message, 697

TSN (Transmission Sequence Number), 348

TTL failure, 66

TTL field, 36

Tunneling, 371, 719–720
  CE (Customer Edge) equipment, 733
  choice of route, 372
  choosing mechanism, 726
  LSPs, 393–396
  Mobile IP, 735
  PE (Provider Edge) equipment, 733
  through IP networks, 720–721
  traffic engineering, 382
  usage, 720–721
  VPNs (Virtual Private Networks), 728

Tunnels, 371–372, 690
  DVMRP (Distance Vector Multicast Routing Protocol), 233
  FAs (Forwarding Adjacencies), 393
  instance of, 459
  IP in IP encapsulation, 722–724
  MPLS, 393–396, 731–733
  qualifying details, 465
  routing protocols, 729
  traffic engineering, 720
  virtual routing adjacencies, 393
  VPNs, 732

type-length-variables. *See* TLVs (type-length-variables)

U

UDP (User Datagram Protocol), xxii, 5, 307, 313
  applications, 578
  BOOTP, 53, 316
  checksums, 314–316
  data integrity verification, 313
  data re-assembly, 313
  destination port identification, 313
  LDP, 429
  LDP Hello message, 403–405
  LMP (Link Management Protocol), 317, 531
  managed delivery to specific port, 336
  mobile nodes, 738
  NFS (Network File System) applications, 317
  NTP (Network Time Protocol), 317
  ports, 316
  protocol identifier, 28
  protocols, 316–317
  versus raw IP, 316
  RSVP, 297
  RTP (Real-time Transport Protocol), 354, 363
  sockets, 579
  source port identification, 313
  versus TCP, 336–337
  TFTP (Trivial FTP), 316, 611
  UDP Lite, 317–318

UDP datagrams
  DNS protocol, 582
  IPv6, 316
  pseudo message header, 315
  receive processes, 315–316
  RIP messages, 148–150
  traceroute, 72
  verifying integrity, 314–316

UDP for IPv6, 317

UDP Lite, 317–318

UDP messages, 313–314

UDP packets, 404

Unicast, 79–84

Unicast addresses, 83

Unicast IP networks, 243

Unicast IPv6 addresses, 101–102

Universal Resource Identifiers. *See* URIs (Universal Resource Identifiers)

Universal Resource Locators. *See* URLs (Universal Resource Locators)

Unix
/etc/hosts file, 579
mrouted program, 232

Unnumbered links, 122–124

Update messages, 486
example, 217
listing of attributes, 211–212
Multiprotocol Reachable Network Layer Reachability Information Extension Attribute, 488
optional attributes, 210
partial attributes, 210
Path Attributes field, 209–210
transitive attributes, 210

Urgent data, 329–330

URIs (Universal Resource Identifiers), 617–618

URLs (Universal Resource Locators), 575, 616–618, 623

USASCII, 591

User agents, 619

User data messages, 350

User Datagram Protocol. *See* UDP (User Datagram Protocol)

User names, 685

V

Van Jacobson compression, 758

Video streaming, 83–84

Virtual links, 174–175, 372

Virtual Private Networks. *See* VPNs (Virtual Private Networks)

Virtual Route Redundancy Protocol. *See* VRRP (Virtual Router Redundancy Protocol)

Virtual routing adjacencies, 393

Virtual routing tables, 729

Virtual wire, 719–720

Voice over MPLS, 749

Voice-over-IP, xxiii, 84, 267, 748–749

VPN IPv4 address, 216

VPNs (Virtual Private Networks), xxiii, 241, 636, 726, 763–764
BGP (Border Gateway Protocol), 216, 730, 733
comparing technologies, 733–734
constructing BGP/MPLS, 489
dedicated links between sites, 727
defining, 727
edge nodes, 729–730
encryption, 731
full reachability information for nodes within, 730
IGP (Interior Gateway Protocol), 729–730
layer-two tunneling solutions, 728–730
MPLS, 731–733
optical, 530–531, 733
popularity, 726
private address spaces, 728
private networks, 727
problems, 387
routing tables, 730
security, 728, 731
solutions using routing protocols, 728–730
tunneling, 719–720, 728
tunnels, 732
virtual routing tables, 729

VRRP (Virtual Router Redundancy Protocol), 243–245

W

W3C (World Wide Web Consortium), 617, 649

wave division multiplexing. *See* WDM (wave division multiplexing)

Waveband, 496

Waveband switching, 493

WDM (wave division multiplexing), 16

WDM (Wave Division Multiplexing) switches, 569

Web browsers, 618

Well-known attributes, 210

Well-known ports, 311, 577–578

WF (Wildcard Filter) style, 464–465

WF (Wildcard-Filter) style, 283

Wide Area Networking technologies, 1–2

Wildcard FEC element, 412

Wildcard Filter reservation style, 292

Window scaling, 336

Wireless networking, 2

Word processors, 616

Working Groups, xxvi

Workstations and Telnet, 591

World Wide Web, 616

World Wide Web Consortium Web site, 633, 674

X

X.25, 2, 4, 30, 31

X.25 networks, 169

XML (Extensible Markup Language), xxiii, 641, 648–650, 652, 660

XML documents, 648–650

XML element, 649

XML-RPC, 650

XNS protocol, 148